WAR WITHOUT MERCY

WAR
WITHOUT
MERCY

RACE AND POWER IN
THE PACIFIC WAR

JOHN W. DOWER

PANTHEON BOOKS

NEW YORK

Copyright © 1986 by John W. Dower

LIBRARY OF CONGRESS CATALOGING-IN-PUBLICATION DATA

Dower, John W.
War without mercy.
Bibliography: pp.
Includes index.
1. World War, 1939–1945—Pacific Area.
2. World War, 1939–1945—Public opinion.
3. Racism.   I. Title.
D767.9.D69   1986   940.53'1   85-43462
ISBN 0-394-75172-8 (pbk.)

Designed by Ann Gold

Manufactured in the United States of America

56789

For

KANA, RISA, and KEN

CONTENTS

Preface   ix

PART I: ENEMIES

1. Patterns of a Race War   3

2. "Know Your Enemy"   15

3. War Hates and War Crimes   33

PART II: THE WAR IN WESTERN EYES

4. Apes and Others   77

5. Lesser Men and Supermen   94

6. Primitives, Children, Madmen   118

7. Yellow, Red, and Black Men   147

   Illustrations   181

PART III: THE WAR IN JAPANESE EYES

8. The Pure Self   203

9. The Demonic Other   234

10. "Global Policy with the Yamato Race as Nucleus"   262

PART IV: EPILOGUE

11. From War to Peace   293

   Notes   319

   Bibliography   367

   Picture Credits   385

   Index   387

PREFACE

Some five years ago, while drafting the opening chapter to a projected book about the occupation of Japan that followed World War Two, I found myself mentioning in passing the race hates and merciless fighting that had been so conspicuous in the war in Asia and the Pacific. One of the impressive features of the occupation, after all, was that the defeated Japanese and victorious Allies, predominantly Americans, worked together so amicably and constructively. War-crimes trials were conducted after Japan's surrender; reports of wartime atrocities preoccupied journalists and jurists for many months; and there was hardly a corner of Japanese society that was not subjected to critical scrutiny. The war hates themselves, however, seemed to disappear almost overnight—so quickly, in fact, that they are easily forgotten now.

In a world that continues to experience so much violence and racial hatred, such a dramatic transformation from bitter enmity to genuine cooperation is heartening, and thus the fading memories of the war pose a paradox. It is fortunate that people on all sides can put such a terrible conflict behind them, but dangerous to forget how easily war came about between Japan and the Western Allies, and how extraordinarily fierce and Manichaean it was. We can never hope to understand the nature of World War Two in Asia, or international and interracial conflict in general, if we fail to work constantly at correcting and re-creating the historical memory. At a more modest level, the significance of the occupation of Japan and postwar rapprochement between the Japanese and their former enemies can only be appreciated against the background of burning passions and unbridled violence that preceded Japan's surrender in August 1945. The importance of remembering that visceral level of the war was what prompted my passing reference in that old draft manuscript on the occupation.

The casual mention of race hates seemed too abrupt to stand without elaboration, however, and my attempt to clarify what this meant marked the genesis of the present book. What occurred next may seem agonizingly familiar to many other historians. The passing comment was expanded to a paragraph, which grew into a section, then became a separate chapter, and finally emerged as a major research project in and of itself. This book is a summing up of some of the places to which this little "elaboration" has led—thus far. Meanwhile, the study of occupied Japan still sits unfinished on the shelf.

This is not the tidiest way to do history, but it is satisfying—for the problem arose naturally, more as a question than a thesis, and unfolded in unanticipated directions. To understand how racism influenced the conduct of the war in Asia has required going beyond the formal documents and battle reports upon which historians normally rely and drawing on materials such as songs, movies, cartoons, and a wide variety of popular as well as academic writings published at the time. In some academic circles these are not respectable sources, and they are certainly difficult to handle. But they are invaluable for re-creating the ethos which underlay the attitudes and actions of men and women during these years. The greatest challenge has not been to recall the raw emotions of the war, however, but rather to identify dynamic patterns in the torrent of war words and graphic images—and to bring such abstractions to earth by demonstrating how stereotyped and often blatantly racist thinking contributed to poor military intelligence and planning, atrocious behavior, and the adoption of exterminationist policies. Beyond this lay a further challenge: to explain how the contempt and hatred of the war years could have been dissipated so easily.

Because distorted perceptions and unrestrained violence occurred on all sides, the Pacific War also provides an excellent opportunity to look at racism and war comparatively—and, as the reader will discover, historically. Eventually, the exegesis on a passing comment led to an examination of perceptions of Self and Other in conflicts between "white" and "colored" peoples dating back to the fifteenth century. At the same time, it became apparent that many of the idioms of "race," on both the

Western and the Japanese sides, are best understood in a larger context of hierarchical and authoritarian thinking. In the war in Asia—and in general—considerations of race and power are inseparable. As it turned out, much that may at first glance appear to be unique in the clash between Japan and the West in the early 1940s was, on the contrary, familiar in practice and formulaic in the ways it was expressed. And much of the explanation of how race hate gave way to an inequitable but harmonious relationship between victors and vanquished lies in appreciating the malleability of political language and imagery in general.

In pursuing the meaning of race hate in such a variety of directions, I have incurred many personal debts. Several are outstanding. Takako Kishima provided invaluable assistance in assembling materials pertaining to Japanese perceptions of themselves and others during the war, and some of the ideas in the Japan chapters—most notably the symbolic wartime use of the "Momotarō" folktale—emerged out of discussions with her. Tom Engelhardt, a friend since student days, proved the best of friends as the editor of this manuscript, for he was severe in his critical comments and generous with his time. Several major sections of the present text were completely revised, or written from scratch, in response to his questions and suggestions. Herbert Bix, who has frequently made me rethink Japanese history, called my attention to the recently discovered secret Japanese government study which became the basis of chapter 10. I was able to explore the world of wartime Japanese cartoons through the generosity of Rinjirō Sodei, who allowed me to copy his collection of wartime issues of the magazines *Manga* and *Osaka Puck*. In the time-consuming task of tracking down pertinent materials from the English-language media and other library resources, I was ably assisted by Julie Bogle and Ken Munz. Yoko Yasuhara provided me with some requested archival materials from Washington.

Over the years, many individuals offered references, suggestions, critical comments, and assistance of one sort or another which also left a mark on the final manuscript. For such help I am grateful to Thomas Archdeacon, Sonja Arntzen, David Bordwell, Paul Boyer, William Brown, Roger Daniels, Daniel Doeppers, Susan Friedman, Mikiso Hane, Milan Hauner, Draper Hill, J. Vernon Jensen, Sandy Kita, Stanley Kutler, Yusheng Lin, Edward Linenthal, James Lorence, Genji Ōkubo, Eric Van Young, Chieu Vu, and Morio Watanabe. Fred Wiemer saved me from several errors with his careful copy editing. For clerical help, I am indebted, again, to Julie Bogle, as well as Karen Delwiche, Catherine Ganshert, Sandra Heitzkey, Kathleen Kisselburgh, and the office staff in general in the Department of History in Madison. Although the end notes reveal my academic debts, it seems appropriate to acknowledge here in one place those authors whose work on racism or the war in Asia has been especially suggestive. Readers who wish to place this present study in an appropriately broader context will find much of interest in the writings of Louis Allen, John Costello, Roger Daniels, George De Vos, Richard Drinnon, Stephen Jay Gould, Saburō Ienaga, Akira Iriye, Stuart Creighton Miller, Richard Minear, Ben-Ami Shillony, Ronald Spector, Christopher Thorne, John Toland, and Hiroshi Wagatsuma.

Finally, as always, I thank my wife, Yasuko. This one, by its nature, was harder than usual.

J.W.D.

Madison, Wisconsin
January 5, 1986

With the exception of these acknowledgments, Japanese personal names are rendered in Japanese order throughout the text, that is, family name followed by given name.

P A R T I
ENEMIES

◄ C H A P T E R 1 ►
PATTERNS OF A RACE WAR

World War Two meant many things to many people.

To over fifty million men, women, and children, it meant death. To hundreds of millions more in the occupied areas and theaters of combat, the war meant hell on earth: suffering and grief, often with little if any awareness of a cause or reason beyond the terrifying events of the moment.

To nations everywhere, World War Two meant technological innovation, bureaucratic expansion, and an extraordinary mobilization of human resources and ideological fervor. Governments on all sides presented the conflict as a holy war for national survival and glory, a mission to defend and propagate the finest values of their state and culture. The Axis powers declared they were creating a virile new world order that both revitalized traditional virtues and "transcended the modern," as some Japanese intellectuals phrased it. Allied leaders rallied their people under the banner of combating tyranny and oppression and defending an ideal moral order, exemplified by the Atlantic Charter and Franklin Roosevelt's "four freedoms." Many individuals gave their lives in the belief that they were sacrificing themselves for such ideals.

At the same time, to most high officials the war meant, above all, power politics at its fiercest. World War Two changed the face of the globe. It witnessed the rise and fall and rise again of empires—the swiftly shifting fortunes of the European powers and the Axis allies, the emergence of the American and Soviet superpowers—and no policymaker was unaware of the stakes involved. Control of territory, markets, natural resources, and other peoples always lay close to the heart of prewar and wartime planning. This was certainly true of the war in Asia, where nationalist aspirations for genuine liberation and independence met resistance from Europeans, Americans, and Japanese alike. In Asia, the global war became entangled with the legacies of Western imperialism and colonialism in a manner that proved explosive, not only at the time but for decades thereafter.

To scores of millions of participants, the war was also a race war. It exposed raw prejudices and was fueled by racial pride, arrogance, and rage on many sides. Ultimately, it brought about a revolution in racial consciousness throughout the world that continues to the present day. Because World War Two was many wars, occurring at different levels and in widely separated places, it is impossible to describe it with a single phrase; and to speak of the global conflict as a race war is to speak of only one of its many aspects. Nonetheless, it is a critical aspect which has rarely been examined systematically.[1]

Apart from the genocide of the Jews, racism remains one of the great neglected subjects of World War Two. We can gain an impression of its importance, however, by asking a simple question: when and where did race play a significant role in the war? The query may seem to border on the simplistic, but it turns out to have no simple answer—not even for the Holocaust. As has become more widely acknowledged in recent years, the destruction of European Jewry itself was neither an isolated event nor a peculiarly Nazi atrocity. The German extermination campaign was not limited to Jews but extended to other "undesirable" peoples as well. At the same time, there occurred a "hidden Holocaust"—that is, a conveniently forgotten one—in which the annihilation of the Jews was actively supported by French and Dutch citizens, Poles, Hungarians, Rumanians, Slovaks, Ukrainians, Lithuanians, and Latvians. It is now also well documented that anti-Semitism in the United States and Great Britain prevented both countries from doing as much as they could have to publicize these genocidal policies or to mount a serious rescue campaign.[2]

The blatant racism of the Nazis had a twofold impact in the anti-Axis camp. On the one hand, it provoked a sustained critique of "master-race" arguments in general, with a wide range of Western scientists and intellectuals lending the weight of their reputations to the repudiation of pseudoscientific theories concerning the inherently superior or inferior capabilities of different races. At the same time, this critique of Nazi racism had a double edge, for it exposed the hypocrisy of the Western Allies. Anti-Semitism was but one manifestation of the racism that existed at all levels in the United States and the United Kingdom. Even while denouncing Nazi theories of "Aryan" supremacy, the U.S. government presided over a society where blacks were subjected to demeaning Jim Crow laws, segregation was imposed even in the military establishment, racial discrimination extended to the defense industries, and immigration policy was severely biased against all nonwhites. In the wake of Pearl Harbor, these anti-"colored" biases were dramatically displayed in yet another way: the summary incarceration of over 110,000 Japanese-Americans.

Such discrimination provided grist for the propaganda mills of the Axis. The Germans pointed to the status of blacks in America as proof of the validity of their dogma as well as the hollowness of Allied attacks on Nazi beliefs. The Japanese, acutely sensitive to "color" issues from an entirely different perspective, exploited every display of racial conflict in the United States in their appeals to other Asians (while necessarily ignoring the white supremacism of their German ally). Racism within the Allied camp was, however, a volatile issue in and of itself regardless of what enemy propagandists said. Although only a few individuals spoke up on behalf of the persecuted Japanese-Americans, both the oppression of blacks and the exclusion of Asian immigrants became political issues in wartime America. Blacks raised questions about "fighting for the white folks," and called for "double victory" at home and abroad. Asians, especially Chinese and Indians, decried the humiliation of being allied to a country which deemed them unfit for citizenship; and for a full year in the midst of the war, the U.S. Congress debated the issue of revising the suddenly notorious Oriental exclusion laws. In such ways, World War Two contributed immeasurably not only to a sharpened awareness of racism within the United States, but also to more radical demands and militant tactics on the part of the victims of discrimination.

This was equally true abroad, especially in Asia, where the Allied struggle against Japan exposed the racist underpinnings of the European and American colonial structure. Japan did not invade independent countries in southern Asia. It invaded colonial outposts which the Westerners had dominated for generations, taking absolutely for granted their racial and cultural superiority over their Asian subjects. Japan's belated emergence as a dominant power in Asia, culminating in the devastating "advance south" of 1941–42, challenged not just the Western presence but the entire mystique of white supremacism on which centuries of European and American expansion had rested. This was clear to all from an early date: to the Japanese; to the imperiled European and American colonials; and, not least, to the politically, economically, and culturally subjugated peoples of Asia.[3]

Japan's Pan-Asiatic slogans played upon these sentiments, and the favorable response of many Asians to the initial Japanese victories against the Americans, British, and Dutch intensified Western presentiments of an all-out race war in Asia. In China, the Japanese had persuaded Wang Ching-wei, formerly a respected nationalist leader, to head their puppet government. After Pearl Harbor, Indian and Burmese patriots both formed independent nationalist armies in collaboration with the Japanese, while in Indonesia pro-Japanese sentiments were expressed by the rousing triple slogan of the so-called AAA movement: Japan the Leader of Asia, Japan the Protector of Asia, Japan the Light of Asia. In the highly publicized Assembly of the Greater East Asiatic Nations convened in Tokyo in November 1943, a succession of Asian leaders voiced support for Japan and placed the war in an East-versus-West, Oriental-versus-Occidental, and ultimately blood-versus-blood context. Thus, Burma's passionately outspoken leader Ba Maw told delegates to the conference, "My Asiatic blood has always called to other Asiatics," and declared that his dreams of Asiatic solidarity had at long last become reality. "This is not the time to think with our minds," Ba Maw exclaimed; "this is the time to think with our blood, and it is this thinking with the blood that has brought me all the way from Burma to Japan." The Burmese prime minister spoke repeatedly of the solidarity of "a thousand million Asiatics," a vision also evoked by other Asian leaders.[4]

Burma and the Philippines, long colonies of Britain and the United States respectively, were granted nominal independence by Japan in 1943. Occupied Indonesia was later also given independence, although the quick end of the war made the transfer of authority untidy. The Tokyo conference of November 1943 was designed to be an inspiring symbol of Pan-Asian idealism and the demise of white colonial rule in Asia; and although it was ultimately a hollow exercise, it fueled both Asian racial dreams and Western racial fears. Officials in the West took the rhetoric of Asian solidarity painfully to heart. During the first year of the war, for example, Admiral Ernest King worried about the repercussions of Japanese victories "among the non-white world" while Roosevelt's chief of staff Admiral William Leahy wrote in his diary about the fear that Japan might "succeed in combining most of the Asiatic peoples against the whites." William Phillips, Roosevelt's personal emissary to India in 1943, sent back deeply pessimistic reports about a rising "color consciousness" that seemed to be creating an insurmountable barrier between Oriental and Occidental peoples. In March 1945, a month before he died, President Roosevelt evoked in a negative way much the same image of Pan-Asian solidarity that the Asian leaders had emphasized in Tokyo in 1943. "1,100,000,000 potential enemies," the president told a confidant, "are dangerous."[5]

The media in the West were frequently even more apocalyptic in their expression of such fears. Thus, the Hearst newspapers declared the war in Asia totally different from that in Europe, for Japan was a "racial menace" as well as a cultural and religious one, and if it proved victorious in the Pacific there would be "perpetual war between Oriental ideals and Occidental." Popular writers described the war against Japan as "a holy war, a racial war of greater significance than any the world has heretofore seen." Spokesmen for the cause of China and a free Asia like Pearl Buck and Lin Yutang were so appalled and alarmed by the way Westerners instinctively saw the fight against Japan in sweeping racial terms that they warned of a Third World War between whites and nonwhites within a generation.

In fact, Pan-Asian unity was a myth, albeit a myth that died hard for all sides. In the end, their own oppressive behavior toward other Asians earned the Japanese more hatred than support. Ba Maw, dreamer of Asian blood calling to Asian blood, eventually became a bitter, scathing critic of Japanese "brutality, arrogance, and racial pretensions"; in his disillusion, as in his dreams, he was typical. As a symbol of Asian audacity, defiance, and—fleetingly—strength vis-à-vis the West, the Japanese commanded admiration throughout Asia. As the self-designated leaders of the Greater East Asia Co-Prosperity Sphere, however, they proved to be as overweening as the Westerners had been before them, and in many instances even more harsh: dominating the political scene, taking over local economies, imposing broad programs of "Japanization," slapping non-Japanese in public, torturing and executing dissidents, exploiting native labor so severely that between 1942 and 1945 the death toll among such workers numbered in the hundreds of thousands. Untold millions of Asian civilians died during the brief existence of the Co-Prosperity Sphere —from fighting, atrocities, disastrous labor and economic policies, and the starvation and disease that followed the war destruction. To some critics, this oppression reflected the fascist nature of the Japanese state. To some, it was better understood as the desperate reflex of an overly ambitious imperialist power that had arrived late on the scene. Still other critics argued that Japanese behavior betrayed a racial supremacism as virulent in its own way as the master-race theories of the Nazis.[6]

That there was a decidedly racist component to the very conception of the Co-Prosperity Sphere is indisputable. Although the Japanese government frequently admonished its officials and citizens to avoid all manifestations of racial discrimination, the operative language of the new sphere was in fact premised on the belief that the Japanese were destined to preside over a fixed hierarchy of peoples and races. An Imperial Army document from the summer of 1942, for example, divided the nationalities of Asia into "master races," "friendly races," and "guest races," reserving the position of undisputed leadership for the "Yamato race." A massive secret study prepared in the civilian bureaucracy in 1942–43 was entitled "Global Policy with the Yamato Race as Nucleus," and expatiated upon the destiny of the Japanese as the "leading race" in Asia and implicitly the world. The Co-Prosperity Sphere, it was argued there, would contribute in both material and psychological ways to maintaining that superiority "eternally." For the Japanese, Pan-Asianism was thus a hydra-headed ideology, involving not merely a frontal attack on the Western colonial powers and their values but also discrimination vis-à-vis the other races, nationalities, and cultures of Asia.[7]

When the struggle in Asia is taken into consideration, it becomes apparent that neither anti-Semitism nor white supremacism in its wider manifestations suffices to illuminate the full impact of racism during World War Two. In the United States and Britain, the Japanese were more hated than the Germans before as well as after Pearl Harbor. On this, there was no dispute among contemporary observers. They were perceived as a race apart, even a species apart—and an overpoweringly monolithic one at that. There was no Japanese counterpart to the "good German" in the popular consciousness of the Western Allies. At the same time, the Japanese themselves dwelled at inordinate length on their own racial and cultural superiority, and like their adversaries, who practiced discrimination while proclaiming they were "fighting for democracy," they too became entangled in a web of contradictions: creating new colonial hierarchies while preaching liberation; singing the glories of their unique Imperial Way while professing to support a broad and all-embracing Pan-Asianism.

The racist code words and imagery that accompanied the war in Asia were often exceedingly graphic and contemptuous. The Western Allies, for example, persisted in their notion of the "subhuman" nature of the Japanese, routinely turning to images of apes and vermin to convey this. With more tempered disdain, they portrayed the Japanese as inherently inferior men and women who had to be understood in terms of primitivism, childishness, and collective mental and emotional deficiency. Cartoonists, songwriters, filmmakers, war correspondents, and the mass media in general all seized on these images—and so did the social scientists and Asia experts who ventured to analyze the Japanese "national character" during the war. At a very early stage in the conflict, when the purportedly inferior Japanese swept through colonial Asia like a whirlwind and took several hundred thousand Allied prisoners, another stereotype took hold: the Japanese superman, possessed of uncanny discipline and fighting skills. Subhuman, inhuman, lesser human, superhuman—all that was lacking in the perception of the Japanese enemy was a human like oneself. An endless stream of evidence ranging from atrocities to suicidal tactics could be cited, moreover, to substantiate the belief that the Japanese were a uniquely contemptible and formidable foe who deserved no mercy and virtually demanded extermination.

The formulaic expressions and graphic visual images which the Japanese relied on to distinguish themselves from others were, on the surface, quite different. Their leaders and ideologues constantly affirmed their unique "purity" as a race and culture, and turned the war itself—and eventually mass death—into an act of individual and collective purification. Americans and Europeans existed in the wartime Japanese imagination as vivid monsters, devils, and demons; and one had only to point to the bombing of Japanese cities (or the lynching of blacks in America) to demonstrate the aptness of this metaphor. In explaining their destiny as the "leading race," the Japanese also fell back upon theories of "proper place" which had long been used to legitimize inequitable relationships within Japan itself.

These dominant perceptions of the enemy on both the Allied and Japanese sides, intriguing in themselves, become even more interesting when it is recognized that they all existed independently of the conflict in Asia. Indeed, both the stereotypes and the explanations used to justify them really had little to do with Americans, Englishmen, Australians, Japanese, or other Asian nationalities per se. They were archetypical images associated with inequitable human relations in general, and their roots traced back centuries on both sides. Where the Western Allies were concerned, the visceral hatred of the Japanese inevitably tapped Yellow Peril sentiments that, before the turn of the century, had been directed mainly against the Chinese. The coarseness and pervasiveness of plain anti–"yellow" race hate throughout the war is as shocking in retrospect as is the popularity of simian imagery; but the Yellow Peril sentiment was itself rooted in earlier centuries. The war words and race words which so dominated the propaganda of Japan's white enemies—the core imagery of apes, lesser men, primitives, children, madmen, and beings who possessed special powers as well—have a pedigree in Western thought that can be traced back to Aristotle, and were conspicuous in the earliest encounters of Europeans with the black peoples of Africa and the Indians of the Western Hemisphere. The Japanese, so "unique" in the rhetoric of World War Two, were actually saddled with racial stereotypes that Europeans and Americans had applied to nonwhites for centuries: during the conquest of the New World, the slave trade, the Indian wars in the United States, the agitation against Chinese immigrants in America, the colonization of Asia and Africa, the U.S. conquest of the Philippines at the turn of the century. These were stereotypes, moreover, which had been strongly reinforced by nineteenth-century Western science.

In the final analysis, in fact, these favored idioms denoting superiority and inferiority transcended race and represented formulaic expressions of Self and Other in general; and this was the case on the Japanese side as well. The Japanese found "proper place" in the Confucian classics they inherited from China, and their notions of "purity" in the rituals of the indigenous Shinto religion. Less obviously, their response to the Americans and Europeans also was strongly influenced by folk beliefs concerning strangers, outsiders, and ambiguous gods or demons whose powers could be either beneficent or destructive. During the war, the Japanese even turned one of their most beloved folk tales into a parable of Japanese destiny and a paradigm of race relations.[8]

These neglected aspects of the war in Asia do more than illuminate general patterns of racial and martial thinking. They also are a reminder of how merciless the conflict was. It was a common observation among Western war correspondents that the fighting in the Pacific was more savage than in the European theater. Kill or be killed. No quarter, no surrender. Take no prisoners. Fight to the bitter end. These were everyday words in the combat areas, and in the final year of the war such attitudes contributed to an orgy of bloodletting that neither side could conceive of avoiding, even though by mid-1944 Japan's defeat was inevitable and plain to see. As World War Two recedes in time and scholars dig at the formal documents, it is easy to forget the visceral emotions and sheer race hate that gripped virtually all participants in the war, at home and overseas, and influenced many actions and decisions at the time. Prejudice and racial stereotypes frequently distorted both Japanese and Allied evaluations of the enemy's intentions and capabilities. Race hate fed atrocities, and atrocities in turn fanned the fires of race hate. The dehumanization of the Other contributed immeasurably to the psychological distancing that facilitates killing, not only on the battlefield but also in the plans adopted by strategists far removed from the actual scene of combat. Such dehumanization, for example, surely facilitated the decisions to make civilian populations the targets of concentrated attack, whether by conventional or nuclear weapons. In countless ways, war words and race words came together in a manner which did not just reflect the savagery of the war, but contributed to it by reinforcing the impression of a truly Manichaean struggle between completely incompatible antagonists. The natural response to such a vision was an obsession with extermination on both sides—a war without mercy.

And yet, despite this, the two sides did have things in common, including not only race hate and martial fury but also battlefield courage and dreams of peace. "Proper-place" theorizing was hardly alien to Western ways of thinking, which also viewed the world in terms of status, inequality, and a hierarchical division of labor and reward. Purity and purification through battle, so conspicuous a part of the carefully cultivated mystique of the Yamato race, were ideals frequently espoused in the West and elsewhere in Asia, where ideologues of the political left and right launched campaigns against spiritual pollution, patriots burned with ardor at the prospects of a holy war, and militarists extolled the purifying nature of life-and-death struggle.[9] No side had a monopoly on attributing "beastliness" to the other, although the Westerners possessed a more intricate web of metaphors with which to convey this.

Even the most basic attitudes toward life and death, which many participants in the war claimed were fundamentally different among Japanese and Westerners, prove on closer scrutiny not to have been so drastically unalike. Many Japanese fighting men died instead of surrendering because they had little choice in the matter, owing not only to pressure from their own side but also to the disinterest of the Allies in taking prisoners. After the initial wave of humiliating Allied defeats and mass surrenders, Allied fighting men also almost never surrendered voluntarily. Indeed, the kill-or-be-killed nature of combat in the Pacific soon made personal decisions about living or dying almost irrelevant for combatants on either side. It is true that Japanese commanders and ideologues attempted with considerable success to make a cult out of dying, as seen in the frenzied banzai charges of imperial land forces in certain battles and the creation of special suicide squads such as the kamikaze in the final year of the war. But Westerners also glorified those who fought to the bitter end, and in several instances Allied leaders at the highest level, including Winston Churchill and Douglas MacArthur, actually ordered their commanders never to surrender.[10] Even as Americans were belittling Japanese who fought to the last man, treating them as virtually another species of being, they were cherishing their own epics of defeat such as the Alamo and the Little Bighorn. On the eve of Pearl Harbor one of Hollywood's most popular offerings was *They Died with Their Boots On,* an Errol Flynn movie commemorating Custer's last stand.

In the heat of war, such points of common ground were lost sight of and the behavior of the enemy was seen as unique and peculiarly odious, with the issue of atrocities playing an exceptionally large role in each side's perception of the other. Savage Japanese behavior in China and throughout Southeast Asia, as well as in the treatment of Allied prisoners, was offered as proof of the inherent barbarity of the enemy. In a similar way, the Japanese stimulated hatred of the Allies by publicizing grisly battlefield practices such as the collection of Japanese skulls and bones, and responded with profound self-righteousness to the terror bombing of Japanese civilians. It is conventional wisdom that in times of life-and-death struggle, ill-grounded rumors of enemy atrocities invariably flourish and arouse a feverish hatred against the foe. This is misleading, however, for in fact atrocities follow war as the jackal follows a wounded beast. The propagandistic deception often lies, not in the false claims of enemy atrocities, but in the pious depiction of such behavior as peculiar to the other side. There is room for debate over the details of alleged incidents of atrocity in the war in Asia; room for discussion about the changing definition of legitimate targets of war; room for argument concerning how new technologies of firepower and air power may have altered the meaning of atrocity in the modern world. However, just as no one can return to Custer and the Little Bighorn any more without observing how vicious the fighting was on both sides, so it is also necessary to acknowledge that atrocious behavior occurred on all sides in the Pacific War. Such acts, and the propagandizing of them, became part of the vicious circle of war hates and race hates and contributed to the deaths of hundreds of thousands of individuals—millions, if the civilian deaths of the Japanese as well as other Asians are counted—long after Japan's defeat was a foregone conclusion.

In these various ways, the "patterns of a race war" become like a palimpsest that continually reveals unexpected and hitherto obscured layers of experience. Centuries-old fragments of language and imagery are pulled to the surface. Harsh words are seen to be inseparable from the harshest of all acts: war and killing. What passes for empirical observation is revealed to be permeated with myth, prejudice, and wishful thinking. A category as seemingly tight as "race" is shown to overflow into categories pertaining to "others" in general.

As the war years themselves changed over into an era of peace between Japan and the Allied powers, the shrill racial rhetoric of the early 1940s revealed itself to be surprisingly adaptable. Idioms that formerly had denoted the unbridgeable gap between oneself and the enemy proved capable of serving the goals of accommodation as well: to the victors, the simian became a pet, the child a pupil, the madman a patient. In Japan, purity was now identified with peaceful rather than martial pursuits, and with the purge of corrupt militaristic and feudalistic influences rather than decadent Western bourgeois values as had been the case during the war. Victory confirmed the Allies' assumptions of superiority, while the ideology of "proper place" enabled the Japanese to adjust to being a good loser. Even the demonic Other, that most popular Japanese image of the American and British enemy, posed no obstacle to the transition from enmity to amicable relations as Japan quickly moved under the U.S. military aegis; for the archetypical demon of Japanese folklore had always had two faces, being not only a destructive presence but also a potentially protective and tutelary being.

To a conspicuous degree, the racial and racist ways of thinking which had contributed so much to the ferociousness of the war were sublimated and transformed after August 1945. The merciless struggle for control of Asia and the Pacific gave way, in a remarkably short time, to an occupation in which mercy was indeed displayed by the conquerors, and generosity and goodwill characterized many of the actions of victor and vanquished alike. That vicious racial stereotypes were transformed, however, does not mean that they were dispelled. They remain latent, capable of being revived by both sides in times of crisis and tension. At the same time, these patterns of thinking also were transferred laterally and at-tached to the new enemies of the cold-war era: the Soviets and Chinese Communists, the Korean foe of the early 1950s, the Vietnamese enemy of the 1960 and 1970s, and hostile third-world movements in general. The patterns persist, even as specific circumstances change. They are only part of the picture, but still a telling and potentially tragic part.

◄ **C H A P T E R 2** ►
"KNOW YOUR ENEMY"

Shortly after the United States entered World War Two, Army Chief of Staff George C. Marshall summoned Frank Capra, the Hollywood director, and asked him to prepare a series of orientation films for viewing by American troops. When Capra demurred on the grounds that he had never made a documentary before, Marshall retorted: "Capra, I have never been Chief of Staff before. Thousands of young Americans have never had their legs shot off before. Boys are commanding ships today, who a year ago had never seen the ocean before." The director apologized, and promised "the best damned documentary films ever made."[1]

The films subsequently produced for the Army by Capra and his team survive as classics of wartime cinematic propaganda—a remarkable accomplishment, in retrospect, since each script eventually had to be approved by some fifty military and civilian agencies in Washington. One of the primary objectives of the series was to combat the isolationist sentiments that lingered in the United States, and with this in mind the seven core films that Capra directed were given the collective title *Why We Fight.* President Franklin Roosevelt was so impressed by the first of these documentaries that he urged it to be shown in public theaters as well as to recruits. This was done, and *Prelude to War* went on to win an Academy Award as the best documentary of 1942. During the course of World War Two, the *Why We Fight* films were required viewing for millions of American soldiers. The series was also distributed abroad, with soundtracks in French, Spanish, Russian, and Chinese.[2]

In a memorandum to one of his aides when the project was still in the planning stage, Capra stated that there were two overriding objectives to the films: to win the war and win the peace. And he quickly hit upon a simple working motto that decisively shaped the style and texture of the films: "Let the enemy prove to our soldiers the enormity of his cause—and the justness of ours." Capra also expressed this more colloquially. "Let our boys hear the Nazis and the Japs shout their own claims of master-race crud," he declared, and our fighting men will *know* why they are in uniform."[3]

What this meant was that extensive use would be made of the enemy's own words and the enemy's own graphics as these were available in the form of confiscated or captured newsreels, propaganda films, commercial movies, and the like. Capra was known for his boldness in the cutting room and his fondness for contrast and counterpoint; the difference now was that he was working with footage taken by others, and indeed in good part by the enemy. He proceeded to collect millions of feet of enemy film, to cut and edit this until the expressions of the Axis powers became lean anti-Axis images, and to juxtapose the menacing faces and words of the enemy against the bright hope and accomplishments of the American people and their allies.

To be inspired with the will to win, Capra told his associates as they embarked on this work, Americans needed to be shown that they were fighting for the existence of their country, and at the same time were carrying the "torch of freedom" for a better postwar world—a world in which conquest, exploitation, and economic evils had been eliminated, and peace and democracy prevailed. This seemed a clear line, and a familiar one to anyone who recalled the idealistic Allied propaganda of World War One. A team of seven Hollywood writers was asked to prepare rough scenarios for a sequence of films conveying this message.

Although the assignment seemed straightforward enough, the draft outlines Capra received upset him greatly, for in his eyes they were "larded with Communist propaganda." He quietly dismissed the seven writers and began again, and *Prelude to War* was the first product of the second start. Although the writers deemed leftists had been dismissed, the film took its basic theme from a speech by one of the most conspicuously progressive political figures on the American scene, Vice President Henry Wallace. The theme, the heart of American propaganda, was that two worlds were locked in mortal combat, the free world and the slave. The corollary, stated outright in this and the later films, was that the enemy was bent on global conquest. One remarkable contrived scene in *Prelude to War* actually depicted "the conquering Jap army" marching down Pennsylvania Avenue in Washington, D.C. "You will see what they did to the men and women of Nanking, Hong Kong, and Manila," viewers were warned. "Imagine the field day they'd enjoy if they marched through the streets of Washington."[4]

This was potent imagery and rhetoric, unambiguous and uncompromising—and yet, as time would prove, free-floating, capable of being turned against other enemies when the winds of war shifted direction. In *Prelude to War*, the "two worlds" were illustrated as literally as can be imagined by drawings of two globes, one black and the other white. The narrative voice here and in all the other orientation films drove home the same message with repeated references to the irreconcilable conflict of "freedom versus slavery," "civilization against barbarism," "good against evil," the Allied "way of life" as opposed to the Axis "way of death," the historic march of democracy and freedom among the Allied nations, including China and the Soviet Union, as opposed to the historic ambition for world conquest seen in Germany and Japan. One of the previews of *Prelude to War* prepared by its producers as a teaser for commercial theaters epitomized the essence of this wedding of Hollywood and the U.S. Army. Here, the trailer exclaimed, was "55 minutes of Democracy's Dynamite! . . . the greatest gangster movie ever filmed . . . the inside story of how the mobsters plotted to grab the world! More vicious . . . more diabolical . . . more horrible than any horror-movie you ever saw!"[5] The only conceivable response to such total evil was total destruction.

In these grandest of overviews, Japan, Germany, and Italy were hardly to be distinguished. They were the slave world, whose histories were swollen with lust for conquest, whose leaders were madmen, and whose people were a subservient mass, "a human herd." Overall, however, the *Why We Fight* films reflected the strategic priorities of the U.S. government and focused primarily on the struggle in the West. Only one film in the series was devoted exclusively to the war in Asia. Titled *The Battle of China* and completed in 1944, this was an epic paean to the resistance of the Chinese people against Japan's aggression. ("One fact was obvious," viewers were told, "China was to be the giant back on which Japan would ride to world conquest.") The Capra touch was displayed in striking scenes of Chinese dignity and heroism amidst an orgy of Japanese destruction and atrocity, and such counterpoint was heightened by a commentary in which Japan's rhetoric of "co-existence and co-prosperity" was recited while the screen showed the devastation of China's cities and the mutilated corpses of its men, women, and children. Viewed by some critics as Capra's most exaggerated portrayal of pure good versus pure evil, *The Battle of China* was temporarily withdrawn because it omitted any mention whatsoever of problems among the Chinese themselves. It was soon returned to circulation, however, and seen by close to four million people before the end of the war.[6]

In 1945, when the *Why We Fight* series was completed and the war in Europe drawing to a close, the Capra team finally turned its full attention to the enemy in Asia. The result again was a film that was withdrawn from circulation, but this time for an entirely different reason. *Know Your Enemy—Japan* was released on August 9, the day Nagasaki was bombed, and withdrawn on August 28, two weeks after Japan had surrendered, upon orders from General Douglas MacArthur's headquarters. Only decades later, in the 1970s, was it exhumed as a "lost" propaganda masterpiece. And a masterpiece it surely is. The late date at which the film was completed may have aborted its usefulness at the time, but makes it all the more valuable in retrospect. For good reason, it has been praised by cinema buffs as a technical tour de force, the crowning accomplishment of over three years spent refining the propagandist's craft.[7] In addition, it is of inestimable value to anyone who seeks to recreate the composite portrait of the Japanese that had emerged in the United States and England by 1945.

Despite its late appearance, *Know Your Enemy—Japan* was not an afterthought. The first script for the film was actually drafted in June 1942. The full explanation for the inordinately long time between start and finish remains obscure, but the delay derived in considerable part from uncertainty and controversy about who the enemy in Japan really was: should the film focus more on the Japanese people or their leaders? Capra as well as the military authorities responsible for approving the script supported the former approach, while some of the scriptwriters were more inclined to emphasize the role of Japan's militaristic leaders, among whom they included the emperor. To the project's more liberal contributers, the attitude promoted by the Army and Frank Capra seemed to border at times on sheer racism.

One early casualty of this disagreement was the Dutch filmmaker Joris Ivens, who had been hired by Capra in the spring of 1942 to produce

the Japan documentary. Ivens' presence in Capra's entourage seemed odd
from the start, since he was known for having produced such left-wing
films as the 1937 documentary *Spanish Earth,* and he lasted with the
project only until the following autumn. By his own account, Ivens was
fired on orders from Washington after producing a script which presented
the emperor as a war criminal and suggested he should be executed after
the war. Over the course of the next year or so, the War Department
rejected a number of draft scripts which attempted to portray the Japanese as ordinary humans victimized by their leaders, and as late as February 1945 the Pentagon was still blue-penciling scripts on the grounds that
the passages in question would evoke "too much sympathy for the Jap
people." As a result of such editing, references to "free-thinking" Japanese were all but deleted from the final shooting script, as were detailed
allusions to specific leaders; on the other hand, greater emphasis was given
to the obedience of the Japanese, their homogeneity, and their sense of
divine mission. Still, the victory of the hard-liners was not a complete one.
Traces of this behind-the-scenes struggle—glimmerings of a more sympathetic approach to the Japanese common people as opposed to their
leaders—can still be discerned, however faintly, in the final product.[8]

Know Your Enemy—Japan followed Capra's rule of thumb (Let the
enemy speak for himself) in an exceptionally evocative manner, for it drew
extensively on original Japanese footage that included not only conventional newsreels and captured propaganda films, but also a variety of
samurai movies and domestic dramas from the 1930s. There was an exotic
fascination in the raw stuff itself, and this was spliced and reassembled in
a montage that did not just set Japanese madmen against Allied torchbear-
ers of civilization, but moved within the Japanese scene to counterpose
the traditional against the modern, the war front against the home front.
Despite the patchwork way in which it had been written, or perhaps even
partly because of it, the narrative was terse and vivid. Beneath its dazzling
surface imagery, however, the message was simple, conveyed in a stark
metaphor and a striking visual image. The audience was told that the
Japanese resembled "photographic prints off the same negative." Visually,
this was reinforced by repeated scenes of a steel bar being hammered in
a forge.[9]

These were stereotypes of a familiar sort among Westerners, and the
Japanese films which the Capra team cannibalized provided ample scenes
of group activity and regimentation to reinforce the impression of a people
devoid of individual identity. The narrative referred to "an obedient mass

with but a single mind," although the point that Capra and the Army were hammering home was not that the Japanese were passive. Rather the collective will which moved the Japanese was shown to be fantastic and fanatic—riddled with the ghosts of history and dead ancestors, taut with emotional tensions, and fired by blind and relentless nationalistic ambitions. Writ small, the Japanese soldier epitomized this. Trained from birth to fight and die for his country, he was a disciplined, proud, and able fighter on the battlefield—and also given to "mad dog" orgies of brutality and atrocity. Writ large, nothing better illustrated the insanity of the collective Japanese mind than the current war, for Japan's single, unified ambition was described, as in the earlier Army films, as being nothing less than to rule the world.

　　Know Your Enemy—Japan was a potpourri of most of the English-speaking world's dominant clichés about the Japanese enemy, excluding the crudest, most vulgar, and most blatantly racist. The filmmakers adopted a strongly historical approach, offering a lengthy survey of those aspects of Japan's past which Westerners believed had made the Japanese a modern menace. They began as almost everyone began in those days, and many still do, with scenes of samurai, echoes of a disciplined killer past. The film then cut to a commentary on the Japanese mind, which was portrayed as being imprisoned in an ideological cage built of two unique elements: the Shinto religion (as perverted by the modern state) and belief in a divine emperor whose role was both sacred and secular. Out of this Shinto-emperor amalgam came Japan's cult of racial superiority, its sense of holy mission, and its goal of placing the "eight corners of the world" under a Japanese roof (encapsuled in the slogan *hakko ichiū*). Warrior ideals of bravery and fanatic loyalty, as well as warrior practices of ruthlessness and treachery, were traced back to the emergence of feudal society around the twelfth century. The lust for overseas conquest was garishly illuminated by the invasion of Korea ordered in the late sixteenth century by Hideyoshi, the megalomaniac who ruled Japan (with the emperor as mere figurehead) and dreamed of an empire embracing Korea, China, and the Philippines. The invasion was abandoned when Hideyoshi died in 1598, leaving a ruined landscape in Korea and a grisly memento in Kyoto in the form of the "ear mound," which contained pickled ears and noses from forty thousand enemy corpses. This became part of the historic memory of the Japanese people, it was explained, an ember that remained alive, waiting only to be fanned into flame again. Three centuries later, that flame licked out: Japan struck against China in 1894 and embarked upon the course of conquest that led to Pearl Harbor.

For most of the three centuries between Hideyoshi and the new imperialism of 1894, the narrative continued, Japan slept, closed off from the outside world under the seclusion policy that was imposed by the Tokugawa shoguns and lasted until the 1850s. To the filmmakers, who followed the best contemporary Anglo-American scholars in this regard, the Tokugawa seclusion was not merely perverse; it was cataclysmic, for it twisted and retarded the development of Japanese society in a manner that made the current war in Asia all but inevitable. In closing their country's doors and windows, the Tokugawa rulers cut Japan off from the spiritual, political, and economic revolutions that shaped the modern world. They proscribed Christianity, with its "revolutionary doctrine of peace on earth," and froze the country in a feudal mold at the very moment when the West was embarking on its great democratic and industrial revolutions. Thus, when Commodore Matthew Perry prodded Japan out of its long slumber in 1853 (offering the hand of friendship in the interest of trade), Japan was woefully ill equipped to compete in the global arena of modern nation-states.

On the surface, for a half century or more, awakened Japan appeared to be modernizing internally and competing internationally with extraordinary speed and skill. This was, alas, but a "cruel joke," for beneath the facade of parliamentarianism and progress persisted feudalistic forms of oppressive control. The modernizing Japanese state was run by militarists (the first team), industrialists (the second team), and political elites (a weak third team of "stooges"). The individual was thoroughly subordinated to the state, with the whole educational system being geared to the mass production of obedient subjects who absorbed what they were told like sponges. Those mavericks and dissidents who managed to resist the stultifying brainwashing of the schools were knocked into line by the regular police, the military gendarmerie, the special thought-control gestapo, the vigilante thugs of the patriotic societies—and, indeed, by the myriad "ghosts" of Shinto and the emperor-system ideology.

Despite the description of the Japanese as prints off the same negative and the overwhelmingly dominant footage of regimentation, fanaticism, and brutality—all of which the U.S. Army insisted upon—the influence of Capra's more generous scriptwriters was apparent in portions of *Know Your Enemy—Japan* that extended sympathy to those at the lowest levels of the social ladder, above all the poor peasants. The film was especially attentive to the miserable plight of rural women, who as adolescents were often contracted out to factories or brothels, and whose assigned role as adults was little more than to perform as "human machines producing rice and soldiers." The comfort of the masses was of scant concern to Japan's modernizing elites, whose eyes were fixed on overseas conquest rather than raising the standard of living.

Abroad as well as at home, the Japanese moved swiftly. China was brought to its knees at the end of the nineteenth century, giving Japan its first colony: Formosa. Russia was humbled in the Russo-Japanese War of 1904–5, placing Japan in Korea and Manchuria. Korea was annexed in 1910. Participation in World War One on the side of the Allies gave the Japanese a seat as one of the victorious Big Five powers at the Paris Peace Conference, as well as control under a League of Nations mandate over the Pacific islands north of the equator formerly possessed by Germany; these were the Marianas, Marshalls, and Carolines, where some of the most terrible battles of the Pacific War would take place.

In retrospect, the film continued, it was clear that these territorial acquisitions were but the first courses on a greedy imperialist menu. It was only in the late 1920s and early 1930s, however, that the world became aware of Japan's insatiable appetite. The sensational Tanaka Memorial, said to have been submitted to the emperor by the prime minister in 1927, was described as "Japan's *Mein Kampf*" in the film, using a familiar comparison of the day. (Most scholars now agree that it was a masterful anti-Japanese hoax).[10] And the record of the final rush into global war was recorded with staccato clips from newsreels and newspaper headlines that most Westerners already had seen many times: Japan's takeover of northern China beginning with the Manchurian Incident of 1931; its withdrawal from the League of Nations in 1933; the China Incident and the Rape of Nanking in 1937; Pearl Harbor in 1941; the Bataan Death March in 1942; the wanton slaughter of civilians in Manila in 1945; the incredible suicide attacks by kamikaze planes in the battles for the Philippines and Okinawa. . . . At home, Japan became a frenzied nation, "turning sweat into weapons of war" and relentlessly forging, constantly hammering out, the most formidable weapon of all: the obedient, fanatical Japanese soldier. On this latter point—the Japanese soldier as Japan's supreme weapon—the documentary was in full accord with the Japanese propagandists themselves. The end, however, was clearly at hand, and the final frames of *Know Your Enemy—Japan* depicted a vast American armada closing in on the little nation of fanatics.

From all that had preceded, however, no American or Englishman could fail to understand that even after the war had been won, the task of winning the peace would remain formidable in Japan. Nothing less would suffice than to overthrow the whole legacy of centuries of militaristic and undemocratic development that had just flashed across the screen in a single, breathtaking hour. More than any other single source from the war years, *Know Your Enemy—Japan* thus captured the passions and presumptions that underlay not only the ferocity of the clash in Asia and the Pacific, but also the sweeping agenda of reformist policies that the Allied powers subsequently attempted to impose upon defeated and occupied Japan.[11]

But let us, in the moviemakers' idiom, fade to a different scene.

On New Year's Day of 1941, Colonel Tsuji Masanobu and a small intelligence unit of the Imperial Army stationed in Formosa began the immense task of preparing a report containing all information pertinent to a Japanese invasion of Southeast Asia. They were given six months to complete the assignment, and threw themselves into the job with great intensity—gathering information from a multitude of sources, undertaking personal reconnaissance missions, participating in practice maneuvers in Formosa, Kyushu, South China, and Hainan Island. Their findings were submitted to the General Staff in Tokyo around July, and provided the basis for the subsequent "move south" that brought about war between Japan and the Allied powers.

Included among the materials submitted to the General Staff was a seventy-page booklet written by Tsuji entitled *Read This and the War Is Won (Kore dake Yomeba Ware wa Kateru)*. Couched in simple, straightforward language, this was designed, as Tsuji put it, to be read by men lying on their backs on hot, crowded ships. All officers and enlisted men were given a copy immediately after embarking for the south, and tens of thousands of fighting men thus already had it in their hands before Pearl Harbor. *Read This and the War Is Won* explained not only how to behave in a tropical combat zone, but also why the Japanese had to fight there. This was, in its limited way, a Japanese counterpart to Frank Capra's *Why We Fight* propaganda—although the words were conspicuously different from the ones Capra selected in pursuing his policy of letting the enemy "speak for himself."[12]

While these activities were going on within the Japanese military, a separate project concerned with domestic indoctrination and morale was underway in the Japanese civilian bureaucracy. This reached the public in August 1941, when the Ministry of Education issued a major ideological manifesto entitled *The Way of the Subject (Shinmin no Michi)*.[13] *The Way of the Subject* told the Japanese who they were—or should aspire to be—as a people, nation, and race. At the same time, it offered a critical analysis of modern Western history and culture. In Japanese eyes, it was the non-Axis West that aimed at world domination and had been engaged in that quest, with conspicuous success, for centuries, and it was the value system of the modern West, rooted in acquisitiveness and self-gratification, that explained a large part of its bloody history of war and repression, culminating in the current world crisis. The Japanese thus read Western history in much the same way that Westerners were reading the history of Japan: as a chronicle of destructive values, exploitative practices, and brutal wars. The picture of the Anglo-American enemy presented here and in the Army pamphlet persisted through the war. Where revision occurred later—during the exhilarating early victories that followed Pearl Harbor, and then during the months of defensiveness and defeat that brought the Allies within bombing range of the Japanese homeland—it was in the direction of calling greater attention to Western hypocrisy and atrocities. The early Western defeats and quick surrenders revealed the flabbiness of Western society, Japanese at home were told. Later, the American bombing of Japanese cities was offered as proof beyond any conceivable question of the bestial nature of the enemy.

The southern region, embarking troops were informed in *Read This and the War Is Won*, was the treasure house of the Far East and a land of everlasting summer. It was also a place where a half million British ruled 350 million Indians, and another few score thousands of Englishmen ruled 6 million Malayans; where two hundred thousand Dutchmen governed a native population of 60 million in the East Indies; where twenty thousand Frenchmen controlled 23 million Indochinese, and a few tens of thousands of Americans ruled over 13 million Filipinos. Eight hundred thousand whites, the tally went, controlled 450 million Asians; if India was excluded, the count was 100 million oppressed by three hundred thousand. "Money squeezed from the blood of Asians maintains these small white minorities in their luxurious mode of life—or disappears to the respective home-countries," the Japanese soldiers were told. The white men were described as arrogant colonials who dwelled in splendid houses on mountainsides and hilltops, from which they looked down on the tiny thatched huts of the natives. They took it as their birthright to be allotted a score or so natives as personal slaves. Ties of blood and color linked the Japanese to these oppressed peoples of Asia. And because the latter had been all but emasculated by generations of colonial subjugation, it was left to Japan "to make men of them again" and lead them along the path of liberation.

Japan had already secured Manchuria against the ambitions of the Soviet Union and freed most of China from Anglo-American exploitation. The next objective was to assist Thailand, Indochina, and the Philippines in becoming independent, and likewise to bring freedom to the rest of Asia, including India—in short, to "liberate East Asia from white invasion and oppression." In the final analysis, this was "a struggle between races." At the same time, the southern advance also had a hard material rationale, for Japan could not survive without the oil, rubber, and tin of the area, and the Western powers were attempting to choke off this lifeline. Gaining control of the resources of the southern region, moreover, would enable Japan to strike a blow at the U.S. military machine by cutting off its access to rubber, tin, and tungsten. All this was a cause worth dying for, and each soldier was advised to prepare himself for this eventuality by writing a will before disembarking and enclosing with it, as a keepsake for relatives back home, a lock of hair and a fingernail paring. The bodies of the dead might never be recovered, but they would not have died in vain. Soldiers and sailors could find solace in a famous verse from the *Manyōshū*, the most ancient of the country's poetic anthologies:

> *Across the sea, corpses soaking in the water;*
> *Across the mountains, corpses heaped upon the grass.*
> *We shall die by the side of our lord.*
> *We shall never look back.*

So central was this sentiment that the poem was quoted not once but twice in Colonel Tsuji's text. And when Prime Minister Tōjō read the imperial rescript declaring war over the radio, his broadcast ended with the playing of the martial song *Umi Yukaba* (Across the Sea), which took as its lyrics the same poem.[14]

This was the preface to the practical instructions contained in *Read This and the War Is Won,* and the booklet was often recovered by Allied soldiers from the bodies of Japanese killed in the Southeast Asian theater —along with another idealistic item of standard issue, the *Field Service Code (Senjinkun)* first issued by the then minister of war, Tōjō Hideki, in January 1941.* *The Way of the Subject* went further in its critique of the enemy, placing the rapacity of the colonial powers in the larger historical context of Western imperialism, beginning with the earliest European voyages of discovery. The Japanese were informed that Western expansion was inspired partly by love of adventure, but more by desire for local resources as well as markets. And they were reminded that the heavy hand of the Occidental expansionists did not fall on Asians alone. Here the Ministry of Education posed two rhetorical questions that would remain effective propaganda to the end of the war: "How were American Indians treated? What about African Negroes?"

Part and parcel of such destructive avarice, *The Way of the Subject* continued, was a modern value system that emphasized individualism, materialism, utilitarianism, and liberalism—all ways of thinking that "regard the strong preying on the weak as reasonable, unstintedly promote epicurean desires, seek a highly expanded material life, and stimulate the competition for acquiring colonies and securing trade, thereby leading the world to a veritable hell of fighting and bloodshed through complicated causes and effects." Such survival-of-the-fittest theories had led almost

---

* "The mission of the Imperial Army," soldiers were instructed in the *Senjinkun,* "lies in making the Imperial virtues the object of admiration through the exercise of justice tempered with mercy." On a matter often violated in practice in ways which outraged the outside world, Japanese soldiers were enjoined to "show kindness to those who surrender." The ultimate objective in fighting for the cause of the Imperial Way was the realization of universal peace, and to this end the Army demanded discipline, unity, cooperation, aggressiveness ("In defense," this section read, "always retain the spirit of attack and always maintain freedom of action; never give up a position but rather die"), and faith in eventual victory. Among the virtues each soldier was to cultivate were loyalty and filial piety; a proper sense of hierarchy (as manifested in saluting); mutual trust and assistance; exemplary behavior on the part of leaders; a sense of the sacredness of each and every duty; the spirit of self-sacrifice for the state; honor, simplicity, and fortitude; and an austere integrity which would enable each soldier to feel no shame in the sight of gods or men.

When the code was issued, War Minister Tōjō explained that it had taken approximately half a year before agreement was reached on the final draft. The basic model for the new code was the 1882 Imperial Rescript for Soldiers and Sailors, and Tōjō noted that outside scholars had been consulted in attempting to clarify the basic meaning of the national polity *(kokutai).* [15]

inevitably to World War One, following which the United States, Britain, and France attempted to impose monopolistic control over the whole world in the hypocritical name of justice and humanity. Other concrete threats to Japan and the peace of the world in general also followed in the wake of the Great War: subversive Communist influences and Comintern intrigues; theories of total war; Western racial discrimination against Japanese and other Orientals; military and economic agreements that were disadvantageous to Japan.

In this setting, Japan's "holy task" was clear. The country was called upon to defend itself, to check the tendency toward world domination by the European and American powers, to stabilize Asia and emancipate its people, and to take the lead in creating a new world order based on moral principles. Where were these principles to be found? Like the twice-told poem in *Read This and the War Is Won*, they were set forth in the ancient classics; and foremost among them were the virtues of loyalty and filial piety under the emperor. In serving the emperor, selfishness was thrown aside, morality was perfected, and private and public life became one. Was this applicable to the whole world? As far as the Ministry of Education bureaucrats and their academic consultants were concerned, yes. And what did this mean then for other countries? That all nations, as the emperor himself had declared in the imperial rescript of September 1940 commemorating the conclusion of the Axis Pact, would find (presumedly like all citizens did within Japan) their "proper place."

Each of these exercises in ideology and propaganda can be seen as a tapestry of truths, half-truths, and empty spaces. When the American and Japanese examples are set side by side, the points each neglected to cover become clearer; and it becomes plain that both sides reveal more about themselves than about the enemy they are portraying. Certainly, no one views a documentary film such as *Know Your Enemy—Japan* decades later to learn about the Japanese in the war; they do so primarily to learn about the Americans. Similarly, *Read This and the War Is Won* and *The Way of the Subject* are of retrospective interest not for what they tell us of Japan's enemies, but for what they tell us about the mind-set of the Japanese at war.

It is helpful to think of such commentaries on the enemy—and the self—as "middle-register" discourse. Whether as film, radio broadcast, or written text, such discourse was ideological and overt, calculated and carefully edited, explicitly designed for public consumption. More refined than visceral expressions of race hate, it was also less frank and densely detailed than the calculations of power and interest made in secret at high levels. Yet it was not simply a tissue of lies or purely cynical manipulation of emotional rhetoric. Speakers, viewers, listeners alike (so long as they were all on the same side) generally took these statements seriously, and there is much to be learned here in retrospect about language, stereotyping, and the making of modern myths. Because World War Two is the context, the consequences of such seemingly abstract concerns emerge with special harshness. To people at war, after all, the major purpose in knowing one's enemies is to be better able to control or kill them.

Several observations are suggested by the three depictions of self and enemy summarized above. *Know Your Enemy—Japan,* for example, serves to remind us of how much both the professional and popular mind was shaped then as now by quick, disjointed images and impressions—by headlines, photographs, newsclips, and cartoons; by "symbolic" items and events such as cinema samurai, Hideyoshi's ear mound, the Tanaka Memorial and the Rape of Nanking, Pearl Harbor and the Bataan Death March; by catch-phrases ("divine emperor," "world conquest," "kamikaze"); by sweeping racial clichés ("regimented," "treacherous," "fanatic," "bestial"). In much the same way, the Japanese saw the Anglo-American enemy at least in part through the prism of the cinema (including gangster and Wild West movies); through the stereotyped persona of the arrogant white colonial with his luxurious house on the hill, and the galling memory of symbolic acts of racial discrimination such as those that occurred at the fledgling League of Nations in 1919 and in the United States in 1924; through such catch-phrases as "economic strangulation" and (everyone's favorite) "world domination"; and through sweeping racial and cultural clichés such as "materialistic," "egoistic," "selfish," and "exploitative."

The gross simplification and reductionism of such disjointed impressions is relatively obvious, their underlying patterns less so. Upon closer examination, however, these portraits of the enemy reveal that stereotypes operated several ways in the war between Japan and the Anglo-American powers. First, they followed predictable patterns of contrariness, in which each side portrayed the other as its polar opposite: as darkness opposed to its own radiant light. Second, the positive self-images of one side were singled out for ridicule and condemnation by the other. Self-stereotypes fed hostile stereotypes: the group became the herd, for example, while the individualist became the egoist. Third, and scarcely acknowledged during the war years, a submerged strata of common values developed in the very midst of the polemics each side employed against the enemy. Each raised the banner of liberation, morality, and peace. Whatever their actual deeds may have been, moreover, they condemned atrocities, exploitation, and theories of racial supremacy.[16] Fourth, policies and practices that became fixated on exterminating the enemy—and verged, for some participants, on the genocidal—followed depiction of the enemy as incorrigibly evil (or base, or mad). Finally, there was a free-floating quality to portrayals of the enemy—a pattern of stereotyping peculiar to enemies and "others" in general, rather than to the Japanese foe or Western foe in particular. This facilitated the quick abatement of hatred once the war had ended—while also facilitating the transferral of the hateful stereotypes to newly perceived enemies. Much of the rhetoric of World War Two proved readily adaptable to the cold war.

On the Anglo-American side, the first of these patterned stereotypes, that of contrariness or mirror opposites, can be seen in the depiction of Japan as a thoroughly militaristic, repressive, irrational nation. Westerners who accepted this, and there were few who did not, commonly also accepted with little question the counterstereotype of modern Euro-American civilization as fundamentally peaceful, democratic, and rational. To think in this black-and-white manner required ignoring huge portions of the Japanese experience and of Western history as well—including the whole modern epoch of imperialism and colonialism, which to the Japanese lay at the heart of the Western experience. In the United States and the United Kingdom, the road to Pearl Harbor was depicted as a one-way street: Japan provoked war, and did so because of the peculiarities of its own history, culture, and collective psychology. External conditions such as the global Depression and the emergence of quasi-autarkic bloc economies all over the world may have abetted and accelerated these trends, but the essential causes of the war in Asia were peculiarly Japanese. After 1941, few Westerners cared to dwell on the rational and possibly legitimate aspects of "Japan's case," or the extent to which Japanese imperialism followed Western precedents.

Such anti-Japanese stereotypes, however, had obvious counterparts in Japan's own propaganda about the Anglo-American enemy, where it was argued and sincerely believed by many that Japan was forced to go to war to defend its honor and very existence against economic and military "strangulation" by the rapacious and hypocritical "white imperialists." As the Army and Ministry of Education tracts both demonstrate, it was hardly necessary to expend much effort rummaging through the European or American past to find good examples of prior Western aggression. The histories of the Western powers provided innumerable examples of rapacity and conquest which could be used to argue that it was *their* lust for land or booty and *their* values and internal dynamics that had finally erupted into the current conflict; a simple glance at the contemporary map of colonial Asia and Africa sufficed to show who had taken the initiative in global expansion and "world conquest." The Japanese made no mention, understandably, of their own energetic activities as a late-developing imperialist and colonial nation—a doubly embarrassing point for them, since the victims of their own imperialism (in Formosa, Korea, and China, including Manchuria) were also, presumedly, their "blood brothers."

In everyday words, this first kind of stereotyping could be summed up in the statement: you are the opposite of what you say you are and the opposite of us, not peaceful but warlike, not good but bad. . . . In the second form of stereotyping, the formula ran more like this: you are what you say you are, but that itself is reprehensible. On the part of the Japanese, this involved singling out the emphasis placed on individualism and profit making in the Western tradition, and presenting this as proof positive that Westerners were fundamentally selfish and greedy, devoted to self-aggrandizement at the expense of the community and the nation as a whole. Westerners, in turn, accepted Japanese emphasis on the primacy of the group or collectivity at face value, and used this as prima facie evidence that the Japanese were closer to cattle or robots than to themselves. One side's idealized virtues easily fed the other side's racial prejudices.

In this regard, Capra's working philosophy of letting the enemy damn himself captured a critical dimension of wartime Allied propaganda: the extent to which many of the Japanese government's own cherished words, shibboleths, images, and values could be taken over almost intact and used against Japan. The image of the Japanese as mere prints off the same photographic negative, devoid of individuality, would appear at first glance to be the crassest sort of Western ethnocentricity and racism, for example; but it was, in fact, not very different from the patriotic slogans promoted by Japan's own ruling groups. During these years the Japanese government's propaganda, for internal as well as external consumption, harped incessantly on "100 million hearts beating as one," "the 100 million people as one bullet," "100 million" as innumerable monolithic entities.[17] Similarly, to describe the Japanese populace as "an obedient mass with but a single mind," as was also done in *Know Your Enemy— Japan*, surely did violence to a complex people and society, and diminished and dehumanized the Japanese in Western eyes. This was the major point of behind-the-scenes controversy among those involved in the production of the film, and some of the writers who struggled in vain to present a more diversified and charitable picture of the ordinary citizens of Japan feared that such stereotyping bordered on racism. Phrases similar to "the obedient mass with but a single mind," however, could have been lifted from the Japanese government's own pronouncements. In the late 1930s, for example, a Spiritual Culture Institute was created by the Ministry of Education explicitly "to perfect and unify the entire nation with one conviction." It was Japan's own newsreels and propaganda films that showed tens of thousands of arms being raised and lowered, in perfect synchronized obeisance to the emperor; and it was Japan's own formal ideological pronunciamentos that declared "history shows clearly that Japan is contrary to individualism."[18]

While this intriguing overlay of hostile stereotypes and positive self-stereotypes draws attention to the manner in which cultural values were idealized as polar opposites during the war in Asia, these idealizations did not necessarily reflect reality. On the contrary, a classic ideological manifesto such as *The Way of the Subject* is especially interesting because it so clearly reveals the class aspect of Japanese war rhetoric. It was not that the Japanese people were, in actuality, homogeneous and harmonious, devoid of individuality and thoroughly subordinated to the group, but rather that the Japanese ruling groups were constantly exhorting them to become so. Indeed, the government deemed it necessary to draft and propagate a rigid orthodoxy of this sort precisely because the ruling classes were convinced that a great many Japanese did not cherish the more traditional virtues of loyalty and filial piety under the emperor, but instead remained attracted to more democratic values and ideals. At several points, *The Way of the Subject* said this directly. In other words, what the vast majority of Westerners believed the Japanese to be coincided with what the Japanese ruling elites hoped they would become.

The most familiar example of this coalescence of stereotypes and self-stereotypes was the relentless emphasis on Japanese "uniqueness" by Anglo-American and Japanese commentators alike. Japan's leaders harped incessantly on the unique and peculiar qualities of the Yamato race, and the Japanese people ultimately paid a terrible price for this racist and ultranationalist raving. For on this point, Japan's enemies were all too willing to accept, at the most general level, what the Japanese ideologues said. They agreed that Japan was "unique"—albeit unique in peculiarly uncivilized and atrocious ways. On neither side did the propagandists offer much ground for the recognition of common traits, comparable acts, or compatible aspirations.

◀ **C H A P T E R   3** ▶

WAR HATES AND
WAR CRIMES

Shortly after World War Two ended, the American historian Allan Nevins, twice winner of the Pulitzer Prize, published an essay entitled "How We Felt About the War." "Probably in all our history," he observed, "no foe has been so detested as were the Japanese." Nevins attributed this to the infamy of the attack on Pearl Harbor, coupled with reports of Japanese atrocities and the extraordinary fierceness of the fighting in the Pacific. "Emotions forgotten since our most savage Indian wars," he went on, "were reawakened by the ferocities of Japanese commanders"—an analogy more telling to us today, perhaps, than Nevins intended.[1]

Nevins' appraisal, which no one at the time would have disputed, is a reminder of the sheer hatred the war in Asia engendered, as it became entangled with an almost spellbinding spectacle of brutality and death. Commentator after commentator in the Anglo-American camp stated flatly that the Japanese were more despised than the Germans, and usually they agreed that there was a good and simple reason for this: the Japanese were uncommonly treacherous and savage.

In retrospect, it is easier to document such sentiments than to fully understand them. For in a war of unprecedented destructiveness, which involved a large part of the world and left a death toll of more than 50 million people, how is it possible to speak of the uncommon savagery of one antagonist in particular? Where the war against Japan is concerned, two more specific questions arise. First, why were the Japanese perceived as being more treacherous and atrocious than the Germans, who attacked neighboring countries without warning or provocation, engaged in systematic genocide against millions of Jews and other "undesirables," killed additional millions of prisoners, especially in the Soviet Union, mobilized slave labor from many countries with the explicit policy of working "antisocial" persons to death, and executed tens of thousands of civilian and military "hostages" in retaliation for the deaths of German officers, not hesitating to obliterate whole villages in such acts of reprisal (the destruction of Lidice and Ležaky in Czechoslovakia in 1942 being but the most famous of these)? And, second, what is one to make of the other side of the coin, namely, Japanese propaganda portraying the Allies as the real barbarians of the modern age, who mutilated Japanese corpses for "souvenirs," killed prisoners on the battlefield, introduced a new crime against humanity in their policy of attacking densely populated areas with incendiary bombs, and did not hesitate to unleash the new force of nuclear destruction against two virtually defenseless cities?

The answer to the first question, why the Japanese were more hated than the Germans despite the latter's orgy of violence, is surely in large part racial—but in ways more complicated than may be apparent at first glance. German atrocities were known and condemned from an early date, but in keeping with their practice of distinguishing between good and bad Germans, Allied critics tended to describe these as "Nazi" crimes rather than behavior rooted in German culture or personality structure. This may have been an enlightened attitude, but it was not a consistent one, for in the Asian theater enemy brutality was almost always presented as being simply "Japanese." So ingrained was this bias that it was maintained even when Japanese behavior was presented as following the German example. In July 1942, for example, the *Washington Post* printed a cartoon entitled "Mimic" which placed Japanese violence in the Philippines in the context of German atrocities in Czechoslovakia. How did the artist choose to do this? By depicting Hitler in the background looming over the ruins of Lidice and Ležaky, while a large gorilla labeled "Japs" trampled Cebu in the foreground.

The distinction between the war in the West and the war in Asia and the Pacific is in itself simplistic, however, for it obscures the fact that the Germans were engaged in several separate wars—on the eastern front, on the western front, and against the Jews—and their greatest and most systematic violence was directed against peoples whom most English and Americans also looked down upon, or simply were unable to identify with strongly. Foremost among these were the eastern Europeans, the Slavs, and the Jews—all of whom, along with Asians, were the target of America's own severe immigration restrictions dating back to the 1920s. Thus, historians of the war in the Western Hemisphere emphasize that the German onslaught against the Soviet Union and eastern Europe was much more savage than the attack to the west; German atrocities on the eastern front were "planned and persistent," while on the western front they were more episodic; and as a consequence, notwithstanding a genuine horror at incidents like Lidice, as well as the normal war hate that simply came from direct confrontation, the response to the Germans in countries like Britain and the United States generally was less violent than elsewhere.[2] Scholars of the Holocaust, in turn, have demonstrated that although the Nazi plan to exterminate the Jews was documented beyond doubt by November 1942, this generally was downplayed by American and British leaders, and was ignored or buried in the mainstream English-language media until after Germany collapsed and Western correspondents actually entered the death camps. Periodicals that regularly featured accounts of Japanese atrocities gave negligible coverage to the genocide of the Jews, and the Holocaust was not even mentioned in the *Why We Fight* series Frank Capra directed for the U.S. Army.[3]

In the English-speaking countries, as everywhere, the fate of one's own countrymen and countrywomen carried an emotional impact greater than reports of the suffering of faceless alien peoples, and the vivid and intimate symbolic incident was more memorable than generalized reports of violence. In this atmosphere, it was not surprising that the Japanese were more hated than the Germans, and were perceived as being treacherous, atrocious, and fanatical in ways peculiar to themselves. They humiliated the United States and Great Britain militarily in unprecedented ways, symbolized by Pearl Harbor and Singapore. They were more brutal to their Anglo-American prisoners than the Germans were (the Germans, in accord with their own racial theories, being more brutal to other races and nationalities than they were to Anglo-Saxons). And after the fortunes of war had turned against them, the Japanese exacted a terrible price in Allied casualties before succumbing, turning hitherto unheard-of places into code words of dehumanization and death: Guadalcanal, Tarawa, Saipan, Peleliu, Iwo Jima, Okinawa, Imphal, Kohima. By the final years of the war against Japan, a truly vicious circle had developed in which the Japanese reluctance to surrender had meshed horrifically with Allied disinterest, on the battlefield and in decision-making circles, in taking prisoners or contemplating anything short of Japan's "thoroughgoing defeat." An analysis of the racial aspects of the war can assume full meaning only in this larger context of violence, atrocity, and hate.

In the wake of Pearl Harbor, the single word favored above all others by Americans as best characterizing the Japanese people was "treacherous," and for the duration of the war the surprise attack on the U.S. Pacific Fleet remained the preeminent symbol of the enemy's inherent treachery.[4] The attack also inspired a thirst for revenge among Americans that the Japanese, with their own racial blinders, had failed to anticipate. In one of his earliest presentations of the plan to attack Pearl Harbor, even Admiral Yamamoto Isoroku, who presumedly knew the American temperament firsthand from his years as a naval attaché in Washington, expressed hope that a shattering opening blow against the Pacific Fleet would render both the U.S. Navy and the American people "so dispirited they will not be able to recover." Colonel Tsuji Masanobu, who planned the brilliant assault on Singapore, recalled similarly that "our candid ideas at the time were that the Americans, being merchants, would not continue for long with an unprofitable war, whereas we ourselves if we fought only the Anglo-Saxon nations [and not the U.S.S.R. as well] could carry on a protracted war."[5] Such hopes were kindled by the rising tide of nationalist propaganda that portrayed Western culture as effete and the average American and Englishman as too selfish to support a long war in a distant place; and the months that followed Pearl Harbor seemed to confirm these prejudices. The Americans were driven from the Philippines, a United Kingdom force of a hundred thousand men surrendered to thirty-four thousand Japanese in Singapore, and throughout Southeast Asia prize after prize dropped like ripe fruit into the laps of the Japanese. Small wonder that, even after they were checked at Midway and Guadalcanal in mid-1942, many Japanese remained convinced that the Anglo-American enemy was indeed psychologically incapable of recovering.[6] In actuality, the contrary was true, for the surprise attack provoked a rage bordering on the genocidal among Americans. Thus, Admiral William Halsey, soon to become commander of the South Pacific Force, vowed after Pearl Harbor that by the end of the war Japanese would be spoken only in hell, and rallied his men thereafter under such slogans as "Kill Japs, kill Japs, kill more Japs." Or as the U.S. Marines put it in a well-known variation on Halsey's motto: "Remember Pearl Harbor—keep 'em dying."[7]

That this exterminationist rhetoric reflected more than just rage at being attacked without warning is apparent, however, in the crudely racist nature of the immediate American response to Pearl Harbor. As *Time* magazine reported it in the opening paragraphs of its coverage, "Over the U.S. and its history there was a great unanswered question: What would the people, the 132,000,000, say in the face of the mightiest event of their time? What they said—tens of thousands of them—was: 'Why, the yellow bastards!' "[8] Such immediate evocations of the "yellow" enemy were utterly commonplace. Even the urbane *New Yorker* magazine responded to the attack on Hawaii with a short story in which the Japanese emerged as "yellow monkeys" in a barroom conversation.[9] There was, however, a curious twist to this generally racist response, reflecting the long-standing assumption that the Japanese were too unimaginative and servile to plan and execute such a stunning military maneuver on their own. Germany, it was widely and erroneously believed, must have put them up to this.[10] In a logical world, such secondhand treachery should have made the Germans doubly treacherous. It did not. The Japanese attack remained the arch symbol of the stab in the back, just as the Japanese soldier soon came to be seen as more barbarous and diabolical than his German counterpart.

Even after Japan surrendered and accepted the Allied dictates of "demilitarization and democratization" with unexpected docility, the memory of a terribly atrocious foe was kept alive. Between 1945 and 1951, military tribunals convened throughout Asia found several thousand former Japanese military men guilty of committing atrocities and other conventional war crimes.[11] At the same time, in the International Military Tribunal for the Far East, which met in Tokyo from early 1946 to mid-1948, the victors accused some of the twenty-eight Japanese military and civilian leaders on trial of actually having engaged in a conspiracy to commit atrocities. They had unleashed, the prosecution charged, the "wholesale destruction of human lives, not alone on the field of battle . . . but in the homes, hospitals, and orphanages, in factories and fields; and the victims would be the young and the old, the well and the infirm —men, women and children alike."[12] By this date, however, at least a small number of Allied observers had concluded that the meaning of "atrocity" had itself become ambiguous in an age of wholesale slaughter. Thus, in the single sweeping dissenting opinion at the Tokyo tribunal, Justice Radhabinod Pal of India dismissed the charge that Japan's leaders had engaged in a conspiracy to commit atrocities, and went so far as to suggest that a stronger case might be made against the victors themselves. The clearest example of direct orders to commit "indiscriminate murder" in the war in Asia, Pal argued in his lengthy dissent, may well have been "the decision coming from the allied powers to use the atom bomb."[13]

Justice Pal's controversial opinion not only challenged the fixation on Japanese or Axis atrocities *in vacuo,* but also called attention to the fact that, in the war in Asia, the portrait of the enemy as a perpetrator of atrocities really began and ended with the bombing of civilians—by the Japanese in China, starting in 1937, and by the United States in Japan in 1944 and 1945, culminating in the nuclear destruction of Hiroshima and Nagasaki. Because air raids against civilian populations had become so commonplace by the end of World War Two, it is easy to forget how shocked the Western powers were when the Japanese began bombing Chinese cities in 1937, and how much Japan's actions at that time served to convince most Europeans and Americans that this was a race and nation still beyond the pale of civilization. Condemnation of Japan by the League of Nations and the U.S. government was explicit on this. On September 28, 1937, one day after a resolution on the subject was unanimously adopted by an advisory committee to the League, the Department of State denounced Japan on the grounds that "any general bombing of an extensive area wherein there resides a large population engaged in peaceful pursuits is unwarranted and contrary to principles of law and of humanity."[14] President Franklin Roosevelt spoke movingly about the barbarity of bombing in his famous "quarantine speech" of October 5, 1937, and the Department of State made further formal condemnations of such activity on March 21 and June 3 of the following year. On the latter occasion, the government's statement included the fighting in Spain as well as in China, but the charge was the same. "When the methods used in the conduct of these hostilities take the form of ruthless bombing of unfortified localities with the resultant slaughter of civilian populations, and in particular of women and children, public opinion in the United States regards such methods as barbarous," the statement read. "Such acts are in violation of the most elementary principles of those standards of humane conduct which have been developed as an essential part of modern civilization."[15] A resolution condemning the "inhuman bombing of civilian populations" also was introduced in the U.S. Senate in June 1938, and the ensuing discussion made it clear that the Japanese were seen as being the major practitioners of this "crime against humanity," pursuing a course "reminiscent of the cruelties perpetrated by primitive and barbarous nations upon inoffensive people."[16]

Although the outcry against the "yellow bastards" who attacked Pearl Harbor tapped an old strain of anti-Oriental sentiment in the United States, by the mid-1930s missionaries and popular writers such as Pearl Buck had helped create a countervailing tide of respect for the long-suffering common people of China. While this mitigated gross color prejudices in some circles, it at the same time heightened anti-Japanese sentiments among Americans as Japan began to step up the pace of its aggression against China in the 1930s. The emotional impact of photographs and newsreels depicting the Chinese victims of Japanese bombing after the Sino-Japanese conflict flared into open war in July 1937 was thus quite spectacular in the West, and helped to freeze two images in the minds of most observers: of the Japanese as indiscriminate killers of women and children; and, more generally, of the horror of all-out war in an age when the technologies of death were developing so rapidly. (Picasso's mural *Guernica*, based on the destruction of the Spanish town by bombing, was completed in April 1937.) When war erupted in Europe in 1939, President Roosevelt immediately followed up on his earlier condemnation of the bombing of civilians with an eloquent plea to all belligerents to refrain from this "inhuman barbarism." "The ruthless bombing from the air of civilians in unfortified centers of population during the course of the hostilities which have raged in various quarters of the earth during the past few years, which has resulted in the maiming and in the death of thousands of defenseless men, women and children," the president began, "has sickened the hearts of every civilized man and woman, and has profoundly shocked the conscience of humanity."[17]

The German bombing of Warsaw in 1939 and Rotterdam, London, and Coventry in 1940 was denounced as wanton terror. Thus, in 1939 the Foreign Office condemned the "inhuman methods used by the Germans in other countries," and declared that "His Majesty's Government have made it clear that it is no part of their policy to bomb nonmilitary objectives, no matter what the policy of the German Government may be." Early in 1940, Winston Churchill, then First Lord of the Admiralty, similarly denounced the bombing of cities as "a new and odious form of attack," while in the same year Roosevelt again pleaded that all parties refrain from bombing civilians, and went on to "recall with pride that the

United States consistently has taken the lead in urging that this inhuman practice be prohibited."[18]

By 1942, the situation had been turned about almost completely, as the Royal Air Force and U.S. Army Air Forces became the apostles of strategic bombing and proceeded to perfect the techniques of massive urban destruction with incendiary bombs, while the Axis powers self-righteously condemned such terror tactics. British and American planners had, in fact, secretly agreed on the desirability of bombing enemy cities many months before Pearl Harbor, and in the summer of 1942 the Royal Air Force began to repay Germany in earnest for the bombings of two years earlier by destroying Hamburg with the newest weapon in the airborne arsenal: incendiaries that created uncontrollable fire storms. From an early date, British leaders supported dense "area" bombing in Germany to destroy civilian morale in addition to more conventional military and industrial targets, and after Pearl Harbor Churchill frequently turned his gift for the vivid image to anticipation of grinding the Japanese to powder, ravaging their cities, or laying their urban areas in ashes. Following the Quebec Conference of August 1943, the British minister of information reported that the Allies intended to "bomb, burn and ruthlessly destroy" both Germany and Japan, and subsequent developments proved him to be a forthright and accurate spokesman.[19]

The prospect of putting Japan's cities to the torch actually had been envisioned in U.S. military circles since shortly before Pearl Harbor, when General George C. Marshall, the chief of staff, instructed his aides to develop contingency plans for "general incendiary attacks to burn up the wood and paper structures of the densely populated Japanese cities."[20] As a general rule, however, even while supporting the RAF in the raids against German cities, U.S. planners tended to express greater reservations than their British counterparts about the deliberate terror bombing of civilians to destroy morale. They presented themselves instead as supporters of the more restrained strategy of high-altitude daytime "precision" bombing of military and industrial targets; and this was, in fact, the general policy followed during the first few months after the U.S. Army Air Forces commenced bombing the Japanese homeland in late 1944.

Precision bombing was abandoned dramatically on the night of March 9–10, 1945, when 334 aircraft attacked Tokyo at low altitude with incendiary bombs, destroying sixteen square miles of the capital city and making more than a million people homeless. Between eighty thousand and one hundred thousand civilians died in the Tokyo raid—"scorched and boiled and baked to death" was how the mastermind of the new strategy, Major General Curtis LeMay, later phrased it. The heat from the conflagration was so intense that in some places canals boiled, metal melted, and buildings and human beings burst spontaneously into flames. It took twenty-five days to remove all the dead from the ruins. With the exception of the fires that raged through Tokyo and Yokohama at the time of the Kanto earthquake in 1923, this was the largest urban conflagration in recorded history. Radio Tokyo referred to the new U.S. policy as "slaughter bombing," and in the days and months that followed, incendiary attacks against urban areas became the primary U.S. aerial strategy against Japan. By May, incendiaries comprised 75 percent of the bomb loads, and in the final reckoning firebombs accounted for close to two thirds of the total tonnage of explosives dropped on Japan. By the time Japan surrendered, sixty-six cities, including Hiroshima and Nagasaki, had been subjected to both precision raids and general urban-area attacks. The exact number of civilians killed by both incendiaries and the atomic bombs is uncertain, but probably was close to four hundred thousand.[21]

Although Allied military planners remained sensitive to the moral issue of bombing civilians (and to the possibility that reliance on obliteration bombing might provoke a public reaction detrimental to the postwar development of the air forces), no sustained protest ever materialized. The Allied air raids were widely accepted as just retribution as well as sound strategic policy, and the few critics who raised ethical and humanitarian questions about the heavy bombing of German cities were usually denounced as hopeless idealists, fools, or traitors.[22] When Tokyo was incinerated, there was scarcely a murmur of protest on the home front. Privately, some insiders did acknowledge the moral ambiguity of the U.S. strategy against Japan, at least in passing. In a confidential memorandum of mid-June 1945, for example, one of General Douglas MacArthur's key aides, Brigadier General Bonner Fellers, frankly described the U.S. air raids against Japan as "one of the most ruthless and barbaric killings of non-combatants in all history."[23] Such thoughts were seldom voiced publicly, however. And when Allied prosecutors sitting in the gutted capital city of Japan in 1946 accused the country's leaders of promoting the indiscriminate destruction of "men, women and children alike," they still did so with little sense of irony. Japan had merely reaped what it sowed.

What Japan sowed among its enemies, and even among erstwhile allies within the Greater East Asia Co-Prosperity Sphere, was death and the seeds of violent loathing. The bombing of Chinese cities was but the first great planting of this hatred, and in the months and years that followed, the Japanese often seemed to go out of their way to call the condemnation of the outside world down upon themselves. Their atrocities frequently were so grotesque, and flaunted in such a macabre manner, that it is not surprising they were interpreted as being an expression of deliberate policy and a calculated exhibition of some perverse "national character." What else was one supposed to make, for example, of the "friendly contest" between two officers in late 1937, avidly followed in some Japanese newspapers, to see who would be the first to cut down 150 Chinese with his samurai sword; or of the rape and murder of nuns in the streets of Hong Kong; or of the corpses of tortured Englishmen hanging from trees in Malaya, with their severed genitals in their mouths; or of the water torture of old missionaries in Korea and Japan, who were then repatriated to tell their tales? No one will ever know how many individuals fell victim to atrocities committed by Japanese troops, or how many Japanese actively participated in such acts. The command responsibility for many such incidents also is destined to remain controversial—particularly if responsibility is understood to include not merely direct orders, but also socialization, indoctrination, and indifference. Many Japanese atrocities were unquestionably "stray" events, as Justice Pal sometimes argued. There can be little dispute about the wide range of conventional Japanese war crimes, however, or about the actual occurrence of certain shocking incidents which were singled out for special publicity in the Allied camp and contributed greatly to the effectiveness of propaganda depicting the Japanese collectively as an inherently savage race. Even skeptics who recalled the unsubstantiated atrocity stories which had been circulated to stir up anti-German passions among the Allies during World War One conceded that most of the wartime reports about atrocious Japanese behavior were essentially true.[24]

Japanese atrocities conformed to several broad categories: massacres of noncombatants, the maltreatment and killing of prisoners, routinized torture, forced labor, and institutionalized murder in the form of lethal medical experiments. The last of these crimes, which took place on a very small scale in Japan proper (notably at Kyushu Imperial University in 1945) and on a large scale in Manchuria (under the murderous contingent of scientists known as "Unit 731") were not exposed until some time after the war ended.[25] By contrast, the other kinds of atrocities were well publicized. Indeed, after Pearl Harbor the reporting of such incidents was, at certain key moments, carefully orchestrated by the American and British governments.

We have already seen how the period embracing the China and Pacific wars opened and closed with the spectacle of civilian populations being slaughtered by aerial bombardment. Massacres of civilians by Japan's ground forces also marked the commencement of this period in 1937, and carried through to its end in 1945. If anything, the massacres mounted in horror, for by the end the Japanese were not only slaughtering their erstwhile Asian compatriots within the Co-Prosperity Sphere, but killing their own kin and countrymen as well.

The Chinese people were the first victims of Japanese massacres. Eradication of Chinese "bandits"—the Japanese euphemism for patriotic resistance groups who opposed them—occurred on various occasions in the early 1930s, but it was in 1937, with the Rape of Nanking, that the killing of noncombatants escalated to a massive scale. Nanking fell on December 12 after heavy shelling and bombing, and for the next six weeks Japanese troops engaged in the widespread execution, rape, and random murder of Chinese men and women both in the captured city and outlying communities. The total number of Chinese killed is controversial, but a middle-range estimate puts the combined deaths from both the shelling and subsequent atrocities at two hundred thousand.[26] Much smaller killings occurred in other Chinese cities that fell into Japanese hands, including Hankow and Canton. In attempting to consolidate their control over northern China, the Japanese subsequently turned to "rural pacification" campaigns that amounted to indiscriminate terror against the peasantry. And by 1941–42, this fundamentally anti-Communist "pacification" campaign had evolved into the devastating "three-all" policy (*sankō seisaku*: "kill all, burn all, destroy all"), during which it is estimated that the population in the areas dominated by the Chinese Communists was reduced, through flight and death, from 44 million to 25 million persons.[27]

Outside of China, massacres small and large by Japanese ground forces were reported from every country that fell within the Co-Prosperity Sphere.[28] After the British surrendered Singapore in February 1942, the overseas Chinese there became an immediate target of Japanese oppression, and upwards of five thousand were summarily executed in the course of a few days. Some were beheaded, others drowned in the ocean, and yet others machine-gunned and bayonetted.[29] For the Japanese enlisted man, the bayonet was the poor man's counterpart to the samurai sword carried by officers; and for the Freudian analyst, the wanton frenzy with which these conscripts plunged this weapon into Allied prisoners as well as defenseless people everywhere in Asia must be of more than passing interest. It certainly caught the attention of observers who reported on the war in Asia to the West, and more than one American propaganda film included an acted-out scene of Japanese soldiers tossing babies in the air and spearing them with their bayonets. In the months following Pearl Harbor, Japanese bayonets cut down scores of Asians and Europeans throughout the new imperium. Foreign Secretary Anthony Eden informed the House of Commons in March 1942 that some fifty British officers and men had been bound and bayonetted during the takeover of Hong Kong, and it was widely reported that the same weapon had been used against doctors, nurses, and hospital patients in Singapore as well as Hong Kong during the takeover. Hundreds of American and Filipino stragglers in the Bataan Death March of April 1942 were bayonetted; and, at a later date, General William Slim's army found Burmese villagers tied to trees and, again, killed by bayonet thrusts. The method was economical, for it saved ammunition. But for many Japanese (including popular graphic artists, who turned it into the Japanese common man's sword of righteousness), the bayonet also possessed a peculiar fascination.[30]

There was, however, variety in the methods of massacre. The Japanese also machine-gunned their victims, decapitated them with swords, drowned them, and occasionally doused them with gasoline and set them afire. In Borneo and other locales within the colonial domain of the Netherlands, upwards of one hundred Dutch civilians were killed early in 1942 as a reprisal for the destruction of the oil fields and other critical installations. Some were maimed and thrown into the ocean to drown.[31] Manila, where random atrocities had occurred during the Japanese takeover of 1941–42, was subjected to a terrible slaughter in February and March of 1945, after land forces of the Imperial Navy refused to surrender the city. Close to a hundred thousand of the city's population of seven hundred thousand were killed by shelling and bombing, by crossfire in the streets, and by Japanese sadists.

Some of the greatest atrocities in Manila took place after MacArthur had announced the liberation of the city, culminating in the torture and murder of some one thousand Filipino hostages held in Christian churches in Intramuros, the old walled quarter of the capital, where the Japanese made their last defense. Carlos Romulo, the distinguished Filipino editor who escaped from Bataan in 1942 and returned with

MacArthur's forces in 1945, described the horror of returning to find Manila "black and gutted and reeking," a "city of the tortured and the dead." "These were my neighbors and my friends whose tortured bodies I saw pushed into heaps on the Manila streets," Romulo recorded, "their hands tied behind their backs, and bayonet stabs running through and through. This girl who looked up at me wordlessly, her young breasts crisscrossed with bayonet strokes, had been in school with my son. I saw the bodies of priests, women, children, and babies that had been bayoneted for sport, survivors told us, by a soldiery gone mad with blood lust in defeat."[32] Once again the world was confronted by the now emblematic mark of the imperial bayonet.

As the Imperial Army and Navy fell on the defensive and began to face certain defeat in all theaters of the war, contingents of the armed forces began to kill their own countrymen and comrades in arms, and to take their own lives in gruesome and desperate acts of suicide. The "banzai charge" and the reluctance of Japanese fighting men to surrender were observed in battle after battle, beginning with Guadalcanal. And on July 9, 1944, Allied observers on Saipan were presented with a horrifying new spectacle as hundreds of Japanese civilians living in the critical island outpost killed their families and themselves rather than surrender. They had been told the Americans would rape, torture, and murder them, and that it was more swift and honorable to take their own lives. Whole families died in full view of the invading Allied forces by killing themselves with hand grenades provided by the Japanese military or leaping from high cliffs into the sea or onto the rocks below. Some, attempting to surrender, were shot or bayonetted by Japanese soldiers. Thousands of noncombatants did in fact defy the Japanese orders and give themselves up to the Americans, but it was the terrible spectacle of the civilian slaughter that impressed itself most deeply on the public consciousness of the Allies. Not only was the story widely reported, but some of the civilian deaths were captured on film by the U.S. military and became part of the regular indoctrination program for Marines.[33] Months later, on Okinawa, local Japanese commanders again ordered the civilian population to commit suicide rather than surrender, and here the agony of flight, entrapment, and death was prolonged for weeks. When the battle of Okinawa ended, ninety-five thousand civilians had been killed by enemy fire, by Japanese soldiers, by loved ones and trusted acquaintances, and by their own hands. As the artist Maruki Toshi observed decades later, after she and her husband Iri had painted a huge mural of the Okinawa tragedy, the Japanese militarists ended up slaughtering the very people they were presumedly protecting.[34]

George Orwell, who spent part of the war years writing propaganda broadcasts for British radio, observed on several occasions in 1942 that while Japanese rhetoric attacking European and American repression in Asia was undeniably "clever" and "inviting," such appealing words were belied by Japan's already demonstrated record as an occupying power in Korea, Formosa, Manchukuo, and China. "To those who say that the cause of Japan is the cause of Asia against the European races," he suggested, "the best answer is: Why then do the Japanese constantly make war against other races who are Asiatics no less than themselves?" Orwell went so far as to argue that for centuries the Japanese had espoused "a racial theory even more extreme than that of the Germans," holding their own race to be divine and all others hereditarily inferior.[35] As time passed, more and more Asians within the new Japanese sphere in southern Asia came to a similar conclusion. They were routinely slapped by Japanese soldiers; ordered to bow to the east, where the Japanese emperor resided; told to learn Japanese; subjected to refined tortures by the hated Kempeitai, or military police; and mobilized for labor projects which proved fatal for tens of thousands of workers. Even collaborators such as Burma's Ba Maw and Sukarno in Indonesia were appalled by the contempt which many Japanese displayed toward other Asians. "The brutality, arrogance, and racial pretensions of the Japanese militarists in Burma," Ba Maw recalled in his outspoken memoirs, "remain among the deepest Burmese memories of the war years; for a great many people in Southeast Asia these are all they remember of the war."[36]

In their penchant for slapping non-Japanese Asians about, Japanese soldiers, especially enlisted men, were treating others in the same way their superiors treated them. Racial arrogance came together here with the all-too-human transfer of oppression; and although such practices made the Japanese hated, these were crude rather than atrocious acts. Torture was another matter, and in this regard the Japanese military police operating in the Co-Prosperity Sphere combined a repertoire of more or less conventional techniques (water torture, beating, starvation, burning, electric shock, pulling joints from their sockets by knee spreads and suspension) with a perverse racial twist: in many overseas locales, the strong-arm work of the Kempeitai was delegated to Korean and sometimes Formosan recruits.[37] For scores of thousands of Asian noncombatants, however, Japan's most brutal wartime policy took the form not of punishment or torture, but of employment under the Japanese.

The war years witnessed at least four sustained acts of criminal Japanese treatment of Asian labor, involving Korean and Chinese workers in Japan proper, Indonesians both within and outside their native land, and Southeast Asian laborers assembled to help construct the notorious Burma-Siam "railroad of death." Between 1939 and 1945, close to 670,-000 Koreans were brought to Japan for fixed terms of work, mostly in mines and heavy industry, and it has been estimated that 60,000 or more of them died under the harsh conditions of their work places. Over 10,000 others were probably killed in the atomic bombings of Hiroshima and Nagasaki. More precise figures are available concerning Chinese laborers mobilized to work in Japan. Of 41,862 men assembled in China for such work between April 1943 and May 1945 (in accordance with a Japanese cabinet decision of November 27, 1942), over 2,800 died before leaving China, close to 600 perished on the boats coming to Japan, and over 200 more passed away before reaching their work assignments in factories throughout Japan. Subsequently, 6,872 Chinese workers were recorded as having died at their Japanese work sites, leaving less than 31,000 to be repatriated after the war ended.[38] Estimates concerning conscripted labor in Southeast Asia vary greatly, although it is well known that Indonesians in particular suffered grievously under the Japanese occupation. Japanese recruitment of Indonesian laborers (rōmusha) was so harsh that some villages were stripped of almost all able-bodied men, causing severe socioeconomic dislocations, while the number of deaths among the rōmusha themselves was in the hundreds of thousands. As many as 300,000 Javanese, Tamil, Malayan, Burmese, and Chinese laborers may have been mobilized to build the Burma-Siam railroad between October 1942 and November 1943; of this number an estimated 60,000 perished in the disease-ridden jungle. In addition to such organized abuse of Asian males, in the war theaters and occupied areas countless non-Japanese (as well as poor Japanese) girls and women were forced to prostitute themselves as "comfort girls" for the emperor's soldiers and sailors.[39]

After World War Two, the story of the Burma-Siam railway became famous in the West through a brilliant book and movie, *The Bridge on the River Kwai*, which told of a captured British officer who became so emotionally involved in helping to complete the construction of the "railroad of death" that he attempted to prevent his own side from destroying it. In defiance of the generally accepted conventions of war governing prisoners, the Japanese did employ POWs on war-related projects, and some 60,000 to 70,000 Allied captives—mostly Australian, British, Indian, and Dutch—were eventually put to work alongside the "native" labor on the Burma-Siam railway. Early in 1945, reports that later proved quite accurate reached the West to the effect that some 15,000 of these prisoners had died.[40] It was this sort of report, concerning atrocities against white troops, which helped confirm Anglo-Americans in their belief that the Japanese were more atrocious than the Germans, although by this time the pattern of special hatred toward the Japanese enemy had already been firmly established.

Although both German and Japanese atrocity stories were covered regularly in the English-language media, three incidents which received special attention in 1943 and the opening weeks of 1944 were widely interpreted as confirming that the Japanese were uniquely barbaric. All three incidents were made known to the English-speaking public through official channels many months after the U.S. and British governments learned about them, and all involved the killing of Caucasian prisoners. This was propaganda of the most sophisticated sort, turning concrete events into icons and symbols; and in evaluating these emotional accounts of Japanese atrocities against white prisoners, it is helpful to keep in mind our earlier observations concerning Germany's several wars. On the eastern front, it is estimated that the Germans took as many as 5.5 million Soviet prisoners, of whom at least 3.5 million were dead by mid-1944. Being more sensitive to the fate of their own countrymen, however, most citizens of the United States and the United Kingdom had a very different picture. Of 235,473 U.S. and U.K. prisoners reported captured by Germany and Italy together, only 4 percent (9,348) died in the hands of their captors, whereas 27 percent of Japan's Anglo-American POWs (35,756 of 132,134) did not survive.[41] No one had such numbers at their fingertips at the time, but the trend was clear. Thus, there was a logical explanation for the perception that the Japanese treated prisoners more brutally than the Germans, but the perception was nonetheless culture-bound and racially biased.

The first truly sensational incident involving Allied POWs occurred in April 1943, when the White House announced that the Japanese government had condemned to death several of the American flyers who participated in the Doolittle raid over Japan one year previously. This raid against Tokyo and several other cities, led by Lieutenant Colonel James

Doolittle from U.S. carriers far off the Japanese coast, had caused negligible material damage but had given a huge psychological boost to the Allies, while shocking Japan's leaders and causing them to reassess their expansionist ambitions. Eight of the flyers were captured when they were forced to land in occupied China, and on August 20, 1942, they were tried for war crimes under a military law which the Japanese had adopted exactly one week previously. The law explicity concerned "enemy flyers who have raided Japanese territories, Manchukuo, or our operational territories," and made it a capital offense to bomb civilians or nonmilitary targets. The law also contained a proviso stating that it was retroactively applicable to acts committed before August 13, and the death penalty was to be carried out by shooting. In extenuating circumstances, enemy flyers found guilty might receive a reduced sentence of from ten years to life imprisonment. The eight Doolittle flyers were sentenced to death under these regulations in a military hearing in China, but when the judgment was reviewed in Tokyo, five of the sentences were commuted to life imprisonment. The remaining three American flyers were executed on October 10.

Both the new regulations and the "severe punishment" meted out to the Doolittle flyers were widely publicized in Japan later in October. The Japanese claimed that the Doolittle raiders killed some fifty civilians, including patients in an easily identifiable hospital and children deliberately machine-gunned in a schoolyard; and, indeed, their condemnation of this "cruel and inhuman act" read like a page from Western texts of four or five years earlier, when the Japanese were bombing the Chinese cities. "Bestial," "evil," "crazed," "inhuman," "lost to all sense of humanity" were some of the phrases used in the press, while the Japanese government's formal statement concerning the Doolittle flyers, dated October 19, stated that "those who ignored the principles of humanity have been severely punished in accordance with military law." Despite the publicity which the new law together with the punishment of the Doolittle flyers received in Japan, all this remained unreported in the West until April 23, 1943, when the White House itself released the information.[42]

President Roosevelt's denunciation of Japan's act was couched in much the same words as Japan's denunciation of the flyers: "barbarous," "uncivilized," "inhuman," "depraved." And, indeed, the response the story provoked in the United States was comparable to the rage that greeted the news of Pearl Harbor. As the British embassy in Washington reported to its home office, the news itself, combined with the emotional response of high American officials, "sharply increased the stimulus of national anger and humiliation which makes of the Pacific front permanently a more burning issue than [the] European front is ever likely to be." On the same day as the British dispatch, the *New York Times* headlined its Sunday review of the incident "Japan's Barbarous Act Has No Parallel in War," with a subhead further explaining "Tokyo Stands Alone as a Cruel Captor in Defiance of Geneva Convention." Not even Germany, the *Times* stated, diabolical as its treatment of enemy civilians had been, had yet been accused of killing uniformed men for performing their duty.[43] In 1944, the torture and trial of the Doolittle flyers became the subject of one of Hollywood's most dramatic war films, *The Purple Heart*, which ended with a memorable prophecy by one of the Americans sentenced to die:

> It's true we Americans don't know very much about you Japanese, and never did—and now I realize you know even less about us. You can kill us—all of us, or part of us. But, if you think that's going to put the fear of God into the United States of America and stop them from sending other fliers to bomb you, you're wrong—dead wrong. They'll blacken your skies and burn your cities to the ground and make you get down on your knees and beg for mercy. This is your war—you wanted it—you asked for it. And now you're going to get it—and it won't be finished until your dirty little empire is wiped off the face of the earth![44]

The Purple Heart was the first major American movie to deal explicitly with the Japanese torture of American prisoners, and its appearance in 1944 followed the carefully planned release of information concerning two other shocking incidents. Early in October 1943, the U.S. government released the translation of an entry in a diary found on the body of a Japanese soldier killed in New Guinea. The passage in question was discovered by language officers in General MacArthur's command, and recorded the beheading of a captured airman the previous March. It was indeed a gripping short document, containing almost poetic references to the composure of the young man ("I glance at the prisoner and he seems prepared. He gazes at the grass, now at the mountains and sea"); passing expressions of compassion ("When I put myself in his place the hate engendered by this daily bombing yields to ordinary human feelings");

jargon concerning the samurai code ("I realize that the emotion I felt just now was not personal pity but manifestation of magnanimity that becomes a chivalrous Samurai"); rage and racism (a Japanese disemboweling the decapitated corpse exclaims, "Here's something for the other day —take that," and then goes on to remark that "these thick-headed white bastards are thick-bellied too"); the gross obscenity of death (the severed head on the ground "like a white doll," the trunk left with "not a drop of blood" in it); and the nonchalance of the casual gossip ("If I ever get back alive this will make a good story to tell. That's why I write it down").[45]

To the Western reader, of course, the soldier's "good story" was, on the contrary, a great tragedy. The *New York Times*, which like many newspapers published the full translation beginning on its front page, editorialized that, like a flashlight in the darkness, the diary illuminated "the real nature of our Asiatic enemy." More terrible even than the murder of the Doolittle flyers, which at least had been cloaked with a pretense at judicial procedure, here there was nothing but "primitive blood lust and brutal butchery"—a naked, tribal savagery which, in fact, was inherent in Japanese culture. "The Japanese," the *Times* explained, appropriating the enemy's own rhetoric, "have kept their savage tradition 'unbroken through ages eternal,' from the fabulous age of their savage gods to the present day." Turning to the samurai code, the *Times* explained that whereas in feudal times the samurai had tested their swords on beggars, Japan's modern samurai "prefer their white enemies, whose necks they consider to be particularly frail."[46]

On January 28, 1944, over three months after publicizing the diary from New Guinea, the U.S. government released information concerning another Japanese atrocity against prisoners of war. This was the most devastating story of all: an account, based on reports from escaped prisoners, of the Bataan Death March of April 1942, during which thousands of Americans and Filipinos died of illness and exhaustion or were summarily killed. The government had possessed this information for over half a year before deciding to release it, and its announcement on January 28 was coordinated with a parallel statement by the British government describing Japanese atrocities against British and Commonwealth prisoners.[47] With this, the floodgates were opened, and a torrent of Japanese atrocity stories poured forth that continued unabated into the months and even years that followed Japan's surrender. No conceivable abuse seemed to be beyond the Japanese. They shot bailed-out pilots in their parachutes, transported prisoners in densely packed "hell ships," starved and beat their prisoners, performed vivisections on them, emasculated them, decapitated them, crucified them, burned or buried them alive, nailed them to trees, used them for bayonet practice.

These brutal acts were not isolated instances, Westerners were informed, nor were they acts common among men at war. Neither could they be dismissed as the frenzies of tormented men stranded abroad and locked in a war they were doomed to lose. The Bataan Death March, after all, occurred at the height of Japan's early victories. Rather, to quote a typical response to the Bataan horror, such atrocities revealed "the true nature of the enemy . . . an enemy that seems to be a beast which sometimes stands erect."[48] Not until May 1945, when the Nazi death camps were exposed, did public horror and indignation against the Germans reach, at least in the United States, a pitch comparable to the feelings directed against the Japanese. And by that time, the Germans had already surrendered.[49]

By that time too, the willingness of the Japanese to accept incredible casualties had persuaded many observers in the Allied camp that this was an enemy that not only deserved to be exterminated, but had to be. Among U.S. fighting men, the idea that every Japanese had to be killed began to take hold after the battle for Guadalcanal, which began as an anticipated minor clash in August 1942 and did not end until February of the following year, after an estimated twenty-four thousand Japanese had given up their lives.[50] In May 1943, one month after the White House made public the fate of the Doolittle flyers, Westerners were informed of the suicidal banzai charges in Attu in the Aleutians of Japanese forces who died almost to the last man rather than surrender; and in the final years of the war, such reports came one after another, culminating in the sensational spectacle of suicide attacks by kamikaze aircraft.

Although the kamikaze pilots were first deployed in the Philippines in October 1944, and were immediately hailed in Japan as pure and selfless martyrs who would ensure the country's victory, for military reasons the news of their appearance and accomplishments was withheld in the West for almost half a year. Reports of the kamikaze were not released in the United States until April 1945, coincident with the death of President Roosevelt and a month after the incendiary bombing of Japanese cities had commenced.[51] Although this intensified the sense on all sides of an inevitable fight to the bitter end, such sentiments were by then deeply rooted. A U.S. Army poll taken in 1943 already indicated that about half of all GIs believed that it would be necessary to kill all Japanese before peace could be achieved.[52] Men in the field were told they faced an enemy unlike any other, and had no choice but to kill or be killed. "You are fighting a shrewd, cruel, merciless enemy, who knows how to kill and who knows how to die," General Sir Thomas Blamey told an Australian unit in Port Moresby in 1942, in a typical sample of Allied battlefield talk. "Beneath the thin veneer of a few generations of civilization he is a subhuman beast, who has brought warfare back to the primeval, who fights by the jungle rule of tooth and claw, who must be beaten by the jungle rule of tooth and claw. Kill him or he will kill you."[53] A terser send-off, laced with black humor, was this briefing for a U.S. Marine unit: "Every Japanese has been told it is his duty to die for the emperor. It is your duty to see that he does so." By the final year of the war, one out of four U.S. combatants stated that his primary goal was not to help bring about Japan's surrender, but simply to kill as many Japanese as possible.[54] Here indeed were the makings of carnage: a losing army and navy ordered not to surrender, and a winning force disinclined to take prisoners and obsessed with the task of slaughter. By the end of the arduous Burma campaign, General Slim calculated that the kill ratio was more than one hundred Japanese for every one of his own men lost, and smaller but nonetheless still incredible ratios were reported from other theaters of the war.[55]

It is understandable that men in battle become obsessed with an-nihilating the foe. In the case of the Japanese enemy, however, the obsession extended to many men and women far removed from the place of battle, and came to embrace not just the enemy's armed forces but the Japanese as a race and culture. How pervasive such sheer genocidal atti-tudes became is hard to say, for on all sides there were always a great number of people who simply desired a quick end to the killing. Public-opinion polls in the United States indicated that some 10 to 13 percent of Americans consistently supported the "annihilation" or "extermina-tion" of the Japanese as a people, while a comparable percentage were in favor of severe retribution after Japan had been defeated ("eye for an eye," "punishment, torture," etc.). In an often-quoted poll conducted in December 1944 asking "What do you think we should do with Japan as a country after the war?," 13 percent of the respondents wanted to "kill all Japanese" and 33 percent supported destroying Japan as a political entity (the identical question asked for Germany on the same date omitted the option of killing all Germans, and found 34 percent of the American respondents in favor of destroying Germany as a nation).[56] Like the soldiers who confessed in 1945 that their goal had become killing rather than simply winning, even after the war ended and the Japanese turned their energies to the tasks of peaceful reconstruction, a surprising number of Americans expressed regrets that Japan surrendered so soon after the atomic bombs were dropped. A poll conducted by *Fortune* in December 1945 found that 22.7 percent of respondents wished the United States had had the opportunity to use "many more of them [atomic bombs] before Japan had a chance to surrender."[57]

Knowledgeable observers who followed American attitudes at the levels where opinions were shaped and policies made certainly concluded that support for an annihilationist policy against the Japanese was extremely strong—probably even more so than the polls indicated. On New Year's Day 1944, for example, several weeks before the news of the Bataan Death March had been released, the weekly report to the Foreign Office by the British ambassador in Washington was already referring to the "universal 'exterminationist' anti-Japanese feeling here."[58] An impressive variety of publicists, politicians, and military figures gave credence to this observation. In the media, for example, the syndicated military analyst Major George Fielding Eliot declared that the Allies' aim must be "the complete and ruthless destruction of Japanese industry, so that not one brick of any Japanese factory shall be left upon another, so that there shall not be in Japan one electric motor or one steam or gasoline engine, nor a chemical laboratory, not so much as a book which tells how these things are made." A 1943 best-seller stated that the fight against Japan had to continue "until not alone the body but the soul . . . is annihilated, until the land . . . is plowed with salt, its men dead and its women and children divided and lost among another people."[59] Carthage, sacked and razed by the Romans in 146 B.C., struck the more historically minded as an apt model for Japan. Admiral William Leahy, Roosevelt's chief of staff, described Japan as "our Carthage" to Henry Wallace in September 1942, meaning "we should go ahead and destroy her utterly." Some months later, *Collier's* ran an editorial entitled "Delenda est Japonia," taking the motto from Cato the Elder's practice of ending every one of his speeches to the Roman Senate for eight years with the line *"Delenda est Carthago,"* or "Carthage must be destroyed."[60]

In May 1943, and for some time thereafter, the Navy representative to the first interdepartmental U.S. government committee that was assigned to study how Japan should be treated after the war revealed himself to be a literal believer in Admiral Halsey's motto "Kill Japs, kill Japs, kill more Japs." He called for "the almost total elimination of the Japanese as a race," on the grounds that this "was a question of which race was to survive, and white civilization was at stake."[61] Prime Minister Churchill, in a triumphant visit to Washington the same month, roused a joint session of Congress with a speech in which he spoke of "the process, so necessary and desirable, of laying the cities and other munitions centers of Japan in ashes, for in ashes they must surely lie before peace comes back to the world."[62] Elliott Roosevelt, the president's son and confidant, told Henry Wallace in 1945 that the United States should continue bombing Japan "until we have destroyed about half the Japanese civilian population."[63] While the president's son was expressing such personal views in private, the chairman of the War Manpower Commission, Paul V. McNutt, told a public audience in April 1945 that he favored "the extermination of the Japanese in toto." When asked if he meant the Japanese military or the people as a whole, he confirmed he meant the latter, "for I know the Japanese people." A week later, McNutt, a former U.S. high commissioner in the Philippines, called a press conference to make clear that his comments reflected his personal views rather than official policy.[64] Several days before the atomic bomb was dropped on Hiroshima, Vice Admiral Arthur Radford was quoted as saying that "the Japs are asking for an invasion, and they are going to get it. Japan will eventually be a nation without cities—a nomadic people."[65]

These were not the only voices in the chorus of opinion concerning Japan. Behind the scenes moderate and conciliatory appraisals of the Japanese were offered by a number of individuals, notable among them a small group of analysts centering around Captain Ellis Zacharias in Naval Intelligence, social scientists including Ruth Benedict and Clyde Kluckhohn in the Office of War Information, and Japan specialists led by Hugh Borton and George Blakeslee in the State Department. Their voices were muted, however, and the overwhelming thrust of public opinion in the United Kingdom as well as the United States demanded, if not the extermination of the Japanese people, then most certainly the country's "thoroughgoing defeat." Support for this came from every part of the political spectrum, and was rationalized, often at considerable length, by three basic lines of argument. In brief, they were these:

1. The "suicide psychology" argument, whereby it was maintained that the Japanese themselves, by their own fanaticism, invited destruction. The political scientist Harold Quigley, one of America's leading experts on China and Japan, turned to this popular thesis in April 1945 when asked if Japan would seek peace once Germany had collapsed. On the contrary, he predicted, in all likelihood "samurai tradition will be followed to the point of national hara-kiri." This argument placed the onus of massive destruction squarely on the Japanese. As the weekly *United States News* put it early in 1945, the proper question was not whether the Japanese should be exterminated, but rather "whether, in order to win unconditional surrender, the Allies will have to kill Japan's millions to the last man."[66]

2. The "lessons of World War One" argument, whereby the rise of the Nazis in Germany was attributed to the incomplete victory of the Allies in World War One. Anything less than thoroughgoing defeat, it was maintained, would permit later nationalists to claim Japan had never really been defeated and, in Admiral Halsey's words, to "use this peace as Germany did before them—to build up for another war."[67] A companion or counterpart thesis to this reading of history was the "hundred-year-war" argument—the widely accepted belief that the Japanese, like "patient" Orientals in general, thought in terms of millennia rather than centuries, and centuries rather than years or decades; and that the current conflict, in the view of Japan's leaders, was but a step in Japan's hundred-year-war plan for world conquest. *Collier's,* for example, ran an editorial entitled "Japan's 100-Year-War Plans" only two weeks before the bombing of Hiroshima—quoting, as often was done, Japanese militarists in support of its thesis. "The Japs have a 2,500 year history, more or less, though their reliable records go back only to about 230 A.D.," the magazine told its readers. "They can therefore take the long view of wars and truces"—and consequently a decisive defeat was essential.[68]

3. The "psychological purge" argument, under which it was argued that great destruction and suffering should be inflicted upon Japan not simply as punishment, or because this was essential to end the war, but rather because only by turning Japan's cities into ashes could the Japanese people as a whole be purged of their fanatic, militaristic sense of national and racial destiny. This was a natural corollary of the "lessons of World War One" argument, as Senator Thomas Hart made clear in the spring of 1945. Hart, a retired admiral who served as commander in chief of the U.S. Asiatic Fleet from 1939 to 1942, warned Americans to beware of

peace offers by the Japanese: "They don't seek real peace—only an armistice to give some years for preparing another attempt to dominate the entire Far East, and then the remainder of the world. Those savages [Japan's militarist leaders] have, for many years, taught the Japanese that such is the divine mission of the Yamato race. It's in their blood and must be washed out." Liberals and leftists also tended to see Japan's thoroughgoing defeat as a psychological necessity which would purge the national psyche of the appeals of militarism and blind emperor worship for years to come—a kind of historical shock therapy, as it were. Thus, the State Department's Alger Hiss stressed the importance of "Japan's being *thoroughly* defeated in the sense that . . . her entire national psychology be radically modified," while the prolific leftist Asia specialist T. A. Bisson argued that without "total victory" it would be necessary to fight the war with Japan "over again a generation hence."[69]

In such ways as these, diverse premises led to the same conclusion: that it was necessary and desirable to bring the war home to every man, woman, and child in Japan. This meant total victory on the battlefield. It meant unconditional surrender by the ruling elites. And it meant terror, heartbreak, and unforgettable memories for every family in Japan. Japanese propaganda concerning "fighting to the bitter end" and, indeed, a "hundred-year war" fueled these hates and passions and, for many, agonizing conclusions. And the clarion call for Japan's "thoroughgoing defeat" in turn reinforced the Japanese militarists as they struggled to rally the Japanese people to die en masse for their country. As one of the major Japanese newspapers put it after the battle of Iwo Jima, "Enemy plans to wipe Japan and the Japanese people off the face of the earth are no propaganda manifestations."[70]

One of the more provocative diversions in doing military history involves imagining things that did not happen, and there are several such hypothetical possibilities that attract students of the war in Asia. What if the Japanese had attacked only the British and European colonies in Southeast Asia, for example, or had been detected en route to Pearl Harbor? What if the U.S. aircraft carriers had been at the Hawaii anchorage as expected, or the Japanese had followed up with a second wave of attacks that included targets such as the fuel storage tanks? Suppose Hitler had not declared war against the United States following Japan's attack (it is still not clear why he did), or the Japanese had changed their naval codes and plugged their disastrous intelligence leaks before Midway, or the Japanese naval command at Leyte had been bolder and more imaginative—how would such developments have affected the course of the war? How long could the Japanese have held out if the United States had adopted a "Pacific first" strategy, as Admiral Ernest King and others consistently urged? On the other hand, how long could they have dragged out the war if they had not overextended themselves? Or again, what if the Allies had been willing and able to temper their demands for unconditional surrender, or the emperor of Japan had been less conservative and more willing to work actively for peace? Could the war have been ended sooner, before the terrible slaughter of the final years? To such familiar counterfactual speculations, we may add another that is more fanciful, though certainly no less provocative: if the Japanese had won, what sort of war-crimes trials would they have conducted?

A reasonable answer can be pieced together from the accusations the Japanese directed against the enemy during the war. It is easy to imagine, for example, that Japanese prosecutors would have adopted some sort of "conspiracy" charge, much as Allied prosecutors in the International Military Tribunal for the Far East did. More precisely, they probably would have focused on four general areas of alleged conspiracy: (1) the long-term Anglo-American ambition to gain hegemony over Asia, dating back to the nineteenth century; (2) more recent and concerted attempts to weaken Japan through military and economic pressure, probably dating from the Versailles and Washington conferences of 1919–22, and in any case from no later than the Manchurian Incident of 1931 (in the Tokyo war-crimes trials, Japan's "conspiracy against peace" was dated from 1928); (3) the wartime conspiracy of the two powers (or three, including China) to permanently reduce Japan to the status of a "third-rate nation" at best, or even a "slave state," as reflected in pronouncements concerning unconditional surrender, dismemberment of the Japanese Empire, and so on that emanated from top-level Allied conferences and were commonplace in the statements of Allied officials; and (4) a "conspiracy to commit atrocities," surely focusing in large measure on the policy of terror bombing of urban areas, culminating in the decision to use nuclear weapons against Japan. In addition to this hypothetical indictment, it is predictable that the Japanese also would have held military trials of Allied servicemen accused of committing atrocities and other conventional war crimes. There is little reason to believe that they would have conducted posthostility tribunals of whatever sort with anything but the harshest exercise of victor's justice. That, however, is not the point. Imagining such war-crimes trials is a useful way of sharpening the focus of Japan's case against the Anglo-American enemy and looking at the issue of atrocities, war crimes, and war responsibility from a different perspective.

Japanese long-range planning was notoriously poor prior to and during World War Two. Military projections were short-term. Occupation plans were drawn up posthaste after the invasion of the southern region had been initiated. Certainly, planning for the "postwar" period had little or no place in a bureaucracy that had lost control of the war by the end of 1942. Nonetheless, in the summer of 1943, a Japanese committee called the Greater East Asia War Inquiry Commission published what amounted to a preliminary prosecutor's brief against the United States and Great Britain. The commission was comprised of prominent civilians drawn from big business, politics, the academic world, and the diplomatic corps, and its "first" (and apparently last) report was published in English in July under the title "The American-British Challenge Directed Against Nippon."[71] After a brief introduction by foreign-policy adviser Arita Hachirō, which spoke of the need "to expose the outrageous words and actions of the enemy nations, words and actions which violate all the principles of justice and humanity," the report launched into a detailed summary of the causes of the present conflict. The Greater East Asia War was described as "the counteroffensive of the Oriental races against Occidental aggression," and the United States was depicted as having been Japan's primary antagonist since the turn of the century, when it hypocritically demanded an open door in China while using the Monroe Doctrine to prohibit outsiders from interfering in the Americas. The decades that followed witnessed a steady increase in anti-Japanese sentiment and activity on the part of the Americans: attempts to neutralize Manchuria and gain U.S. railroad rights there after the Russo-Japanese War; criticism of Japan's position in China at the peace conference at Versailles in 1919; pressure to force Great Britain to give up the Anglo-Japanese alliance in the early 1920s; the imposition of an unfavorable naval ratio at the 1921–22 Washington Conference; anti-Japanese immigration and commercial policies; support, along with Great Britain, of Chiang Kai-shek's attack on Japan's legitimate rights and interests in Manchuria and China, especially after the 1931 Manchurian Incident; and the ABCD (American, British, Chinese, Dutch) encirclement that began at the end of the 1930s, involving both economic strangulation and the strengthening of the Anglo-American military presence in Asia and the Pacific, most notably in Singapore and the Philippines. "The arrogant

Anglo-Saxons, ever covetous of securing world hegemony according to the principle of the white man's burden," the commission declared in commenting on the ABCD encirclement, "thus dared to take recourse to measures designed to stifle Nippon to death. It is small wonder that Nippon had to rise in arms."

Much of this lengthy report dealt in detail with the "villainous character of the encirclement ring" in the years just prior to Pearl Harbor, when trade with Japan was embargoed and Japanese assets were frozen. The longer-term "conspiracy" also was amply itemized, however, with much of the historical argument against the Anglo-American powers actually being taken from the standard English-language text of the time, A. Whitney Griswold's *The Far Eastern Policy of the United States*, published in 1938. The commission also argued that the current conflict with Japan was inseparable from two fundamental developments in American history: westward expansion and racial struggle. They called attention to the relocation or annihilation of the American Indians as the pioneers moved west, briefly mentioned the rise of Yellow Peril sentiments, and concluded that "when the problem is considered in this light . . . understanding is secured for the first time in regard to the United States' practically morbid jealousy of the Empire of Nippon, the sole first-class power among the colored nations of the world." British policy toward Japan was fundamentally the same as that of the United States, the report observed, differing only in that it was "not as vulgarly exhibitionistic." If Japan had not risen to break the encirclement ring, "the only paths that lay ahead of her were suicide or annihilation. Nippon chose to rise in self-defense."

The Greater East Asia War Inquiry Commission did not address developments after Pearl Harbor, but charges that the Allied powers were plotting to reduce Japan to insignificance as a power, and had engaged in the planned atrocity of massacring civilians through air power, came from all sides within Japan. Prime Minister Tōjō himself had described Allied policy as announced at the Cairo Conference, where the "unconditional surrender" formula was first mentioned, as being to reduce Japan to the status of a "slave state"; and the bombing of civilians and nonmilitary targets, as already seen, was made a capital offense in the wake of the Doolittle air raid.[72] Where conventional war crimes and atrocities were concerned, Japan's case against the enemy would have dwelled upon what it meant to be on the Japanese side of a war governed by such slogans as "Kill or be killed" and "No quarter, no surrender."

Since the 1880s, the Japanese military had been enjoined to exemplify true valor and avoid reprehensible behavior against the enemy. The important Imperial Precepts to Soldiers and Sailors, issued by the emperor in 1882 and memorized by servicemen during World War Two, stated in the third of its five articles that military men should behave in such a way as to earn the esteem of the enemy. "If you affect valor and act with violence," the precepts stated prophetically, "the world will in the end detest you and look upon you as wild beasts. Of this you should take heed." The *Senjinkun (Field Service Code)* which Japanese servicemen carried in their pockets similarly admonished them not to stain the honor of the Imperial Way by atrocious behavior.

The Japanese public was not completely unaware of brutal behavior by Japanese troops abroad. The press carried accounts of the "friendly contest" to cut off the heads of 150 Chinese, and the diarist who described the beheading of an airman in New Guinea had looked forward to recounting the episode back home. Accounts of massacres such as the Rape of Nanking, the Bataan Death March, and the sack of Manila, however, appear to have been successfully censored, and even withheld from relatively well-placed individuals. Sidney Mashbir, one of General MacArthur's intelligence officers, for example, described how a high Foreign Ministry official became visibly shaken right after Japan's surrender when he was informed of the sack of Manila and shown corroborating reports and photographs.[73] To the majority of Japanese, as to the Anglo-Americans, atrocities committed by one's own side were episodic, while the enemy's brutal acts were systematic and revealed a fundamentally perverse national character.

Some of the rumors concerning Allied atrocities which circulated among Japanese servicemen and civilians were sensational and quite imaginary. The Chinese were reported to roast their captives and cut out their hearts.[74] Young American men, it was said, qualified for the Marine Corps by murdering their parents, and routinely raped and killed women in Asia (this was one of the rumors behind the mass suicides by Japanese civilians on Saipan and Okinawa).[75] The Allies killed prisoners on the battlefields by laying them on the ground and running them over with tanks and bulldozers, and intended to drastically depopulate Japan itself if they won. In perhaps the most fanciful rumor of all, it was said the Allies planned to turn Japan into an international park and kill all but five thousand attractive women, who would serve as guides.[76] Other reports, however, were not imaginary. The Japanese accused the Allies of mutilating Japanese war dead for souvenirs, attacking and sinking hospital ships, shooting sailors who had abandoned ship and pilots who had bailed out, killing wounded soldiers on the battlefield, and torturing and executing prisoners—all of which did take place.

There is a popular belief that men who have experienced combat and been fortunate enough to survive return home to regale their cronies with war stories. In fact, many have seen and done such terrible things that they choose not to recall them at all. They turn to the building of a new life and attempt to bury the past. It is only after the passing of years that the past resurfaces and demands to be reencountered. Certainly, this was true of many veterans of the war in Asia, and in the most honest of these retrospective accounts one confronts not only the dehumanization that occurred on all sides in the jungles and on the atolls where the Pacific War was fought, but also acknowledgment of Allied atrocities. Thus, J. Glenn Gray, in his reflective 1959 study *The Warriors,* recalled how a few years earlier a veteran reminisced before a class of students about how his unit had unexpectedly "flushed" an isolated Japanese soldier on an island that had already been secured, and amused themselves by shooting at him as he dashed frantically about the clearing in search of safety:

> The soldiers found his movements uproariously funny and were prevented by their laughter from making an early end of the unfortunate man. Finally, however, they succeeded in killing him, and the incident cheered the whole platoon, giving them something to talk and joke about for days afterward. In relating this story to the class, the veteran emphasized the similarity of the enemy soldier to an animal. None of the American soldiers apparently even considered that he may have had human feelings of fear and the wish to be spared. What puzzled the veteran in retrospect was why his comrades and he found the incident so humorous. Now, a few years later, it appeared to him grisly and cruel enough; at the time, he had had no conscience about it whatever.[77]

This solitary death is not identical to the execution of the Allied airman in New Guinea. It lacks the diarist. The Japanese soldier was technically not a prisoner, although he was helpless. There was no ritual. But the human tragedy is much the same, and this emerges in many other recollections by Allied participants as well. A Marine interviewed almost four decades after the event, for example, recalled the fate of a Japanese soldier on Guadalcanal who responded to an appeal to surrender and emerged from a pillbox with his hands over his head: "Now, I'm ashamed to say this, but one of our men shot him down. Not only was this a vicious thing to do but it was asinine. You can bet your life that none of the others are going to come out."[78] The popular American writer William Manchester, in *Goodbye, Darkness,* his 1980 memoir of fighting in the Pacific, recalled a young American soldier on Okinawa, crazed by the death of a revered commander, who "snatched up a submachine gun and unforgivably massacred a line of unarmed Japanese soldiers who had just surrendered."[79] The military historian Denis Warner, in a book about Japanese suicide units published in 1982, introduced in passing his own firsthand experience on Bougainville, where wounded Japanese attempting to surrender were ordered shot by the Australian commander:

> "But sir, they are wounded and want to surrender," a colonel protested to [a major general] at the edge of the cleared perimeter after a massive and unsuccessful Japanese attack.
> "You heard me, Colonel," replied [the major general], who was only yards away from upstretched Japanese hands. "I want no prisoners. Shoot them all."
> They were shot.[80]

In a thoughtful memoir published by Presidio Press in 1981, Professor E. B. Sledge, an American biologist, painfully recalled what it was like to be a young frontline Marine at two of the fiercest battles of the Pacific, Peleliu and Okinawa, where both sides were possessed by "a brutish, primitive hatred." Sledge, deeply religious and patriotic, watched his comrades go over the edge: severing the hand of a dead Japanese as a battlefield trophy, "harvesting gold teeth" from the enemy dead, urinating in a corpse's upturned mouth, shooting a terrified old Okinawan woman and casually dismissing her as "just an old gook woman who wanted me to put her out of her misery." More terrifying still, Sledge found himself coming close to accepting such conduct as normal. "Time had no meaning, life had no meaning," he writes at one point. "The fierce struggle for survival . . . eroded the veneer of civilization and made savages of us all. We existed in an environment totally incomprehensible to men behind the lines—service troops and civilians."[81] Another Marine account of the fighting in the Pacific described this hell on earth similarly: "Death was as common as head colds. . . . I had resigned from the human race. . . . I just wanted to kill."[82] And these are the reminiscences of men who fought on the winning side.

The Japanese themselves bore no little responsibility for the reluctance of Allied soldiers to take prisoners, for early in the war they established a practice of booby-trapping their dead and wounded, and using fake surrenders to ambush unwary foes. Here again, certain incidents were elevated to symbolic status, and became accepted as exemplifying the ineffable and unvariable national character of the enemy. It would have been a rare Marine indeed, for example, who did not "know" the enemy —perhaps even before he had even seen a Japanese—through the story of the "Goettge patrol," concerning over twenty Marines who responded to what appeared to be a Japanese attempt to surrender, and were ambushed, shot, and bayonetted to death. The incident occurred on August 12, 1942, at the very outset of the Guadalcanal campaign, and the psychology of "Kill or be killed" ruled the battlefield thereafter.[83] Although the slogan became well known to civilians on the home front in the United States and the United Kingdom, however, few could appreciate what this really meant; and, indeed, few really wanted to know. "What kind of war do civilians suppose we fought, anyway?" asked Edgar L. Jones, a former American war correspondent in the Pacific, in the February 1946 issue of *Atlantic Monthly*. "We shot prisoners in cold blood, wiped out hospitals, strafed lifeboats, killed or mistreated enemy civilians, finished off the enemy wounded, tossed the dying into a hole with the dead, and in the Pacific boiled the flesh off enemy skulls to make table ornaments for sweethearts, or carved their bones into letter openers." Jones went on to speak of such practices as adjusting flamethrowers so that they did not kill their Japanese targets instantly. At the same time, he also took care to attribute such behavior to the nature of modern war itself, and to emphasize that it was done by all sides, but by no means condoned by all or even most fighting men.[84]

On the Allied side, some forms of battlefield degeneracy were in fact fairly well publicized while the war was going on. This was especially true of the practice of collecting grisly battlefield trophies from the Japanese dead or near dead, in the form of gold teeth, ears, bones, scalps, and skulls. For some servicemen, gold teeth and severed ears became a fetish even before they had engaged in combat. In *Guadalcanal Diary*, a best-seller published late in 1942, the journalist Richard Tregaskis recreated the conversation of young men bolstering their courage before encountering their first Japanese. "They say the Japs have a lot of gold teeth. I'm going to make myself a necklace," said one. "I'm going to bring back some Jap ears," another declared. "Pickled."[85] In the diary of a seaman, published after the war, we find tucked away in an entry in July 1944 the casual mention of a Marine who had already collected seventeen gold teeth, the last from a Japanese soldier on Saipan who was wounded and still moving his hands.[86] Sledge, in his memoir of Peleliu and Okinawa, records an even more excruciating scene of a wounded Japanese thrashing on the ground as a Marine slit his cheeks open and carved his gold-crowned teeth out with a kabar.[87]

Despite the attention given in Allied propaganda to Hideyoshi's three-and-a-half-century-old ear mound, in the current war in Asia it was Allied combatants who collected ears. Like collecting gold teeth, this practice was no secret. "The other night," read an account in the Marine monthly *Leatherneck* in mid-1943, "Stanley emptied his pockets of 'souvenirs'—eleven ears from dead Japs. It was not disgusting, as it would be from the civilian point of view. None of us could get emotional over it."[88] Even as battle-hardened veterans were assuming that civilians would be shocked by such acts, however, the press in the United States contained evidence to the contrary. In April 1943, the *Baltimore Sun* ran a story about a local mother who had petitioned authorities to permit her son to mail her an ear he had cut off a Japanese soldier in the South Pacific. She wished to nail it to her front door for all to see. On the very same day, the *Detroit Free Press* deemed newsworthy the story of an underage youth who had enlisted and "bribed" his chaplain not to disclose his age by promising him the third pair of ears he collected.[89]

Scalps, bones, and skulls were somewhat rarer trophies, but the latter two achieved special notoriety in both the United States and Japan when an American serviceman sent President Roosevelt a letter opener made from the bone of a dead Japanese (the president refused it), and *Life* published a full-page photograph of an attractive blonde posing with a Japanese skull she had been sent by her fiancé in the Pacific. *Life* treated this as a human-interest story, while Japanese propagandists gave it wide publicity as a revelation of the American national character.[90] Another well-known *Life* photograph revealed the practice of using Japanese skulls as ornaments on U.S. military vehicles. For practical reasons, however, skulls were not popular as personal trophies, for, as we learn from the gruesome details of contemporary accounts, they were cumbersome to carry and the process of removing the flesh from a severed head (by boiling it, sometimes in lye, or setting it out for the ants to eat) was smelly and offensive.

Most combatants did not engage in such souvenir hunting, and *Leatherneck* itself published a cartoon which expressed contempt and pity for all scavengers of the dead.[91] At the same time, most fighting men had personal knowledge of such practices and accepted them as inevitable under the circumstances. It is virtually inconceivable, however, that teeth, ears, and skulls could have been collected from German or Italian war dead and publicized in the Anglo-American countries without provoking an uproar; and in this we have yet another inkling of the racial dimensions of the war.

Of greater interest is what the reminiscences cited earlier reveal: that many men in the field participated in or at least witnessed the killing of helpless, wounded, or captured Japanese. Here again, behavior which was presented to Western audiences as revealing the unique and inherent savagery of the Japanese occurred on both sides. Even Westerners who acknowledged this, however, usually went on to depict such Allied acts as a just retribution in the Old Testament sense. A familiar subject of anti-Japanese graphics, for example, was a white airman in a parachute being gunned down by a Japanese pilot. "And how are your ethics today?" ran the heading of an advertisement which used this scene.[92] Japanese, however, suffered the same fate when the tables were turned. "A few Japs parachuted when they were hit," a young seaman wrote in his diary late in 1943, "but a few sailors and Marines on the 20 mm opened up on the ones in the chutes and when they hit the water they were nothing but a piece of meat cut to ribbons." The gunners, he went on, were mildly chastised by their superiors and in the same breath praised for their good shooting. In any case, he added, it was the Japanese themselves who started doing this.[93]

Some massacres of Japanese, like that of the wounded soldiers attempting to surrender on Bougainville, were ordered to take place by Allied officers, or at least received tacit support from superior officers after the event. A U.S. submarine commander who sank a Japanese transport and then spent upwards of an hour killing the hundreds and possibly thousands of Japanese survivors with his deck guns, for example, was commended and publicly honored by his superiors even though he included an account of the slaughter in his official report. To Navy colleagues, many of whom were repulsed by this action, the fact that the officer received high praise rather than censure was interpreted as an endorsement of such practices by the submarine high command.[94] An equally grim butchery took place on March 4, 1943, the day after the three-day battle of the Bismarck Sea, when U.S. and Australian aircraft systematically searched the seas for Japanese survivors and strafed every raft and lifeboat they found. "It was rather a sloppy job," a U.S. major from the 5th Bomber Command wrote in his official battle report, "and some of the boys got sick. But that is something you have to learn. The enemy is out to kill you and you are out to kill the enemy. You can't be sporting in a war."[95]

The slaughter on the Bismarck Sea is of particular interest for two reasons. First, the theater of operations was close to New Guinea, where the beheading of the Allied airman which so aroused popular rage against the Japanese "savages" occurred. (By coincidence, the sea battle and the beheading even took place in the very same month.) And second, the killing of Japanese survivors was no secret. The Allied press followed military censorship stipulations faithfully, and apparently was not placed under severe restrictions in its coverage of this action. Thus, *Time,* in a good example of Old Testament fervor, informed its readers on March 15, 1943, that "low-flying fighters turned lifeboats towed by motor barges, and packed with Jap survivors, into bloody sieves. Loosed on the Japs was the same ferocity which they had often displayed. This time few, if any, Japs in battle green reached shore." When, two weeks later, *Time* published a single letter to the editor questioning the morality of such "cold-blooded slaughter," this triggered a spate of subsequent letters ridiculing the notion that "brotherly love" had any place in the current conflict. One respondent began with a list of Japanese atrocities, and then asked if the original letter writer would be "remorseful about killing a helpless rattle-snake after he had spent his 'strike.' " Another wrote: "Thoroughly enjoyed reading of the 'cold-blooded slaughter.' . . . Another good old American custom I would like to see is nailing a Jap hide on every 'backhouse' door in America." Still another stated that if the Americans did not treat the Japanese as atrociously as they treated others, "we would have lost 'face' " in their eyes.[96]

The kill-or-be-killed psychology was of course a vicious circle, and this should be kept in mind when considering one of the most potent beliefs of the war years: that Japanese fighting men did not surrender. There were occasions when fair numbers of Japanese were taken prisoner, but it is true that in the jungle and island battles of the Pacific, most Japanese fought until they were killed, or committed suicide. They did so for many reasons, prominent among them the fact that they were socialized to sacrifice themselves for the emperor and the state, and ordered not to surrender by their commanders. The Japanese were told they were fighting a holy war against a demonic foe, and many died believing they were giving their lives for a noble cause—"mad dogs" to their enemies, but martyrs in their own eyes and heroes in the eyes of their countrymen and countrywomen. Mass psychology and mass frenzy may have played a part in these deaths, even inebriation in some of the banzai charges, but so did duty, honor, and obedience in ways familiar everywhere: Japanese fighting men also died simply because their country or sovereign called upon them to do so. Still others fought to the bitter end because they believed, with good reason, that surrender would bring ostracism upon their families.

What is often overlooked, however, is that countless thousands of Japanese perished because they saw no alternative. In a report dated June 1945, the U.S. Office of War Information noted that 84 percent of one group of interrogated Japanese prisoners (many of them injured or unconscious when captured) stated that they had expected to be killed or tortured by the Allies if taken prisoner. The OWI analysts described this as being typical, and concluded that fear of the consequences of surrender, "rather than Bushido," was the motivation for many Japanese battle deaths in hopeless circumstances—as much as, and probably more than, the other two major considerations: fear of disgrace at home, and "the positive desire to die for one's nation, ancestors, and god-emperor." Even those Japanese who were willing to risk surrendering anyway found it difficult to do so. A summary report prepared for the OWI immediately after the war ended, for example, noted that documents pertaining to Japanese prisoners were "full of accounts of ingenious schemes devised by POWs to avoid being shot while trying to give themselves up," due to the fact of "surrender being made difficult by the unwillingness to take prisoners" on the part of Allied fighting men.[97]

As the American analysts themselves acknowledged, these Japanese fears were not irrational. In many battles, neither Allied fighting men nor their commanders wanted many POWs. This was not official policy, and there were exceptions in certain places, but over wide reaches of the Asian battleground it was everyday practice. The Marine battle cry on Tarawa made no bones about this: "Kill the Jap bastards! Take no prisoners!"[98] —and certain U.S. units became legendary for living up to this motto wherever they fought. An article published by a U.S. Army captain shortly after the war, for example, carried the proud title "The 41st Didn't Take Prisoners." The article dealt with the 41st Division under MacArthur's command, nicknamed "the Butchers" in Tokyo Rose's propaganda broadcasts, and characterized the combat in the Pacific in typical terms as "a merciless struggle, with no holds barred." Prisoners were taken primarily when it suited military needs for intelligence purposes. Thus, we learn that in a mission that rescued several hundred Allied prisoners at Aitape in 1944, a task force of the 41st Division "even took forty-three prisoners, mostly labor troops, despite the division staff officer's complaints that they had enough prisoners already." In a small but costly battle at Wakde Island off Dutch New Guinea the same year, "the general wanted a prisoner, so we got him a prisoner."[99] The reputation of not taking prisoners also became associated with Australian troops in general. In many instances, moreover, Japanese who did become prisoners were killed on the spot or en route to the prisoner compounds.

Stories of this nature frequently emerge in conversations with veterans of the Pacific War, often—like J. Glenn Gray's veteran—in a tone almost of disbelief concerning the blind savagery of those days. No source, however, captures the war hates and war crimes of this merciless struggle more soberly than Charles Lindbergh's diary. For over four months in mid-1944, Lindbergh lived and flew as a civilian observer with U.S. forces based in New Guinea, and as the weeks passed he became deeply troubled, not by the willingness to kill on the part of the soldiers, which he accepted as an inherent part of the war, but by the utter contempt in which Allied fighting men held their Japanese adversaries. The famous "Lone Eagle," whose isolationist sentiments had placed him among the conservative opponents of President Roosevelt's policies, really hearkened back to what Gray has called the more chivalrous tradition of the professional militarist, who accepts the necessity of war while maintaining respect for his adversary, recognizing courage as courage and duty as duty, irrespective of the uniform worn. Lindbergh found no such sentiments among the Allied forces in the Pacific, where officers and enlisted men alike saw the enemy simply as animals and "yellow sons of bitches," and his detailed journal may be the most forthright firsthand account available of the "other" side of the Pacific War.

On May 18, 1944, about two weeks after Lindbergh had tied in with a Marine unit, he recorded that the camps were full of reports of Japanese torture and the beheading of captured American pilots. A month later, on June 21, he summarized the conversation of an American general who told how an unsuspecting Japanese prisoner was given a cigarette and then seized from behind and had his throat "slit from ear to ear" as a demonstration of how to kill Japanese. Lindbergh's objections were treated with tolerant scorn and pity. The journal entry for June 26 told of a massacre of Japanese prisoners and of Japanese airmen being shot in their parachutes. Of several thousand prisoners taken at a certain place, Lindbergh was informed, "only a hundred or two were turned in. They had an accident with the rest. It doesn't encourage the rest to surrender when they hear of their buddies being marched out on the flying field and machine guns turned loose upon them." The Japanese deserved such treatment, it was explained to Lindbergh, for they mutilated prisoners and shot airmen in their parachutes. The entry for July 28 spoke of kicking in the teeth of Japanese, sometimes before and sometimes after executing them.

On July 13, Lindbergh wrote, "It was freely admitted that some of our soldiers tortured Jap prisoners and were as cruel and barbaric at times as the Japs themselves. Our men think nothing of shooting a Japanese prisoner or a soldier attempting to surrender. They treat the Japs with less respect than they would give to an animal, and these acts are condoned by almost everyone." On July 21, he wrote again about the desire to ruthlessly exterminate all Japanese. "A Japanese soldier who cuts off an American soldier's head is an Oriental barbarian, 'lower than a rat,' " he observed, whereas "an American soldier who slits a Japanese throat 'did it only because he knew the Japs had done it to his buddies.' " Lindbergh still believed that "Oriental atrocities are often worse than ours," but the line was increasingly hard to draw. One day later, he wrote of being told by a U.S. infantry colonel that "our boys just don't take prisoners." On July 24, he visited a battle site where Japanese corpses had been ransacked for gold teeth, others had been dumped in garbage pits, and a cave was filled with dead Japanese who had tried to surrender but been told to "get the hell back in and fight it out."

On August 6, Lindbergh described the blackboard in the pilots' alert tent, with a naked girl chalked in at the bottom and a Japanese skull hung on the top. A few days later, he wrote that when the word went out to take Japanese prisoners, and was accompanied by material inducements, prisoners were brought in in great numbers, but usually there was no incentive for doing this. He reported the slaughter of all inmates of a Japanese hospital, and went on to mention that the Australians often threw Japanese out of airplanes on their way to prison compounds and then reported that they had committed hara-kiri. At the same time, however, reports of Japanese castrating prisoners and even engaging in cannibalism persuaded Lindbergh that "barbaric as our men are at times, the Orientals appear to be worse." Another journal entry in early August mentioned a patrol unit that had taken up the hobby of making penholders, paper knives, and the like out of the thigh bones of dead Japanese. On August 30, Lindbergh visited Tarawa, recalled the terrible casualties there, and told of a naval officer who lined up the few Japanese captured, kept those who could speak English for questioning, and had the rest killed. In early September, he noted that on some islands Marines actually dug up dead bodies in their search for gold teeth. Elsewhere they collected noses as well as ears, teeth, and skulls. When Lindbergh finally left the Pacific islands and cleared customs in Hawaii, he was asked if he had any bones in his baggage. It was, he was told, a routine question.[100]

In the opening days of 1943, almost a year and a half before Lindbergh arrived on New Guinea, General Blamey gave an emotional speech to his exhausted Australian troops, who were just beginning to turn the tide against the Japanese on that same bitterly contested island. "You have taught the world that you are infinitely superior to this inhuman foe against whom you were pitted," he said. "Your enemy is a curious race —a cross between the human being and the ape. And like the ape, when he is cornered he knows how to die. But he is inferior to you, and you know it, and that knowledge will help you to victory." The general went on to compare his men to the courageous Roman legionnaires of ancient times, and to tell them that although the road ahead was long and hard, they were fighting for nothing less than the cause of civilization itself. "You know that we have to exterminate these vermin if we and our families are to live," he concluded. "We must go on to the end if civilization is to survive. We must exterminate the Japanese." In an interview around the same time that was reported on page 1 of the New York Times, Blamey, visiting the Buna battlefield, was quoted in much the same terms. "Fighting Japs is not like fighting normal human beings," he explained. "The Jap is a little barbarian. . . . We are not dealing with humans as we know them. We are dealing with something primitive. Our troops have the right view of the Japs. They regard them as vermin." The general even went on to refer to the enemy as simply "these things."[101]

One cannot imagine a more categorical distinction than this between the superior self and inferior other, but General Blamey had no monopoly on such rhetoric. Japanese leaders spoke in analogous ways, calling on their "pure" countrymen to drive the Anglo-American devils out of Asia, even to annihilate them completely, and calling also on their own history for near-legendary models of fortitude and bravery. In their castigation of the enemy, they offered close counterparts to the Blamey text. An editorial on the American firebombing of Japanese cities, for example, stated that "this is most emphatically not war," but rather an "attempt at the terrorization of the civilian population through the most horrible means ever conceived by a fiendish mind." By these immoral acts, the Americans had shown themselves once and for all to be "utterly lacking in any ability to understand the principles of humanity. Whatever may be the state of their material civilization, they are nothing but lawless savages in spirit who are ruled by fiendish passions and unrestrained lust for blood. Against such enemies of decency and humanity, the civilized world must rise in protest and back up that protest with punitive force. Only through the complete chastisement of such barbarians can the world be made safe for civilization."[102]

There are many such parallel declarations in the propaganda of both sides, and these become even more suggestive when we consider another passage in General Blamey's speech. "You have lost many comrades," he told his men, "but you have learnt that it is the highest and sweetest achievement of us all that we should die for our country." Such words could have been placed in the mouth of a Japanese commander almost without change (they would not have said "sweet"); but when the Japanese did speak of the nobility of dying for emperor and country, their enemies offered this as evidence of their peculiar fanaticism, irrationality, even collective psychosis and death wish. The Japanese, in turn, belittled the Allied dead. Holy wars permit scant space for reflecting on a common humanity, whether the commonality lie in bravery and idealism, or obedience and helplessness, or arrogance, oppression, and atrocity.

Most of the propaganda the Allies and Japanese engaged in concerning the enemy's atrocious behavior was rooted in actual occurrences, and the horror, rage, and hatred this provoked on all sides was natural. Of greater interest now, however, is the way such behavior was offered as confirmation of the innately inferior and immoral nature of the enemy— a reflection of national character—when, in fact, the pages of history everywhere are stained with cruelty and unbridled savagery. The "civilization" which both the Allies and the Japanese claimed to be defending had failed to stem these impulses, and World War Two simply witnessed new as well as old ways of carrying out mass destruction and individual violence. Allied propagandists were not distorting the history of Japan when they pointed to much that was cruel in the Japanese past. They had to romanticize or simply forget their own history, however, to turn such behavior into something uniquely Japanese—to ignore, for example, the long history of torture and casual capital punishment in the West, the genocide of the Indian population in the Western Hemisphere by the sixteenth-century conquistadores,[103] the "hell ships" of the Western slave trade, the death march of American Indians forcibly removed from the eastern United States in the 1830s, the ten thousand or more Union prisoners of war who died at Andersonville during the U.S. Civil War, the introduction of "modern" strategies of annihilation and terrorization of civilians by Napoleon and Lee and Grant and Sherman, and the death marches and massacres of native peoples by the European colonialists in Africa and Asia, right up to 1941.[104] In their genuine shock at the death rituals which the Japanese military engaged in, moreover, the Westerners tended to forget not only their own "epics of defeat" (immortalized in such names as Roland, Thermopylae, the Alamo, and Custer), but also the self-sacrifice against hopeless odds of thousands of Allied fighting men. To give but one example, the number of United Kingdom airmen who gave their lives in World War Two was ten times greater than the number of Japanese who died as kamikaze pilots. The acceptance of certain death by the latter did indeed set them apart, but the difference can be exaggerated.[105]

In this milieu of historical forgetfulness, selective reporting, centralized propaganda, and a truly savage war, atrocities and war crimes played a major role in the propagation of racial and cultural stereotypes. The stereotypes preceded the atrocities, however, and had an independent existence apart from any specific event. Seemingly casual expressions—General Blamey's reference to the infinite superiority of his men, and his call to exterminate the inhuman Japanese, the apes, the vermin; or Japanese references to their purity, and their call to chastise the fiendish foe or kill the Anglo-American devils—such expressions, in actuality, were not at all random. They belonged to webs of perception that had existed for centuries in Western and Japanese culture, and the atrocities were taken as simply confirming their validity. It is these more fundamental perceptions that are the subject of the chapters that follow.

PART II

THE WAR IN WESTERN EYES

◄ **C H A P T E R   4** ►
APES AND OTHERS

Despite the kill-or-be-killed nature of the fighting in the Pacific, hundreds of Japanese did become prisoners. Many were ill, wounded, or unconscious when captured. Others were taken by surprise and offered little resistance. Still others took the initiative to surrender, usually at considerable risk. And with few exceptions, their behavior as prisoners confounded initial expectations. The ferocious, fanatic foe suddenly revealed himself to be exceedingly mild and cooperative. Since most had been told they would be killed or tortured if they fell into Allied hands, they expressed gratitude at receiving good treatment. About four out of every five prisoners actually demonstrated "remarkable cooperation," in the words of an internal U.S. report, in such ways as providing military information and offering to assist in trying to persuade other Japanese to surrender.[1]

Presumedly, such behavior should have jarred those on the other side who encountered it, and forced them to rethink their stereotypes of the enemy. To some extent this did happen. Intelligence analysts in Washington, as well as in MacArthur's command after the return to the Philippines, concluded that a serious psychological-warfare campaign directed to the Japanese could expedite surrenders in the field and hasten the end of the war; but such ideas had little impact.[2] The war was so savage and war hates ran so deep that even individuals who encountered the Japanese as prisoners ordinarily found it impossible to change their views. General Blamey's kind of war words were gospel: the Japanese were subhuman.

There may be no better witness to this than the journalist Ernie Pyle, whose down-home style earned him the status of a folk hero among American war correspondents. He was, in American terms, a humanist: he not only gave the names of the soldiers he wrote about, but also the streets on which they lived in the United States and the numbers of their houses. Pyle gained his fame covering the war in Europe, and was transferred to the Pacific in February 1945, three months before Germany surrendered. By this time, his dispatches were carried by almost seven hundred newspapers and reached an estimated fourteen million readers.

What Pyle told this impressive audience, right away, was that the enemy in Asia was different. "In Europe we felt that our enemies, horrible and deadly as they were, were still people," he explained in one of his first reports from the Pacific. "But out here I soon gathered that the Japanese were looked upon as something subhuman and repulsive; the way some people feel about cockroaches or mice." To Pyle himself, this seemed a perfectly appropriate response, for he went on to describe how, soon after arriving, he had seen some Japanese prisoners in a fenced-in enclosure. "They were wrestling and laughing and talking just like normal human beings," he wrote. "And yet they gave me the creeps, and I wanted a mental bath after looking at them."[3]

So commonplace was this attitude that a popular American scientific magazine could publish a short entry in 1945 entitled "Why Americans Hate Japs More than Nazis" without first demonstrating that this was the case. No one questioned such an observation. And although the explanation offered may have been simplistic (the Japanese were more hated because of their greater outward physical differences), the very manner in which the magazine phrased the problem was suggestive in unintended ways. In addition to using the conventionally pejorative "Japs" for Japanese, the article followed the telltale phrasing of the war years by speaking not of the Germans and the Japanese, but of the Nazis and the Japanese. A well-publicized wartime book by a New York Times correspondent who had been assigned to both Germany and Japan followed this pattern with a chapter entitled "Nips and Nazis." A poster by the Veterans of Foreign Wars sharpened the distinction even further, in a familiar way, with the warning, "Remember Hitler and the Japs are trying to get us fighting among ourselves." Songwriters caught the same bias in a patriotic song called "There'll Be No Adolf Hitler nor Yellow Japs to Fear."[4]

The implications of perceiving the enemy as "Nazis" on the one hand and "Japs" on the other were enormous, for this left space for the recognition of the "good German," but scant comparable place for "good Japanese." Magazines like *Time* hammered this home even further by frequently referring to "the Jap" rather than "Japs," thereby denying the enemy even the merest semblance of pluralism. Indeed, in wartime jargon, the notion of "good Japanese" came to take on an entirely different meaning than that of "good Germans," as Admiral William F. Halsey emphasized at a news conference early in 1944. "The only good Jap is a Jap who's been dead six months," the commander of the U.S. South Pacific Force declared, and he did not mean just combatants. "When we get to Tokyo, where we're bound to get eventually," Halsey went on, "we'll have a little celebration where Tokyo was." Halsey was improvising on a popular wartime saying, that "the only good Jap is a dead Jap," and his colleagues in the military often endorsed this sentiment in their own fashion. Early in 1943, for example, *Leatherneck,* the Marine monthly, ran a photograph of Japanese corpses on Guadalcanal with an uppercase headline reading "GOOD JAPS" and a caption emphasizing that "GOOD JAPS are dead Japs."[5]

Hollywood movies of the war years practically canonized these contrasting perceptions of the enemy. The closest counterparts to good Germans and bad Germans which they seemed able to muster for Asia were good nationalities (the Chinese, the Filipinos) and bad (the Japanese). That this distinction between the enemy in Asia and the enemy in Europe derived less from the events of the war than from deep-seated racial bias was reflected in the opening months of 1942, when the U.S. government incarcerated Japanese-Americans en masse, while taking no comparable action against residents of German or Italian origin. Indeed, U.S. citizens of Japanese extraction were treated with greater suspicion and severity than German or Italian aliens—despite the fact that the German-American Bund (with an estimated membership of twenty thousand) had agitated on behalf of Hitler in the United States prior to the outbreak of war, and despite the fact that there never was, at Pearl Harbor or later, any evidence of organized subversion among the Japanese community.

In fact, the treatment of Japanese-Americans is a natural starting point for any study of the racial aspects of the war, for it reveals not merely the clearcut racial stigmatization of the Japanese, but also the official endorsement this received.[6] Under Executive Order 9066, signed by President Roosevelt on February 19, 1942, more than 110,000 persons of Japanese ancestry were removed from California, Oregon, and Washington and interned in ten camps in the interior of the United States. The president of the United States, the secretary of war, the U.S. military establishment, the Department of Justice and eventually the Supreme Court, and the U.S. Congress—all actively participated in enacting and upholding this policy. Similar internments were carried out in Canada, Mexico, and Peru. Such official consecration of anti-Japanese racism was profoundly symbolic: if every man, woman, and child of Japanese origin on the western coasts of the Americas was categorically identified by the highest quarters as a potential menace simply because of his or her ethnicity, then the real Japanese enemy abroad could only be perceived as a truly faceless, monolithic, incorrigible, and stupendously formidable foe.

Obviously, "blood told" where the Japanese—but not the Germans or Italians—were concerned, a point clearly articulated by some of the white Americans who supported the relocation of the Japanese. "Blood will tell," declared the mayor of Los Angeles in a public statement urging the government to move against Japanese-Americans on the grounds that they were "unassimilable," and his West Coast counterparts agreed almost to a man; of all the mayors of large cities in the three westernmost states, only one (the mayor of Tacoma, Washington) opposed forced relocation. Secretary of War Henry Stimson, who assumed major responsibility for the decision to go ahead with Executive Order 9066, recorded in his diary for February 10, 1942, that in his estimation second-generation Japanese-Americans were even more dangerous than their immigrant parents. They either had to be removed from the coastal areas as part of a general evacuation, he continued, "or by frankly trying to put them out on the ground that their racial characteristics are such that we cannot understand or trust even the citizen Japanese. This latter is the fact but I am afraid it will make a tremendous hole in our constitutional system to apply it."

Such blood-will-tell racism was encoded in a variety of formulaic images and expressions. The *Los Angeles Times*, for instance, turned to reptilian metaphor: "A viper is nonetheless a viper wherever the egg is hatched—so a Japanese-American, born of Japanese parents, grows up to be a Japanese not an American." In a telephone conversation shortly before the order for evacuation was signed by President Roosevelt, John J. McCloy, the influential assistant secretary of war, agreed with the more prosaic summation of the problem made by Lieutenant General John L. De Witt, commander of the Western Defense Command, to the effect that whereas Germans and Italians could be treated as individuals, "a Jap is a Jap." General De Witt, who administered the evacuation, still found this phrasing felicitous over a year later when called upon to testify before a congressional committee as to why the incarcerated Japanese-Americans, even bonafide citizens, still could not be allowed to return home. "A Jap's a Jap," he reiterated in public testimony in April 1943. "You can't change him by giving him a piece of paper." Indeed, in General De Witt's view, the menace posed by the Japanese could only be eliminated by destroying the Japanese as a race. In his testimony of early 1943, the general went on to state frankly that he was not worried about German or Italian nationals, "but the Japs we will be worried about all the time until they are wiped off the face of the map." This was, by then, familiar rhetoric in the nation's capital. A day before the president signed the executive order of February 19, a member of the House of Representatives had declared that the Japanese should be removed "even to the third and fourth generation." "Once a Jap, always a Jap," exclaimed John Rankin of Mississippi. "You can't any more regenerate a Jap than you can reverse the laws of nature."[7]

Another manifestation of this most emotional level of anti-Japanese racism was the routine use of racial slang in the media and official memoranda as well as everyday discourse. "Nip" (from Nippon, the Japanese reading of the country's name) and especially "Jap" were routinely used in the daily press and major weeklies or monthlies such as *Time, Life, Newsweek,* and *Reader's Digest.* "Jap" was also extremely popular in the music world, where the scramble to turn out a memorable war song did not end with the release of tunes such as "The Remember Pearl Harbor March" and "Good-bye Mama, I'm Off to Yokohama." "Mow the Japs Down!" and "We've Got to Do a Job on the Japs, Baby" are fair samples of the wartime songs, although titles with internal rhymes on "Jap" were even more popular. These included "You're a Sap, Mister Jap," "Let's Take a Rap at the Jap," "They're Gonna Be Playing Taps on the Japs," and "We're Gonna Have to Slap the Dirty Little Jap." There was no real counterpart to this where Germany and Italy were concerned. "Nazis" was the common phrase for the German enemy. Cruder epithets for the Germans (heinies, Huns, Jerrys, Krauts) were used sparingly by comparison.[8]

A characteristic feature of this level of anti-Japanese sentiment was the resort to nonhuman or subhuman representation, in which the Japanese were perceived as animals, reptiles, or insects (monkeys, baboons, gorillas, dogs, mice and rats, vipers and rattlesnakes, cockroaches, vermin —or, more indirectly, "the Japanese herd" and the like). The variety of such metaphors was so great that they sometimes seemed casual and almost original. On the contrary, they were well routinized as idioms of everyday discourse, and immensely consequential in their ultimate functions. At the simplest level, they dehumanized the Japanese and enlarged the chasm between "us" and "them" to the point where it was perceived to be virtually unbridgeable. As Pyle matter-of-factly observed, the enemy in Europe "were still people." The Japanese were not, and in good part they were not because they were denied even the ordinary vocabularies of "being human."

For many Japanese-Americans, the verbal stripping of their humanity was accompanied by humiliating treatment that reinforced the impression of being less than human. They were not merely driven from their homes and communities on the West Coast and rounded up like cattle, but actually forced to live in facilities meant for animals for weeks and even months before being moved to their final quarters in the relocation camps. In the state of Washington, two thousand Japanese-Americans were crowded into a single filthy building in the Portland stockyard, where they slept on gunnysacks filled with straw. In California, evacuees were squeezed into stalls in the stables at racetracks such as Santa Anita and Tanforan. At the Santa Anita assembly center, which eventually housed eighty-five hundred Japanese-Americans, only four days elapsed between the removal of the horses and the arrival of the first Japanese-Americans; the only facilities for bathing were the horse showers, and here as elsewhere the stench of manure lingered indefinitely. Other evacuees were initially housed in horse or cattle stalls at various fairgrounds. At the Puyallup assembly center in Washington (which was called Camp Harmony), some were even lodged in converted pigpens. The only redeeming touch of grace in these circumstances lay in the dignity of the victims themselves.[9]

Looking upon the Japanese as animals, or a different species of some sort, was common at official levels in Washington and London before Pearl Harbor. A year and a half before the outbreak of the war, for instance, Churchill told Roosevelt that he was counting on the president "to keep that Japanese dog quiet in the Pacific." Secretary of War Henry Stimson picked up much the same image in October 1941 when arguing, as he had long done, in support of economic sanctions against Japan. When President Woodrow Wilson took a hard line against the Japanese in 1919, Stimson reminded the U.S. cabinet, they had retreated "like whipped puppies." During the war, "mad dogs" as well as "yellow dogs" were everyday epithets for the Japanese among the Western Allies. An American who spent considerable time in Japan between 1936 and late 1941 wrote a wartime article describing the evolution of one of his Japanese acquaintances from a moderate newsman into a "mad dog" ultranationalist military officer. "Mad dogs," he concluded, "are just insane animals that should be shot."[10]

After his repatriation from Japan in the first half of 1942, former U.S. Ambassador Joseph Grew, whom some Westerners regarded as an oracle on things Japanese, drew equally upon the insect and animal kingdoms in his lectures about the enemy. He never attempted to conceal his personal respect and affection for certain "moderate" members of the cultured upper classes in Japan, but his most often-quoted statements about the Japanese people in general were those which also basically depersonalized them. For instance, Grew described Japan as a bustling hive of bees all servicing the queen (in real life, the emperor), and this image of the busy, buzzing swarm or its grounded counterpart the anthill was also popular with many other Western writers. An American sociologist explained on a wartime radio broadcast sponsored by General Electric that the Japanese were "a closely disciplined and conformist people—a veritable human bee-hive or ant-hill," in sharp contrast to the "independent and individualistic" Chinese. This, he continued, made Japan a "totalitarian" nation long before the word was invented to describe the fascist and Nazi systems. When Japanese ground forces lost the initiative in Southeast Asia and the Pacific, the antlike imagery was evoked in a somewhat different fashion. One reporter described the mid-war battles as a time when "the Japs turned into ants, the more you killed the more that kept coming." General Slim, Great Britain's commander in the epic Burma campaigns, used a similar metaphor in describing how his own forces finally seized the offensive. "We had kicked over the anthill," he wrote in his memoirs; "the ants were running about in confusion. Now was the time to stamp on them."[11]

Former Ambassador Grew also spoke of the Japanese as sheep, easily led, which easily led one awkward publicist for the U.S. Navy to compare the frenzy of obedient Japanese soldiers to "angry sheep." *Yank*, the weekly magazine of the U.S. Army, referred to the "sheep-like subservience" of the Japanese (whom the magazine also called "stupid animal-slaves"), but by and large the sheep metaphor did not become a dominant one for the Japanese (in Churchill's menagerie, as in Stalin's, it was the Germans who were sheep). The more general description of the Japanese as a "herd," or possessing a "herd mentality," however, was routine. With various turns of phrase, the herd was one of the pet images of a group of distinguished Far Eastern experts assembled by Britain's Royal Institute of International Affairs to give advice on enemy Japan at the end of 1944. An Australian war correspondent went further, explaining that Japanese enlisted men not only behaved like, but also looked like, cattle. "Many of the Japanese soldiers I have seen have been primitive oxen-like clods with dulled eyes and foreheads an inch high," he wrote in a 1944 book directed to American readers. "They have stayed at their positions and died simply because they have been told to do so, and they haven't the intelligence to think for themselves."[12]

Other, more random metaphors reinforced the impression of a sub-human enemy. Westerners writing about their personal experiences in Japan, for example, frequently described the Japanese as "hissing," a snakelike impression whether witting or not. As the Japanese extended their overseas imperium, even prior to Pearl Harbor, cartoonists depicted the country as an octopus grasping Asia in its tentacles. In *Know Your Enemy—Japan,* Frank Capra's team enlisted animators from the Walt Disney studio to present this as a central image, with the tentacles of octopus-Japan reaching out to plunge daggers into the hearts of neighboring lands, and groping toward the United States itself. The bucktoothed Japanese became a standard cartoon figure, prompting comparison to the Looney Tune creation Bugs Bunny; the Warner Brothers studio followed up on this with a short animated cartoon titled *Bugs Bunny Nips the Nips.*

Without question, however, the most common caricature of the Japanese by Westerners, writers and cartoonists alike, was the monkey or ape. Sir Alexander Cadogan, the influential permanent undersecretary of the British Foreign Office, routinely referred to the Japanese in his diary as "beastly little monkeys" and the like even before the war began (or alternatively, in February 1941, as "yellow dwarf slaves"). During the early months of the Japanese conquest of Southeast Asia, Western journalists referred to the "apes in khaki." The simian image had already become so integral to Western thinking by this time that when General Yamashita Tomoyuki's troops made their lightning move down the densely jungled Malay Peninsula to capture Singapore, rumors spread that they had accomplished this breathtaking advance by swinging from tree to tree. In mid-January of 1942, *Punch,* the celebrated British satirical magazine, drew upon the same utterly conventional image in a full-page cartoon entitled "The Monkey Folk" that depicted monkeys swinging through the jungle with helmets on their heads and rifles slung over their shoulders. In much the same way, U.S. Marines in the combat zones made jokes about tossing a grenade into a tree and blasting out "three monkeys —two bucktooths and a real specimen," a witticism that the *New Yorker* carried to its upper-class readership in cartoon form late in 1942 and *Reader's Digest* reproduced for its own huge audience soon after. It portrayed white riflemen lying in firing position in a dense jungle, where the trees were full of monkeys along with several Japanese snipers. "Careful now," one white soldier is saying to another, "—only those in uniform." An American radio broadcaster informed his audience early in the war that it was appropriate to regard the Japanese as monkeys for two reasons: first, the monkey in the zoo imitates his trainer; secondly, "under his fur, he's still a savage little beast."[13]

Among the Allied war leaders, Admiral Halsey was the most notorious for making outrageous and virulently racist remarks about the Japanese enemy in public. Many of his slogans and pronouncements bordered on advocacy of genocide. Although he came under criticism for his intemperate remarks, and was even accused of being drunk in public, Halsey was immensely popular among his men and naturally attracted good press coverage. His favorite phrase for the Japanese was "yellow bastards," and in general he found the color allusion irresistible. Simian metaphors, however, ran a close second in his diatribes. Even in his postwar memoirs, Halsey described the Japanese as "stupid animals" and referred to them as "monkeymen." During the war he spoke of the "yellow monkeys," and in one outburst declared that he was "rarin' to go" on a new naval operation "to get some more Monkey meat." He also told a news conference early in 1945 that he believed the "Chinese proverb" about the origin of the Japanese race, according to which "the Japanese were a product of mating between female apes and the worst Chinese criminals who had been banished from China by a benevolent emperor." These comments were naturally picked up in Japan, as Halsey fully intended them to be, and on occasion prompted lame responses in kind. A Japanese propaganda broadcast, for example, referred to the white Allies as "albino apes." Halsey's well-publicized comment, after the Japanese Navy had been placed on the defensive, that "the Japs are losing their grip, even with their tails," led a zookeeper in Tokyo to announce he was keeping a cage in the monkey house reserved for the admiral.[14]

The variations on the simian theme were endless. Americans learned from Ernie Pyle that Marines in the Marianas had coined the word

"Japes," a combination of "Japs" and "apes." A comparable neologism was "monkeynips." As early as February 1942, *Leatherneck* ran an unusually wild comic strip in which an unkempt white soldier—infuriated when a canteen of liquor is shot out of his hands by the "slant-eyed jerks" and "jaundiced baboons"—plunges into the jungle and emerges with four dead creatures with monkeys' bodies and Japanese faces, tied by their tails and hanging from his shoulders. "They're a bit undersized," he exclaims, "but I got four of 'em!!" A booklet prepared by the U.S. Navy Pacific Command during the final months of the war, in anticipation of the occupation of Japan, related these stereotypes to Japanese atrocities. When Westerners learned of these atrocities, it was explained, they scrapped their picture of the average Japanese "as a comical little person and substituted a blood-soaked beast—half man and half monkey." (The Navy guide, it should be noted, was devoted to repudiating such gross stereotypes.) The Army's *Infantry Journal* took a different tact in warning of the danger of overconfidence that might come from thinking of the enemy as merely "a buck-toothed, near-sighted, pint-sized monkey." (He was better seen, it was suggested, as "a robot-like creature.") Following Japan's capitulation, General Robert Eichelberger, one of MacArthur's key commanders, wrote to his wife that "first, monkeys will come to Manila," in reference to the impending Japanese mission to MacArthur's headquarters to arrange the surrender procedures.[15]

One of the better-known American cartoons of the war years was published in April 1943, after the news of the execution of some of the Doolittle pilots was released. It depicted the Japanese as a slavering gorilla labeled "Murderers of American Flyers"—with the huge pistol of "Civilization" pointing at its head—and can be taken as a concrete illustration of the U.S. Navy's explanation that such animal imagery was directly related to Japanese atrocities. This explanation, however, is too simple. Reports about Japanese atrocities undoubtedly contributed greatly to the Western perception of the Japanese as beasts, but the simian personification existed independently of such associations. This was perhaps the most basic of all metaphors traditionally employed by white supremacists to demean nonwhite peoples. It was more often used in a way that portrayed the colored subject as ridiculous rather than savage. And it was a racist archetype that thoroughly obsessed Westerners, as any survey of the popular graphics of the war soon reveals. Even when one reviews the political cartoons of wartime America and Britain with foreknowledge of the fondness for apish imagery in depicting the Japanese enemy, the extensiveness of such representation is startling—as is also the fact that the Japanese were portrayed, not just as apelike but as apes plain and simple. While Hitler and the Nazis also occasionally emerged as simians, this was a passing metaphor, a sign of aberration and atavism, and did not carry the explicit racial connotations of the Japanese ape.[16]

The simian image was ubiquitous in the American and British media, appearing in publications both conservative and liberal, popular and highbrow. The *American Legion Magazine*'s contribution to the genre was a cartoon depicting monkeys in a zoo who had posted a sign in their cage reading, "Any similarity between us and the Japs is purely coincidental." *Collier's* featured several full-color covers by the British artist Lawson Wood portraying Japanese airmen as apes, and *Time* ran a cover portrait pertaining to the Dutch East Indies in which a Japanese apeman dangled from a tree in the background. The esteemed antifascist cartoonist David Low, whose work appeared in the *Evening Standard* in London and was widely reproduced, contributed some of the most blunt and memorable graphics of this sort. In July 1941, months before Pearl Harbor, Low produced a cartoon depicting three stalwart white servicemen standing stripped to the waist beneath a palm tree and gazing out into the Pacific; they were identified as the United States, Britain, and the U.S.S.R. Hanging by its tail from the tree was a monkey labeled "Jap," wearing eyeglasses, clutching a dagger, and contemplating which white man to stab in the back. In October, Low portrayed Tōjō's assumption of the premiership with a drawing of a gorilla in admiral's uniform taking command of the Japanese ship of state. Immediately after the outbreak of war, Low presented the Japanese army, navy, and air force as three monkeys on a beach outside Singapore. In March 1942, he returned to the imagery of the previous July to render Japan's grab for power in Asia once again as a monkey suspended by its tail—in this case with an armful of coconuts, precariously reaching for more (representing India and Australia.)[17]

The *New York Times* found the latter cartoon so effective that it reproduced it on the front page of its Sunday book-review section, as an illustration for a review of books on Japanese policy. The *Times*'s practice of featuring political cartoons from other newspapers in its Sunday edition provides a convenient source through which to gain an impression of the thoroughly conventional nature of the simian fixation. Thus, in mid-1942, Japanese soldiers in the Aleutians (who died almost to the last man) were depicted as an ape on a springboard. Later that year, the Japanese took the form of a monstrous King Kong figure with a bloody knife. In 1943, they were portrayed squatting in the trees among monkeys, and on a wanted poster in a cartoon entitled "It All Depends on the Neighborhood." In the latter, Hitler was "Public Enemy No. 1" for England and a jug-eared, monkey-faced Japanese was Hitler's counterpart for the Allies in the Pacific. In 1944, as the U.S. Pacific offensive gained momentum, readers were offered a monkey labeled "Japs" with coconuts falling on its head. At the end of 1944, when the bombardment of the Japanese homeland was commencing, the *Times* reproduced a cartoon of a bandaged, bawling ape with horn-rimmed eyeglasses and buckteeth. Early in 1945, in a column of random clever observations regularly featured in its Sunday magazine, the *Times* called on its own staff for the following entry:[18]

Obviously, the depiction of groups and individuals by nonhuman forms or symbols is not in itself inherently demeaning. The American eagle and British lion are ample proof to the contrary. The Japanese, on their part, celebrate "Boys' Day"—and "manly" struggle against adversity —with the symbol of a carp leaping against the current (a rather unusual choice by Western standards), and medieval warriors had adopted heraldic emblems depicting wildlife as various as hawks, horses, deer, pigeons, and plovers, as well as butterflies and dragonflies. What we are concerned with here is something different: the attachment of stupid, bestial, even pestilential subhuman caricatures on the enemy, and the manner in which this blocked seeing the foe as rational or even human, and facilitated mass killing. It is, at least for most people, easier to kill animals than fellow humans. Indeed, it may be easier for many hunters to kill animals by closing their minds to the fact that they are sentient beings that know fear and feel pain. Thus, in a rather rare document, a diary kept by an ordinary American seaman during the entire course of the Pacific War, we find breathless descriptions of what Marines told the sailors when they came on board: "Fighting the Japs is like fighting a wild animal. . . . The Japs take all kinds of chances, they love to die." A profile of the Japanese fighting man in a serviceman's magazine also argued that "he isn't afraid to die. In fact, he seems to like to die." Indeed, this article went on to note that "when they die," it was said that the Japanese enemy "turn over on their backs and smile and face the sun."[19] By such reasoning, it was almost a favor to kill the Japanese. Beyond this, of course, being beasts, they deserved to die.

This linguistic softening of the killing process was accomplished most often through two general figures of speech: the metaphors of the hunt, and of exterminating vermin. The evocation of the hunt appears everywhere in American writing about combat in the Pacific, sometimes with an almost lyric quality, evoking images of the Old West and physical pleasures that have always been part of the picture of the good life in the more rural American consciousness. Advertisers played up this theme. A magazine advertisement for the brewing industry, for example, depicted a hunter and his companions with a fine deer trophy, identified as one of the "little things" (along with beer and ale) that meant a lot to a Marine on leave, and went on to note that "he's been doing a different kind of hunting overseas." An advertisement by a cartridge company carried a headline reading "Now Your Ammunition Is Getting *Bigger* Game," and juxtaposed a painting of a hunter sighting in on a mountain sheep with a scene of ammunition stores on Guadalcanal. An ad for telescopic sights showed a Japanese soldier crouched on his hands and knees, with the cross hairs fixed behind his shoulder. "Rack up another one," the heading read. Cards for display in automobile windows proclaimed "Open Season for Japs."[20]

"Good luck and good hunting" was a common sendoff for men embarking on a combat mission, as moviegoers learned from the 1944 Hollywood film *Destination Tokyo*. Sometimes the imagery chosen was of a general nature: of Marines descending from the ridges "to hunt out their prey," for example, or simply shooting "animals" or "predatory animals." Sometimes the hunt was violent. General Slim divided the decisive battle of Imphal-Kohima into four stages, the last of which was pursuit—"when the Japanese broke, and, snarling and snapping, were hunted from the field." At another point, Slim recalled that "relentlessly we would hunt them down and when, desperate and rabid, they turned at bay, killed them." The hunt also could be a joke. A satirical article on mopping-up operations on Guadalcanal described the place as a "hunter's paradise . . . teeming with monkey-men." Very frequently, however, the hunt was pastoral, almost lazy, and the quarry small and easy. A cover story in *Life,* showing GIs walking through the jungle with rifles ready, looking for Japanese snipers, explained that "like many of their comrades they were hunting for Japs, just as they used to go after small game in the woods back home." A 1943 book giving a firsthand account of the combat explained that "every time you hit a Jap [with rifle fire] he jumps like a rabbit." The battle of the Philippine Sea in June 1944, in which the Japanese lost three carriers and over 345 aircraft, compared to a loss of seventeen planes on the Allied side, became immortalized as "the great turkey shoot." "Duck hunting" was another popular figure of speech, and naturally brought up references to both dead ducks and sitting ducks. Killing Japanese reminded others of shooting quail. "Tanks are used to flush the Japanese out of the grass," a Pulitizer Prize-winning journalist reported from Guadalcanal, "and when they are flushed, they are shot down like running quail."[21]

In its confidential weekly summaries of the social and political climate in the United States (mostly written by the historian Isaiah Berlin), the British embassy in Washington commented in passing at one point on the popular American perception of the Japanese as a "nameless mass of vermin." The observation was accurate, and its implications were clear: vermin must be exterminated. Especially during the last few years of the war, "exterminationist" figures of speech did indeed become a stock way of referring to the killing of Japanese, not only in battle but also in the cities of Japan's home islands. In the steaming combat zones, the Japanese came to be regarded as almost another form of jungle pest. "Well, which would you druther do—exterminate bug-insecks or Japs!?" asked a sergeant in a comic strip in *American Legion Magazine*. A squad mate spraying bugs replied there wasn't much difference, "but slappin' Japs is more satisfyin'!" A more sophisticated series of comic graphics in *Leatherneck* depicted common afflictions suffered by the Marines in the Pacific and concluded with the "Louseous Japanicas," a grotesque insect with slanted eyes and protruding teeth. The first serious outbreak of this pestilence was noted on December 7, 1941, at Honolulu, it was explained, and the Marines had been assigned "the giant task of extermination. Extensive experiments on Guadalcanal, Tarawa, and Saipan have shown that this louse inhabits coral atolls in the South Pacific, particularly pill boxes, palm trees, caves, swamps and jungles. Flamethrowers, mortars, grenades and bayonets have proven to be an effective remedy. But before a complete cure may be effected the origin of the plague, the breeding grounds around the Tokyo area, must be completely annihilated." Other cartoonists picked up the same theme by depicting the Japanese as ants awaiting an application of ant poison, as spiders about to be stepped on, or as "Japanese beetles" being exterminated with the spray gun of American air power.[22]

Another vivid and familiar expression of this exterminationist sentiment involved depiction of the Japanese as rodents, most often trapped or cornered rats. Allied forces picking apart routed Japanese troops were described as being "like terriers onto rats." Reporters spoke of the "beady little eyes" of critically wounded Japanese, and Japanese soldiers pinned down in caves and tunnels on the Pacific atolls were likened to rats caught in their holes. The hero in *The Purple Heart* told his Japanese captors that they were just "cornered rats"; and in March 1945, *The Nation* used exactly the same image to illustrate the categorical difference between the death in battle of a Japanese fighting man and an American on Iwo Jima. A Japanese soldier's death was "the rat's death, defiant in a corner until all fails," *The Nation* explained, while the Marine's death was "a proud man's death, in the open, advancing, for such simple, noble, and old-fashioned reasons as love of comrades and of corps or ambition to set the flag atop bloody Suribachi." One of the most awesome weapons of extermination employed by the Allied forces in their exhausting battles against the last-ditch resistance of the Japanese on the Pacific islands was the flamethrower, which sprayed a long stream of oil burning at a temperature of 2,000° F. In February 1945, when the battle of Iwo Jima was taking place, the *New York Times* ran an illustrated advertisement by a U.S. chemical company showing a GI blasting a path "through stubborn Jap defenses" with a flamethrower. The ad bore the heading "Clearing Out a Rat's Nest."[23]

On Iwo Jima itself (where U.S. casualties were six thousand killed and twenty-five thousand wounded, while the Japanese defense force of twenty thousand was virtually annihilated), many Marines actually went into battle with the legend "Rodent Exterminator" stenciled on their helmets. Like much of the morbid humor of the war, this reflected the fear, fury, and protective black jokes of combat. Something else was also involved, however, for the metaphor of killing rats was not peculiar to the battlefield. It was also part of everyday life on the home front, among civilians who in many cases had never encountered a Japanese man or woman. After Pearl Harbor, many eateries on the West Coast placed signs in their windows reading "This Restaurant Poisons Both Rats and Japs." Right-wing vigilante groups distributed pamphlets with titles like *Slap the Jap Rat,* and placed stickers with the slogan "Remember a Jap Is a Jap" and the picture of a rat with a Japanese face on the windshields of their automobiles. When concrete plans were broached to evacuate the Japanese-Americans to camps in other states in the interior, or to allow camp inmates to attend nearby educational institutions, the governor of Idaho opposed having any of the evacuees brought into his state and declared that "a good solution to the Jap problem would be to send them all back to Japan, then sink the island. They live like rats, breed like rats and act like rats." If loyal neighbors of Japanese extraction at home could be so summarily categorized as vermin, it is—once again—easy to imagine how such an exterminationist sentiment could be applied not merely to Japanese combat forces in Asia and the Pacific, but to the men, women, and children of the Japanese homeland itself. For a perfect expression of this, we need only attend a patriotic parade in New York City in mid-June of 1942. This mammoth display of martial might and patriotic spirit was the largest parade in the history of New York to that date, and one of its most popular entries was a float called "Tokyo: We Are Coming." As the press described it, this depicted "a big American eagle leading a flight of bombers down on a herd of yellow rats which were trying to escape in all directions." The crowd, it was reported, "loved it."[24]

The scene is worth dwelling on, for at the symbolic level much was captured here: the Manichaean dimension of caricature (the eagle versus the rat); the numerous and undifferentiated pack, devoid not merely of humanness and individuality but even of gender and age; the yellowness of the vermin, as well as their dwarfed size—suggesting not only the "little Japs" but also the yellow hordes of Asia; and also the diminished stature of human targets in the eyes of the bombardier (and in the eyes of the audience on the home front as well). The float was suggestive in another direction also, in that whereas the grand conflict was depicted metaphorically, the technology of the conflict was portrayed realistically: bombers were bombers. Looking back on this expression of grass-roots patriotism, we are reminded that while the expressive forms of race hate remained relatively conventional, a revolution was taking place in military technology and strategy—giving the Allied powers, among other things, the flamethrower, the B-29 Superfortress bomber, napalm, the concept of strategic bombing, the identification of civilian morale as an important and legitimate target in war, the tactical perfection of low-level saturation bombing raids over urban centers, and, finally, nuclear weapons. In the course of the war in Asia, racism, dehumanization, technological change, and exterminationst policies became interlocked in unprecedented ways.

◄ **C H A P T E R   5** ►

LESSER MEN
AND SUPERMEN

The dehumanization of the Japanese was challenged by a variety of Western commentators, many of whom came from the ranks of the "old Japan hands" who had acquired firsthand knowledge of Japan as missionaries, journalists, diplomats, and military officers. They spoke as experts and professionals, offering commentaries that ranged from anecdotal observations to detailed explanations of Japanese history and culture. Neither biological determinism nor the mark of the beast had a significant place in this view of the Japanese, and the commentaries were frequently informative. Just as frequently, however, they were ethnocentric and condescending, and perpetuated in their own way a variety of racial or cultural stereotypes about the Japanese.

Some of the favorite observations about the Japanese character which such experts offered during World War Two bore a striking similarity to the earliest European commentaries on the Japanese, written four centuries previously. Beginning in the mid-sixteenth century, the Jesuits in particular wrote voluminously about the Japanese—whom they categorized, incidentally, as "white"—and generally agreed with the great pioneer missionary in Japan, Francis Xavier, that these were the most promising and accomplished of the heathen. In the end, however, even these sanguine early proselytizers despaired of understanding Japan—in itself an omen of things to come. Their frustrations, as well as many of their conclusions, were perpetuated virtually unchanged by succeeding centuries of Western observers.[1]

The most important and enduring of the Jesuit conclusions was that the Japanese were inscrutable. "Among the Japanese it is considered a matter of honor and wisdom not to disclose the inner self, to prevent anyone's reading therein," wrote Francisco Cabral, head of the Jesuit mission from 1570 to 1581. "They are trained to this from childhood; they are educated to be inscrutable and false." The second grand conclusion was that Westerners could make a start at scrutinizing the inscrutable by recognizing that the Japanese mind, and everything that emanated from it, was upside down. Here is Father Cabral's successor, Alessandro Valignano, writing in the 1580s: "They have rites and ceremonies so different from those of all the other nations that it seems they deliberately try to be unlike any other people. The things which they do in this respect are beyond imagining and it may truly be said that Japan is a world the reverse of Europe, everything is so different and opposite that they are like us in practically nothing. . . ."[2]

Westerners have always been intrigued and baffled, not just by Japan, but by Asian or "Eastern" cultures and the "Oriental mind" in general. When Rudyard Kipling produced his famous dictum that "East is East and West is West, and never the twain shall meet," it is easy to imagine heads nodding ruefully in mission houses and trading companies and consular offices all the way from Egypt to Japan. Still, those who became professionally engaged with Japan were with few exceptions uncommonly zealous in insisting upon their subject's "uniqueness" and its unparalleled predisposition to the "irrational" and the "illogical." The English scholar-diplomat George Sansom, the most esteemed Western expert on Japanese culture in the years prior to Pearl Harbor, was attracted to Japan because it was "so peculiarly *sui generis.*" John Embree, an American anthropologist who wrote a classic study of a Japanese village in the 1930s, agreed that "Japan and the Japanese are different from other nations, or rather, as Japanese nationalists phrase it, they are 'unique among the peoples and cultures of the world.' "[3] Compton Pakenham, an English military officer raised in Japan, who knew Konoe Fumimaro, later prime minister, as a boy and spent a half year attached to a Japanese Army regiment before the war, contributed a long series of articles on Japanese psychology to *Newsweek* magazine in 1945. The series was prefaced with the observation that while Westerners did share certain ideas and customs with the Chinese, Indians, and Arabs, Japan was "an absolutely unique nation . . . utterly different from any other in the world." Their warped psychology and sinister cynicism, Pakenham wrote, made it "almost im-

possible for a foreigner to exchange opinions or reach an understanding
with a Jap." Ellis Zacharias, the U.S. Navy's top intelligence expert on
Japan, referred to the Japanese personality as "that strange, inscrutable,
and peculiar phenomenon."[4]

Such comments came from every direction. In a book-length critique of Japanese militarism published in 1943, Gustav Eckstein informed
his readers that "the Shintoists look different, more boiling, more dangerous, more self-contained." A U.S. military officer who traveled with the
Japanese Army in North China for over four years just prior to Pearl
Harbor declared that the Japanese "neither look, think, nor act like other
people on earth." Otto Tolischus, the *New York Times*'s correspondent
in Japan at the time the war began, agreed that the Japanese were "unlike
any other people on earth." Barbara Tuchman, who would later become
one of America's most honored historians, contributed a "clinical note"
on Japan to the journal *Foreign Affairs* in 1936, even before the outbreak
of open war with China, in which the impression of the unique and
inscrutable Japanese was expressed in almost Jesuitic terms: "So completely divorced is the Japanese mental process from the Occidental, so
devoid of what Westerners call logic, that the Japanese are able to make
statements, knowing they present a false picture, yet sincerely believing
them. How this is accomplished it is impossible for a foreigner to understand, much less to explain." Small wonder that *Fortune* magazine informed its wartime readers that the Japanese "have confused all who have
tried to study them."[5]

Among many Westerners with long personal experience in Japan,
it even became a sort of badge of expertise to say that you knew from long
and vain endeavor that it was futile to try to penetrate the Japanese mind.
As Robert Craigie, the British ambassador to Japan at the time the war
broke out, put it: "The 'old Japan hand' will tell you that the longer you
live among the Japanese, the more incomprehensible they become."
Three days before Japan laid down its arms, the *New York Times* resurrected a 1941 conversation with an American businessman who had lived
in Japan for twenty-five years. "When I first came here I thought I would
be able to understand the Japanese mind," the anonymous expert
confided. "Today I realize that no Westerner can really penetrate the
recesses of Japanese psychology. The mistake Americans and British make
is that we try to forecast Japanese policies on the basis of what we consider
logic and common sense. Consequently, our guesses nearly always go
wrong." Joseph Grew, whose tenure as U.S. ambassador to Japan ran from

1932 until Pearl Harbor, emphasized in his innumerable wartime speeches about the Japanese that "their psychology and logic are peculiarly their own," and consequently to attempt "to measure their thinking processes or their sense of rationality by Western yardsticks would be misleading and inaccurate." This exasperation was shared by Grew's fellow Asian experts in the State Department. In its special report of Japan's surrender, *Newsweek*, without even a footnote to Alessandro Valignano, S.J., featured an article on the "Topsy-Turvy Mind of the Jap" devoted to the thesis that "the viewpoints of Jap and American have nothing in common." The Americans about to occupy Japan, the article began, "will pass through the looking glass into an upside-down world where, without music, 'The Mikado' might be played as straight philosophical drama."[6]

Imagery in the operatic mode was in fact one of the few benign impressions of Japan which lingered in Western minds during the years of war—not only the buffoonery of *The Mikado* ("Our attitude's queer and quaint—You're wrong if you think it ain't"), but also the romantic exotica of *Madama Butterfly* (ending, it must be remembered, in Cio-Cio-San's suicide, which by 1945 simply added femininity to Western battlefield impressions of the Japanese as a people with a compulsive death wish). Before the crisis in Asia exploded, there had been almost a minor cottage industry in the English-speaking world devoted to conveying impressions of an exotic Japan to foreigners. The Japanese government itself endeavored to promote Anglo-American appreciation of "cultural Japan" by sponsoring a variety of English-language publications as well as lectures, films, exhibitions, and performances of the Japanese arts abroad, and such official propagandizing was actually accelerated in the late 1930s under the aegis of the Society for International Cultural Relations (Kokusai Bunka Shinkōkai) and its New York offshoot, the Japan Institute.

The effect of such programs was, at best, negligible. At worst, the woodblock prints, tea ceremonies, flower arrangements, and poems that ended after three or five lines reinforced Western stereotypes of a little country with a shallow cultural heritage. "The Japanese have lost much irreparably by not having a great art, a great poetry, a great drama, to introduce to the Western world," wrote Willis Lamott, a missionary who became well known as an interpreter of Japan during the war years. "They have lost by introducing, often in a bungled and naive fashion, cultural forms that exhibit the strangeness, the difference, and the peculiarities of the Japanese people. In doing this they have created a clientele in the West that looks upon them as 'delightful little people,' 'charming, quaint, and very artistic' but they have not interpreted to the West the intense human possibilities of the Japanese as a race." William Henry Chamberlin, in a small textbook on modern Japan that was published under the auspices of the Institute of Pacific Relations in 1942, struck a similar note. "The Japanese are great in small things and small in great things," he wrote. Japan's contributions lay in "some of the slighter cultural accomplishments" such as prints, lacquerwork, gardening, and haiku, Chamberlin observed, but the country had produced no great philosophical or religious thinkers comparable to those of India and China and no literature comparable to the best in the Greco-Roman and European traditions. The lengthy *Guide to Japan* issued by the U.S. Navy around September 1945, almost simultaneously with Japan's surrender, captured these familiar sentiments when it observed that even premodern Japan had been a "third-hand culture," having acquired most of its early high civilization from China by way of Korea. The response of the Japanese to the modern world had been to hustle around the globe, "borrowing this and copying that, never inventing, but always adapting western machines, western arms, and western techniques to their own uses." Even in the art of war, the guide commented, Japan had not invented a single weapon or introduced any new method other than the suicide attack.[7]

Here was a curiosity indeed: unique and *sui generis*, yet exceptionally imitative, creative only in the "lesser accomplishments." Even after Japan seized Manchuria in 1931, withdrew from the League of Nations and the naval arms-limitation agreements, and then launched full-scale war against China, most Westerners found it difficult to take the Japanese really seriously. They were obviously causing great destruction in China —bombing, killing, looting, raping—but militarily they also seemed to be performing less than impressively. Despite the threat of the Japanese government to "annihilate" China following the outbreak of the China Incident in 1937, the Japanese military had become bogged down after occupying the coastal regions, unable to finish off a poorly equipped and poorly trained (and, of course, purely Asian) foe.

Military and other professional observers shared this disparaging view of Japan's military potential, and the practical repercussions of this were incalculable. Prior to Pearl Harbor, Westerners greatly underestimated Japan's intentions and capabilities. They rated the country, as one high U.S. military officer later summarized it, as "no better than a class-C nation." Then, shocked and stunned by the military successes of the Japanese in the months that followed the outbreak of war, they erred in the opposite direction by exaggerating the enemy's material and psychological strength. In 1942, many of these English and American military experts became almost morbidly obsessed by the specter of a seemingly invincible foe, capable of undreamed-of military feats. The Japanese were soon being called a more formidable adversary than the Germans; and in response to such paranoia, there emerged in turn a campaign in both journalistic and official circles devoted to debunking "the myth of the Japanese superman." These transitions and juxtapositions in the Western image of the Japanese were abrupt and jarring: from subhuman to superhuman, lesser men to supermen. There was, however, a common point throughout, in that the Japanese were rarely perceived as being human beings of a generally comparable and equal sort.[8]

The contempt for Japanese capabilities prior to the actual outbreak of war was shared equally by the English and the Americans; and in retrospect, the calamitous consequences of such arrogance have overtones of a bleak, contemporary morality play. For the British, the play culminated in the fall of Singapore, and the lines recited to that point by actors great and small are resonant with the hubris of a waning empire. They are at the same time, however, conspicuously lacking in the elegance that makes for tragedy.

Here, for example, is General Robert Brooke-Popham, commander in chief of the U.K. forces in the Far East, reporting on a tour of Hong Kong in December 1940 during which he observed Japanese troops across the border in occupied China: "I had a good close-up, across the barbed wire, of various sub-human specimens dressed in dirty grey uniform, which I was informed were Japanese soldiers," he reported to General Hastings Ismay in London. "If these represent the average of the Japanese army, the problems of their food and accomodation would be simple, but I cannot believe they would form an intelligent fighting force." At almost the same moment, the British Chiefs of Staff sent a message to Brooke-Popham which stated that the Japanese "should not be over-estimated." In February 1941, Brooke-Popham reported that one of his battalion commanders had lamented, when reviewing his troops, "Don't you think they are worthy of some better enemy than the Japanese?" Another officer, eager for battle, told Brooke-Popham, "I do hope, Sir, we are not getting too strong in Malaya, because if so the Japanese may never attempt a landing."

While some British intelligence officers (and many Australians) warned against such overconfidence, their views were all but ignored. The British military attaché in Tokyo, for example, visited Singapore in April 1941 and told officers in the garrison there that he regarded the Japanese as a first-class fighting force, well trained, well officered, and possessing high esprit de corps. At the end of his talk, the head of the Malaya Command, Lieutenant General Lionel Bond, rose to declare that such talk of Japanese efficiency was "far from the truth." General Bond told his officers that he had access, among other intelligence data, to confidential Japanese cables, which merely confirmed his low regard for the Japanese. "I do not think much of them," he declared, "and you can take it from me that we have nothing to fear from them."[9]

Cecil Brown, an American radio broadcaster for the CBS network, was assigned to Singapore from August 1941 and kept a daily log in which notations about the British confidence that "we can handle those Japs without very much trouble" appear time and again, right up to the very last moment. When the civilian colonial governor of Singapore was awakened by General A. E. Percival in the early hours of December 8 and informed that the Japanese had commenced hostilities by attacking Kota Bharu on the northeast coast of the Malay Peninsula near Siam, his immediate response was marvelously cool and serene. "Well," he replied, "I suppose you'll shove the little men off!" In Singapore, the city was still ablaze with lights and the headquarters of the civilian Air Raids Precautions organization was unmanned when the first Japanese bombers appeared at 4 A.M. The Order of the Day issued by the British later that morning (which had been drafted the previous May) read in part: "We are ready. We have had plenty of warning and our preparations are made and tested. . . . We are confident. Our defenses are strong and our weapons efficient." It then went on to depict Japan as a weak and demoralized country "drained for years by the exhausting claims of her wanton onslaught on China." In Burma, the British took the Japanese threat so lightly that when the war broke out their troops had virtually no training in jungle tactics and included only one individual capable of handling the Japanese language.[10]

The extent to which racist anti-Japanese myths overrode rational intelligence gathering prior to the fall of Singapore was epitomized in the swift, terrible fate of the *Repulse* and the *Prince of Wales*. These two British battleships were dispatched to Singapore in the fall of 1941 upon Churchill's insistence that this meager show of sea power, combined with the U.S. military presence in the Philippines, would deter Japan from advancing to the south. Two days after the Japanese called this feeble bluff by attacking Pearl Harbor and the Philippines, they sank the two great vessels in the South China Sea with astonishing ease, losing only three planes in the process. Coupled with the destruction of the U.S. fleet at Pearl Harbor, this cleared the Pacific of the last force of capital ships that might have interfered with Japan's naval operations. In his memoirs, Churchill described this as his greatest shock of the war, and the remarkable notebook of Cecil Brown—who had been invited to sail aboard the doomed *Repulse*—pointedly captured the last moments of British wishful thinking concerning Japanese incompetence. At 1:20 P.M. on December 9, Pacific time, the day before battle was joined, the flag-deck officer on the *Repulse* laughed when asked about the report that a Japanese capital ship, three heavy cruisers, and a number of destroyers were nearby. "Oh, but they are Japanese," he declared reassuringly. "There's nothing to worry about." Brown's notes for five hours later on the same day read as follows:

We are at dinner listening to the BBC. Heavy fighting is going on in Malaya. The fighting is still confused, but BBC says reinforcements should reach there during the day.

BBC says there is no truth in the Japanese reports that an attack was made on Singapore. The Japs have entered Bangkok. . . .

We sat around in the wardroom. There must have been twelve or fifteen officers discussing the news.

"Those Japs are bloody fools," one of them said. "All these pinpricks at widely separated points is stupid strategy. The Japs should have sent over three hundred planes over Singapore, not eleven."

"Bloody fools!" another snorted.

"Those Japs can't fly," one of the officers said. "They can't see at night and they're not well trained."

"They have rather good ships," one of the officers remarked, "but they can't shoot."

When Brown suggested that the British officers might be underestimating the enemy, his wardroom companions mulled this over for a moment before returning to their confident appraisal of the situation. "We are not overconfident," was the general rejoinder. "We just don't think the enemy is much good. They could not beat China for five years and now look what they are doing out here, jumping all over the map instead of meeting at one or two places. They cannot be very smart to be doing that." Shortly after noon on the following day, the *Repulse* and the *Prince of Wales* were sunk by a succession of perfectly executed air attacks launched from Japanese carriers.[11]

The factual trappings of such smug overconfidence are noteworthy. Prejudice masqueraded as fact. It rested on innumerable minuscule and presumedly empirical observations. Thus, Westerners did not simply dismiss the Japanese out of hand as militarily incompetent. They "knew" that the Japanese were not a serious threat because it had been reported over and over again that they could neither shoot, sail, nor fly. When Japan proved incapable of making good its threat to crush China after 1937, it was natural to assume that these certainties had simply been reconfirmed. One need not inquire about such practical matters as the formidable logistics of war in China's vast territorial reaches, or the unexpectedly tenacious resistance of the Chinese.

The concrete and detailed manner in which this thesis of Japanese military incompetence was presented deserves elaboration, for such rumors gained credence because they were so precise—so "logical," to use one of the Westerners' favorite terms of self-description and self-praise—in pointing out exactly where and why the Japanese were inept. A classic analysis of this sort, which in one form or another emerged in many publications prior to and immediately after Pearl Harbor, was offered by the American military commentator Fletcher Pratt in 1939. Japan's military strengths, Pratt explained, were offset by "four weaknesses." First, scarcity of iron and steel had forced the Japanese to compensate in unfortunate ways in naval construction, notably by overarming smaller vessels and relying on welding instead of rivets. The results were top-heavy ships (what the media sometimes took pleasure in referring to as ships with "pagodalike" superstructures) and vessels with inherent structural weaknesses. As evidence, Pratt cited an overburdened Japanese torpedo boat that capsized in sea trials in 1934, and a cruiser that sprang leaks at the welded joints after firing a heavy barrage.

Japan's second weakness, the analysis continued, was in the air, where both planes and pilots were conspicuously inferior. The Japanese "can neither make good airplanes nor fly them well," Pratt explained, "in spite of the most heroic efforts." And while the Japanese were daring, "every observer" agreed they were incompetent. Although there was controversy concerning why this was so, four main theories had been advanced:

According to the first postulate the Japanese as a race have defects of the tubes of the inner ear, just as they are generally myopic. This gives them a defective sense of balance, the one physical sense in which an aviator is not permitted to be deficient.

The second explanation places the blame on Bushido and the Japanese code that the individual life is valueless. Therefore, when the plane gets into a spin or some other trouble, they are apt to fold their hands across their stomachs and die cheerfully for the glory of the Empire, where Westerners, with a keener sense of personal existence, make every effort to get the plane out of trouble, or bail out at the last minute. This explanation has been advanced by several aviation instructors who have been in Japan.

The psychological theory points out that the Japanese, even more than the Germans, are a people of combination. "Nothing is much stupider than one Japanese, and nothing much brighter than two." But the aviator is peculiarly alone, and the Japanese, poor individualists, are thus poor aviators.

Finally, the educational explanation points out that Japanese children receive fewer mechanical toys and less mechanical training than those of any other race.

Both the third and fourth of Japan's military weaknesses, the analysis continued, were psychological. The Japanese were short-tempered on both a small and large scale, and in battle were inclined to waste men unnecessarily when operations did not go well. Finally, and most important of all, the Japanese would simply never dare to provoke a war with the United States.[12]

A comparable and even more extensive catalog of comforting "intelligence" observations permitted British military observers to belittle the Japanese threat to southern Asia. The Japanese Army was reported to be ill equipped, especially in automatic weapons. Its drivers and mechanics were said to be poor. Its troops were supposed to be weak in unit training —and, despite their own propaganda to the contrary, low in morale. The officer corps was analyzed as being weak at the junior level, while strategy and tactics were stereotyped and inflexible. The Japanese were said to be untrained in guerrilla warfare and jungle combat—and, indeed, culturally and tempermentally unsuited for this. Cecil Brown, for example, was told by one middle-echelon British officer that the Japanese were afraid of the jungle because they believed it was full of ghosts and demons. A British general told the CBS reporter that even if the Japanese were so foolhardy as to invade the Malay Peninsula, they would not get far because the hills near the Siamese border were full of iron ore and would throw the compasses of the unwary invaders out of whack.[13]

The British also maintained that the Japanese avoided night operations on land because they were simply incapable of carrying them out well, while they avoided nighttime aerial attacks, as well as dive-bombing, for the same reasons Pratt had presented: their pilots were poor and their aircraft inferior. The persistence of this belief up to the end of 1941 is especially surprising, since from August 1940 some Japanese pilots in China had been flying the world's most advanced fighter plane, the Mitsubishi Zero, developed under the Imperial Navy. The first actual combat test of the Zero occurred in September 1940, when thirteen of the planes downed twenty-seven Chinese aircraft in ten minutes. Between that engagement and August 31, 1941, when the revolutionary new fighter began to be mass-produced by Nakajima Aircraft, approximately thirty Zeros accounted for 266 confirmed kills in China. Yet the plane remained all but ignored in the West—to the astonishment, among others, of its designer, Horikoshi Jirō, who vainly scanned Western aviation magazines for reports about its extraordinary performance.

Neglect of the Zero by the Western media, and indeed by top military planners, did not derive from lack of available information. The plane received a great deal of publicity in Japan following its spectacular initial victories (secrecy became tighter around January 1941), and both the Americans and the British possessed accurate intelligence reports on its capabilities. Claire Chennault, the retired U.S. Army Air Corps officer who headed the flamboyant "Flying Tigers" squadron and helped rebuild the Chinese Air Force after 1937, sent detailed reports on the Zero to British and Australian, as well as American, authorities. In mid-1941, moreover, the British actually obtained possession of a downed Zero and prepared, at the lower levels of the military, an accurate and potentially valuable analysis of the plane. Like Chennault's reports, this was ignored. As Horikoshi later observed, it was not so much the success of the Japanese Navy in shrouding the Zero in secrecy that made its "sudden" appearance against the Westerners so shocking in December 1941 as the blindness of most high-ranking Allied officers, who simply could not conceive of Japan independently designing and manufacturing an aircraft of this caliber.[14]

The belief that the Japanese were poor pilots because the race as a whole suffered from myopia and inner-ear defects surfaced in countless ways in the years and days before war came—sometimes dressed with bizarre expertise. No devotee of Western cartoons can have failed to notice the ubiquitous caricature of the Japanese squinting through owlish horn-rimmed glasses—in nearsightedness, as in everything, homogeneous. Military observers on all sides accepted this notion. Only a week before the outbreak of war, for example, Canadian officers attending a briefing by a British officer in Hong Kong were informed that Japan's aircraft were mostly obsolete, its air force had little practice in night flying, and its pilots were myopic and thus unable to carry out dive-bombing attacks. One reason there was no one in Singapore's Air Raid Precautions headquarters on the night Japan attacked was that shortly before that fatal date an RAF officer had informed the air-raid wardens that Japanese could not fly in the dark. A particularly ingenious exercise in scientific explanation attended myopia's twin myth: that the Japanese suffered widespread inner-ear damage. What caused this? Japanese motherhood, in the opinion of one Western expert, who apparently rejected Pratt's explanation of congenitally defective "tubes." The practice of strapping babies to their mother's backs, it was explained, caused their heads to bounce about and permanently impaired their sense of balance.[15]

Such complacency naturally turned into astonishment and disbelief when the Japanese launched their bold, unorthodox, and meticulously executed attacks on the Western powers in December 1941. As is well known, the first electronic sightings of the Japanese attack force moving against Pearl Harbor were not taken seriously. When Japanese aircraft swooped in on the Philippines nine hours after Pearl Harbor and wiped out General Douglas MacArthur's air force on the ground, the general was caught by surprise and refused to believe that the pilots could have been Japanese. He insisted they must have been white mercenaries. At almost the same moment, the British defenders of Hong Kong were voicing similar incredulity as they came under pinpoint low-level fire from Japanese planes. They "firmly believed," as the official British history of the war in Asia put it, "that Germans must be leading the sorties." (In the Soviet Union, Stalin joined this early chorus that placed Germans in Japan's cockpits). In some quarters, disbelief that the Japanese could really master the weapons of modern war persisted long after they had presumedly proven their mettle. When battle-hardened GIs, accustomed to the light-arms combat of the jungles and island atolls, moved on to Okinawa in April 1945 and found themselves suddenly pinned down by accurate heavy-artillery fire, the rumor quickly spread that "German experts are directing the Jap artillery." In this respect, the war in the Pacific ended much as it had begun: in American underestimation of the technical capability of the Japanese.[16]

Comparable rumors flourished concerning the Japanese mind. It was the *sine qua non* of virtually all Western commentaries that the Japanese did not think as other peoples did, and were certainly not guided by "reason" or "logic" in the Western sense. They were often said to "feel" rather than think, or to think with their "whole being" rather than just their brains. Their minds were described as "pre-Hellenic, prerational, and prescientific"—labels which were also commonly employed in discourse concerning the inferiority of the female mind. On occasion, this equation was made explicit. "The Japanese mind works in a more elemental way," wrote Otto Tolischus, "as a woman's is supposed to do—by instinct, intuition, apprehension, feeling, emotion, association of ideas, rather than by analysis and logical deduction."[17]

There was, to be sure, a positive variant of this attitude, promoted by many Japanese and other more mystically inclined Asians, which lauded the "intuitive" or "spiritual" powers of the Easterner. British and American readers of middle-brow magazines were vaguely familiar with Zen Buddhism and its challenge to "common sense," and the writings of D. T. Suzuki, Zen's most fluent and prolific interpreter to the West, were always available for a quotation concerning the Japanese reliance on intuition rather than the manipulation of concepts. Although Suzuki and the Zen teachings he espoused were avidly embraced by Westerners after World War Two, most of his major books had already been translated into English in the 1920s and 1930s. Western intellectuals such as Carl Jung had called attention to Zen insights before the war, but the war years themselves were hardly a time when the "wisdom of the East" was taken seriously. On the contrary, Eastern spiritualism and emphasis on the nondiscursive were generally perceived as an irrational oddity at best, and at worst as an alien and ominous threat. This derived not merely from a vague and unsettling impression that Oriental religions such as Zen gave their devotees special "occult" powers and a special sense of unity, but also from the more specific recognition of the relationship between Zen discipline and martial practices. Zen, as the Canadian historian of Japan E. H. Norman wrote during the war years, facilitated killing.[18] The "spiritual strength" of Japanese fighting men did indeed impress many Westerners as the war dragged on, but usually as evidence of a blind savageness that is, and should be, shucked off in the course of civilization and progress.

The manner in which Westerners turned Japanese emphasis on "intuition" or nondiscursive communication into evidence of Japanese "irrationality" is an excellent example of the way in which one party's self-congratulatory self-images can be turned into negative and derogatory stereotypes by others. In this instance, it was but a short step for the Westerners to argue that the Japanese had inferior brains. Thus, one rumor that circulated in the West held that the Japanese relied on emotion and intuition more than logic and analysis because their brain was "whiter" and more primitive than the "gray matter" of the Occidentals. That, it was said, explained why Caucasian physicians in Japan were not allowed to perform autopsies on Japanese. More sophisticated theories tended to prevail, however. The British Admiralty and naval officers at the Staff College appear to have been strongly influenced by a report prepared by the naval attaché in Tokyo in 1935, which not only advanced the theory that the Japanese had "peculiarly slow brains," but went on to explain in detail why this was so. The reason was essentially cultural rather than physiological, being "fundamentally due to the strain put on the child's brain in learning some 6,000 Chinese characters before any real education can start." As a consequence of such cramming, the Japanese tended to be "a race of specialists," incapable of switching their minds quickly from one subject to another. Such stultifying training carried over to Japan's Naval College, the attaché had been informed by an English instructor there, in the form of physical over-training and additional mental over-cramming, "the finished product being a thoroughly over-tired human being." As a result of such considerations, the British report continued, all of the foreign naval attachés in Japan had concluded that the unwillingness of Japanese authorities to show their ships and weapons to others "is due rather to the barrenness of the cupboard than to any secrets it may contain."[19]

The question of whether the heavy burden of rote memorization required to learn a cumbersome writing system had deleterious effects on Japanese analytical capabilities was something that eminent Japanese (such as Mori Ōgai, the turn-of-the-century scientist and man of letters) had themselves debated. It surfaced during the immediate postwar occupation of Japan, moreover, when Allied reformers, along with some Japanese supporters, unsuccessfully called for the abandonment of ideographs and adoption of a phonetic script for writing Japanese. The question was thus neither a frivolous nor an exclusively ethnocentric one, but there was ample evidence—not least the enormous strides the country had made in industrialization and modernization since the overthrow of the feudal regime in 1868—to suggest that this was hardly a people of impaired mental ability and inflexible fixations. Westerners, however, tended to find essentially what they started out expecting to find—and in the case of the president of the United States, as Professor Christopher Thorne has revealed, this turned out to be a brain that was not so much peculiarly slow as peculiarly small. For this expert information, President Roosevelt was indebted to the curator of the Division of Physical Anthropology at the Smithsonian Institution, who, in a lengthy correspondence, explained that the Japanese were "as bad as they were" because their skulls were "some 2,000 years less developed than ours." The president's receptivity to this bogus empiricism reflected the durability of presumedly discredited nineteenth-century racist theories. And how could the Japanese escape this unfortunate biological curse? After they had been defeated, Roosevelt once privately suggested, they should be encouraged by every means possible to intermarry with other races.[20]

It is in the milieu of such assumptions that the initial multipronged Japanese attack on Hawaii and Southeast Asia seemed so incredible in every sense of the word: for beyond the sheer audacity of the assault, few Westerners credited the Japanese with the mental or physical ability to formulate such complex military plans or carry them out so brilliantly. However optimistic Anglo-American leaders may have been in the summer and early autumn of 1941 concerning the possibility of forcing the Japanese to abandon their ambitions in Asia, by late November it had become clear to the top leadership that an attack was imminent. It was still assumed, however, that such an attack would be directed against the European colonies in Asia rather than the U.S. forces in Hawaii or the Philippines; and, in any case, like their British counterparts, few Americans at the command or popular level believed the Japanese would prove to be a formidable foe.

Top-level U.S. military planners were by no means unaware of their relative weaknesses vis-à-vis the Japanese in 1941. On the contrary, one of the major arguments against taking a hard line on Japanese expansion in Asia at that time was that the United States was not yet adequately prepared for war. Its naval construction programs in particular were far from complete (which, from Japan's perspective, was one reason for striking quickly). Such sober appraisals, however, did not dispel a general attitude of contempt for Japan's military capabilities, and the record of pre-Pearl Harbor commentary about Japan on the American side is only slightly less embarrassing in retrospect than that of the British before the fall of Singapore. (The best comparison may be to Japan's own arrogant overconfidence vis-à-vis China in 1937.) Early in the fatal year of 1941, for instance, the assistant naval attaché in the U.S. embassy in Tokyo cockily told a group at the American Club, "We can lick the Japs in twenty-four hours." His superiors in Washington unquestionably would have qualified this, but to what extent? In an off-the-record conversation in March 1941, a conservative member of the Military Affairs Committee of the House of Representatives informed newsmen about recent secret testimony by Secretary of War Stimson and General George Marshall. Japan's intentions were described as "a question mark," as one reporter summarized the briefing in a confidential background report to his editor: "Indications here are that she is scared to death by the British and American attitudes. Our naval people hold the Japanese to be very inferior, and I gather they would like to knock them off any time—which would, of course, mean that we wouldn't need a two-ocean Navy. Chances are she would not live up to her Axis commitment unless England appeared to be hopelessly beaten. Even then she'd hesitate a long while before coming to grips with the American fleet." Two months later, in another background letter containing not-to-be-published material, this time following confidential briefings by Admiral Ernest King, the same reporter observed: "Incidentally, Navy people have a good deal of interest in the Japanese situation. They feel we should have knocked off the little brown brother years ago, and they still favor it as a step previous to entering the Battle of the Atlantic."[21]

While the lively language of such background briefings was not divulged to the general public, the overall impression of Japanese weakness and vulnerability was widely broadcast. Thus, the November 1941 issue of *Reader's Digest* reprinted an article from the *American Mercury*, by a journalist who lived in Japan for thirteen years, describing Japan as a disorganized country with low popular morale, negligible physical resources, and a basically "obsolete or obsolescent" air force with the highest accident rate in the world. According to German officers who had trained them, it was said, Japanese pilots lacked the individual initiative to fly high-speed planes in combat. A concerted attack "from Siberian, British, Dutch and Philippine bases," the article continued, "would annihilate or ground the Japanese air force within a few weeks." On December 4, three days before the Pearl Harbor attack, Secretary of the Navy Frank Knox dined with a group of Washington power brokers. Over after-dinner cigars, the secretary agreed that war with Japan might start at any minute, and when it did it would be pretty much a Navy show. "We're all ready for them, you know," Knox placidly declared. "We've had our plans worked out for twenty years. . . . It won't take too long. Say about a six months' war." Even in the immediate wake of Pearl Harbor, most Americans remained optimistic that the war would be a short one. Early in 1942, Admiral Leahy, President Roosevelt's chief of staff, still calculated that the war could be over within the year. In the estimation of the Speaker of the House of Representatives, the American people at first assumed it would take about six weeks to defeat Japan. He detected serious alarm among the public when this deadline passed with no end to the war in sight.[22]

In immeasurable ways, the outrage of Americans over the surprise attack at Pearl Harbor was compounded by this long tradition of belittlement. It was, to begin with, preposterous for these comic-opera people to presume they could take on a white giant, and outrageous that they chose to do so in such an insulting way. The Australian journalist Hugh Byas, well known since the early 1920s for his coverage of Japan, wrote in his diary entry for December 9, while in New York: "People here are wild at the insolence of the 'little Japs,' whom they thought of as comic figures." Two months later, Fortune observed in a similar vein that "the Honorable Enemy has shown himself to be much more complicated than our casual impressions had painted him—a bowing, smirking, bespectacled, bandy-legged little man who leaves his shoes on the porch and wears his hat in the temple; who has a passion for arranging flowers and constructing thirty-one-syllable poems; who never invented anything important of his own, but copied everything he saw, complete with leaky fuel lines and broken glass; who couldn't shoot or fly straight and whose flashy warships were all top-heavy, underarmored, and undergunned. . . ." On the third anniversary of Pearl Harbor, the chief of the State Department's Division of Japanese Affairs gave a speech in which he recalled the shocked astonishment that the Japanese attack had caused among the general public. Westerners "either did not believe that the supposedly 'nice little Japanese,' whom they associated only with cherry blossoms and geisha, could really build up such a [military] machine," he told a Kiwanis

Club audience, "or they shrugged off the growing danger with the easy assumption that one American, or one Briton, or one Australian is equal in fighting qualities to five or ten Japanese." This latter assumption, turned about, was essentially the same as what the war planners in Tokyo counted on, equally erroneously, to guarantee their own victory. Among them, it was an article of faith that the "spiritual strength" of the Japanese fighting man made him more than a match for any number of effete and self-indulgent Caucasians.[23]

Because the Pearl Harbor attack came so unexpectedly—so literally out of the blue, as the saying goes—most Westerners also regarded Japan's initiation of war as high folly, an incredible miscalculation of America's pride, its wrath, and its bountiful resources. The attack thus managed to reinforce existing impressions of the Japanese as unpredictable and fundamentally irrational—even though, upon calmer appraisal, it might as easily have been interpreted as evidence of the relentless logic of Japanese war planning. While Westerners talked about the personality disorders of the Japanese, Japan's leaders were preoccupied with the global disorder of the Western-dominated imperialist system. By 1941, they had concluded that their country could only survive by controlling an autarkic bloc in Asia which included access to the raw materials of Southeast Asia. It followed from this that Japan must control Singapore and the Philippines; and from this in turn followed the terrible logic of the necessity of mounting a swift, secret attack not only against the European and American colonial outposts in Southeast Asia, but also against the U.S. fleet in Pearl Harbor.

Even after the technically brilliant attack on Pearl Harbor, after the Japanese wiped out MacArthur's air force in Manila, and after they sent the *Prince of Wales* and the *Repulse* to the depths, some white men still found it hard to take them seriously. They were still the little men. Thus *Time,* in its distinctive prose, reported on the next to last day of 1941 that "big only in their fury . . . the little men," barefoot or wearing rubber sneakers, were advancing down Malaya "on a miniature scale," using "tiny one-man tanks and two-man gun carriers. The British even said that their doctors cut miniature Japanese bullets out of miniature British wounds." Two weeks later, *Life* quoted a British soldier who told Cecil Brown in Singapore that "a British soldier is equal to ten Japanese, but unfortunately there are eleven Japanese."[24]

Two months into the new year, Singapore surrendered to a Japanese force one third the size of the British Army. And two months after Singapore, a combined U.S.-Filipino army of seventy-eight thousand men surrendered on Bataan. By then, a new creature roamed the fertile fields of the Anglo-American imagination: the Japanese superman.

The superman came from land, sea, and air, as well as from the nightmares of the Westerners. He also came from lay pulpits in Washington and London, where public figures sought to cover their blunders and gird their people for a long struggle. Pearl Harbor, Manila, the British battleships at the bottom of the South China Sea—all attested to the exceptional competence of the Japanese Navy and its air arm. Singapore, Bataan, and Japan's knifelike thrust into Burma revealed an extraordinarily potent Imperial Army. The catastrophe of the two warships alone, on the second day of the war, the British history of these events records, "led to a belief in the invincibility of Japanese air power, a belief which was given strength by the ease with which the enemy outmatched the obsolescent Allied aircraft. It created the myth of Japanese superiority in all three Services, which took a long time to die."[25]

The unexpected appearance of the Zero—the best fighter plane in Asia, manned by skilled pilots—inspired shocked admiration, and a similar awe greeted the Japanese advance down the presumedly impassable Malay Peninsula. "Suddenly, instead of being treacherous and cunning, the Japanese had become monstrous and inhuman," writes a later chronicler of the fall of Singapore. They became "invested in the eyes of both civilians and soldiers with superhuman qualities." In Burma and other tropical areas, the Japanese soldier—who was supposed to be night-blind and afraid of supernatural creatures in the jungle—suddenly became transformed in Allied eyes to what *Yank*, the Army weekly, referred to as "a 'born' jungle and night fighter." In General Slim's words, they became the "superbogeymen of the jungle," while the British forces fell into a massive "inferiority complex"—an experience unprecedented in the history of the British Empire. Indeed, the marvels that occurred in this imaginary world beggared belief, as is implicit in a newspaper headline during the months when sentiment against the Japanese-Americans was being pumped up. "Caps on Japanese Tomato Plants Point to Air Base" trumpeted the *Los Angeles Times* in an article purporting to uncover local farmers plotting to guide Japanese attack planes to their targets. Gone in a flash were the nearsighted, wobbly Japanese flyers of yesterday. Now they were men with telescopic vision, and infernally clever to boot.[26]

In the United States, prominent figures contributed to turning the one-time "little man" into a Goliath. A month after Pearl Harbor, Secretary of War Stimson gave a widely reported speech warning Americans that the Japanese were tough, well disciplined, and well equipped. Former ambassador to Japan Joseph Grew returned to the States on the repatriate ship *Gripsholm* in September 1942, and immediately became the most quotable oracle of grim tidings concerning the enemy in the Pacific. In an exhausting round of speeches, broadcasts, films, and publications (including his 1942 book *Report from Tokyo*), the former ambassador presented a terrifying picture of the Japanese foe. He was "sturdy," "Spartan," "clever and dangerous." His will to conquer was "utterly ruthless, utterly cruel and utterly blind to any of the values which make up our civilization." If Japan succeeded in consolidating its Co-Prosperity Sphere, "the billion men of an enslaved Asia, and all the resources of the East" would be poised to strike at the Western Hemisphere—in five years' time, or ten, or fifty. Indeed, it was Japan's ultimate goal to "bivouac on the White House lawn" after bombing America's major cities—and she might succeed in doing this. The Germans had cracked in 1918, and would crack again, but not so the enemy in Asia. "The Japanese will not crack," Grew told Americans almost as soon as he had disembarked from the *Gripsholm.* "Only by utter physical destruction or utter exhaustion can they be defeated." The alternative for Americans was to pass into slavery.[27]

This was a potent dose indeed of Yellow Peril rhetoric from the country's most esteemed Japan expert, and the media traveled along the same track. Huge Japanese figures moved into the editorial cartoons: Asian giants filling the horizon, huge shadows falling out of the East over the globe, an imperial sun eating the world. Where color was used, the graphics made vivid use of yellow. "All the world knows that Hitler's European New Order is failing," said *Time* in April 1942, many months before Grew returned to lend his aura of officialdom to the same thought, "but it will be a long time before the world knows how Japan's New Order will fare in Asia, for the Japanese have a genius for suppression." And also a genius for guile, hatred, torture, inscrutability—and, as the war dragged on, for dying for their cause.[28]

In the wake of the early defeats, a number of publishers rushed to resurrect the writings of an older generation of Yellow Peril writers, especially Homer Lea, who in 1909 had predicted Japan's global conquest. Lea's apocalyptic vision, presented in a ponderous tome entitled *The Valor of Ignorance,* was distinguished by its reluctant but glowing esteem for Japan's racial vigor and martial spirit, and a correspondingly bleak, even despairing, perception of American heterogeneity and lack of discipline. In 1942, indeed, Lea's vision of an ascendent Japan sounded so much like a prophecy of American doom that the Japanese themselves resurrected him for their own propaganda purposes. The Japanese counterpart to Allied panic concerning the suddenly risen superman was the "victory disease" of overoptimism which swept the country.[29]

To a certain degree, the perception of the Japanese superman flourished because of deliberate acts on the Allied side. The adoption of a "Europe first" policy, for example, meant that the Japanese were given a freer hand than the Germans to consolidate their early conquests and attempt to push on to—where? Australia? India? Madagascar? The Near East? Hawaii and the continental United States? All of these possibilities were spoken of as feasible in the early stages of the war, and the fear of Japanese attack and invasion persisted in the United States for some time after Pearl Harbor. The great American New Year's Day rite, the Rose Bowl football game, was transferred from its traditional setting in Pasadena, California, to North Carolina to avoid a spectacular Japanese outrage, and West Coast cities practiced blackouts until well into 1942. The West Coast from Mexico to Canada was strung with barbed wire, and women in certain coastal areas received instructions in "How to Kill a Jap" in case of invasion—much like the Japanese women who were mobilized to defend their homeland in 1945 and were branded as suicidal fanatics by the Allies. As late as June 1943, around half of Americans questioned still expressed fear of a Japanese attack on the West Coast. The relocation and incarceration of West Coast Japanese-Americans reflected this fear—while at the same time feeding it by giving official endorsement to the belief that the Japanese were a far greater menace to the United States than the other Axis powers.[30]

The Allies' own propaganda mills also contributed to the creation of the new superman. Lingering concern about the isolationist sentiment that had prevailed in the United States prior to Pearl Harbor prompted a campaign to ensure that the will to fight did not flag. However contemptuous of the Japanese the Allied leadership may have been before December 7, they quickly realized an arduous struggle lay ahead. To awaken their compatriots to the same realization required stimulating all the image-making machinery the state and society had to offer; and in the eyes of some observers, the government went too far. In its endeavors to revise the old stereotypes of the "little men" of Japan, the critics argued, Allied leaders themselves promoted an exaggerated caricature that was as harmful to the national purpose as the contemptuous old distortions. Lieutenant Colonel Archie Roosevelt, the son of Theodore Roosevelt and a veteran of the fighting in New Guinea, for example, sent an angry letter to the undersecretary of war declaring that "I feel very strongly that there has, in the United States, been an entirely wrong emphasis put on the prowess of the Jap." In War Department pamphlets and training programs, Roosevelt claimed, the Japanese soldier "has been built up, officially and unofficially, as a sort of superman-superdevil, in ability, ferocity, and training. This resulted in U.S.-trained soldiers coming into battle with an inferiority complex." Roosevelt went on to suggest that a great deal of the hyperbole about Japanese prowess originally came from the British, who were attempting to cover up the "shameful mess" of their own performance in Malaya by exaggerating the formidable capability of the foe. In a vignette that suggests something of what Roosevelt was talking about, after the war one Marine recalled his astonishment, upon encountering his first Japanese soldiers in the flesh, to discover that they were physically small.[31]

In the best dialectical manner, the mythic new Japanese superman soon provoked a myth-debunking vogue. Military events became defined, that is, in terms of how they destroyed a certain corner of the mystique of Japanese invincibility. There emerged the journalistic cult of "the first." Coral Sea and Midway, in May and June 1942, were Japan's first naval defeats. Guadalcanal was the first real test of the superman on land. The battle of Tenaru River in August was Japan's first defeat in jungle combat. At Cape Esperance in August, the Japanese experienced their first defeat in a night battle. By year's end, war correspondents were reporting for the first time that the myth of the "invincibility of the Zero" was finally being destroyed, along with the myth of the Japanese as "unbeatable" jungle fighters.[32]

Yet such myths proved remarkably tenacious, even after the Japanese had fallen on the defensive. The *New York Times Magazine* had entered the fray as early as the spring of 1942 with an article entitled "Japanese Superman: That Too Is a Fallacy," but the bloody resistance of Japanese fighting men in the months and years that followed helped keep the fallacy alive, and a year later the *Times* was still addressing the topic "How Tough Are the Japanese?" After the war, Admiral Halsey went so far as to suggest that his unrestrained abuse of the "monkeymen," which he really let loose in full force at the beginning of 1943 and kept up until the war ended, had been partly motivated by a conscious concern to discredit "the new myth of Japanese invincibility" and boost the confidence of his men. In retrospect, we know that Japan was at the end of its tether by mid-1945, its merchant marine sunk, its cities shattered, its labor force disrupted. It could not have survived much longer, and some military leaders such as Curtis LeMay did argue this at the time. So powerful was the mystique of the superman, however, that prior to the dropping of the atomic bombs, Allied military planners still anticipated that the Japanese could and would hold out for another year or even more.[33]

The war did not create the image of the superman, but rather brought it to the surface—conjured it up, not from some pool of past impressions of the Japanese, but rather from the great Western reservoir of traditional images of the Other. For like the mark of the beast and the numerous traits of the lesser men, in times of fear and crisis "superhuman" qualities too are commonly ascribed to despised outsiders. The great and strong have no monopoly here. Special powers assigned to avowedly lesser men and women take many forms, including physical prowess, sexual appetite, intuitive genius or "occult" skills, fanaticism, a special capacity for violence, monopolization of certain forms of knowledge or control, even an alleged capacity for "evil." Such uncomfortable evocations of the superhuman also may rest on sheer numbers: an impression of the enemy or Other as being quantitatively huge, and consequently a serious and even unfair threat as a collectivity. Apes and other subhuman species are not menacing in themselves. Neither are "lesser men." When the bearers of such pejorative labels suddenly pose an unexpected challenge and perform acts they were not believed capable of undertaking, however, then one looks for special powers—and invariably finds them.

The subhuman and superhuman share in common the ascription of being nonhuman, but there is more to the story than this. Where the treatment of Japan was concerned, they also meant inhuman, in the moral sense. And they coexisted easily. Subhuman and superhuman were not mutually exclusive, as might be expected, but complementary. The visual images associated with each might appear or recede in accordance with fortunes on the battlefield, but the Japanese ape and the Japanese giant went through the war together in the imagination of their Anglo-American enemies. And along with them went certain other archetypical figures as well.

Some of these archetypical companions were variations on the lesser man, and three variations in particular. The Japanese also were described as being primitives or savages in a tribal (as well as just "uncivilized") sense. They were portrayed as children and subjected to theories concerning childhood traumas and adolescent behavior. They also were treated as near lunatics, a race suffering from severe collective psychological disorders. These three caricatures were paraded across the war scene clothed in "empirical" observations of a more serious nature than was the rhetoric of subhumans and superhumans. They too were paradigmatic concepts, with a history in European and American thought that extends far beyond the narrow domain of images of the Japanese per se, and are the subject of the next chapter.

At the same time, however, it is obvious that if the lesser man has many faces, this is equally true—or perhaps even more true—of the superman. As many quotations have already revealed, the superman image was much bigger than the Japanese alone. It entailed visions of Japan leading the "billion" other Asians against the West, and apprehensions of special occult or "Oriental" powers that were simply beyond the grasp of the Europeans and Americans. This was, of course, the old phantom of the Yellow Peril, in all its sinister ambiguity; and that too is a subject that requires separate treatment.

◄ **C H A P T E R 6** ►
PRIMITIVES, CHILDREN, MADMEN

In both the Allied and Axis camps, World War Two witnessed an unprecedented mobilization of resources. Government, industry, and the scientific and intellectual community came together everywhere to forge and set in motion their formidable war machines. For obvious reasons, we tend to think of this primarily in terms of manpower and technology, but ideas also were mobilized. In trade books and popular magazines, in universities and professional journals, in the intelligence arms of the services, and in governmental agencies such as the U.S. Office of War Information and the British Ministry of Information, a variety of experts turned their attention, among other concerns, to analyzing enemy behavior in a manner that would facilitate both accurate military planning and long-term policy-making for the postwar period. Where the enemy in Asia was concerned, these experts and specialists treated their subjects in human terms that were in sharp contrast to the popular idioms of the subhuman and superhuman, and some features of the personality profile of the Japanese that was drawn in the early 1940s have carried over to contemporary approaches to the same elusive subject.[1]

At the academic level, these contributions to understanding the enemy came out of a larger vogue of interdisciplinary "culture and personality" studies that drew heavily upon the methodologies and vocabularies of anthropology, psychology, and psychiatry. The "applied" behavioral and social sciences received unprecedented government support and public attention during the war, offering many academics an exhilarating opportunity to take theory out of the classroom and wed it to causes that seemed simultaneously practical and noble—involving nothing less than understanding the enemy, hastening the end of the war, and laying the groundwork for a more tolerant and peaceful postwar world. Hopes were voiced for the creation of a truly "scientific humanism" or a "humanistic science," and some of the best-known English and American anthropologists, along with their peers in sister disciplines, contributed energetically to this cause as theorists and proselytizers. Notable among them were Margaret Mead, Gregory Bateson, Ruth Benedict, Clyde Kluckhohn, Alexander Leighton, and Geoffrey Gorer. Mead once suggested that country-oriented studies could be most accurately described as focusing on "cultural character structures." Gorer would have preferred the phrase "social character" if that had not already acquired other technical connotations. As it was, these inquiries became best known as the studies of "national character." They were one of the more conspicuous offspring of the wedding of war and the social and behavioral sciences in the West.

Ruminating upon the distinctive character of a country or people had a long and occasionally distinguished tradition in the world of letters. One thinks immediately of de Tocqueville on America or, on Japan, the early European missionaries and Lafcadio Hearn, and even the vivid passages about the "people of Wa" in the ancient Chinese chronicles. The national-character studies differed from these earlier and more literary descriptions in being avowedly "scientific." They also were shaped by the war circumstances in which they developed, with the subject peoples being studied from a distance and the research itself being explicitly designed for use in psychological warfare. The original wartime U.S. national-character studies dealt with Japan, Germany, Burma, Siam, and Rumania, and those on Japan are generally regarded in retrospect as being by far the most interesting.[2]

A fundamental premise of the national-character approach was "the psychic unity of humankind"—the assumption, as Margaret Mead later expressed it, that "all human beings share in a basic humanity." This reflected the antiracist influence of Franz Boas, who had been the immensely influential teacher of Mead and Ruth Benedict, among many others. Boas played a leading role in repudiating the theories of biological determinism, or "scientific racism," which dominated the mainstream of European and American anthropological teaching throughout the nineteenth century. Many of the scholars who became associated with the national-character studies went out of their way to emphasize that the most recent and reliable work on racial differences by anthropologists in no way supported theories of biologically engendered superiority or inferiority in intellect or character. On the contrary, the historical and anthropological record demonstrated that the different racial stocks were all capable of creating and participating in highly developed and civilized pursuits.

The "scientific antiracism" associated with Boas and his disciples was spelled out *in extensio* by Ruth Benedict, who introduced the basic premises of the "culture and personality" approach to a wide audience in 1934 with her popular book *Patterns of Culture,* and over a decade later, after the war had ended, emerged as the best-known Western interpreter of the Japanese national character with the publication of *The Chrysanthemum and the Sword.* In 1940, Benedict published a book-length critique of racism that was revised and reissued during the war. In the preface to the 1945 edition of this work, she observed that the war had made many Americans realize for the first time how guilty their own nation had been of grave racial injustices. And should the war end leaving the impression in Asia, Africa, and the Near East that it had been waged for the benefit of a "white man's world," then there would be little hope of winning the peace. In addition to this work, Benedict also coauthored a wartime pamphlet entitled *The Races of Mankind.* Published in October 1943, this became a center of controversy when it was banned by the U.S. Army and the USO (the civilian United Service Organizations, which sponsored recreational facilities for U.S. servicemen), and denounced by the Military Affairs Committee of the House of Representatives for reflecting "all the techniques . . . of Communist propaganda."[3]

The uproar over this pamphlet is a reminder of the Red baiting which liberal critics of racism frequently had to endure in wartime America. It also places the issue of the Japanese enemy in a broader political and racial perspective, for the antiracist academics were always aware of being engaged in a cause that touched home in intimate ways. Boas and many of his colleagues and successors were Jewish, and acutely sensitive to anti-Semitism in all its guises. Their work also challenged antiblack discrimination in the United States, which is why some members of Congress and the military attacked *The Races of Mankind.* It was within this highly charged domestic context that the experts attempted to offer a more balanced and empirical analysis of the Japanese national character —always aware that biased perceptions of the Japanese were part of the larger problem of American and English racism in general. Race, they consistently argued, was not a determining factor in behavior. Rather, integrated cultural patterns, the unconscious logic of sentiments and assumptions, and the processes of "enculturation" were the keys to understanding all people participating in a common milieu. Culture was inherited from the past, but had to be learned by each generation. Culture also was capable of being altered in innumerable ways, small and large.

The insights that derived from applying such an approach to enemy Japan were substantial and provocative. Highlighted on the one hand was the wholeness of Japanese culture, the tight weave of often unarticulated and, at first glance, random patterns of behavior. At the same time, however, Japan was also shown to be a society encumbered by heavy psychic burdens, taut with enervating anxieties at both the individual and societal levels—all of which was contrary to the holistic "harmony" of a formidably unified and indomitable people exalted in Japanese propaganda and usually taken at face value by Western observers. Seemingly paradoxical behavior such as extreme politeness and extreme brutality was presented as two sides of the same culturally minted coin. By the same token, Japan's aggression against other countries, and the atrocious or fanatic behavior of its fighting men, were seen as predictable outcomes of restrictive domestic pressures and controls (as opposed to being a psychobiological inheritance). There was no reason to assume, however, that Japan was unlike other societies and nations and lacked the capacity for change, even change of a relatively abrupt and drastic nature.

Such observations helped to open a lively discussion of many politically significant issues, including the nature of Japan's basic value system; the emotional stability of individual Japanese and sociopolitical stability of the body politic as a whole; the possibility of bringing about a Japanese surrender by either cracking morale or appealing to indigenous values; whether it was worthwhile for an outside power even to contemplate trying to promote fundamental changes in a defeated Japan—and, if extensive postwar reform of Japan was deemed feasible as well as desirable, whether this should be accomplished by making positive use of established cultural patterns or by attacking traditional values head-on.

Although the anthropologists and other social and behavioral scientists did not speak with one voice on these matters, the single most important recommendation that emerged from the entire multicountry corpus of wartime national-character studies pertained to Japan and was, given the temper of the times, extraordinarily tolerant. Briefly, the recommendation was this: that the Allies refrain from attacking the emperor and the imperial institution, the consumate symbols of the culture system as a whole. To do otherwise would harden Japanese resistance to surrender, for attacking the throne would be seen as a threat to destroy the entire Japanese "way of life." Looking beyond the surrender, this argument continued, it was possible that retention of the throne could even hasten rather than hinder postwar change in a more peaceful and moderately "democratic" direction. To critics—ranging from the exterminationists to most liberals and virtually everyone on the political left—this was tantamount to advocating retention of the very linchpin of all the ideological indoctrination, fascist regimentation, and militaristic ultranationalism that led Japan to war in the first place. In theory, and in practice where the Japanese emperor was concerned, the anthropologists thus made a case—seemingly quite against the predominant currents of the time—for both cultural tolerance and subtle cultural manipulation.[4]

Despite this respect for cultural differences and appreciation of the subtle dynamics of cultural change, however, many writings in the national-character mode still tended, however unwittingly, to reinforce a whole series of assumptions about the Japanese that also were commonplaces of racist thinking. Although these studies may have helped make the Japanese a more complex people in Western eyes, they also gave a patina of scholarly credibility to the impression that the Japanese were unique in unattractive ways, almost totally lacking in diversity or individuality (the very notion of "national character" reinforced the impression of an undifferentiated mass), culturally and socially primitive, infantile or childish as individuals and as a group, collectively abnormal in the psychological and psychiatric sense, and tormented at every level by an overwhelming inferiority complex (not, it was usually indicated, without good reason). They remained odd and alien—and, in rather precise ways, stunted. Out of a welter of theory and detail, in fact, three rather simple sets of code words soon emerged as central to any definition of the Japanese national character. One was phraseology usually associated with primitive and tribal peoples. Another involved the rubric of childishness and immaturity, extending to concepts of adolescent delinquency and gang behavior. And the third drew upon the clinical vocabularies used in the diagnosis of mental and emotional illness.

To a considerable degree, these jargonistic biases were inherent in the disciplines that had greatest influence on the national-character studies. The very genesis of cultural anthropology in fieldwork among "primitive" peoples, for example, predisposed the disciples of that discipline toward concepts based on studying the web of tribal behavior, communal cults, and the like. When such points of focus were carried over to an industrialized country like Japan, they reinforced the impression that the Japanese were dressed-up primitives—or "savages" in modern garb, as the war rhetoric had it—who still conformed to a tribal mode, however far they might have traveled in matters of literacy, technology, and bourgeois trappings.

Alongside such a predisposition to concepts of primitivism, many of the academics involved in national-character studies appeared on the scene as fledgling Japan specialists already persuaded that a people's basic values and patterns of behavior were profoundly shaped by child-rearing practices and early childhood experiences. Given such an orientation, it is not surprising to find that in certain extremely influential accounts toilet training became the key to illuminating most Japanese behavior, including (in the classic exposition, described below) a compulsive need to conquer and control the whole world. To the plainer anthropological perceptions of enduring traumas and insecurities engendered by Japanese child-rearing practices, moreover, stricter Freudian apostles added the more dramatic conceptualization of collective psychic blockage at an infantile (anal or genital) stage of development. From this perspective, Japanese overseas aggression became explicable in terms of penis envy or a castration complex, depending on whether the external enemy was perceived as strong or weak, male or female.

The Freudian analysis was extreme, but at the same time it was symptomatic of the compelling place that concepts of childishness held in both popular and academic perceptions of the Japanese. Superficially, there was a simple explanation for this perception of the Japanese as children: to Westerners, Oriental adults in general looked younger than their actual years. At an average height of five feet three inches, the Japanese soldier was considerably shorter than his English or American foe. Thus, the rubric of the "little men" also had a plain, physical side to it. Japanese men were also less hirsute than their Caucasian antagonists. In the opening weeks of the war, the short stature and relatively beardless faces of Japanese fighting men actually gave rise to a rumor that the force invading Southeast Asia was composed mostly of inexperienced and poorly trained youngsters.

Like other exemplary metaphors in the lexicon of unequal relationships, however, childishness ultimately had nothing to do with appearance and everything to do with assigned status. To the Freudians, it meant the psychic and emotional blockage of the Japanese people as a race. To other social scientists, the term connoted that Japanese personality structure, culture, and institutions were, in various ways, as yet immature. Childishness was a cognate of primitivism, albeit with softer connotations—for the child can become an adult more surely than the primitive can become thoroughly civilized.

The insights—and biases—of psychiatry and clinical psychology were also strongly apparent in the third major line of emphasis that emerged out of the national-character studies: the thesis that the Japanese were collectively unstable. Ruth Benedict, perhaps the most graceful and subtle of the wartime analysts of Japan, once described culture as "individual psychology thrown large on the screen"; and, as Benedict herself appreciated, such a conceptual leap was fraught with peril. What was involved in this transfer—implicit in the very notion of "national character"—was the application to whole nations and cultures of an analytical language that had been developed through personal case studies. The very premise that this was a valid way of understanding whole societies was itself questionable. When this language derived primarily from vocabularies developed by psychiatrists and psychologists for the diagnosis of sick, abnormal, emotionally disturbed individuals, moreover—as was in good part the case where the wartime studies of the Japanese enemy were concerned—then the tools of analysis themselves became almost inherently deprecatory.[5]

The single most influential academic analysis of "Japanese character structure" that was presented during the war was undoubtedly a paper delivered before an academic audience in the United States in March 1942, and published in abbreviated form in a scholarly journal near the end of 1943. The author was Geoffrey Gorer, an English social anthropologist; and despite the narrow forums he chose to publicize his ideas, he reached a significant and varied audience. Gorer was close to the American academics involved in the development of "culture and personality" studies, and briefly associated with the analysis of Japanese behavior being conducted under the Foreign Morale Analysis Division of the Office of War Information. In addition, his theories were quickly picked up in the popular press. His seminal paper, entitled "Themes in Japanese Culture" in its original presentation, was recapitulated in *Time* under the heading "Why Are Japs Japs?"[6]

Gorer began his analysis by observing that on the surface Japan appeared to be "the most paradoxical culture of which we have any record," illustrating this with a familiar catalog of contradictions. In spite of having adopted many trappings of modern society, he went on, the country still retained a worldview "more consonant with an isolated and primitive tribe than with a major industrial nation." The explanation for this was not to be found in genetic peculiarities but rather in socialization, especially habits and attitudes ingrained in early childhood. Although Gorer acknowledged the limited nature of his data base and noted that this data applied primarily to middle- and higher-income groups in Japan's urban areas, his conclusions were widely accepted as applicable to all Japanese.

Gorer was especially concerned with the brutal, often sadistic aggressiveness of Japanese males at war, and linked such behavior directly to "ethics peculiar to the Japanese," reflected most conspicuously in their extreme concern with ritual and tidiness. In the casebooks of contemporary psychology and psychiatry, individuals preoccupied with ritual, cleanliness, and order were identified as "compulsive neurotics." Because such behavior was statistically common rather than unusual in Japan, Gorer preferred to describe the Japanese character as simply compulsive or obsessive (leaving aside the technical question of whether it should also be labeled neurotic). Whatever the label, such behavior (or ethics, or national character) was unsavory, and Gorer's significant conceptual contribution lay in offering a clear hypothesis as to its origins as well as its implications.

Although the focus on cleanliness and ritual purity was intimately associated with Shinto, Japan's indigenous religion, Gorer argued that in actual practice such preoccupations derived from "learning associated with the control of the gastro-intestinal tract," that is, "drastic toilet training." From this followed several conclusions seductive in their simplicity. The whole Japanese value system was depicted as situational; there were no overarching codes of behavior, no "sin" applicable everywhere. "If this cleanliness training lies at the bottom of the value system of the society," the argument ran, "it would follow that there would be no absolutes, no 'right' or 'wrong,' but instead very strong emphasis on doing the right thing at the right time." This went far toward explaining the seemingly contradictory behavior exhibited by Japanese in different settings, where their status might differ or where there was no clear prescription concerning the "right thing" to do. Furthermore, the compulsively ritualistic behavior manifest in the national character, as known through clinical cases of individual obsessives, "covered a deeply hidden, unconscious and extremely strong desire to be aggressive."

It would be difficult to devise a more intimate explanation for international conflict and war atrocities than this: Japanese aggression and barbaric behavior abroad derived from the value system and national character, which in turn were profoundly influenced by forced control of the sphincter muscle in early childhood. Alien and unfamiliar situations were terrifying to the Japanese, for there were no clear rituals of behavior to follow. By the same token, however, in such contexts the collapse of customary prescribed rituals of behavior meant the collapse of the subliminal restraints against aggressive impulses, with catastrophic consequences. Frustration and rage pent up by the regimented rituals of social interaction within Japan exploded with appalling savagery against enemies abroad.

Gorer elaborated upon this analysis by also relating Japan's international behavior to discriminatory sexual socialization (beginning with the different attitudes encouraged toward the mother and father), as well as to early learning associated with control of one's body, emotions, and immediate environment (culminating in a collective psychological need to control the world). The patterns of male dominance and female passivity and subservience inculcated in early relations with parents, siblings, and one's small social sphere were extended by mature Japanese to the world of nation-states as well. Consequently, contemporary Japanese viewed other races and societies "as either male or female: as groups to be followed and obeyed implicitly, or as groups to be forced to yield to aggression or threats of aggression."

Previous writers had already called attention to the way Japanese leaders perceived the external world sexually. In *Inside Asia*, published in 1939, for example, John Gunther recorded a conversation with a prominent Japanese statesman who described Japan's relation to China as that of male to female. If China disobeyed Japan, Gunther was told, she obviously must be severely punished (in the "statesman's" metaphor, by having her arms and legs cut off!). As Gorer saw it, in recent decades the Japanese had revised their sexual categorization of the Anglo-American powers, which had been perceived as virile and indubitably male in the nineteenth century, but were now regarded as soft, indecisive, and consequently feminine. This transformation in sexual identification probably began with Japan's defeat of Russia in 1905, an immensely gratifying victory over a "white" power. The bickering and vacillating policies of the

English and Americans in the Far East in the years thereafter, culminating in their "feminine" response to the Manchurian Incident and its aftermath (threats and complaints unbacked by forceful action), completed Japan's new perception of itself as the genuinely male force in world affairs—opposed to, and intrinsically superior to, not only a female China but also a feminine United States and Great Britain.

What emerged from this pioneer hypothesis was the picture of a country superficially arrogant and self-confident, but in actuality shot through with an enervating sense of inferiority and insecurity. The "desire for a controlled universe" was overwhelming at the individual level and catastrophic at the level of the collective Japanese psyche, for in the final analysis the Japanese were literally driven psychologically to try to conquer the world. "Owing to the methods by which, and the society in which, the Japanese are brought up, no Japanese can feel safe and secure unless the whole environment is understood and as far as possible controlled." This explained the attempt to "control" the unknown world by excluding it during the centuries of the feudalistic Tokugawa seclusion; the frantic attempts to comprehend and master Western learning once the country had been opened up to the outside world; the repressive controls imposed by the Japanese government upon its own society; the "almost continuous history of aggressive warfare" that characterized Japan's last eighty years —and the current quest for world conquest. "The Japanese can never feel safe," Gorer concluded, "unless, as some of their more bombastic military speakers have proposed, the Mikado rules the whole earth."

This remarkable odyssey from rectal fixation to conquest of the world was, by almost any reckoning, a tour de force of suggestive generalization. In this single early paper on the psychocultural structure of the Japanese, Gorer articulated many of the basic ideas that assumed a central place in the analyses of other Western intellectuals: the notion of a clinically compulsive and probably collectively neurotic people, whose lives were governed by ritual and "situational ethics," wracked with insecurity, and swollen with deep, dark currents of repressed resentment and aggression. In addition, despite his assumption that the Japanese were psychologically driven to place the whole world under the rule of the emperor, Gorer was also one of the first Western intellectuals to argue that "neither the Mikado nor the abstract Throne should be attacked" by the Allied powers, and indeed "should never be mentioned other than respectfully"—having reached this conclusion in an unpublished report prepared in the weeks immediately following the attack on Pearl Harbor.

The Japanese could not conceive of living without a ritual head, Gorer reasoned, any more than medieval Catholics could contemplate the elimination of the pope. To commit the "foolish sacrilege" of attacking the emperor would only excite anger among the Japanese. On the other hand, to acknowledge "the sacred dignity of the Mikado" would make it possible to attack the wielders of power in Japan for betraying their august sovereign.[7]

Subsequent commentators on the Japanese often acknowledged their debt to Gorer, and many found his thesis buttressed by John Embree's booklet *The Japanese,* which was published in January 1943 as part of the War Background Studies of the Smithsonian Institution.[8] Although Embree was more temperate and balanced than Gorer in his evaluation of Japanese personality and society, the portion of his study that attracted most attention also dealt with the importance of severe toilet training in early childhood, along with the abrupt withdrawal of maternal indulgence when a new child was born. This, Embree felt, created in the Japanese child an early sense of insecurity as well as rage which persisted into adult life, emerging as tantrums in infancy and behavior bordering on the "paranoic" in adulthood. Many of the elaborate social rituals which Occidentals found so bizarre, such as the use of go-betweens and the reliance on group rather than personal responsibility, reflected an abiding fear of losing face and being subjected to ridicule and rejection, and could be attributed to the traumatic and contradictory experiences of the toddler. Embree went so far as to argue that assassination, so conspicuous a part of the Japanese political scene, was "the adult manifestation of the temper tantrum resulting from lack of attention or fancied slight," while suicide was a manifestation of the deep shame felt from real or threatened loss of face, and fierce expressions of racial and cultural pride were at least partly to be explained by the insecurities induced by childhood traumas.

Elsewhere in the Smithsonian booklet, Embree agreed that Japanese soldiers behaved with exceptionally brutal lack of restraint abroad, and he attributed this almost offhandedly to the "Japanese male character structure." In their borrowing from the West, he declared, the Japanese had adopted virtually nothing of substance in the realm of culture and ideology. On the contrary, they developed a "defense reaction" that asserted the superiority of the Japanese way. Like Gorer, albeit in a milder way, Embree asserted that the Japanese truly believed it was their "divine duty to bring the Japanese way to all the world." At the same time, he emerged as by far the most consistent exponent of pure cultural tolerance and cultural relativism, arguing in the Smithsonian study and elsewhere that the Allies neither could nor should attempt to impose any sort of reforms whatsoever on Japan once victory was attained. Embree rested hope instead on latent and indigenous traditions of democratic practice in Japan, especially at the village level.[9]

Embree was at this time the only formally trained Western anthropologist who had done fieldwork in Japan. His research in 1935–36 for his doctoral dissertation at the University of Chicago had resulted in the sympathetic village study *Suye Mura* (1939), and by comparison to many of his colleagues his descriptive style was plain. Embree was never associated with the "national-character" vogue per se, and in the immediate postwar years he let fly some sharp attacks on the ethnocentric biases of these presumedly value-free attempts to "know the enemy."[10] Yet during the war years, his own writings were generally interpreted as supporting some of the more degrading aspects of the national-character theories. One review of *The Japanese* was entitled "Jap Cruelty Traced to Childhood." Another described Embree's book as a cogent analysis of Japan's "national psychosis." The *New York Times Magazine*, without directly mentioning Embree or his study, had this to tell its readers in August 1943, under the heading "Jap Bullies":

> The anthropologists tell us why the Jap soldier is a truculent and vengeful bully. From his birth his mother pets him inordinately until the arrival of his little sister, after which she dismisses him as her chief interest in life and hands him over to the indifferent care of servants. It injures his nervous system at a critical time in his development, and he never gets over the shock. If birth control were practiced in Japan he might grow up a gentleman. Better yet, he might not be born at all. . . . The subject, however, is a dangerous one, and we drop it like a hot potato. Right here.[11]

Gorer, who had no firsthand experience in Japan, described his own theoretical approach as deriving from the disciplines of social anthropology, psychoanalysis, and stimulus-response psychology. He had a much more rigid and psychologically oriented sense of causality than Embree, but skirted the use of a really vigorous Freudian framework. That such a framework also found the diagnostic key to the Japanese national character (and, to a milder degree, the German personality too) in the "primitive phases" of infantile or childhood development was spelled out in an article in the *Psychoanalytic Review* by Dr. Judith Silberpfennig in early 1945.[12]

In the Silberpfennig analysis, the "inferiority-superiority complex" frequently observed in Japanese (and Germans) was related to the behavior of children in the phallic stage of development as well as to neurotic patients whose difficulties centered on an inability to resolve or transcend conflicts of the phallic stage. To the psychoanalyst, there were striking analogies between the "paradoxa" of the enemy and the obnoxious "little boy who suffers from fears and night terrors," who manifests "paranoid, criminal, grandiose" behavior, and who is not only envious of his father and other males who possess a bigger phallus, but also suffers "phantastic fears of castration" at the hands of the weak, deprived, and feminine. Silberpfennig drew upon Gorer in emphasizing the significance of the severe early anal training to which Japanese children were subjected, as well as the importance of male-female distinctions in Japanese culture. Thus, she pointed to the manner in which the four-year-old Japanese male was encouraged in "anal-sadistic forms of aggression against his mother," and also called attention to the deep latent fear which the "superclean" Japanese "supermale" felt toward "unclean" women and, by extension, the "unclean" foreigner.

Pursuing this line of analysis, Dr. Silberpfennig went on to suggest that unresolved tensions of the phallic stage lay behind the Japanese ideology of racial superiority: "Earlier overevaluation of the body and the consequent overevaluation of the phallus find an universal expression in the overevaluation of the race. The Yamato race is divine, and the weak foreigners are jealous of their strength and harbor sinister schemes to rob the strong males." "Phantastic fears" combined with "an infantile disregard for reality" led the Axis enemy to embark upon ceaseless attempts to attain security by amassing territory, the Japanese appearing to be even more irrational and fanatic in their racial fears and prejudices than the Germans. In part, this could probably be explained by the fact that the Japanese emperor embodied the "phantasies of a strong father" in a more abstract and irrational way than the Führer. Beyond this, serious thought obviously need be given to "whether the Germans of today have not regressed to the attitude of the disturbed phallic phase, while the Japanese never came out of it." (Whatever one may think of Freudian analysis, to the extent that it drew attention to early childhood and family relations as a major source of emotional tension and trauma, there was an unintended but ironic aptness in its wartime application to Japan, where the

romanticized ideology of "family," "familial harmony," and the beneficent parent-child relationship lay at the heart of ruling-class orthodoxies.)

Gorer's pioneer analysis had been based on a fairly extensive survey
of Western-language sources on Japan plus interviews with some twenty
informants, while Dr. Silberpfennig's speculations rested on a slight bibliography in which only five sources, including Gorer's essay, dealt directly
with Japan. As the war unfolded, however, academics with ties to the U.S.
government gained access to a wide range of new materials as they attempted to draw a more detailed portrait of the Japanese national character. One voluminous source of raw data consisted of open, intercepted,
or captured Japanese-language materials (newspapers and magazines,
radio broadcasts, captured documents, diaries and letters found on Japanese prisoners or war dead). These were translated in massive quantities
within the government. Interrogation of captured prisoners provided additional insight into both individual and collective attitudes. In addition,
under the U.S. War Relocation Authority, a program of "community
analysis" was established in the ten camps in which Japanese-Americans
were incarcerated. Staffed primarily by trained anthropologists, with a
sprinkling of sociologists (over thirty scholars were involved at one time
or another), these research projects focusing on first- and second-generation Japanese-Americans, plus youngsters of the third generation, contributed in both direct and indirect ways to the burgeoning vogue of
national-character studies. Observations based on work with these persecuted and uprooted Americans were superimposed upon the growing
collective portrait of the Japanese enemy, and several social scientists who
worked in the camps went on to participate directly in psychological-
warfare planning pertaining to Japan.[13]

By 1944, a considerable number of social and behavioral scientists
had thus turned their attention to Japan; and by and large they agreed
that, in one way or another, "immaturity" was a critical concept for
understanding Japanese behavior. This was certainly the impression conveyed in December 1944, when over forty distinguished social scientists,
psychiatrists, and Japan specialists met for two days in New York under
the auspices of the Institute of Pacific Relations specifically to discuss
"Japanese character structure."[14] The working minutes from this conference summarized the discussions as follows: "The most conspicuous new
insight which developed was the comparison between Japanese character
structure and behavior which is characteristic of the adolescent in our
society. This comparison makes it possible to invoke our knowledge of

individual adolescent psychology and of the behavior of adolescents in gangs in our society, as a systematic approach to better understanding of the Japanese."

Although participants in these discussions offered various opinions concerning the manner in which this "adolescent" quality was manifested by the Japanese, it was recorded that there was "very little disagreement with the diagnosis itself." Indeed, much of the attractiveness of this line of analysis lay in its apparently wide range of applicability. At an early point in the discussions, the sociologist Talcott Parsons observed that the manner in which the Japanese found security and stability by "fitting into a system of culturally defined patterns of group life" was "analogous to the conformism of our adolescent patterns." Margaret Mead agreed that this "conscious conformity" lay at the heart of the adolescent quality in Japan, and went on to note that "whereas in the United States system this is limited to our adolescents, in Japan it permeates all through society." Parsons picked up the ball again by stating that the "compulsive conformity" of the Japanese to their own standards amounted to "a revolt against conformity to adult standards."

Participants in the New York conference were in agreement that Japanese conformity to prescribed norms generally lacked personal or individual conviction; and such "conformity without conviction," as one political scientist put it, "is the perfect clinical picture of adolescence." One of the several psychiatrists invited to the conference pointed out that Japanese behavior conformed to such "clinical samples" of adolescent immaturity as "vacillation between different attitudes, differing emotional reactions, the use of fantasy, and the disorganization of the personality." He called attention to differences in Western and Japanese child-rearing practices, while also suggesting that differences in national character structures reflected differences in stages of human development, and "the gangster phase of the Japanese is a particular phase of boyhood development." The anthropologist Gordon Bowles dwelled on "adolescence in Japanese political life," by which he meant social, political, and linguistic legacies from feudal times. Frank Tannenbaum, a historian, found particularly fascinating "the typical gang psychology in Japan where you have security in the group and complete individual insecurity outside the group." The day after the conference ended, Tannenbaum followed up this notion in a letter to Margaret Mead, one of the coordinators of the conference, in which he provided a list of twenty-eight points of analogy between Japanese behavior and "the character structure of the American gangster."

When the experts later turned their attention to the proper attitude which the Anglo-American powers, and especially the United States, should adopt in attempting to bring about the surrender and subsequent reform of Japan, the discussion proceeded along the same conceptual track. The United States should assume an "elder brother" pose vis-à-vis "younger brother" Japan, it was suggested, and assure the defeated country a future place in the "family of nations."

While calling attention to the childishness or immaturity of Japanese culture and personality, Western commentators also argued that the Japanese suffered from innumerable emotional maladies and anxieties. Conspicuous among these was a massive inferiority complex, which the Westerners tended to treat as not inappropriate under the circumstances: the Japanese, after all, had good reason to feel inferior. Two of the West's most distinguished anthropologists, Margaret Mead and her husband Gregory Bateson, for example, took this line. At the December 1944 conference, Mead agreed that Japanese culture was "childish" and "pathological." Previously, in a 1942 book on Bali, she and Bateson already had dealt in passing with Japan's savage treatment of other Asians in the current war. They related this behavior to Japan's long history of unhappy cultural contacts, and observed that "the Japanese, lacking respect for their own culture, perceive their inevitable inferiority and feel insulted when they meet this self-respect in others."[15]

Mead and Bateson wrote as individuals with deep emotional ties to Southeast Asia, but many others echoed these sentiments. An almost identical opinion was expressed by Edgar Snow, Mao Tse-tung's early biographer and one of the West's most articulate chroniclers of China's struggle. Japan's "pronounced inferiority complex," Snow explained, derived in large measure from the fact that subconsciously "the individual Japanese is aware of his unfortunate intellectual and physical inferiority to individual Koreans and Chinese, the two peoples subject to his god-Emperor. He is forever seeking ways of compensation"—and finding such compensation in the humiliation, brutalization, and wanton slaughter of others. Helen Mears, one of the most iconoclastic of the journalistic commentators on Japan during the war years and after, suggested that the Japanese susceptibility to indoctrination and mythic mumbo jumbo about racial superiority could be seen as "a kind of incantation and self-hypnosis, a technique to bolster their sense of inferiority—economic and military inferiority in relation to the genuinely powerful Western powers, and psychological inferiority in face of the scientific achievements of the West, and the humiliation of Western insistence on 'colored' inferiority."[16]

In the Western diagnosis, manifestations of a collective inferiority complex were but one symptom of a larger psychological disorder that pervaded all of Japanese society; and this disorder was, in fact, usually presented as inseparable from the traits of primitivism and immaturity previously mentioned. The three concepts—primitivism, immaturity, and mental and emotional instability—were woven into almost all extended discussions of the Japanese character, as integrated rather than separate characteristics of the enemy. A group of British Far Eastern specialists meeting at almost exactly the same time as the New York conference on Japanese behavior, for example, prepared an important report on long-term planning for Asia in which they spoke of "the present immaturity of Japanese development," and typically characterized the Japanese people as a whole as "primitive and emotionally repressed." Ruth Benedict, then working for the Office of War Information, was developing a more tempered equation between childish behavior and emotional disorder in the Japanese case. The acute sensitivity of the Japanese to "trifles," she observed (in the postwar reworking of her wartime studies), "occurs in American records of adolescent gangs and case-histories of neurotics."[17]

As Margaret Mead later observed, Benedict herself was uncomfortable with rigid psychological and psychiatric concepts, and used them sparingly. Gorer too, although more sympathetic to Freudian analysis, had hesitated in his seminal essay to describe the Japanese as collectively neurotic. Many Western analysts and commentators, however, felt no such constraints, and "neurosis" or "compulsive neurosis" was probably the single most popular diagnostic phrase borrowed from the psychiatrists and clinical psychologists and applied to the Japanese en masse. At the December 1944 conference, this line of analysis was introduced enthusiastically by Douglas Haring, a respected anthropologist who had lived in Japan for many years as a missionary. Haring described how he had read a chapter in Karen Horney's *The Neurotic Personality of Our Time* to a Western acquaintance who also had spent a long time in Japan, substituting the word "Japanese" in every place where Horney had written "neurotic." His acquaintance, Haring declared, said that it was "the most perfect description of the Japanese" he had ever heard.[18]

That the Western experts were capable of moments of self-critical introspection is revealed by the sentence in the conference notes immediately following Haring's comments. "Someone suggested," it was recorded, "that almost the same results could be achieved by substituting the word 'American' for 'neurotic.'" Such wry self-reflection was rare, however. More often, the Japanese as a collectivity were diagnosed as suffering not merely from an inferiority complex, or emotional repression, or neurosis, but from the whole gamut of mental and emotional disorders found among maladjusted individuals in the West. Willis Lamott captured this attitude in the early pages of his 1944 book *Nippon*. "Modern Japan is undeniably a psychological case," he wrote. "Her national psychosis, her neurosis, her schizophrenia, and her paranoia have been described so many times already as to make repetition unnecessary. Call it what you will, her mental condition is abnormal." Or as another expert on the Far East observed, "what would be the lunatic fringe in any other country . . . comes close to being the norm in Japan."[19]

The thesis that the Japanese were collectively ill in a clinical sense received its most elaborate scholarly expression at the very end of the war in a famous analysis of the Japanese character structure published by Weston La Barre in August 1945 and based on the author's observations as a "community analyst" among Japanese-Americans in the Topaz (Utah) relocation camp.[20] La Barre, a Yale-trained anthropologist, took as his task correcting the simplistic notion that people everywhere are just people, which he felt various misguided idealists were attempting to foist on the American people. On the contrary, he declared, Americans needed to be reminded of "cultural-psychological differences" among peoples of the world. The collective American psychology, he suggested, showed an early mix of feudal and democratic strains, but "on the whole, freedom and democracy has . . . clearly been the major motif," along with "rugged individual self-reliance"; "humor, confidence and exuberance"; and "a sense of the law, of equal applicability to all men, which is entirely foreign to India and China and Japan." Americans were neither absurdly litigious like the Indians, nor did they suffer the "spiritual hemophilia" of the Chinese. The most striking contrast of all to the American character, however, was posed by the Japanese, whom La Barre concluded were "probably the most compulsive people in the world ethnological museum."

La Barre was unfamiliar with Gorer's pioneer analysis when he prepared his own paper, a surprising oversight given the wide impact of that earlier study in professional circles. Like Gorer, however, he too related the compulsive personality of the Japanese to the anal level of development, "in which the child is forced to relinquish primary gratifications and to take on culturally colored conditioning of the sphincters." He then proceeded to list nineteen basic traits of the compulsive personality, and devoted the remainder of his long article to discussing how each occurred "with great consistency in the typical Japanese character structure." The nineteen traits were these: "secretiveness, hiding of emotions and attitudes; perseveration and persistency; conscientiousness; self-righteousness; a tendency to project attitudes; fanaticism; arrogance; 'touchiness'; precision and perfectionism; neatness and ritualistic cleanliness; ceremoniousness; conformity to rule; sadomasochistic behavior; hypochondriasis; suspiciousness; jealousy and enviousness; pedantry; sentimentality; love of scatological obscenity and anal sexuality."

La Barre, like most commentators, accepted without question that the Japanese—all Japanese—did indeed desire to rule the world. He discussed this under the compulsive trait of self-righteousness, in which there was little ego examination of severe superego demands. "As with the Nazis in similar circumstances," La Barre observed, "the Japanese have manifested a sort of puzzled, hurt shock that other people did not accept their doctrine and domination, when their motives of civilizing the world under the divine ordainments of Amaterasu Omikami and her line were so pure and so self-evident." In both the German and Japanese cases, such self-righteousness was "part of a tribal theology of racial superiority and consequent divine mission." Unlike the majority of his anthropologist colleagues, however, La Barre concluded that this racist and militaristic sense of mission could only be expunged from the Japanese psyche by a direct and thoroughgoing attack on the mystique of the imperial institution. In this respect, he was a maverick among his peers, and far more in sympathy with those more politically radical analysts who analyzed Japan's dilemma from a historical and fundamentally socioeconomic perspective.

The wartime opportunity to engage in "applied" social and behavioral sciences was seductive, and has remained so for countless scholars and professionals ever since. However, when we ask to what extent the experts actually challenged prevailing opinions and influenced policy in a specific case—here the case of understanding the Japanese and dealing with them before and after they surrendered—the answer must be a qualified one. Some of the analyses done on Japanese behavior, often under the government's aegis, were sophisticated and provocative, and certain predictions about Japanese responses to defeat proved impressively close to the mark. Prior to Japan's surrender, however, it is difficult to point to a single area where the wartime studies brought about a major change in public opinion or government policy. On the other hand, certain lines of emphasis, such as the paradigmatic concepts discussed in this chapter, actually reinforced rather than repudiated popular prejudices concerning the Japanese; it can be argued that they even bore, like the mark of Cain, the sign of incipient racism.

There were perhaps three major areas where the scholars and intelligence experts who worked on Japan during the war did offer significant theories that ran against the grain of conventional opinion. The first was the conclusion, reached before 1945, that Japanese morale was cracking and a serious psychological-warfare campaign directed against Japanese fighting men, the civilian population, and the Japanese leadership itself had a good chance of increasing battlefield surrenders and hastening an early capitulation. Social scientists in the Foreign Morale Analysis Division of the Office of War Information concluded as early as April 1944 that the morale of Japanese fighting men was not "virtually impregnable" as was commonly believed. On the contrary, they could be persuaded to surrender if a serious effort were mounted to this end. This conclusion was based on analysis of captured diaries and interrogation of the small number of Japanese who had been captured, but the low-ranking experts in Washington found it virtually impossible to convince commanders in the field of either the value of prisoners or the possibility of taking them in larger numbers. In an article on psychological warfare in the Pacific published in the last month of the war, Edgar Jones observed that until the final stage of the invasion of Okinawa, "psychological warfare seldom was employed against the Japanese, who were regarded popularly as too inhuman to be propagandized. . . . While learned authorities on Far Eastern matters were busy in Washington planning detailed propaganda programs for use against the Japanese, the commanders in the field disregarded paper weapons [that is, psychological-warfare leaflets] and stuck to their guns."[21]

By late 1944, moreover, the OWI analysts had reached the further conclusion that Japanese home-front morale also was deteriorating rapidly. They issued their first major internal report to this effect on January

5, 1945, and in subsequent reports cited mounting evidence of defeatism, apathy, fear, and social disintegration. The conclusions of the Foreign Morale Analysis Division on this critical issue were summarized in a lengthy analysis of "Current Psychological and Social Tensions in Japan" issued on June 1—a month and a half before the successful test of the atomic bomb at Alamogordo. This report identified fifteen major areas where social and political conflict were already conspicuous, and concluded that an intensive psychological-warfare campaign against the homeland—one which offered assurances that the imperial system would not be destroyed and innocent people would not be punished—would turn the country against its militarist leaders and hasten Japan's surrender. Again, such conclusions contradicted prevailing impressions of a Japanese citizenry girding for and even welcoming a fight to the bitter end, and the analysts found their conclusions dismissed even by higher officials within the OWI itself. No U.S. official in a policy-making position appears to have read any of the findings of the OWI social scientists assigned to analyze Japanese behavior, and one of the rationales advanced by Secretary of War Stimson for using the atomic bombs was that there was no indication that the Japanese resolve to go on fighting was cracking. Looking back on these activities, the sociologist and psychiatrist Alexander Leighton, who headed the OWI team working on Japan, turned to a saying popular at the time: "The administrator uses social science the way a drunk uses a lamppost, for support rather than for illumination."[22]

The two other major conceptual breakthroughs by the wartime social scientists involved their sanguine appraisal of the emperor and the imperial institution, and their elaboration of the concept of situational ethics. The anthropologist Clyde Kluckhohn, who also worked with the Foreign Morale Analysis Division, expressed the sentiment of many participants in stating that the group's position on the emperor was its most significant contribution. Kluckhohn belittled the vulgarized theories of Japanese character structure that overemphasized the traumatic effects of harsh toilet training. To insiders, he later confided, this was known as the "Scott Tissue interpretation of history." The most important insight that the social scientists offered, in his view, was that the emperor was the single universally respected symbol in Japan, and thus had to be retained as both the rallying point for surrender and the vehicle for postwar change. If the throne were to be abolished, this could only be done by the Japanese themselves. For the Allies to attempt to do so by fiat would only provoke violent resistance.

That the throne was an ambiguous symbol—equally adaptable to war, surrender, and peace—was consistent with the "situational" nature of Japanese ethics and values in general. In contrast to the absolute morality that characterized the Judeo-Christian tradition, the Japanese adjusted to whatever situation they found themselves in. Thus, as was well known to the experts, who worked closely with prisoner reports, while the Japanese fighting men who did fall into Allied hands generally proved to be docile and cooperative, even to the point of volunteering information and helping with propaganda, they also remained firmly devoted to the emperor and the imperial institution. To the academics, the implications of this were crucial and obvious: if the Allies made positive use of the emperor instead of appearing to threaten both him personally and the throne as an institution, the Japanese people would readily accept surrender and peace.[23]

This argument too had negligible impact on the formulation of Allied war policy, despite the fact that the U.S. government did refrain from making the emperor a direct target of propaganda attacks (and the Imperial Palace a deliberate bombing target) on the grounds that this would merely stiffen Japanese resistance—and despite the fact that retention of the imperial institution, and even Emperor Hirohito personally, became a key feature of the postsurrender U.S. occupation policy. To offer guarantees concerning the throne while the war was underway violated both the Allied demand (since 1943) for "unconditional surrender" and the widespread belief that the emperor and the imperial institution were the nucleus of a fascist and militarist state. Only after Japan had capitulated did maintenance of the emperor become feasible—especially after General MacArthur emerged as a confirmed believer in using the throne to maintain stability. In the fury of the war, however, when the Japanese militarists and ideologues were so clearly in control of the potent imperial symbol, such moderate ideas were politically unpalatable.

What was not unpalatable in the heat of war was expert opinion that could be interpreted as confirming existing prejudices. Policymakers tend to hear what they wish to hear, as Leighton ruefully concluded. And scholars, on their part, often discover what popular sentiment wishes them to discover. It is here that the important place which the Japanese national-character exercises assigned to primitivism, childishness, and emotional disturbance becomes of more than esoteric interest. For these categories, like apes and vermin, and lesser men and supermen, were also in one form or another the coinage of everyday opinion about the Japanese.

From the beginning of the war to its end, for instance, primitivism and its cognates (savagery, barbarism, tribalism) were not only central to everyday Allied commentary on the Japanese enemy, but also usually offered as if they were genuinely historical or anthropological observations. This emerges in both passing comments and more sustained discourse on the British side, for example, where the war in Asia was a decidedly secondary concern. Sir John Pratt, one of the most highly regarded Far Eastern experts in the Foreign Office, spoke in familiar terms when he referred in a mid-war book to "the ferocity of the primitive savage, which is never far below the surface in Japan." That this was close to the orthodox view is apparent from a pamphlet on the Japanese published in April 1942 by the Ministry of Information, Britain's counterpart to the OWI. "Smoking chimneys, policemen and traffic lights, taxis hurrying little men in black coats and bowler hats to offices that might well be in New York," the pamphlet observed, "bear witness to Japan's modern technique and disguise her primitive heart." The following year, in a publication entitled *The Japanese People*, the ministry referred to "these mediocre people" as being similar to the Germans in such matters as pseudoreligions, tribalism, brutality, and negation of God, but different from their Axis ally in that "Germany is a heretic, relapsed from universal standards that Japan has never known."[24] This mode of expression, incidentally, was virtually *de rigueur* whenever the Japanese and Germans were discussed together in American or British writings: the Germans were bad, but the Japanese were worse; the Germans were compulsive, but the Japanese were the most compulsive people in the world; the Germans had regressed to a phallic stage, while the Japanese never came out of it; the Germans, as in this case, had lapsed from standards the Japanese never knew.

In April 1945, as Germany crumbled and the British began to turn greater attention to the battle in Asia, the Ministry of Information developed some of these ideas about Japanese primitivism in a new publication entitled *A Diagnosis of Japanese Psychology*. The analysis began with the observation that the same people who displayed an exquisite love of nature "will in a moment become savage barbarians, taking to any outrage and cruelty with both gusto and enthusiasm." The ministry attributed such contradictory behavior to "a racial background" in which ancient influences had persisted tenaciously down to modern times. These included the "fierce, excitable" character traits of a prehistoric "Malayan strain"; the practice of Ancestor Worship (always capitalized in the pamphlet), a religious activity that all advanced peoples transcend; the survival along-side this of ancient communal cults and mores that suppressed individual-ism and denied all privacy whatsoever—the legacies, in general, of a primitive "group ideology," sanctified by archaic communal religion and reinforced by centuries of tyranny. The dependence of Japanese on the group and their emotional instability as individuals was similarly singled out as reflecting "one of the chief distinctions between a primitive and an advanced society."[25]

The Ministry of Information "diagnosis," which was passed by the British Censor and made available to the public "as a basis for articles, speeches, broadcasts, etc.," had innumerable nonofficial counterparts on the American side, where primitivism also was a favorite concept in the mass media. In a famous photo feature that appeared in *Life* a few weeks after Pearl Harbor under the title "How to Tell Japs from Chinese," Prime Minister Tōjō was offered as a "typical" Japanese, whose squat long-torsoed build, massively boned head, flat pug nose, and yellow-ocher skin "betrays aboriginal antecedents." *Asia and the Americas* informed readers that the Japanese were "a kind of freak survival in the modern world." The *American Legion Magazine* described Shinto as a "wicked, bloody demonology" that "has not budged an inch since the days of cave-dwelling cannibals." The same monthly also referred to the Japanese as a people possessed "with brutal desires still fresh from the dark period through which all races must pass to the light of civilization." The widely quoted Otto Tolischus informed Americans that "Japanese military and police followed traditions reaching back to primitive ages"; Edgar Snow spoke of contemporary Japan's "feudal world of tribal gods, superstitions, taboos and fetishes"; and *Reader's Digest* dismissed the Japanese enemy as "creatures of the jungle." General Marshall, in an internal draft memo-randum agonizing over the maltreatment of Allied prisoners, suggested that the Japanese be warned that "the future of Japan as a nation—in fact, of the Japanese race itself—depends entirely and irrevocably upon their capacity to progress beyond their aboriginal barbaric instincts."[26]

One functional consequence of the pseudohistorical or pseudoan-thropological notion of Japanese primitivism was to remove the percep-tion of a savage enemy from the battlefield per se; to place it on the people, race, and culture as a whole; and to rationalize and legitimize thereby one's own savage acts of reprisal and retribution. Thus, in a memorandum of January 1942, in the early moments of the war, we find Admiral Leahy quoting the common belief that "in fighting with Japanese

savages all previously accepted rules of warfare must be abandoned."
Three-and-a-half years later, as the war neared its violent end, President
Truman learned of the successful test of the atomic bomb while at
Potsdam and immediately decided to use it against Japan. This was
regrettable but necessary, he wrote in a makeshift diary he was keeping
at the time, because the Japanese were "savages, ruthless, merciless, and
fanatic."[27]

That the Japanese were also childish—or, more gently, childlike—
was a commonplace that from an early date had dominated the commentaries even of those Westerners who were perceived to be admirers of
Japan. Lafcadio Hearn, the romantic turn-of-the-century popularizer of
things Japanese, concluded that "the charm of Japanese life is largely the
charm of Childhood," and this more innocent side of Japan attracted
many foreigners in the years before war came.[28] Sometimes the perception of the Japanese as children was revealed almost unconsciously—as in
August 1941, when Churchill and Roosevelt agreed the best policy toward
the Japanese for the time being would be to "baby them along"; or in
December of the same year, when the Japanese invasion force in Southeast Asia was rumored to be comprised of "half-trained 16-year-old kids."
Most often, however, the allusion to the Japanese as childish was straightforward and clearly intended to signify their inherent immaturity. As on
so many other points pertaining to Japan, Joseph Grew gave the imprint
of authority to the popular cliché. "The Japanese are really children," he
wrote in his diary a little over a week before Pearl Harbor, "and should
be treated as children." The diary was published with considerable publicity in 1944. Another old Asia hand, an Englishman with long service in
China, informed readers of the venerable *Asia* that Japan's "national
psychological impulses remain those of infancy." *Newsweek*'s old Japan
hand Compton Pakenham introduced Americans to "the child mind of
the Jap conscript," and the prolific Japan specialist Willard Price entitled
a chapter in one of his wartime books "Japan: The Last to Grow Up."[29]

The pervasive Western image of the physically and emotionally
immature Japanese found vivid expression in a report prepared for propaganda purposes in General MacArthur's Southwest Pacific Command in
the summer of 1944. In a truly startling observation, it was suggested that
the diminutive size and childish nature of the Japanese could even be seen
as having caused the war. "In every sense of the word the Japanese are
little people," the document stated. "Some observers claim there would
have been no Pearl Harbor had the Japanese been three inches taller. The

archipelago itself is a land of diminutive distances. Japanese houses are artistic but flimsy and cramped. The people, tiny in stature, seem to play at living. To a Westerner they and their country possess the strange charm of toyland. Centuries of isolation have accentuated the restrictive characteristics of their outlook on life. Being *little people*, the Japanese dreamed of power and glory, but lacked a realistic concept of the material requirements for a successful world war. Moreover, they were totally unable to envisage the massive scale of operations in which the United States is now able to indulge."[30]

Frequently, the metaphor of the child was used in a manner that highlighted the overlapping nature of immaturity, primitivism, violence, and emotional instability as key concepts for understanding the Japanese. A writer in the liberal monthly *American Mercury*, for example, neatly combined primitivism and childishness by referring to Japan as "a half-savage urchin in the family of nations." Others linked childishness to delinquent behavior, just as the experts did in their unpublicized New York conference on Japanese character structure in 1944. Thus the *New York Times Magazine* carried an account of the Japanese in the Philippines by a former American POW, who characterized his military guards as practicing "the pettiest kind of senseless oppression—the sort of thing you might expect from a gang of bad boys." A British prisoner in Singapore who was tortured by the Kempeitai was quoted as saying his tormenters behaved like "spoilt boys of fourteen." In the autumn of 1944, readers of *Science Digest* were treated to an excerpt from an American aviation magazine which described the average Japanese pilot as having "a cultural finish roughly corresponding to that of a Dead End child in lower Manhattan." *Reader's Digest*, in its issue dated the month the war ended, informed its huge audience that "the Japanese have been the problem children of the world" for three quarters of a century.[31]

From the diagnosis of the Japanese as problem children and juvenile delinquents, it was but a small step to see them as emotionally maladjusted adolescents and, finally, as a deranged race in general. The "temper tantrum" explanation of Japanese violence which had been offered by Gorer and Embree proved extremely attractive to those who engaged in popular psychologizing about the Japanese. The Ministry of Information's 1945 pamphlet, for example, explained that the social controls that had been built up over the centuries in Japan had "resulted in the Japanese as an individual reacting to the problems of life much as would be expected from a strictly brought up and constantly repressed child. Their behavior after defeat in the Philippines, when all restrictions had clearly gone by the board, was typical; it was strictly comparable to that of a disappointed child, who, losing his temper and with it all control, smashes his toys and kicks his companions or anyone near him." The other side of the temper tantrum, which kept the Japanese subservient to their leaders, the ministry went on to explain, was the "herd instinct." At the end of the war, the U.S. Navy borrowed much the same explanation for its guidebook on Japan that was to be issued to personnel being assigned there for occupation duty. A Japanese, the GIs were informed, responds to humiliation "like a petulant child," and "will sulk and brood in a corner and unless petted a little and soothed may decide to commit suicide or kill the man who made him lose face." Other popular commentaries were blunter. The Japanese soldier, Hugh Byas wrote in a 1943 article, was "a moronic individual." In the words of a Marine author, the Japanese were simply "plain crazy, sick in the head, that's all." The *American Legion Magazine* titled another Marine's war story "These Nips Are Nuts." This was crude, but it was not in essence different from what the Japan experts and social and behavioral scientists were saying with their own more clinical diagnostic vocabularies.[32]

By 1943, most Japanese fighting men in Asia and the Pacific were trapped and doomed and knew it. Many died of illness or hunger. Scores of thousands of others fought with fanatic tenacity, and frequently they went berserk in the final battles, allowing themselves to be mowed down in hopeless attacks, blowing themselves up with hand grenades while they were still plentifully supplied with ammunition that could have been used against the foe, engaging in bizarre and almost ritualistic dances in the line of fire, charging to their deaths screaming not only the emperor's name but also outlandish phrases in English.[33] The vision of this battlefield frenzy and death agony naturally stunned Allied soldiers and war correspondents. By his atrocities, the enemy had become identified as a savage. By these banzai charges and mass deaths, he became known as a madman. And from these battlefield hell scenes emerged the picture of an entire race whose growth was stunted in every way: in cultural evolution and in mental and emotional development, both as individuals and as a group.

In Western eyes, fixed on the war in Asia, madness itself became culture-bound, as the lingo of the battlefield revealed. In Marine jargon, GIs who suffered shell shock and battle fatigue and went out of their minds were said to have "gone Asiatic." What the academics and Asia specialists tried to do was put things in better perspective—to call attention to a web of fundamentally cultural forces that contributed to Japanese violence and tightly regimented group behavior; to demonstrate that even the war fanaticism was not inevitable, and rational appeals could be made to the Japanese to surrender; and to point out that Japanese culture contained within itself the potential for change and constructive peace. This was a notable accomplishment in such a caldron of intense race hate, although on purely intellectual grounds the fundamentally anthropological and psychological approach to the problem left a great deal of territory still thinly covered: serious analysis from the perspectives of history and political economy, for example; questions of class and state power; and areas where fruitful comparisons rather than contrasts might have been drawn between Japanese behavior on the one hand and European and American behavior on the other (areas such as imperialism, colonialism, racism, and battlefield conduct).

In retrospect, however, there is another aspect of the analysis of Japanese national character—and of the entire spectrum of concepts used to characterize the Japanese enemy—which compels attention. We have seen that important aspects of the analysis offered by the experts actually reinforced popular stereotypes, but the problem runs deeper and perhaps can be suggested by two final quotations written in the midst of war:

> In wisdom, skill, virtue and humanity, these people are as inferior to the [English and Americans] as children are to adults and women to men; there is as great a difference between them as there is between savagery and forbearance, between violence and moderation, almost—I am inclined to say—as between monkeys and men.

Or again:

> Although these barbarians are not altogether mad, yet they are not far from being so. . . . They are not, or are no longer, capable of governing themselves any more than madmen or even wild beasts and animals. . . . [Their stupidity] is much greater than that of children and madmen in other countries.[34]

These quotations were, in fact, written in the early sixteenth century by Spaniards rationalizing the devastation of the Indian populations in the

New World as a just war; and the bracketed "English and Americans" in the first statement reads "Spaniards" in the original. We can perform comparable sleights of hand with other quotations of both historical and contemporary origin—substituting "Japanese" not only for the names of other races and peoples, but also for references to non-Christians, to women, to the lower classes, and to criminal elements. This is not a mere conjurer's trick. Rather, it points to the basic categories through which male-dominated Western elites have perceived and dealt with others over the centuries. Like the mark of the beast, the categories of the primitive, the child, and the mentally and emotionally deficient enemy—which in World War Two often seemed to be so specifically applicable to the Japanese, and even to entail new intellectual breakthroughs peculiar to the Japanese—were basically formulaic concepts, encoded in the Western psyche and by no means reserved for the Japanese alone.

Racism was but one form of prejudice which relied on this ritualized language (religion, class, and gender being others), and the larger racial context of the war in Asia is the subject of the chapter that follows. Here the analysis is carried in two further directions: first, suggesting through a historical overview how the war words directed against the Japanese coincided with a deeper white-supremacist outlook; and second, demonstrating how, during World War Two itself, anti-Japanese sentiment in the Anglo-American camp became entangled with larger fears concerning Asians in general (the Yellow Peril) and "colored" peoples as a whole.

◄ **C H A P T E R   7** ►
YELLOW, RED, AND BLACK MEN

Over four centuries of intimate contact between white and non-white peoples preceded the war in Asia, beginning with the European age of expansion. The Japanese survived this encounter more successfully than other nonwhites, being neither conquered nor enslaved nor turned into a colony or neocolony. On the contrary, they succeeded in shutting the Westerners out for several centuries; and when they opened their doors in the mid-1800s, good fortune, hard work, and shrewd leadership enabled them to escape being swallowed up by the Western imperialists. Instead, they became imperialists themselves, taking their first colony in 1895 (Formosa) and the second in 1910 (Korea), and recording in between those dates the first modern military victory of a nonwhite nation over a white power. When Japan defeated czarist Russia with dramatic victories on both land and sea in 1904–5, her accomplishment not only stunned the West but also electrified nationalists throughout Asia. By 1919, the Japanese appeared to have attained not merely equality but eminence on the global scene, sitting at the Paris Peace Conference as one of the Big Five victors after World War One and helping to reapportion the world. When the Japanese expanded onto continental Asia, their most cosmopolitan officials spoke of the need to emulate British colonial models. When they came under fire for accelerating their expansion in the 1920s and 1930s, they invoked the rhetoric of a "Monroe Doctrine for Asia." They were patriots and nationalists, of course, and thus believed their country possessed unique virtues, but until late in the game they also believed themselves to be just good, practical imperialists, like their European and American teachers.

These accomplishments naturally drew special attention and consideration to the Japanese from Europeans and Americans, even murmurs of admiration; but they did not bring them genuine respect. In spite of their accomplishments in Western ways, including modern uses of technology and power, the Japanese remained firmly placed among the nonwhite "others"—the cleverest of the pupils of the West, perhaps, but still primarily perceived in terms of color and culture. When war erupted in the Pacific, it became clear just how enduring and universal the old images that had been attached to nonwhite peoples since the sixteenth century really were—for if we go back to the early encounters of whites and nonwhites, we find a volcabulary remarkably similar to that used against the Japanese in World War Two. The two quotations from the early 1500s in the preceding chapter were not exceptional. They were the rule, already part of a rich symbolic world which white Europeans and Americans relied on over the ensuing centuries to put others in their place.

It is revealing, for our present purposes, to note that in good part these prototypical race words were also war words. The European age of expansion was bloody and cruel in ways that still stagger the imagination, even after two world wars; and the blacks of Africa, the Indians of the "New World," the many peoples of Asia all entered the Western consciousness amidst scenes of extraordinary violence. Those violent images remained ever present, but often residual, like a great underground stream that bursts to the surface when the earth shakes. And the conflicts between whites and nonwhites were, indeed, interrupted and serial in nature. Looking back from the anti-Japanese rhetoric of the Pacific War, for example, it is possible to trace a suggestive legacy of racial war words through two great military struggles in particular: the conquest of the Indians in the Americas, and the U.S. conquest of the Philippines at the turn of the century. This was not, however, a solitary stream, but one fed by two others: one that we may call slave words and colonial words, drawn from the experience of blacks and Chinese "coolies" in America, and from the colonial enterprise everywhere; and another stream of language which deserves the label "intellectual words," involving the rationalization of racism beginning with the great debates among Spanish theologians and philosophers at the time of the conquistadores, and carrying through the "scientific racism" of the nineteenth century right up to the Pacific War.

The image of the nonwhite in European eyes was initially shaped by the simultaneous encounter with black peoples in Africa and the natives of the Americas. The two were not treated identically. Blacks were enslaved, but until the eighteenth century were not seen as subjects capable of conversion to Christianity. The Indians were massacred, but after learned debate among ecclesiastics were also soon accepted as humans fit for conversion. Both blacks and Indians, however, confronted Europeans with the common question of "savagery," and it is this concept that lies at the base of much modern racist thinking, as scholars such as Winthrop Jordan and Richard Drinnon have demonstrated.[1]

By chance, these great early racial confrontations coincided with a small discovery that fascinated Europeans: the orangutan, which became the inspiration for the apish stigmata quickly assigned to blacks, and eventually to nonwhites in general (as well as to "inferior" whites, like the Irish in English eyes). In the capitals of seventeenth-century Europe, both blacks and Native Americans were exhibited side by side with apes and baboons, and the mark of the beast enriched the languages of the conquerers in a myriad of forms. Naked savages pranced through playwrights' scripts as "Monkeys, Baboons, and Marmosites," while writers on Africa described the people they encountered there as creatures possessed of "Barbarous, Wild, and Savage Natures," "neer beasts," hybrids halfway between white men and apes. The third president of the United States, Thomas Jefferson, was one of those who later endorsed the hybrid thesis. Other early characterizations of black peoples may also strike the student of World War Two as anything but archaic. Supporters of slavery in the United States characterized blacks as deceitful and false, cruel and treacherous, "devoid of reason." They were "Creatures of a Kind somewhat inferior," explained a more moderate soul in 1764. The Negro, argued a defender of slavery at a debate at Harvard in 1773, was a "child," an "ideot," a "madman." Out of the terrible mortality rates that slavery brought, there also emerged another theory concerning nonwhites that carried through the centuries and was sometimes used to explain massive Japanese deaths in the Pacific late in the war: they did not feel pain as severely as the more sensitive whites did, and life was cheap to them.[2]

From the time of the earliest Spaniards who addressed the nature of the Indians of the New World, nonwhites were treated as polar opposites of their conquerers: as savages, children, madmen, and beasts; and, of course, as pagan and evil as opposed to Christian and good. And for these sins (along with their gold), many of them were tortured and exterminated. The Spanish conquest of the Indians, however, was not undertaken casually. It provoked intense learned discussions in Europe concerning the true nature of the Indians, culminating in a justly famous debate between Bartolomé de Las Casas and Juan Ginés de Sepúlveda in 1550; and out of these deliberations we have our first inkling of the manner in which intellectual discourse at the highest levels would serve as a legitimization of racism over the centuries that followed. The problem of savagery became comprehensible in terms of the theological and philosophical theory of a Great Chain of Being—a fixed hierarchy of existence extending from God down to the basest of creatures. Even more precisely, in the debates concerning the nature of the American Indians, Aristotle was found to provide the key in his concept of the "natural slave," as set forth in the first book of the *Politics,* in which it was declared that some men are by nature free and others by nature slaves. The natural slave was in this argument not a beast, but a lesser human, a "barbarian"; by the same reasoning, women and children were also natural slaves, and some would argue that so also were peasants.[3]

What the Spaniards had to say about the Indians who fell within their empire was repeated, with a good deal less philosophical agonizing, by the British and others who encountered the native populations of North America. The "Salvages" [savages], in a phrase from the 1630s, were "a dangerous people, subtill, secreat and mischeivous." The Pequots were "barbarians, ever treacherous," who deserved "severe execution of just revenge." (They were slaughtered in 1637). The Mohawks, in Roger Williams' view, were "mad dogs." Timothy Dwight's epic poem *The Conquest of Canäan* (1785) spoke of the "childish rage" of the savages. The Declaration of Independence enshrined the phrase "merciless Indian Savages." The first president of the United States described the Indians as "beasts of prey," similar to the wolf "tho' they differ in shape." Thomas Jefferson, on the other hand, addressed them as "Children" or "My Children," and briefly entertained the idea of improving their racial stock by encouraging miscegenation with whites—much as Franklin Roosevelt reportedly did when musing about what to do with the Japanese after the war.

There were indeed paternalistic and even heroic aspects to the American perception of the Indian—the latter emerging in the literary persona of the Noble Savage—but the overwhelming view was much closer to Washington's than Jefferson's. Francis Parkman, one of America's most honored nineteenth-century historians, captured the dominant image in his monumental lifework *France and England in North America,* published serially beginning in the 1860s and not completed until 1893. Parkman's bestial Indian was "man, wolf, and devil all in one," a race doomed to die and deserving of such a fate. The twenty-sixth president of the United States agreed. Before he became president, Theodore Roosevelt publicly identified himself as a supporter of the virtual extermination of the American Indian. "I suppose I should be ashamed to say that I take the Western view of the Indian," he stated in a speech in 1886. "I don't go so far as to think that the only good Indians are dead Indians, but I believe nine out of every ten are, and I shouldn't inquire too closely into the case of the tenth. The most vicious cowboy has more moral principle than the average Indian."[4]

With Theodore Roosevelt's frank statement, we stand not only on the eve of the twentieth century, but also on the eve of America's first war in Asia: the conquest of the Philippines, which began in 1898. And how did Americans characterize their enemy in this conflict, in which an estimated twenty thousand Filipino "insurgents" were killed and as many as two hundred thousand civilians may have died of hunger and disease that accompanied the destruction (with U.S. combat deaths being slightly more than four thousand)? They were people who engaged in "base treachery, revolting cruelty," in the words of the secretary of war. They were "gorillas" who hid in the bush, in the report of one general— "savages, habitually violating all the laws of war as known to civilized nations" in the words of another. A third U.S. general, vexed by the difficulty of separating enemy soldiers from the native population as the war dragged on, wrote in 1901 that "the problem here is more difficult on account of the inbred treachery of these people, their great number, and the impossibility of recognizing the actively bad from the only passively so"—words very similar to those used to justify the incarceration of Japanese-Americans in 1942. Theodore Roosevelt expressed a popular sentiment when he characterized the U.S. victory in the Philippines as a triumph of civilization over "the black chaos of savagery and barbarism." Rudyard Kipling's famous poem "The White Man's Burden," written in 1899 in response to the war in the Philippines, enshrined for all time the Western perception of Filipinos and their fellow Asians as "fluttered folk and wild . . . sullen peoples, half devil and half child."

In the jargon of American troops, as Stuart Creighton Miller has documented in great detail, the Filipinos were "niggers," "treacherous savages," and "treacherous gugus" (or "goo-goos")—the latter reemerging in World War Two as "gook"—and the fighting was called "Injun warfare." One American soldier told a reporter that "the country won't be pacified until the niggers are killed off like the Indians"; another explained "the only good Filipino is a dead one. Take no prisoners; lead is cheaper than rice." In fact, there was a general policy of not taking prisoners in many areas, often justified on the grounds of enemy atrocities. "No more prisoners," one participant declared; "They take none, and they torture our men, so we will kill wounded and all of them." A U.S. private reported on the "goo goo hunt" as follows: "The old boys will say that no cruelty is too severe for these brainless monkeys, who can appreciate no sense of honor, kindness or justice. . . . With an enemy like this to fight, it is not surprising that the boys should soon adopt 'no quarter' as a motto, and fill the blacks full of lead before finding out whether they are friends or enemies." When General Arthur MacArthur was asked by a congressional committee why fifteen Filipinos were reported killed for every one wounded, he replied that "inferior races" succumbed to wounds more easily than Anglo-Saxons.[5]

For many Americans, the link between fighting Indians on the Western frontier and Filipinos in Asia was anything but figurative or symbolic: they personally fought both enemies, moving to the Philippines from frontier posts in the western territories of the United States. Arthur MacArthur, the father of Douglas MacArthur, was one of the more conspicuous U.S. Indian fighters who was reposted further west in this way. That his son commanded U.S. forces in the Pacific in World War Two is as good a reminder as any of how close in time the Indian wars, the war in the Philippines, and World War Two really were. War correspondents and GI combatants certainly kept the analogy in mind, for jungle combat against the Japanese was often characterized as "Indian fighting." The U.S. Army publication *Infantry Journal* informed its readers that the Japanese enemy were "as good as Indians ever were" at infiltration. The *New York Times Magazine,* however, in a short note to its Sunday readers (entitled "The Nips"), suggested that the analogy was an injustice to the Indians:

> The Japanese are likened to the American Indian in their manner of making war. Our fighting men say that isn't fair to the Indian. He had honor of a sort. Moreover, even a dead Jap isn't a

good Jap. His loving comrades mine him and set him. It grieves us to think of K. Nippo, our poetic ex-contributor, stretched cold and still and beautiful beneath a palm in the Marshalls with a booby trap in his inside. Yet such are the Nipponese. In death as in life, treacherous.[6]

No one thought the Indians had much honor at the time they were being fought, of course; but such a use of history would have been too subtle for the war years. Of greater interest is the fact that when white people at the turn of the century spoke of "inferior races," they were now able to defend their prejudice with more than Great-Chain-of-Being theologizing and the Aristotelian postulation that some people were natural slaves; for by this date the mainstream of Western science had placed itself behind the theory of racial inequality. The academic racism of the nineteenth century drew support from such disciplines as anatomy, phrenology, biological evolution, ethnography, psychology, social psychology, theology, and linguistics to provide proof that the traits attributed to nonwhites by Europeans in earlier centuries—primitiveness, immaturity, and mental, moral, and emotional deficiency—were indeed inherent characteristics of colored peoples. The old faith in a hierarchy of existence was confirmed, with "Mongol" peoples placed between the lowly blacks and the lofty whites. The impression that nonwhites remained, in effect, "natural slaves"—that is, persons destined to serve and subordinate themselves to the superior whites—was thus implicitly revitalized by the mainstream of Western rational inquiry and empirical investigation, a welcome finding indeed in an age of intensified empire building. Even with all the new theoretical language, scientific racism had a familiar ring. Here, for instance, is a well-known example of how nineteenth-century scholars used the concept of childishness to explain the characteristics of Asians and their place in the hierarchy of races: "As the type of the Negro is foetal, that of the Mongol is infantile. And in strict accordance with this we find that their government, literature and art are infantile also. They are beardless children, whose life is a task, and whose chief virtue consists in unquestioning obedience."

The argument that the races of the world conform to a scale of development comparable to stages in the individual life cycle was pioneered in the mid-nineteenth century by scholars such as the anatomist Étienne Serres and is known to specialists as recapitulationist theory.

Recapitulationist theory postulated that the childhood of the white race was a counterpart to primitivism or savagery on the evolutionary scale, while adults of "inferior" groups were at the mental or emotional level of white male children or adolescents. "Inferior" groups by no means referred only to nonwhite races. Women, criminals, the poor and dispossessed, and despised nationalities in general could be and were all relegated to subordinate status under this theorizing—and it was exactly this sort of pseudoscientific dogma that Franz Boas and his disciples sought to repudiate with their great emphasis on culture, enculturation, and socialization.[7]

In the United States, attitudes nurtured in the harshness of slavery and Indian fighting, reinforced by the new scientific racism, also shaped perceptions of another group of Asians in the latter half of the nineteenth century: the Chinese, whom many Americans first encountered as immigrants brought over to help build the transcontinental railway. The writer Robert Louis Stevenson, traveling that same railway in the 1890s, offered a moving picture of how white people now grouped the Chinese with the unfortunate remnants of the Indian tribes. His fellow Caucasian passengers, Stevenson recorded, treated the Native Americans and Chinese almost identically as "despised races." They never really looked at the Chinese, listened to them, or thought about them, "but hated them *a priori*. . . . They declared them to be hideous vermin, and affected a kind of choking in the throat when they beheld them."[8]

Could there not be a rational explanation for this apart from plain racism—a class explanation, for example? For these Chinese were for the most part uneducated laborers; and they were laborers, moreover, who were willing to work more cheaply than others, and thus had drawn the full fury of white workers and organized labor against themselves. Stevenson himself considered this, but in the end turned for an explanation to "old, well-founded, historical hatreds"—and confessed that he "was ashamed for the thing we call civilization." And, indeed, shameful acts had been quickly visited on the Chinese in America. As early as 1854, they were barred from testifying in court cases involving whites in California, on the grounds that Indians were already barred and Indians and Chinese were of the same race. In 1879, the new state constitution of California denied suffrage to all "natives of China, idiots, and insane persons." Three years later, all further Chinese immigration to the United States was prohibited.[9]

These events occurred in tandem with the rise of scientific racism, which left little doubt about how the Chinese were to be perceived. As early as 1839, before the first Chinese emigrants even arrived in the United States, Samuel George Morton, whose pioneer work on the measurement of crania became a central prop for theories of biological determinism, wrote of the Chinese that "they have been compared to the monkey race, whose attention is perpetually changing from one object to another." Rather than contradict such demeaning impressions, Westerners who could claim to know the Chinese firsthand in their native land —the diplomats, missionaries, and traders of the nineteenth century— also dismissed them with contempt. To these world travelers, the Chinese were "depraved and vicious," and "on a level with the rudest tribes of mankind." They were "pagan savages," "idolatrous savages," and "almond-eyed heathens"; a nation of "children or idiots" who lived in an "imbecile world"; "a poor, miserable, dwarfish race of inferior beings." Their attacks on foreigners in China (who, among other enterprises, were bringing vast quantities of opium into their country) led them to be accused of "vicious treachery" and "fiendish and demonic atrocities," and to be condemned as a "lawless pack of wolves." Following a tour of China in 1873, the Englishman Sir Halliday Macartney reported that "the Chinaman is a low animal."[10]

As Kipling had noted, however, the Asians were not only half savage in Western eyes, but also half child. In the United States as well as in the colonial areas, the Asian half child filled a clearly defined role. He or she became the natural servant—the obedient child of recapitulationist theory, the modern metamorphosis of Aristotle's natural slave. "Boy" became a ubiquitous word for Asian males, just as it had long been for blacks in the United States. Even amidst the vilest allegations of Asian depravity, the image of the child persisted, and the most cosmopolitan of men endorsed this. Around the same time that Stevenson was crossing the American continent by rail, for example, his acquaintance Henry Adams, the famous educator, was traveling in Asia and finding it, by and large, amusing and difficult to take seriously. In Hawaii, he and his traveling companion were told that the Chinese and Japanese working on the sugar plantations were "great children." In Samoa, Adams observed that "the natives, like all orientals, are children, and have the charms of childhood as well as the faults of the small boy." He found Japan, which he visited in 1886, to be "a child's country. . . . The whole show is of the nursery."

In other musings, Adams veered in other familiar directions. In a letter to John Hay, later famous as the author of the "Open Door" policy in Asia, Adams confessed that he found most of what he had encountered in Japan to be "primitive," and "cannot conquer a feeling that Japs are monkeys, and the women very badly made monkeys."[11]

Even Henry Adams, however, worried that "the dark races are gaining on us," and in this apprehension, just as much as in his contempt, he caught a new temper in the times: the fear that white supremacy was imperiled. This came from several directions in the nineteenth century, one of which was China; for despite the disdain shown China and the Chinese, there was also awe at the country's vast size and population, and apprehension that it was a sleeping giant about to awaken. In the United States, the first of numerous novels depicting a Chinese invasion appeared as early as 1880, and it was not long before the phrase "Yellow Peril" was known throughout the world. The first great iconographic rendering of the imagined threat from the East actually came from Germany in the 1890s, in a painting of the *Gelbe Gefahr* commissioned by Kaiser Wilhelm II. In this work, the nations of Christendom, personified by figures in the heroic mold, gaze apprehensively toward a dark billowing cloud in the East, wherein reposes a Buddha in a nimbus of flame. The Boxer Rebellion in China in 1900, which saw the foreign legations in Peking and Tientsin besieged by thousands of frenzied Chinese associated with a mystical secret society, became another memorable icon in this developing fantasy, offering the concrete image of a violent and heathen Orient on the verge of engulfing the smaller Christian enclave.[12]

These multiple associations were inherited by Japan. After 1882, the Japanese replaced the Chinese as the major wave of Asian immigrants into the United States, and came to suffer the burden of deflected stereotypes. By the time of the Boxer Rebellion, moreover, Japan had already defeated China in the first Sino-Japanese War and established itself as the real rising power in Asia. This did not, however, simply shift the focus of Yellow Peril fears from China to Japan. Rather, it multiplied those fears. While sensational writings imagining Japan's conquest of the United States or the world now appeared on the scene, the great bogey of the menace from China remained alive and well in the popular consciousness. For the vision of the menace from the East was always more racial rather than national. It derived not from concern with any one country or people in particular, but from a vague and ominous sense of the vast, faceless, nameless yellow horde: the rising tide, indeed, of color.

The Yellow Peril was naturally the stuff of fantasy and cheap thrills, a fit subject for pulp literature, comics, B-movies, and sensational journalism. But fantasy and sensationalism shape the mind in ways beyond measure, undoubtedly a great deal more than most scholarship does; and there were many who addressed the alleged threat from the East in a manner that made a significant impact. Some, like the Hearst newspapers, warned of a "Yellow Peril" led by Japan as early as the 1890s, and maintained an unwavering editorial policy of anti-Oriental polemics over the next half century.[13] Others, like the visionary military writer Homer Lea, offered a forecast of Japan's destiny so apocalyptically compelling that the Japanese themselves were flattered and quickly prepared a translation. Still others, like the best-selling novelist Sax Rohmer, created a fictional persona of Oriental genius so flamboyantly sinister that even people who did not read the novels or see the films based on them could recite not merely the name of the villain, but the name bracketed by marvelously venomous appendages, like some titled Prince of Darkness: "The Insidious Dr. Fu Manchu, the Evil Genius."

Homer Lea and Sax Rohmer constitute, for our purposes, a suggestive coupling—a complementary yin-yang of the mind, as it were, conveying by their very differences both the richness and the elusiveness of the Yellow Peril vision as a whole. In *The Valor of Ignorance*, first published in 1909, Lea identified Japan as the most virile young power in the world and introduced his readers to *bushido*, the way of the warrior, with the tense fervor of a reluctant convert. Lea's grudging admiration of Japan was all the more effective because he devoted almost equal space to decrying the growing softness and decadence of his own country. He was an unabashed example of a white supremacist who feared that Anglo-Saxon purity was threatened by rot within as well as enemies at the gate. Unless the United States recovered its martial ardor and sense of purpose, he warned, "Japan, militarily supreme in the Pacific," would become "industrially the controlling factor in Asia. And in due time, with the mastery of the major portion of the undeveloped wealth of the earth, Asiatic militance and industrialism shall reign supreme in this world and the Mikado shall become the Mikado of kings." Either the Japanese would have to be virtually wiped out, Lea warned, or they "would become the samurai of the human race and the remainder of man shall toil and trade for them and their greatness."

Homer Lea enjoyed a revival in the United States in the months following Pearl Harbor, when his vision of Japanese supermen suddenly seemed prophetic. Secretary of War Stimson wrote about him in his diary. Congresswoman Clare Boothe Luce, wife of the publisher of *Time, Life,* and *Fortune,* published a two-part essay about him in the *Saturday Evening Post* ("The cloth is being cut much too close to the author's pattern," she said); and uncounted magazines ranging from *Time* to *American Rifleman* followed suit with their own resurrections of the rediscovered prophet. In 1942, *The Valor of Ignorance* was reprinted by a prestigious publishing house with the congresswoman's essay as an introduction.[14]

As Clare Boothe Luce noted, however, Homer Lea was an oracle only in retrospect. His book went out of print in 1922, after eighteen thousand copies had been sold; and to the historian, the revival of this apocalyptic work in 1942 is of equal if not greater interest than its first interlude in the sun. Had Lea been widely remembered, after all, there would have been less racist complacency about the "little men" of Japan. What carried through over these prewar decades was not so much a clear sense of a specific threat from the Orient, but rather a vague premonition of future peril; and it is in this regard that the fictional "evil genius" Fu Manchu is an excellent counterpoint to Homer Lea.

The first Fu Manchu novel was published in 1913, the tenth in 1941. The author was British, and popular in both his own country and the United States, where his work usually was serialized in *Collier's* before appearing in book form. Several of the novels also were reworked as film thrillers, and the advertisement for a 1932 MGM production (starring Boris Karloff) suggests the flavor of these popular offerings. In *The Mask of Fu Manchu,* Hollywood declared the evil Chinese doctor conveyed "menace in every twitch of his finger . . . terror in each split second of his slanted eyes." Although Rohmer's villain was Chinese, the hordes of every exotic place in Asia were at his beck and call. He was more brilliant than any Westerner who went against him (his antagonist, Nayland Smith, was a tenacious bore), for not only had he mastered the languages and sciences of the West, but he also commanded the secrets of the Orient. Better than any other single individual, Sax Rohmer succeeded, through the figure of Fu Manchu, in drawing together in a flamboyant but concrete way the three main strands of an otherwise inchoate fear: Asian mastery of Western knowledge and technique; access to mysterious powers and "obscure and dreadful things"; and mobilization of the yellow horde ("shadowy," in one episode, "looking like great apes"). Whether led by China or Japan, this was the essence of the Yellow Peril.

Sax Rohmer and Homer Lea shared, in addition to an awe of Asia's potential, a fondness for overripe prose. The creator of the Chinese doctor of doom bombarded his readers with references to "the menace of the Yellow Doctor," "the man who dreamt of an universal Yellow Empire," "the titanic genius whose victory meant the victory of the yellow races over the white," and "the breath of the East—that stretched out a yellow hand to the West" (an unusually potent breath indeed!). As the years passed, moreover, Rohmer also began to flirt with the most explosive racial fears and phobias of all: not merely a clash of white and yellow, but a union of yellow and black peoples against the whites, and the ultimate eradication of color distinctions. In the tenth Fu Manchu novel, published in 1941, the evil genius was placing advanced weaponry in the Caribbean, working with blacks, harnessing the power of Haitian voodoo to create an army of zombies, and engaged in laboratory experiments aimed at altering skin pigmentation. These wild imaginings, in which Rohmer's evil Asian was already experimenting with yellow white men and "white Nubians," amounted to symbolic miscegenation and touched on the ultimate white-supremacist fear: the obscuring and eventual obliteration of color lines.[15]

There were counterimages to the insidious Fu Manchu in American popular culture. The wise Chinese-American detective Charlie Chan, created by Earl Derr Biggers, appeared in magazines, novels, and movies beginning in the 1920s. When Earl Derr Biggers died in the mid-1930s, his publishers, seeking someone who could create a new Oriental sleuth, settled on John Marquand and found themselves sponsoring the debut of a surprising new protagonist in 1936: Mr. Moto, the efficient and patriotic, but essentially moderate, Japanese secret agent.[16] Humble Chinese commoners found eloquent voice in the writings of Pearl Buck, who was rewarded with the Nobel Prize for literature in 1938. Beginning in the 1930s, Lin Yutang conveyed the "wisdom of the East" in a succession of best-sellers. Such writings helped to counter prejudice and foster respect toward Asians; and sympathetic media coverage of China's resistance to the Japanese created an even greater surge of pro-Chinese sentiment after Pearl Harbor. The response to Japan's attack exposed such a virulent anti-"yellow" animus in the United States and Great Britain, however, that Pearl Buck and Lin Yutang and those who shared their concerns

became among the most dire prophets of a potential race war themselves.[17]

As such individuals saw it, the Western fixation on the Japanese as
a "yellow" or Oriental menace threatened to become a self-fulfilling
prophecy, for such blatant white supremacism could easily turn the peoples of China and all Asia against the Americans and British and create
what the Japanese were calling for: a solid, antiwhite racial bloc. Both
Pearl Buck and Lin Yutang warned of this danger repeatedly during the
war, and the former proved adept at turning some of the Westerners'
favorite clichés about the enemy against themselves. In her novel *The
Promise,* published in 1943 and dealing with Chinese and British forces
fighting together against the Japanese in Burma, it was the British who
were the most cruel and casual about the lives of others, clearly unable
to believe that nonwhites "were altogether human as they were." In a
speech in Los Angeles the same year, Pearl Buck stated frankly that the
Japanese spoke the truth when they declared that "it is white peoples who
have the deepest race prejudices." Most white people were a century
behind the colored races in their view of the future, she observed, for the
latter recognized that colonialism had become an anachronism. Indeed,
the average white American, in his or her smug contempt for nonwhite
peoples, could only be likened to "a spoiled child" about to encounter the
real world. "Although we may not be willing to know it," she declared in
an earlier lecture, "it is possible that we are already embarked upon the
bitterest and the longest of human wars, the war between the East and
the West, and this means the war between the white man and his world
and the colored man and his world." If the race barriers that the whites
had erected were not quickly destroyed, one could only gird for Armaged-
don:

> . . . then we must prepare for a future of nothing but struggle and
> war on a stupendous scale, particularly for the white man. We shall
> have to make up for our inferiority in numbers by military prepara-
> tion of the most barbarous and savage kind. We must prepare
> superweapons, we must not shrink from chemical warfare on a mass
> scale, we must be willing to destroy all civilization, even our own,
> in order to keep down the colored peoples who are so vastly our
> superior in numbers and our equals in skills. Is this a future which
> any human being wants to face?[18]

Lin Yutang, whom middle-class Americans had previously known as a gentlemanly guide to Asian high culture, was comparably pessimistic and caustic. In 1942, he told a conference on global racial problems convened by the socialist League for Industrial Democracy that war pitting the peoples of Asia and Africa against the predominantly white nations, including Germany, might erupt within twenty-five years; and the fault would lie in large part with the English and Americans, who tended to pass master-race theories off on the Nazis and ignore their own racial arrogance. In his 1943 best-seller, *Between Tears and Laughter*, Lin even commented bitterly that the average white man seemed to think "that if he shot a few yellow men on earth after his missionaries had saved their souls for heaven, that ought to make it even."[19]

What horrified these critics was the flood of Anglo-American commentary that wittingly or unwittingly placed Japanese aggression in the context of a race war against Oriental peoples and values in general. Thus, the *Saturday Evening Post*, exhumer of Homer Lea, responded to Pearl Harbor with an editorial on how "the Yellow Serpent struck on our Western side." Artists and cartoonists followed suit with thrashing dragons, huge figures labeled "Jap Hordes," and colored graphics saturated with yellow. *Time*'s cover for December 22, 1941, depicting Admiral Yamamoto, was entirely yellow in color—and prompted predictable letters to the editor concerning the personification of Satan, "yellow ape," "mad dog," and the "most inhuman likeness of Homo Sapiens I have ever seen." One of the Hearst papers, in an editorial entitled "Peril Exposed," characterized the war in Europe as "a family fight," that is, a conflict "between white nations" which did not challenge Occidental civilization; whereas Japan, "an enemy of unexampled ferocity and greed," was fighting for Oriental ideals. Another Hearst paper declared that "The war in the Pacific is the World War, the War of Oriental Races against Occidental Races for the Domination of the World." A popular book titled *Blood for the Emperor*, published in 1943, characterized the conflict in Asia as "a holy war, a racial war of greater significance than any the world has heretofore seen." Such rhetoric was also heard on Capitol Hill, where segregationist congressmen and others were quick to identify the war in Asia as a "race war," and to evoke the specter of Genghis Khan and the prospect that the white races "may be liquidated."[20]

Winston Churchill, who worried about the "pan-Asian malaise" and the looming "shadow of Asiatic solidarity," was himself inordinately fond of the racial slurs that were guaranteed to alienate Asian peoples. His Chinese allies remained "little yellow men" to him, even as the same phrase became an everyday expression in discussions of the Japanese enemy. Hanson Baldwin, the respected military analyst, used this in a commentary on the Japanese fighting man; so did an American weapons manufacturer, whose advertisement for its submachine gun proclaimed, "It's blasting big red holes in little yellow men." Near the end of the war, an advertisement by a U.S. shipbuilder recalled how, in 1941, "a pagan and treacherous enemy spilled out of his homeland and overwhelmed the rich and peaceful islands of the South Seas"; now, however, the tide had turned and "the swollen yellow empire is shrinking." *Reader's Digest* featured an essay on Japanese psychology by a lieutenant colonel in the U.S. Army who had lived in Japan as a military attaché and spoke Japanese, which moved into its subject with the comment, "Let us look into one of these yellow heads and see what it contains." "Yellowbellies," "yellow bastards," "yellow monkeys" were all standard phrases. In one American newsreel, the Japanese were simply reduced to "the LYBs," shorthand for "little yellowbellies." Songwriters followed the fashion with such titles as "We're Gonna Find a Fellow Who Is Yellow and Beat Him Red, White, and Blue" and "Oh, You Little Son of an Oriental." Other songs were crass in other ways: "The Japs Don't Have a Chinaman's Chance," for example, and "To Be Specific, It's Our Pacific."[21]

Such demeaning and exclusionary rhetoric—so obvious to Asians, and so casually tossed off by the Western Allies—took other forms as well. Eyes, for example, were used in a manner analogous to color, as Asians were lumped together through such slang as "slant-eye," "slant," "squint eyes," and "almond eye." "Slopey" or "slopie" was GI jargon for the Chinese (a Chinese woman was a "slopie gal"). A patriotic advertisement in Melbourne in early 1942 exhorted Australians to "get ready to fight. Get ready to show these slant-eyed slash and grabs that Australians don't lie down!" Even "gook," the most popular word used by American fighting men to describe Asian people or things (as an adjective in the latter case)—which derived from "goo-goo," the ethnic label attached to Filipinos at the turn of the century—suggested both eyes ("goo-goo eyes" became famous in a popular American song of the 1920s) and craziness (as in a similar slang expression, "gaga"). In a different direction, exclusionary war words took the form of defining Allied war aims in ethnocentric terms as a defense of Christian, or Western, values. Lord Halifax, the

British foreign secretary, for example, aroused the ire of the Chinese by repeatedly declaring that the Allies were engaged in a struggle to save Christian civilization. Apart from insulting non-Christian allies and supporters, such crusading references had the doubly counterproductive effect of provoking Asians to call attention to the recklessness of the Christian world. "It is perhaps necessary to remind ourselves," wrote a Chinese professor in an American magazine, "that the most destructive wars in the world's history have been waged by the Christian countries."[22]

Underlying such images was not merely racist bias, but also the three elements of racial fear that had been exemplified by that consummate symbol of the Yellow Peril, Fu Manchu. The most immediate and alarming aspect of the Yellow Peril was always the vision of the vast multitudes of Asia uniting and advancing on Europe and the Western Hemisphere like the reborn hordes of Genghis Khan. Japan's Pan-Asianism and the huge expanse of its occupied territories seemed to indicate that this aspect of the Peril had materialized. As the East began to industrialize, moreover, the Yellow Peril assumed a second ominous aspect, namely, the prospect that the peoples of Asia could eventually combine their vastly superior numbers with mastery of Western military technology. When Japan's carriers and fighter planes smashed their way to victory in 1941–42, this nightmare too suddenly seemed to have materialized. The horde was organized and effectively armed. Nor was this all. From an early date, a third aspect of Yellow Peril fears had been the attribution of vague, nondiscursive, "occult" powers to the Oriental; and this also seemed to be present in the Japanese fighting men, with their incredible endurance and perseverance under the most forbidding conditions, and their apparent willingness to die—for reasons that were all but incomprehensible to Westerners. It was such presentiments as these that account for the especially forbidding quality that was associated with Japan's avowed war aims by the Allies, and created an ambience different from that associated with Hitler's proclaimed new order. The Imperial Way, the Greater East Asia Co-Prosperity Sphere, the Hundred-Year War, the New World Order; in the context of a half century of Yellow Peril sentiment, such slogans seemed to herald the doom of white supremacy—as, indeed, they were meant to do. It is in this context that rousing but alarmist speeches by Allied spokesmen such as former Ambassador Grew are to be understood. Germany would crack—but would Japan? At the level of ominous rumor, it was frequently reported during the war that the Axis Alliance was a marriage of convenience for both the Germans and Japanese; and if and when an Axis victory was attained, Germany would be next on the Japanese menu.[23]

Shortly after Pearl Harbor, a debate arose in the United States which continued for over a year and drew attention, in unanticipated ways, to the fact that anti-Oriental sentiment not only had deep roots in American history, but also was imbedded in the laws of the land. The debate began with the recognition of an anomalous fact: that even as the Nationalist government of China was being praised in Congress for its "gallant resistance" against the Japanese and elevated to the status of one of the "Big Four" Allies by President Roosevelt, the country and its people had been singled out for discrimination in two conspicuous ways. In accordance with the provisions of extraterritoriality imposed by the imperialist powers under the unequal-treaty system almost a century earlier, China still could not try American or British nationals in Chinese courts for crimes committed on Chinese soil. In addition, Chinese were prohibited from emigrating to the United States under a series of restrictive immigration laws dating back to 1882. The unequal-treaty provisions were abrogated by the United States and Britain in 1942 as a symbolic gesture toward China's equality, but the immigration issue dragged on until the final weeks of 1943. For many observers, this latter issue provided a revealing introduction to both the depth and indiscriminate breadth of anti-Oriental race hate in the United States.[24]

U.S. immigration law was labyrinthine, but there was no question about where the labyrinth led—or, more accurately, did not lead—when Asian peoples were concerned. Although revisions of the basic immigration law in 1924 had established a quota system under which subsequent immigration was controlled (the quota for each nationality was set at 2 percent of the population from those nations resident in the United States in 1920), even this narrow "quota" door was closed to Asians (as well as Arabs). This was possible because the law also stipulated that no one could enter the United States as a permanent resident who was not eligible to become a naturalized citizen, and under prior regulations Asians already had been designated ineligible for naturalization. As was noted during the congressional debates of 1942–43, the naturalization law amounted to a pure "color" law, and placed a "stigma of biological inferiority" on the yellow races.[25]

This was an uncomfortable matter to dwell on for a nation that was waging war against the Japanese in Asia under the banners of the "Four Freedoms" and the slogans of liberty, democracy, and equality; and the longer the discussion dragged on, the more embarrassing the revelations became, especially where China and India, the two most populous Asian allies, were concerned. It was revealed, for example, that the Chinese had been singled out by name as undesirable immigrants in no less than fifteen federal laws, or parts of laws, passed between 1882 and 1913—a dishonor done to no other nationality. Those who followed the debate also had their attention called to the adoption of a pure "white immigration" policy in 1917, through the creation of the "Asiatic barred zone." Under this act, passed by overwhelming congressional majorities over the veto of President Woodrow Wilson, a vast area of Asia and the Pacific was simply blocked out on the map as being subject to exceptionally severe immigration restrictions. In continental Asia, the "barred zone" extended from Indochina across all of southern Asia to Arabia; it also included all islands adjacent to continental Asia with the exception of the Philippines and Guam, which were both U.S. possessions. China and Japan were not included for the simple reason that immigration was restricted by other agreements, as was true also concerning emigration from the Philippines. The Supreme Court had upheld the special provisions barring Asians from becoming U.S. citizens in 1922 (the Ozawa case) and 1923 (the Thind case), and the major revision of the immigration laws in 1924 simply codified in one place the established policy of excluding Asians.[26]

Where the Chinese in particular were concerned, as one politician summarized the situation when these matters were reopened in 1942, thirty Congresses over a period of sixty years had actively or passively found exclusion appropriate. That was the cold fact, but it took on increasingly emotional overtones as the human side of the story emerged in both the congressional hearings on the subject and essays in the media. The Christian press in the United States was especially active in exposing the indignities to which the Chinese in America had been subjected. It was revealed, for example, that fear that Chinese might attempt to enter the country illegally or under false pretenses had promoted a vigilance on the part of U.S. authorities that frequently shaded over into outright oppression. Chinese seamen attempting to take shore leave in U.S. port cities were routinely arrested, while merchants who had conducted business in Mexico and wished to sail for China from a California port had to travel with a guard from the Mexican border to the point of departure, and pay this unwanted chaperone out of their own pocket. Chinese eligible to enter the country on a temporary basis, such as merchants and students, were required to obtain special certificates and could enter only at specific designated ports. American-born Chinese (who were citizens by birth) had to fill out a special form when applying for a U.S. passport, and were subjected to grueling questioning by immigration officials upon both departure and reentry. Incoming Chinese, including U.S. citizens, were placed in detention without any exceptions if their papers were deemed to be not in order, and in many cases this imposed grave hardships. Detention and interrogation often lasted for weeks, and in some cases, especially when China-born wives and children were attempting to join a husband or father with American resident status, it could continue for months or even more than a year. Youngsters were not excluded; indeed, their confinement, like that of any other entering Chinese, could be prolonged if their answers to a lengthy list of questions did not correspond to the answers to the same questions given separately by two other Chinese supporting their admission. Such procedures, understandably called an inquisition by one Chinese-American as these matters were being debated in 1942, were not only humiliating and psychologically destructive, but also costly, since in the end Chinese attempting to enter the country often found it necessary to obtain legal assistance to clarify their eligibility. No other national group was treated so harshly by immigration authorities, and in these circumstances it comes as little surprise to find Chinese speaking of U.S. immigration officials as "gestapo," or to learn that in 1942 a distraught Chinese woman who had come to join her merchant husband committed suicide in the San Francisco detention center after being incarcerated and questioned for several months without any prospect of being released.[27]

Although there was general agreement that such humiliating treatment of a now-esteemed ally was unfortunate, this did not mean that the situation could be rectified easily. Why? Because any attempt to redress the insult to China would draw further attention to the larger anti-Oriental context of U.S. immigration policy. If the fifteen explicitly anti-Chinese exclusion laws were abrogated, all but a handful of Chinese would still be prohibited under the 1924 law from emigrating to the United States and becoming naturalized citizens. They would remain, in the formal realm of the law, an inferior and undesirable people. If, on the other hand, the Chinese were put on the quota system which applied to non-Asian peoples under the 1924 law, that would be tantamount to placing them in a position superior to all other Asians—including, as one congressman put it, America's own special colonials, "the race of the little brown men of Manila." When it was claimed that the latter argument was not really valid since, apart from Japan, China was the only "sovereign" country in Asia, this too evoked embarrassing recitations from recent history. For, apart from Korea and Formosa, it was not Japan that had suppressed independence in most of Asia, but the European and American colonial structure that had existed since the nineteenth century. Where India, the second most populous country in Asia was concerned, the issue thus called renewed attention not only to British imperialism (a *bête noire* of many American conservatives as well as liberals), but also to the fact that the United States also relegated Indians to an inferior position.

Once this issue started unraveling, there seemed to be no end to it. As can be easily imagined, Japanese propagandists found the debate valuable ammunition in their appeals to other Asians, and the campaign to revise the exclusion laws gained many alarmed adherents whose primary concern was to "spike" Japan's propaganda guns. At times, the issue thus took on an almost surreal dimension, with criticism of the laws in the United States providing ammunition for the Japanese, which in turn provided further ammunition for the critics of the laws. Where the target was so vulnerable, the Japanese scored well. They informed their Asian audiences not only about the exclusion policy itself, but also about the harassment of Chinese at detention centers (where, a Tokyo broadcast to China declared, they were "practically treated like a class apart from the rest of humanity"), the social pressures that forced Chinese into ghettoized "Chinatowns" in the poorer residential areas, and the discrimination that relegated most of them to "the most menial of occupations, despised and mistreated and at best patronizingly tolerated with a contemptuous humor."[28]

One congressman referred to this as "drivel" dished out by "chattering monkeys," another spoke of "the childish fury of this propaganda," but virtually no one, including President Roosevelt, denied its potential effectiveness. A retired Navy officer told the congressional hearings inquiring into the issue that the anti-Chinese legislation was worth "twenty divisions" to the Japanese Army. Many others agreed that placing China under the normal quota system for immigration would not only right a historic injustice but also help avert a potential disaster ("combine canniness with good manners," as the *Saturday Evening Post* phrased it), for there was no reason to believe that China's will to resist the Japanese was unshakable. The Chinese Nationalists had fought long. They had suffered grievously. They had seen the United States and England supply military goods to Japan until almost the eve of Pearl Harbor and pursue a "Europe first" policy thereafter. They had listened to Churchill proclaim his intention to restore the British Empire, and listened in vain for a clear American disavowal of support for this plan to reconstruct the *status quo ante* of the white man's imperium. Lawmakers such as Walter Judd of Minnesota and Mike Mansfield of Montana, who were respected by their colleagues for their special expertise on Asia, spelled this out carefully, and the implications were well understood. Despite all the hoopla about the close relationship between Chiang Kai-shek's Nationalist regime and the United States, it was not difficult to envision the Nationalists' morale cracking—and if China fell from the Allied side, the consequences would be incalculable.[29]

In this manner, a rather arcane debate about immigration laws soon came to involve the old visions of the Yellow Peril, but now in a concrete setting that pointed to the way in which China might tip the scales one way or another in a global conflagration. "If this war or its aftermath develops into a race struggle there will be about half a billion more people on the side of the colored races than on our side," declared Representative John Vorys of Ohio in a typical speech on the subject. "In such a crisis the fact that the most numerous colored race on earth has had unique relations of friendship with the United States, that single fact, may prove the salvation of the white race." Vorys' colleague in the House, Carl Curtis of Nebraska, spoke in a similar vein: "Suppose the Chinese do capitulate and join Japan, then all Asia is apt to go with her. Then you will have a race struggle in which we are hopelessly outnumbered that will last, not for 1 year or 5 years, but throughout the generations to come." Walter Judd, who had recently been elected to the House after ten years as a medical missionary in China, agreed that the future hinged on China: "There cannot be a great war between the white and colored races in the next 10 years, or the next 100 years, or the next 300 years, if we keep ourselves—the white people—and the Chinese, the largest and strongest of the colored peoples, on the same side—the side of freedom and democracy." To suggest how delicate the balance was, however, Judd quoted the recent words of an individual with rare credentials: Paul Yu-pin, the Roman Catholic bishop of China. In the July 1943 issue of the Catholic journal *Commonweal,* the bishop had responded as follows when asked what the consequences would be if the United States failed to repeal the anti-Chinese exclusion laws:

> Certainly China will keep in the fight until Japan is defeated. In this defeat, you of course will play a great part. But if your attitude of superiority continues, if the Far East becomes convinced that the United States has forfeited her moral right to leadership, and is fixed in her determination to look down upon the colored races, I can foresee only a prospect which makes me tremble at its horrors.
>
> In that case the next war would almost inevitably be a war between races, and that would mean a war in which not only armies are pitted against each other, armies and industries, but a war in which child is against child, woman against woman, grandfather against grandfather. In such a war there would not even be talk of mercy and decency. It would literally be to the death, and we would not hear of unconditional surrender, but of annihilation. What Christian can envisage such things without being tempted to despair![30]

Using a Chinese Christian to help make his case was a sign of Judd's astute understanding of one of the ironies of this debate, that popular esteem for China and the Chinese in the United States was entangled with the perception that China might hold the key to whether white Christian civilization would survive. Thus, we find a supporter of the bill to put China on a normal immigration quota, Representative Robert Ramspeck of Georgia, defending his position in terms of "doing justice to a valiant ally whose fighting in this war may well be the balance of power between victory and defeat for the forces of Christian civilization." In this context, one can also appreciate some of the marvelous commentary exhumed by Professor Christopher Thorne, such as the Chicago newspaper that referred to China in 1943 as "our 'white hope' in the East," and the pro-Chinese lobbying group that argued in a widely distributed pamphlet that to lose China's goodwill through continuing discrimination was to "incur the risk of another war in which white supremacy may be openly challenged by the Oriental races."[31]

Even the most liberal and best-intentioned friends of the Chinese
were not immune to the colonial mind-set, and as a result, the final
disposition of the mid-war exclusion controversy was, unsurprisingly, ambivalent. In December 1943, amidst fanfare as well as the protests of such
groups as the American Legion, the Veterans of Foreign Wars, and the
American Federation of Labor, the Chinese exclusion laws were revised
to permit a maximum of 105 Chinese eligible for naturalization to immigrate into the United States each year. Seventy-five percent of these had
to come from China proper; the rest could already be in the United States
as temporary residents. The basic Immigration Act of 1924 remained
unaltered insofar as any other Asians were concerned. In this, Congress
followed the argument of President Roosevelt, who stated that while
extension of the privilege of citizenship "would give the Chinese a preferred status over certain other oriental people, their great contribution
to the cause of decency and freedom entitles them to such preference."[32]

China remained a problem to U.S. and British leaders to the end
of the war, but its importance in the eyes of many Americans was certainly
enhanced by these exercises in imagining what might happen if the
Chinese joined the enemy camp; the legacy of such thinking, of course,
carried over to the furor over the "loss of China" that wracked the United
States after the war. Although there was some confusion over statistics,
there was little disagreement concerning the fact that China's size was
awesome. Estimates of the Chinese population ranged from 350 million
to 500 million, and with such impressive figures to play with, it is not
surprising that discussions about "holding" or "losing" China frequently
assumed a hyperbolic tone. Such numbers also inspired several concrete
considerations that continued well into the postwar years to arouse both
hope and terror in the hearts of many Western observers: hope in the
form of a rekindled dream about the fabulous potential of the "China
market," and fear that Japan's defeat in itself would mean little if the rest
of Asia, led by China, continued to wave the banner of national and racial
liberation.

By 1943, many Americans were already worrying about postwar
economic conversion from a war economy to peacetime production. As
Collier's put it in an editorial supporting a standard immigration quota
for the Chinese, China's vast population and great potential for rapid

industrialization once hostilities were ended offered "appetizing postwar possibilities" for American business. Such evocations of the fabled China market were a conspicuous feature of the 1942–43 debate over Chinese exclusion. It was, in this context, "good business," "good hard business sense," "enlightened selfishness" to repeal the humiliating immigration restrictions. Many observers felt that once Japan had been eliminated as both a military drain and a ruthless economic rival, China's potential for economic growth would prove substantial. Congressman Noah Mason of Illinois, who as a member of the House Committee on Immigration and Naturalization took an active part in these deliberations, did not hesitate to go so far as to declare that China offered "the only real post-war market for American manufactured goods":

> China is awakening from her long sleep. She is on the verge of an industrial revolution. She will need billions of dollars worth of machine tools after this war is over to help in her industrial development. She will need railroads built, railroad engines and railroad equipment for those railroads, farm machinery for modernizing her agricultural methods, road-building machinery to build the vast system of hard roads that will be required, and mining machinery to develop her vast mineral resources. Best of all, China will have the raw materials and consequent international credits to pay for these things. So, Mr. Chairman, our potential trade with China after this war is over should furnish jobs to hundreds of thousands, if not millions, of our boys when they return from the war.[33]

China would also, it was anticipated, take over the textile markets formerly dominated by Japan, and provide a major market for U.S. agricultural products such as cotton. Conversely, of course, if this great potential market were closed off, the whole process of postwar U.S. economic reconversion could be imperiled. From this perspective, old words took on new connotations. The "Yellow Peril" could be turned about and seen as a "negative peril"—the denial of access to Asia deemed critical to a capitalist economy that virtually everyone believed would confront a monumental crisis of overproduction and underemployment once the war ended. Similarly, there emerged dawning awareness of a double entendre in the debate on "exclusion," as politician after politician suddenly seemed to become aware of the possible connection between past domestic policies of excluding Chinese from the United States and future prospects of being excluded from the postwar China market.[34]

Beyond this loomed the larger and more conventional Yellow Peril specter of China breaking with the Anglo-American powers and throwing its weight behind a Pan-Asian and antiwhite movement. In the war on hand, this would not simply have added the several million troops who comprised Chiang Kai-shek's nationalist forces to the ranks of the enemy, but would have freed an estimated two-million additional Japanese troops to fight against the Allies. Even assuming the Nationalists stayed the course in the battle against Japanese imperialism, however, it still remained to be asked where China and the rest of Asia would stand thereafter—whether there would develop what William Phillips, a personal representative of President Roosevelt to India in 1943, perceived as a burgeoning "white against colored complex in the East." To the end of the war, the notion persisted in many circles that Japan could still "win by losing." This could happen, warned Robert S. Ward, an experienced U.S. foreign-service officer stationed in Chungking in May 1954, simply because "it is in the Japanese identification of imperial aims with the appeal to a race revolt that the real peril lies." The peoples of the East, he continued, had been exposed to "a virus that may yet poison the whole soul of Asia and ultimately commit the world to a racial war that would destroy the white man and decimate the Asiatic, with no possible future gain."[35]

Such presentiments of "World War Three" in the midst of World War Two betrayed a pessimism that contrasted sharply with the dream of the World War One years that that war might be the "war to end all wars." As World War Two progressed, moreover, apprehension concerning the next global war developed in another area as well, as tensions mounted between the Soviet Union and its British and American allies. "Which War Comes Next?" asked H. C. McGinnis in *Catholic World* in July 1945, between Germany's and Japan's surrenders; and he concluded that the two hypothetical wars which then dominated popular consciousness, the race war and the struggle between Russia and the West, were not in fact mutually exclusive. On the contrary, one could easily envision the two conflicts becoming one. "Russia is also an Asiatic power," he observed—an observation that others had voiced as well, among them Joseph Stalin himself. Certainly, it was reasonable to anticipate that a revolt against white imperialism beginning in Asia and spreading to other parts of the globe would receive Moscow's support. So, as

World War Two built to its ferocious climax, the vision of a Yellow Peril and a Red Peril began, at least for some observers, to fuse in an absolutely overpowering way:

> Together with China, India and Japan, Moscow can arrange that millions of colored warriors be equipped. With Russia's expert mechanized forces spearheading an invasion of Europe and, according to current Red tactics, with stupendous concentrations of Red artillery blasting holes in white defenses through which literally scores of millions of hate-infuriated colored warriors will pour to wreak vengeance for the thousands of injustices heaped upon their people, Europe would probably become a veritable shambles. Perhaps the Americas too, for the Bering Strait is not wide. There is no hatred or no fury comparable to that engendered by racial injustices. Such a war would be altogether too horrible to even imagine.
>
> It is now much later than the average white man thinks. . . .[36]

Like a stone cast into the water, the race issue made itself felt in ever-widening circles. Just as attacks on the Japanese enemy carried over into animosity toward Asian peoples in general, so also did the Yellow Peril sentiment pass on into even larger fears concerning the rise of "colored" peoples everywhere. For the English, the colored problem evoked a multitude of unsettling images linking the war to the clamor for independence from colonial rule in India, Burma, Malaya, and, though still muted there, Africa. For white Americans, "color" was a blunt reminder that the upheaval in Asia coincided with rising bitterness, impatience, anger, and militance among blacks at home.

The alarm which accelerating black demands for equality caused in U.S. military and civilian circles during the war cannot be underestimated. Secretary of War Stimson agonized over the "explosive" and seemingly insoluble race problem, and confided to his diary early in 1942 that he believed Japanese and Communist agitators were behind Negro demands for equality. General Marshall confidentially told reporters in August 1943 that he "would rather handle everything that the Germans, Italians and Japanese can throw at me, than to face the trouble I see in the Negro question." A white Southern moderate writing in *Atlantic Monthly* early in 1943 painted a doomsday picture of race riots erupting throughout the United States, incited by both radical blacks and reactionary whites, with blacks soon coming to the conclusion that they had little to lose by a Japanese victory. "Like the natives of Malaya and Burma," he stated, "the American Negroes are sometimes imbued with the notion that a victory for the yellow race over the white race might also be a victory for them." At the same time, the article went on, should the United States erupt in racial violence, this probably would have "far-reaching and heavily adverse effects upon the colored peoples of China, India, and the Middle East."[37]

In parts of the American South, fears among white people of a Japanese-Negro alliance were apparently fairly commonplace from the 1930s on, and wartime opinion surveys did indicate that at least some black Americans were willing to admit that they were reserving judgment about the Japanese. A confidential poll conducted by black interviewers found that 18 percent of blacks queried admitted "pro-Japanese inclinations," while a mid-war book on the theme "inside Black America" concluded from a survey of editorials and letters to the editor in the black press that blacks as a whole neither supported nor condemned Japan, but rather viewed the war in Asia from a "neutralized" stance. Gunnar Myrdal, whose massive pioneer study of black Americans was published in 1944, emphasized their "thoroughly American" outlook and their loyalty in the current war. As a whole, he concluded, they were as prodemocratic and antifascist as most white groups. At the same time, Myrdal also observed that a modest number took "vicarious satisfaction in imagining a Japanese (or German) invasion of the Southern states"; and he warned that if black grievances remained unredressed after the war, it was difficult to predict how they would react "if later a new war were to be fought more definitely along color lines."[38]

Beginning in the 1930s, the Japanese did attempt to influence black opinion in the United States, but their efforts to this end were desultory and largely ineffective. In the mid-1930s, working through an agent identified as Major Takahashi Satakata, they established a connection with the radical antiwhite Black Muslim movement led by Elijah Muhammad. Prior to his deportation from the United States in the late 1930s, Takahashi apparently had succeeded in persuading a splinter group of Black Muslims known as the Development of Our Own to rally behind the cause of the emperor. In a 1942 raid on three militant Negro cults (the Temple of Islam, the Peace Movement of Ethiopia, and the Brotherhood of Liberty for Black People of America), the FBI arrested twelve black leaders, including Elijah Muhammad, for allegedly seditious activities including voicing support for a Japanese victory, and also imprisoned a number of their followers for draft resistance. Before the war, the Japanese also established a relationship with Robert O. Jordan, a charismatic black sometimes called "Harlem's Hitler," who also was arrested after Pearl Harbor; estimates of Jordan's followers ranged from five hundred to five thousand. In addition, it was later revealed that, working through a Caucasian agent named Joseph Hilton Smyth, the Japanese government had attempted to penetrate the U.S. media by gaining control of several magazines (including two reputable publications, *Living Age* and *North American Review*) and founding, in 1940, a rather ineffectual press service named the Negro News Syndicate. Well into the war, Stimson and other top-level leaders remained convinced that the Japanese and Germans were conducting a "systematic campaign" to stir up black demands for equality, and that "a good many" black leaders were receiving payments through the Japanese ambassador in Mexico.[39]

Japanese propaganda directed at the United States during the war did indeed attempt to appeal to nonwhites by emphasizing racial discrimination, but the real impact of the war on black opinion did not come from clandestine activities or the effectiveness of enemy radio broadcasts. It came from the very nature of the war. The struggle against both the Germans and the Japanese was accompanied by attacks on master-race theories in general, and thus cut at the roots of white supremacism and discriminatory laws and institutions in the United States. At the same time, however, blacks were still denied good jobs in the defense industries and were drafted to fight for freedom in a military establishment where even the blood plasma was segregated.[40] They were called apes by white soldiers and described in military orders as "akin to well-meaning but irresponsible children." Most skilled military positions were closed to them, and the prospects of advancement were negligible. Such circumstances politicized many blacks and sharpened their grasp of the contradictions in their own society.[41]

At the same time, the Japanese attack had memorable symbolic aspects for black people. While Japanese propaganda hammered at the practices of white racism, it was Japan's actions rather than its words that really altered the worldview of many nonwhites. The Japanese dared to challenge the dominant white establishment directly. Their initial victories humiliated the Europeans and Americans in unforgettable ways, forever destroying the myth of white omnipotence, or even white efficiency. By the same token, the Japanese victories demonstrated the capacity of nonwhites to develop and handle the advanced technologies of the modern world. As the black leader Roy Wilkins put it, the disaster at Pearl Harbor was due at least partly to the stupid habit of white people looking down on all nonwhite nations. A conversation with a black taxi driver in a northern U.S. city, reported about a year after Pearl Harbor in a magazine survey of racial problems and the war, conveyed similar sentiments in lively everyday language:

DRIVER. "Man, those Japs really do jump, don't they? And it looks like everytime they jump, they land."
PASSENGER. "More they land, the worse it's going to be for you and me. . . ."
DRIVER. "I know it's gonna be a long war. But one thing you've got to give those Japs, they showed the white man that a brown hand could handle a plane and a machine gun too."
PASSENGER. "Yes, Hitler believes that they're fit to be allies of the great Nazis."
DRIVER. "Well, I reckon one's bad as the other, but they still can fight, and they've already knocked out a lot of the white man's conceit. And that's something."[42]

Comparable anecdotes and rumors concerning the black response to the war sometimes assumed an almost folklorish quality, being repeatedly evoked in publications that catered to a predominantly white audience. Right after Pearl Harbor, for example, it was reported that an elderly black sharecropper had occasion to talk to his white boss and murmured, upon leaving, "By the way, Captain, I hear the Japs done declared war on you white folks." In various versions, this became a favorite story in the American press. Another often-told story concerned a young black who, upon being inducted into the Army, requested that his epitaph read: "Here lies a black man killed fighting a yellow man for the protection of the white man." *The Nation,* the liberal weekly, told of a young man who declared he intended to get his eyes slanted, so that he could fight back the next time he got shoved around by a white man. Other sources picked up on black resentment at the way white Americans tended to frame the war in Asia in derogatory color terms. "All these radio announcers talking about yellow this, yellow that," a Harlem resident was quoted as saying. "Don't hear them calling the Nazis white this, pink that. What the hell color do they think the Chinese are anyway! And those Filipinos on

Bataan! And the British Imperial Army, I suppose they think they're all blondes?''

As the war dragged on, magazine articles began to appear in the United States under such titles as ''Fighting for White Folks?'' or ''Fighting a White Man's War''—and it is a sign of the tensions of the times that there was no way of telling by the title alone whether the article was primarily concerned with the attitude of American Negroes or the anguished concerns of Asian supporters of the Allied powers. The potentially explosive nature of the situation became most apparent, however, when blacks began appropriating the Allied rhetoric of ''fighting for democracy'' as their own and drawing practical lessons from the war.[43]

The conflict in Asia itself provided several sometimes contradictory models for black leaders, including the example of Japanese militance, the inspiration of Chinese resistance against the Japanese, and the tactics of nonviolent resistance exemplified by Gandhi in his struggle against British colonial rule in India. But the ''good war'' against the oppressive Axis powers was inspiration enough in itself for many American blacks, and campaigns for civil rights were organized during the war under such slogans as ''Double Victory,'' ''Victory at Home as Well as Abroad,'' and ''Defeat Hitler, Mussolini and Hirohito by Enforcing the Constitution and Abolishing Jim Crow.'' A well-publicized civil rights rally at Madison Square Garden in June 1942, attended by eighteen thousand persons, provided an example of what such slogans meant to many blacks. The highlight of the evening was a skit in which a black man who had just been drafted had the following lines: ''I want you to know I ain't afraid. I don't mind fighting. I'll fight Hitler, Mussolini and the Japs all at the same time, but I'm telling you I'll give those crackers down South the same damn medicine.'' There was, it was reported, ''bedlam'' when these words were spoken, and the audience called for the actor to repeat them.[44]

Left-wing black leaders like A. Philip Randolph did not hesitate to speak of a global union of ''the darker races'' emerging out of the war, and to couple this with a call for democratic revolution by repressed peoples everywhere. Neither the vision nor the warning, however, were confined to politically radical circles. Walter White, head of the traditionally non-militant National Association for the Advancement of Colored People, struck a similar chord in a small book titled *A Rising Wind*, devoted exclusively to the black and the war, and published just after Japan's defeat. Plainspoken through most of its pages, White's book ended with a sweeping warning. ''World War II,'' he wrote, ''has given to the Negro a sense of kinship with other colored—and also oppressed—peoples of the world. Where he has not thought through or informed himself on the racial angles of colonial policy and master-race theories, he senses that the struggle of the Negro in the United States is part and parcel of the struggle against imperialism and exploitation in India, China, Burma, Africa, the Philippines, Malaya, the West Indies, and South America. The Negro soldier is convinced that as time proceeds that identification of interest will spread even among some brown and yellow peoples who today refuse to see the connection between their exploitation by white nations and discrimination against the Negro in the United States." White spoke of "the inevitability of world-wide racial conflict unless the white nations of the earth do an about-face on the issue of race." (Here he quoted with respect, as black leaders often did, Pearl Buck's wartime warnings and entreaties concerning the possibility of a future race war.) And he concluded by warning that if "Anglo-Saxon practices" of racism and imperialism were not revised drastically and immediately, much of Asia, including China and India, might "move into the Russian orbit as the lesser of two dangers." The "rising wind" (the title came from a phrase in a speech by Eleanor Roosevelt), he intimated, could easily develop into a hurricane.[45]

In various ways, racial hurricanes did arise out of World War Two and change the landscape of the postwar world. They did not sweep the globe in a single violent blast, as the most dire prophets feared. They did not destroy white supremacy worldwide, although they weakened it. They took the form of national and racial liberation movements in Asia and later Africa, and the civil rights and black-power movements in the United States. They would have happened eventually, but the war accelerated them in ways beyond measure.

The contribution of the Japanese to this rising tide of racial politicization was substantial. It was they, after all, who tripped the wire that brought the United States into the conflict and turned the separate wars in Europe and Asia into a single global conflagration. They destroyed the myths of white supremacism and shattered the European and American colonial structure in Asia in a way that proved—after long postwar agony, as the colonials tried to reimpose control—to be beyond repair. The Japanese inspired countless millions of Asians with their audacity, even as they inspired hatred by their own overweening arrogance. For the

Japanese were as racist as their Anglo-American adversaries, and their slogans of Asian liberation, coexistence, and coprosperity were as propagandistic (and as sincere, to some) as the rhetoric of "four freedoms" and "fighting for democracy" was to the Anglo-American powers.

The problem of racism is often approached as if it were a one-way street named White Supremacism. That is understandable, since whites themselves coined the phrase, imposed their supremacy over most of the globe and most of the darker races, and spent over four centuries writing about the inferiority of nonwhites. The many attitudes that come together to comprise racial consciousness, however—including pride in one's native place and culture and bloodlines—are hardly a monopoly of white peoples. When racial consciousness is also recognized as an expression of status and power vis-à-vis others—comparable to class consciousness, to nationalism and great-power chauvinism, and to gender arrogance —then it becomes clear that there is a place for serious comparative study here.

There must be, a priori, an imbalance in such a study, deriving from the fact that Europe and the United States have dominated the modern political economy. The industrialized world did not borrow a great deal from outside itself. The later developers, like Japan, did. Because Japan borrowed from the West, Japanese attitudes toward others have been mixed. They could never look upon the Westerners and call them "little men," for example. They could not really call them apes, since they had not gone through the Western voyages of discovery and later bastardization of evolutionary theory. It would not have made sense to characterize the Westerners as children, since the Westerners were initially stronger and taught them a great deal. (On the other hand, it made good sense to call weaker and less developed peoples, like other Asians, "children".) There were certainly no great impediments to hating or denigrating the Westerners, but the idioms had to fit: strong and threatening, beneficent and evil. They settled on demons, albeit demons with a human face.

The Japanese found the demon in their own folk culture, just as they found there the mechanisms and metaphors for relegating other Asians to inferior status. At the same time, they also spent an inordinate amount of time working on their own self-image. Since they were taking on their former teachers, and taking on an unprecedented role as well, the task of making a persuasive case for their own superiority was no small undertaking. As a consequence, the Japanese spent much more time than their

Anglo-American enemies did in identifying and belaboring—largely for home consumption—their own unique and superior qualities. In the end, they focused on their "purity," in the sense of both bloodlines and morality.

These matters are the subjects of the chapters that follow, where it will be seen that Japanese racism worked in different ways from that of the Anglo-Americans. The idioms were different. The preoccupations were different. The psychology was different, and more complex. While the Japanese denounced the Western Allies in no uncertain terms, their attitude toward Europeans and Americans remained ambiguous; and while they preached Pan-Asianism and devoted much energy and propaganda to glorifying the "common culture" of the East, in actual practice they could hardly conceal their contempt for other Asians. Despite such differences, however, the end results of racial thinking on both sides were virtually identical—being hierarchy, arrogance, viciousness, atrocity, and death.

THROWING IN AN EXTRA CHARGE

1. This cartoon by the *Chicago Tribune*'s Carey Orr, published three days after Pearl Harbor, is an unequivocal reminder of how the surprise attack became an indelible symbol of Japanese treachery in the United States, and inspired an immediate commitment to a vengeful war without mercy. Japanese military planners, obsessed with operational issues and misled by disdainful stereotypes of Americans as decadent and egocentric, gave virtually no thought to the psychological consequences of their decision to attack the U.S. fleet.

EAST OR WEST?

2 and 3. The famous political cartoonist David Low offered this stark contrast (above) between the Japanese "monkey-men" and the white powers in July 1941, when it was still being debated whom Japan was most likely to attack. A *Washington Post* cartoon one year later, comparing Japanese atrocities in the Philippines to German ones in Czechoslovakia, illustrates sharply contrasting American images of the enemy—an ape representing all "Japs" imitates "Hitler."

Mimic

THE MONKEY FOLK

"Always pecking at new things are the bandar-log. This time, if I have any eyesight, they have pecked down trouble for themselves."—*The Jungle Book*.

4. Taking its caption from Rudyard Kipling's *Jungle Book,* this full-page illustration was published in *Punch* in mid-January 1942, as the Japanese were advancing down the Malay Peninsula toward Singapore.

"KNOCK HIM OFF THAT SPRINGBOARD"

THE ALEUTIANS

5

5, 6, 7, and 8. The Japanese attempt to seize control of the Aleutians in 1942–1943 prompted a typically apish cartoon in the *Philadelphia Inquirer* (figure 5). When the Japanese garrison at Attu fought to virtually the last man, the U.S. media offered this as further evidence of the subhuman nature of the foe (while the same event inspired the Japanese to eulogize their war dead as "shattered jewels"). *Collier's* turned to the British cartoonist Lawson Wood, famous for his animal graphics, for its May 1943 cover, depicting two downed Japanese airmen as a ludicrous monkey and chimpanzee (figure 6). Depiction of the Japanese as apes also implied that they were vicious jungle creatures who had to be exterminated, as in this April 1943 *New York Times* response to the execution of captured Doolittle fliers—captioned with a line from *The Mikado*: "Let the punishment fit the crime" (figure 7). Exterminationist sentiment also was reinforced by depicting the Japanese as vermin. "Louseous Japanicas" (figure 8) appeared in the U.S. Marine monthly *Leatherneck* in March 1945, the same month that the United States adopted the policy of low-level incendiary bombing of Japanese cities.

Collier's
TEN CENTS
MAY 8, 1943

6

7

8

Louseous Japanicas

The first serious outbreak of this lice epidemic was officially noted on December 7, 1941, at Honolulu, T. H. To the Marine Corps, especially trained in combating this type of pestilence, was assigned the gigantic task of extermination. Extensive experiments on Guadalcanal, Tarawa, and Saipan have shown that this louse inhabits coral atolls in the South Pacific, particularly pill boxes, palm trees, caves, swamps and jungles.

Flame throwers, mortars, grenades and bayonets have proven to be an effective remedy. But before a complete cure may be effected the origin of the plague, the breeding grounds around the Tokyo area, must be completely annihilated.

The words "September", "The", "Leatherneck", "MAGAZINE OF THE MARINES", "15c", and the signature "FRED LASSWELL" appear on the cover.

9. The cover of *Leatherneck*'s September 1945 issue, celebrating Japan's surrender, revealed the malleability of wartime stereotypes, as the simian caricature was almost immediately transformed into an irritated but already domesticated and even charming pet.

A British commentary on the Japanese soldier.

How Tough Are the Japanese?

**They are not tougher than other soldiers, says a veteran
observer, but brutality is part of their fighting equipment.**

10. Following Japan's spectacular early victories, the perception of the Japanese as supermen emerged alongside the images of apes and lesser men. This British graphic was used
to illustrate a mid-1943 article in the *New York Times Magazine*.

THE HEROIC ROLE
"And so brave Jack defied the Giant Ogre, and.."
JACK THE GIANT
....THE LAD WHO GREW UP TO PLAY THE PART...
JAP HORDES
AMERICAN FIGHTER IN THE PHILIPPINES
ORR

11

11, 12, and 13. The image of the Japanese superman immediately evoked more traditional visions of the Yellow Peril and menacing Asian "horde," as in Orr's January 1942 cartoon for the *Chicago Tribune* (figure 11). In the original, the face and hands of the "Jap hordes" were bright yellow—a routine feature of virtually all colored depictions of the Japanese. The *Tribune* evoked the specter of the Yellow Peril even more explicitly in a graphic published two weeks after Pearl Harbor (figure 12). The sexual fears underlying Yellow Peril and anti-"colored" sentiments are revealed in the poster of a Japanese soldier carrying off a naked white woman (figure 13). Submitted to a "This Is the Enemy" contest in 1942, this was exhibited at New York's Museum of Modern Art and reprinted in *Life*.

"ANOTHER PUZZLER FOR WORLD SCHOLARS"

14. The Western perception of the Japanese as "little men" or "lesser men" meshed easily with images of the enemy as primitive, childish, moronic, or emotionally disturbed. This graphic, originally published in the *Detroit News* on the occasion of Japan's surrender in August 1945, reached a much larger audience when it was reprinted in the Sunday *New York Times*.

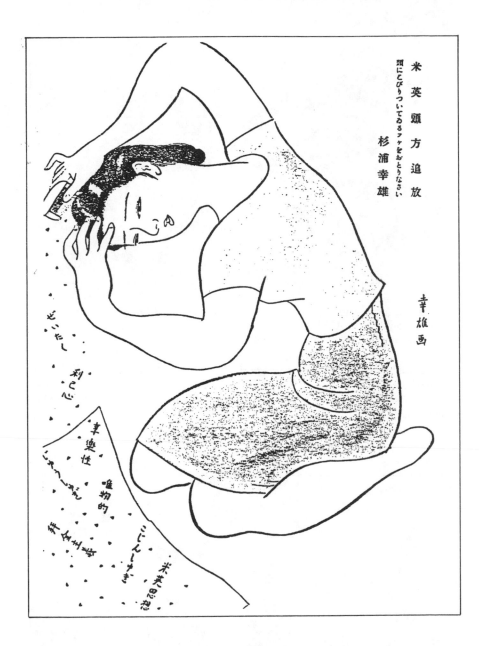

15. The wartime Japanese fixation on purity and purification was expressed in an original manner in this May 1942 cartoon from the officially sponsored humor magazine *Manga* —entitled "Purging One's Head of Anglo-Americanism," with a further admonition "Get rid of that dandruff encrusting your head!" The scurf being combed out is identified as extravagance, selfishness, hedonism, liberalism, materialism, money worship, individualism, and Anglo-American ideas.

16 and 17. In its January 1942 issue, *Manga* responded to the outbreak of war with an exuberant graphic by Ikeda Eiji. The purifying sun of Japanese glory dispels the "ABCD" powers. America and Britain are thugs (the crown of Jewish—"J"—plutocracy is falling from America's head). China is a sprawling figure with Chiang Kai-shek's face—and a stubby tail, a bestial mark often attached to the Nationalist Chinese. All that remains of the Dutch is a wooden shoe. Ikeda's rendering of the Allied leaders as Napoleonic megalomaniacs, trampling the oppressed (and typically dark) natives of Asia underfoot, appeared in *Manga* in mid-1942.

馬脚狸尾
近藤日出造

18

18 and 19. In "Horse's Legs, Badger's Tail" (above), published in January 1942, the famous cartoonist Kondō Hidezō applied familiar folk idioms for exposing deceptive appearances to the outbreak of the war. Japan's planes have revealed that the pious Churchill really has the hindquarters of the cunning badger and is clothed in death, while Padre Roosevelt has a horse's backside (like the English "cloven hoof") and a crucifix for a dagger, and his real clothing is the almighty dollar. In Kondō's "Vespers" (below), from July 1942, Roosevelt and Churchill, their helpless offspring Chiang at their feet, pray against a field of slaughtered bodies in a parody of Millet's famous painting "The Angelus." The two leaders are chained together, and a flag of surrender hangs from the pitchfork.

19

近藤日出造 晩鐘

民主義

獨裁

スラトキ

神女の由自のき嘆

小野佐世男

2601
SASEO.

20. In Ono Saseo's "Grieving Statue of Liberty," Roosevelt, waving the slogan "democracy" while holding the club of "dictatorship," appears in the classic guise of a demon. America's decadence is represented by the figures on Liberty's crown: the carousing "antiwar" sailor; the fettered figure of "military action"; the strident worker waving a "strike" placard; and the clownish "Jew," inflating the balloon of profits disguised as the American flag. The "2601" above the artist's signature is the year (1941) in the new nationalistic calendar adopted by the Japanese, based on the divine origins of the imperial line; the cartoon appeared in January 1942.

21

22

21, 22, and 23. Most graphic renderings of the demonic foe bore the face of the U.S. president or British prime minister. In the original Japanese caption to figure 21, a horned Roosevelt proclaims, "The demon is me! The demon is me!" Figures 22 and 23 appeared in October 1944, when Japanese propaganda concerning alleged Allied atrocities was accelerating. The latter portrays Roosevelt and Churchill as debauched ogres carousing within sight of Mount Fuji, and was accompanied by an exhortation to kill the "devilish Americans and British."

23

米國の「米」の字

24

24 and 25. "The Ideograph for America" (left) is a visual pun which turns one of the characters used in writing *Beikoku*, or America, into a Roosevelt crucified by Japan. The *Osaka Puck* graphic below exemplifies the fondness for the bayonet as, in effect, a wartime rendering of the pure sword of Japanese righteousness confronting and exterminating the enemy. Published in February 1942, the heading reads "India! Now is the time to rise!!" The flag bears the motto "Greater East Asia Holy War," and the demonic nature of the enemy is revealed by Churchill's (or John Bull's) telltale small horns.

25

イ ンド よ 今 こそ 起ち 上る 時 だ!!

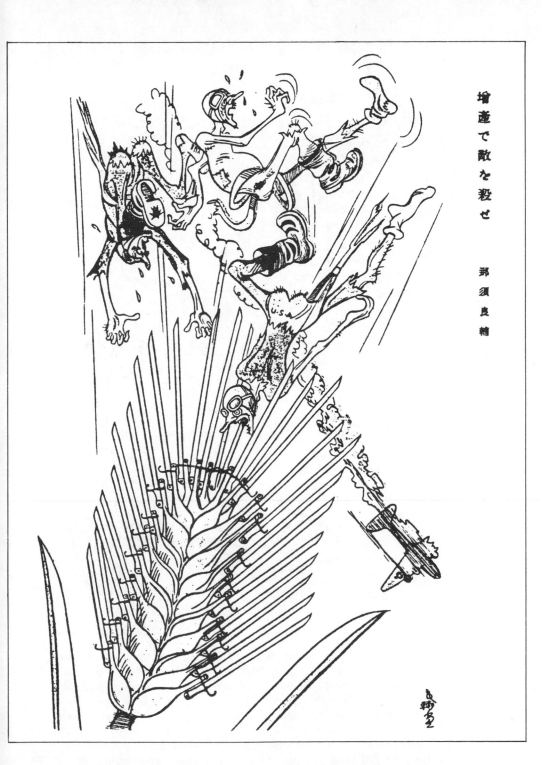

増産で敵を殺せ

郡須良輔

26. This grotesque cartoon, which appeared in *Manga* in July 1944, reveals the increasing desperation of the Japanese as the war turned decisively against them. Entitled "Kill the Enemy by Increasing Production," ludicrous American flyers are impaled on a head of rice bristling with blades of righteousness.

27 and 28. In this classic folkloric rendering (above), Japan's wartime mission is associated with the divinely born Momotarō (the "Peach Boy"), who with the aid of a dog, pheasant, and monkey subdued threatening demons from a distant land. The banner reads "Establish the East Asia Co-Prosperity Sphere," while the lapels on Momotarō's overgarment identify him as "First in the world." The humorous boxing sequence on the opposite page is a "modernized" version of this story. Chiang Kai-shek is on the ropes. Roosevelt and Churchill, flabby and elderly, step in to save him but are roundly defeated by an exemplary Momotarō-type symbol of Japan: young, clean, wearing a Rising Sun headband. In the final panel, black Americans cheer lustily at Japan's victory, while whites are shocked and chagrined.

南方の人　岸丈夫

29. "People of the Southern Region" appeared in *Osaka Puck* in December 1942 as part of a "before-and-after" sequence depicting Asia under Western domination and after Japanese liberation. It reveals many of the ways the Japanese signified their superiority vis-à-vis other Asians. Here, the familiar purifying sun (labeled "Co-Prosperity Sphere") beams down on Indonesia, driving out the Dutch, while the Japanese hand clasps the native's as that of an unmistakable patriarch—indeed, literally as the hand of God (a conceit Western illustrators also used). The Japanese hand is far lighter in color than the dark-skinned native's, and a jacket cuff is in evidence, whereas the "southern person," obviously a manual laborer, is half-naked and implicitly half-civilized. Not only is his inferior "proper place" as a race, nation, and culture absolutely clear, but so also is his subordinate role in the division of labor within the Greater East Asia Co-Prosperity Sphere.

PART III
THE WAR IN JAPANESE EYES

◄ C H A P T E R 8 ►
THE PURE SELF

During the war, the Japanese routinely referred to themselves as the leading race *(shidō minzoku)* of the world. Like their American and Commonwealth adversaries, they called on a variety of metaphors, images, code phrases, and concepts to affirm their superiority—ranging from expressions that demeaned non-Japanese to elaborate affirmations of their own unique qualities. And as also happened to their enemies, their prejudices affected their war conduct: the way they evaluated, and frequently misjudged, Allied capabilities; the attitudes and policies they adopted toward other Asians within the Co-Prosperity Sphere; and how they fought and died.

While there were many similarities between Japanese and Western attitudes in this regard, substantial differences existed in the way the Japanese set themselves apart from others. These reflect the influence of cultural and historical developments that have shaped Japanese modes of perception over the centuries; and while the influences themselves cannot be analyzed in detail here, it is essential to point out some of the more dramatic ways in which they were revealed during the years of global conflict. Distinctive and richly symbolic patterns of color perception; concepts of purity and pollution firmly rooted in folk religion; and traditional social distinctions between "insiders" and "outsiders" or strangers —such originally indigenous and inner-directed ways of thinking and seeing all played a role in later attempts by the Japanese to distinguish themselves from foreigners. Peculiarities of both written and spoken Japanese also contributed to conspicuous differences in the manner in which the Japanese and Westerners proclaimed their superiority. The ideographic writing system, for example, permitted visual "puns" that reinforced, even at a subliminal level, the Japanese affirmation of their status as a chosen people. At the same time, the language was conducive to rendering modern slogans in an archaic mode that tended to reinforce a sense of deep-seated and abiding racial and cultural uniqueness.

Japan's modern experience itself generated an indebtedness to the West which made a Japanese equivalent of white supremacism improbable if not impossible. In addition to the rapid and often enthusiastic "Westernization" which took place in Japan during the decades that followed the overthrow of the feudal regime in 1868, moreover, one must take into consideration two further factors. First, the half century or more during which the Japanese initially turned to the West for education coincided almost exactly with the period when scientific racism dominated the natural and social sciences in Europe and the United States. In Japan, that is, the very process of Westernization involved being told that the racial inferiority of the Japanese was empirically verifiable, thus placing Japanese scientists and intellectuals in the awkward position of either ignoring such arguments or attempting to repudiate their ostensible teachers. Second, by the 1930s the Japanese had been forced to endure racial slights and outright discrimination by both Americans and Europeans in a variety of highly public forms, including the unequal treaties of the nineteenth century, discriminatory immigration policies in the United States and elsewhere, and humiliation in the founding moments of the League of Nations, when Japan's request for a simple declaration of "racial equality" was rejected. To an immeasurable degree, there was thus a reactive cast to the anti-Western rhetoric of the Japanese during the years under discussion—a clear sense of revenge for past indignities and maltreatment which, again, has no precise counterpart in the racism of white supremacists.[1] The situation was compounded further by a decided assumption of Japanese superiority vis-à-vis the other races of Asia —a condescending attitude which rested in good part upon Japan's successful adaptation of Western machines.

Whatever reasons may be offered to explain differences between the racial and racist thinking of the Japanese and that of their Western enemies during World War Two, one overarching generalization seems difficult to challenge: whereas racism in the West was markedly characterized by denigration of others, the Japanese were preoccupied far more exclusively with elevating themselves. While the Japanese were not in-adept at belittling other races and saddling them with contemptuous stereotypes, they spent more time wrestling with the question of what it really meant to be "Japanese," how the "Yamato race" was unique among the races and cultures of the world, and why this uniqueness made them superior.

This intense self-preoccupation ultimately led to the propagation of an elaborate mythohistory which emphasized the divine origins of the Japanese imperial line and the exceptional racial and cultural homogeneity of the Japanese people. For modern Japan, history played a role somewhat comparable to the sciences and social sciences in the West as a vehicle for affirming racial superiority; and the essence of the superiority alleged was, in the final analysis, moralistic. The Japanese declared themselves to be neither physically nor intellectually superior to others, but rather inher-ently more virtuous. Although this moral superiority was frequently ex-pressed in set phrases extolling the supreme virtues of filial piety and loyalty as expressed under the influence of the divinely descended Japa-nese imperial line, these qualities themselves were meant to reflect an even more sublime virtue: purity. In countless ways, the Japanese pre-sented themselves as being "purer" than others—a concept that carried both ancient religious connotations and complex contemporary ramifica-tions.

On the day of the Pearl Harbor attack, the Japanese government approved a document entitled "An Outline of Information and Propa-ganda Policies for the War between Japan and the Anglo-American Pow-ers."[2] It should be made absolutely clear to the Japanese people, this stated, that the enemy's "selfish desire for world conquest" made war unavoidable, and Japan's cause was a moral one. The country's goal was to create a "new world order" which would "enable all nations and races to assume their proper place in the world, and all peoples to be at peace in their own sphere." In pursuing this great goal, the utmost care should be taken to avoid implying in any way that this was a race war between colored and white peoples. The outline went on to describe the conflict as a holy war for the establishment of eternal world peace which traced back to the founding of the Japanese state by the Emperor Jimmu 2,600 years previously. (It was from the name of the locale where this mythic progenitor eventually established his court, Yamato, that the designation of the Japanese as the "Yamato race"—*Yamato minzoku*—derived.) The war would be a long one, and would involve full mobilization of all material and spiritual resources in accordance with the requirements of "total war." Confidence should be instilled among the Japanese populace by informing them of Japan's strategic and economic advantages and the superiority of the Imperial Army, but care should be taken not to create a mood of irresponsible optimism. The purpose of domestic propaganda was to spiritually mobilize the Japanese for a protracted conflict and inspire them to take up "shield and spear" to destroy evil, bring about justice, and protect the country's "shining history" of 2,600 years.

The key phrase in this document—and in the Japanese vocabulary of discrimination between Self and Other in general—was "proper place." What makes this early bureaucratic guide to propaganda policy so useful, however, is that it embraces in a brief format many of the other emotional elements that were intimately wrapped up with the concept of proper place and integral to the Japanese designation of themselves as the "leading race." We have here moral righteousness, mythical legitimization, global vision, and the evocation of a "shining history"—an image of brightness that will be found recurring in many forms. We also have an explicit repudiation of racial categories as appropriate for explaining the war.

Throughout the war, it was common for official Japanese documents to repeat this admonition to avoid describing the war as a conflict between the white and colored races. As the same propaganda policy statement went on to make clear, there was a simple reason for doing so, for such sentiments were incompatable with Japan's alliance with Germany and Italy. At the same time, some policymakers and public figures also criticized race-war rhetoric on more idealistic grounds. This was, they declared, simply inconsistent with the high moral ideals for which Japan was fighting. Scholars associated with one of the most philosophical of Japan's nationalistic wartime groups, the Kyoto School (Kyoto Gakuha), for example, took care to stress this point.[3]

Such admonitions were easily ignored. On the surface, the situation Japan's leaders confronted may seem comparable to that faced by the Allies, who also feared that the war effort would be imperiled by crass rhetoric that treated the conflict as a struggle between whites and non-whites. In actual practice, the alliance between Japan and the European Axis was not as delicately balanced as that between the Anglo-American powers and China. In the latter case, there was a real possibility that the

Nationalist regime might crumble and be absorbed into the Co-Prosperity Sphere, with disastrous consequences to the Allied war effort in Asia. Thus, the explosion of anti-"yellow" sentiments in the West posed a real danger of alienating an already precarious ally.

There was no comparable danger in the Axis camp, where the alliance was purely expeditious from the start. While Germans such as Karl Haushofer and General Erich von Ludendorff admired Japan's racial homogeneity, its purely national religion, and its militaristic esprit, Hitler and most of his Aryan supremacists were embarrassed by their alliance with one of the *Untermenschen.* The Japanese humiliation of the British at Singapore actually appears to have caused the Führer considerable distress. The Japanese, in turn, had to purge their translations of *Mein Kampf* of the worst racial slurs, and engaged in a great deal of vacuous rhetoric to try to disguise the hollowness of their relationship with Germany. Privately, the Japanese—with conspicuous exceptions among die-hard fascists—often expressed contempt for their German allies (they appear to have generally ignored the Italians). Indian nationalists such as Mohan Singh reported that Japanese officers were contemptuous of the Germans and regarded them as but temporary allies. On a more anecdotal level, reports out of Batavia (Djakarta) in 1943 claimed that one of the most popular captured films among Japanese officers was Charlie Chaplin's satire of Hitler, *The Great Dictator.* Whether positively or negatively, Germany and the Germans did not have the hold over popular consciousness in Japan that China and the Chinese did in the United States. In any case, the Germans hardly cared what the Japanese thought about race issues; and there certainly was no danger that antiwhite sentiments in Japan might drive the Nazis into the arms of the Allies.[4]

The official prohibitions thus did little in practice to curb antiwhite rhetoric, which had a history extending back many decades. Since early in the twentieth century, Japanese patriots had turned the Yellow Peril ravings of the Westerners around and condemned the "White Peril" in Asia. *Read This and the War Is Won,* the booklet soldiers were given upon embarking for the southern areas, explicitly identified the enemy as the white Europeans and Americans. Japanese propaganda leaflets dropped over China declared in Chinese that "to liberate Asia from the white man's prison is the natural duty of every Asiatic! All of you Asiatics who have groaned under the yoke of the white man, unite!" A representative propaganda leaflet distributed in Malaya and Singapore similarly proclaimed that the Japanese had come to liberate local peoples from "many years of tyranny under white rule." Despite strict censorship at home, magazines regularly resorted to color-oriented invectives.[5]

Frequently, the color issue was raised in indignant diatribes which dwelt at length on the enemy's white supremacism. The Japanese were well informed about segregation and the lynching of blacks in the United States, for example, and the more blatantly racist statements of U.S. officials were invariably publicized. A notorious quotation of the latter sort which became well known in Japan came from a congressman who declared that if God had really intended the Japanese to rule Asia, He would have made them white. The Anglo-Americans, readers of one popular monthly were informed, "regard colored peoples as races meant to serve them like domestic animals."[6] In much the same vein, Osaka Puck, a wartime humor magazine, offered its readers excerpts from an imaginary notebook written by an American, which included such snippets as the following clumsy prayer: "That the world exists for the happiness of us Anglo-Americans is an unmistakable truth. Is not peace what occurs when all black men and yellow men serve us? Ah God! Has God fallen asleep? Amen."[7]

Despite such examples, however, references to "white people" did not dominate the rhetoric of wartime Japan, and color did not play the role in Japanese perceptions of the conflict in Asia that it did in the West. The grand white-yellow-black schemata which so dominated Western racist thinking simply did not work very well as a means by which to mobilize the Japanese and Asian sense of solidarity. Although the Japanese did occasionally refer to themselves as "yellow" or "colored," there was no rubric of "yellow supremacism" or "colored supremacism" comparable to white supremacism in the West. One reason this did not emerge undoubtedly was because the Japanese themselves looked down on all the other "colored" races. At the same time, intriguingly, they themselves had esteemed "whiteness" since ancient times—not only in an individual's complexion, but also as a more abstract symbol of purity.

The peculiar circumstances by which color connotations, skin pigmentation, and racial attitudes intermingled may be one of history's crueler jokes. As Herman Melville recounted so memorably in Moby Dick, in the chapter called "The Whiteness of the Whale," whiteness has many connotations in the Western tradition. It is by no means unambiguously good—but by and large, in popular usage, white is associated with pureness and cleanliness. Even where the association is more ambiguous, even ominous, white tends to carry an aura of mystery and power. At the same time, yellow is associated with unpleasant circumstances in the West (while black since ancient times has carried even more negative connotations). Yellow is the color of illness, especially jaundice; and from this comes an association with weakness and, by extension from physical weakness, cowardice. In traditional Christian painting, yellow was the color of treason; and in some places during the Inquisition, heretics were required to wear yellow clothing.[8]

In Japan also, white has been admired since ancient times. It is, to begin with, the color of purity. Thus, the Shinto priest, who performs the rites of purification, wears white robes. Whiteness or lightness of complexion is also associated with personal beauty as well as high social status, as the ancient literature and painting of the country make amply clear. From at least the Heian period (790–1185) on, the pale patrician has been idealized in Japan; and any reader of the eleventh-century *Tale of Genji* is aware of the scorn to which dark-complexioned individuals might be subjected. In the ancient society, heavy applications of cosmetics did the job, but the class and caste connotations of a fair complexion are obvious: dark-skinned people were the laboring class, who worked in the sun.[9]

In some writings of the early 1940s, examples can be found where the pigmentation of the Japanese is given positive emphasis. Usually, this was presented in a clinical way, however, in the context of listing those physical attributes which made the Japanese more capable of adapting to tropical climates than the Caucasians.[10] Far more common, however, was the tendency among Japanese to try to distance themselves physically from the "darker" peoples of Asia. One of the most compelling early examples of this can be found in the woodblock prints depicting the first Sino-Japanese War at the end of the nineteenth century. In these brilliantly colored graphics from the final decade of "reportage" through the woodblock medium, just before journalistic photography came on the scene, Japanese combatants—officers and enlisted men alike—were portrayed as essentially Caucasian figures: tall and fair-complexioned, with long, almost rectangular faces, and invariably dressed in Western garb. By contrast, the Chinese usually appeared in the prints as short, round-faced, yellow-skinned figures—bearing considerable resemblance, in fact, to the stereotyped caricature of the Oriental that Westerners loved to draw.[11]

Evidence that the Japanese continued to indulge in "Caucasianization" of themselves vis-à-vis other Asians during World War Two, even in the midst of all the rhetoric about Pan-Asianism, is available in numerous forms. Japanese servicemen dispatched to the southern theater, for example, were known to be reluctant to acknowledge that their skin color was the same as that of natives in the occupied territories; as a result, it is said, they fell into the habit of repeatedly emphasizing how sunburned they were.[12] Like pallid copies of the old Sino-Japanese War prints, Japanese cartoons during World War Two frequently depicted the peoples of southern and southeastern Asia as dark-skinned, while the Japanese standing among them were light. (The Japanese also delighted in cartoons depicting dark and thick-lipped blacks—South Sea islanders—who were essentially identical to the cannibal-like stereotypes found in the American popular media.)[13] Among pejorative clichés in the Japanese vocabulary were several which equated ugliness with Southeast Asians, and implicitly but unmistakably evoked the impression, again, of dark skin. About an unattractive Japanese woman, for example, it might be said that "she could be a beauty in the South Seas" (*Nanyō jya bijin*).[14]

There were other, less direct ways of appropriating whiteness, however. These involved internalizing the color, equating it with moral qualities, and transforming it into a more abstract ideal of brightness or radiance—brightness in the sense of purity, that is, and of an intensity unique to the Japanese race. At the same time, the Japanese also associated themselves with another color which carried highly spiritual connotations: red. A crude but vivid example of such color consciousness appeared in an editorial in the government-sponsored humor magazine *Manga* in March 1943. Picking up on the previously mentioned comment by an American congressman to the effect that if God had intended the Japanese to be leaders of Asia, He would have made them white, the magazine went on to observe that the god before whom such a stupid individual "made the sign of the cross" was indeed then an unfortunate deity. The sort of person who felt compelled to boast of his white skin in such a manner was obviously someone whose soul was completely black. On the other hand, the historic Buddha had been black-skinned. What mattered was not skin color but rather the color of one's spirit, and the color of the Japanese spirit was unmistakable. "Behold," the editorial enthused, "the red heart of the yellow Japanese!"[15]

In this instance, the writer may have become carried away by his metaphor (the editorial went on to talk about the enemy turning "green" when they beheld the red hearts of the Japanese). The color consciousness, however, was conventional. Indeed, the original Japanese translated here as "red heart" (*sekishin*) is a literal rendering of a common Japanese word composed of two ideographs whose dictionary definition is "true heart, faithful mind." A companion word in the lexicon of Japanese moral values is "sincerity" (*sekisei*), which similarly incorporates the ideograph for red (*seki*), and literally means "red truth." The equation of blood with the giving of life, and this in turn with sincerity, is straightforward, and the association of redness with sincerity thus seems quite natural. This is not peculiar to Japan; on the American side, we need only recall Stephen Crane's classic war novel *The Red Badge of Courage.* Yet such symbolism was surely more deeply ingrained on the Japanese side, and the impression was deepened by the visual richness of written Japanese. In Japanese, to read "sincerity" involves seeing an ideograph meaning "red" and intimating blood; and to encounter the ideograph for red, or the color itself, in turn evokes vague intimations of purity and sincerity in ways that simply do not occur in the alphabetic languages or the color perceptions of Europeans and Americans.

In the January 1942 issue of *Bungei Shunjū,* one of Japan's most popular middle-class monthlies, war with the Allied powers was greeted in racial terms that relied on much the same sort of abstract and color-suffused language.[16] The outbreak of the war, it was stated in an article entitled "Establishing a Japanese Racial Worldview," had clarified the Japanese character, whose basic traits were brightness, strength, and up-righteousness. These qualities made the Japanese "the most superior race in the world," and it followed that all the other countries and peoples of Asia should be assimilated into the Greater East Asia Co-Prosperity Sphere in accordance with their particular abilities. Under no circumstances was it appropriate to think in terms of "formal equality," since no one else could equal the "bright and strong" moral superiority of the Japanese. Thus, the legalistic liberal worldview of the European and American powers had to be replaced by a racial worldview emanating from Japan. And the foundation for this racial worldview, in turn, would necessarily be a level of "spiritual and physical purity" that the Japanese alone were capable of attaining.

This was the rhetoric of "proper place" that runs like a deep current through all Japanese discussions of their role as the "leading race," but the *Bungei Shunjū* article was unusually zealous in defining the metaphors which linked race, status, morality, purity, and color in the Japanese worldview. Thus, it went on to declare that national power could be born only from a "brightness that leaves no corner untouched," and spoke of the joyous state of unalloyed pureness that had marked the initiation of war with the Anglo-Americans. "Brightness," the article went on, was in and of itself an "active power"; it was purity, a creative "cleanliness of life." And this could be expressed in color terms as well. Here "Establishing a Japanese Racial Worldview" spoke of the melding of whiteness and redness in a most evocative way:

> The conception of purity associated with Shinto has been thought of hitherto as something pure white, as if it were something that had been thoroughly washed clean, like the white robes of a Shinto priest. The experience of the day the war broke out, however, has shown the error of such thinking; and this error is indeed apparent to those who have actually engaged in the rite of purification *(misogi)*. The color of purification is faint red, tinged with the pinkness of blood; it is the color of life itself. It is this very warmth of life which has made the cherry blossom the symbol of the Yamato spirit.

Passages such as this, as esoteric as they may seem at first glance, can serve as a magnet that draws together many scattered impressions that are associated with Japan at war. One thinks immediately, for example, of the Rising Sun flag as well as the ensigns of the Imperial Army and Navy, all of them red and white. Neither the Stars and Stripes nor the Union Jack can be said really to tap the depths of subliminal symbolism that is present in Japan's national emblems. The sun itself became a dominant presence in the Japanese imagery of war, in its whiteness, its brightness, or its redness. On the global maps which all Japanese schoolchildren came to know, the homeland almost invariably was colored red. The young pilots about to embark on suicide missions during the final year of the war live vividly in the mind's eye wearing white headbands with the red Rising Sun emblem; and like countless other civilian and military patriots, the kamikaze pilots were intimately associated with the cherry blossoms. The nationalism of the Rising Sun and the graceful falling of the cherry blossoms are fairly straightforward symbols, but to many observers, certainly in the West, the color connotations of the symbols—the whiteness of purity and redness of both blood and sincerity—may not have been so readily apparent.

Such intimations of purity were conveyed in countless other ways in Japan before and during the war. Ancient texts were ransacked to provide slogans for modern times, suggesting the unsullied survival of traditional and indigenous wisdom. Warships of the Imperial Navy took their names from the enduring verities of myth, nature, or the unforgotten past: from mythological objects or creatures (carriers); the names of ancient provinces (battleships); mountains (heavy cruisers and small battleships), rivers (light cruisers), weather in its more poetic guises (destroyers), and flowers, fruit, and trees (small destroyers, from 1944). As new places fell under Japanese control, they were rechristened with names which, again, frequently conveyed the impression of purity. Singapore, for example, was renamed Shōnan, or "Radiant South." As the *Bungei Shunjū* effusion reminds us, moreover, for many Japanese intellectuals and men of letters, the outbreak of war was perceived as a "cleansing" experience—an act which dispelled at a stroke the miasma of uncertainty that had hovered over the country for years. All-out war gave clarity to present and future tasks. It cleared the mind and lifted the individual to a higher plane of moral consciousness and behavior by dispersing selfish and materialistic preoccupations.[17]

The extent to which the ideal of purity and radiance penetrated popular consciousness in wartime Japan is also reflected with great consistency in popular songs. Although the Japanese lexicon of war included a fair range of invectives denigrating the enemy, such abuse rarely intruded upon the songwriter's world. There appear to be no Japanese counterparts to the racist lyrics that constituted a conspicuous strain in American songwriting during World War Two. In fact, Japanese songs of the late 1930s and early 1940s rarely mention the enemy by name at all (just as Japanese films rarely show them). Where allusion to the foe did occur, it was usually abstract: a simple reference to "the enemy" (*teki*), or, even more indirectly, an intimation of a darkness which was being dispelled by the light of Japan. The popular lyrics of these years are by no means all of a piece. Some are melancholy, some romantic, some comic and even satirical. Most, however, reveal an almost painfully self-conscious aspiration for transcendence, and are suffused with an aura of whiteness, brightness, and redness.

"Flowers of Patriotism," for example, which was popular in 1938, the year after the China Incident, gave four stanzas to four flowers: cherry blossoms on the slopes of "pure white" Mount Fuji, red plum blossoms in winter, crimson camellias, and "sparkling" chrysanthemums.[18] In 1942, right after the outbreak of global war, a patriotic song entitled "Divine Soldiers of the Sky" extolled parachute troops descending on the enemy like "pure white roses" from heaven.[19] A bittersweet and extremely popular tune of the same year, with no overt military connotations, was entitled "Pure Snow"; another rhapsodized about the "white lily of the valley" as the flower of dreams, love, and song—and, in its bell-like shape, a reminder of the limits of life.[20] In 1940, "2,600 Years Since the Nation's Founding," an officially sponsored song commemorating the anniversary of the founding of the nation by Emperor Jimmu, captured many of the prevailing visual images of transcendence with ornate and appropriately archaic lyrics about "the glorious light of Japan," "pure gratitude burning like a flame," "the glistening national power," and "the rising sun of everlasting prosperity."[21] "Praying in the Dawn," a rougher song from the war in China that also became popular in 1940, told of mountains and rivers "stained with the red blood of loyalty."[22] "Do You Leave Tomorrow?", composed in 1942, was a song of friendship that came to be sung at farewell parties for men departing for the front. The sorrow of parting was tempered here by the vision of the draftee as a "brave man of Yamato" who would be leaving on a noble mission "bathed in sunlight."[23] "Song of the Young Eagles," popular in 1943, eulogized young Navy pilots with "hearts like flaming jewels."[24] "Companion Cherry Blossoms" of 1944, which took its lyrics from a composition in a schoolgirls' magazine, perfectly epitomized this sentiment of ultimate transcendence. Here is the first of its four stanzas:

> You and I, companion cherry blossoms,
> Flowered in the garden of the same military school.
> Just as the blossoms calmly scatter,
> We too are ready to fall for our country.

So pervasive was this abstract, elegiac mood in the music world that at one point the molders of public sentiment deemed it necessary to toughen up patriotic spirit by encouraging more specifically anti-Anglo-American songs. Thus, in April 1943 a nationwide competition was announced for a "lively, sturdy tune" in march tempo. The prescribed title was "Down with Britain and America."[25]

Among its least significant accomplishments, the war revealed the Japanese to be inveterate slogan makers. Scarcely a week passed without several new exhortations or mottoes emanating from private as well as public quarters: Think as one; Act as one; Build a new Japan; Construct a new Asia; Remember that savings accounts mean tanks and guns; Practice frugality; Have large families; Support neighborhood associations; Beware of spies; and on and on. Many of these slogans are typical of the propaganda of any modern nation at war, but here too it is noteworthy that the Japanese exhortation to sacrifice was interwoven with, first, a sense of absolute solidarity epitomized in the recurrent phrase "the one hundred million" (*ichioku*)—a "transcendant" phrase in itself, since the population of Japan at the time was slightly over seventy million; and, second, the same sense of purity of purpose, again reflected most conspicuously in recurrent references to brightness. Like the wartime songs, the more formal Japanese slogans rarely mentioned the enemy by name. During the first eight months of the war, for example, one monthly magazine printed patriotic slogans in the margin of every page, but only one of these referred explicitly to the enemy—and that was a reference to Chiang Kai-shek.[26] The prevailing sentiment was conveyed in one of the most popular of all the wartime slogans, officially introduced to the Japanese public the day after the attack on Pearl Harbor: "One hundred million advancing like a ball of flame."[27]

This emphasis on collective as well as individual purity, so central to the Japanese sense of racial separateness and superiority, occurred at several distinct levels. To begin with, the Japanese portrayed themselves as being historically purer than other peoples genetically and morally— an assertion they buttressed with theories about the divine origins of the Yamato race.

The heritage of such celestial genetics, however, was neither absolute nor unassailable. Rather, it was portrayed as being a blessed but vulnerable legacy, subject to corrupting influences and requiring constant refinement and revitalization. Twentieth-century Japanese were told that their goal must be to attain a higher state of perfection and purity; or, as it was sometimes phrased, that the task of the present was to restore a past racial and spiritual purity largely lost in recent times. In the 1930s and early 1940s, this ideal was emphatically linked to the conduct of war: the Japanese were indoctrinated to see the conflict in Asia and the Pacific as an act which could purify the self, the nation, Asia, and ultimately the whole world. All Japanese were to participate in this process, not merely those on the battlefield; but the purest accomplishments, of course, entailed the greatest sacrifices, culminating in the supreme sacrifice of life itself. For the Japanese during World War Two, that is, the "sacrifices" of war were portrayed as being truly sacerdotal, a bath of blood becoming the supreme form of spiritual cleansing.

Like apostles of war in other nations and at other times, the Japanese often eulogized martial conflict in an extremely general and abstract way. A famous pamphlet published by the Imperial Army in 1934 described war as the father of creation and the mother of culture, and one of the fundamental tenets of the wartime Kyoto School of philosophers and historians was that the conventional dichotomy of war versus peace was fallacious. War, as this highly visible quartet of Kyoto Imperial University professors explained it, "is eternal," and should be recognized as being "creative and constructive." War was central to the ongoing historical process of "purification of sins"; it was correctly seen as being in itself "a philosophical struggle."[28] Such sentiments found zealous Japanese adherents even after U.S. bombers began to destroy Japan's cities. A huge *Study of Protracted War* prepared by the Total War Research Bureau of the Japanese cabinet in March 1945, for example, attempted to demonstrate with extensive historical data that war was constructive and protracted war inevitable—and, indeed, that protracted war required the thoroughgoing exercise of a nation's "unique racial power."[29]

Despite the general nature of such paeans to war, however, the Japanese invariably regarded them as applying to themselves alone. For all practical purposes, they nationalized and racialized purity, treating this ultimate ideal as if it could only be truly appreciated, and attained, by Japan and the Japanese. Thus, the report of the Total War Research Bureau moved almost imperceptibly from rational commentary on the nature of modern warfare to near-mystical effusions about the unprecedented spiritual potency of Japan's "imperial war." Neither this nor any other comparably important ideological tract of these years suggested that war could be simultaneously ennobling and purifying for the enemy. Quite the contrary was the case, for the enemy had no just or moral cause. And how then were Japan's antagonists to be viewed? As unclean and wrong-hearted men, as beasts, and ultimately—in the most prevalent Japanese idiom of all—as demons. In the final analysis, the Japanese dehumanized the Anglo-American enemy just as the enemy dehumanized them; but the conceptual roads taken to this end, the symbols juggled and vocabularies used, differed in many ways.

Of these various affirmations of a purity unique to the Japanese, the most simplistic rested on the argument that the Japanese were a homogeneous race who traced their origin, or at least the origin of their imperial line, back to the gods. No other people in the world could claim such divine descent. None were able to boast of such a wedding of blood and morality. The orthodox version of history which the Japanese government had adopted prior to World War Two—emphasizing the founding of the Japanese state in 660 B.C. by Emperor Jimmu, the direct descendent of the Sun Goddess—strongly encouraged this line of thinking. Blunter expressions of the same ideas were heard on the political hustings. "There are superior and inferior races in the world," Nakajima Chikuhei, a major industrialist and political party leader declared in 1940, "and it is the sacred duty of the leading race to lead and enlighten the inferior ones." The reason that Japan was "the sole superior race in the world," Nakajima went on, was twofold: the Japanese were pure-blooded, and they had descended from the gods. The Greater East Asia War was thus no ordinary conflict but rather a divine mission.[30] Many other such statements could be quoted, and needless to say they made their way into the anti-Japanese propaganda of the West, where they were presented as proof that the Japanese, like the Nazis, regarded themselves as a master race.[31]

It is difficult to know how seriously the mythohistorical explanations of the origins of the Japanese people and the imperial state were taken by the average Japanese, however, and easy to exaggerate the extent to which the thesis of divine origins was accepted as literal truth. Despite the government's intense indoctrination concerning Jimmu and the founding of the nation, the theory of biological evolution never became taboo in Japan, even during the war years. Scholars continued to publish on the subject, and evolution was taught in the public schools. Moreover, even while paying homage to Japan's "2,600-year history," serious researchers attached to the government accepted the argument that the Japanese were originally of mixed stock. Such academic considerations existed as a steady counterpoint to the mystique of Japan's divine origins.

A revealing illustration of how the Japanese handled scientific theories of evolution and the question of physical differences among races during this period of ultranationalism can be found in a collection of essays published for a popular audience in the spring of 1944 by a well-known anatomist, Professor Adachi Buntarō. The collection, entitled *Studies in the Physical Constitution of the Japanese People*, was a revised edition of a book originally published in 1928 and containing essays dating back to before World War One. The new edition included a short patriotic preface by the author condemning Europeans and Americans for conceitedness and arrogance concerning their own racial superiority, and claiming that publication of the author's own findings in German many decades previously had forced international academic circles to reconsider some of these discriminatory theories. It was his hope, Adachi declared, that republication of the essays would help boost Japanese pride in the midst of the war crisis and serve as one building block in the construction of a brilliant Greater East Asian culture.

Adachi's main thesis, however, was not that the Japanese or Asian races in general were superior, but rather that all races possessed relatively more or less developed physical characteristics, and absolute assertions of superiority were scientifically unfounded. In developing this argument, moreover, he offered (and left unrevised in the 1944 edition) a number of observations that were certainly less than complimentary to the Japanese and other Asians. Human beings, as Adachi described them for the general reader, were *Mammalia* like the apes, and could be usefully compared to the orangutan, gorilla, chimpanzee, and gibbon. Blood tests, he observed in an essay originally published in 1912, not only showed a relationship between humans and apes, but also revealed that certain races had a closer blood relationship to the apes than others. Specifically, Adachi found Malay blood to be closest to monkey blood in his limited test sample, Dutch blood to be most dissimilar, and Chinese blood to be somewhere between the two, and in fact closer to Dutch blood than to Malay. He did not offer blood-test results for the Japanese themselves. In a 1914 essay comparing the musculature and blood vessels of Japanese and Westerners, Adachi stated flatly that the Japanese were inferior. According to him, the British had the best muscle structure of all Westerners and the Russians the worst, being in fact closer to the Japanese than they were to other Europeans on this score. Adachi did not find cause for distress in this, but he was chagrined to have to report the "extremely dishonorable" fact that Negroes ("black slaves," in the ideographs he chose) were also superior to the Japanese in musculature. He sought to explain this away by suggesting that since most Negroes were actually half-breeds, their muscular superiority in all likelihood was a result of the European admixture.

The most clear-cut balance sheet offered by Adachi in comparing the physical attributes of the Japanese and Westerners appeared in an essay that was originally delivered as a lecture as early as 1907. There was no conspicuous difference in the brain weight of Japanese and Westerners, he stated; and since Japanese were on the average physically smaller than Westerners, the ratio of their brain weight to the rest of their body was comparatively higher. If one took the orangutan as the standard by which to measure the development of different races—relative "superiority" being indicated by greater departure from the apish norm—then in the overall picture the Japanese might be said to be slightly inferior to the Westerners, but in certain areas they demonstrated superior development. Physical features that placed the Japanese as a whole closer to the apes than the Westerners included shorter noses; protruding teeth; a higher incidence of a certain tiny cartilage in the corner of the eye; peculiarities of the upper-arm muscles, upper-breast muscles, and blood vessels; and a general tendency to underdevelopment of the female labia. The "superior" anatomical characteristics of the Japanese, on the other hand, were their relatively flattened forehead-to-nose profile (Adachi claimed to have discovered that the irregular profile of Westerners was closer to that of the apes); their shorter ratio of arm length to body length (longer Western arms again being more apish); their lack of a peculiar bone spur in the upper arm which Westerners and animals both possess; their relative lack of body hair; and their relatively mild body odor (he equated the body smell of Caucasians, and even stronger odor of Negroes, with animalistic sexual desires).

Although Adachi's findings may look outlandish today, the conclusion he drew from them is revealing. "While race A may be superior to race B in certain points," he emphasized, "in certain other respects race A may be inferior to race B. It can never be argued that race A is superior or inferior to race B in all respects."[32] An almost identical argument was offered in another popular book on racial issues that was also published in Tokyo in 1944. Readers of *A History of Changing Theories about the Japanese Race* by Kiyono Kenji were again reminded of the various physical features of the Japanese which Westerners commonly offered as proof of Japanese inferiority: relatively short stature, shorter and flatter noses, single-edged eyelids, protruding teeth, and the so-called "Mongolian blue spot" (a speckling found permanently in monkeys and temporarily in Orientals up to around the age of twelve, but rarely in Caucasians). As physical features which on the contrary placed the Europeans closer to monkeys and other animals than the Japanese, Kiyono offered this Adachi-esque list: "high" noses, hairiness, relatively long arms, lower brain-to-body-weight ratio, thick fingers, and strong body odor of the sort associated with the generative function in certain animals. Kiyono also reminded his readers of Westerners' preoccupation with skin color, and their use of proximity to whiteness as a evaluative code, under which the yellow races were more highly esteemed than the black simply because they were relatively lighter in pigmentation. If one carried Western thinking to its logical extreme, Kiyono suggested sarcastically, it would entail arguing that white rabbits were more advanced than black ones, and herons, on grounds of color alone, were superior to crows. On the contrary, it was necessary to recognize that all races had strong points and shortcomings. The great challenge was to bring the races of the world together in such a way that they supplemented and complemented one another.

From such idealistic sentiments, Kiyono proceeded to a romanticized portrayal of the Greater East Asia Co-Prosperity Sphere as a noble undertaking in which each race would be given its "proper place" and "suitable work" in accordance with its special qualities. He also emphasized the necessity of giving "superior races" special support, including encouragement in increasing their population. In this, he was perfectly consistent with official government policy, in which it was made clear that in the final analysis the most superior race was the Japanese, and the "proper place" of the Japanese was one of absolute leadership.[33]

The general theory of evolution was endorsed even in popularized science books directed to young readers during the war. A text entitled *Evolution of Life* that was published a year after Pearl Harbor, for example, informed young Japanese that virtually all reputable biologists accepted evolution. According to such teachings, the ancestor of all humankind was not a human being, and may well have been some kind of creature living in water. The human fetus, floating in its own fluid, seemed to be a reenactment of these ancient origins, and in many other ways as well the evolution of life appeared to be recapitulated in the human experience. Thus, the fetus was monkeylike, the first cry of the child was catlike, infants crawled like animals before walking, babies sometimes had tail-like protuberances when born, and the ability of humans to wiggle their ears suggested the persistence of an animal muscle. Many people found the notion of evolution from lesser creatures repugnant, the young readers were informed, and certainly much research remained to be done on the subject. Nonetheless, following Darwin, it seemed entirely natural to view such a development as honorable and deserving of pride, for it showed the human race to be advancing in a progressive and positive direction.[34]

Despite exposure to such theories, however, even well-educated Japanese did not hesitate to proclaim, like Nakajima Chikuhei, that Japan's destiny as the "leading race" in the world was divinely as well as genetically preordained. The government's doctrinaire teachings on this score were couched in vague and often extremely ambiguous language, and certainly gave great attention to cultural factors, but the orthodoxy unmistakably encouraged an assumption of inherent racial superiority. Thus, the widely disseminated gospel of official thinking about what it meant to be Japanese—*Cardinal Principles of the National Polity* (*Kokutai no Hongi*), issued by the Thought Bureau of the Ministry of Education in 1937— explicitly declared that the Japanese were "intrinsically quite different from the so-called citizens of Occidental countries," and went on to explain why they were at the same time superior to other Asians as well. What set the Japanese apart from all other peoples was an "original condition" that was comprised of a spirit of loyalty and filial piety inseparably wedded to veneration of the divinely descended sovereigns of Japan. Moreover, it was virtually impossible to describe this original condition without reference to the dominant quality of purity—the "pure and clear state of mind that belongs intrinsically to us as subjects," for example, or "our national character that is cloudless, pure, and honest." "Our nation has, since its founding," *Cardinal Principles of the National Polity* explained, "developed on the basis of a pure, unclouded, and contrite heart; and our language, customs, and habits all emanate from this source." To focus on the individual and the self, as was the practice in Western culture, led to "the corruption of true spirit and the clouding of knowledge." It created a heart that was "filthy and impure." To practice filial piety at a particularistic level, as was done in China and India, was commendable by contrast with Western immorality, but still fell woefully short of the transcendent expression of loyalty and filial piety that the Japanese had attained through identification with the "deity incarnate" who ruled them. The task of the moment for the Japanese was to bring forth the "clear, bright heart" within, which formed "the basis of our national spirit." And while this higher Japanese morality could and should be extended to other races and nations, the latter could only hope to assume their "proper place" and "appointed duties" under the canopy of Japanese virtue.[35]

Cardinal Principles of the National Polity drew upon the ancient writings of Japan to illustrate the divine descent of the imperial line and the recognition by wise men of yore of the superiority of the Yamato race. Because of these textual trappings, the tract can serve for the modern scholar as a little source book of racial and nationalist thinking in the premodern period. Thus, the emperor's mid-twentieth-century subjects were reminded that the fourteenth-century *Records of the Legitimate Succession of the Divine Sovereigns* (*Jinnō Shōtōki*) had opened with this proud and ringing declaration:

> Japan is the divine country. The heavenly ancestor it was who first laid its foundations, and the Sun Goddess left her descendants to reign over it forever and ever. This is true only of our country, and nothing similar may be found in foreign lands. That is why it is called the divine country.[36]

"The Inherent Character of the People," a key chapter in *Cardinal Principles of the National Polity*, began with a quotation from the seventeenth-century scholar Yamaga Sokō: "The Land of Japan stands high above the other nations of the world, and her people excel the peoples of the world." From the early-nineteenth-century nationalist scholar Fujita Tōko came a poem whose opening lines told how "The sublime 'spirit' of the universe / Gathers pure over this Land of the Gods."[37]

While *Cardinal Principles of the National Polity* went so far as to state outright that "our country is a divine country governed by an Emperor who is a deity incarnate," it did not claim that all of the Japanese people were originally of divine descent. Rather, it was suggested that in ancient times Japan had been peopled by divinely descended clans "of one blood and one mind" under the emperor, to whom subordinate groups of unrelated blood were affiliated. In time, however, all merged into one under the emperor.[38] In more popular renderings, the argument that the Yamato race as a whole was divinely descended was presented less hesitantly. For example, a text entitled *History of Japan* which was translated into English by one of the government's own tourism agencies in 1939 spoke of the "consanguineous unity" of the nation, and the emergence over the centuries of "a race of admirable tendencies" which was so thoroughly assimilated "that the imperial blood may be said to run in the veins of all Japanese, who have thus become kinsmen with one another, descended from a common ancestor." And who was that progenitor?

> That common ancestor, or ancestress, is Amaterasu Omikami [the Sun Goddess]. The relations between the Imperial House and the people today may therefore be likened to those between the trunk

and branches of a gigantic tree, for if we were to trace the genealogy of each Japanese subject, we would find that he belongs to a family which centuries ago was either a direct or an indirect offshoot of the Imperial Family. . . . In other words, the Imperial Family and the people having a common ancestor in Amaterasu Omikami, our sovereign and his subjects are completely united like one man to form the Japanese nation and state.[39]

Readers of the English-language *Japan Times and Mail* were treated to a similar argument on February 11, 1940, in a special edition commemorating the 2,600-year anniversary of the national founding. The paper described the anniversary as a watershed in the "racial history" of the Japanese people as they looked back on the heritage of the past and forward to the "promise of even greater attainments, a promise that is found in the deep consciousness of racial destiny that moves the soul of the race. . . ." When Emperor Jimmu founded the Japanese state 2,600 years earlier, the *Japan Times and Mail* explained, the land was inhabited by at least five different races. Jimmu declared that they should unite under "one roof," and in obedience to that command the races became "as brothers of one family."[40] Although the newspaper did not press the point, it was this same account of Jimmu extending his sway over the diverse peoples of ancient Japan, based on a passage in the earliest written chronicles of Japan, dating from the eighth century, which inspired Japan's World War Two slogan about the country's divine mission to bring all races and nations of the world under "one roof."

While official and semiofficial statements on these matters tended to be couched in an abstract vocabulary that even moderately well-educated Japanese sometimes found difficult to understand, the themes of racial solidarity, purity, and destiny also had a host of popular interpreters who expressed themselves in plainer language. A fair sample of the nonofficial approach was offered by the famous writer Tokutomi Iichirō in his 1944 book *A Citizen's Reader for Certain Victory.*[41] Tokutomi began by dismissing Darwin's theory of the origin of species as probably correct but not really relevant to current concerns. The history of mankind, he went on, offered the spectacle of a constant movement of humans from place to place, and it was a striking fact that of all the great peoples, the Japanese alone had remained in one place since earliest times, always under the emperor. No one could say for sure where the first Japanese came from. Scholars could not agree on the matter, and one might just as well take the accounts of the "Age of the Gods" in the ancient chronicles at face value. What mattered was that Japan had never been conquered in its long history. On the contrary, the "imperial virtue" had attracted other races to Japan and then completely absorbed them. The fact that Japan alone had survived like a great rock in the turbulent seas of history, one nation and one people, was proof that the country "did not exist only for itself, but rather for the two billion people of the world." Both Japan and the Japanese, state and people together, bore the heavy responsibility of being "the model, the pattern, the standard for the world." It was Japan's destiny "to lead the whole world along the path of virtue."[42]

Tokutomi went on to inform his readers about why the United States was unqualified to perform such a leadership role. The American people, he explained, derived from two primary strains of immigrants. One was the Puritans, who struggled mightily for their own freedom, but did not hesitate to oppress others in the process. The second and probably more dominant strain—a psychological "temper" really, as Tokutomi presented it—was made up of Anglo-Saxon pirates and adventurers who settled primarily in the South. Where the northern Puritan strain was self-righteously arrogant toward others, the southern pirate-adventurer strain was haughty and contemptuous. Each contributed, in its own way, to the contemporary ideology of "American as Number One." Tokutomi described how from an early date Americans had been internal imperialists, plundering and stealing the land from the native Indians as well as from earlier Spanish settlers. He also reported how in American eyes the Japanese were a contemptible "yellow race," who could be treated any way the Americans desired. As evidence of American contempt toward the Japanese, he called attention to the way even President Roosevelt referred to the Japanese as "Japs." As evidence of American hatred and inhumanity, he reminded his readers of a notorious photograph from the Pacific theater in *Life*, which they had already surely heard about from other Japanese sources as well. The photograph depicted a Japanese skull with a helmet on it, displayed on the turret of a tank.[43]

While the Americans were fighting to preserve their own luxury, Tokutomi declared, the Japanese were fighting for their very existence, for the liberation of Asia, and ultimately for the construction of a new global order. The three aims were like three concentric circles: Japan must first save itself, then Asia, but ultimately the whole world from the oppression of the English and the Americans. Tokutomi then moved on—his own argument more like a contracting rather than expanding circle—to an anti-Semitic tirade. While Americans spoke of government of, by, and for the people, he explained, in reality they practiced government of the rich, by the rich, and for the rich; and the *deus ex machina* behind this was the "evil and ugly plutocracy" of the Jews. Like most other Japanese polemicists, Tokutomi also drew upon the ritual language of Shinto purification ceremonies in describing the current conflict. "For the Japanese," he wrote, "the Greater East Asia War is a purifying exorcism, a cleansing ablution."[44]

Such acts of spiritual cleansing were important to the Japanese. As *Cardinal Principles of the National Polity* phrased it, while the "inherent character of the people" may have been a "pure and cloudless heart," in actuality this was an ideal from which the people as a whole had strayed. Thus, *Cardinal Principles* was only in part a self-congratulatory tract which identified the superior qualities of the Japanese; it was also a catechism of proper behavior, an exhortation to the Japanese people to "bring into being our original condition." While the war may have been described as a divine mission to spread the Imperial Way throughout the world, it was simultaneously perceived in Japanese ruling circles as a life-or-death engagement through which the Japanese themselves would hopefully recover a vanished state of moral excellence.

The most extreme statement of this may well have been a booklet published in February 1942 by the Imperial Rule Assistance Association (IRAA), the sprawling quasi-governmental political organ which absorbed all of Japan's legal political parties in 1940. Written by Professor Fujisawa Chikao of Kyoto Imperial University, the head of the IRAA Research Bureau, this document was made available in an English translation by the Japanese themselves under the imposing title *The Great Shinto Purification Ritual and the Divine Mission of Japan*.[45] Fujisawa began by explaining that the Japanese emperor (whom he repeatedly referred to by the exalted title Sumera Mikoto, or August Sovereign) embodied a cosmic life-force, and with impressive aplomb he went on to state that Japan (referred to as Sumera Mikuni, or the August Land) had been the true cradle of civilization in ancient times. Recent linguistic and archaeological evidence, Fujisawa declared, revealed the existence of a prehistoric "world-wide family system" in which Japan had been revered as the "parent land," while other countries (including Babylonia, Egypt, and China) were known as the "lands of children" or "branch lands." Among other acts of evidential legerdemain, Fujisawa suggested that the Sumerian civilization of ancient Mesopotamia took its name, and culture, from the August Sovereign, Sumera Mikoto.

Readers who staggered through these extraordinary assertions learned that individuals trained by the IRAA for work at home or abroad routinely underwent the ritual of purification by water (*misogi*). More importantly, these patient readers were informed that the key to the Japanese (and cosmic) spirit was the Ōharai or Great Purification Ritual performed twice annually by the emperor, and that the current war amounted to a struggle to rid the world of moral impurities such as individualism and its twin offspring, capitalism and Marxism. Within Japan too, many individuals, especially the young, were still in the grip of such false ideas.

The world system envisioned by Fujisawa and his IRAA sponsors would be a "fundamental vertical order," in keeping with the family model of "perfect concord and consummate harmony." Japan and the Japanese emperor naturally would be venerated as the family head of this global community, while other nations assumed their "due places." Given Japan's ancient role as the parent land and source of world civilization, moreover, it was not unreasonable to expect other peoples and cultures to eventually come to appreciate the "great justice" which Japan was now in the process of extending to the far corners of the world. Japan's holy war for the construction of a new world order might also awaken the sleeping memories in other cultures of their ancient debt to Japan. After all, Fujisawa observed, carrying his remarkable hypothesis to its logical conclusion, "It is very likely that similar rituals observed by the Chinese, the Hindus, and the Jews derive from the O-harai of Sumera Mikuni, the sacred motherland of all human races." Christians too would find intimations of the Great Purification Ritual in their own holy teachings, especially the writings of the apostle John in the New Testament.

While Fujisawa and kindred ideologues in such strategically situated places as the IRAA and the Ministry of Education were attempting to portray the war as a process of restoring ancient virtues and relationships, Fujisawa's colleagues at Kyoto Imperial University who were associated with the Kyoto School were taking a very different tack by arguing that Japan was engaged in a struggle to "transcend the modern" and create an entirely new world order. The Kyoto School scholars (Kōsaka Masaaki, Kōyama Iwao, Suzuki Shigetaka, and Nishitani Keiji) conveyed their views to the general public in a series of influential articles and roundtable discussions that began several weeks before Pearl Harbor and continued into 1943. Their line of argument was more abstract than Fujisawa's, and certainly more sophisticated; and with one singular exception noted below, it did not involve reliance on the evocative vocabularies of Shinto folk practices and the ancient Japanese classics. On the contrary, the Kyoto School dealt with such broad and amorphous concepts as "perpetual war" and "total war"; "living space" and "historical space"; the "eternal task of founding the state"; the "racial nation-state" as a creative subjective entity that transcended narrow nationalism and racism and became an agent of mediation between the past and the future; and the "nation-state race," which went beyond the common ties of land, blood, language, and religion to embrace as well moral energy and subjective self-awareness.[46]

For all their abstract theorizing, however—and despite acknowledged borrowing from such non-Japanese scholars as Leopold von Ranke —the Kyoto School also made it clear that the current conflict represented Japan's ascension as the leading "world-historical race." To them as to all other Japanese patriots, the war in Asia and the Pacific was a "holy war," and represented an unprecedented struggle for the attainment of a transcendent Great Harmony (Taiwa). This near-mystic Great Harmony, which lay at the core of the Kyoto School's theorizing, was reinforced from a different direction by the writings of Suzuki Daisetsu (D. T. Suzuki), who had already emerged as one of the best-known interpreters of Zen Buddhism to the West. Like his counterparts in the Kyoto School, Suzuki did not simply repudiate all Western influence. Instead, he devoted his attention to identifying an intuitive sense of harmony and "oneness" that he declared to be characteristic of Oriental thought. In a book written for general readers in 1942 and titled *Oriental "Oneness"* (*Tōyōteki "Ichi"*), Suzuki warned against national or cultural chauvinism, but went on to endorse Japan's attempt to take the lead in restoring the consciousness of oneness among the peoples of Asia. The Taiwa concept was also emphasized in *Cardinal Principles of the National Polity*, as well as in basic military texts such as the *Field Service Code* (*Senjinkun*) issued to all Japanese soldiers beginning in January 1941.

As used in these years of conflict, the ideal of a transcendent oneness or Great Harmony was the close conceptual counterpart to Fujisawa's Great Purification—and the fundamentally racial focus of this ideal was reinforced in a subtle, almost subliminal, manner. Because of the linguistic peculiarities of written and spoken Japanese, the two ideographs used to write Taiwa (大和) were also used to write Yamato, the site of the mythic founding of the imperial line by Emperor Jimmu and the most resonant of all designations for the Japanese people as a race. Indeed, Emperor Jimmu's name too (神武) carried a similar visual pun, being written with the characters for "god" and "martial arts" or "military affairs"—in effect, "divine military." It is entirely possible that many and perhaps even most Japanese never consciously dwelt on these associations. Subconsciously, however, they existed as ever-present messages that the race was identical with the highest ideals, and charged with a holy mission.[47]

Despite their intellectual abstruseness, treatises such as *Cardinal Principles of the National Polity*, *The Great Shinto Purification Ritual*, and the writings and discussions of the Kyoto School had a large audience in wartime Japan. Over two million copies of *Cardinal Principles of the National Polity* were published and the text was required reading in the schools, while one of the major forums for the Kyoto School was the mass-circulation monthly *Chūō Kōron*. If the average Japanese citizen had been asked what "purification" meant during these years, however, he or she undoubtedly would have answered in less abstract terms. At the everyday level, purification was understood to mean (1) expunging foreign influences, (2) living austerely, and (3) fighting and, if need be, dying for the emperor.

The first of these prescriptions was the simplest, involving a catalog of proscribed "Western" influences ranging from products in the marketplace and popular cultural fashions such as jazz and Hollywood movies to "dangerous thoughts." The single most corrupting feature of Western thought was identified as being preoccupation with the self, or the individual, as opposed to the larger collectivity. From this egocentrism and individualism stemmed most of the ills of the modern age: utilitarianism, materialism, capitalism, liberalism, socialism, and communism among them. Innumerable public and private statements of the sort already encountered explained the rationale for purging Japan of these degenerate and corrupting influences,[48] but no source captures the popular level of the campaign more concisely (or has been more neglected by academics) than wartime cartoons.

For example, a December 1941 *Osaka Puck* cartoon portrayed advertising figures associated with Japanese products holding their ground in the marketplace while a variety of Western products were sent scurrying, among them movies and phonograph records, automobiles, Lipton tea, Lucky Strike cigarettes, and Coty perfume.[49] One lighthearted rendering of the cleansing theme, as literal as can be imagined, had a woman's bathwater being warmed up by burning pictures of Western movie stars. Another offered a housewife vigorously wielding a broom to sweep away a pile of Hollywood characters including Popeye, Mickey Mouse, and Charlie Chaplin.[50] In another issue of *Osaka Puck,* early in 1942, a soldier drawn in the heroic mode also wields a broom as he strides out of Japan into greater Asia, sweeping Uncle Sam and John Bull off the globe.[51] Another version of the same theme portrayed Japan and Asia sweeping the world clean of liberalism and democracy while a Nazi figure looked on approvingly in the background; the caption stressed that this cleansing was creating a "new world order."[52] A simpler graphic rendering of the cleansing of Asia represented Japan as a gigantic roller-type blotter removing the dirty spots of the Western presence from the map.[53]

Many cartoons also depicted the purge of Western ideas. Typically, animated books with *Liberalism, Democracy, Anarchism, Communism,* and similar titles on their spines are sent scurrying.[54] In one unusually harsh rendering, kimono-clad figures with the faces of Roosevelt and Churchill were pinned like insects to a tome entitled *Anglo-American Thought.*[55] A graphic rendering in *Manga* in May 1942 was virtually comprehensive in its depiction of unclean influences, and certainly original in its chosen image. It personified Japan as a woman combing her hair and shaking out the dandruff of Anglo-American influences: extravagance, selfishness, hedonism, liberalism, materialism, individualism, worship of money, and Anglo-American thoughts in general.[56] Another cartoonist introduced the notion that the English language itself was unclean and polluting by drawing a student speaking English into a rubbish bin. His mother stands by with a container of salt, the traditional purgative agent in Shinto rituals, to purify the spot.[57] A droll variant on the same theme was recounted after Japan's surrender by a man recalling the wartime rationing of cigarettes. He managed to get enough smokes by rolling his own, using a page from his pocket English-Japanese dictionary for each cigarette. Not only did the thin paper make for a good smoke, he said, but it made him feel that every puff was a patriotic puff.

The last anecdote offers a reminder that many Japanese were capable of taking the heavy dosages of wartime indoctrination with a grain of salt (as it were). It also points to the second aspect of the war experience that Japanese intellectuals and ideologues attempted to turn into a "purifying" experience: the material deprivation which the average Japanese had to endure. There can be no question that many, probably most, citizens simply accepted material deprivation as inescapable and attempted to make the best of a hard situation. "Extravagance," trumpeted one of the government's favorite slogans long before Pearl Harbor, "is the enemy." More popularly, the saying was simply that every day was a work day. Like the soldier and sailor, every citizen was now on constant call, and after Pearl Harbor the militarization of civilian life was lightly symbolized by transferring a slogan about the Imperial Navy to the populace as a whole. The phrase was originally the title and refrain of a popular song of 1940 about life in the navy, where there were no longer weekends or days of rest. Rather, the seven days of the week now consisted of "Monday, Monday, Tuesday, Wednesday, Thursday, Friday, Friday."[58]

In the Western idiom, this might be called a Spartan existence or referred to by such phrases as "tightening one's belt." In Japan, however, a concerted attempt was made to elevate such self-denial and self-control into morally pure qualities which set the Japanese apart from all others. One of the government's more restrained propaganda organs, the English-language monthly *Contemporary Japan,* for example, regularly included essays that touched in one way or another on what such purity entailed. Thus a 1943 essay by Hasegawa Nyozekan, a well-known critic, identified the essence of the Japanese character as being an inbred capacity for "emaciated endurance," conveyed in the phrase *yase-gaman.* This, Hasegawa declared, was the core of the samurai spirit; it was both a moral ideal and a pragmatic force; and its uniquely Japanese symbolic expression was to be found in the Shinto act of *misogi,* or ablution with water, a ritual representing the attainment of both mental and bodily purification. "Emaciated endurance" was a positive attitude contrary to the "negative character of mental endurance" found in the religion and philosophy of India, China, and Greece. In a phrase very popular in Japan's wartime English-language propaganda, it was the essence of Japan's "virile national mentality"—a notion also sometimes rendered as "racial virility." Hasegawa wrote in the same vein for Japanese audiences, and elsewhere went on to point out that Japan was also distinctive in that its virile qualities penetrated all classes of society. A less abstract and more personal expression of such sentiments came from the poet Takamura Kōtarō, who told acquaintances he was able to reconcile himself to the war situation only after he had come to recognize how hardships could purify his mind and soul. Once he had awakened to this fact, even living through the bombings of Tokyo became a positive—indeed, elevating—experience.[59]

If material sacrifices could simultaneously purify the individual and the Japanese race as a whole, then it followed that near-perfect purity could be attained by the ultimate sacrifice of all, the offering of one's own life. In the ancient folk tradition, death had been the supreme defilement, and one of the early passages in the first written mythohistories of Japan portrays the god Izanagi bathing himself after beholding the putrefying body of his dead spouse. Once war and dying well became established as honorable practices, however, death assumed connotations of purity and transcendence, and the ablution that purified could be the bath of blood itself. The falling cherry blossom was a traditional symbol of this; and in 1943, as the tides of military fortune shifted against them, the Japanese leadership introduced a dramatic new phrase which had the effect of graphically presenting mass deaths in combat as an act of collective purification.

The new expression was coined in the aftermath of the battle of Attu in the Aleutians in May 1943, where twenty-five hundred Japanese soldiers fought to virtually the last man against an American force that outnumbered them five to one. It was reported in the West that the Japanese defenders charged the Americans screaming such incredible lines in English as "Japanese drink blood like wine!"; and a poem found on the body of one Japanese casualty was later translated as reading, "I will become a deity with a smile in the heavy fog. I am only waiting for the day of death." Attu stunned Westerners by its spectacle of Japanese fanaticism, and was used by many of them as proof of the irrational and subhuman nature of the enemy. Thus, *Time* magazine gave its coverage of the battle the headline "Perhaps They Are Human," and concluded with the statement that nothing on Attu indicated that this was the case; the article was reprinted under the same title in *Reader's Digest*. [60]

While Westerners were portraying the Japanese at Attu as dying like rabid animals at bay, the Japanese leadership reached into the Chinese classics for an expression that would convey the transcendent moral quality of such sacrifice. What they came up with was a stunning phrase, *Attu gyokusai*—*gyokusai* being a word composed of two ideographs that literally meant "jewel smashed." The expression derived from a line in the sixth-century Chinese history *Chronicles of Northern Ch'i*, where it was stated that on matters of principle, the man of moral superiority would break his precious jade rather than compromise to save the roof tiles of his home. After the war, a former officer in the Japanese Imperial Army recalled how moved he and others had been when the government introduced this phrase to describe their fallen comrades. No one thought of the dead as having suffered a defeat, he said; rather, it simply seemed "as if their spirits had been further purified."[61]

Gyokusai was not a familiar word at the time it was introduced, but it quickly became part of the daily lexicon of war, understood to mean choosing to die heroically in battle rather than surrender, or, more simply, choosing death over dishonor. As the war situation worsened and the military turned to increasingly desperate tactics, other symbolic equations of self-sacrifice and purity were introduced. The suicide units known collectively as the Special Attack Forces (Tokkōtai) were created near the end of 1944, and virtually every act in which they engaged in one way or another connoted purity. The falling cherry blossom became the best known symbol of the young flyers, appearing in their poems, their songs, their farewell letters, and in the hands of the virgin schoolgirls who assembled to see them off on their final missions in the spring of 1945. The first Special Attack Forces unit, formed in the Philippines, took the name Divine Wind (Shimpū; or, more popularly in the West, kamikaze), and was divided into four groups whose names all derived from this seventeenth-century poem: "The Japanese spirit is like mountain cherry blossoms, radiant in the morning sun." In addition to their white Rising Sun headbands and white scarfs, the pilots often wore white *senninbari* or "thousand-stitch belts," long strips of cloth in which one thousand women had each sewn a stitch—and thus, symbolically, joined the men as they sacrificed themselves. They donned clean clothes for their last flights, and some units drank a ritual cup of water as a further act of purification. Vice Admiral Ōnishi Takijirō, with whom the idea of the Special Attack Forces originated, often inscribed this line when asked for a sample of his fine calligraphy: "The purity of youth will usher in the Divine Wind."[62]

In a poem published on the front page of the *Asahi* newspaper, the well-known poet Hino Ashihei likened the self-sacrificing Tokkōtai pilots not to cherry blossoms but to "fire-arrow deities" sacrificing their lives to cleanse a polluted world, and as early as December 1944 the populace as a whole was exhorted by officials and the press alike to think of themselves as a collective suicide unit. *Ichioku Tokkō*, the new slogan went: "the hundred million as a Special Attack Force."[63] In the spring of 1945, after the United States had initiated the policy of low-level saturation bombing of Japan's urban centers, the *gyokusai* phrase too was extended to embrace every man, woman, and child of the Yamato race. Beginning around April, a new slogan appeared: *ichioku gyokusai*, "the shattering of the hundred million like a beautiful jewel."[64] The supreme sacrifice and ultimate state of purification, by this terrible logic, had finally come to mean readiness to embrace extermination.

◄ **C H A P T E R   9** ►

THE DEMONIC OTHER

Since ancient times, consciousness of purity and pollution combined with other attitudes within Japanese society to shape in-group
behavior toward outsiders or strangers. Professor Yamaguchi Masao has
gone so far as to argue that in the eyes of Japanese villagers until the mid-
nineteenth century, there really existed "only two major categories of
people: the insider and the outsider." At the same time, however, outsiders themselves were ambiguous figures, for usually they were believed to
possess both beneficent and malevolent powers. The stranger or outsider
might have skills pleasing or valuable to the community and be the
harbinger of good fortune in general, but he or she could equally well be
the bringer of calamity, the bearer of evil.[1] Although such attitudes
developed as ways of buttressing intimate in-group consciousness within
Japan, thereby contributing to the development of a highly fragmented
and compartmentalized society, they also came to operate on a larger scale
whereby the Japanese saw themselves collectively as insiders, while non-
Japanese assumed some of the ambiguous roles traditionally associated
with the stranger.

   Whether viewed as a bearer of blessing or misfortune, the outsider
usually was ascribed mystical and supernatural powers which specialists in
Japanese folk religion often relate to the traditional perception of the gods
as possessing a dual nature—a gentle spirit (*nigitama*) as well as a violent
spirit (*aratama*). Within this frame of reference, outsiders might be associated with kindly "visiting gods" (known as *marebito* in ancient times).

Equally, or perhaps even more often, however, they were equated with animal spirits or demonic forces—foxes or badgers in human form, vengeful ghosts (*goryō*), goblins, ogres, and the like. The malevolent or demonic being was explicitly associated with pollution and danger, and exorcised in a variety of ritual ways. In addition, Japanese folk beliefs also related threats from outside (such as epidemics or other calamities) to alien forces within the community—much as the crisis of the 1930s and early 1940s would be equated with both external enemies and internal corruption by foreign influences.[2]

Complex discriminations between insiders and outsiders were hardly peculiar to folk beliefs and rural society, however. From early times in Japan's towns and cities, there existed exclusive groups based on blood ties (the *uji* clans) as well as occupations (the *be* "corporations"). The seventh-century law codes distinguished between "good people" (*ryōmin*) and unfree "base people" (*senmin*), while a millennium later the seventeenth-century feudal authorities attempted to define a frozen four-tier society composed, from the top down, of the ruling samurai class, peasants, artisans, and merchants (the so-called *shi-nō-ko-shō* hierarchy). The class arrogance of the ancient ruling elites was vividly expressed by the Heian court nobility's designation of itself as the "good people" (*yoibito*), as opposed to the common, ill-bred riffraff. Within the elites, further insider-outsider distinctions were drawn on the grounds of kinship and pseudokinship, factional or feudal affiliation, place of origin or geographic base of power, and other bonds of common identity.[3]

A formal caste system also contributed to the complex patterns of insider and outsider identification that existed in traditional Japan. The "base people" of the seventh-century codes evolved over the centuries into a diversified spectrum of legally stigmatized hereditary outcastes, many of whom were collectively identified from around the ninth century as "nonhumans" (*hinin*). Included among these medieval outcastes were intinerent priests, shamans, diviners, troubadours, entertainers, and certain artists and craftsmen—all of whom possessed conspicuous skills and in one way or another filled the role of the liminal or socially marginal "strangers" who were believed to embody both constructive and destructive forces. Another general group of pariahs was composed of individuals more directly associated with impurity and pollution, such as butchers, tanners, leatherworkers, falconers, executioners, undertakers, caretakers of cemeteries, and even the makers of footwear and straw matting (both of the latter being associated with dirt).[4] Some anthropologists argue that since ancient times the Japanese imperial house also has represented a force "outside" the society as a whole, with ambiguous symbolic connotations that conform to the classic pattern of the stranger and even the outcaste. In this analysis, both the myth cycles concerning the origins of the imperial line and the actual manipulation of the imperial symbol over the centuries reveal elements of disruption as well as stability and order —or, as Professor Yamaguchi puts it, "both demonic force and the authority of kingship."[5]

Such observations reveal a traditional society, and even a traditional mythology, that was far less harmonious and homogeneous than the romanticized picture offered by the propagandists of the war years. While modern communications helped foster a sense of national identity in the period that followed the overthrow of the feudal regime in 1868, moreover, the process of accelerated industrialization and diversification simultaneously created innumerable new social compartments and cleavages. In the process, many of the traditional attitudes toward strangers, outsiders, and "others" in general that divided the Japanese among themselves were perpetuated or transformed.

The structures of discrimination between Self and Other, or core group and outsiders, which have long characterized relationships among the Japanese proved to be readily transferrable to the European and American foreigners. Like the outsiders of the folk beliefs, Western imperialists who intruded so abruptly on Japan in the mid-nineteenth century were ambiguous strangers who brought gifts and danger simultaneously. They could be (and were) viewed, virtually at one and the same time, as humans, as gods or at least creatures with superior powers, and as a demonic and menacing presence. In the metaphoric language and iconography of World War Two, the demon or devil was in fact probably the most popular Japanese characterization of the English and American enemy. It is important, however, to keep in mind the alternative and more positive faces and facets of the outsider as well, for otherwise the abrupt dissolution of Japanese hatreds after the war ended is almost incomprehensible.[6]

At the same time, when it came to stereotyping the enemy in World War Two the Japanese also had a limited but colorful vocabulary of more explicitly antiforeign appellations upon which they could draw. The same eighth-century writings in which the myth of Emperor Jimmu was recounted also told of the suppression by the early imperial rulers of "barbarians in far-off places"—tribes variously identified as the Ebisu, Emishi, Ezo, and Kumaso. ("Ebisu," incidently, is a good example of the god-demon ambiguity, being both the name of the god of wealth and of a purportedly savage tribe).⁷ It was in the late-eighth-century campaigns against these peoples that the title shogun—literally "barbarian-quelling great generalissimo" (*seii tai shōgun*)—first appeared, later to be appropriated by the feudal leaders of the country between the late twelfth and the mid-nineteenth centuries. The ideograph for "barbarian" (*i*) in "barbarian-quelling great generalissimo" was the same as that used to designate the Ebisu, and in the nineteenth century it was applied to the Westerners who were knocking on Japan's closed doors, as seen in the famous rallying cry "Expel the barbarians" (*jōi*).

The first strangers from the West whom the Japanese encountered were not the nineteenth-century imperialists, but Portuguese and Spanish seafarers and clergy in the mid-sixteenth century. It was believed for a while that they came from Tenjiku, an old name for India which had connotations of being a remote and heavenly land (*ten* is written with the ideograph for heaven). Their best-known early name, however, linked their arrival from the south with less-than-heavenly characteristics: they were called the "southern barbarians" (*nanbanjin*). This name, which became associated with a whole genre of painting portraying European subjects, especially on folding screens (the *nanban byōbu*), was borrowed directly from the Chinese classics, where the ancient Middle Kingdom was said to be surrounded by barbarians in all four directions, north, east, south, and west. These early Western intruders were indeed welcomed by many Japanese as men bearing material and spiritual gifts, but like the ambiguous stranger of folk tradition they were at the same time rumored to practice witchcraft and black magic. They could control the weather, it was said, and make grass and trees wither at a touch. Outsiders themselves, they attracted outcastes to them—beggars, lepers, and other "base rabble"; and with their occult arts, they reportedly made them clean and well again. They could also, the rumors went, perform acts of sheerly exuberant magic: turn towels into horses, dust into flowers, mud into jewels.⁸

As fear of this first wave of European intruders mounted in Japan, the demonic persona was pulled more sharply to the surface. Thus, it was said that the Christian missionaries upset proper relations between man and woman, parent and child, elder and younger, and thereby turned this world "into the Realm of Beasts." They practiced "demonic trickery," a Zen Buddhist priest declared. Hayashi Razan, the famous Confucian tutor to the Tokugawa shoguns, castigated them as "shrike-tongued monsters," while a late-seventeenth-century tract described the place that the southern barbarians came from as "a land of beasts who merely look human." The most lively and unrestrained anti-Christian polemic from this first tragic encounter between Japan and the West was a popular illustrated chapbook entitled *Tale of the Christians (Kirishitan Monogatari)*, which was published in 1639 and is doubly interesting in retrospect—for it would not really have been entirely out of date in the early 1940s. When the first trading ship of the southern barbarians arrived in Japan, this polemic began, an extraordinary creature disembarked from it, looking partly like a human but more like a combination of a long-nosed goblin (*tengu*) and a certain giant demon worshiped by mountain ascetics (Mikoshi Nyūdō). The creature's nose was like a conch shell. Its eyes were as big as spectacles, but all yellow where they should have been white. It had claws on its hands and feet, and teeth longer than a horse's. It was over seven feet tall, and black all over—except for the nose, which was red. Its voice was like the screech of an owl. All Japanese who saw it agreed that this was the most terrifying demon imaginable. It was, it turned out, a creature called a Christian padre.[9] It was also, we can say in retrospect, a ludicrous creature, meant to evoke derisive laughter as well as terror. This touch too, what in modern times would be called the element of burlesque, was also conspicuously present in Japanese caricatures of the enemy in World War Two.

The clawed hand, a subtle mark of the beast that proved popular among Japanese cartoonists in World War Two, emerged in other Japanese accounts of the first Europeans. Among the apocrypha that became attached to the Jesuit superior Alessandro Valignano, for example, was that he rode horseback standing in the saddle, hypnotized birds in the trees, and lit his tobacco by striking fire from his own claws. More sobering, however, were the accounts of atrocities by these Europeans. Converts to Christianity, it was said, were soon initiated into the practice of self-flagellation, and lacerated themselves until they were drenched in blood. Worse, the missionaries ate children, and disemboweled dying people to extract poisons from their bodies.[10] Such accounts were, of course, a mixture of truth and fantasy, for some Christians did practice self-abuse, and the Church outside Japan did subject heretics to torture and execution. In Japan itself, however, it was the Christian missionaries and converts who were heretics and were subjected to persecution, torture, and execution. The issue of atrocities was thus present on both sides from the earliest contacts between Japan and the West.

With the exception of a small Dutch enclave on the artificial island of Deshima in the harbor of Nagasaki, the Europeans were expelled from Japan in the 1630s and the feudal authorities adhered to a strict policy of seclusion for over two centuries. During these years of isolation, various other characterizations of the white strangers were nurtured. The Westerners were known as "red hairs" (kōmō, or kōmōjin), for example, and the prevalence of beards among them also led from an early date to their being called "hairy foreigners" (ketō, or ketōjin), another term which suggested the mark of the animal. The fact that after long sea voyages the foreigners stank did nothing to dispel these animal associations; and their fatty diets perpetuated the impression that, judging by smell alone, they approximated the animals. During the Tokugawa period, it was widely said of the Dutch that they were exceedingly tall and big-nosed, with odd eyes and doglike feet that did not touch the ground in back (which was why they wore wooden heels on their shoes). They had blunt penises like dogs, were as lascivious as dogs, and lifted their legs like dogs when urinating. Even Hirata Atsutane, a passionate nationalist scholar of the early 1800s who called attention to the superior scientific skills of the Dutch, gave credence to such dehumanizing reports.[11]

The designation "barbarian," which had been codified in the term nanbanjin, continued into the final centuries of feudal rule under the Tokugawa shoguns, although alternate ideographs for ban, or barbarian, were used. In the first, abortive century of contact, Christianity had been known as "the barbarian sect" (banshū).[12] In the Tokugawa period (1600–1868), Western studies were sometimes known as "barbarian studies" (bangaku), and the central government's own bureau for translating Western books was called the Barbarian Works Investigation Bureau (Bansho Shirabesho). In the turbulent years after 1853, when Commodore Matthew Perry forced the Tokugawa regime to open Japan's doors to the West, dissident samurai rallied under the slogan "Revere the emperor, expel the barbarian." Since the shogun had failed to live up to his title and quell the incursion of new American and European barbarians, he was fair game for being deposed; and so it happened, with a surprising minimum of violence, in 1868. In the midst of all the rhetoric that surrounded the overthrow of the ancien régime, a variety of fairly original slurs were attached to the Western imperialists. Aizawa Seishisai, for example, one of the best known of the mid-nineteenth-century ideologues, declared that cosmology proved that Japan resided at the center of the universe, while Western countries were peripheral and palsied.

"Today," exclaimed Aizawa, "the alien barbarians of the West, the lowly organs of the legs and feet of the world, are dashing about across the seas, trampling other countries underfoot, and daring, with their squinting eyes and limping feet, to override the noble nations. What manner of arrogance is this!"[13]

What manner of arrogance this was became clear in time; and in responding to the twentieth-century foreign challenge, the Japanese fell back on some of the basic patterns of identifying strangers and outsiders just described. There was nothing in their tradition identical to the concept of the "savage" that had emerged in the West beginning with Columbus at the very end of the fifteenth century. "Barbarian" was a term borrowed from China, and the Japanese had no genuinely visceral sense of primitivism or of wild men. The Japanese storehouse of language differed in other notable ways as well. There were no brutal, dominant metaphors comparable to the apish stigmata, and no metaphors of the hunt that came naturally to the whole male population and could be easily transferred to the killing of humans. In fact, during World War Two the Japanese use of caricature in the animal or reptilian mode appears to have been almost entirely random. It is true that Japanese pilots were called eagles in songs and slogans; and it is hardly happenstance that the greatest Japanese fighter plane, Mitsubishi's Zero, was known as the Mitsubishi Eagle. It even became a cliché to describe Japanese pilots dispersing the enemy as eagles swooping down on a flock of sparrows.[14] No one, however, would have pointed to the eagle as a basic symbol of the Japanese fighting man (it was, of course, America's symbol, as the lion was Britain's and the bear Russia's). In a similar way, Japanese cartoonists sometimes depicted India or Burma as elephants trampling the British colonists or the ABCD powers. This was a natural representation for southern Asia, but had a larger, patterned significance only in an oblique and surely subconscious way—in that the elephant was seen as a tamed creature, understood to be responsive to Japan's bidding.[15]

The Anglo-American enemy flitted from bird to beast form, reptile to worm. A cartoon early in the war depicted the British and Americans in southern Asia as an alligator and a serpent respectively. Another had them as grubs—with Churchill's and Roosevelt's faces, no less—being plucked from the flowering bush of Asian prosperity by Prime Minister Tōjō, while Japan's Axis partners looked on approvingly. Elsewhere, the

United States was depicted as a *kappa,* or water imp, with "Democracy" written on its back, futilely trying to defy the sun; or a grotesque frog adrift in the sea, again under a blazing Japanese sun; or an octopus with gunlike tentacles menacing the Pacific; or a beached whale (with Roosevelt's face), dead from having tried to digest the world. In mid-1942, two fish bearing the faces of the British and American leaders were grilled by a cartoon housewife over the caption "One hundred million as a ball of fire," a homey and rather unexpected twist on the famous slogan. An American who lived in Hayama prior to the war (where children threw pebbles at him while yelling "foreign devil") recalled lounging on the beach and eavesdropping on the conversation of his high-class Japanese fellow bathers, who were discussing his sickly white coloring and comparing him to a squid.[16]

In his diary for February 1943, the critic Kiyosawa Kiyoshi noted that some newspapers had adopted a new way of referring to the American and British enemy, whereby the former was now designated by three ideographs that could be read *Mei-ri-ken* ('merican) and literally meant "misguided dog." The British emerged from the same lexiconic revision in a rendering of *An-gu-ro* (Anglo) that made them look "dark-stupid-foolish." Earlier, following Japan's victory at Singapore, it was the British Navy that was ridiculed as a "once-bitten stray dog," yapping as it turned tail and ran away. Where apishness was concerned, educated Japanese were capable of cleverly turning the tables. Thus, several Westerners reported before the war challenging Japanese acquaintances concerning the myth of the divine descent of the Japanese race, only to be told: We know from where we come, and we understand you have your own theories concerning your own evolution. This was upper-class wit, however. The apish stigmata had no significant place at the popular level.[17]

One of the rare occasions when Japanese cartoonists did portray the enemy as an ape involved not English or Americans but Chiang Kai-shek, who was depicted as a gorilla on a leash held by Churchill.[18] Poor Chiang (who was usually depicted simply as a gaunt, battered figure covered with bandages) also appeared in one political cartoon as a trapped rat, and in another as a donkey being ridden by the imperialists. In a huge cartoon published the month after the outbreak of World War Two in Asia, Japan was depicted as a scorching sun driving off the ABCD powers. Here America was a fleeing thug whose jeweled crown (marked "J," presumedly for Jews) was falling off; Britain was a sprawling, cigar-chewing figure clutching a dagger; and the Dutch were but a wooden shoe flying through the air. China alone, however, was singled out for the subtle mark of the beast, being a figure with Chiang's face and a short, stubby tail.[19]

Not only was the use of specific animal imagery by Japanese cartoonists sparse, random, and bland, but even where used it tended to be highly personalized. The creatures chosen to represent the enemy, that is, more often than not bore Roosevelt's face, or Churchill's, or Chiang's—quite in contrast to the thoroughly depersonalized and dehumanized graphic images of the Japanese which flooded the media in the United States and Britain. At the same time, however, both verbally and pictorially the Japanese did use three highly generalized kinds of images for the Anglo-American enemy: that of beastliness in general; of monsters, demons, or devils; and of fellow—but deranged or degenerate—humans. Where these general references occurred, they were often accompanied by specific allusions to English or American oppression of other races or to atrocities in battle.

In a remark that has since been widely quoted, the novelist Dazai Osamu greeted the news of Pearl Harbor with the jubilant declaration that he was "itching to beat the bestial, insensitive Americans to a pulp." The outburst is of interest not simply because it was made by this famous writer, but because in one form or another it was said by so many Japanese. As a typical overseas radio broadcast of the war years put it, in words often heard and presumedly widely believed in Japan, the Americans were "nothing but brutes, wearing the mask of humanity." At the end of 1942, some sectors of the Japanese printed media endorsed the thesis of the enemy as beast in an ingenious way that was once again peculiar to the ideographic writing system: to the usual characters for America (米) and Britain (英), they added a conventional "radical," or part, denoting bestiality (犭). Thus, America and the Americans became 猍, while Great Britain and the British became 獌 .[20]

The most common animal invectives leveled against the Anglo-American foe were simply "brute" (*kedamono*) and "wild beast" (*yajū*), and innumerable wartime speeches and essays spelled out in detail why the behavior of the enemy made such labels appropriate. A long philippic published in a popular magazine at the end of 1944 exemplifies such propaganda, and at the same time illustrates how well informed the Japanese public was about white supremacism. The article was, beyond any doubt, thoroughly introduced. The title was "The Bestial American People." Below this ran a subtitle: "Beat the Americans to Death!" Above the title was the warning "This Is the Enemy!" And tucked amidst these typographic leaders was a caricature of a sweating Roosevelt, mysteriously wearing headphones—perhaps intended to suggest he was listening to the moral indignation of the Japanese. Evidence of the bestial nature of the enemy, the article explained, was overwhelming. It could be seen in the Americans' preoccupation with sex, their fixation on creature comforts, and their strong instinct for conquest. Negatively, the absence of a basic humanity was revealed by American incomprehension concerning such virtues as goodwill, gratitude, and filial piety. The uncivilized nature of the Americans was blatantly apparent in their race hate. Readers were informed about the history of anti-Japanese racism in the United States, including the depiction of Japanese as monkeys. They also were informed that American children were now brainwashed to "kill Japs." The authors and editors did not see any equivalence here to their own exhortation to "Beat the Americans to Death!" Rather, they too spoke in terms of kill-or-be-killed.

The real meaning of American individualism, readers of "The Bestial American People" were informed, was that power determined everything. In fact, the Americans desired to destroy "the divine state of Japan" simply to gratify their insatiable carnal desires. Their cruelty and bestiality were revealed in countless ways. They killed deformed babies by drowning them, and some American mothers even practiced infanticide by bashing their baby's head against a wall. American soldiers killed Japanese prisoners of war, and practiced the law of the jungle in general in the present conflict. They drove tanks over wounded Japanese, wrapped malaria-wracked prisoners in barbed wire and tossed them into rivers to drown, and took pleasure in playing with the sacred bones of the Japanese war dead. Only beasts and barbarians could do such things. Certainly, humans could not.

Racism, it was explained, lay at the root of American atrocities against the Japanese, for white Americans were simply incapable of accepting colored peoples as humans. They could treat them only as animals, or as commodities; and in the present war, infuriated by the racial aspects of the necessary attack on Pearl Harbor, the United States had resolved to remove the Yamato race from the face of the earth. The article went on to quote a "top-secret" document, which, it was claimed, had been obtained from a captured American officer, telling how to treat Japanese prisoners. They should first be kicked in the knees, then in the face when they doubled over, then struck in the chin with one's elbow and in the eyes with one's boot. Then they should be stomped to death, or battered with something like a stone. This tirade concluded with a familiar gratuitous Naziism, associating Roosevelt with the "Jewish plutocracy."[21]

Such unleavened propaganda conveys a sense of how the enemy was presented by more rabid circles to the home front in Japan. A cartoon sequence which appeared in another popular magazine, *Hinode* (Sunrise), in November 1944 offered a graphic version of similar themes. Entitled "Brutality of the Americans," this two-page spread portrayed the Americans as burglars, unshaven capitalists, and unregenerate racists. As evidence of the American love of bloodletting, the Japanese were presented with a sketch of a boxing match replete with cheering female spectators. As examples of American racism, they were offered several graphics: a Negro child being stoned to death while swimming; Negroes as the targets of a ball-throwing game in an amusement park; and a Negro being lynched, upside down. The cartoon montage also included an episode that received much publicity in wartime Japan, the American bombing of a hospital ship. In addition, it squeezed in the information that the American appetite for murder and lynching was whetted by Hollywood, and concluded with the dry observation that "it is mysterious how such a race could behave so pompously on this earth." For more educated readers, books were available in Japanese dealing with the tragic history of the Negro in America.[22]

In popular illustrations, the marks of the beast were claws, fangs, animal hindquarters, sometimes a tail, sometimes small horns—all of which, however, also marked a transition from the plain beast to the quasi-religious demon or devil. This latter stereotype was the dominant metaphor in Japanese propaganda against the enemy during World War Two—the closest equivalent on the Japanese side to the Anglo-American fixation on the apish stigmata and yellow vermin. Here too, as in the plain bestiary, the vocabulary was generally limited and rudimentary: the Anglo-Americans were described as demons (*oni*), devils (*kichiku*), evil spirits (*akki* and *akuma*), and monsters (*kaibutsu*). More elaborate variations were offered on occasion, such as "hobgoblins" and "hairy, twisted-nosed savages," but the basic image remained intact—as did the natural response to being confronted by such forces of evil. Before the war, individuals such as Foreign Minister Matsuoka Yōsuke had actually gone so far as to declare that "the mission of the Yamato race is to prevent the human race from becoming devilish, to rescue it from destruction and lead it to the world of light."[23] The demons had to be exorcised—and in the midst of all-out war it was often argued that they had to be utterly destroyed. Exterminationist logic was not an English or American monopoly.

Many popular wartime writings and drawings fell into this pattern of the demonic Other, and in some instances their kinship to the traditional perception of the ambiguous outsider, half superhuman and half subhuman, was overt. In the spring of 1941, for example, when the United States and Japan were still struggling to resolve their disagreements diplomatically, America was depicted as a country in which good and evil forces were locked in combat—personified, in one case, by a droll cartoon of a boxing match in which an angelic albeit potbellied Roosevelt, fully equipped with wings and halo, was taking a pounding from a demonic Roosevelt, identifiable by his telltale horns.[24]

Two months after Pearl Harbor, when Japan appeared to be sweeping through Southeast Asia like a typhoon, Kondō Hidezō, one of the country's most energetic nationalist cartoonists, depicted Roosevelt and Churchill as padres whose robes had been pulled up by small Japanese planes flying overhead. Roosevelt was revealed to have the hindquarters of a horse, while Churchill was exposed as possessing a badger's behind—thus accounting for the cartoon's title, "Horse's Legs, Badger's Tail." Both euphemisms meant "betraying one's true nature." The inner lining of Churchill's robe was revealed to have a skull-and-bones pattern, while Roosevelt's was decorated with a dollar-sign design; and the crucifix in the American leader's hand had turned into a dagger. In the same vein, later in the war, a journalistic account of the historical background to the conflict in Asia was accompanied by an illustration of Uncle Sam as a sharp-nailed, sharp-toothed clergyman with the tail of a fox, preaching from the "Bible" of duplicitous "Open Door" theology. On another occasion, Roosevelt was depicted as a padre with a bushy tail peeping from beneath his robes and tiny fangs protruding from his lower jaw, standing among armaments, money bags, and chains, before an "altar of blood." Among the grotesque objects before him were a candle made out of Chiang's head and a decapitated pig's head representing Churchill.[25]

Depiction of the enemy as demons or beasts or simply despicable people who had to be destroyed began to appear in various forms as soon as Japan commenced war against the Allied powers. The artist Katō Etsurō, for example, responded to the outbreak of war with several exceedingly harsh graphics which portrayed the purifying Japanese bayonet cleansing the world of this vile Other. A well-known poster by Katō depicted a bayonet with the Rising Sun emblem on its mount sinking into the stomach of a Roosevelt with bestial hindquarters, behind whom loomed a smaller demonic Churchill. The poster's legend read: "The death of these wretches will be the birthday of world peace!" Similarly, the full-color cover of *Osaka Puck*'s February 1942 issue, also done by Katō, featured a huge upright bayonet on which both Roosevelt and Churchill were skewered, with the American president still clutching now broken shackles in his hand. Here the slogan exclaimed: "Administer the *coup de grâce* to the disturbers of world peace!" From the outset of the war, the image of the demonic enemy was frequently reinforced by concrete allegations of Allied atrocities. In the opening weeks of 1942, for example, a report that beleaguered U.S. forces on Mindanao had machine-gunned some seventy interned Japanese was published under the headline "Cruel Devilish U.S. Defense Garrison Massacres Our Detained Countrymen." A large subheading in the same report denounced the "Enemies of Humanity!" The Doolittle raid in April 1942, as already seen, provoked a similar outburst of condemnation of the "devilish" and "demonic" enemy, as did charges on several occasions that the Americans had deliberately sunk Japanese hospital ships. At a more prosaic level, the Japanese counterpart to such U.S. slogans as "Every war bond kills a Jap" was that savings accounts helped kill the Allied devils.[26]

Depiction of the enemy as a demonic force crystallized in its final form after the Americans captured Saipan in mid-1944, for thereafter it was no longer possible for the Japanese leadership to deny that the war had turned disastrously against them. Possession of Saipan enabled the Americans to reach the Japanese home populace with shortwave propaganda broadcasts, to commence soon thereafter incendiary bombing raids against Japanese cities, and to begin laying concrete plans for the invasion of the home islands. It was in this desperate setting that the tactics of suicidal resistance became formalized within the Japanese military and then urged upon the general populace through such slogans as "The hundred million as a Special Attack Force." While the mystique of the pure Self was one part of this exhortation to embrace death, the demonic nature of the enemy was its essential counterpart.

The government's formal propaganda policies made this explicit. Thus, a policy paper for guiding public opinion approved by the cabinet in October 1944 declared that in light of the drastically worsening war situation, concerted efforts must be made to incite much stronger feelings of hostility against the enemy. The public had to be informed that a decisive battle was inevitable, but that ultimate victory was certain if the entire populace embraced the "spirit of Yamato" (*Yamato damashii*). At the same time, however, it was essential to constantly remind the public about the cruel nature of the enemy, especially as revealed in their atrocious deeds during the current war. This policy was reaffirmed the following January, at which time the cabinet adopted a further policy of informing the people of Japan that there were only two choices before them: to be victorious, or perish.[27]

A lively magazine entry from October 1944 captures some of the rhetoric of these post-Saipan days, when the Anglo-American foe emerged full-blown as the demonic Other. Under the title "Naming the Western Barbarians," and accompanied by a drawing of an ogre with a necklace of skulls removing a smiling Roosevelt-faced mask, this little exercise in popular phrasemaking ran as follows:

> It has gradually become clear that the American enemy, driven by its ambition to conquer the world, is coming to attack us, and as the breath and body odor of the beast approach, it may be of some use if we draw the demon's features here.
>
> Our ancestors called them Ebisu or savages long ago, and labeled the very first Westerners who came to our country the Southern Barbarians. To the hostile eyes of the Japanese of former times they were "red hairs" and "hairy foreigners," and perceived as being of about as much worth as a foreign ear of corn. We in our times should manifest a comparable spirit. Since the barbaric tribe of Americans are devils in human skin who come from the West, we should call them *Saibanki*, or Western Barbarian Demons [a pun on *Saipanki*, demons from Saipan].

Readers of this same magazine were also offered, in another feature entitled "Devilish Americans and English" a large drawing that depicted Roosevelt and Churchill as drunken ogres carousing within sight of snow-covered Mount Fuji. How could the Japanese respond to such a diabolical threat? By extermination. "Beat and kill these animals that have lost their human nature!", the panel exclaimed. "That is the great mission that Heaven has given to the Yamato race, for the eternal peace of the world!" The same illustrated feature, which covered two pages, continued with a familiar litany about the true face of the enemy: recounting the gruesome lynchings of Negroes in white America, the way whites looked upon colored peoples in general as simply "races who should serve them like domestic animals," and how liberalism and individualism amounted to little more than survival-of-the-fittest philosophies that justified big fish eating little fish. Through skill in science, the enemy had developed materially, but without morality or true godliness, and this could no longer be tolerated. "Temporarily, we may have let them play around in the Pacific," the polemic concluded, "but the blood of the Divine Country's three thousand years cannot allow these beasts to run rampant."[28]

By the time this article appeared, phrases such as "devilish Americans and English" (*Kichiku Bei-Ei*) and "American devils" (*Beiki*) were firmly in place as everyday Japanese war words, and the juxtaposition of a pure and sacred homeland imperiled by bestial and demonic outsiders was sharply drawn. The vocabularies of pureness, pollution, defilement, beastliness, and demonism became thoroughly integrated. Classrooms displayed posters exhorting students to "kill the American devils," and already in 1943 a unique opportunity for involving schoolchildren in the ritual destruction of the enemy had arisen in the form of a debate over what to do with some twelve thousand blue-eyed dolls that had been given to Japanese schools in 1927 as a gesture of goodwill by American charity groups. Eventually, almost all of the dolls were destroyed.[29] It is against this background that the heightened fanaticism of the post-Saipan propaganda offensive took place, and the rhetoric of both the pure Self and the demonic Other became inseparable from visions of inevitable slaughter.

There are countless illustrations of this. A magazine article about the struggle in the Philippines in the closing months of 1944, for example, typically described the Americans as both beasts and demons, and declared that "the more of them that are sent to hell, the cleaner the world will be." U.S. air raids over the homeland in January 1945 were described as attacks by wild beasts which "polluted" the grounds of the shrine of the Sun Goddess at Ise, and Prime Minister Koiso Kuniaki similarly denounced the "vulgar barbarians" for having "polluted" the Imperial Palace in the air raids of March 1945. The tactic of bombing Japanese cities with incendiaries, first employed in the March air raid on Tokyo, was naturally presented as conclusive proof of the "inhuman" nature of the enemy. That same month, government-sponsored newsreels described Iwo Jima (where over twenty thousand Japanese and six thousand Americans eventually died) as "a suitable place to slaughter the American devils." To extirpate evil required the mass death of the Other, just as purifying the Self required acceptance of mass self-slaughter.[30]

The virulence of Japanese propaganda in the last, desperate year of the war—and the plausibility of such propaganda as well—are well illustrated by a typical issue of *Hinode*, which was a monthly aimed at less well educated Japanese (the magazine contained *furigana* readings next to every single ideograph, telling how to pronounce it). *Hinode*'s November 1944 issue opened with a pious page on the "divine land," followed by a full-page drawing by the famous artist Itō Shinsui, depicting serene women and children praying at the edge of a cliff "in the Marianas" (clearly Saipan) before throwing themselves into the sea below rather than submit to the foe. Following this, a two-page drawing depicted laughing U.S. sailors on a surfaced submarine shooting shipwrecked Japanese in the water. A poem accompanying this drew upon a famous Chinese line to the effect that the two sides could not possibly coexist under the same heaven. Yet another large illustration followed, depicting exhausted but resolute Japanese soldiers on Guadalcanal. Here the accompanying verse spoke of how they ate grass roots, leaves, even dirt, but still retained their indominable spirit. They held on like gods.

Cartoons in *Hinode* depicted the Americans as gangsters lusting after overseas lands and commiting racist outrages at home. In one extraordinary panel, the righteous bayonet of "the divine country Japan" speared cartoon-thug America in the posterior as he tried to lasso Mount Fuji. Among feature stories, a roundtable discussion with five Japanese men, many of whom had lived for a long time in the United States, ranged widely over the many forms of barbaric behavior which Americans engaged in behind the masks of humanism and due process. The discussants mentioned, among other things, reports that American fighting men sometimes cut noses off captured Japanese, blinded them, and castrated them; and they related this to past behavior against the American Indians. One of the illustrations which accompanied this portion of *Hinode* was a copy of the *Life* photograph of the young woman who had been sent a Japanese skull by her fiancé. Another illustration was a reproduction of an English-language card laid out as if it were an advertisement to join the U.S. Marines. This took the form of a "Japanese Hunting License," announcing "open season" on the foe and promising "free ammunition and equipment—with pay!" Japanese readers were told that such items were found in every American city, amply revealing how in American eyes the Japanese were no more than animals. Another article in the same issue featured an interview with two women—one a resident of Saipan and the other a dancer who had been entertaining the troops abroad—who had been aboard ships torpedoed in separate incidents by U.S. submarines. It was the story of the former about how the submarine then circled among the survivors while laughing crew members shot them which inspired the magazine's opening illustration of atrocity on the high seas. The woman, who was the sole survivor of the incident, recalled how her little sister called for their mother as the submarine bore down on them, and was told, "That's a ship with terrible demons on it, so pretend you are dead." She died in her sister's arms, still in the ocean, shortly thereafter.[31]

The pure Self and demonic Other were such polar extremes that they made the work of many polemicists and artists fairly easy. In cartoons, for example, Japan was often represented by highly idealized non-human symbols, such as the purifying sun or the sword (or, more frequently, bayonet) of righteousness.[32] By contrast, the Anglo-American enemy commonly took the form of the *oni*, a huge horned creature well known in the folktales of Japan since ancient times and variously rendered in English as "demon," "ogre," "devil," or "fiend." The *oni* was the most straightforward graphic representation of the demonic Other, and the link to verbal assaults on "devilish Americans and English" and "American devils" was absolutely clear-cut: the same ideograph used to write *oni* appeared (in two alternate phonetic readings) in both of these popular phrases.

Even in and of itself, however, the *oni* was not a simple creature, for in traditional folk belief it also possessed what has been described as "a benevolent, tutelary face as well as a demonic one." It was, indeed, most often associated with violence and destruction, appearing, among other places, in the Buddhist hell as a fiendish torturer. At the same time, however, the *oni* could be subdued and brought over to one's own side. An account of such a happening appears in the twelfth-century *Konjaku Monogatari*, Japan's earliest great collection of folktales; and this potentially positive side of the demon was reflected in certain local festivals in Japan, where someone made up to resemble an *oni* marched at the head of the festival procession and drove away evil influences. In this regard, the *oni* was like the ambiguous stranger of Japanese folk belief in possessing powers that might be used for evil or good.

A striking instance of the persistence of this belief was, in fact, included in the late-1944 issue of *Hinode* just described. As the shadow of the Allied advance fell over Japan and even the popular press frankly reported that their heroic fighting men were eating grass and dirt, it became necessary to find ever more dramatic images to describe the ferocious tenacity of their resistance. *Hinode* found such an image in a vivid old concept, namely, "the protective demons of the country" (*gokoku no oni*); and thus its November issue also featured a story about Japanese combatants entitled, literally, "Demon Gods" (*kijin*, or in an alternative reading, *kishin*). There was no sense of contradiction vis-à-vis the demonic enemy here; there are simply times when a terrible strength is deemed needed for the cause, and clearly there could be no more perilous time than the present. What this self-appropriated demon-god image reveals in retrospect, however, is how rich, subtle, and adaptable some of the core images of these years were. To anticipate but briefly, it should be kept in mind that after the Japanese surrendered it was the Americans who became the protectors of their country.[33]

As a popular symbol of the American and British enemy during the years in question here, it was the violent and evil nature of the *oni* that was overwhelmingly dominant. The potential of being pacified or tamed was always latent, however, and the wartime graphics themselves offered several noteworthy variations which indicated that this demonic foe could be subdued short of extermination, and even turned into an amiable ogre. One of these variations can be called the "Momotarō paradigm," after the famous folktale figure of that name. The other entailed the forthright recognition of demons with a human face.

The story of Momotarō, the Peach Boy, is the best-known of all Japanese folk tales. It tells of an old couple who found a peach floating in a river, out of which a miraculous youngster emerged. As Momotarō grew older, he exhibited prodigious strength; and before long, he took it upon himself to free Japan from a menace that had long threatened it, namely, the periodic incursions of *oni* who lived on a distant island. Momotarō donned warrior's garb for his noble mission, and tied a white headband around his brow. His elderly parents provided him with "the best dumplings of all Japan,"—or in some versions, the best in the whole world—to sustain him on his way.

En route to the distant land of the demons, Momotarō encountered, in turn, a dog, a monkey, and a pheasant—each of whom asked what he was carrying and became his follower after being given one of the marvelous dumplings. At the fortress of the demons far across the sea, the three retainers assisted Momotarō in accordance with their specific skills. The pheasant flew over the fortress and reported the demons' disposition; the monkey climbed the wall and opened the gate from within. In the battle that ensued, the dog and the monkey distracted the foe by running among them biting and scratching, while the pheasant swooped down and pecked their faces. Momotarō then subdued the demons, and the victors returned to Japan with a cart full of treasures, pulled by the dog and pheasant and pushed from behind by the monkey. Momotarō naturally preceded them, as befitted a conquering hero.

No Japanese youngster was unfamiliar with this fable. Indeed, it was included, with colored illustrations, in the basic textbook for elementary language instruction issued by the Ministry of Education between February 1941 and September 1945. Like any such product of the oral tradition, there were different versions of the Momotarō story, and the appealing richness of the subject is suggested by the fact that during the war Japan's greatest folklorist, Yanagita Kunio, published a book of over five hundred pages on the Peach Boy. One of the most intriguing points in the story's variant versions lay in its end: what happened to the demons? In some versions, Momotarō killed them all with his sword; in others he annihilated all but the leader; in yet others he killed none, but rather forced them to surrender and pledge to mend their ways. The official version adopted in school texts followed the most moderate of these resolutions. After Momotarō bested their leader in combat, the *oni* were left to themselves (albeit stripped of their treasures) after promising that "from now on, we will never harm people or steal things again."[34]

This would be of peripheral interest to an understanding of Japanese attitudes during World War Two were it not for the fact that, in one form or another, the Momotarō image was worked into the war effort over and over again. At the simplest level, Japanese educators regarded the stalwart Peach Boy as an exemplary model for young Japanese—being himself youthful, vigorous, positive, and unwavering in his determination to bring about justice by subduing the forces of evil. (There was even controversy among educators concerning whether such an exemplary pure soul should return with booty.) On the one hand, Momotarō was divinely descended, making him a perfect symbol for Japan and the Japanese; as the folklorists pointed out, he was what was known as an *arahitogami* in traditional Shinto: a deity in human form. At the same time, his adoptive parents were eminently human, and toward them he displayed warm affection and filial piety. Such lessons went considerably beyond the school texts, how-

ever, and also beyond the elementary-school audience, as Momotarō conquering the *oni* became an irresistible parable for Japan conquering the
demonic Anglo-American foe.

Momotarō appeared in many wartime cartoons and magazines. Animated films, meant for all ages, were devoted to the story. Copies of the
tale were included among books distributed to servicemen, and it was
translated into other languages. A typical example of Momotarō's many
uses was a single-panel cartoon in the February 1942 issue of the adult
magazine *Manga* depicting Momotarō with his three small retainers driving off the demons Roosevelt and Churchill. The dog held aloft a banner
heralding the establishment of the Co-Prosperity Sphere, while the lapels
of Momotarō's own overgarment bore the phrase "First in the World"
(*Sekai Ichi*). This was a perfect expression of the most simple symbolic
use of the old folk tale: divine Japan and its lesser Asian followers driving
out the white imperialists and establishing their supremacy. In Indonesia,
the Momotarō story was adapted to the local youth theater, where the
great conquering hero from Japan again led other Asians in expelling the
devilish Europeans and Americans.[35]

Momotarō made his debut as a modern war hero in a short film
entitled *Momotarō of the Sky,* released in the late 1930s, in which the
divine boy and his three followers defended—of all places—the South
Pole and its resident penguins against assault by an evil eagle. In 1942,
and again in 1945, he returned to take on the Americans and the British
in two pioneer undertakings by the Japanese film industry. Near the end
of 1942, the Geijutsu film company released *Momotarō and the Eagles of
the Ocean,* a half-hour movie billed as Japan's first full-length cartoon.
Here Momotarō and his three retainers piloted planes and handled machine guns, and the "Island of Demons" was Hawaii. The final months
of the war saw the release of an even more ambitious cinematic undertaking, produced by a major studio, Shōchiku, in collaboration with the
Ministry of the Navy. Initiated in the latter part of 1944, the film was
released in April 1945 under the title *Momotarō—Divine Troops of the
Ocean.* [36]

In this innovative seventy-four-minute animated film, Momotarō
and his followers were presented as the prophesied "divine troops from
an eastern land" who were destined to liberate the peoples of southern
Asia from their enemies and oppressors. The film was a fascinating exercise in both transparent and subtle symbolism, in which Momotarō was
the great commander (and essence) of Japan—youthful and plump-

cheeked, stern yet caring, and absolutely beyond questioning. His familiar retainers in this case were the Japanese fighting men themselves: charming, well-clothed, and well-disciplined creatures (dogs, monkeys, pheasants, and—an addition to the prototype—bears), each of whom performed clear military tasks. The peoples of southern Asia emerged in this rendering as simple and good-hearted, but unruly and generally unclothed, wild beasts (baboons and proboscis monkeys, deer, tigers, leopards, elephants, rhinoceroses, kangaroos, and the like). These creatures of jungle and field performed manual labor and were taught Japanese, while Momotarō and his completely trustworthy air crew reconnoitered the enemy and readied for battle.

The enemy was not engaged or even mentioned until very late in the film—following the conventions of Japan's wartime cinema (and the preoccupation with the Self in general), where the focus was on the attractive side of one's own character. When at long last the foe appeared, they were gangly and pale human figures soon revealed to have the telltale horn of the demon. They spoke, or rather stuttered and whined, British English—with subtitles appearing in none-too-simple Japanese. One enemy soldier was skewered by a bayonet thrust by one of the divine troops who parachuted into the fortress of the foe. A few fell to bullets. The rest capitulated abjectly, their leaders caving in entirely after being told by Momotarō that their only choice was between unconditional surrender or continued slaughter. In the final frames, the children or young siblings of the divine troops back home in Japan celebrated the great victory by playing at parachuting themselves—jumping out of trees and landing on an outline of the United States drawn in the dirt.

Momotarō—Divine Troops of the Ocean would have been a major propaganda undertaking at any time during the war. The late date of its production and release makes it all the more remarkable; for although the Japanese did demand the unconditional surrender of the British at Singapore and the Americans in the Philippines in 1942, this hardly seemed an appropriate theme to dwell on in April 1945—to say nothing of intimations of invading the United States. The film in itself was highly romantic; and such obliviousness to the actual war situation at the time it was produced conveys a sense of men who were now truly living in a world of fables and fantasy. The Momotarō paradigm in general is all the more engaging because of this durability. Like the *Know Your Enemy— Japan* film completed by the U.S. Army near the end of the war, Shōchiku and the Imperial Navy drew together here many of the assumptions concerning themselves and the enemy that had emerged as central as the war unfolded. Apart from the obvious pitting of good against evil, these included the divine origin and righteous mission of the Yamato race; the "proper place" and assigned tasks of all good-hearted Japanese; the lower status and menial functions of the less civilized peoples of the rest of Asia; and the demonic and craven nature of the white enemy.

The adaptability of these folk elements to the war situation did not stop at this point, however, for neither Momotarō nor the demonic Other proved to be hard and fast symbols. We have seen that the depiction of the enemy as demons, devils, or ogres permitted the rise of an exterminationist rhetoric in Japan comparable to the metaphors of the hunt or of exterminating vermin in the West. Like the official textbook version of the Momotarō story, however, the 1945 film offered a less sanguinary model for coming to terms with the demonic foe. Indeed, a noteworthy feature of the film was that both Momotarō and his Caucasian adversaries were depicted in human form. Although the latter were groveling and contemptible figures who bore the demons' horns and besmirched the map of their conquered areas with demons' names in English (Ogre's Island, Lake Devils, The Devil's Strait, etc.), in this presentation they obviously were not demons through and through. Momotarō and the Caucasians thus confronted each other as figures who partook of supranatural as well as human qualities; and in this regard they were actually closer to each other than was apparent at first glance.

The common human quality shared by the archetypical Momotarō and the demons was highlighted in a great deal of the cartoon work by Japanese artists, and points to an important alternative to the sense of Self and Other as polar opposites. This amounted to the humanization or naturalization of the Momotarō paradigm—involving, on the one hand, the depiction of Japan and the Japanese as a youthful and vigorous, but not necessarily innately superior, figure; and, on the other hand, the portrayal of the Americans and English as demons with a human face. The demon with a human face, in turn, often shaded off into a portrayal of the white foe as plain, albeit depraved, human beings whose behavior may have been atrocious and "inhuman," but whose nature was not necessarily intrinsically so. Such symbolic ruptures of the original Momotarō-demon polarity, even if not explicitly recognized or acknowledged at the time, helped prepare the ground for discarding the antipodal stereotypes of the pure Self and the incorrigibly evil Other once Japan had acknowledged its defeat; for the conflict was thereby returned, in effect, to a struggle of man against man. This intimation of essential equality, however latent, was almost completely lacking in Western representations of the conflict with Japan.

A most important aspect of this naturalized Momotarō figure was the evocation of youthful vigor. It is true that much of Japanese propaganda and indoctrination involved the attempt to evoke a sense of Japan's unique and immutable virtues by exhuming both heroes and catchphrases from ancient times and archaic texts. This is one of the features of Japanese wartime behavior that Westerners seized upon and turned to their own uses when they described Japan as an essentially primitive country. What the Westerners usually overlooked, however, was the comparable or even greater energy which Japanese publicists and polemicists devoted to evoking the image of a dynamic, "new" Japan. A sense of change, of entering a new epoch, was certainly one of the most compelling ideals in Japan in the 1920s and 1930s, expressed in an almost limitless variety of settings. The Japanese public not only was bombarded with grand visions of a new political structure and a new economic structure at home, and a new order in Asia and throughout the world; they also were immersed in a culture in which countless familiar aspects of everyday life were being wedded to the prefix "new" (*shin* or *shinkō*)—the new poetry, for example, and the new photography, new theater, new zaibatsu, new bureaucrats, and, indeed, new man and new woman.[37] These influences came from many directions, including the ideological left, and in the cultural realm in particular they often were at odds with the state orthodoxy. The overall ideal of a fresh start was widely shared, however, and in this setting it was not at all unnatural for the Momotarō-type figure to become adopted as a popular symbol of Japan and the Japanese in the years leading up to the war in Asia. It was a familiar and comfortable figure. It had been uniquely Japan's since ancient times. At the same time, it was unmistakably associated with youth, vigor, and the promise of a new era.

This naturalized Momotarō figure was easily recognizable: a fresh-faced youth or young man, erect of bearing, steadfast of gaze, frequently wearing a Rising Sun *hachimaki*, or headband. He graced the illustrated covers of both children's and adult's magazines, appeared in wartime posters, and eventually moved touchingly and tragically into the camera's eye in the form of the young pilots in the Special Attack Forces, tying on their headbands and preparing to depart on their first and last great missions. In cartoon art, the Momotarō type emerged in several roles and guises. He was the clear-faced liberator of Asia. He was also sometimes depicted confronting the Anglo-American enemy in simple man-to-man combat such as a boxing match—a trim and youthful figure asserting his superiority over an old, flabby antagonist.[38] In another variation, the Momotarō type represented the good Self that existed within each Japanese, but was at war with the demons of temptation.

In the latter rendering, of course, it was not only the Momotarō archetype that was internalized, but also the demonic Other in its most negative sense. Like Westerners who since medieval times had agonized over "the wild man within," the Japanese too sometimes acknowledged that their external demons were partly a projection of their own inclinations and impulses. In the war years, this was interpreted as meaning primarily an attraction toward Western influences, or toward undisciplined, indulgent, and egocentric activity in general. A cartoon panel in the major government-sponsored humor magazine in mid-1943, for instance, portrayed this internal struggle in a light and good-natured manner. Here a factory worker's temptation to absent himself from work and go fishing was represented by a leering Roosevelt, with the telltale small horns of the *oni*, lurking in the worker's heart; the temptation to go carousing after work took on the face of Churchill. On the other hand, the worker's good impulses were represented by a Momotarō type who also resided in his breast—a youthful, muscular figure who sported not only the familiar Rising Sun headband, but also an angel's wings.[39]

The horned Roosevelt of this comic sequence was in fact typical. It was the demon with a human face—indeed, a readily identifiable face—depicted, moreover, with a wry touch. This contrasts sharply to the war art of Japan's enemies in the West, where it was conventional to attack the Japanese as a people, rather than just their leaders—and where the Japanese were usually portrayed as outright beasts or ridiculous, depersonalized humans. More often than not, Japanese renderings of the demonic Other retained the human touch by being combined with the features of Roosevelt and Churchill. In this way, they gave a sense—however small —of personality and individuality as well as humanity to the enemy. To a certain degree, the popular graphics that accompanied this demonology may also have socialized the Japanese to associate the demonic nature of the enemy with the enemy leadership.

The demon with a human face merged almost imperceptibly with another large category of Japanese depictions of the enemy, which simply portrayed them as humans with depraved, degenerate, or demonic impulses. From this perspective, the enemy were at least recognizably human, although assuredly still not humans "like ourselves." A careful study of English-language Japanese radio propaganda broadcasts in Southeast Asia and the South Pacific during the war reveals that the Japanese had a set vocabulary of descriptive terms for the Americans that included "satanic" and "diabolical" among the favored invectives, but hardly rested with this. The other odious character traits most frequently ascribed to the Americans were that they were mercenary, immoral, unscrupulous, vainglorious, arrogant, luxury-loving, soft, nauseating, superficial, decadent, intolerant, uncivilized, and barbarous.[40]

The cartoonists, once again, had a heyday with such traits; and as a consequence, their wartime graphics of the enemy are as a whole more diversified and less ethnocentric and culture-bound than the general output of their Western counterparts—and frequently more witty and artistically sophisticated as well. They did quite a bit with images of lunacy and megalomania, for example, often turning to figures from the West's own history to make their points: Roosevelt and Churchill as Don Quixote and Sancho Panza, for instance, or as larger and smaller versions of Napoleon. Drunkenness and debauchery also were popular motifs, symbolizing both the hedonism and flabbiness of the decadent West. Vivid graphics were offered contrasting the European and American colonial oppression of Asians to the liberation that was to come under the Co-Prosperity Sphere. Japanese artists also were fond of illustrated excursions through history, such as a chronological "train of aggression" of Western imperialism.[41]

These mass-oriented graphics also offered strains of both anti-Semitic and anti-Christian sentiment that were more vicious than is usually recognized. Especially in the early years of the war, there appears to have been an outburst of anti-Jewish race hate which has no explanation beyond mindless adherence to Nazi doctrine. Even the gifted illustrator Ono Saseo joined this anti-Semitic chorus.[42] The anti-Christian sentiment emerged in a variety of forms. Monkish renderings of Roosevelt and Churchill were defrocked and exposed as demons and warlocks. The Pietà was made a mocking (albeit sophisticated) parable of political futility, with Roosevelt as the Virgin Mary, Churchill the slain Christ, and Chiang a grieving disciple. The cross or crucifix was transmogrified. It became a bloody dagger, or a sign of death alone, just the marking on a grave. An unusually harsh cartoon in the government humor magazine several months after the war with the United States began combined the form of the cross with the ideograph for America to offer a crucified Roosevelt as the new meaning of "United States."[43]

The final rendering of the enemy that emerged more forcefully in graphics than in words was the portrayal of English and Americans as old and decrepit. And at this point, we return not only to the Momotarō paradigm, with its youthful Japan-signifying hero, but also to the point at which the double-edged ambiguity of this sort of symbolism becomes clearer. Whether the foe was personified by Roosevelt and Churchill or Uncle Sam and John Bull (the line between them was often obscure), they were clearly elderly, a declining force in the face of the new Japan and the emerging new global order. Their time had passed. They awaited only the *coup de grace* from the rising Axis powers.

That final blow, of course, never came. What remained after 1945 was the image of the Anglo-American powers and Japan as elder and younger modern nation-states respectively—the younger now chastised and put back in its place. Once the fact of defeat, or failure, had been accepted, the Japanese still had a familiar patterned way of seeing international relationships to hold on to. Younger submitted to older, and redefined in more modest and traditional terms its "proper place" in the family of nations.

Much as happened in the case of the Americans and the English, Japanese at all levels allowed themselves to be misled by distorted perceptions of both their own strengths and the purported weaknesses of their enemies. They exaggerated their social cohesiveness and supposedly unique spiritual and moral qualities, while at the same time grossly underestimating the material strength and moral fiber of the other side.

This was most conspicuous in the year preceding and the year following Pearl Harbor. The decision to attack the Pacific Fleet in its Hawaii anchorage was not reached easily, nor was it irrational once the decision had been made that Japan could not survive without control of the southern region. As researchers such as Michael Barnhart and others have demonstrated, however, the brilliance of the military's operational plans for the opening stage of the war was offset by an astonishing lack of serious intelligence analysis of a psychological and economic nature. Prior to 1940, the Imperial Army virtually ignored the United States and Great Britain altogether in its intelligence gathering, being more focused on China and the Soviet Union; English was not even taught in the Army schools. Neither the Imperial Navy nor other key government organs made a major investigation of U.S. productive capacity before initiating the war. Because the plan to attack Pearl Harbor was so secret, moreover, Naval Intelligence was kept out of the planning (which was done by the Operations section), and no serious evaluation of the probable psychological effects of a surprise attack were undertaken. Admiral Yamamoto himself, as previously noted, hoped the attack would discourage the Americans and destroy their will to respond.[44]

This blithe assumption reflected an arrogance and ineptitude every bit as great as that displayed toward the Japanese by the British and Americans in the period prior to December 1941; and in a similar fashion such wishful thinking rested on disdainful racial and cultural stereotypes. Briefly put, Westerners were assumed to be selfish and egoistic, and incapable of mobilizing for a long fight in a distant place. All the "Western" values which Japanese ideologues and militarists had been condemning since the 1930s, after all, were attacked because they were said to sap the nation's strength and collective will. More concretely, it was assumed that Great Britain would fall to the Germans, and the U.S. war effort would be undercut by any number of debilitating forces endemic to contemporary America: isolationist sentiment, labor agitation, racial strife, political factionalism, capitalistic or "plutocratic" profiteering, and so on. Such simplistic impressions of the "national character" of the projected enemy had disastrous consequences at the most practical levels. To give but one striking example, Japanese naval strategists assumed that Americans were too soft to endure the mental and physical strains of extended submarine duty, and thus never developed an effective antisubmarine capability—a failure of monumental significance given the decisive role submarines later played in the war of attrition against Japan.[45]

For a half year or more after Pearl Harbor, this impression of a soft enemy appeared to be true. The huge size of the U.K. force that surrendered without much of a fight at Singapore was incredible by anyone's reckoning, and the combined U.S. and Filipino army that capitulated on Bataan was twice as large as the Japanese expected. (They expected forty thousand prisoners, or possibly many fewer, and approximately seventy-eight thousand men surrendered.) Japanese casualties were light, and Japanese euphoria knew no bounds. For the Western Allies, these were the months of humiliating defeat that spawned the myth of the Japanese superman; to the Japanese, they were months of glorious victory that once and for all confirmed their innate superiority. It was during these months that there emerged in Japan what after the war was called the "victory disease," the fatal hubris of invincibility. Even the most cautious of military leaders were not immune to such wishful thinking. On the eve of the decisive battle of Midway, for example, Admiral Nagumo Chūichi's intelligence concluded that Americans did indeed "lack the will to fight."[46]

These sentiments persisted long after the war turned against Japan —partly because Japanese propagandists lied a great deal about the outcomes of battles, partly because myths die hard. The Japanese did not change their codes when they should have done so, because they did not think the Westerners could break them. In the field, they frequently left important papers behind, apparently on the assumption that Westerners could never figure out how to read them. And to the end of the war, they continued to believe that the more they showed themselves willing to die, the better chance they would have to persuade the Allies to agree on a compromise peace—as if the Allied leaders paid no attention to public rage and the desire to repay a blood debt.

It is possible that Japan's early victories compounded the arrogance already inherent in believing one's own people to be the "leading race." Certainly, they did nothing to temper this, as almost all non-Japanese who encountered the imperial forces and their civilian cohorts discovered. Tens of thousands of Allied prisoners learned that while the "leading race" preached magnanimity, it practiced brutality. Hundreds of millions of Asians learned a similar lesson: that when the Japanese spoke of creating a "new order" in which each race and nation assumed its proper place, it was taken for granted that the proper place of everyone else was below the Japanese. Such practice conformed not merely to the effusions of the ideologues and the paradigms of the popular culture, but to the dictates of official policy as well. Once the European and American demons were expelled from Asia, the Japanese were to take their places as the new and destined overlords.

◄ C H A P T E R   1 0 ►

"GLOBAL POLICY WITH THE YAMATO RACE AS NUCLEUS"

One of the most often repeated stories about the time between Japan's surrender in mid-August of 1945 and the arrival of the U.S. occupation forces two weeks later tells how the skies over Tokyo were gray with smoke as the billowing infernos caused by air raids were replaced by the bonfires of bureacrats destroying their files. Although the reports of smoke-filled skies may be fanciful, the rest of the story is not. In the wake of the capitulation, Japanese officials hastily destroyed huge quantities of paperwork, and much of the documentary record that survived the fire-bombings did not survive the cease-fire. The fragmentary papers that remain from the war years on the Japanese side thus have come to carry a heavy burden of suggestiveness for scholars—much like the broken artifacts unearthed by archaeologists that become the basis for recreating a vanished world.

By far the most impressive endeavor to collect the official and semi-official Japanese materials that did survive both the presurrender and postsurrender destruction was undertaken in conjunction with the war-crimes trials conducted in Tokyo between 1946 and 1948. Since then, a variety of additional documents have come to the attention of scholars. One of these, discovered in a used-book store in Tokyo in 1981, is a massive report that sheds more light on Japanese racial attitudes than any other single document that has survived from this period. Consisting of almost four thousand pages divided into eight volumes, this report was written during the first half of the Pacific War by approximately forty researchers associated with the Population and Race Section of the Research Bureau of the Ministry of Health and Welfare. The first two volumes, entitled *The Influence of War upon Population* and dated December 1, 1942, analyzed the probable demographic impact of the war in Asia against the historical background of prior conflicts, beginning with the first Sino-Japanese War at the end of the nineteenth century. The six remaining volumes, totaling 3,127 pages, are of greater interest. They bore the completion date July 1, 1943, and were collectively entitled *An Investigation of Global Policy with the Yamato Race as Nucleus.* [1]

The report was not a polemical work meant for public consumption, but rather a practical guide for policymakers and administrators. One hundred copies, classified secret, were circulated within the government. There is no reason to believe it was especially influential at the time, for the Ministry of Health and Welfare was not a powerful arm of the bureaucracy, and top policymakers in the midst of all-out war do not pause to read four-thousand-page documents. This relative detachment from the day-to-day concerns of actually administering the occupied areas is, however, precisely what gives the report much of its special value as a historical document. Spelled out in impressive detail here are many of the common assumptions that were expressed cryptically elsewhere, including the rationale behind policies that were actually adopted toward other races and nationalities. At the same time, the researchers had the rare opportunity of offering a long-range vision of Japan's projected global "new order" —a grand view most harried officials simply had no time to articulate.

This sort of detailed, long-term projection is a critical complement to what actually took place in the Greater East Asia Co-Prosperity Sphere —for the sphere itself, proclaimed in 1940 and dead by the summer of 1945, only lasted a little more than five years. During this period, Japan's activities were frantically devoted to imposing military control, harnessing the resources of the southern area to the immediate war effort, and responding to the crisis of imminent Allied victory. Later apologists for the Japanese have argued that the extraordinary demands of the war distorted Japan's true aims and prevented the Japanese from putting their generous ideals of "coexistence and coprosperity" into effect; and those who take this position can indeed find idealistic statements which seem to support their argument in the secret 1942–43 report. The study as a whole, however, supports an entirely different conclusion: that the subordination of other Asians in the Co-Prosperity Sphere was not the unfortunate consequence of wartime exigencies, but the very essence of official policy. It was the intention of the Japanese to establish permanent domination over all other races and peoples in Asia—in accordance with their needs, and as befitted their destiny as a superior race.

Portions of the report confronted the issue of racism directly, in what at first glance would appear to be a balanced tone. All peoples, it was stated, tended to adopt a racial view of the world peculiar to their own group, and in the modern age nationalism and racial consciousness often went hand in hand. The tendency to look upon the members of different tribes or races as beasts, demons, or enemies, however, can be found in the earliest stages of history among Asians and non-Asians alike. Among Asians, for example, Westerners who were recognized as being humane and civilized as individuals were depicted as barbarians when seen as a rival collectivity. The white races, on their part, had a tradition of asserting physical and cultural superiority over the colored races; although buttressed by modern accomplishments, this condescending attitude actually had roots in ancient times. In support of this assertion, the researchers offered a brief synopsis of racist attitudes expressed by such Western philosophers as Aristotle and Plato, as well as Comte, Oppenheimer, Herder, and Fichte. The task of the present day, the report went on, was to transcend such racism, and there were three places where transcendent values might be found: in ideas unique to Japan, ideas common among the Asian races, and ideals shared by all mankind.[2]

These were idealistic sentiments, and in one form or another they cropped up throughout the ministry report. They, were however, buried by the nationalistic and racist weight of the study as a whole, for the dominant theme in these pages was that the peoples or races of the world formed a natural hierarchy based on inherent qualities and capabilities. Exaggerated declarations of equality obscured the reality of inescapable inequalities, and true morality and justice entailed treating peoples in accordance with their varying characteristics and abilities. In the flowery words of the report itself: "To view those who are in essence unequal as if they were equal is in itself inequitable. To treat those who are unequal unequally is to realize equality."[3]

From this perspective, it followed that each ethnic or national group had its "proper place" in the regional or global scheme of things. The report rendered this critical concept in several different ways, but was unequivocal about the proper place of the Japanese. They were the "leading race" of Asia and implicitly the whole world. What is more, they were destined to remain so "forever"—provided, that is, that they pursued an intelligent policy of overseas expansion. For psychological as well as economic and strategic reasons, it was emphasized, it was essential that a carefully coordinated policy be adopted for planting Japanese blood on the soil of all Asia, while simultaneously avoiding intermarriage and preserving the purity of the Yamato race. Much of the ministry report was thus devoted to both summarizing existing policies concerning the Greater East Asia Co-Prosperity Sphere and outlining blueprints for consolidating the inferior peoples of Asia in an autarkic bloc, with Japan in its proper place as their political, economic, and cultural head.

The report bears all the earmarks of a committee project patched together over the course of many months. It is a sprawling and redundant document, and the analysis which follows can convey neither its nuances nor its rambling style. What hopefully will come through are the several ways in which this mammoth bureaucratic undertaking can be an eye-opener to anyone interested in the comparative study of racism and war. The report is, to begin with, an exceptionally detailed example of empirical racism in the hands of well-educated Japanese practitioners. In addition, it is an unusually frank statement of the relationship between Japan's expansionist policies and its assumption of racial and cultural supremacy —that is, of the assumptions of permanent hierarchy and inequality among peoples and nations that lay at the heart of what the Japanese really meant by such slogans as "Pan-Asianism" and "co-prosperity." Finally, the report shows Japanese racism and ethnocentrism to be far from a unique and *sui generis* phenomenon, as it is sometimes said to be. The affirmation of Japanese supremacy reflected Western intellectual influences as well as Western pressures. Perhaps most interesting, even where the language used to set the Japanese apart as the "leading race" seems to differ conspicuously from the Western models of racism, closer analysis suggests that the patterns of supremacism are analogous.

The overlap between borrowed ideas and indigenous attitudes in Japanese racism can be illustrated by two popular phrases in the ministry report: "blood and soil" and "proper place," the first a transparently alien expression and the second, on the surface, almost quintessentially "Oriental." The blood-and-soil rhetoric reflected indebtedness to Nazi sloganeering (the words, in fact, were almost always placed in quotation marks); and the impression of a general affinity with Nazi thought is reinforced by other aspects of the report, such as demands for "living space," affirmations of a "family"-centered morality transcending bourgeois law, and an emphasis on "organic" relationships, especially in the form of a racially bonded organic community or *"Volk."* The fact that the government's researchers were obviously familiar with Nazi doctrine and sympathetic to some of it, however, does not necessarily mean that they were decisively influenced by it. They did not, for instance, carry their racial prejudices to formal policies of genocide as their Nazi allies did. Moreover, for concepts such as the family system or the organic community, they were not really beholden to the Nazis at all. Here it is more accurate to speak of conceptual affinities rather than influences.

Coming from the opposite direction, "proper place" had a long pedigree in the history of Asian thought going back to early Confucianism in China. While the concept flourished for centuries as a pure product of the Confucian tradition, however, and later came to assume the coloration of Japanese family-system ideologies as well, it is misleading to see it as peculiarly Asian. For practical purposes, "proper place" was the functional equivalent of the Great Chain of Being in Western thought, and like that potent concept served in the mundane world to rationalize and reinforce disparate status and power relationships among people, races, and countries. Just as master-race theories could sprout from the soil of the Great Chain of Being in the West, so the Japanese perception of themselves as the leading race was fully consistent with traditional philosophic concepts of "proper place." At less theoretical levels too (such as parent-child metaphors and the depiction of other peoples as relatively childish and immature), the Japanese again will be found engaging in familiar or analogous forms of self-serving ratiocination. The most meaningful level of comparison is thus not between "Nazism" and "Japanism," but between the hierarchic patterns of thinking that governed the worldviews of Europeans, Americans, and Japanese alike.

In the modern world, the Japanese researchers repeatedly observed, racism, nationalism, and capitalist expansion had become inextricably intertwined. The Greater East Asia Co-Prosperity Sphere, as they described it in the abstract, would break this pattern by creating an autarkic community governed by reciprocity and harmonious interdependence. When it came to proposing concrete policies for the new autarkic bloc, however, the real meaning of "proper place" became unmistakably clear. It meant division of labor—an international and interracial allocation of tasks, chores, and responsibilities that was based on a gradient of national "qualities" and "abilities" determined in Tokyo, and that was so structured economically and politically as to ensure that the relationships of superior and inferior would be perpetuated indefinitely.

In their theoretical explanation of "race," the Japanese researchers drew a distinction between the narrow and more biologically oriented concept (*Rasse* in German, *jinshu* in Japanese) and the broader, more culturally influenced perception of a race as a people or nationality (*Volk* in German, *minzoku* in Japanese). *Minzoku*, or *Volk*, was the core word. The report most often identified the Japanese themselves as the *Yamato minzoku* ("Yamato people" or "Yamato race"), rather than simply the "Japanese" (*Nipponjin*), but the same general rubric applied to other peoples as well. The Chinese, for example, were identified as the *Han minzoku* ("Han people" or "Han race," from the historic designation dating back to the ancient Han dynasty). Although "blood" was undeniably important, strictly biological considerations tended to receive peripheral attention from the report's writers. Similarly, the great color categories of white, yellow, and black which so fascinated Caucasians were mentioned only rarely. At one point, the report explicitly referred to this as an Anglo-American fixation that should be avoided by the Japanese, and made the familiar point that such color prejudice was incompatible with Japan's alliance with Germany and Italy.[4]

In distinguishing between *jinshu* and *minzoku*, *Rasse* and *Volk*, the Japanese cited the writings of a variety of Westerners, and as their attentiveness to the *Volk* concept attests, German theorists were conspicuous among these authorities. While the Nazi view of the Jews was recapitulated with little criticism, the government researchers predictably ignored the anti-Oriental aspects of German and Nazi racism. Just as the Japanese translation of *Mein Kampf* omitted Hitler's derogatory references to the Japanese, so the writers of the Ministry of Health and Welfare report mentioned the theory of Aryan supremacy only fleetingly. Their overriding concern was to formulate an approach to peoples and races which encompassed the kinds of practical information that would be useful in consolidating Japanese control throughout Asia.[5]

As the Japanese defined them, *Volk* or *minzoku* were "natural and spiritual communities which shared a common destiny." They were organic collectivities that transcended their individual members and gave rise to distinctive national characters, representing *in toto* a fluid conjunction of blood, culture, history, and political form. Although innumerable variables might enter the picture, the basic factors which came together to shape the national character of a people would thus usually include a shared genetic and historical base, association with a particular geographic place, a common language and sociocultural heritage, and the influence of some form of political centralization.[6]

In the modern era, the analysis continued, the nation-state had come to assume a conspicuous role in this configuration, and of course many states asserted control over diverse races and peoples. This was especially true of the capitalist Western powers in the age of imperialism. Although it was possible to create a sense of spiritual community that transcended blood bonds, the cohesion of such a community was fragile; racial homogeneity was more conducive than racial heterogeneity to national strength. And although the instinct for self-preservation was characteristic of all peoples, this could pull in opposite and sometimes conflicting directions: toward preservation of traditional ways on the one hand, and toward adaptation to challenge and external stimuli on the other. No race, people, or nationality—no *minzoku*, no *Volk*—could remain unchanging and survive.[7]

Having drawn fine distinctions between *Rasse* and *Volk*, or *jinshu* and *minzoku*, the Ministry of Health and Welfare researchers nonetheless went on to emphasize that blood mattered. Biology was not destiny, but a common genetic heritage could contribute immensely to forging the bonds of spiritual consciousness and cultural identity that were so crucial to the survival of the collectivity. What they were arguing, in effect, was that "blood told"—not in the strict sense of inherited capabilities, but in the realm of consciousness and ideology. Blood mattered psychologically.[8]

At this point, the report became more concrete and interesting, for it went on to discuss, over several thousand sometimes meandering pages, the superiority of the Japanese and the reasons that their survival as a people depended on overseas expansion; the ideals of creating a larger "collective racialism" or "racial community" in Asia; and Japan's destiny to lead such a collectivity "eternally."[9]

Like many educated individuals in wartime Japan, the government researchers were obliged to weave some of the better-known propagandistic strains of officially sanctioned "knowledge" into their account—thus speaking, for example, of the "2,600-year history" of their country and the early consolidation of the state by the Emperor Jimmu.[10] On the racial makeup of the Japanese, however, their position was quite sober. In their preliminary theoretical discussion, they endorsed the thesis of certain Western scholars that no modern races were pure. Elsewhere they explicitly acknowledged that this was true of the Yamato race itself. Concerning the racial origins of the Japanese, they cited with approval the speculations of Erwin Baelz, a well-known German medical doctor who had lived in Japan in the late nineteenth century, to the effect that the modern Japanese probably represented the intermingling of three racial strains: Ainu, Malay, and Mongoloid.[11]

Despite these diverse origins, it was still possible to speak of the Japanese (and other races as well) as being "pure" in all practical senses. In addressing this provocative notion, the drafters of the report appear to have exercised greater restraint than their predecessors in the Ministry of Health and Welfare, who two years earlier had been quoted as confirming that the Japanese were the purest of the races. According to accounts in the Japanese press in August 1941, a major survey of hereditary mental illness conducted in several prefectures had determined that despite a notable increase in known cases in the last decade, only 6 percent of the Japanese population suffered from mental disorders, as compared to an average of 20 percent in the United States, Great Britain, Germany, and Italy. The respected *Asahi* newspaper reported these findings under a headline reading " 'Japanese Purity' Finally Proven." The scientific findings were especially noteworthy given current concerns about a "race war," the *Asahi* noted, for they "proved that the 'purity of blood' of the Yamato race is unsurpassed in the world." This was no doubt due to the fact that historically the Japanese had had little crossbreeding with other races, the article continued. At the same time, however, the recent increase in hereditary mental illness was alarming, and had prompted the Ministry of Health and Welfare to enact a National Eugenics Law.[12]

In the 1943 report, the researchers cited with approval Hitler's concern with identifying the "Germanness" of his own people, and rested content with arguing that even in ancient times there had been a "main line" or "main race" among the peoples who came together to form the Japanese race. This main line could be called the original Japanese, and by a process of natural selection and assimilation it gradually absorbed the other racial strains into a single "enduring structure." The isolation of the Japanese archipelago facilitated this assimilation, which was completed in the centuries of relative seclusion which followed the end of the Heian period in the twelfth century. Thus, to acknowledge the diverse ancient origins of the Japanese by no means implied that they could be considered a "mongrel" race. As the German geopolitician Karl Haushofer observed, they had become a uniform racial state.[13]

Over the centuries, various influences had impinged on the Japanese to shape their national character. The report touched on these in an impressionistic manner. Geographic isolation coupled with frequent natural disasters had created a sense of social cohesion as a "suffering-sharing community," it was argued at one point. In addition, the distinct seasonal variations of the land probably helped explain why adaptability had become so conspicuous a part of the national character as a whole. The fact that Japan was an island nation was also immensely consequential. The surrounding seas both separated the archipelago from other lands and connected it to them, and the effect of this on the national character was twofold: the Japanese, much like the British, were traditionalistic and conservative on the one hand, and progressive and cosmopolitan on the other.

In developing their thoughts concerning geography as destiny, the Japanese suggested that islands rather than continents had become the great bearers of initiative and influence in modern times. Just as British civilization had come to influence all Europe, so Japan was destined to spread its values and ideals over all Asia. And what was the essence of these values? Fundamentally: the best of East and West. "Japanism" (*Nipponshugi*) had come to consist of "purified Orientalism plus the merits of Western civilization"—a synthesis made transcendent by Japan's own indigenous moral qualities. The time had now come to "pay back old debts" by assimilating others under this superior culture.[14]

Affirmation of present superiority did not mean the Japanese race was perfect, however, or that Japanese expansion abroad was first and foremost the unfolding of a benevolent mission. On the contrary, the report repeatedly emphasized that "qualitative as well as quantitative improvement" of the Japanese population was crucial, and made it absolutely clear that permanent expansion and colonization abroad was essential to the psychological dynamism, not just the security and material well-being, of the Yamato race.[15]

To bring about the qualitative improvement of the Japanese, the report called for improved eugenic programs. On this matter, Nazi-like attitudes were exposed, albeit in passing, in criticism of the prevailing concern of the medical profession with illness and infirmity. Instead of concentrating on the sick and weak, it was declared, "we should actively improve our physical capacity eugenically by promoting such methods as mental and physical training as well as selective marriages."[16]

On the quantitative side of the matter, it was argued that the birth rate had been declining in Japan due to a combination of liberal ideas concerning birth control coupled with declining family size associated with rising urbanization. At the time the Ministry of Health and Welfare study was done, the total Japanese population was approximately 73 million. Drawing upon certain Western theories concerning the "coefficient of pressure" exerted on a people by neighboring populations, the study called for a drastic spurt in population growth. It was urged that the number of Japanese be increased to more than 100 million "as rapidly as possible."[17]

There was nothing secret about this concern with improving the race qualitatively and quantitatively. Programs to improve physical fitness traced back to the late 1930s, when the Japanese government belatedly acknowledged how physically ravaged the poorer classes were. Tuberculosis and other diseases and infirmities made untold thousands of young men and women unfit to be workers or soldiers. After the China Incident of 1937, agencies such as the Ministry of Health and Welfare (which was created in January 1938) took the lead in promoting social-welfare legislation that improved working conditions, created new medical facilities, and provided national health insurance. In January 1941, the government announced a population policy in which the twin goals of qualitative and quantitative improvement were spelled out in detail, and it was stated forthrightly that this policy was essential for maintaining Japan's leadership throughout East Asia. The target date for reaching a population of 100 million Japanese was set at 1960, two decades ahead; and to achieve this, it was announced, a concerted effort would be made to accelerate the birth rate by lowering the average marriage age by three years over the course of the next decade.

The goal established in 1941 was an average of five children per family, to be encouraged by tax incentives, loans, rationing privileges, and other material inducements—as well as by educational programs which discredited individualistic concerns and placed primary emphasis on the family and the Japanese race. Birth control and abortion were to be prohibited, and it was hoped that the atomizing effects of urbanization could be reversed by locating more factories and schools in the countryside and holding about 40 percent of the total population in the agrarian sector. Qualitative improvement of the Japanese race was also to be promoted by marriage counseling and tighter coordination of the various organizations which were involved in arranging marriages. One of the many domestic campaigns launched by the Japanese government prior to

Pearl Harbor was the "propagate and multiply movement," and healthy-baby contests were a familiar, and happy, feature of the early 1940s in Japan.[18]

Although such racial goals were well publicized in the late 1930s and early 1940s, *An Investigation of Global Policy with the Yamato Race as Nucleus* contained proposals that went further in explicitly linking the qualitative and quantitative advancement of the Yamato race to overseas expansion and colonialism. As a general principle, it was stated, island nations must expand to ensure their security and survival. As another general principle, moreover, it had been cogently argued by some Westerners that overseas expansion and colonization usually involves the most energetic and dynamic members of a population, and contributes directly to the "regeneration"—the "social evolution" and "racial development" —of the colonizing people as a whole. Indeed, it was predictable that any race or people whose vital powers were not energized by such external challenges would eventually decline.[19]

Obviously, the current military crisis in Asia demanded increased manpower to secure and defend the new Co-Prosperity Sphere. The Tokyo bureaucrats, however, were more concerned with the long-term requirements of the imperium, and to this end engaged in a variety of illuminating speculations. They observed that in recent times there had been debate over whether a successful colonial policy required planting a good-sized contingent of people from the colonizing country abroad, and concluded that expert opinion in the West agreed such overseas settlements were essential. In support of this, they cited not merely the Germans, but also General Smuts in South Africa and the Royal Institute of International Affairs in London.[20]

Exactly what did Japanese officials have in mind when they spoke of the new imperium? The Ministry of Health and Welfare bureaucrats acknowledged that this had never been clearly defined. As presumedly commonplace assumptions, however, they offered an ambitious schedule concerning the stages of expansion of the Greater East Asia Co-Prosperity Sphere, along with a chart projecting the number of Japanese settlers who ideally would be living abroad by 1950. The preciseness of these two "blueprints" is rather exceptional among surviving documents from the war years, and helps explain why the bonfires blossomed so ubiquitously in Tokyo in the days and weeks after Japan's capitulation.

The Japanese were determined to revise the Eurocentric cartography of the West and place Japan and Asia at the center of the map. In October 1942, the government took a step in this direction by announcing that hereafter the term "Far East" (*Kyokutō*) would not be used at all, since it was so transparently Eurocentric. Indeed, the formal rhetoric of Japan's "Greater East Asia War" and "Greater East Asia Co-Prosperity Sphere" had already signified the new cartography. There were wilder redraftings of the map, however. Shortly after the fall of Singapore, for example, one of Japan's leading geographers, Professor Komaki Tsuneki-chi of Kyoto Imperial University, delivered a series of radio broadcasts which became notorious in the West, although they were directed primarily at the domestic Japanese audience. In these broadcasts, and in numerous popular writings as well, Komaki designated both Europe and Africa as part of the Asian continent, while rechristening America as the "Eastern Asia Continent" and Australia as the "Southern Asia Continent." Observing that all the great oceans of the globe were connected, Komaki proposed that henceforth they all be known under a single name as the "Great Sea of Japan."[21]

The more staid bureaucrats in the Ministry of Health and Welfare, drafting their report a year after Komaki had refashioned the map, were slightly less radical, although they did identify Africa as an appendage of Asia and speak of America as Asia's "eastern wing," the two continents having once been joined.[22] Their understanding of what "East Asia" comprised was also amazingly expansive, as a section of the report entitled "Stages in the Enlargement of the Sphere of the East Asia Cooperative Body" reveals:

Stage 1. Japan, Manchuria, Mongolia, North China, major islands off the China coast, Central and South China under the Wang Ching-wei regime.

Stage 2. Remaining areas of China, French Indochina, Thailand, British Malaya, Burma, Dutch East Indies, New Guinea, British Borneo, New Caledonia, Australia, New Zealand, South Sea Islands with the exception of the Philippines.

Stage 3. Soviet territory east of Lake Baikal, peripheral regions of China, the Philippines, India and its coastal islands.

Stage 4. Assyria, Turkey, Iran, Iraq, Afghanistan and other central Asian countries, West Asia, Southwest Asia.

The report went on to note that these stages were not fixed and immutable, but might have to be revised in accordance with changing international conditions.[23]

Immediately following these projections, in a section dealing with the fundamental political, economic, diplomatic, and intellectual policies of the East Asia Cooperative Body, the report offered an even more expansive vision. "The ultimate ideal of the Cooperative Body is to place the whole world under one roof," it was stated, "and to bring about the existence of a moral, peaceful, and rational prosperity in which all peoples of the world assume their proper place."[24] This was an improvisation on the popular slogan of "the eight directions under one roof" (hakkō ichiu), which Westerners often interpreted as signaling Japan's plan for world conquest; and while the 1942–43 report does not substantiate such an interpretation in the literal sense of military conquest, certain comments here and elsewhere indicate that at least some Japanese did envision Japan using the East Asian bloc as a stepping stone to world leadership. Policies concerning transportation and communications, for example, were described as being critical not merely for successful prosecution of the war in Asia, but also "to establish the Japanese empire's subsequent leading position in the creation of a new world order."[25] Similarly, the section of the report dealing with mining, industry, and electrical power in East Asia stated that in addition to promoting the overall economic strength of Asia and establishing the productive base for the autonomous military defense of the area, such economic policies should also be understood as being designed to "establish the superiority of East Asia in a new global economy."[26] The opening pages of the 1943 study contained the flat assertion that the war would continue "until Anglo-American imperialistic democracy has been completely vanquished and a new world order erected in its place."[27]

Whatever form Japan's future world leadership might take, the pressing challenge for the present was to consolidate an autarkic bloc in Asia dominated by Japan. To ensure effective control of that bloc, it was essential that the "blood of the Yamato race" be "planted in the soil" of the various countries that comprised the Greater East Asia Co-Prosperity Sphere. Here was the notorious Nazi phrase—albeit with an odd twist, whereby "soil" meant not the homeland but the lands within the new imperium. And how much Yamato blood—if all went well—needed to be planted abroad? On this, the report was precise. The Population and Race Section estimated that by 1950 the Japanese population would have increased to approximately 86.8 million (it is not clear how they calculated projected war casualties). Of this number, an impressive 14 percent—12,090,000 individuals—should be living abroad as permanent settlers, with the majority engaged in agricultural pursuits. The projected distribution of these settlers throughout the Co-Prosperity Sphere—which in this particular reckoning included Australia and New Zealand—was as follows:[28]

Country	Total Japanese Population	Population Engaged in Agriculture
Japan	74.7 million	27.4 million
Korea	2.7 "	1.35 "
Taiwan	0.4 "	—
Manchukuo	3.1 "	2.5 "
China	1.5 "	1.0 "
Indochina		
Thailand		
Burma	2.38 "	1.0 "
Philippines		
East Indies		
Australia		
New Zealand	2.0 "	2.0 "

This was a dramatic projection; and in spelling out the details of this planned exodus, the Japanese revealed a great deal of what they really had in mind in speaking of the Yamato race as a superior *minzoku* destined to lead Asia forever. The Japanese sent abroad as permanent settlers naturally would be carefully screened by the government. They would play leadership roles in the areas to which they migrated, serve as role models, and ensure the cooperation of native peoples with Japan. To facilitate close coordination among these colonists, as well as between them and the Japanese homeland, they would be concentrated in compact settlements throughout Asia; the report recommended establishing "Japan-towns" (*Nippon-machi*) in each region. Intermarriage with native peoples was to be avoided at all costs—not merely because mixed-blood children were generally inferior, but also because intermarriage would destroy the psychic solidarity of the Yamato race.[29]

In the summer of 1943, almost simultaneously with the completion of this secret report, a Ministry of Health and Welfare official presented some of the same ideas in a popular journal. Writing in the July 1943 issue of *Nippon Hyōron,* Furuya Yoshio, a medical doctor who headed a research department in the ministry, acknowledged that the war had impeded progress in the directions set forth in the January 1941 population policy. It was thus now all the more imperative for Japan to increase its population and "reinforce its racial integrity and creative faculty," with particular attentiveness to consolidating the country's position in the countries to the south. While due respect should be shown to the customs and aspirations of other peoples within the Co-Prosperity Sphere, Furuya continued, no one could deny that "no nation in this part of the Orient can stand comparison with Japan in point of racial virility and organizational ability. The racial vigor of Japan is the most potent factor that has enabled it to attain its present distinguished position in the polity of nations." Furuya cautioned that the Japanese sent to settle in the southern areas should take care to maintain their cultural values and avoid miscegenation, with all the vexing "biological and social" problems that intermarriage would cause. At the same time, however, he also expressed hope that the other countries of Asia would be inspired by Japan's example to develop their own sense of racial vigor and sharpen their organizational skills. By serving as a racial role model in this manner, the Japanese would reveal their "sincerity of purpose and purity of intention" as leaders of the Co-Prosperity Sphere.[30]

The mixture of racial pride and idealism evident in this article was typical—and typically misleading. The ministry's secret report also was so thoroughly peppered with the apparently sincere vocabulary of "morality" and "liberation" and "respect for native customs" that it can legitimately be offered as a provocative contrast to the cynical race hate that seeped through the public and private pronouncements of Japan's German allies. In their references to "blood" and "soil," and their fulminations against mixed marriage, however, the Japanese researchers also revealed their Nazi affinities. Often idealistic and racist attitudes were so completely jumbled together that they became, for all practical purposes, inseparable. Thus, a lengthy discussion of "the problem of mixed blood" began with reference to the literal spilling of Japanese blood in the current war to liberate Asia, and then moved immediately to the vision of Japanese blood being planted abroad in the form of colonial settlers to ensure Japan's permanent leadership over "liberated" Asia:

We, the Yamato race, are presently spilling our "blood" to realize our mission in world history of establishing a Greater East Asia Co-Prosperity Sphere. In order to liberate the billion people of Asia, and also to maintain our position of leadership over the Greater East Asia Co-Prosperity Sphere forever, we must plant the "blood" of the Yamato race in this "soil."

The passage then went on to warn that those Japanese settlers who planted their country's blood abroad in this manner should take care not to mix it with that of other races.[31]

"Purity of blood" emerged as a concern of many Japanese officials during the war, in reference to the indigenous populations of the occupied areas as well as the Japanese themselves. In Indonesia, for example, the Japanese found "half-breeds" or "mixed-breeds" to be a particularly difficult group to deal with, and went so far as to establish eight different categories for Eurasians, depending on their percentage of European blood. Many were incarcerated during the war (along with almost all white people in Indonesia), and according to some estimates as many as 10 percent died in prison. Concerning overseas Japanese, admonitions against racial intermarriage were a standard part of policy documents, and the 1943 report spelled out the rationale for this: intermarriage would destroy the "national spirit" of the Yamato race. Even though the first generation of emigrants would be carefully selected to ensure complete loyalty to the Japanese state, long-term detachment from the homeland could dilute the consciousness of being Japanese. This problem would become more acute among the subsequent generations of overseas Japanese, and in this regard the report recommended not only that the settlers live in closely knit communities, but also that their offspring return to Japan for education. By the second and third generation, one could anticipate a truly serious crisis of identity among overseas Japanese, and rigorous policies would have to be adopted to "ensure that they remain aware of the superiority of the Japanese people and proud of being a member of the leading race."[32]

In promoting the development of unassimilable Japanese communities strategically located throughout Asia, the government researchers flirted with another Nazi concept: *Lebensraum.* "Expansion of living space," "securing the living space of the Yamato race," "the broader living sphere of the Yamato race"—such phrases wove in and out of the general discussion of the Greater East Asia Co-Prosperity Sphere. At one point, *Lebensraum* for Japan was explicitly presented as the first of a trinity of basic goals—to be followed by Asian liberation and the consolidation of a new order. Of these three goals, the report identified the first as being of greatest importance, and then proceeded to devote many pages to an analysis of German "occupation" policies.[33]

The simplest rationalization for Japan's need for expanded living space in Asia was overpopulation. Japan's 73 million people constituted approximately 5 percent of the world's population, it was noted, and even taking into account the colonial territories of Korea and Formosa, they were squeezed into roughly one half of 1 percent of the world's land. Japan was already the most densely populated country in the world—and, of course, destined to experience a dramatic population boom in the immediate future if current policies to boost the birth rate materialized. The government's demographers, it will be recalled, had calculated that a population of at least 100 million—over one third larger than existed at the time—was the minimum necessary to ensure a margin of security vis-à-vis the United States, the Soviet Union, and China. If the present Japanese population was already pushing at the seams of the home islands, the anticipated population simply could not fit. Nor could it be fed from existing home resources, or accommodated by existing home industries.[34]

Such seemingly relentless demographic imperatives merged with broader military and economic considerations in such a way that, in Japanese eyes, the Co-Prosperity Sphere naturally came to be seen as simultaneously providing a secure defense zone, a self-sufficient economic bloc, and a new living space which could accommodate Japan's excess population. Dreams of autarky merged easily with dreams of new *Lebensraum* for the Yamato race; and this seemed a happy convergence for numerous reasons. The Co-Prosperity Sphere would solve Japan's overpopulation problem, the permanent overseas Japanese population would play a leading role in both controlling and developing the Co-Prosperity Sphere, and the very sense of mission which this colossal undertaking demanded would invigorate the Japanese sense of cohesion and self-importance. In spreading out geographically, the Yamato race would draw closer psychologically. In the realm of racial consciousness, expansion meant contraction.

A comparable sort of logic characterized the core vocabulary that was used to define racial relations within the Co-Prosperity Sphere, for here the set phrases that suggested interracial bonding among the peoples

of Asia went hand in hand with code words denoting permanent separa-
tion and discrimination. The vocabulary of bonding was quite standardized, and provides yet another example of the similarity between Japanese
and German thinking. Relationships within the autarkic bloc were most
often described as being, ideally, "organic";[35] and the most popular set-
phrase denoting interracial harmony within the Co-Prosperity Sphere was
one that can be written with variant ideographs and rendered in several
ways in English: *minzoku kyōdōtai*, a "collectivity of peoples," "racial
community," or "racial cooperative body."[36] The report also spoke of
"racial harmony" (*minzoku kyōwa*—a concept that had been heavily
emphasized since the 1930s among Japanese in Manchuria), "racial consanguinity," and the possibility of creating a "collective racialism." There
was even passing reference to bonds of "heart" and "love."[37]

Such references to emotional ties uniting the peoples of Asia were
introduced in the context of the most benign of all metaphors of inequality: the family. This was, in addition, the metaphor which most clearly
revealed how the mystique of the Japanese as the leading race within the
Co-Prosperity Sphere was intimately linked to the language and ideology
used to reinforce hierarchy within Japan. During World War Two, this
model of familial relations often was presented by Japanese spokesmen
(and Western experts as well) as one of the abiding legacies of traditional
Japan. In fact, it is better understood as an ideological construct carefully
and even brilliantly nurtured for modern times. In the feudal era, the
values associated with the patriarchal "family system" were most closely
associated with the ruling samurai elite, and did not have deep popular
roots in the rural community or among the urban masses. It was not until
the late nineteenth century that the Japanese oligarchy and emerging class
of big industrialists began to vigorously promote the family system to
buttress the patriarchal state headed by the emperor, legitimize social
inequality, and obscure the harsh realities of class (and gender) exploitation. In other words, when the ruling groups of postfeudal Japan belatedly
began to introduce "traditional family morality" in their laws, textbooks,
and sweatshops, they were shrewdly resurrecting an old elite concept for
purposes of modern mass control. Within the family, each individual was
to have his or her proper place, culminating at the top in the single
patriarch or family head, whose authority was to be unquestioned. The
family was the archetypical "organic" entity, whose inner relationships
were inequitable but in theory complementary and harmonious.[38]

It was not until the 1930s that this "unique" familial model became formally adopted—first, as a ruling-class orthodoxy delineating the proper place of all Japanese within their overarching family-nation, and then, before much time had passed, as a ruling-state and leading-race ideology applicable to the whole world. This critical late development can be illustrated with some precision. The manifesto which enshrined the family system as a domestic ideology was *Cardinal Principles of the National Polity* (*Kokutai no Hongi*), issued by the Ministry of Education in 1937. This was supplemented by two later Education Ministry publications, *The Way of the Subject* (*Shinmin no Michi*, 1941) and *The Way of the Family* (*Ie no Michi*, or more formally, *Senji Katei Kyōiku Shidō Yōkō*, 1942). That the essence of these teachings was the family paradigm, and the essence of the family paradigm in turn was the concept of "proper place," is apparent in the following passage from *Cardinal Principles of the National Polity*:

> In our country, under a unique family system, parent and child and husband and wife live together, supporting and helping each other. . . . [T]his harmony must also be made to materialize in communal life. . . . In each community there are those who take the upper places while there are those who work below them. Through each one fulfilling his position is the harmony of a community obtained. To fulfill one's part means to do one's appointed task with the utmost faithfulness each in his own sphere; and by this means do those above receive help from inferiors, and inferiors are loved by superiors; and in working together harmoniously is beautiful concord manifested and creative work carried out. This applies both to the community and to the State.[39]

The extension to the global sphere of this domestic model for age, gender, and class relationships took place in 1940, in conjunction with Japan's announcement of a Greater East Asia Co-Prosperity Sphere and, immediately following that, its conclusion of the Axis Pact with Germany and Italy. On August 1, 1940, the day the Co-Prosperity Sphere was introduced, Foreign Minister Matsuoka Yōsuke delivered a brief statement which—in the Foreign Office's own English translation—began as follows:

> I have always said that the mission of Japan is to proclaim and demonstrate the *kōdō* (Imperial way) throughout the world. Viewed

from the standpoint of international relations, this amounts, I think, to enabling all nations and races to find each its proper place in the world. . . .[40]

Almost two months later, in its formal announcement of the Tripartite Alliance, the Foreign Office spoke similarly (here again in its own translation):

The Governments of Japan, Germany and Italy, considering it as the condition precedent of any lasting peace that all nations of the world be given each its own proper place, have decided to stand by and co-operate with one another in regard to their efforts in Greater East Asia and the regions of Europe respectively wherein it is their prime purpose to establish and maintain a new order of things calculated to promote mutual prosperity and welfare to all of the peoples concerned. . . .[41]

On September 27, 1940, in his brief imperial rescript announcing the fatal alliance, the emperor declared in almost identical words that the monumental task for the future was "to enable all nations and races to assume their proper place in the world, and all peoples to be at peace in their own sphere."[42] Thereafter, the concept of a global hierarchy of nations and races, each in their proper place, was treated as holy writ in official plans, pronouncements, and publications. In March 1941, the Ministry of Education's new edition of history textbooks for primary-school children used the emperor's own phrasing to describe the significance of the Axis Pact, and emphasized that Japan's mission was to bring peace not merely to Asia but throughout the whole world.[43]

In addition to the philosophizing and moralizing that undergirded it, the modern family-system ideology also involved mythologizing at two levels. Domestically, in the world of everyday affairs, it romanticized relationships in the actual kinship network, the work place, and the nation as a whole. In other words, the romanticized family metaphor helped to perpetuate the myth of harmony in a society where social tensions were severe and class conflict by no means absent. Refashioned for export, the same family metaphor was evoked to reinforce the myth of complementariness and reciprocity in what in actual practice was a grossly inequitable imperialistic power structure.

At the same time, the mystique of the family also drew sustenance from the myths found in the earliest writings of Japan. It drew, that is, on genuine mythology, treating ancient legends as history and ascribing the origins of the moral ideal of family relationships to the earliest progenitors of the Japanese imperial family. No one could deny that much of the vocabulary of social hierarchy and familial relationships had come to Japan from China in the form of Confucianism. By turning to their own mythohistory, however, the Japanese were able to argue that such relationships actually predated Confucius and had been theirs since earliest times in the form of a figure unique to the Yamato people—the emperor, the purest *pater familias* of all. Japan's adaptability may have permitted it to absorb the best of Oriental and Occidental civilizations over the centuries. What enabled the Japanese to transform such outside influences into a synthesis that represented a higher plane of culture, however, was their unique embodiment of this emperor-centered familial ideal. Indeed, in espousing the familial ideal to his subjects at war, the contemporary emperor, Hirohito, was recreating the idealized persona of his mythical progenitors.

For all their sober academicism, the bureaucrats who drafted the 1943 report also fell back on such mythohistory in explaining Japan's proper place as a world leader. Under the family-system ideology within Japan, every Japanese was assigned his or her proper place in accordance with the rules of patriarchy. Abroad in Asia, however, these same Japanese became transformed into collective patriarchs; as a race, they were the self-proclaimed head of the family of peoples gathered under the Co-Prosperity Sphere. In a long section devoted to "the characteristics of the Japanese race as a leading influence," the government researchers thus dwelt in familiar terms on the "family-nation" nature of the Japanese polity, in which the emperor was a father to his children-subjects, and the guiding ethos rested on family spirit. They then paid obeisance to the mythic Emperor Jimmu, quoting a line from the ancient classics attributed to him to legitimize the argument that once such a moral ideal had been established within the country, it was destined to be carried abroad. Japan's modern history since the first Sino-Japanese War of 1894–95 represented the realization, over two-and-a-half millennia later, of Jimmu's great vision.[44] In this way, myth, morality, and mission were wedded, with a concreteness and vivacity the Nazis could only have envied.

Just as family spirit and the family-nation had triumphed over individuality in the Japanese moral order, the report went on, so in the contemporary world a "new order of morality" was replacing the old order of individual states governed by international law. This emerging new order, exemplified by the Greater East Asia Co-Prosperity Sphere, was unprecedented in world history. It did not rest on the force and oppression that the old imperialist powers relied on, nor on the outmoded and only superficially "rational" legalistic premises of equality, but rather on the moral principle of "enabling all nations and races to assume their proper place in the world." The phrasing adopted by the researchers was thus identical with that canonized by the emperor and officialdom beginning in 1940, and read by the primary-school pupils as well—although "proper place" was also rendered in various other ways in the same study.[45] The report also stated explicitly that if the Co-Prosperity Sphere was a "pseudo-family," it should never be forgotten that Japan was the indisputable "family head."[46] In keeping with the highest expression of paternalism, the authority of the family head should be tempered by love. The guiding phrase here was a righteous old maxim that saw heavy service during these years: "combining benevolence and stern justice" (oni heiyō).[47]

In the final analysis, morality thus took precedence over both science and law; this morality was "organic," and its essence could be found in microcosm in the idealized family; and no nation or people embodied this ideal more perfectly than Japan and the Japanese. As other Japanese writers put it at this time, the outmoded "rule of law" of the bourgeois West was being replaced by a more moral and realistic "rule of man."[48]

There were many variations on the familial model. In the most high-flown statements, the Japanese described their goal as being to bring the whole world together as one happy family under the emperor. "Under the glory of the Throne," students were told in their wartime ethics textbooks, "it is our fixed aim that people of the world should become one big family." More often, the family metaphors were applied to relations within the Co-Prosperity Sphere. A booklet titled The Greater East Asia War and Ourselves (Dai Tōa Sensō to Warera), published by the government in 1942, explained that the various countries of East Asia would be bound together in reciprocal relationships like "parent and child, elder and younger brother."[49] The puppet state of Manchukuo, often cited as a model for Japan's relationships with other Asian countries, was described as a "branch family" in the ministry study and a "child country" in other sources.

In some schemes, Japan was denoted the parent, the role of elder brother or brothers was assigned to the core countries of the Co-Prosperity

Sphere (China, Manchukuo, Korea, and Formosa), and the peoples and nations of the south were relegated to the status of younger brothers. Propaganda addressed to the West sometimes attempted to blunt criticism of such slogans as *hakkō ichiu* ("the eight directions under one roof") by equating this with the English phrase "universal brotherhood," but in the Japanese idiom brotherhood itself was inherently hierarchic. Thus, the report of the Ministry of Health and Welfare itself at one point offered the relationship between elder and younger brothers as a model for relations between the Japanese and other Asians. While the spirit of "the eight directions under one roof" might lead to assimilation in the remote future, for the foreseeable future it was important not to misinterpret the rhetoric of coexistence and coprosperity as meaning that mentally and culturally inferior peoples should be treated as equals. To treat kindergarten children as college students, the report observed, was of no help to the kindergarten children.[50]

In the thousands of pages devoted to Japan's future relations with other races and nationalities, the researchers also made it amply clear that any sort of "assimilation" within the Co-Prosperity Sphere could only involve other countries gradually being lifted up toward Japan's level. It was crucial that the process not move in the other direction, thus pulling Japan down to an inferior level. While local customs should be respected if they did not disrupt the larger goals of the Co-Prosperity Sphere, and while "common Oriental cultural ideals" naturally should be emphasized, the new order was to be constructed in accordance with Japanese characteristics. Japanese would become the common language of the bloc, and Japan would "assimilate other races into Nipponism." Indoctrination (called "thought leadership") would be effected through extensive control of the channels of information. Art, sports, and tourism that heightened a consciousness of East Asian solidarity would be promoted. Propaganda about Japan's culture as well as its national power would be widely disseminated. A new history of the world would be taught, focusing on East Asia with Japan at its center, rather than on the West or China as heretofore. The emerging native elites would be trained by the Japanese.[51] There was nothing in this sprawling cultural agenda to suggest that the Japanese had anything to learn from other Asians. Nor was there any suggestion whatsoever that they would ever relinquish their role as the "leading race"—or ever even reach a point of sharing power equitably. In the family-system paradigm, there could be but a single family head.

·　·　·

In the course of the brief life of the Co-Prosperity Sphere, certain Japanese emerged as genuine friends of the peoples of Southeast Asia. The names of two middle-echelon officers of the Imperial Army in particular have come to exemplify the spirit of Asian brotherhood and true liberation that Japan's slogans proclaimed: Major Fujiwara Iwaichi, who through his F Agency (F Kikan) helped organize the Indian National Army under Mohan Singh in 1941; and Colonel Suzuki Keiji, whose Southern Agency (Minami Kikan) played a similar role in supporting the "Thirty Comrades" in Burma in forming the Burmese Independence Army. Other Japanese officers have been remembered with respect if not comparable affection as individuals sensitive to the aspirations for true equality among Southeast Asian nationalists, and a number of Japanese civilians who flocked to the occupied areas took the ideals of "elder brother" or "elder sister" to heart in the best of ways, and impressed the non-Japanese they dealt with with their altruism and warmth. Decades after the war, for example, one Indonesian woman who was a schoolgirl at the time still fondly recalled the kindness, dedication, enthusiasm, and exuberant Pan-Asian idealism of her female Japanese instructors.[52]

For every such positive account, however, there are countless others that speak of the oppression and outright brutality of the Japanese in Southeast Asia; and in the light of Japan's own prior history of interacting with other Asians, this is hardly surprising. The record of the Japanese as colonial or neocolonial administrators in Formosa, Korea, Manchukuo, and occupied China varied depending on the place and circumstances, but the basic assumption of Japanese superiority was invariable. Certainly, the Koreans could have told the new members of the Co-Prosperity Sphere what to expect. Their outspoken nationalist leaders had been tortured and executed in 1919. Their government, commerce, industry, and agriculture had been almost totally taken over by the Japanese. Over six thousand of their countrymen and countrywomen living in Japan had been tortured and massacred by both the police and rampaging Japanese citizens in the wake of the 1923 Kanto earthquake, in a horrendous outburst of sheer race hatred. First- and second-generation Koreans resident in Japan (who numbered close to 2 million by 1945) were denied full citizenship and subjected to every conceivable form of discrimination— their treatment being very similar to that accorded blacks in the United States, despite the fact that many Koreans could pass physically for Japanese.[53]

The Chinese too had been regarded with disdain since the late nineteenth century, when they were defeated in the first Sino-Japanese War. By the 1930s, such contempt had thoroughly permeated the China section of the Imperial Army intelligence arm—which had its own colloquial equivalents to such popular English racial slurs as "chinks"—and this goes far to explaining why the Japanese so badly underestimated China's will and capacity to resist Japanese aggression after 1937.[54] In part, it helps explain as well the violent outrages which Japanese soldiers committed against Chinese civilians when their offensive met unexpectedly stiff resistance. In Southeast Asia, overseas Chinese were, after the white colonials, the target of the severest Japanese treatment. Whether in colonial Korea and Formosa, in "independent" Manchukuo, or in occupied China, moreover, the Japanese made amply clear that the only *modus operandi* they were comfortable with in dealing with other Asian nations was that of puppet master to puppet.

These earlier colonies and conquests not only provided models for Japanese behavior in Southeast Asia, but also many of the same overbearing administrative personnel. Ba Maw, the Burmese premier, for example, referred to the most vicious elements of the Japanese military officialdom in Southeast Asia as the "Korea clique," comprised largely of men who "had learnt in Korea, Manchukuo, and China to believe that the Japanese were the master race in Asia and to deal with the other Asian races on that footing." For such men, he went on, "there was only one way to do a thing, the Japanese way; only one goal and interest, the Japanese interest; only one destiny for the East Asian countries, to become so many Manchukuos or Koreas tied forever to Japan. These racial impositions— they were just that—made any real understanding between the Japanese militarists and the peoples of our region virtually impossible."[55]

Ba Maw's appraisal of Japan's brief interlude as overlord of Asia is the most common one among Asians who encountered the Japanese, and the "racial impositions" of which he spoke took numerous forms. One was spontaneous: the visceral racism exhibited by Japanese soldiers of all ranks toward non-Japanese in the form of slapping and other verbal and physical abuse upon the slightest provocation. A second "racial imposition" was the more formal policy of "Japanization," which the Japanese attempted to impose throughout the Co-Prosperity Sphere. Native peoples were required to bow to all Japanese, of whatever rank (just as POWs had to salute all Japanese soldiers). They were also forced to perform the *saikeirei* or ritual bow toward the emperor in Tokyo at public assemblies. Local calendars were changed to Japanese mythohistorical time; thus, 1942 became the year 2602 (following the founding of the imperial state in 660 B.C.). Purely Japanese holidays became Co-Prosperity Sphere holidays, including the "Foundation Day" of the imperial line (*Kigensetsu,* celebrated on February 11), the birthday of the current emperor (April 29), and the anniversary of the birth of the Emperor Meiji (November 3). Western languages and books were proscribed in certain places, while Japanese was promoted everywhere as the "lingua franca" of the new imperium. Many edicts to local Japanese commanders in the occupied areas called for respect for local customs and traditions so long as these did not conflict with Japanese interests, but the essence of basic cultural policy was the promotion of grass-roots "Japanization."[56]

The most persuasive evidence of the permanent rather than temporary nature of Japan's "racial impositions" is to be found in the basic financial and economic policy adopted toward the Co-Prosperity Sphere. Policy guidelines established early in 1942 for the military governments in the southern area made it absolutely clear that the Japanese were to assume the dominant financial and economic roles formerly played by the European and American colonial powers, and to refashion these in a manner which ensured Japan's permanent supremacy in Asia. This was articulated in a basic "Outline of Economic Policies for the Southern Areas" adopted immediately after Pearl Harbor, in which Japan's long-term objective was described as "the attainment of an autarkic Greater East Asian Co-Prosperity Sphere, with the major goals being to assist the economic expansion of the Japanese people in the southern areas on the basis of overall national planning, and to advance economic changes within the Co-Prosperity Sphere." A basic guideline for military administrations adopted by the Ministry of the Navy the following March spelled out what this meant in greater and franker detail. "As our financial institutions are established and strengthened," it stated, "they shall gradually assume the financial hegemony hitherto held by the enemy institutions." Concerning industrial development, the Navy observed that "in keeping with the policy of utilizing the southern areas as a supplier of raw materials for our country and as a market for our products, the fostering of manufacturing industries in occupied areas shall be discouraged." Japanese businessmen were brought in to handle the pressing requirements of the Japanese war machine, but it was taken for granted that in due time they would assume permanent control of all key sectors of the local economies. While criminal abuse of native labor such as the scores of thousands of Indonesian *rōmusha* who died working for the Imperial

Army may be attributed to the war circumstances, it was general Japanese policy that "wages shall be held down as much as possible." It was also general policy, wherever possible, to maintain the administrative structures established by the former colonials, and to rely on local labor bosses as well as the local elites.[57]

This policy of creating an economic structure which would ensure the permanent subordination of all other peoples and nations of Asia to Japan clarifies the key elements in the Japanese worldview in a concrete way: when the Japanese applied the concepts of "proper place" or familial relationships to their relations with other Asians, they were in fact talking about a practical division of labor within an autarkic bloc totally dominated by themselves. They naturally analyzed this bloc in conventional economic terms concerning the optimum mobilization of available resources, but racial and ethnic issues were also integral to these calculations. In this regard, the secret 1942–43 report which has been the focus of this chapter is again illuminating, for it illustrates the central place which racial considerations held in the long-term vision of the Co-Prosperity Sphere. The planners looked not only at the natural resources and strategic placement of each area, but also at the character traits of the indigenous populations. They engaged, that is, in much the same sort of "national character" commentaries that were preoccupying many Westerners during the same period.

In this appraisal, none of their fellow Asians fared very well. The Han Chinese were characterized as fundamentally phlegmatic. The overseas Chinese, whose business acumen was undeniable, were basically flunkies, for sale to the highest bidder. It was recommended that the Japanese "utilize" them for the time being, "but gradually expel them." Burmese, Annamese, Malays—indeed, "southern peoples" in general— were all characterized as lazy. With few exceptions (such as the Lao), they lacked any business sense. The Filipinos may have been superior to other Asians, but they still could not be called genuinely civilized. For good or ill, they had been profoundly influenced by the Americans, and the catalog of their qualities was a mixed but generally unflattering one. As the Japanese described them, the Filipinos were materialistic, extravagant, duplicitous, imitative, litigious, poor at figures, weak in analytical skills, and, at the ruling-class level, hopelessly corrupt and dependent on the United States.[58] Certain of these negative qualities (duplicitous, imitative, lacking in analytic skills) were identical to character traits that Westerners said the Japanese possessed.

Concerning the Koreans and Formosans, the report was exceedingly harsh. They were described as being especially suitable to carry out the heavy physical work of a protracted war. Given their high birth rates, resistance to Japanization, and strategic locations, special care had to be taken to prevent them from becoming "parasites" within the empire. Once the war was over, Koreans living within Japan proper should be sent home; those living near the Soviet border should be replaced by Japanese settlers; and, in general, Koreans should be encouraged to emigrate to harsh and thinly populated places such as New Guinea. Far from the Greater East Asia Co-Prosperity Sphere meaning the lifting of the colonial yoke from Korea and Formosa, it was recommended that the Japanese presence in each country be increased until it amounted to 10 percent of the total population.[59]

While public speakers called for Pan-Asianism, racial harmony, and liberation from the white colonial yoke, privately the Japanese managers of the new imperium were advised to pay careful attention to relations among the different races and countries under their leadership. They were told to "take advantage of enmity and jealousy among these peoples" and pursue, wherever feasible, a shrewd "divide-and-rule" policy. They were also warned to be particularly cautious in dealing with the mixed-blood offspring of Southeast Asians and Caucasians or overseas Chinese.[60]

To borrow the terminology of a later generation of social scientists, the Japanese plan for the Co-Prosperity Sphere amounted to an almost perfect model of "center-periphery" relationships, all designed to ensure the supremacy of the Japanese as the leading race. In this scheme, Japan was the towering metropole, the overwhelmingly dominant hub of the great autarkic bloc. All currency and finance would naturally be tied to the yen. All major transportation and communication networks, whether on land or by sea or air, were to center on Japan and be controlled by Tokyo. All war-related industrial production, energy sources, and strategic materials would likewise be centralized and controlled by Japan, and, in general, Japan would be responsible for the production of high-quality manufactures and finished products in the heavy-industry sector. While Japan would provide capital and technical know-how for the development of light industry (generally for local consumption) throughout the Co-Prosperity Sphere, most countries would remain in their familiar roles as producers of raw materials and semifinished goods. To the extent possible, trade within the bloc would take the form of barter. The basic policy toward the farming populations throughout the bloc would simply be to encourage them to work hard. There were no immediate plans, it was indicated, to "reform management" in the agrarian sector—presumedly meaning there were no plans for land reform, or the breaking down of the Western colonial plantations.[61]

Naturally, there would be gradations within the bloc—critical "semiperipheral" areas, as it were. As the civilian planners saw it, the "core region" of the Co-Prosperity Sphere for a long while to come would remain the Japanese home islands plus Manchukuo, along with North China and Mongolia, with genuine "self-sufficiency" only gradually coming to embrace Central and South China, Southeast Asia, and India. At one point, the report spoke colorfully of the Japan Sea and East China Sea serving as a great "inland sea" for Greater East Asia. In the southern regions, the special economic importance of Hong Kong and Singapore was acknowledged—and was indeed taken as sufficient reason for withholding independence from Hong Kong and Malaya indefinitely.[62]

It was naturally hoped that this division of labor would benefit all members of the bloc, but the prime beneficiaries would always be the Japanese. On this, the report did not mince words. The long-term goal of Japanese policy, it acknowledged at one point, was to create "an inseparable economic relationship between the Yamato race, the leader of the East Asia Cooperative Body, and other member peoples, whereby our country will hold the key to the very existence of all the races of East Asia."[63] A policy guideline issued previously in Singapore expressed much the same sentiment in even more positive terms: "Japanese subjects shall be afforded opportunities for development everywhere, and after establishing firm footholds they shall exalt their temperament as the leading race with the basic doctrine of planning the long-term expansion of the Yamato race."[64]

PART IV
EPILOGUE

◄ C H A P T E R 1 1 ►
FROM WAR TO PEACE

It has long been observed that it is easier to begin wars than to end them, and the war in Asia not only confirmed this truism but gave it new meaning for the modern age. Although the Japanese committed themselves to hostilities with grave misgivings, they gave virtually no serious thought to how the conflict might be terminated. Somehow, before too long, they hoped, the Allies would tire of the struggle and agree to a compromise settlement which left the Co-Prosperity Sphere essentially intact. The American and British leaders, on their part, recognized that the war would be long and arduous, and quickly came to an agreement that the struggle against Germany had to take priority over that against Japan. They were not only confident of ultimate victory, however, but also assumed from the start that this must entail grinding the Japanese to powder and laying their cities in ashes, as Churchill so vividly phrased it. They were not speculating about Japanese psychology when they made these predictions, but simply acknowledging what they felt to be the nature of war itself.

And so it happened. There may be disagreement as to which battle or battles proved to be the decisive turning point in the war: the Coral Sea and Midway in mid-1942? Guadalcanal, where Allied victory was assured by the end of 1942? Imphal, the Philippine Sea, Saipan, Tinian, and Guam—Japan's major defeats on land and sea—in mid-1944? Leyte Gulf, which effectively eliminated the Imperial Navy as a serious threat in October 1944? In any case, by the autumn of 1944 it was absolutely clear to leaders on both sides that Japan was doomed. And yet the struggle dragged on for another year.

This final year of agony dramatically revealed the altered nature of modern war. The traditional psychological factors which made ending wars difficult—pride on all sides, desperation and mental paralysis on the part of the losers, the winners' drive for revenge and unequivocal victory —were now wedded to unprecedented forces of destruction. War hates were not new to the mid-twentieth century, nor were race hates or the killing of noncombatants. Holy wars were surely not new. The techniques of mobilizing and sustaining such sentiments at fever pitch had, however, advanced by quantum leaps in the twentieth century—now involving not only the sophisticated use of radio, film, and other mass media, but also a concerted mobilization and integration of the propaganda resources of the whole state apparatus. Such developments went hand in hand with breathtaking advances in the technologies of destruction, especially in air power and firepower. Simultaneously, there occurred an erosion of "old-fashioned" constraints on the legitimate targets of war.

Just as these new technologies permitted killing at greater and greater distances, so also did there take place an increasing psychological distancing between one's own side and the enemy. The enemy became remote, monolithic, a different species, ultimately simply large numbers to tally up gleefully on one's growing list of estimated enemy dead. The new capability for rapidly killing large numbers of people was accompanied, almost inevitably, by a general acceptance of the belief that in the "total war" of the modern age it was necessary and even proper to do so, with little distinction made any longer between combatants and noncombatants. It is possible to obscure what war is about, as we have seen, by denying enemies their humanity and seeing them as beasts, vermin, demons, or devils. Numbers all too often contribute to much the same psychic numbing, and may even serve the further function of rendering more abstract, and somewhat easier to accept, the losses on one's own side.

Yet now, at a distance, the numbers have a capacity to shock as well as inform; and it is sobering to observe not only how many men, women, and children died in Asia, but also how many of these deaths occurred in the final year of the conflict, after Japan's defeat was already assured. China aside, as many or more individuals died after the outcome of the war was clear as perished while there was still reasonable doubt about how events would unfold. Accurate mortality figures are impossible to obtain, especially for Asian victims of the war (other than the Japanese themselves); and the task becomes next to impossible when civilian deaths are included, extending to "peripheral" victims such as conscript laborers worked to death and ordinary people who starved or died of epidemic diseases as a consequence of the war's ravages. Still, the approximate human toll can be suggested.

It is often stated that close to 55 million people died in World War Two, although usually it is difficult to ascertain the precise figures which lie behind this appalling toll. In fact, cumulative estimates of the human costs of the war by Westerners have tended to neglect Asian deaths other than Chinese and Japanese, and to ignore the millions of Asians who fell victim to the economic chaos that accompanied the rise and fall of the misnamed Co-Prosperity Sphere. When the situation in Asia is taken fully into account, the total death count for World War Two may be even higher than has previously been appreciated.

Several countries and races bore an overwhelming share of the burden of loss in World War Two. The Soviet Union suffered by far the heaviest casualties, with military and civilian deaths now estimated at 20 million or more. Close to 6 million Jews were murdered; estimated military and civilian deaths among the Germans were in the neighborhood of 5.6 million; some 3 million Poles died, not counting the Polish Jews; and perhaps 1.6 million civilians and military perished in Yugoslavia. Seven other countries in the West account for another 2 million military and civilian deaths, each nation having losses in the range of a quarter to a third of a million individuals: Austria, Britain, France, Italy, Hungary, Rumania, and the United States. Losses by the remaining belligerent countries in the West come to another million. In the Soviet Union and the West alone, and including the genocide of the Jews, the many separate wars of these barbaric years thus claimed at least 39 million lives.[1]

In Asia, estimates of the human toll in China range from several million to 15 million deaths. The official figure for Chinese soldiers killed in action against the Japanese over eight years of war, from 1937 to 1945, is 1.3 million, although other sources place battle deaths higher. The greater difficulty lies in calculating civilian deaths. A United Nations report in 1947 estimated that 9 million Chinese were killed in the war, and "an enormous number" died of starvation or disease in 1945 and 1946 in the prolonged famine that occurred as a result of Japan's final devastating offensive in China, which began in late 1944 and swept through the rice-producing regions from Hunan to Kwangtung, Kwangsi, and Kweichow provinces. The Chinese representative to the postwar Far Eastern

Commission, which had a nominal oversight role concerning policy toward occupied Japan, estimated total Chinese casualties—including killed, wounded, and disabled—to be 11 million. In 1948, another Chinese spokesman stated that the war cost China $50 billion and the lives of 15 million people, while leaving an additional 60 million homeless. So great was the devastation and suffering in China that in the end it is necessary to speak of uncertain "millions" of deaths. Certainly, it is reasonable to think in general terms of approximately 10 million Chinese war dead, a total surpassed only by the Soviet Union.[2]

The human cost of the war in Indonesia also was severe, and is likewise extremely difficult to ascertain with any precision. By one official account, some 130,000 Europeans were interned in Indonesia by the Japanese, of whom 30,000 died in prison. Another report indicated that these deaths included 4,500 European women and 2,300 children. Between 300,000 and 1 million Indonesians (as well as many Chinese residents of Indonesia) were mobilized as forced labor by the Japanese, with many being sent outside the country to work on the construction of the Burma-Siam "railroad of death." Estimates of total deaths among these workers range from many tens of thousands to a half million. After the war, the United Nations accepted a figure of 300,000 deaths among Indonesian forced laborers during the Japanese occupation, but went on to indicate that this was but a small part of the total tragedy of the war for Indonesians. Many laborers became so malnourished that they were unable to work after Japan's defeat. According to the U.N.'s Working Group for Asia and the Far East, "the total number who were killed by the Japanese, or who died from hunger, disease and lack of medical attention is estimated at 3,000,000 for Java alone, and 1,000,000 for the Outer Islands."[3]

Civilians elsewhere in Asia also suffered grievously. Malayan officials after the war claimed, possibly with exaggeration, that as many as 100,000 residents, mostly Chinese, may have been killed by the Japanese; of 73,000 Malayans transported to work on the Burma-Siam railway, 25,000 were reported to have died. Human losses in the Philippines amounted to almost 30,000 Filipino battle deaths as well as civilian losses of over 90,000, most of whom were killed in the sack of Manila in 1945. The French sought postwar reparations from the Japanese on the grounds that during the Japanese interlude in Indochina, 5.5 percent of the European population and 2.5 percent of the native population had died. Until 1945,

the Japanese had exercised control over Indochina through the administrative apparatus of the Vichy French, and the country was spared the
ravages of direct combat. As in China, however, the final stages of the war
also witnessed to a devastating famine. The combination of monopolistic
Japanese rice policies (to feed Japanese troops) and U.S. air raids and naval
blockade from late 1944 (which disrupted internal communications) contributed greatly to the starvation of 1945, in which over a million Vietnamese died in Tonkin and Annam. India later estimated its total war
casualties at 180,000 (the number of war dead may have been around
40,000) and also argued that Japan's war policies were at least partly
responsible for the severity of its own famine in Bengal, which took a
million-and-a-half lives. Because the war disrupted rice production in
Burma (half of Burma's rice acreage fell out of cultivation), India was
unable to respond to the Bengal crisis with its usual imports of Burmese
rice. Although Korea was not a theater of combat, perhaps 70,000 Koreans
died during the war—as victims of the atomic bombings of Hiroshima and
Nagasaki, manual laborers in Japan, and conscripts in the Imperial Army.
Approximately 30,000 Australians were killed in combat, while New Zealand troops suffered combat losses of over 10,000 men.[4]

Compared to the situation for most other Asian countries, estimates
of Japanese war casualties are fairly precise. Here too, however, there
remain areas of uncertainty, and the total is higher than is usually acknowledged. By the Japanese government's own calculations, military war dead
between 1937 and 1945 break down as follows:

China War, 1937–41		185,647
Imperial Army, 1941–45		1,140,429
Against U.S. Forces	485,717	
Against British and Dutch Forces	208,026	
China	202,958	
Australian Combat Zones	199,511	
French Indochina	2,803	
Manchuria and U.S.S.R.	7,483	
Other Overseas	23,388	
Japan Proper	10,543	
Imperial Navy, 1941–45		414,879
Total Military Deaths		1,740,955

Civilian deaths in the air raids against Japan's cities which commenced in late 1944 were estimated conservatively after the war, especially in the case of Hiroshima and Nagasaki. Using the official figures for conventional bombing fatalities and current revised estimates of atomic-bomb victims, the number of civilians killed in Japan proper was approximately as follows:

Tokyo	97,031
Hiroshima	140,000
Nagasaki	70,000
63 other cities	86,336

Almost all of these deaths occurred after early March 1945, when the U.S. Air Forces adopted the strategy of saturation bombing with incendiaries.[5]

The total of over 2,100,000 military and civilian Japanese deaths amounts to 3 percent of the total Japanese population at the time, but this does not convey the full picture on the Japanese side. It is estimated that only one third of the military deaths occurred in actual combat, the majority being caused by illness and starvation. Over 300,000 men were wounded severely enough to qualify for government pensions during and after the war. In 1945 alone, some 4,470,000 of the Japanese troops repatriated to Japan immediately after the surrender—the vast majority of the total fighting force—were found to be suffering from illness or injury. The condition of the imperial forces was so wretched by war's end that over 81,000 Japanese died overseas after the cease-fire before they could be repatriated by their Allied captors (other than the Soviets)—a startling figure in itself, although it went virtually unnoticed at the time and survives only as a forgotten historical footnote.[6]

The standard listings of Japanese war victims also generally neglect other deaths, both military and civilian, that occurred after as well as during the period of actual fighting. As many as 10,000 Japanese civilians may have perished on Saipan, while a recent study of the last great battle of the war, on Okinawa in the spring of 1945, places civilian deaths (including citizens recruited for war work) at 150,000—one third of the island's population. For hundreds of thousands of Japanese, moreover, the war did not end in 1945. Scores of thousands of soldiers became absorbed by Chinese armies engaged in the civil war that wracked the mainland after Japan's defeat; thousands of others were held as Allied prisoners in Southeast Asia until as late as October 1947; and an immense number fell into the hands of the Soviet Union. The Japanese government estimated that over 1.3 million Japanese soldiers and civilians surrendered to the U.S.S.R. in Manchuria and northern Asia in August 1945, but over the course of the next four years only 1 million were repatriated to Japan— leaving more than 300,000 unaccounted for and presumed to have died after August 1945. Countless Japanese civilians, many women and children among them, failed to survive the chaos that followed the end of the war in continental Asia. In Manchuria in the winter of 1945–46 alone, it is estimated that well over 100,000 Japanese soldiers and civilians perished from hunger, cold, and epidemics.[7]

When such neglected figures are added to conventional tallies, the human cost of the war for the Japanese themselves appears to be at least 2.5 million individuals—much smaller than China's losses and less than half the combined military and civilian deaths suffered by the Germans, but twenty-five times greater than American combat deaths in the Pacific theater, and eight or nine times greater than the total number of Americans killed in World War Two. For both sides, moreover, the final year of the war was the most deadly one. Although estimates of Japanese and Allied combatants killed in action in each battle vary, the approximate toll for the final savage year of conflict is calculable and sobering: almost 30,000 of the emperor's men were sacrificed on Saipan (slightly less than ten times the U.S. death count); over 10,000 were ordered to fight to the end on Guam in the weeks that followed (1,400 were killed on the Allied side); between 8,000 and 10,000 Japanese were killed on Tinian at almost exactly the same time (with less than 400 deaths on the U.S. side); 10,500 Japanese sailors and airmen were killed in the naval battle of Cape Engaño in October 1944 (with 2,800 U.S. deaths); 10,000 or more Japanese died on Peleliu, in the ferocious fighting of September to November 1944 (with American dead being between 1,000 and 2,000); between 20,000 and 23,000 Japanese gave their lives on Iwo Jima in the second and third months of 1945 (at a cost of close to 6,000 U.S. dead and 20,000 wounded); at least a third of a million Japanese men were expended in the futile defense of the Philippines between October 1944 and the end of the war (compared to slightly more than 20,000 U.S. battle fatalities in all services). On Okinawa, where the battle raged on land, air, and sea from the beginning of April to the latter part of June, more than 110,000 Japanese fighting men died—approximately ten times more than perished on the American side.[8]

By any count, late summer of 1944 to late summer of 1945 was the killing year. This was obviously true for the Japanese forces, who were

thrown by their desperate generals and admirals into one hopeless confrontation after another. On the U.S. side, over half of all losses suffered
in the Pacific (including prisoners of war who died in captivity) occurred
between July 1944 and July 1945, as the following figures indicate:[9]

U.S. MILITARY CASUALTIES IN THE PACIFIC THEATER

	Total Casualties	Total Deaths	Casualties from 7/1944	Deaths from 7/1944
Army & Air Forces	157,573	50,380	96,561 (61%)	26,092 (52%)
Navy	59,057	31,032	30,446+ (52+%)	12,631+ (41+%)
Marines	74,913	19,585	58,418+ (78+%)	14,627+ (75+%)
All Services	291,543	100,997	185,425+ (64+%)	53,349+ (53+%)

It was in this frenzy of violence that the kamikaze were born in
October 1944, the consummate symbol of the pure spirit of the Japanese
that would turn back the demonic onslaught. And it was in this atmosphere that precision bombing of Japanese military targets was abandoned
by the United States and the "madmen" and "yellow vermin" of the
homeland became primary targets. The atomic bomb, born at Alamogordo in July 1945, was in this setting but a more efficient way of killing,
and its use marked the beginning of the end of the long, unnecessary
death agony. Hiroshima was destroyed on August 6; Nagasaki, with hardly
a pause for a measured Japanese response, on August 9. On August 15,
the cease-fire was finalized.

On August 10, the day after the Nagasaki bomb (and two days after
the Soviet Union declared war on Japan), the Japanese government made
clear it intended to surrender, although the terms remained to be ironed
out. Between then and the actual end of the war, two now-forgotten
happenings took place that symbolize the war hates and race hates which
had driven both sides so far, so disastrously. After the saturation bombing
of Japanese cities began in March 1945, the Japanese military in the home
islands commenced summarily executing the small number of U.S. airmen
who fell into their hands. On August 12, eight were executed in Fukuoka;
on August 15, the formal cease-fire a whisper away, eight more were killed
by the military command in the same city—marking Japan's last moment
of war with a final atrocity. While this was taking place, General Henry

H. Arnold, one of the major planners of the U.S. bombing strategy, was desperately attempting to arrange "as big a finale as possible" to end the war. It was his dream to hit Tokyo with a final 1,000-plane air raid—and on the night of August 14 he succeeded in collecting such a force and sending it against the already devastated capital city. A total of 1,014 aircraft—828 B-29 bombers and 186 fighter escorts—bombed Tokyo without a single loss. President Truman announced Japan's unconditional surrender before all of them had returned to their bases.[10]

Japan lay in ruins; but even amidst a shattered landscape, racial pride and determination held strong—at least among those who were now adapting war words to peace. The emperor's rescript announcing the surrender to his subjects concluded with the plea that "the entire nation continue as one family from generation to generation, ever firm in its faith of the imperishableness of its divine land, and mindful of its heavy burden of responsibilities, and the long road before it." The *Asahi*, Japan's premier newspaper, concluded its editorial on the surrender by reaffirming "the superiority of our race." The *Mainichi*, one of the *Asahi*'s distinguished competitors, observed on the same day that history offered examples of superior races regenerating themselves after setbacks.

After such a merciless war, how can one explain the peaceful nature of the Allied occupation of Japan, and the genuine goodwill that soon developed between the Japanese and the Americans in particular? How could the race hates dissipate so quickly?

There are many answers, the simplest of them being that the dominant wartime stereotypes on both sides were wrong. The Americans were not demons, as the Japanese discovered when they were not raped, tortured, and murdered as wartime propaganda and rumors had forecast. And the Japanese were more diversified and far more war-weary than their enemies had been led to believe. The analysts in the Foreign Morale Analysis Division of the Office of War Information, ignored by men in power while the war raged, proved to be accurate in their predictions of both Japanese exhaustion and Japanese adaptability. Liberal and leftist scholars in the West, who had tried with little success during the war to call attention to democratic and progressive traditions in prewar Japan, also turned out to have been more perceptive than the propagandists and most of the war planners. The Japanese people—unlike their militarist leaders—welcomed peace.

That is the simplest and perhaps most important answer, but it is not sufficient in itself. The abrupt transition from a merciless racist war to an amicable postwar relationship was also facilitated by the fact that the same stereotypes that fed superpatriotism and outright race hate were adaptable to cooperation. Here we confront the reason why certain code words and pet images of everyday life survive extreme vicissitudes: they are usually remarkably flexible and malleable, and can be turned about, even turned almost inside out, to legitimize a multitude of often contradictory purposes. This can be demonstrated with virtually all of the core metaphors or images that dominated the racial perceptions of each side during the war.

Take, for example, the crudest of Western images of the Japanese: the simian. Like most of the Western media, the Marine magazine *Leatherneck* used this to heap scorn on the Japanese during the war. The cover of *Leatherneck*'s September 1945 issue, immediately following Japan's capitulation, however, introduced a subtle and significant metamorphosis: it depicted, in full-color illustration, a smiling Marine with an appealing but clearly vexed monkey on his shoulder, dressed in the oversized uniform of the Imperial Army. David Low's monkey looking for a white man's back to stab or a Co-Prosperity Sphere coconut to grab; *Punch*'s simian invader swinging from tree to tree; the *New Yorker*'s monkeymen snipers in the jungle; the King Kong monster that emerged when the Japanese superman was in vogue; the blood-soaked gorilla that symbolized the American response to news of the execution of the Doolittle-raid flyers; the *New York Time*'s apish symbol of the Missing Link—all were now abruptly transformed, as *Leatherneck* sensed immediately, into the clever, imitative, domesticated pet. The wartime side of the simian image was bestiality and jungle law. The other side—quick to emerge in a peaceful milieu—was charm and mimicry. Thus, *Newsweek*'s feature article on the Japanese surrender, published at the same time *Leatherneck*'s suggestive cover appeared, described the defeated foe as "Curious Simians."[11]

This was still contemptuous, of course, but it was a more benign face of racism. A softer version of the same process took place in the perpetuation of the image of the Japanese as lesser men, but in this case men (and women) whom one could teach: good at imitation, good at learning—in short, good pupils. The "good pupil" was an absolutely central image in the minds of many Americans who participated in the occupation of Japan, and naturally invokes—transformed—the wartime metaphor of the Japanese as children. During the war, Western social scientists had used childishness in precise academic ways to diagnose the pathology of the Japanese: they were collectively blocked at the anal or phallic stage; their behavior as a people was equivalent to adolescent behavior among Westerners; they could be analyzed by essentially the same methodology used for dealing with juvenile delinquents or adolescent gangs in America. In occupied Japan, the more generous and paternalistic side of the child metaphor was pulled to the fore, and the Japanese were now perceived as children to be guided toward maturity—or, even more positively, as apt, willing, and attractive pupils in the school of Western-style democracy. During the war, Westerners were told of the "child mind of the Jap conscript." After the war, the same newspapers and magazines spoke of "Seventy-Million Problem Children"; and cartoonists had a field day depicting the Japanese as infants in the crib or, more often, children attending General MacArthur's School of Democracy.[12]

Such paternalism was unquestionably the essence of MacArthur's attitude toward the Japanese—and Oriental people in general. His guiding philosophy during the occupation, he stated in widely publicized Senate hearings in 1951, after President Truman had recalled him from Asia, had been to treat the Japanese as twelve-year-olds. This was not an incautious remark, for the former supreme commander went on to expound his position at some length, explaining in the process why he believed the Japanese might be more receptive to American-style democratic ideas than the "mature" Germans. "The German problem is a completely and entirely different one from the Japanese problem," MacArthur informed the senators. "The German people were a mature race. If the Anglo-Saxon was say 45 years of age in his development, in the sciences, the arts, divinity, culture, the Germans were quite as mature. The Japanese, however, in spite of their antiquity measured by time, were in a very tuitionary condition. Measured by the standards of modern civilization, they would be like a boy of 12 as compared with our development of 45 years. Like any tuitionary period, they were susceptible to following new models, new ideas. You can implant basic concepts there. They were still close enough to origin to be elastic and acceptable to new concepts. . . ."

In his distinctive way, MacArthur meant this as a compliment of sorts, in that he was attempting to convey why he believed democracy might take firmer root in postwar Japan than in Germany. The bluntness of the metaphor embarrassed the general's Japanese admirers, however, and—in one of history's smaller losses—prompted some of them to abandon plans for a Statue of Liberty-sized statue of the general in Tokyo Bay. The comment was not only a fair reflection of the supreme commander's outlook, however, but also helps illuminate the kind but frequently condescending premises of U.S. occupation policy in general. Such parent-child or teacher-student paternalism was reminiscent of Japan's own now discredited Co-Prosperity Sphere rhetoric, and had obvious roots in the Western colonial tradition exemplified by such phrases as "white man's burden" and "little brown brother." It was certainly not an attitude reserved for the Japanese alone, although MacArthur's imposing paternal presence made it especially conspicuous in the Japanese case. In the midst of the war, for example, when addressing the problem of how to deal with the colonial areas in the future, the U.S. State Department and the British Foreign Office spent considerable time playing with the concept of the dominant Western powers as "Parent States" or, as one diplomat put it, "adult states."[13]

This process of turning well-established negative images about so that they provoked a constructive rather than destructive response carried over to the companion metaphors to that of the child which were so conspicuous in the anti-Japanese war rhetoric. Thus, the Japanese "savage" or "primitive" was to be civilized. The fanatic or madman was to be calmed down and cured. In the former case, much of the reformist agenda of the occupation was thus phrased in terms of eliminating the more primitive, tribal—and, especially, "feudal"—legacies of the Japanese past. For General MacArthur, as for his staff, Japan's pernicious "feudal" legacy was the key to defining the targets of the reformist agenda; where "child" guided his understanding of the psychology of the Japanese, "feudal" guided his critical approach to their institutions.

In an analogous way, the perception of the Japanese as collectively neurotic, or in some way mentally and emotionally unstable, also evoked a conspicuously different response in peace than it did in war. The sick Other now became not an ominous threat but a troubled patient, and the victors unhesitatingly assumed the role of analyst and healer. In the controlled environment of unconditional surrender, one cut away the diseased parts of the body politic (as in the purge of militarists and ultranationalists, the amputation of the military, and the repudiation of the existing constitution); laboriously evoked, confronted, and transcended the negative influences of the past (as in the war-crimes trials, the critical reevaluation of Japanese history, and the general critique of existing institutions that accompanied each reform); and arrived at a new level of stability and equanimity (through the creation, literally, of a less re-pressed society). In a time of peace, in a word, the extremely negative wartime images of the Japanese as primitives, children, and madmen summoned forth the victor's more charitable side: as civilized mentor, parent, doctor, therapist—and possessor, without question, of superior power.

Such postwar attitudes on the part of the victors dovetailed neatly with the mind-set of the defeated Japanese, for the basic metaphors through which they viewed the world also proved easily adaptable to the postwar circumstances. The Japanese philosophy of "proper place," for example, facilitated the superficially drastic transition from leading race to defeated power. It had been foolhardy for the Japanese to step out of line and challenge the older and more powerful imperialist powers, the postwar line of reasoning went. Now, confronted with a ruined landscape and undeniable defeat, Japan had no choice but to redefine its proper place. And what was that? To be a "good loser," counseled Suzuki Kantarō, the octogenarian last prime minister of wartime Japan and an occasional Taoist sage. This was not entirely discouraging, as Suzuki's attentive pupil, Yoshida Shigeru, perceived. Yoshida, prime minister of Japan for most of the occupation period (1945–52) and two years thereafter, took as his guiding motto another old saying that rested comfortably beside the "good loser" aphorism: History provided many examples, as Yoshida put it, of losing wars and winning the peace.[14]

Acceptance of this new, and lesser, "proper place" subservient to the United States was made easier for the Japanese because other staples of wartime racist imagery were also malleable. Noteworthy here was the positive or beneficent side of the outsider, stranger, or demon that was so deeply imbedded in Japanese folk culture. The stranger or outsider always possessed double powers: the capacity to destroy, but also gifts that were entertaining and pleasant, and gifts that could contribute to one's own self-strengthening. The demon—the overwhelmingly dominant persona of the Anglo-American enemy during the war—was also the demon with a human face, the potentially tutelary deity. In occupied Japan, and for many years thereafter, this is the side of the demon that prevailed: large, powerful, human, protective, awkward, vaguely forbidding, generally but not entirely trustworthy.

Purity and purification too assumed new meaning for the Japanese in the postwar era. They remained fixations, albeit with drastically altered content. The Japanese were sick of death, and purification through self-destruction now seemed absurd. Discredited too was the wartime goal of purging and purifying the country of decadent, bourgeois Western influences. After August 1945, the goal became instead to cleanse Japan of corrupt traditional, feudalistic, militaristic elements. "Purity" remained the touchstone, but its political import had been turned upside down. Now purification entailed purging reactionary individuals from public life, getting rid of traditional institutions, sweeping out old customs and ideas which had succored militarism and oppression.

This was not the abrupt turnabout it might appear to be at first glance. On the contrary, it was compatible with the spirit, if not the content, of renovationist sentiments that had flourished in wartime Japan. The ideal model of "young Japan," exemplified by the vigorous Momotarō image, proved to be transferable with little difficulty to the "new Japan" of the American-dominated occupation period. If one takes seriously the power of vaguely defined but strongly held ideals, this was not a frivolous or superficial transition. The quest for a "new order" abroad and a "new structure" at home was at the most obvious level an ideological campaign of the late 1930s and early 1940s to create an autarkic bloc dominated by Japan in Asia, while constructing a quasi-fascist Japanese state under the emperor. It also reflected, however, a commitment to experimentation and drastic change that had marked Japan's response to the Western challenge ever since the mid-nineteenth century. Once the war experiment proved to be an unmitigated disaster, the quest continued in new and more democratic and pacifistic channels. The Momotarō image of a vibrant young Japan, with Rising Sun headband and rolled-up sleeves, was readily adaptable to the new directions charted after the guns had been stilled. Now one simply went to work for reconstruction, for a more democratic society—and for strength and eminence through peaceful pursuits.

There were also more conspicuously manipulative ways in which the wartime core concepts eased the transition to a drastically altered world. Shortly after Japan's capitulation, for example, the ruling groups who had recently been calling upon the "hundred million" to die en masse for the country urged (in the so-called *ichioku sōzange ron*) that the hundred million now reflect on their collective guilt—a conspicuously self-serving dismantling of the formerly sacrosanct hierarchies of responsibility, but at the same time a way of emphasizing the society's unity and using old formulas to move in new directions. As is well known, the elites also immediately devoted themselves to a concerted and highly successful campaign to portray the emperor as a man of peace, instrumental in the final acceptance of the Allied surrender terms—thus turning him overnight, as many of the Western social scientists had anticipated, from the deified centerpiece of the militarist ideology into a secular symbol of peaceful pursuits. In peace as in war, the emperor remained the quintessential symbol of the Japanese people's pure heart.

The secularized emperor of postsurrender Japan was a less potent symbol than his previous incarnation as the divine descendent of a line unbroken since ages eternal. Emperor Hirohito dismounted from his famous white horse, shed his customary austere military uniform forever, and in a succession of carefully planned appearances actually walked as a concerned monarch among the common people. The imperial reign remained unbroken, however, and the retention of the emperor as an individual and the throne as an institution posed a significant counterpoint to the wholesale purge of individuals and critique of basic institutions that characterized the early years of the occupation of Japan. While almost two hundred thousand individuals were purged from public activity after the war for having been military officers or associated with ultranationalist organizations, the very person in whose name they had acted remained untouched; and while the Imperial Army and Imperial Navy were abolished, the imperial nation-state remained.

This entailed very subtle forms of symbolic manipulation indeed, as the emperor came to exemplify not just national unity but retrospective disunity as well: he remained the emblem of the pure spirit of the Yamato race, but those who had just yesterday acted in his name abruptly became today's internal scapegoats and demonic forces. The militarists and superpatriotic ideologues were now portrayed—by the Japanese civilian elites and their American conquerors alike—as corrupt influences who had distorted the pure essence of the Imperial Way. They were outsiders who had somehow muscled their way into close proximity to the throne; and, like the archetypical outsider of the folk tradition, their apparent power to do good had revealed itself to be, in the end, fundamentally destructive. The war was their war, an aberration in Japan's modern history which had involved the conspiratorial manipulation of the imperial institution to legitimize aggression; and to perceive the truth of this, the reasoning went, one had only to observe the painfully sincere individual who stepped out from behind the brocade curtain after August 1945. When U.S. occupation authorities lent their support to this almost magical transformation of political responsibility, the way was paved for arguing that neither the disastrous war nor the reforms of the occupation itself had fundamentally altered Japan's unique and superior "national polity." The throne and allegedly unchanging *kokutai* remained both an unassailable fortress in which the old nonmilitary elites could take refuge, and an ambiguous rallying point for present and future pride in being a member of the Yamato race.

At more mundane levels, the manipulation was crasser. Thus, in August 1945, in anticipation of the arrival of the occupation forces, the Home Ministry endeavored to protect the "good" women of Japan by exploiting the poor—more precisely, the female poor—in the name, once more, of "purity." The powerful ministry, bastion of the wartime police state, ordered local associations of "special prostitutes" to be organized explicitly to serve the foreigners. We have already seen how the Japanese elites utilized traditional vocabularies of virtue and "proper place" to legitimize their domination of a new empire in Asia. When the empire collapsed, the hierarchical ideals likewise contracted and became focused more exclusively, once again, on reaffirming inequality within Japanese society. In a small but vivid example of the pious rhetoric that accompanied both class and gender oppression, lower-class women—many orphaned or widowed by the war, and previously recruited to work in the war factories—were now told to serve the country by servicing the GIs. In Tokyo, the "special prostitutes" association was even given a formal inauguration in front of the Imperial Palace, during which some thirty young women pledged, in extremely ornate language, to sacrifice themselves to "maintain and cultivate the pure blood of the race for hundreds of years into the future," thereby contributing to the tranquillity of the society and helping to ensure the preservation of the national polity. The women had no previous experience as prostitutes—but, of course, the young men chosen only a short while earlier to protect the purity of the Yamato race as kamikaze pilots also had had no prior experience of being expended for the country's sake. Here again, in peace as in war, the ruling groups proved themselves masterful at wedding demands for self-sacrifice to appeals to youthful idealism and ultimately racial concerns.[15]

The easy transition from antagonistic to congenial images on all sides was facilitated not only by the malleable and double-faceted nature of the dominant wartime stereotypes, but also by the monolithic aspect of such images. The Other remained, essentially, homogeneous. The demonic Westerners could suddenly become transformed into their tutelary guise, extirpating evil feudalistic and militaristic influences from

Japan, and leading the folk procession along the road to democracy. The Japanese, on the other hand, retained in Western eyes characteristics of the herd, the undifferentiated mass. Formerly "all bad," they now became all (or almost all)—what? Diligent, peace-loving, pro-American—and anti-Communist.

With the "anti-Communist" allure of postwar Japan, one moves on to a fuller appreciation of the true resilience of code words concerning the Other. Not only are such concepts capable of evoking constructive as well as destructive responses; they are also free-floating and easily transferred from one target to another, depending on the exigencies and apprehensions of the moment. The war hates and race hates of World War Two, that is, proved very adaptable to the cold war. Traits which the Americans and English had associated with the Japanese, with great empirical sobriety, were suddenly perceived to be really more relevant to the Communists (deviousness and cunning, bestial and atrocious behavior, homogeneity and monolithic control, fanaticism divorced from any legitimate goals or realistic perception of the world, megalomania bent on world conquest). Indeed, as influential American spokesmen such as George Kennan and John Foster Dulles occasionally pointed out at the height of the cold war, the Russians were really an Asiatic, or Oriental, people. They were, as Churchill liked to say even before the war ended, the real menace from the East.[16]

Enemies changed, with wrenching suddenness; but the concept of "the enemy" remained impressively impervious to drastic alteration, and in its peculiar way provided psychological continuity and stability from the world war to the cold war. If this was true in the shaping of anti-Soviet sentiments, the transferral became even more vivid when China joined the Communist camp and Japan and China changed places in the eyes of the Americans and the British. Heralded by Americans during the war for their individualism and love of democracy, the Chinese suddenly inherited most of the old, monolithic, inherently totalitarian raiments the Japanese were shedding. They became the unthinking horde; the fanatics; the 500 (or 600 or 700) million blue ants of Asia; the newest incarnation of the Yellow Peril—doubly ominous now that it had become inseparable from the Red Peril. The Chinese, like the Russians, explained the diplomat O. Edmund Clubb, one of America's leading China specialists, in April 1950, "do not think like other men." On the contrary, they acted out of a "madness born of xenophobia." To the nonmilitarist conservatives who inherited power in postsurrender Japan, this was a decidedly fortuitous development. Their cartoonists went ahead and drew the Communists with horns on their heads, as befitted the new demons. And the Japanese leadership set about the task of replacing China as a "free world" ally in American eyes.[17]

To policymakers in Washington, the Japanese and Chinese had already changed places by 1948, even before the Chinese Communists consolidated their victory and established the People's Republic of China. By 1950, before the Korean War broke out, the policy of rearming as well as economically rehabilitating Japan was on the docket. This does not mean, however, that the recent war hates and racial tensions were gone. Rather, they were sublimated, and emerged in less blatant guises. The more enlightened paternalism of the early occupation period, which saw the Japanese as capable of developing a freer society through their own efforts, guided and abetted by the victors, was certainly a form of repudiation of wartime racial contempt. Neither the impressive support which the postsurrender reform agenda received from the majority of the Japanese people, however, nor the fervid anticommunism of the Japanese leadership fully persuaded the American policymakers that the Japanese could really be trusted. Thus, even as plans were being made for the remilitarization and economic reconstruction of Japan, the granting of a generous and nonrestrictive peace settlement, and the conclusion of a bilateral U.S.-Japan security treaty—all in the period from 1948 to 1952 —nagging doubts persisted concerning the true nature and intentions of the Japanese. Westerners worried, for example, that Japan's Oriental identity would, in the end, prove decisive and lead to some kind of accommodation between the Japanese and the Chinese Communists. "Every ethnic argument is on my side," thundered Senator Everett Dirksen during hearings on the Japanese peace treaty in 1952, "when I say they are Asiatics and they will be Asiatics." John Foster Dulles, who orchestrated the peace settlement as a special ambassador for President Truman, shared similar misgivings. "The Oriental mind, particularly that of the Japanese, was always more devious than the Occidental mind," he declared privately in 1951—in a conversation with, rather astonishingly, the Nationalist Chinese ambassador, Wellington Koo. The Japanese character had not been altered by the occupation, Dulles went on, and he himself feared that on the issue of relations with the People's Republic of China, Japan might be "playing a double-faced policy vis-à-vis the United States."[18]

The Americans dealt with these doubts about the character of their emerging ally in the Pacific very practically. When the issue of Japan's trustworthiness came up in conversations with the British early in 1951, Dulles suggested that the United States and England should make every effort to assure Japan's allegiance by exploiting the Japanese feeling of superiority toward other Asians. The Western alliance, as Dulles described it, was essentially "an elite Anglo-Saxon club," and it could be hoped that the Japanese would be more attracted to the "social prestige" of being associated with the Anglo-Saxons and their accomplishments rather than with the less developed masses of Asia. "I have a feeling that the Japanese people have felt a certain superiority as against the Asiatic mainland masses," Dulles explained, and "anything we can do to encourage that feeling will set up an attraction which is calculated to hold the Japanese in friendly association with us. . . ." More concretely, the United States resolved the dilemma of needing Japan as a remilitarized ally while still mistrusting the Japanese by structuring the U.S.-Japan security alliance in such a manner that it ensured Japan's permanent military insubordination to the United States. In fact, the bilateral security pact which the two countries agreed upon at the end of the occupation was the most inequitable formal arrangement which the United States entered into in the postwar period—an "unequal treaty" in the old style which was not revised until 1960.[19]

The lessons to be drawn from the war in Asia and its aftermath concerning perceptions of enemies and others are both encouraging and ominous. It is impossible not to be impressed by the speed with which a war of seemingly irreconcilable hatred gave way to cordial relations once the fighting had ceased; and the manner in which the most basic idioms of contempt and sheer race hate proved to contain nuances which permitted constructive rather than destructive relationships is encouraging in a qualified way. The very same developments, however, are ominous in two respects. First, the war hates and race hates did not go away; rather, they went elsewhere. To pursue this thoroughly would involve comparing the war words of World War Two not only with the language of the cold war, but also the Korean War, the war in Indochina, and those contemporary conflicts which pit the dominant Western powers against peoples in the Middle East, Latin America, and Africa. Race colors all these conflicts, and in ways that often find expression in language, imagery, and purportedly empirical analysis that is identical or closely analogous to that discussed in the present study.

There is, at the same time, the legacy of residual racism. As the transition of Japan and the Western powers from war to peace demonstrated, the hard idioms have a soft underside; but by the same token, the softer idioms often conceal a hard and potentially devastating edge. Racial undertones, however muted, have been present on all sides in the postwar relationship between the former belligerents, and it is predictable that harsher racist attitudes reminiscent of the war years will again arise at times of heightened competition or disagreement.

Nothing illustrates this better than the relationship between Japan and the Western powers since the late 1970s. To the historian, there is certainly a humorous side to the reincarnation of the Japanese "superman" in a business suit four decades after he was first observed in military uniform in the skies of the Pacific and the jungles of Southeast Asia. Certainly no one in the immediate postwar period anticipated that Japan, stripped of its empire, could ever reemerge as a dominant power on the world scene. Even as practiced a visionary of apocalyptic developments as John Foster Dulles, who from an early date saw Japan as the key to the balance of power in Asia, had no inkling of the country's true potential. A few days before the outbreak of the Korean War in June 1950, for example, Dulles was in Tokyo suggesting that the Japanese turn their thoughts to developing the U.S. market as a partial alternative to China. What could they export to America? Why, shirts and pajamas, Dulles suggested; and they might also look into cocktail napkins.[20]

This was the old five-and-dime-store view of the Japanese as imitative "lesser men" in the world of high commerce and industry. When this gave way to the recognition of a dynamic economic boom in the 1960s, Westerners still had a reassuring negative idiom to fall back upon; now the Japanese became "economic animals"—aggressive, even impressive, but still a species apart. It was only in the 1970s, when Westerners confronted the unexpected spectacle of Japanese victory upon victory in the global trade wars, that the image shifted again—drastically, much as had occurred at the outset of World War Two in Asia—and a new Japanese superman was suddenly perceived looming on the horizon.

Like his predecessor in khaki, the current version of the superman has inspired the emergence of a veritable cottage industry of commentary on Japan. That is only to be expected. More tantalizing is the fact that many of these presumably expert accounts end up speaking of "secrets" and "miracles" which ultimately trace back to some nondiscursive realm of intuition and quasi-mystical bonding unique to the Japanese. Even in the capitalist marketplace and on the frontiers of high technology, the Japanese are presented as being different from all other races and nations engaged in the same practical, profit-making endeavors. It is not only non-Japanese commentators who dwell on these myths of extraordinary singularity. Many Japanese also attribute their impressive accomplishments fundamentally to the unique and ineffable spirit of the Yamato race —as if no one else had ever tasted victory in the entrepreneurial wars of the modern industrial age.

It is possible to respond to some of this with a tired smile, but there is very little that is amusing about other ways of thinking and seeing that have been dredged up from the war years and are heard widely in both Western and Japanese society. In the United States, "Japan bashing" became a national pastime when the balance of trade began to get out of hand; in private circles at all levels, the expression is usually simply "Jap bashing." Even as the new entrepreneurial superman causes tremors in political and economic circles in the West, moreover, the old pejorative stereotypes are resurrected—just as during World War Two the specter of a superhuman Japanese enemy prowled the Western imagination hand in hand with the image of an alien, subhuman, contemptible foe. The head of a congressional trade delegation to Japan in 1983, for example, referred in a Democratic Party gathering to "the little yellow men, you know, Honda"—a comment that became well known in Japan. The White House chief of staff, a former secretary of the treasury, likened the Japanese to his sheepdog, which had to be "whacked over the head" to get its attention—a figure of speech that calls to mind Henry Stimson in the fall of 1941, speaking of the Japanese as puppies who would back down before the whip. Representatives of industrial sectors which have fared poorly in the new levels of competition argue that the Japanese have simply competed unfairly, and wartime images of treachery have been resurrected for the present day. Many Westerners do indeed give the Japanese credit for hard work, farsighted planning, and high standards of production; but as economic imbalances mount, so also does the tendency among Japan's competitors to attribute Japanese success to deviousness. In a poll conducted among Australian executives in October 1984, for example, a remarkable 89 percent stated that the Japanese were untrustworthy and unethical.

It is natural for the language of war to be applied to the battlefields of commerce. There is not, after all, an infinite variety of lively words to go around. The rhetoric of the present economic conflict, however, is historically specific: it is the rhetoric of World War Two. Thus, in 1985, in a typical American commentary, a Republican presidential aspirant took the occasion of the fortieth anniversary of the end of World War Two to clarify "two facts": "First, we're still at war with Japan. Second, we're losing." A U.S. senator described a Japanese decision to export more automobiles to the United States as "an economic Pearl Harbor." Around the same time, a White House staff member was attracting attention by evoking the war in even more abrupt terms. "The next time B-52s fly over Tokyo," he declared, also responding to the trade issue, "we better make sure they carry bombs."

Individuals who were involved in the war against Japan four decades earlier have reemerged as commentators on the current conflict, and the link between the 1940s and 1980s is frequently drawn in bold, emotional, personal strokes. A distinguished American writer who covered the formal Japanese surrender ceremonies on the U.S.S. *Missouri,* for example, was called upon for a major article on the fortieth anniversary of the war's end. Under the title "The Danger from Japan," he argued that the Japanese had taken unfair advantage of America's generous postwar policy and were now bent on dominating the world economy. An Australian former prisoner of war of the Japanese, currently a successful writer and lecturer in England, linked past and present even more dramatically with a 1983 book entitled *Japan against the World, 1941–2041: The 100-Year War for Supremacy.* The publisher's sensational send-off spoke of the hundred-year plan as "Japan's 'Mein Kampf,' " worked in the Japanese killing of Allied prisoners during the war, and described the Japanese as "a new master race" determined to make their country the most powerful in the world. On the cover, the Western Hemisphere (like the Manichaean globes in Frank Capra's wartime propaganda film *Prelude to War*) was entirely covered by the blood-red Rising Sun.

Japan's competitors have no monopoly on such reinvocation of the old war words and images, however. Japanese public figures and commentators frequently fall back on comparably provocative racial and martial idioms; and as the barbs move back and forth across the Pacific, each side quoting the other, the conflict begins to take on its own internal dynamic. As apparent victors in the economic wars, the Japanese (like the British a half century or more ago) occasionally show a touch of wit and irony in their expressions of national pride. This is apparent in an anecdote popular in Tokyo in 1984 and subsequently picked up by the U.S. media. A perhaps apocryphal Japanese businessman was quoted as offering his foreign acquaintances a vision of the future world economy dominated by Japan. Australia would become Japan's mine, and America its granary, he explained, while Europe would become Japan's boutique. "Proper place" for the twenty-first century!

The more usual expressions of Japanese pride, however, lack this whimsy. Late in 1982, for example, a high Japanese official was quoted on the front page of the *Wall Street Journal* as stating that "the Japanese are a people that can manufacture a product of uniformity and superior quality because the Japanese are a race of completely pure blood, not a mongrelized race as in the United States." Predictably, this provoked several harsh letters to the editor. On the anniversary of Hiroshima in 1983, Prime Minister Nakasone Yasuhiro, a staunch patriot frequently quoted in the West for his references to Japanese superiority and "the eclipse of European races," stated that "the Japanese have been doing well for as long as 2,000 years because there are no foreign races" in their country. Prior to becoming prime minister, Nakasone authored a pamphlet (in 1978) offering the vision of a peaceful "new civilization" in the world. In the Asia-Pacific area, in his projection, Japan would take charge of general economic management, while the less developed countries concentrated on production.

The prime minister's passionate sense of "one country/one race" was representative, although rarely expressed so forthrightly. The annual white paper of Japan's Defense Agency in 1983 struck a similar note when it attempted to evoke patriotic sentiments by referring to "one race, one state, and one language." The nationality of mixed-blood children, who so preoccupied the Japanese planners of the Co-Prosperity Sphere, remains a controversial legal issue in contemporary Japan; so also does the registration (and fingerprinting) of non-Japanese resident "aliens," including hundreds of thousands of second- and third-generation Koreans. In Japanese popular culture, the contemporary racial counterpart to the West's "little yellow people" is "queer foreigner" (*hen na gaijin*, literally "queer outside-person"), a term used with particular reference to Caucasians who presume to have an understanding of Japanese language and culture.[21]

Reflected in these quotations and small points, which could be extended indefinitely, are a new and an old phenomenon. What is new is the perception that the West is no longer materially and technologically preeminent. From this, it follows that the paternalistic pose which the United States and European powers have hitherto adopted toward nonwhite and less developed peoples has had the ground cut out from under it. More precisely, Japan's postwar accomplishments have shattered the parent-child or teacher-pupil model which defined U.S.-Japan relations after the war; and neither side has yet determined its new role. This development has certain historic precedents for Japan and the West, but in the final analysis it is extraordinary. It is the third time Japan has challenged the myths of Western and white supremacy—the first being 1904–5, against Russia, and the second 1941–42—and by its very nature, this time the challenge is a permanent one. Now the Japanese are competing at the cutting edge of management and technology. Their formidable challenge has already altered the nature of the modern world and rung the death knell for a world system dominated by the Atlantic community.

Despite the revolutionary nature of this change, however, the questions it has raised and the tensions it has provoked have thrown people on all sides back to the past. This is the more familiar side of the issue. In both the United States and Japan, where national and racial tensions are most raw, there has been not only a revival of old war words to describe current economic tensions, but also a revival of historical interest in World War Two in Asia. This is a natural response to any great event as it recedes into the past, but in this instance there is an unusual sense of linkage as well as detachment. The potential for misreading and misusing the war for current political purposes is immense.

At a conspicuous public level, each side already engages in the ritual reenactment of patriotic anger. Americans, for example, generally use the anniversary of Pearl Harbor as an occasion for recalling Japanese treachery. Although Hiroshima remains this century's great symbol of the horror of modern war, for some Japanese the commemoration of those who died there and at Nagasaki also serves—increasingly, as time goes by—as a nationalistic reminder of the suffering the Yamato race has long been called upon to endure. Smaller examples of the patriotic use of the past by both public figures and the mass media are apparent everywhere: as paeans to the high ideals and heroic sacrifices of one's own side, and as recollections or re-creations of the violence and double standards of the other side. It is in such a milieu that classic propaganda films from the war years such as *Know Your Enemy—Japan* and *Momotarō—Divine Troops of the Ocean* have been rediscovered and have enjoyed a revival in their countries of origin—as marvelous sources for understanding the past, to be sure; but also, for some, as occasions for recalling "the good war."

To return to that terrible conflict of four decades ago is thus inevitable and essential—and fraught with peril. It can teach us many things, but can also fan the fires of contemporary anger and self-righteousness. In whatever way, World War Two in Asia has become central to our understanding not only of the past, but of the present as well.

NOTES

CHAPTER 1: PATTERNS OF A RACE WAR

1. The most notable exception to this statement is the wide-ranging analysis of World War Two in Asia by Christopher Thorne, who has been as sensitive to the problem of racism as he has to other critical and often neglected aspects of the war. See *Allies of a Kind: The United States, Britain, and the War against Japan, 1941–1945* (1978: Oxford University Press), esp. 3–11, 725–30; "Racial Aspects of the Far Eastern War of 1941–1945," *Proceedings of the British Academy* 66 (1980): 329–77; and "Britain and the Black G.I.s: Racial Issues and Anglo-American Relations in 1942," *New Community: Journal of the Community Relations Commission* 3.3 (Summer 1974): 262–71. Akira Iriye has also been attentive to racial issues in his numerous writings on U.S.-Asian relations; for an earlier period, see especially his *Pacific Estrangement: Japanese and American Expansion, 1897–1911* (1972: Harvard University Press). Iriye's recent *Power and Culture: The Japanese-American War, 1941–1945* (1981: Harvard University Press) adopts a comparative approach to the war just as this present study does, but touches on racism only in passing while emphasizing the more positive points of convergence on the U.S. and Japanese sides; for an extended review of this important work, see John W. Dower, "Rethinking World War Two in Asia," *Reviews in American History* 12.2 (June 1984): 155–69. Louis Allen has called attention to racial issues involving the British and their colonial subjects in India and Malaya, and devoted an entire chapter to "The Factor of Race" in *Singapore 1941–1942* (1977: Davis-Poynter), 247–63; see also Allen's essay "The Indian National Army" in installment 107 of *Purnell's History of the Second World War* (n.d.), 2984–86. In a recent appraisal of American intelligence on Japan before Pearl Harbor, David Kahn argues that "disbelief in a Japanese attack was reinforced by belief in the superiority of the white race"; Ernest R. May, ed., *Knowing One's Enemies: Intelligence Assessment Before the Two World Wars* (1984: Princeton University Press). For more general studies see Hugh Tinker, *Race, Conflict, and the International Order: From Empire to United Nations* (1977: St. Martin's Press); also Rubin Francis Weston, *Racism in U.S. Imperialism: The Influence of Racial Assumptions on American Foreign Policy, 1893–1946* (1972: University of South Carolina Press).

2. Theodore S. Hamerow, "The Hidden Holocaust," *Commentary*, March 1985,

32–42; David S. Wyman, *The Abandonment of the Jews: America and the Holocaust, 1941–1945* (1984: Pantheon).

3. For examples of Western racial concerns regarding Asia prior to Pearl Harbor, cf. Bradford A. Lee, *Britain and the Sino-Japanese War, 1937–1939* (1973: Stanford and Oxford university presses), 94; Thorne, "Racial Aspects," 338–39; and chap. 5 below.

4. The major speeches delivered at the Assembly of the Greater East Asiatic Nations are reprinted in *Contemporary Japan* 12.11 (November 1943): 1339–86.

5. Thorne is excellent on these pervasive racial fears; cf. *Allies of a Kind,* esp. 8, 157–58, 175, 291, 359–60, 401, 433, 539, 594–95. For Admiral King, see Ernest J. King and Walter Muir Whitehall, *Fleet Admiral King: A Naval Record* (1952: Norton), 382. Phillips' numerous dispatches to both the president and the secretary of state appear in U.S. Department of State, *Foreign Relations of the United States, 1943,* 4: esp. 197, 217–22, 229, 231; cf. ibid., *1945,* 6: 249–51.

6. "Peril Exposed," *San Francisco Examiner,* January 25, 1943; Walter B. Clausen, *Blood for the Emperor: A Narrative History of the Human Side of the War in the Pacific* (1943: D. Appleton-Century), 331; Ba Maw, *Breakthrough in Burma: Memoirs of a Revolution, 1939–46* (1968: Yale University Press), 180. The Western fears of a global race war are discussed throughout the present book, but especially in chap. 7. On Japan's actions in the Co-Prosperity Sphere, see chaps. 3, 10, and 11.

7. For "master races" (*shūjin minzoku*), "friendly races" (*yūjin minzoku*), and "guest races" (*kigū minzoku*), see the August 6, 1942, "Plan for Leadership of Nationalities in Greater East Asia" in Joyce C. Lebra, ed., *Japan's Greater East Asia Co-Prosperity Sphere in World War II: Selected Readings and Documents* (1975: Oxford University Press), 118–21. The "leading race" (*shidō minzoku*) concept and secret document of 1942–43 are discussed at length here in chap. 10, where the use of *minzoku,* which can also be translated "people," is defined.

8. The manner in which Japanese ways of thinking governing inequitable domestic relationships were transferred to the international scene is discussed in chap. 10. Although the historical antecedents of the anticolored war words of the Western Allies are discussed in chap. 7, the resonance of this language and imagery with anti-Semitic and sexist or misogynist thinking, or the structural denigration of the lower classes, is not developed. A classic representation of the Jews as vermin, for example, was the notorious German propaganda film *The Eternal Jew.* On the myth of the psychopathology of Jews (and blacks and women), see Sander L. Gilman, "Jews and Mental Illness: Medical Metaphors, Anti-Semitism, and the Jewish Response," *Journal of the History of the Behavioral Sciences* 20 (April 1984): 150–59. There were many other parallels between anti-Semitism and anti-Japanese racism, including the direct association of Jews with "Asiatic" origins; the charge of Jewish conspiracy, as symbolized by the bogus *Protocols of the Elders of Zion* (which had its Japanese counterpart in the forged Tanaka Memorial); and the association of Jews with "feminine" qualities. Cf. George L. Mosse, *Toward the Final Solution: A History of European Racism* (1978; 1984: University of Wisconsin Press).

For commentaries on women as the Other which suggest comparison with the anti-Japanese idioms, cf. Frances Power Cobbe's well-known feminist essay of the mid-nineteenth century, "Criminals, Idiots, Women, and Minors: Is the Classification Sound?" *Fraser's Magazine,* December 1868; Kristin Herzog, *Women, Ethnics, and Exotics: Images of Power in Mid-Nineteenth-Century Fiction* (1983: University of Tennessee Press); and Jung's "amina type," in Violet Staub de Laszlo, ed., *The Basic Writings of C. G. Jung* (1959: Modern Library), esp. 175–82, 540–41. Describing the Other as "subhuman" and inherently primitive, childish, irrational, given to hysterical outbursts, and the like is also immediately recognizable as commonplace in elite characterizations of the lower classes virtually everywhere.

9. The pervasiveness of concepts of purity and purification in modern societies— developed here in chap. 8 only for the Japanese side—is again a subject that could be pursued comparatively in many directions (apart from the obvious but somewhat mislead-

ing comparison to Nazi thought). The avid response of European intellectuals to World War One as a "rite of purification," for example, is strikingly similar to the response of many Japanese intellectuals and ideologues to the outbreak of World War Two; cf. Noel Annan's review essay "Patriot" in *New York Review of Books*, September 24, 1981. Another rarely observed point of comparison would be the campaign against "spiritual pollution" in China in the 1930s—and, indeed, in much of Europe—by forces associated with both the political right and left; see, for example, Paul Pickowicz's study of spiritual-pollution themes in prewar Chinese films forthcoming in *Modern China*.

10. The take-no-prisoners practice is discussed in chap. 3. Churchill told his commanders in Malaya that Singapore had to be "defended to the death," and that "no surrender can be contemplated." The battle, he ordered in another directive, "must be fought to the bitter end. Commanders and officers should die with their troops." General Archibald Wavell conveyed these orders in similarly unequivocal terms: "Commanders and senior officers must lead their troops and if necessary die with them. There must be no question or thought of surrender. Every unit must fight it out to the end and in close contact with the enemy." MacArthur reportedly intended to die with his men on Bataan in 1942. After he was ordered to escape, he radioed Major General Jonathan Wainwright that he was "utterly opposed under any circumstances or conditions to the ultimate capitulation of this command." See John Toland, *The Rising Sun: The Decline and Fall of the Japanese Empire, 1936–1945* (1970: Random House), 273, 290, 292; John Costello, *The Pacific War, 1941–1945* (1981: Quill Trade Paperbacks), 192, 200, 212, 227.

CHAPTER 2: "KNOW YOUR ENEMY"

1. Frank Capra, *The Name above the Title: An Autobiography* (1971: Macmillan Co.), 327.

2. The *Why We Fight* series is discussed in Capra, 325–43; Thomas William Bohn, *An Historical and Descriptive Analysis of the "Why We Fight" Series*, Ph.D. dissertation in Speech, University of Wisconsin-Madison, 1968 (reprinted by Arno Press, 1977); David Culbert, " 'Why We Fight': Social Engineering for a Democratic Society at War," in K. R. M. Short, ed., *Film and Radio Propaganda in World War II* (1983: University of Tennessee Press), 173–91; Richard W. Steele, " 'The Greatest Gangster Movie Ever Filmed': *Prelude to War*," *Prologue* 11.4 (Winter 1979): 221–35; William Thomas Murphy, "The Method of *Why We Fight*," *Journal of Popular Film* 1 (1972): 185–96. Although Winston Churchill liked the films, his Ministry of Information did not and prevented their wide showing in Great Britain; Culbert, 177–78.

3. Capra, 330–32; Bohn, 100.

4. Capra, 335; Steele, 230; Bohn, 122, 130, 140.

5. Steele, 233–34; Bohn, 129–31, 140–48.

6. Culbert, 176, 184. The U.S. government's own catalog to the films simply notes that *The Battle of China* was withdrawn; National Audiovisual Center, *Documentary Film Classics Produced by the United States* (n.d.), 25. The reference to using China as a springboard to world conquest reflected the film's use of the Tanaka Memorial, discussed in n. 10 below.

7. The sophistication of *Know Your Enemy—Japan* in both content and technique is even more obvious when the film is compared to an earlier propaganda film prepared by the U.S. Navy and released several years earlier under a similar title, *The Japanese Enemy*. Two other propaganda films which did not get much viewing because the war ended sooner than anticipated were *Two Down, One to Go* and *On to Tokyo*.

8. William J. Blakefield, "A War Within: The Making of *Know Your Enemy—Japan*," *Sight and Sound: International Film Quarterly* 52.2 (Spring 1983): 128–33, provides an analysis of these behind-the-scenes disagreements. On the key issue of sympathy for the Japanese people, Blakefield writes:

Capra personally made several revisions that tended to erode many of the ideas included by earlier writers. First, the pervasive influence of the militarists upon Japanese domestic and foreign policy was downplayed, and a lengthy passage providing the names of those "Hakko Ichiu gentlemen" was eliminated. Secondly, an attempt was made to associate the Japanese *people* with militarism by adding such lines as ". . . they feel themselves as soldiers with a divine mission." Finally, direct references to "free thinking" Japanese who might not be willing to conform to their government's edicts were all but eliminated. Allowed to stand were characterizations of their society as "an obedient mass with but a single mind." In reference to the Japanese soldier, Capra himself added what was later to become one of the most quoted lines in the film: "He and his brother soldiers are as much alike as photographic prints off the same negative."

From early in 1942, it was official U.S. policy to direct propaganda against the enemy people as a whole, and not just their leaders. Although in theory this applied to all Axis people, in practice the policy was most rigidly adhered to in the case of the Japanese. As reported in the show-business journal *Variety* on May 20, 1942, newsmen, radio broadcasters, and Hollywood filmmakers all were requested not to concentrate on leaders such as Hitler and Emperor Hirohito, but rather "to use a wider symbol than a single individual for the Nazis and the Japs." Various explanations were given for this policy. The war would go on even if the conspicuous leaders of the enemy died, and the public should not be misled into believing otherwise. In the case of Japan, moreover, the emperor's status as a "deity" in the eyes of his subjects posed special reasons for not singling him out for abuse. This would be blasphemous and "not in keeping with democratic principles of freedom of religion." More practically, it would backfire, for any attack on the emperor would be sure to enrage the Japanese and drive them to even greater heights of religious fanaticism. After all was said and done, however, the basic objective of the decision to turn the public eye away from the enemy leaders and toward the enemy people as a whole was something quite different from practical theology: "Americans, the theory is, will be better haters— and thus better fighters and workers—if they are not beclouded with the false idea that the enemy is a bunch of poor, misguided people, who deserve more pity than bullets and bombs." Despite such avowed policies, Western filmmakers and publicists found a place for the "good German" in their propaganda, but no comparable counterpart for the Japanese.

9. Among the scriptwriters who worked on the film were Irving Wallace, later a best-selling novelist; Theodor Geisel, who became famous after the war as the author and illustrator of the whimsical "Dr. Seuss" children's books; and Carl Foreman, who later worked on such Hollywood films as *High Noon, The Bridge on the River Kwai,* and *The Guns of Navarone;* Blakefield, 130.

The "prints off the same negative" line was fairly typical wartime rhetoric. Wilfrid Fleisher, for example, one of the most prolific journalistic commentators on Japan at this time, was fond of the image. In March 1945 he told a "Town Meeting of the Air" radio audience that through its control of education, the Japanese government "provides an official negative from which millions of prints are made," and he repeated this in a popular book published shortly thereafter; Andrew Roth, *Dilemma in Japan* (1945: Little, Brown), 275, and Wilfrid Fleisher, *What to Do with Japan* (1945: Doubleday, Doran & Co.), 132. Similarly, a Navy pamphlet being prepared just as Japan surrendered, for use as a guide for occupation forces, traced the eradication of individualism to the late feudal age and observed that "just as a giant press stamps out of sheet metal thousands and thousands of identical pieces, so the Japanese shoguns stamped out millions of Japanese all alike"; *Guide to Japan* (CINPAC-CINCPOA Bulletin no. 209-45, September 1, 1945), 44.

10. The notorious memorial was reprinted in the United States in 1942: Carl Crow, ed., *Japan's Dream of World Empire: The Tanaka Memorial* (1942: Harper & Brothers). The bogus nature of the document is discussed in John J. Stephan, "The Tanaka Memorial

(1927): Authentic or Spurious?" *Modern Asian Studies* 7.4 (1973): 733–45. In a long essay written in 1940 and published in 1941, however, Leon Trotsky argued that the Tanaka Memorial was a genuine Japanese document which had been obtained from the Ministry of the Navy through Soviet espionage; "On Japan's Plans for Expansion" and "The Tanaka Memorial," both reprinted in *Writings of Leon Trotsky, 1939–40* (1973: Pathfinder Press), 168–80.

11. The film cut a proposed moderate ending to the effect that "as surgeons, without hatred, we must eradicate this evil cancer of brutal, stupid war-loving militarism that has caused the peoples of the world so much pain. And out of the bitterness and humiliation of crushing defeat, our hope is that the people of Japan will accept their rightful place among the peace loving peoples of the world"; Blakefield, 131.

12. A more literal translation would be *If You Read Only This, We Shall Win*. I have followed here the excellent translation of Tsuji's memoirs, as well as the booklet, by Margaret Lake: Masanobu Tsuji, *Singapore: The Japanese Version* (1962: Constable & Co.). The original Japanese edition of the memoirs was entitled *Shingaporu: Unmei no Tenki*. For the booklet, see also *Reports of General MacArthur* (1966: Government Printing Office), vol. 2 *(Japanese Operations in the Southwest Pacific Area)*, pt. 1, 9–12. In John Toland's influential account of the war, Tsuji emerges as the most racist and atrocious of Japanese officers; *The Rising Sun: The Decline and Fall of the Japanese Empire, 1936–1945* (1970: Random House), 295, 301, 317–18, 399.

13. The official translation of *Shinmin no Michi* was included as an appendix to Otto Tolischus' important wartime book *Tokyo Record* (1943: Reynal & Hitchcock), 405–27.

14. *Reports of General MacArthur*, 2, 1:43. The Japanese reading of this most famous of war poems is: *"Umi yukaba mizuku kabane / Yama yukaba kusamusu kabane / Ogimino henikoso shiname / Kaerimiwaseji."*

15. The *Senjinkun* was a pocket-size booklet of thirty-four text pages. See *Asahi Shimbun*, January 8, 1941, for coverage of its adoption. An official English translation was published by Japanese occupation forces in the Philippines: Bureau of Publicity, Department of General Affairs, Japanese Military Administration [Philippines], ed., *The Official Journal of the Japanese Military Administration*, 3:237–42, (May 11, 1942).

16. This is a central theme in Akira Iriye's *Power and Culture: The Japanese-American War, 1941–1945* (1981: Harvard University Press). Cf. also the interesting chart of "In-Group Out-Group Stereotypes Used by the Japanese" in L. D. Meo, *Japan's Radio War on Australia, 1941–1945* (1968: Melbourne University Press), 134.

17. The phrase "hundred million" *(ichioku)* was poetic license, and carried a classical and heroic aura fully in keeping with the wartime ideology. Japan's population at the time was upwards of 70 million.

18. Quoted in Willis Lamott, *Nippon: The Crime and Punishment of Japan* (1944: John Day Co.), 97, 152.

CHAPTER 3: WAR HATES AND WAR CRIMES

1. Allan Nevins, "How We Felt About the War," in Jack Goodman, ed., *While You Were Gone: A Report on Wartime Life in the United States* (1946: Simon & Schuster), 13.

2. Cf. Peter Calvocoressi and Guy Wint, *Total War: Causes and Courses of the Second World War* (1972; 1974: Pelican), 259–60, 565.

3. David W. Wyman, *The Abandonment of the Jews: America and the Holocaust, 1941–1945* (1984: Pantheon), especially x–xi, 19–21, 61, 321–30. Wyman notes that the Holocaust was virtually ignored by *Time, Life, Newsweek*, and most other mass-circulation U.S. magazines, as well as by the popular commercial newsreel *March of Time*, until after Germany surrendered.

4. Seventy-three percent of Americans polled in July 1942 agreed that the Japanese were treacherous. Next in order among the adjectives listed were "sly" (63 percent),

"cruel" (56 percent), "warlike" (46 percent), and "hard working" (39 percent). Hadley Cantril, ed., *Public Opinion, 1935–1946* (1951: Princeton University Press), 501.

5. Admiral Yamamoto's statement appears in his plan of January 7, 1941, reproduced in Sanematsu Yuzuru, ed., *Gendai Shiryō 35: Taiheiyō Sensō 2* [Contemporary Documents 35; Pacific War 2] (1969: Misuzu Shobō), 127. Tsuji's summary of Japanese assumptions goes on as follows: ". . . that after we had achieved some great victories in the south the Republic of China would be willing to conclude an unconditional peace treaty based on the principles of an East Asia Co-Prosperity League; that Russia would break away from her western allies; and that after conclusion of peace with China it would be possible for us to move a million troops from that country to Manchuria, which would be sufficient to deter Russia from any further adventure in that direction or to deal with any attack which might develop there"; Masanobu Tsuji, *Singapore: The Japanese Version* (1962: Constable & Co.), 21. For a critique of the woeful shortcomings of Japanese intelligence, especially on the psychological and economic potentialities of the enemy, see Michael A. Barnhart, "Japanese Intelligence before the Second World War: 'Best Case' Analysis," in Ernest R. May, ed., *Knowing One's Enemies: Intelligence Assessment before the Two World Wars* (1984: Princeton University Press), 424–55.

6. Cf. John J. Stephan's chapter on "Victory Disease" in his *Hawaii under the Rising Sun: Japan's Plans for Conquest after Pearl Harbor* (1984: University of Hawaii Press), 122–34; also ibid., 86, 92, 119.

7. James M. Merrill, *A Sailor's Admiral: A Biography of William F. Halsey* (1976: Crowell), 53, 92, 111, 202; William F. Halsey and Joseph Bryan, *Admiral Halsey's Story* (1947: McGraw-Hill), 123. The slogan is incorporated in a blunt illustration of a slant-eyed Japanese soldier in the cross hairs of a gunsight in *Leatherneck* 25.3 (March 1942): 48.

8. *Time*, December 15, 1941, 17.

9. *New Yorker*, December 20, 1941, 19.

10. In a public-opinion poll conducted three days after Pearl Harbor, asking why Japan attacked the United States, 48 percent of the Americans surveyed responded that Japan was "urged by Germany" to do this. Two months later, in February 1942, an even larger number (68.5 percent) agreed that Japan's attack "was part of German strategy." Cantril, 1078.

11. Philip R. Piccigallo, *The Japanese on Trial: Allied War Crimes Operations in the East, 1945–1951* (1979: University of Texas Press). Summary figures are on p. xi. A total of 920 Japanese were sentenced to death, while approximately 3,000 others received prison terms.

12. From the chief prosecutor's presentation by Joseph B. Keenan, in R. John Pritchard and Sonia Magbanua Zaide, eds., *The Tokyo War Crimes Trial: The Complete Transcripts of the Proceedings of the International Military Tribunal for the Far East* (1981: Garland Publishing), 1:390.

13. Radhabinod Pal, *International Military Tribunal for the Far East, Dissentient Judgment* (1953: Sanyal & Co., Calcutta), 620–21. A British officer serving on the defense in one of the regional trials offered a comparable argument, citing the atomic bombing of Hiroshima as an example of the illogicality of prosecuting Japanese military men for crimes against civilians; Piccigallo, 115.

14. U.S. Department of State, *Foreign Relations of the United States: Japan, 1931–1941* (1943: Government Printing Office), 1:506.

15. Ibid., 379–83 for the "quarantine speech"; *New York Times*, June 4, 1938, for the statement of June 3.

16. U.S. Congress, Senate, *Congressional Record*, 75th Cong., 3rd sess., 1938, 83, pt. 8: 8922, 9134, 9523–26.

17. *The Public Papers and Addresses of Franklin D. Roosevelt, 1939 Volume: War —and Neutrality* (1941: Macmillan Co.), 454, 511–12, 587–89. The first appeal, dated September 1, was sent to Great Britain, France, Italy, Germany, and Poland. In December, much the same appeal was sent to the Soviet Union and Finland.

18. Robert Batchelder, *The Irreversible Decision, 1939-1950* (1961: Houghton Mifflin), 172-73; *Catholic World* 159 (May 1944): 103.

19. Wesley Frank Craven and James Lea Cate, eds., *The Army Air Forces in World War II* (1948: University of Chicago Press and U.S. Office of Air Force History), 1: 135-50, 591-611; Denis Richards and Hilary St. George Saunders, *Royal Air Force, 1939-1945* (1954: Her Majesty's Stationery Office), 2: esp. 117-40; Max Hastings, *Bomber Command* (1979: Dial), 94-99, 123-40; also the chapter on "Mass Bombing" in Calvocoressi and Wint, 489-508. For Churchill's comments, see his *The Grand Alliance* (1951: Houghton Mifflin), 510-12; U.S. Department of State, *Foreign Relations of the United States: Conferences at Washington, 1941-1942, and Casablanca, 1943*, 34-35; Christopher Thorne, *Allies of a Kind: The United States, Britain, and the War Against Japan, 1941-1945* (1978: Oxford University Press), 372. The statement by the minister of information, Brendan Bracken, is quoted in A. Marjorie Taylor, *The Language of World War II*, rev. ed. (1948: H. W. Wilson Co.), 41. Britain was persuaded of the efficiency of bombing in weakening enemy morale not only by its own experience under German attack in 1940, but also by its earlier use of aerial bombardment to put down colonial uprisings in India and Iraq—a point often neglected in discussions of the early debate on the morality of bombing; cf. R. J. Overy, *The Air War, 1939-1945* (1980: Europa), 14.

20. Quoted in John Costello, *The Pacific War. 1941-1945* (1982: Quill Trade Paperbacks), 105. The statement was recorded November 19, 1941.

21. Craven and Cate, vol. 5, chap. 20 on "Urban Area Attacks" against Japan. General LeMay's description appears in his memoirs: Curtis E. LeMay with MacKinlay Kantor, *Mission with LeMay: My Story* (1965: Doubleday), 387. Of a total of 153,000 tons of bombs dropped on Japan, 98,000 were firebombs; U.S. Strategic Bombing Survey, *Final Report Covering Air-Raid Protection and Allied Subjects in Japan* (Report 11), 200. See also Costello, 547-53, on the firebombing of Tokyo. The total number of Japanese killed in air raids, including Hiroshima and Nagasaki, was estimated by the U.S. Strategic Bombing Survey in 1947 to be 257,769, but this greatly underestimates the death toll in Hiroshima (71,379 here) and Nagasaki (13,294 here). The best available estimates of atomic-bomb casualties put the number of persons killed at 130,000 to 150,000 in Hiroshima and 60,000 to 80,000 in Nagasaki. The total number killed in the numerous raids on Tokyo was calculated by the Strategic Bombing Survey to be 93,056, but this also may be on the low side. See U.S. Strategic Bombing Survey, *Effects of Air Attacks on Japanese Urban Economy (Summary Report)* (Report 55). For the effects of the atomic bombs, see Committee for the Compilation of Materials on Damage Caused by the Atomic Bombs in Hiroshima and Nagasaki, *Hiroshima and Nagasaki: The Physical, Medical, and Social Effects of the Atomic Bombings* (1981: Basic Books; originally published in Japanese in 1979 by Iwanami Shoten), esp. 113, 115, 367-69.

22. On the general issue of bombing and ethics, see Batchelder, esp. 170-89; George F. Hopkins, "Bombing and the American Conscience During World War II," *The Historian* 28.3 (May 1966): 451-73; and Ronald Schaffer, "American Military Ethics in World War II: The Bombing of German Civilians," *Journal of American History* 67.2 (September 1980): 318-34, with an exchange on this article appearing in ibid., 68.1 (June 1981): 85-92. See also Calvocoressi and Wint, 490, on the difficulties endured by the bishop of Chichester when he questioned the morality of area bombing. The major criticism of the Allied bombing policy was a pamphlet by the British writer Vera Britain, published by the Christian and pacifist Fellowship of Reconciliation with the endorsement of twenty-eight clergymen and pacifists, before the air raids against Japan were commenced: "Massacre by Bombing: The Facts Behind the British-American Attack on Germany," *Fellowship* 10.3 (March 1944): 50-64. In the same periodical, cf. R. Alfred Hassler, "Slaughter of the Innocent," 10.2 (February 1944): 19-21, and Charles Inglehart, "America's War Casualties," 11.7 (July 1945): 119-22. The hostile response to Britain's pamphlet by the U.S. media is briefly summarized in Hopkins, 467-70. Schaffer, however,

demonstrates that the pamphlet caused considerable concern among U.S. military planners at the time (323).

23. Fellers' memorandum to Lt. Col. Greene, June 17, 1945, Bonner Frank Fellers Collection, Hoover Institution, Box 3.

24. The most recent analysis of the problems of atrocities and war responsibility, which looks at Allied as well as Japanese behavior, is Ienaga Saburō, *Sensō Sekinin* (1985: Iwanami Shoten). An accessible reprint of the majority judgment is B. B. A. Roling and C. F. Ruter, eds., *The Tokyo Judgment: The International Military Tribunal for the Far East (I.M.T.F.E.), 29 April 1946–November 1948,* vol. 1 (1977: APA-University Press Amsterdam BV); this is cited below as *The Tokyo Judgment.* Vol. 2 reprints dissenting opinions. The most extensive documentation of Japanese atrocities remains the IMTFE proceedings plus local military tribunals covered in Piccigallo.

25. On Unit 731, see Morimura Seiichi, *Akuma no Hōshoku* [The Devil's Gluttony] (1981: Kobunsha); John W. Powell, "Japan's Germ Warfare: The U.S. Cover-Up of a War Crime," *Bulletin of Concerned Asian Scholars* 12.4 (October–December 1980): 2–17; and Powell's "Japan's Biological Weapons, 1930–1945: A Hidden Chapter in History," *Bulletin of the Atomic Scientists* 37.8 (October 1981): 44–52. The experiments at Kyushu Imperial University involved vivisection of eight American airmen and took place in May and June 1945; this and Unit 731 are briefly discussed in Saburo Ienaga, *The Pacific War, 1931–1945* (1978: Pantheon), 188–90.

26. The Japanese debate over the Rape of Nanking is conveniently summarized in John Burgess, "Rewriting the 'Rape of Nanking,' " *Washington Post National Weekly Edition,* February 11, 1985, 18. The official Chinese figure for the Nanking death toll is 300,000. The International Military Tribunal for the Far East estimated the number of civilians and prisoners of war murdered during the six weeks to be around 200,000 (see chap. 8 in the trial "Judgment"). The figure of 200,000 combined combat and atrocity deaths is offered by Hora Tomio.

27. Chalmers Johnson, *Peasant Nationalism and Communist Power: The Emergence of Revolutionary China, 1937–1945* (1962: Stanford University Press), 41, 48, 55–56, 58, 194–95, 207–8.

28. *The Tokyo Judgment,* 396–401.

29. Louis Allen, *Singapore 1941–1942* (1977: Davis-Poynter), 34–36; Victor Purcell, *The Chinese in Southeast Asia* (1951: Oxford University Press), 369–70. Purcell cites the postwar testimony of a Japanese lieutenant colonel who claimed he was originally told upon entering Singapore that some 50,000 Chinese were to be killed.

30. Contrived scenes of Japanese spearing babies with their bayonets appear in the 1943 RKO film *Behind the Rising Sun* as well as a U.S. War Department film promoting war bonds, entitled *Every War Bond Kills a Jap* (Official War Film, Misc. 1099). The Hong Kong, Singapore, and Bataan bayonettings were widely reported, and picked up in the Tokyo war-crimes trials. For General Slim's report, see William Slim (Field Marshal the Viscount Slim), *Defeat Into Victory* (1961: David McKay Co.), 405.

31. *The Tokyo Judgment,* 396–97.

32. Ibid., 400; Carlos P. Romulo, *I See the Philippines Rise* (1946: Doubleday, Doran & Co.), 221–23; Rafael Steinberg et al., *Return to the Philippines* (1979: Time-Life Books), 136–43. Romulo, an intimate friend of MacArthur who held the title of brigadier general during the war, believed that the Japanese harbored special hatred toward the Filipinos because of their Christianity: "To them our faith was the mark of our trust in the white race to whom we were united in religion and ideology" (224). Photographers under MacArthur's command made an extensive graphic record of the sack of Manila, including tortured and executed Filipinos.

33. The use of films of the civilian suicides on Saipan in Marine indoctrination is noted in Henry Berry, *Semper Fi, Mac: Living Memories of the U.S. Marines in World War Two* (1982: Arbor House), 216–17. For typical coverage of the civilian deaths on Saipan, see Robert Sherrod's coverage for *Time* (August 7, 1944), reprinted in *Reader's Digest,*

October 1944, 83–84. A contrary interpretation, stressing the large number of Japanese civilians who disregarded Japanese military pressures and did surrender, was presented in an article entitled "Japs Don't Want to Die" in *Collier's*, October 21, 1944.

34. Ota Masahide, ed., *Sōshi: Okinawa-sen* (1982: Iwanami Shoten), 219; when civilians attached to the military are included, total deaths among Okinawans was 150,000, or one third of the island population. As in Nanking and Manila, it is not possible to break down the causes of civilian deaths with great precision. For the Marukis' work linking the great atrocities of the mid twentieth century—including Hiroshima and Nagasaki, Nanking, Auschwitz, and Okinawa—see John W. Dower and John Junkerman, eds., *The Hiroshima Murals: The Art of Iri Maruki and Toshi Maruki* (1985: Kodansha International).

35. W. J. West, ed., *Orwell: The War Broadcasts* (1985: British Broadcasting Company/Duckworth); see Orwell's transcripts for broadcasts of January 17, April 4, and July 25, 1942.

36. Ba Maw, *Breakthrough in Burma: Memoirs of a Revolution, 1939–1946* (1968: Yale University Press), 172–86 (esp. 177, 180–81), 265, 276–79; Sukarno, *Sukarno: An Autobiography* (as told to Cindy Adams) (1965: Bobbs-Merrill), 169, 174, 180–82, 186–94; Harry J. Benda, *The Crescent and the Rising Sun: Indonesian Islam Under the Japanese Occupation, 1942–1945* (1958: W. van Hoeve, The Hague and Bandung), 122–23.

37. *The Tokyo Judgment*, 406–9; Sukarno, 181–82; Ba Maw, 277–79, 282–83. Scholars working on Southeast Asia are frequently told by informants of the particular role played by Koreans attached to the Kempeiti during the war.

38. For Korean and Chinese workers, see Kawahara Hiroshi and Fujii Shōzō, eds., *Ni-Chū Kankei Shi no Kiso Chishiki* (1974: Yuhikaku), 367–69. Estimates of Koreans killed by the atomic bombs are given in *Hiroshima and Nagasaki* (n. 21 above), 462–75, esp. 474.

39. A 1956 study concluded that as few as 70,000 of some 300,000 Indonesian *rōmusha* may have survived; W. F. Wertheim, *Indonesian Society in Transition: A Study of Social Change* (1956: W. van Hoeve, The Hague and Bandung), 263–66. A more recent appraisal puts the total number of impressed Indonesian workers at over half a million, of whom "not more than a small fraction returned home alive after the war"; B. R. O'G. Anderson, "Japan: 'The Light of Asia'," in Josef Silverstein, ed., *Southeast Asia in World War II: Four Essays* (1966: Monograph Series no. 7, Southeast Asia Studies, Yale University), 29. See chap. 11, n. 3 below for even larger estimates. *The Tokyo Judgment* accepted a figure of 60,000 deaths among Asian laborers on the Burma-Siam railroad project (403–6). On Asian women forced into prostitution by the Japanese, cf. Ienaga, *The Pacific War*, 158–59, 170, 174, 184, 190–91.

40. Costello, 397; *New York Times*, February 4, 1945, 14.

41. The estimate of Soviet prisoners killed is from Calvocoressi and Wint, 256; of Anglo-American prisoners of the Germans, Italians, and Japanese, from *The Tokyo Judgment*, 385. See also chap. 11, n. 3 below.

42. The general chronology of events, including the text of the August 13 law, are given in the IMTFE judgments: see *The Tokyo Judgment*, 394–96, and Justice Pal's dissent, 676–78. The Japanese government's formal statements concerning the new regulations and punishment of the flyers were printed in *Contemporary Japan* 11.11 (November 1942): 1669. For the banner-headline press coverage in Japan, see *Japan Times Advertiser*, October 20, 1942. The story first made headline news in the West on April 22, 1943, almost exactly one year after the raid.

43. H. G. Nichols, ed., *Washington Despatches, 1941–1945: Weekly Political Reports from the British Embassy* (1981: University of Chicago Press), 180 (report for April 25, 1943). *New York Times*, April 25, 1943, News of the Week section.

44. John Gassner and Dudley Nichols, eds. *Best Film Plays of 1943–1944* (1945: Crown), 147. This Twentieth Century-Fox production was conceived in 1943 but delayed by the U.S. government until the time was deemed appropriate to emphasize the Japanese

328 ◄ NOTES FOR PAGES 51–56

torture of prisoners of war; Colin Shindler, *Hollywood Goes to War: Films and American Society, 1939–1952* (1979: Routledge & Kegan Paul), 82.

45. Most major newspapers printed the diary excerpt, although some omitted the term "bastards."

46. *New York Times*, October 6, 1943, 22.

47. Approximately 66,000 Filipino soldiers and 10,000 to 12,000 Americans surrendered at Bataan, of whom one third or so were sick or wounded. The Japanese had anticipated between 25,000 and 40,000 prisoners, and had made plans for an orderly evacuation in a "friendly manner," but in fact the evacuation and subsequent treatment of the prisoners was disorganized and generally vicious. More than twice as many Americans died in prison camps in the two months after the march as died or were killed on the march itself; and when the war ended, only about 4,000 of the Americans who surrendered at Bataan were still alive. The fate of the Filipinos is not clear. For recollections of the Death March by American survivors, with a useful brief introduction by Stanley L. Falk, see Donald Knox, *Death March: The Survivors of Bataan* (1981: Harcourt Brace Jovanovich). The first reports of the fate of the survivors reached the U.S. government in April 1943.

48. *Time*, February 7, 1944, 12.

49. Nichols, *Washington Despatches*, 553 (British embassy report of May 6, 1945).

50. Debs Myers, Jonathan Kilbourn, and Richard Harrity, eds., *Yank—the GI Story of the War*, with articles by the staff of *Yank, the Army Weekly* (1947: Duell, Sloan & Pearce), 256–57.

51. Richard O'Neill, *Suicide Squads* (1981; 1984: Ballantine), 158. The news of the kamikaze planes was censored until April 13, 1945, presumedly to prevent the Japanese from evaluating the effectiveness of the suicide attacks; cf. Denis Warner and Peggy Warner, *The Sacred Warriors: Japan's Suicide Legions* (1984: Avon), 114, 224.

52. The poll actually indicated that more GIs in the European theater (58 percent) than in the Pacific theater (42 percent) believed it would be necessary to kill all Japanese; cited in William J. Blakefield, "A War Within: The Making of *Know Your Enemy— Japan*," *Sight and Sound: International Film Quarterly* 52.2 (Spring 1983): 130.

53. George H. Johnston, *The Toughest Fighting in the World* (1943: Duell, Sloan & Pearce), 207, for the quotation from General Blamey.

54. *Time*, March 19, 1945, 32.

55. Slim, 437.

56. In Cantril's *Public Opinion, 1935–1946*, see the comparative figures for Germany and Japan for polls taken on June 17, 1942 (1112-#8 and 1118-#1), February 1944 (1115-#17 and 1118-#2), and December 20, 1944 (1114-#14 and 1118-#3).

57. *Fortune*, December 1945, 305.

58. Nichols, *Washington Despatches*, 299 (British embassy report of January 1, 1944).

59. Both cited in *Christian Century*, May 5, 1943, 535. The best-seller was George Waller's *Singapore Is Silent* (1943: Harcourt, Brace & Co.); see p. 5.

60. Henry A. Wallace, *The Price of Vision: The Diary of Henry A. Wallace, 1942– 1946*, ed. John Morton Blum (1973: Houghton Mifflin), 115. *Collier's*, July 31, 1943, 74.

61. Captain H. L. Pence, quoted in Akira Iriye, *Power and Culture: The Japanese-American War, 1941–1945* (1981: Harvard University Press), 123. By 1944, Pence had modified his views; ibid., 202.

62. Thorne, 372.

63. Wallace, 448 (diary entry for May 16, 1945).

64. *New York Times*, April 6, 1945, 5, and April 14, 1945, 10.

65. *Time*, August 4, 1945, 28.

66. *United States News*, March 23, 1945, 24, and April 13, 1945, 38; the April 13 and April 20 issues of this weekly contain opinions by a range of experts on Japan's likely actions. On "suicide psychology," cf. also *American Mercury*, July 1945, 14–15, and *Wall Street Journal*, August 7, 1945, 5; even after the atomic bombing of Hiroshima, the latter

editorialized that there was reason to doubt that the Japanese would not continue to resist to the last man, woman, and child.

67. *Collier's,* April 28, 1945, 19.

68. *Collier's,* June 23, 1945, 82. The hundred-year-war concept, immensely popular in the Western media, did have supporters among Japan's militarists, although some officers condemned it as defeatist; cf. Barnhart, 452.

69. Hart and Bisson were quoted in *United States News* on April 13, 1945, 37, and April 20, 1945, 40, respectively; for Hiss, see Iriye, 167. By "total victory," "thoroughgoing defeat," etc., liberals and leftists were particularly concerned with adhering to the "unconditional surrender" demands and refusing to offer the Japanese any guarantees concerning the future of the emperor or the imperial institution.

70. Warner and Warner, 176.

71. Greater East Asia War Inquiry Commission, ed., *The American-British Challenge Directed Against Nippon* (1943: Mainichi Publishing Co.). Twenty-five well-known individuals were listed as members of the commission, and another twelve, many from industry and finance, were cited as "contributors" to the publication. Four additional volumes were identified as being in preparation but do not appear to have been completed. The 1943 volume was 128 double-column pages in length.

72. *Fortune,* April 1944, 211–12. On December 8, 1943, Tōjō said that unconditional surrender as announced at the Cairo Conference would reduce Japan to the status of a third-rate nation; Iriye, 163. During the war, the Japanese did execute scores of captured American flyers, presumably under the provisions of the regulations adopted after the Doolittle raid. This occurred both in the home islands and in occupied areas, with most of the executions in the former case being carried out during the final months of the war; *The Tokyo Judgment,* 395–96.

73. Sidney Forrester Mashbir, *I Was An American Spy* (1953: Vantage Press), 333–34. The Japanese official was Okazaki Katsuo.

74. Edgar Snow, *The Battle for Asia* (1942: World Publishing Co.), 193.

75. The rumor that young men qualified for the Marines by killing their mother and father was apparently spread among civilians on Saipan by the Japanese military; James J. Fahey, *Pacific War Diary, 1942–1945* (1963: Houghton Mifflin), 192.

76. Mashbir, 284.

77. J. Glenn Gray, *The Warriors: Reflections on Men in Battle* (1959; 1970: Harper & Row), 178–79.

78. Berry, 72.

79. William Manchester, *Goodbye, Darkness: A Memoir of the Pacific War* (1980: Dell), 439. Manchester went on to tell of a Marine unit on Okinawa which heard voices coming from a cave and ordered those inside to come out. "When they didn't, flamethrowers moved in, killed them all"—and only then did they discover that their victims were eighty-five schoolgirls who had been mobilized as nurses and had fled to the cave to hide.

80. Warner and Warner, xi, 36.

81. E. B. Sledge, *With the Old Breed at Peleliu and Okinawa* (1981: Presidio Press), esp. 34, 121–24, 152–53, 199, 287–88. Sledge also is interviewed in Studs Terkel, *"The Good War": An Oral History of World War Two* (1984: Pantheon), 59–66.

82. S. E. Smith, ed., *The United States Marine Corps in World War II* (1969: Random House), 662, 680.

83. Sledge, 33–34; Smith, 201–7; Berry, 74–75.

84. Edgar L. Jones, "One War is Enough," *Atlantic Monthly,* February 1946, 48–53, esp. 49.

85. Richard Tregaskis, *Guadalcanal Diary* (1942: Random House), 15–16.

86. Fahey, 192.

87. Sledge, 120. The kabar, or K-bar, was the Marine fighting knife.

88. *Leatherneck* 26.2 (June 1943): 29.

89. Both press reports are cited in *Christian Century,* May 5, 1943, 535.

90. The *Life* photo appeared in the issue of May 22, 1944, 35, with the caption "Arizona war worker writes her Navy boyfriend a thank-you note for the Jap skull he sent her." For the Japanese response, see Ben-Ami Shillony, *Politics and Culture in Wartime Japan* (1981: Oxford University Press), 143–46. Roosevelt announced on August 9, 1944, that he had refused to accept a letter opener made of the bone of a Japanese; particularly among church groups, this prompted protests against such desecration; *New York Times*, August 10 and October 14, 1944.

91. *Leatherneck* 28.3 (March 1945): 11.

92. *Collier's*, November 13, 1943, 46. For a serious artistic rendering of the same theme, see the lithograph by James Hollins Patrick entitled *This Is Our Enemy* in Ellen G. Landau, *Artists for Victory: An Exhibition Catalog* (1983: Library of Congress), 91.

93. Fahey, 68.

94. Clay Blair, Jr., *Silent Victory: The U.S. Submarine War Against Japan* (1975: Lippincott), 384–86. The submarine was the *Wahoo*, and the episode occurred off the north coast of New Guinea in January 1943. One of the officers on the *Wahoo*, recalling the occasion, spoke of the commander's "overwhelming biological hatred of the enemy"; George Grider and Lydel Sims, *War Fish* (1958: Little, Brown), 101. The submarine commander, following this mission, was awarded both the Navy Cross and, from General MacArthur, an Army Distinguished Service Cross.

95. Martin Caidin, *The Ragged, Rugged Warriors* (1966: Dutton), 36–37. Samuel Eliot Morison acknowledged "the sickening business of killing survivors in boats, rafts or wreckage" in his official history of U.S. naval operations, but went on to describe this as "a grisly task, but a military necessity," since the Japanese did not surrender and might have made it to shore and joined the garrison there. He then proceeded to mention that some of the survivors swam to Papua, thus providing the natives there with "open season on Nips"; *History of the United States Naval Operations in World War II* (1950: Little, Brown), 6: 62.

96. *Time*, March 15, 1943, 20; March 29, 1943, 4; April 19, 1943, 10.

97. Foreign Morale Analysis Division, Bureau of Overseas Intelligence, Office of War Information: *Japanese Use of American Statements and Acts, Real or Alleged, in Propaganda to Create Fear* (Report no. 21, June 15, 1945), 4–7; *Principal Findings Regarding Japanese Morale During the War* (Report no. 26, September 20, 1945), 8–10. U.S. National Archives, R.G. 208 (OWI), Box 444. For a sample of such ingenuity, cf. Ernie Pyle, *Last Chapter* (1946: Henry Holt & Co.), 25.

98. Tom Bailey, *Tarawa* (1962: Monarch Books), 38.

99. George S. Andrew, Jr., "The 41st Didn't Take Prisoners," *Saturday Evening Post*, July 27, 1946, 22ff.

100. Charles A. Lindbergh, *The Wartime Journals of Charles A. Lindbergh* (1970: Harcourt Brace Jovanovich), 797–923. Lindbergh's sense of "chivalry" in war, in the specific context of the Pacific conflict, emerges in the chapter entitled "The Man on the Beach" in his *Autobiography of Values* (1978: Harcourt Brace Jovanovich).

101. Johnston, 228. *New York Times*, January 9, 1943, 1.

102. *Nippon Times*, March 29, 1945, 4.

103. It is estimated that in the half century after 1500 the Indian population of the Americas declined from 80 million to 10 million as a consequence of the European onslaught; Tzvetan Todorov, *The Conquest of America: The Question of the Other*, translated from the French by Richard Howard (1982: Harper & Row), 127–45, esp. 133. This suggestive work focuses, like the present study, on the problem of the Other.

104. On the Western, particularly American, "strategy of annihilation" and "strategy of terror," cf. Russell F. Weigley, *The American Way of War: A History of United States Military Strategy and Policy* (1973: Indiana University Press), 127, 133–35, 149–152. On the annihilation of the American Indians, see ibid., 153–63. In a little-known atrocity of 1941, French troops razed villages in the Mekong Delta in Indochina, arrested as many as 8,000 civilians, including old people and children, chained them together by running

wires through their palms or heels, and transported them on barges for days under the tropical sun; Chieu Vu, "Political and Social Change in Viet-Nam between 1940 and 1946," Ph.D. dissertation in history, University of Wisconsin-Madison, 1984, chap. 3.

105. For an imaginative case study of the Western "epic of defeat," see Bruce A. Rosenberg, *Custer and the Epic of Defeat* (1974: Pennsylvania State University Press). This can be read as a counterpoint to Ivan Morris' *The Nobility of Failure: Tragic Heroes in the History of Japan* (1976: Meridian Books). U.K. aircrew killed in World War Two numbered 55,573 men, over 38,000 of them from the RAF; Max Hastings, *Bomber Command* (1979: Dial), 11. The number of kamikaze pilots who gave their lives was in the neighborhood of 5,000. A recent source gives the precise figure of 4,615 (2,409 from the Imperial Navy and 2,206 from the Imperial Army); O'Neill, 278. It is often observed, in passing, that during the early stages of the war Allied fighting men who faced hopeless situations often sacrificed themselves in what amounted to suicide attacks, including crashing their planes onto enemy warships; cf. Manchester, *Goodbye, Darkness*, 291.

CHAPTER 4: APES AND OTHERS

1. Foreign Morale Analysis Division, Office of War Information, *The Attitudes of Japanese Prisoners of War: An Overall View* (Report no. 31, December 29, 1945), esp. 15–16; and the same unit's *Wartime Analysis of Japanese Morale* (n.d., but late 1945 or early 1946), esp. 5; U.S. National Archives, R.G. 208, Boxes 443 and 445. The reports of this unit contain many studies of prisoners, and the general findings are summarized by Alexander H. Leighton, former head of the unit, in *Human Relations in a Changing World: Observations on the Use of the Social Sciences* (1949: Dutton); on Japanese prisoners, see 303–4, 321–22. See chap. 6, n. 1 below for a fuller citation to these materials.

2. See chap. 6, especially the concluding section.

3. Ernie Pyle, *Last Chapter* (1945: Henry Holt & Co.), 5. For circulation figures, see Jack Goodman, ed., *While You Were Gone: A Report on Wartime Life in the United States* (1946: Simon & Schuster), 367.

4. *Science Digest* 17.3 (March 1945): 5; Otto Tolischus, *Tokyo Record* (1943: Reynal & Hitchcock), chap. 28; the poster is in the G. William Gahagan papers, Hoover Institution; for the song, see the sheet music illustration in Anthony Rhodes' interesting *Propaganda, The Art of Persuasion: World War II* (1976: Chelsea House), 164.

5. James M. Merrill, *A Sailor's Admiral: A Biography of William F. Halsey* (1976: Crowell), 111; *Leatherneck* 26.2 (February 1943): 12; cf. ibid., 27.2 (February 1944): 10.

6. On the Japanese-American experience and wartime "relocation," see the major studies by Roger Daniels: *The Politics of Prejudice* (1968: Atheneum), *Concentration Camps USA: Japanese Americans and World War II* (1971: Holt, Rinehart & Winston), and *The Decision to Relocate the Japanese Americans* (1975: Lippincott); also Carey McWilliams, *Prejudice: Japanese-Americans—Symbol of Racial Intolerance* (1944: Little, Brown); Audrie Girdner and Anne Loftis, *The Great Betrayal: The Evacuation of the Japanese-Americans During World War II* (1969: Macmillan Co.); Stetson Conn, "The Decision to Evacuate the Japanese from the Pacific Coast (1942)," in Kent Roberts Greenfield, ed., *Command Decisions* (1959: Harcourt, Brace & Co., for the Office of the Chief of Military History, Department of the Army), 88–109; Stetson Conn, Rose C. Engelman, and Byron Fairchild, *Guarding the United States and Its Outposts* (1964: Office of the Chief of Military History, Department of the Army), 115–49; Eugene V. Rostow, "The Japanese American Cases—A Disaster," *Yale Law Journal* 54.3 (June 1945): 489–533; Commission on Wartime Relocation and Internment of Civilians, *Personal Justice Denied* (December 1982).

7. Cf. Daniels, *Concentration Camps*, 61–62; Daniels, *The Decision to Relocate*, 97; Girdner and Loftis, 17, 24, 101; McWilliams, 116, 251; *Henry L. Stimson Diaries* (Yale University Library microfilm), reel 7: 512 (entry for February 10, 1942).

8. For song titles, see Rhodes, 147, 148, 164; A. Marjorie Taylor, *The Language of*

World War II, rev. ed. (1948: H. W. Wilson Co.), 232–38; Colin Shindler, *Hollywood Goes to War: Films and American Society, 1939–1952* (1979: Routledge & Kegan Paul), 35; *Time*, December 29, 1941, 46; Geoffrey Perrett, *Days of Sadness, Years of Triumph: The American People, 1939–1945* (1973: Coward, McCann & Geoghegan), 241.

9. Cf. *Personal Justice Denied*, 139–40; Girdner and Loftis, 151–52.

10. Churchill is quoted in Francis L. Lowenheim et al., eds., *Roosevelt and Churchill: Their Secret Wartime Correspondence* (1975: Saturday Review Press), 95. For Stimson, see Dorothy Borg and Shumpei Okamoto, eds., *Pearl Harbor As History: Japanese-American Relations, 1931–1941* (1973: Columbia University Press), 51; cf. 281. *Leatherneck* 27.7 (June 1944): 63; cf. Daniels, *Concentration Camps*, 32. "Mad dog" was also used in the U.S. Army film *Know Your Enemy—Japan*. For an earlier reference to Orientals in general as "frightened hares," see Stephen Roskill, *Hankey: Man of Secrets, Volume 2, 1919–1931* (1972: William Collins, Sons & Co.), 250–51; cf. also 244.

11. Waldo Heinrichs, *American Ambassador: Joseph C. Grew and the Development of the United States Diplomatic Tradition* (1966: Little, Brown), 370; see also Grew in *United States News*, April 6, 1945, 20. *Science Digest* 12.5 (November 1942): 33–34, and 15.3 (March 1944): 54–56; *Leatherneck* 28.3 (March 1945): 23; William Slim (Field Marshal the Viscount Slim), *Defeat Into Victory* (1961: David McKay Co.), 401. In an interesting guide to Japan prepared by the U.S. Navy when Japan surrendered, the country was described as a "monstrous beehive"; *Guide to Japan* (CINCPAC-CINCPOA Bulletin no. 209–45, September 1, 1945), 65.

12. *Guide to Japan*, 51; Debs Myers et al., eds., *Yank—the GI Story of the War* (1947: Duell, Sloan & Pearce), 148; Winston Churchill, *Triumph and Tragedy* (1953: Houghton Mifflin), 637; Milovan Djilas, *Conversations with Stalin* (1969: Pelican), 79; Chatham House, *Japan In Defeat* (1944: Royal Institute of International Affairs), 8, 71, 119; George H. Johnston, *Pacific Partner* (1944: Duell, Sloan & Pearce), 205.

13. David Dilks, ed., *The Diaries of Sir Alexander Cadogan, 1938–1945* (1971: Cassell & Co.), 353, 358, 392, 416, 445; John Goette, *Japan Fights for Asia* (1943: Harcourt, Brace & Young), 36; William Manchester, *American Caesar: Douglas MacArthur, 1880–1964* (1978: Dell), 264; *Punch*, January 14, 1942; S. E. Smith, *The United States Marine Corps in World War II* (1969: Random House), 247, 252; *New Yorker*, September 12, 1942, reproduced in *Reader's Digest*, December 1942, 248; Edward Tabor Linenthal, *Changing Images of the Warrior Hero in America: A History of Popular Symbolism* (1982: Edwin Mellen Press), 131.

14. Merrill, 35, 65–66, 73–74, 82–83, 85, 88–89, 106, 111, 142, 202, 209–10, 232, 246; William F. Halsey and Joseph Bryan III, *Admiral Halsey's Story* (1947: McGraw-Hill), 141–42, 206; Foreign Morale Analysis Division, *Japanese Use of American Statements and Acts, Real or Alleged, in Propaganda to Create Fear* (Report no. 21, June 15, 1945), esp. 9; U.S. National Archives, R.G. 208, Box 444.

15. Taylor, 114; Lester V. Berrey and Melvin Van Den Bark, *The American Thesaurus of Slang*, 2nd ed. (1953: Crowell), 385; *Leatherneck* 25.2 (February 1942); *Guide to Japan*, 40; *Infantry Journal*, March 1945, 23–24, and August 1945, 41; Robert Eichelberger, *Dear Miss Em: General Eichelberger's War in the Pacific, 1942–1945*, ed. Jay Luvaas (1972: Greenwood Press), 300, 303.

16. *New York Times*, April 25, 1943.

17. *American Legion Magazine*, October 1942, 56; *Collier's* covers of April 18, 1942, and May 8, 1945; *Time* cover of January 26, 1942; David Low, *Years of Wrath* (1946: Simon & Schuster).

18. *New York Times*: Sunday Book Review section, May 17, 1942; Sunday News of the Week in Review section, December 21, 1941; May 17, June 28, and November 8, 1942; April 4 and April 25, 1943; February 6 and November 12, 1944. *New York Times Magazine*, May 2, 1942, and February 25, 1945. Another excellent cartoon source is the *Chicago Tribune*, which published its major graphics from the first year of the conflict

in *War Cartoons by McCutcheon, Orr, Parrish, Somdal: December 8, 1941–September 28, 1942* (1942: Chicago Tribune).

19. James J. Fahey, *Pacific War Diary, 1942–1945* (1963: Houghton Mifflin), 45–46; *Leatherneck* 26.1 (January 1943): 45.

20. *American Legion Magazine*, November 1944, 31; *Leatherneck* 26.7 (July 1943): 3; *American Rifleman*, July, August, and September, 1944; cf. ibid., June 1943 and January 1945; McWilliams, 131; *Time*, December 22, 1941, 13.

21. *Time*, November 2, 1942, 30; *Newsweek*, February 7, 1944, 25; *American Rifleman*, January 1945, 47; *Reader's Digest*, January 1945, 88; Slim, 254, 277; *Leatherneck* 26.8 (August 1943): 24–25; *Life*, September 6, 1943, cover, 18, 43; *Science Digest* 12.6 (December 1943), 53; *American Legion Magazine*, November 1942, 55, and August 1943, 20, 48; S. E. Smith, 223, 332, 598. The prize-winning journalist was Ira Wolfert.

22. H.G. Nichols, ed., *Washington Despatches, 1941–1945: Weekly Political Reports from the British Embassy* (1981: University of Chicago), 558 (May 13, 1945); cf. 299 (January 1, 1944). *American Legion Magazine*, October 1944, 52; *Leatherneck* 28.3 (March 1945): 37; Chicago Tribune, *War Cartoons; New York Times*, March 7, 1943.

23. Slim, 392; *Time*, February 15, 1945, 25; Richard Tregaskis, *Guadalcanal Diary* (1942: Random House), 71; *The Nation*, March 3, 1945, 240. Merrill, 138, 210; *New York Times*, February 7, 1945, 36.

24. *Time*, March 19, 1945, 32; Richard Polenberg, *War and Society: The United States, 1941–1945* (1972: Lippincott), 65; McWilliams, 131, 163–64, 237, 241. The parade is reported in the *New York Herald Tribune*, June 14, 1942, 1, 2, which described this as "a grim and bristling war pageant that streamed up Fifth Avenue for eleven hours." A half million people participated, and estimates of the crowd ranged from 2.5 to 5 million. A "Pearl Harbor" float in the same parade "showed a Japanese diplomat smilingly negotiating with Uncle Sam while a Japanese general, urged on by Hitler, prepares to knife Uncle Sam in the back"; cf. Polenberg 135.

CHAPTER 5: LESSER MEN AND SUPERMEN

1. On the early encounter between Europeans and the Japanese, see Charles R. Boxer, *The Christian Century in Japan, 1549–1650* (1961: University of California Press); Michael Cooper, S.J., ed., *They Came to Japan: An Anthology of European Reports on Japan, 1543–1640* (1965: University of California Press); George Elison, *Deus Destroyed: The Image of Christianity in Early Modern Japan* (1973: Harvard University Press).

2. Elison, 16; Cooper, 229.

3. George Sansom, *The Western World and Japan* (1950: Knopf), 3; Sansom's classic, *Japan: A Short Cultural History*, was published in 1931. John F. Embree, *The Japanese* (Smithsonian Institution War Background Studies no. 7, January 23, 1943), 34.

4. *Newsweek*, June 11 and July 2, 1945 (pp. 48 and 33 respectively). Pakenham's boyhood relationship with Konoe was not pleasant, for he claims Konoe stole his dog, initially denied doing so, and later acknowledged the act with the comment "My mother tell me to misstate to a foreigner is not to lie." Pakenham later played an interesting backstage role during the postsurrender occupation of Japan when, still associated with *Newsweek*, he became associated with the American Council on Japan lobby that advocated abandonment of the initial program of extensive reform. Prior to that, he was temporarily banned from Japan by General MacArthur's headquarters, which took umbrage at some of his early reports on occupation policy. For Zacharias, see Ellis M. Zacharias, *Secret Missions: The Story of an Intelligence Officer* (1946: Putman), 62.

5. Eckstein is quoted in Helen Mears, *Mirror for Americans: Japan* (1948: Houghton Mifflin), 79. The military officer was John Goette: *Japan Fights for Asia* (1943: Harcourt, Brace & Young), 182. Tolischus' comment appears in the foreword to his *Through Japanese Eyes* (1945: Reynal & Hitchcock). Tuchman's essay was published as Barbara

Wertheim, "Japan: A Clinical Note," *Foreign Affairs* 14.3 (April 1936): 521–26, and is reprinted in her *Practicing History: Selected Essays* (1981: Knopf), 93–97. The *Fortune* quotation appears in the February 1942 issue, 169. Some of the most sophisticated popular writing on Japan during the war appeared in *Fortune*, especially a special issue of April 1944, and was later reprinted by the U.S. government and used in training Japan specialists in the United States: The Editors of *Fortune*, eds., *Japan and the Japanese: A Military Power We Must Defeat, A Pacific Problem We Must Solve* (1944: Infantry Journal).

6. Robert Craigie, *Behind the Japanese Mask* (1946: Hutchinson & Co.), 157; *New York Times*, August 12, 1945, E3; Joseph C. Grew, "The People of Japan," in U.S. Office of Education, *Introducing the Peoples of the Far East* (Bulletin 1945, no. 7), 1; *Newsweek*, September 3, 1945, 23. Cf. Wilfrid Fleisher, *What to Do with Japan* (1945: Doubleday, Doran & Co.), 7; *United States News*, April 6, 1945, 20 ("Men who have been longest in Japan are quickest to admit they have no way of knowing what will be the Japanese reaction to anything"); and, for the postsurrender continuity of such befuddlement, U.S. Department of State, *Foreign Relations of the United States 1946*, 8: 192 (for April 10, 1946).

7. Willis Lamott, *Nippon: The Crime and Punishment of Japan* (1944: John Day Co.), 191–95; William Henry Chamberlin, *Modern Japan*, ed. Maxwell S. Stewart (1942: American Council, Institute of Pacific Affairs and Webster Publishing Co.), 14–15; *Guide to Japan* (CINCPAC-CINCPOA Bulletin no. 209–45, September 1, 1945), 26. Cf. Peter De Mendelssohn, *Japan's Political Warfare* (1944: George Allen & Unwin), 96–99, 139–40; Douglas Gilbert Haring, *Blood on the Rising Sun* (1943: Macrae Smith Co.), 159–61.

8. The "class-C nation" comment was by Admiral Halsey; James M. Merrill, *A Sailor's Admiral: A Biography of William F. Halsey* (1976: Crowell), 74. The underestimation of Japanese capabilities is noted by virtually all contemporary accounts as well as the basic military and diplomatic histories of the war, including the following: S. W. Kirby, *The War against Japan* (1957: Her Majesty's Stationery Office), vol. 1; S. W. Kirby, *Singapore: The Chain of Disaster* (1971: Cassell & Co.); Louis Allen, *Singapore, 1941– 1942* (1977: Davis-Poynter); Cecil Brown, *Suez to Singapore* (1942: Halcyon House); Noel Barber, *Sinister Twilight: The Fall and Rise Again of Singapore* (1968: William Collins, Sons & Co.); Christopher Thorne, *Allies of a Kind: The United States, Britain, and the War against Japan, 1941–1945* (1978: Oxford University Press); William Slim (Field Marshal the Viscount Slim), *Defeat Into Victory* (1961: David McKay Co.); essays by Peter Lowe and David Kahn, on Great Britain and the United States respectively, in Ernest R. May, ed., *Knowing One's Enemies: Intelligence Assessment before the Two World Wars* (1984: Princeton University Press); John Toland, *The Rising Sun: The Decline and Fall of the Japanese Empire, 1936–1945* (1970: Random House); John Costello, *The Pacific War, 1941–1945* (1982: Quill Trade Paperbacks); H. P. Willmott, *Empires in the Balance: Japanese and Allied Pacific Strategies to April 1942* (1982: Naval Institute Press).

9. Allen, 50–54; Kirby, *Singapore*, 73–75; Kirby, *The War against Japan*, 1: 166–67.

10. Brown, 140–42, 168, 170, 176, 240, 249, 269, 307–08; Kirby, *Singapore*, 134; Kirby, *The War against Japan*, 1: 183–84, 525; Barber, 39–40; Slim, 21, 97, 191–92.

11. Costello, 108–10, 159, 619; Willmott, 126–29; Kirby, *The War against Japan*, 1: 193–99, 251; Brown, 304–8.

12. Fletcher Pratt, *Sea Power and Today's War* (1939: Harrison-Hilton), 175–80. Pratt, an isolationist prior to Pearl Harbor, was a consultant to *Time* magazine and the *New York Post*. Before the war, some Westerners also refused to book passage on Japanese ships on the grounds that their officers were poorly trained; Jesse Steiner, *Behind the Japanese Mask* (1943: Macmillan Co.), 6. The belief that the Japanese could not construct seaworthy vessels appears to have derived from mishaps of the early 1930s which were reported in such standard military references as *Jane's Fighting Ships*; cf. the early evaluation of the Japanese by MacArthur's later psychological-warfare chief, Bonner Fellers, *The*

Psychology of the Japanese Soldier (1934–35: Command and General Staff School, Fort Leavenworth), 37; in Bonner Frank Fellers Collection, Hoover Institution, Box 1.

13. Kirby, *The War against Japan*, 1: 116–17; Kirby, *Singapore*, 74, 94; Brown, 168, 170–71, 176.

14. Jirō Horikoshi, *Eagles of Mitsubishi: The Story of the Zero Fighter* (1980: University of Washington Press; translated from the 1970 Japanese ed. by Kappa Books), esp. 93–109; Claire Lee Chennault, *Way of a Fighter: The Memoirs of Claire Lee Chennault*, ed. Robert Holz (1949: Putnam), 89, 92–94; Denis Richards and Hilary St. George Saunders, *Royal Air Force, 1939–1945* (1954: Her Majesty's Stationery Office), 2: 11; Kirby, *The War against Japan*, 1: 240; Kirby, *Singapore*, 73–74, 102, 121.

15. Kirby, *The War against Japan*, 1: 116–17; Barber, 45; Tolischus, 144. It was also rumored that the Japanese could not shoot straight because their eyes were slanted; after Pearl Harbor, Westerners then argued that the Japanese themselves had deliberately and deviously fostered this rumor; cf. Joseph Rosenfarb, *Highway to Tokyo* (1943: Little, Brown), 7–8; Steiner, 6.

16. William Manchester, *American Caesar: Douglas MacArthur 1880–1964* (1978: Dell), 188; Kirby, *The War against Japan*, 1: 147; Anthony Eden, *The Eden Memoirs: The Reckoning* (1965: Cassell & Co.), 292–93; Toland, 248; Debs Myers et al., eds., *Yank —the GI Story of the War* (1947: Duell, Sloan & Pearce), 254.

17. Otto Tolischus, *Tokyo Record* (1943: Reynal & Hitchcock), 208; cf. Ernest T. Nash, "Japan's Schizophrenia," *Asia*, September 1942, esp. 528.

18. Suzuki, born in 1870, had published three major volumes of essays and at least seven other books about Japanese Buddhism in English by the mid-1930s. For a serious wartime treatment of these themes by a philosopher who taught in Japan from 1936 to 1941, see Karl Löwith, "The Japanese Mind," *Fortune*, December 1943. Norman's comment was made in a review of Tolischus' *Tokyo Record* in *Far Eastern Survey*, April 19, 1943, 81–83.

19. Tolischus, *Tokyo Record*, 208; Stephen Roskill, *Naval Policy Between the Wars* (1976: William Collins), 2: 188–89.

20. Thorne, 158–59, 167–68.

21. Tolischus, *Tokyo Record*, 19 (entry for February 14, 1941); Glen C. H. Perry, *"Dear Bart": Washington Views of World War II* (1982: Greenwood Press), 10, 13, 15.

22. James R. Young, "Japan Risks Destruction," *Reader's Digest*, November 1941, 29–33; Bruce Catton, *The War Lords of Washington* (1948: Harcourt, Brace & World), 9, for the quotation from Knox; William D. Leahy, *I Was There: The Personal Story of the Chief of Staff to Presidents Roosevelt and Truman Based on His Notes and Diaries Made at the Time* (1950: McGraw-Hill), 79; Henry A. Wallace, *The Price of Vision: The Diary of Henry A. Wallace, 1942–1946*, ed. John Morton Blum (1973: Houghton Mifflin), 61 (entry for March 31, 1942). For public-opinion polls on the duration of the war, see Hadley Cantril, ed., *Public Opinion 1935–1946* (1951: Princeton University Press), 1097–1100.

23. Hugh Byas, *The Japanese Enemy: His Power and His Vulnerability* (1942: Knopf), 12; *Fortune*, February 1942, 53; Erle Dickover, in *Vital Speeches of the Day* 9.6 (January 1, 1945): 178.

24. *Time*, December 29, 1941, 13; *Life*, January 12, 1942, 32.

25. Kirby, *The War Against Japan*, 1: 199.

26. Barber, 58; Myers, *Yank*, 256 (*Yank* was attempting to correct this erroneous notion); Slim, 95–97, 154, 160–61, 213, 310; Roger Daniels, *Concentration Camps USA: Japanese Americans and World War II* (1971: Holt, Rinehart & Winston), 33.

27. Joseph C. Grew, *Report from Tokyo* (1942: Simon & Schuster), esp. viii, 17, 29, 30; *Time*, January 12, 1942, 17–18, and September 28, 1942, 34. Grew's first speech upon his return to the United States is reproduced in *New York Times*, August 31, 1942.

28. *Time*, May 18, 1942, 26; cf. April 20, 1942, 18, for a vivid example of the metamorphosis of the Japanese from the "funny, myopic, bucktoothed, bandylegged,

pint-sized Jap" to an individual who suddenly appeared "taut-muscled, courageous, vastly menacing." See also ibid., December 22, 1941, 24; February 15, 1943, 24; May 3, 1943, 19.

29. Homer Lea's *Valor of Ignorance,* discussed in chap. 7, was republished in 1942 by Harper & Brothers in the United States and by Hokuseido in Japan. For samples of the Lea boom, cf. *American Mercury,* April 1942, 473–78; *American Rifleman,* September 1942; *Christian Science Monitor,* March 7, 1942 (an interesting account by a boyhood acquaintance of Lea); *Saturday Review of Literature,* April 4, 1942; *Contemporary Japan* 11.7 (July 1942): 1099–1103. *Life* resurrected Hector Bywater, another early prophet of a Pacific war, in its issue of December 22, 1941.

30. Geoffrey Perrett, *Days of Sadness, Years of Triumph: The American People, 1939–1945* (1973: Coward, McCann & Geoghegan), 205–6; *Life,* January 12, 1942; Cantril, 1067–68 for public-opinion polls.

31. Denis Warner and Peggy Warner, *The Sacred Warriors: Japan's Suicide Legions* (1982: Avon), 63; Henry Berry, *Semper Fi, Mac: Living Memories of the U.S. Marines in World War II* (1982: Arbor House), 46, 49, 79.

32. George H. Johnston, *The Toughest Fighting in the World* (1943: Duell, Sloan & Pearce), 134–37, 233; S. E. Smith, ed., *The United States Marine Corps in World War II* (1969: Random House), 219.

33. Nathaniel Pfeffer, "Japanese Superman? That, Too, Is a Fallacy," *New York Times Magazine,* March 22, 1942; Hugh Byas, "How Tough Are the Japanese?" ibid., May 2, 1943. James M. Merrill, *A Sailor's Admiral: A Biography of William F. Halsey* (1976: Crowell), 72–74. For another sample of debunking "the myth of the Jap as a fighting superman," cf. Sydney Greenbie, "Misconceptions About the Japanese," *American Mercury,* May 1944, 533–38. *Infantry Journal* was still addressing the superman notion in 1945; cf. Colonel A. G. Foxx, "Your Enemy: The Jap" in the March 1945 issue, 23–24. LeMay did not oppose using the atomic bomb, but thought Japan could be brought to quick capitulation by continued conventional bombing; cf. Wesley Frank Craven and James Lea Cate, *The Army Air Forces in World War II* (1953: University of Chicago Press; 1983: Office of Air Force History), 5: 711. U.S. military plans at the time the decision to use the atomic bombs against Japan was made anticipated (under the "Olympic-Coronet" plan) invasion of Kyushu in late 1945, followed by invasion of the Kanto area of Honshu in the spring of 1946.

CHAPTER 6: PRIMITIVES, CHILDREN, MADMEN

1. Much of the basic analysis of Japan conducted by American and British social scientists during the war was carried out under the auspices of the Foreign Morale Analysis Division, Bureau of Overseas Intelligence, U.S. Office of War Information (OWI). FMAD papers on Japan, including regular reports beginning in 1944, are available in R.G. 208 in the National Archives; see especially Boxes 443, 444, 445. Individuals involved at one time or another with FMAD's analysis of Japanese wartime morale included Alexander Leighton, Clyde Kluckhohn, Morris Opler, Ruth Benedict, John Embree, Frederick Hulse, Dorothea Leighton, Hermann Spitzer, Iwao Ishino, and Marion Levy, Jr.

The most famous work to emerge out of these OWI intelligence activities was Ruth Benedict's *The Chrysanthemum and the Sword* (1946: Houghton Mifflin), based on a sixty-page report written in the summer of 1945 and issued immediately after Japan's surrender: *Japanese Behavior Patterns* (Report no. 25, September 15, 1945). Also of particular interest are *Japanese Use of American Statements and Acts, Real or Alleged, in Propaganda to Create Fear* (Report no. 21, June 15, 1945); *Bibliography of Articles and Books Relating to Japanese Psychology* (Report no. 24, August 25, 1945); *Principal Findings Regarding Japanese Morale During the War* (Report no. 26, September 20, 1945); *The Japanese Emperor* (Report no. 27, October 31, 1945); *Japanese Personality and Reactions as Seen in Soldiers' Diaries* (Report no. 30, December 19, 1945); *The Attitudes of Japanese Prisoners of War: An Overall View* (Report no. 31, December 29, 1945); and *Pro-American Sentiment Among the Japanese During the War* (Report no. 32, December 31, 1945). Benedict later offered a nutshell summary of her thesis in " 'The Japanese Are So Simple'," *Asia and the Americas,* November 1946, 500–503.

The activities and principal findings of FMAD were summarized after the war by the former chief of the division, Alexander Leighton, in his *Human Relations in a Changing World: Observations on the Use of the Social Sciences* (1949: Dutton); this work includes a personnel list for FMAD and the complete reprint of one of the division's most important special reports: *Current Psychological and Social Tensions in Japan* (Special Report no. 5, June 1, 1945). Clyde Kluckhohn, vice chief of FMAD, discussed the wartime work on Japan in his *Mirror for Man: The Relation of Anthropology to Modern Life* (1949: McGraw-Hill). Basic materials pertaining to wartime intelligence work on Japan are excerpted in William E. Daugherty and Morris Janowitz, eds., *A Psychological Warfare Casebook* (1958: Johns Hopkins University Press, for the U.S. Operations Research Office). For a general study of psychological warfare by another participant in the wartime activities, see Paul M. A. Linebarger, *Psychological Warfare* (1948: Infantry Journal Press). Other retrospective pieces by FMAD social scientists are Alexander Leighton and Morris Opler, "Psychological Warfare and the Japanese Emperor," in Robert Hunt, ed., *Personalities and Cultures: Readings in Psychological Anthropology* (1967: Natural History Press; originally published in 1946), 251–60; Hermann M. Spitzer, "Psychoanalytical Approaches to the Japanese Character," *Psychoanalysis and the Social Sciences* 1 (1947): 131–56.

For general studies of the OWI, see Allan M. Winkler, *The Politics of Propaganda: The Office of War Information, 1942–1945* (1978: Yale University Press); also Robert Lee Bishop, "The Overseas Branch of the Office of War Information," Ph.D. dissertation in mass communications, University of Wisconsin-Madison, 1966. The British counterpart to the OWI devoted its energies primarily to the war in Europe; cf. Ian McLaine, *Ministry of Morale: Home Front Morale and the Ministry of Information in World War II* (1979: George Allen & Unwin), esp. 158–59, 273–74, 299 for Asia.

For military intelligence, several reports in the voluminous Bonner Frank Fellers Collection in the Hoover Institution at Stanford University summarize concisely the intelligence evaluations General MacArthur was receiving in the Southwest Pacific Command. These include Fellers' staff paper of 1934–35 written for the Command and General Staff School at Fort Leavenworth and entitled *The Psychology of the Japanese Soldier* (of which Fellers wrote in November 1944 that "today I'd not change a line in this study"); *Answer to Japan* (July 1, 1944); and *Basic Military Plan for Psychological Warfare Against Japan, with Appendices and Minutes of the Conference on Psychological Warfare Against Japan,* Manila, May 7–8, 1945 (Boxes 1 and 4). For postwar reminiscences by intelligence personnel, see Ellis M. Zacharias, *Secret Missions: The Story of an Intelligence Officer* (1946: Putnam); Ladislas Farago, *Burn after Reading The Espionage History of World War II* (1961: Walker & Co.), 276–302; Sidney Forrester Mashbir, *I Was An American Spy* (1953: Vantage Press). The best published collection of Allied propaganda leaflets dropped on Japanese troops and over the homeland in the latter part of the war is Suzuki Akira and Yamamoto Akira, eds., *Hiroku: Boryaku Senden Bira—Taiheiyō Sensō no Kami Bakudan* [Propaganda Leaflets—Paper Bullets of the Pacific War] (1977: Kodansha). The Hoover Institution has an excellent selection of these leaflets in both the Bonner Frank Fellers Collection (Boxes 4 and 13) and "U.S. Army Forces in the Pacific, Psychological Warfare Branch" (1 box plus scrapbook).

2. The theories and premises underlying national-character studies were explained by Margaret Mead in a number of postwar essays: "The Study of National Character," in Daniel Lerner and Harold D. Lasswell, eds., *The Policy Sciences: Recent Developments in Scope and Method* (1951: Stanford University Press), 70–85; Margaret Mead and Rhoda Metraux, eds., *The Study of Culture at a Distance* (1953: University of Chicago Press), esp. 3–53, 397–400; "National Character," in A. L. Kroeber, ed., *Anthropology*

Today: An Encyclopedic Inventory (1953: University of Chicago Press), 642–67; "Anthropological Contributions to National Policies During and Immediately After World War II," in Walter Goldschmidt, ed., *The Uses of Anthropology* (1979: American Anthropological Association), 147–57. See also Geoffrey Gorer in Mead and Metraux, 57–82, 401–2; Victor Barnouw, "Childhood Determinism and the Study of National Character," in his *Culture and Personality* (1963: Dorsey Press), 120–36.

3. Ruth Benedict and Gene Weltfish, *The Races of Mankind,* included in Benedict's *Race: Science and Politics,* rev. ed. (1945: Viking); the 1945 edition includes a comment on the debate about the pamphlet. Cf. also *New York Times,* March 6, 8, and 16, 1944; Judith Schachter Modell, *Ruth Benedict: Patterns of a Life* (1983: University of Pennsylvania Press), 247–55. For general appraisals of scientific racism—and, more specifically, racist anthropology—cf. Stephen Jay Gould, *The Mismeasure of Man* (1981: Norton); Marvin Harris, *The Rise of Anthropological Theory* (1968: Crowell), esp. chaps. 4 and 5; Morton H. Fried, *The Study of Anthropology* (1972: Crowell), esp. chap. 3.

A few years before Pearl Harbor, several major academic associations formally denounced the theories that had dominated their disciplines in earlier generations and contributed so obviously to Nazi racism. In 1938, for example, the American Anthropological Association passed a resolution deploring the distortion and misinterpretation of data "to serve the cause of an unscientific racialism rather than the cause of truth." The anthropologists declared that the "psychological and cultural connotations" of race, "if they exist, have not been ascertained by science." That same year, the executive committee of the American Psychological Association issued a lengthy statement emphasizing that "in the experiments which psychologists have made upon different peoples, no characteristic, inherent psychological differences which fundamentally distinguish so-called 'races,' have been disclosed." This included, they emphasized, any conclusive evidence linking race or nationality to native intelligence. The psychologists went on to state that racial and national attitudes could not be understood apart from their economic, political, and historical backgrounds. The following year, biologists at the International Genetics Congress in Edinburgh issued a manifesto which criticized "the unscientific doctrine that good or bad genes are the monopoly of particular peoples or of persons with features of a given kind." They too emphasized the need to eliminate the political and socioeconomic conditions that created inequality and fostered antagonism among "peoples, nations, and 'races.' " These resolutions and manifestos are reproduced in Benedict, *Race,* 195–99.

4. This is summarized in the publications of Kluckhohn, Leighton, and Opler cited in n. 1 above. Cf. also Mead in Lerner and Lasswell, 75, and in Mead and Metraux, 399. The same point was made independently at an early date by General MacArthur's intelligence personnel; see the concluding section of *Answer to Japan,* Bonner Frank Fellers Collection, Box 1. This document (prepared in July 1944), contains some remarkable rhetoric, including the observation that "there must be no weakness in the peace terms. However, to dethrone, or hang, the Emperor, would cause a tremendous and violent reaction from all Japanese. Hanging of the Emperor to them would be comparable to the crucifixion of Christ to us. All would fight to die like ants. The position of the gangster militarists would be strengthened immeasurably. The war would be unduly prolonged; our losses heavier than otherwise would be necessary." The origins of General MacArthur's later unhesitating decision to retain the emperor and the imperial institution in postsurrender Japan are to be found in such documents as this. See also n. 30 below.

5. The emphasis here on primitivism, childishness, and collective psychological disorder is my own, but the national-character approach has been criticized by others from an early date—including John Embree, one of the social scientists associated with FMAD (see n. 10 below). For critiques of the general methodology involved, cf. Alfred R. Lindesmith and Anselm L. Strauss, "A Critique of Culture-Personality Writings," *American Sociological Review* 15.5 (October 1950): 587–600; Barnouw, op. cit.; Harris, esp. chaps. 9, 10, 15, and 16. For Japanese responses to Ruth Benedict's consummate summa-

tion of the wartime approaches to Japan, see John W. Bennett and Michio Nagai, "The Japanese Critique of the Methodology of Benedict's *Chrysanthemum and the Sword,*" *American Anthropologist* 55.3 (August 1953): 404–11.

Peter T. Suzuki has been severely critical of the research methods and methodologies employed in using Japanese-Americans in the relocation camps as subjects in drawing conclusions concerning the wartime character of the Japanese enemy: "A Retrospective Analysis of a Wartime 'National Character' Study," *Dialectical Anthropology* 5.1 (May 1980): 33–46; "Anthropologists in the Wartime Camps for Japanese Americans: A Documentary Study," *Dialectical Anthropology* 6.1 (August 1981): 23–60. Richard H. Minear broke ground on some of the issues discussed here in three articles: "The Wartime Studies of Japanese National Character," *Japan Interpreter,* Summer 1980, 36–59; "Cross-Cultural Perception and World War II: American Japanists of the 1940s and Their Images of Japan," *International Studies Quarterly* 24.4 (December 1980): 555–80; "Helen Mears, Asia, and American Asianists," Occasional Papers Series no. 7, Asian Studies Committee, International Area Studies Program, University of Massachusetts-Amherst, 1981.

6. Geoffrey Gorer, "Themes in Japanese Culture," *Transactions of the New York Academy of Sciences,* 2nd ser., 5.1 (November 1943): 106–24. The published version was a condensation of a paper prepared for the Committee on Intercultural Relations under the title "Japanese Character Structure and Propaganda." "Why Are Japs Japs?" *Time,* August 7, 1944, 66.

7. Mead and Metreaux, 399, 402.

8. John F. Embree, *The Japanese* (Smithsonian Institution War Background Studies no. 7, January 23, 1943).

9. Embree, 12; cf. his "Democracy in Postwar Japan," *American Journal of Sociology* 50.3 (November 1944): 205–7.

10. "Applied Anthropology and Its Relationship to Anthropology," *American Anthropologist* 47.4 (October–December 1945): 635–37; "Anthropology and the War," *Bulletin of the American Association of University Professors* 32.3 (Autumn 1946): 485–95; "A Note on Ethnocentrism in Anthropology," *American Anthropologist* 52.3 (July–September 1950): 430–32; "Standardized Error and Japanese Character: A Note on Political Interpretation," *World Politics* 2.3 (April 1950): 439–43.

11. *Science Digest* 13.4 (April 1943): 42; *Science News Letter,* February 13, 1943, 103; *New York Times Magazine,* August 1, 1943, 17 (the ellipses are in the original). During the war, Embree also wrote an article on Japanese-Americans in the relocation camps that was published under an unfortunate title which tended to confirm the most negative stereotypes of people of Japanese origin: "Resistance to Freedom—An Administrative Problem," *Applied Anthropology* (July–September 1943): 10–14; cf. Suzuki, *Dialectical Anthropology* 6. 1: 26.

12. Judith Silberpfennig, "Psychological Aspects of Current Japanese and German Paradoxa," *Psychoanalytic Review* 32.1 (January 1945): 73–85.

13. The use of incarcerated Japanese-Americans as subjects for "community analysis" posed methodological and moral problems comparable to anthropological use of the American Indians and colonial peoples as subjects for field work. Cf. Suzuki's essays cited in n. 5 above; also George M. Foster, *Applied Anthropology* (1969: Little, Brown), chap. 9; Talal Asad, *Anthropology and the Colonial Endeavor* (1973: Ithaca Press).

14. "Provisional Analytic Summary of Institute of Pacific Relations Conference on Japanese Character Structure, December 16–17, 1944," Box 92, Institute of Pacific Relations Papers, Butler Library, Columbia University. Cf. related materials in Box 197. Embree criticized this conference immediately after the war with the comment that "at a recent meeting of persons interested in Japan, some of the social 'scientists' present made remarkable generalizations about the 'adolescent' and 'gangster' qualities of our Asiatic enemy—overlooking for the moment the youth of American culture, and such little matters as American lynching parties and race riots. To explain the causes of war in terms of individual behavior or even cultural patterns is to ignore the whole complex of socio-

economic developments that lead to international conflicts." *American Anthropologist* 47.4 (October-December 1945): 635–37; also Embree in ibid., 52.3 (July–September 1950): 430–32.

15. Gregory Bateson and Margaret Mead, *Balinese Character: A Photographic Analysis* (1942: Special Publications of the New York Academy of Sciences, vol. 11), 263.

16. Edgar Snow, *The Battle for Asia* (1942: World Publishing Co.), 65–70; Helen Mears, *New Republic*, March 29, 1943, in a review of Otto Tolischus' *Tokyo Record.*

17. Royal Institute of International Affairs, *Japan in Defeat: A Report by a Chatham House Study Group* (1945: Oxford University Press), xii, 129; Benedict, *The Chrysanthemum and the Sword*, 108; cf. 165.

18. Margaret Mead, *Ruth Benedict* (1974: Columbia University Press), 57–59. Haring was also a prolific writer on Japan during the war, producing among other contributions a book entitled *Blood on the Rising Sun* (1943: Macrae Smith Co.); see the selections on Japanese national character in his *Personal Character and Cultural Milieu: A Collection of Readings*, 3rd rev. ed. (1956: Syracuse University Press).

19. Willis Lamott, *Nippon: The Crime and Punishment of Japan* (1944: John Day Co.), 11; book review by Nathaniel Peffer in *Asia and the Americas*, January 1943, 6.

20. Weston La Barre, "Some Observations on Character Structure in the Orient," *Psychiatry: Journal of Biology and the Pathology of Interpersonal Relations* 8.3 (August 1945): 319–42.

21. Leighton, 55; Edgar L. Jones, "Fighting with Words: Psychological Warfare in the Pacific," *Atlantic Monthly*, August 1945, 47–51. Cf. *Life*'s coverage of the belated use of psychological warfare in the Okinawa campaign in its issue of July 9, 1945—under the revealing title "Jap Surrenders Are Increasing—Psychological Warfare Proves Effective."

22. Leighton, 58–75, 89–95, 120–28; the quotation is on 128. The important June 1, 1945, report is reprinted in ibid., 227–89. Similar conclusions about the possibility of persuading the Japanese to surrender were reached independently by Naval Intelligence analysts working under Captain Ellis Zacharias, and by Colonel Sidney Mashbir in General MacArthur's intelligence corps. These were more oriented to the possibility of persuading the top leadership in Tokyo to surrender, and both Zacharias and Mashbir were given permission to direct radio broadcasts to Japan in the final months of the war. Like Leighton, they felt a more serious Allied psychological-warfare campaign could have succeeded in bringing about an earlier Japanese surrender. The bureaucratic as well as political, intellectual, and ideological intricacies of these activities are a separate study in themselves, about which there is considerable scattered material in English. See the books by Zacharias and Mashbir cited in n. 1 above.

23. Kluckhohn, 171–78, 200.

24. John T. Pratt, *War and Politics in China* (1943: Jonathan Cape), 242; Pratt was referring specifically at this point not to Japanese atrocities, but to the insurrection of young military men in Japan in 1936. Ministry of Information, *Japan: The Place and the Population* (April 1942) and *The Japanese People* (1943); quoted in McLaine, 158–59. Former ambassador to Japan Robert Craigie similarly found the main cause of the war to be "a primitive lust for power and dominion" among Japan's "warrior caste"; *Behind the Japanese Mask* (1946: Hutchinson & Co.), 162.

25. Ministry of Information, *A Diagnosis of Japanese Psychology* (April 27, 1945).

26. *Life*, December 22, 1941, 81; *Asia and the Americas*, January 1943, 6; *American Legion Magazine*, April 1944, 19, 34; ibid., November 1942, 6; Tolischus in *Time*, March 23, 1942, 22; Snow, *Battle for Asia*, 66; *Reader's Digest*, January 1945, 88; Denis Warner and Peggy Warner, *The Sacred Warriors: Japan's Suicide Legions* (1982: Avon), 37.

27. William D. Leahy, *I Was There* (1950: McGraw-Hill), 79. Truman's Potsdam diary is reprinted in *Diplomatic History* 4.3 (Summer 1980): 317–26; see esp. 324.

28. Setsuko Ono, *A Western Image of Japan: What Did the West See through the Eyes of Loti and Hearn?* Thèse no. 235, Institut Universitaire de Hautes Études Interna-

tionales, Université de Genève, 1972, 104. This is an illuminating content analysis of writing on Japan by two of that country's most famous Western interpreters, Pierre Loti (whose *Madame Chrysanthème* became the basis for Puccini's *Madama Butterfly*) and Lafcadio Hearn.

29. For Churchill and Roosevelt, see U.S. Department of State, *Foreign Relations of the United States: Japan 1931–1941*, 2: 355. *Life*, January 12, 1942, 26, on "16-year-old kids"; cf. John Toland, *The Rising Sun: The Decline and Fall of the Japanese Empire, 1936–1945* (1970: Random House), 246. Grew's comment was presented as something said to him by a Japanese acquaintance, with which the ambassador agreed; see his diary entry for November 29, 1941, in *Ten Years in Japan* (1944, Simon & Schuster), 484. The British commentator, Ernest T. Nash, was born in China and worked in the Shanghai municipal government for twenty-five years; "Japan's Schizophrenia," *Asia*, September 1942, 526–28. *Newsweek*, July 30, 1945, 35; Willard Price, *Japan and the Son of Heaven* (1945: Duell, Sloan & Pearce), chap. 19.

30. *Answer to Japan*, Bonner Frank Feller Collection, Box 1. Emphasis in original.

31. *American Mercury*, November 1942, 32, reprinted in *Reader's Digest*, January 1943. *New York Times Magazine*, March 4, 1945, 10; Noel Barber, *Sinister Twilight: The Fall and Rise Again of Singapore* (1968: William Collins, Sons & Co.), 297; *Science Digest* 15.6 (December 1944): 57, reprinted from *Flying*, October 1944; Willis Church Lamott in *Reader's Digest*, August 1945, 26.

32. Ministry of Information, *A Diagnosis of Japanese Psychology*. Guide to Japan (CINPAC-CINPOA Bulletin no. 209–45, September 1, 1945), 46, 51. Hugh Byas, "How Tough Are the Japanese?" *New York Times Magazine*, May 2, 1943, 6. *Science Digest* 14.6 (December 1943): 53; cf. ibid., 15.6 (December 1944): 57. Herman Kogan, "These Nips Are Nuts," *American Legion Magazine*, February 1945, 88–89.

33. As reported in the Western press, Japanese battlefield English was remarkably fluent and colloquial—implicitly reinforcing the impression that many Japanese were Japanese-Americans who had shown their true colors by joining in the battle against the United States. Thus, the folklore of the combat zones has the Japanese uttering such cries as the following: "Marines, you die!" "Marines, we will kill you!" "U.S. Marines be dead tomorrow!" "Japanese boys kill American boys!" "Japanese drink blood like wine!" "Blood for the Emperor!" "One, two, three, you can't catch me!" "To hell with Babe Ruth! To hell with Babe Ruth!" Japanese refusing to surrender were quoted as yelling, "Shut up, you American bastards" and even "Come and get me, you souvenir-hunting sonuvabitch." *Yank*, the U.S. Army magazine, went so far as to have the Japanese screaming, "Banzai, the f------ Marine will die!" At Kiska, *Yank* also reported, the victorious Allies came upon a hand-lettered sign saying, all in capital letters, "We shall come again and kill out separately Yanki-joker." Also on Kiska they came upon an English placard of a very different sort. Placed near the wreckage of an American P-40, it read: "Sleeping here a brave hero who lost youth and happiness for his motherland, June 25." Debs Myers et al., *Yank—The GI Story of the War* (1947: Duell, Sloan & Pearce), 42–46, 69, 126. Cf. *American Legion Magazine*, February 1945, 88–90; S. E. Smith, *The United States Marine Corps in World War II* (1969: Random House), 262, 267, 320, 397, 538, 548–49, 646–47; *Reader's Digest*, September 1943, 74, excerpted from *Time*, July 5, 1943; Toland, 381, 427.

34. Juan Ginés de Sepúlveda and Francisco de Vitoria, both quoted in Tzvetan Todorov, *The Conquest of America: The Question of the Other*, translated from the French by Richard Howard (1984: Harper & Row), 150, 153. See also Anthony Pagden, *The Fall of Natural Man: The American Indian and the Origins of Comparative Ethnology* (1982: Cambridge University Press), 116–17.

CHAPTER 7: YELLOW, RED, AND BLACK MEN

1. Winthrop D. Jordan, *White over Black: American Attitudes toward the Negro, 1550–1812* (1968: University of North Carolina Press); Richard Drinnon, *Facing West:*

The Metaphysics of Indian-Hating and Empire-Building (1980: New American Library). The potential range and variety of materials which can be brought to bear on a historical and comparative study of racism, violence, oppression, and power is almost limitless, and I have relied here on several studies which are especially attentive to the language with which Europeans and Americans defined their relationship to the Other. For the earliest contacts with the peoples of Africa and the Western Hemisphere, see the studies by Tzvetan Todorov and Anthony Pagden cited in chap. 6, n. 34; also Margaret T. Hodgen, *Early Anthropology in the Sixteenth and Seventeenth Centuries* (1964: University of Pennsylvania Press), esp. chaps. 9 and 10. V. G. Kiernan offers an overview of race and imperialism in *The Lords of Human Kind: Black Man, Yellow Man and White Man in an Age of Empire* (1969: Little, Brown). "Color and Race" was the subject of a special issue of *Daedalus* (Spring 1967), and the question of color in the Portuguese Empire was addressed by C. R. Boxer in "The Color Question in the Portuguese Empire," *Proceedings of the British Academy* 47 (1962): 113–38. Thomas F. Gossett offers a broad overview of racial thought in the United States in *Race: The History of an Idea in America* (1963: Southern Methodist University Press). For the American Indian, see Robert F. Berkhofer, Jr., *The White Man's Indian: Images of the American Indian from Columbus to the Present* (1978: Knopf), and Evan S. Connell's graphic *Son of the Morning Star: Custer and the Little Bighorn* (1984: North Point Press). Stuart Creighton Miller has studied two critical periods in the formation of American attitudes toward Asian peoples: *The Unwelcome Immigrant: The American Image of the Chinese, 1785–1882* (1969: University of California Press), and *"Benevolent Assimilation": The American Conquest of the Philippines, 1899–1903* (1982: Yale University Press). The themes of scientific racism from the mid-nineteenth century have been lucidly presented by Stephen Jay Gould in *The Mismeasure of Man* (1981: Norton). Although not developed in the present text, many of the themes concerning European stereotypes of the Islamic world addressed by Edward Said in *Orientalism* (1978: Pantheon) apply to the ethnocentric perceptions of the "Far East" as well. These would include the depiction of the "East" as a threat; what Said calls the virtual obliteration of the "Oriental" as a human; and the portrayal of Near Eastern peoples as irrational and childlike, unchanging, fatalistic, inherently despotic, and in general exotic and bizarre.

2. Hodgen, 417–18; Jordan, 28–32 and 234–39 on the mark of the ape; cf. ibid., 199–200, 233, 305, 308, 309, 490; Gould, 71, 125–26. On the projection of black and apish images (the "prognathous visage" among them) upon the Irish by the English, cf. L. Perry Curtis, Jr., *Apes and Angels: The Irishman in Victorian Caricature* (1971: Smithsonian Institution), which includes many cartoons from the late nineteenth century which take on new meaning in the light of World War Two cartoons depicting the Japanese; also Richard Ned Lebow, *White Britain and Black Ireland: The Influence of Stereotypes on Colonial Policy* (1976: Institute for the Study of Human Issues).

3. See Tzvetan Todorov's table of "oppositions," *The Conquest of America: The Question of the Other,* translated from the French by Richard Howard (1984: Harper & Row), 153; on the "natural slave," see Anthony Pagden, *The Fall of Natural Man: The American Indian and the Origins of Comparative Ethnology* (1982: Cambridge University Press), esp. 38, 42–45, 67, 97–99, 107, 116–18, 122–23. For the great debate, see Lewis Hanke, *All Mankind Is One: A Study of the Disputation between Bartolomé de Las Casas and Juan Ginés de Sepúlveda in 1550 on the Intellectual and Religious Capacity of the American Indians* (1974: Northern Illinois University Press); Bartolomé de Las Casas, *In Defense of the Indians: The Defense of the Most Reverend Lord, Don Fray Bartolomé de Las Casas, of the Order of Preachers, Late Bishop of Chiapa, against the Persecuters and Slanderers of the Peoples of the New World Discovered across the Seas,* trans. and ed. Stafford Poole (1974: Northern Illinois University Press).

4. Drinnon, 19, 40, 42–43, 50, 53, 65–66, 81, 85, 95–99. Hermann Hagedorn, *Roosevelt in the Badlands* (1921: Houghton Mifflin), 355.

5. Miller, *"Benevolent Assimilation,"* 176–95, 251; Drinnon, 308–10, 313, 321.

Kipling's seven-stanza "The White Man's Burden," which bears the subheading "The United States and the Philippine Islands," is an almost perfect expression of the mix of missionary sentiment and racial contempt that characterized the colonial endeavor; the poem is in *Rudyard Kipling's Verse: Definitive Edition* (1940: Doubleday, Doran & Co.), 321–23.

6. *Infantry Journal*, October 1942; reprinted in *Science Digest* 12.6 (December 1942): 52–56. *New York Times Magazine*, February 13, 1942, 2.

7. For a general summary of such "recapitulationist" theorizing, see Gould, esp. chap. 4. The quotation appears in "Race in Legislation and Political Economy," *Anthropological Review* 4 (April 1866): 120.

8. "Across the Plains," in *The Travels and Essays of Robert Louis Stevenson* (1924: Scribner's), esp. 139–43.

9. Gossett, 290; Frank F. Chuman, *The Bamboo People: The Law and Japanese-Americans* (1976: Publishers, Inc.), 9. The "natives of China, idiots, and insane persons" stipulation appears in Article 2 of the May 7, 1879 constitution.

10. Gould, 56; Miller, *The Unwelcome Immigrant*, 55, 74, 94, 105, 136–138, 149; cf. Kiernan, 146–72, esp. 149 (on Karl Marx and China's "hereditary stupidity"), 153 ("They are only Asiatics . . . treat them as children"), 160 (Macartney), and 163 (on the imperviousness to pain of the Chinese).

11. John La Farge, *Reminiscences of the South Seas* (1916: Doubleday, Page & Co.), 61 (La Farge was Henry Adams' traveling companion); Harold Dean Cater, comp., *Henry Adams and His Friends: A Collection of His Unpublished Letters* (1947: Houghton Mifflin), 200; Worthington Chauncey Ford, ed., *Letters of Henry Adams (1858–1891)* (1930: Houghton Mifflin), 269, 373, 377. The fuller passage on "child's country," also written to John Hay from Yokohama, reads as follows: "Of startling or wonderful experience we have had none. The only moral of Japan is that the children's story books were good history. This is a child's country. Men, women, and children are taken out of the fairy books. The whole show is of the nursery. Nothing is serious; nothing is taken seriously. All is toy; sometimes, as with the women, badly made and repulsive; sometimes laughable, as with the houses, gardens and children. . . ." (Ford, 369). Adams' repugnance toward Japanese women is quite striking, and contrary to the response of most Western males to Japanese women; and he even found the landscape in the beautiful Nikko area to be "ridiculous" (ibid., 369). Such idiosyncrasies, however, do not alter the conventional nature of his comments on Japanese childishness. Indeed, his "all is toy" phrase is strikingly similar to the observation of General MacArthur's intelligence staff in July 1944 to the effect that the "little people" and their country "possess the strange charm of toyland"; see chap. 6, n. 30. The Western view of Asians as natural servants was applied to the Japanese in one of the first Hollywood movies to appear after Pearl Harbor, Warner Brothers' *Across the Pacific*, starring Humphrey Bogart and depicting a Japanese conspiracy to destroy the Panama Canal. Bogart remarks of the Japanese that "they all look alike anyway," and comments as a ship's steward leaves his cabin that "Japanese make great servants."

12. Drinnon, 242. On the Yellow Peril in American literature, see William F. Wu, *The Yellow Peril: Chinese Americans in American Fiction. 1850–1940* (1982: Archon Books). Wu offers many themes and quotations from the early anti-Chinese popular literature in the United States which reemerged virtually intact in the anti-Japanese polemics of World War Two. Thus, late-nineteenth-century novels depicting a Chinese invasion of the United States dwelled on the puppetlike mass obedience of the Chinese, their "stoic indifference to pain," their diabolical deviousness, and their disdain for human life (chaps. 2 and 3). Readers were told that "their general expression was one of simian cunning and a ferocity that was utterly devoid of courage" (100), while praise was reserved for those Chinese who displayed an attitude of obedience and servitude toward Caucasians (80). One of the later fictional clones of Fu Manchu in American pulp literature even bore the name Ssu Hsi Tzu, which readers were informed was Mandarin for "Ruler of Vermin"

(193). For a reproduction of the famous German painting of the *Gelben Gefahr,* done by Hermann Knackfuss, see Werner Conze and Volker Hentschel, eds., *Pletz: Deutsche Geschichte* (1980: Verlag Ploetz); Kiernan, facing 161.

13. On the occasion of Japan's surrender in 1945, the Hearst newspapers ran a large advertisement summarizing their warning about Japan dating back to the 1890s; cf. *Business Week,* September 1, 1945.

14. Homer Lea, *The Valor of Ignorance,* with an introduction by Clare Boothe Luce (1942: Harper & Brothers). The 1919 edition of Lea's work contains an interesting introductory note on the way the Japanese translation was advertised in Japan in 1912. "More interesting than a novel, more mysterious than philosophy," the Japanese translator concluded, "this is really excellent reading matter for Oriental men with red blood in their veins." The "Mikado of kings" quotation appears on p. 189 of the 1919 edition. Clare Boothe Luce began her introduction by referring to an October 1941 conversation in Manila with Charles Willoughby, then and later one of MacArthur's key aides, who recalled reading Lea at West Point. On the revival of Lea after Pearl Harbor, see chap. 5, n. 29. Stimson's February 10, 1942, diary entry moved, all in one paragraph, from commenting on the dangerous "racial characteristics" of the Japanese-Americans, through recording that "I think it is quite within the bounds of possibility that if the Japanese should get naval dominance in the Pacific they would try an invasion of this country; and, if they did, we would have a tough job meeting them," to resurrecting Homer Lea. "The people of the United States have made an enormous mistake in underestimating the Japanese," the secretary of war confided to his diary. "They are now beginning to learn their mistake. Many times during recent months I have recalled meeting Homer Lea when I was Secretary of War under Mr. Taft. He was a little humpback man who wrote a book on the Japanese peril entitled 'The Valor of Ignorance'. In those days the book seemed fantastic. Now the things which he prophesied seem quite possible." *Henry L. Stimson Diaries* (Yale University Libraries microfilm), reel 7: 512.

15. For a listing of the Fu Manchu books and films, see Janet Price, *The Black Book of Villains* (1975: David & Charles), 52–55. A bibliography of Rohmer's writings is also included in Cay Van Ash and Elizabeth Sax Rohmer, *Master of Villainy: A Biography of Sax Rohmer* (1972: Bowling Green University Popular Press). The quotations are from the Pyramid editions of the first, second, and ninth Fu Manchu novels: *The Insidious Dr. Fu Manchu* (1913), 71, 104; *The Return of Dr. Fu Manchu* (1916), 34, 87, 162; *The Drums of Fu Manchu* (1939), 46. *The Island of Fu Manchu* (1941) was the tenth in the series. In the fourth novel, *The Daughter of Fu Manchu* (1931), one of Rohmer's characters observed that "a great federation of Eastern States affiliated with Russia—a new Russia—is destined to take the place once held by the British Empire." In the eighth novel, *President Fu Manchu* (1936), the evil genius was plotting to seize the presidency of the United States through a front organization. In *The Drums of Fu Manchu,* the ninth in the series, the extraordinary plot hinged on saving a thinly disguised Hitler from assassination by Fu Manchu and his legions of colored henchmen. For the MGM teaser, see Miller, *The Unwelcome Immigrant,* 9. Another example of Rohmer's flirtation with racial taboos was a theme introduced in the fourth novel, *The Daughter of Fu Manchu,* involving the sensuality of Oriental females and the emergence of a romantic liaison between Fu Manchu's daughter and the Caucasian protagonist.

16. Charlie Chan and Mr. Moto were the answer of the *Saturday Evening Post* to the serialization of Fu Manchu in *Collier's.* On Marquand as a successor to Earl Derr Biggers, see the introduction to J. P. Marquand, *Thank You, Mr. Moto and Mr. Moto Is So Sorry* (1977: Curtis Publishing). Mr. Moto is an intriguing figure in American popular culture of the late 1930s, representing a rational antidote to the entirely negative stereotype of the subhuman monkeymen and militarists—capable of killing for his country as well as dying for it, but desiring to do neither. Such a person could be a valuable ally as well as an implacable foe. In one of the early Mr. Moto novels (*Thank You, Mr. Moto,*

1936, chap. 5), Marquand's American narrator actually delivered a little pro-Japanese speech about realpolitik to an Englishman in China:

"Furthermore," I told him, "imperialism is not a new or even an interesting phenomenon. My country has practised it and certainly yours has. If Japan wishes to expand she is only following every other nation from the time of Babylon; furthermore, I cannot see why outsiders should be so greatly worried. I think it would be better if everyone were to recognize what is an actual fact—Japan's ability to control the mainland of Asia. I have never seen how anything is to be gained by diplomatic quibble. Japan is a world power and a growing power; we may as well admit it."

Even as he was about to exit from the literary scene, Mr. Moto expressed hopes for a more amicable future. In the last novel (set, like Fu Manchu's last prewar appearance, in the Caribbean, where the Japanese secret agent was endeavoring to obtain what amounted to a prototype radar instrument for fighter planes), Mr. Moto addressed his American adversaries with typical courtesy. "So sorry there should be trouble between America and Japan—two such very nice nations," he said. "It is all a cultural misunderstanding" (from chap. 13 of *Last Laugh, Mr. Moto,* 1941). The movie role of Mr. Moto helped launch the career of Peter Lorre. For Marquand's thoughts on stereotyping just prior to the war, see his "These Are People like Ourselves," *Asia,* July 1941, 361–64.

17. In addition to her numerous novels, Pearl Buck was an indefatigable essayist and lecturer, often using the magazine *Asia* (later *Asia and the Americas*) as her forum. Her sympathy with the lower classes in China—and corresponding distance from and even scorn for the Chinese elites, including the intelligentsia—is worthy of note, and sets her apart from Lin Yutang; this emerges vividly in an exchange between Pearl Buck and a Chinese critic in the *New York Times Book Review,* January 15, 1933. Christopher Thorne portrays Pearl Buck as, in effect, a cultural imperialist in his *Allies of a Kind: The United States, Britain, and the War against Japan, 1941–1945* (1978: Oxford University Press), cf. 715; and, in fact, in a moment of deep despair, as the Japanese and Chinese sank into wanton slaughter in the late 1930s, this famous friend of the Chinese penned one of the most negative Yellow Peril essays imaginable—depicting the "Oriental mind" as the antithesis of the Western tradition, in that Asians had no counterpart to Western humanism and were cruelly indifferent to human welfare and the worth of the individual life; "Western Weapons in the Hands of the Reckless East," *Asia,* October 1937, 672–73. Overall, however, no Westerner did more than Pearl Buck to give dignity and individuality to the Chinese; and no one criticized white supremacism and called attention to American and British double standards more frankly and consistently.

Lin Yutang was more attracted to Chinese high culture and elite society than Pearl Buck, but he shared her sensitivity to Western racism, her wartime pessimism, and her almost apocalyptic vision of a future race war. Like her too, in 1937 he also endorsed some of the most negative stereotypes about Asian peoples. The "insensitivity to pain" of the Chinese soldier, he told Westerners, "is almost amazing. Life is cheap to him"; *New York Times Magazine,* August 29, 1937. For a useful survey of English-language best-sellers about Asia in the prewar and postwar periods, see Daniel B. Ramsdell, "Asia Askew: U.S. Best-Sellers on Asia, 1931–1980," *Bulletin of Concerned Asian Scholars* 15.4 (October–December 1983): 2–25.

18. Pearl Buck, *The Promise* (1942–43, *Asia* magazine; 1945: Sun Dial Press); cf. 31, 113, 126, 146, 206–7, 237–38, 240. Also "Tinder for Tomorrow," *Asia,* March 1942, 153–56; "Postwar China and the United States," *Asia and the Americas,* November 1943, 613–15; "An Appeal to California," *Asia and the Americas,* January 1944, 21–23; "The Race Barrier 'That Must Be Destroyed'," *New York Times Magazine,* May 31, 1942.

19. *New York Times,* May 10, 1942, 33; cf. Lin in *Survey Graphic,* November 1942, 533–34 and 560–61; *Between Tears and Laughter* (1943: John Day Co.), esp. 22, 213.

20. *Saturday Evening Post,* January 3, 1942, 24; Chicago Tribune, *War Cartoons by McCutcheon, Orr, Parrish, Somdal* (1942: Chicago Tribune); "Peril Exposed," *San Francisco Examiner,* January 25, 1943, 6; Carey McWilliams, *Prejudice: Japanese Americans —Symbols of Racial Intolerance* (1944: Little, Brown), 234; *Blood for the Emperor* excerpt in *Science Digest,* 14.6 (December 1943): 91; U.S. Congress, House of Representatives, *Congressional Record,* 78th Cong., 1st sess., 1943, 8631 (October 21, 1943); also cited in Thorne, *Allies of a Kind,* 291.

21. For Churchill, cf. Thorne, 7–8, 191, 277, 356–57, 726, 730. Baldwin in S. E. Smith, *The United States Marine Corps in World War II* (1969: Random House), 101; *American Rifleman,* February 1943, 3; Warren J. Clear, "Close-Up of the Jap Fighting Man," *Reader's Digest,* November 1942, 125. The "LYB" phrase appears in a newsreel excerpted in the NBC documentary film *Guilty by Reason of Race* (1972). For songs, see chap. 4 n. 8.

22. On "gook," cf. Harold Wentworth and Stuart Berg Flexner, eds., *Dictionary of American Slang,* 2nd supplemented ed. (1975: Crowell), 223. The Australian advertisement is reproduced in L. D. Meo, *Japan's Radio War on Australia, 1941–1945* (1968: Melbourne University Press), facing 136. Bingham Dai, "Some Chinese Fears," *Asia and the Americas,* November 1943, 611–19; this article dwells on "American race prejudice and the American grandiose conception of the Christian religion." For a similar criticism by an Indian scholar, see Haridas T. Muzumdar, "Asians Ask Some Questions," *Asia,* July 1942, 416–18.

23. On the Axis alliance between Japan and Germany, see chap. 8, n. 4 below.

24. Abrogation of the unequal treaties was announced on October 9, 1942, and became effective on January 11, 1943. For clarification of the complex immigration laws, see E. P. Hutchinson, *Legislative History of American Immigration Policy, 1798–1965* (1981: University of Pennsylvania Press), esp. 166–67, 180, 430–33, and chap. 14; also useful is Chuman, *The Bamboo People.*

25. U.S. Congress, House of Representatives, *Congressional Record,* 78th Cong., 1st sess., 1943, 8588–89, 8632; this source, covering debates in October 1943, is cited below as *CR.* For committee hearings in the same session of the House (in May and June 1943), see Committee on Immigration and Naturalization, *Repeal of the Chinese Exclusion Acts.* Committee documents submitted to the whole House are *Repealing the Chinese Exclusion Laws: Report* (Report no. 732, October 7, 1943); *Repealing the Chinese Exclusion Laws: Minority Report* (Report no. 732, pt. 2, October 7, 1943); *Message from the President of the United States Favoring Repeal of the Chinese Exclusion Laws* (Document no. 333, October 11, 1943).

26. The fifteen laws are itemized in the committee report to the House. For the Asiatic Barred Zone, see Hutchinson, 166–67, 180, 431–32; also, U.S. Congress, Senate, *Congressional Record,* 64th Cong., 1st sess., 1916, 12926–28. Cf. "Repeal Chinese Exclusion!", *Asia,* February 1942, 92–94.

27. Cf. "Justice to Our Allies," *Commonweal,* June 5, 1942, 150–53; "How We Grill Our Allies," *Asia,* September 1942, 520–23; and "Repeal Chinese Exclusion Now," *Asia and the Americas,* January 1943, 4. *Christian Century* carried many editorials and letters on this issue between March 1942 and December 1943, and was one of the most persistent voices supporting repeal of the exclusion laws. A letter to the editor in the December 9, 1942, issue observed that whereas Hitler stressed "blood," "with us it is 'color' that counts." An editorial in the February 17, 1943, issue observed that "behind the loud professions of noble purposes with which we are fighting the war in the Pacific there leers a grinning death's head. It is the racial injustice which we have done to the Asiatic billion." In a June 9, 1943, editorial, *Christian Century* declared that "to do justice, we must remove the stigma that we regard the Asiatic *as such* as a lower order of human being."

28. *CR,* 8629 ("little brown men"); "Repeal Exclusion Laws Now," *Asia and the Americas,* June 1943, 322–23.

29. *CR*, 8596, 8580, 8576, 8579. *Saturday Evening Post*, October 23, 1943, 112. *CR*, 8591–92 and 8695 for Judd and Mansfield statements.

30. *CR*, 8629, 8597, 8633; "A Strong China, A Strong Church—An Interview with Bishop Paul Yu-pin," *Commonweal*, July 2, 1942, 266–69.

31. *CR*, 8631; Thorne, *Allies of a Kind*, 172, 731.

32. Roosevelt's comment appears in his October 11 message cited in n. 25 above.

33. *Collier's*, October 9, 1943, 82; U.S. Congress, *Appendix to the Congressional Record*, 1943, 89, pt. 2: A4468–69; *CR*, 8592–8593, 8581–82, 8583–84 (the Mason quotation); cf. *CR*, 8627, 8630.

34. *CR*, 8592 (cotton market). Reports by knowledgeable people evaluating the postwar China market received wide dissemination during the war. Lawrence K. Rosinger submitted a cautious report on "China as a Post-War Market" to the January 1945 Hot Springs conference of the Institute of Pacific Relations; reprinted in *Foreign Policy Report* 20.20 (January 1, 1945): 250–63. Donald M. Nelson, following an official mission to China in 1945 to evaluate the country's industrial potential, predicted that China would replace Japan in textile exports and in the process become a market for U.S. textile machinery. Hydroelectric projects on the Yangtze, he anticipated, would permit development of fertilizer and metallurgical industries. Unless China developed as a market for American capital goods, Nelson concluded, "we may be in a serious way"; *Collier's*, May 12, 1945. Eric Johnston, president of the U.S. Chamber of Commerce, used the pages of *Reader's Digest* in June 1945 to offer an extremely optimistic vision of China and other backward countries as postwar fields of investment for U.S. "surplus capital that remains idle." In China, Johnston observed, the United States had already identified some one thousand projects in mining, manufacturing, and other areas which offered a potential investment of one billion dollars. "The Chinese Government itself," he went on, "has projects which it believes could profitably use an investment of $4,000,000,000 in each of the ten years after the war. . . . I see profit in that thar hill . . . profit for the dividends of American investors and profit for the wages of American workingmen"; "America's World Chance," *Reader's Digest*, June 1945, 5–9. See also U.S. Department of State, *Foreign Relations of the United States, 1944*, 6: 1076, 1079–80, 1082; ibid., *1945*, 7: 1348–51.

35. William Phillips in *Foreign Relations of the United States, 1943*, 4: 197. In a personal cable to the president in April 1943, Phillips observed that "as time goes on, Indians are coming more and more to disbelieve in the American gospel of freedom of oppressed peoples." He went on, after linking India, Burma, and China, to emphasize that "color consciousness is also appearing more and more and under present conditions is bound to develop. We have, therefore, a vast bloc of Oriental peoples who have many things in common, including a growing dislike and distrust of the Occidental"; ibid., 218–19; cf. 221. In another cable in May, Phillips informed the president that "the peoples of Asia—and I am supported in this opinion by other diplomatic and military observers—cynically regard this war as one between fascist and imperialist powers"; ibid., 222; cf. 229–31. Robert S. Ward, "Can Japan Win by Losing?" *Asia and the Americas*, May 1945, 234–38.

36. H. C. McGinnis, "Which War Comes Next?" *Catholic World*, July 1945, 329–35. Stalin's comment on the Russians being an "Asiatic" people was made to Foreign Minister Matsuoka Yōsuke in 1940, at the time of the conclusion of the Japan-U.S.S.R. neutrality pact. It was frequently quoted thereafter; cf. Pearl Buck in *Asia and the Americas*, January 1944, 2.

37. *Henry L. Stimson Diaries*, (Yale University Libraries microfilm), reel 7: 740 (entry for May 12, 1942). For Marshall, see Glen C. H. Perry, *"Dear Bart": Washington Views of World War II* (1982: Greenwood Press), 184. Virginius Dabney, "Nearer and Nearer the Precipice," *Atlantic Monthly*, January 1943, 94–100.

38. Roi Ottley, *'New World A-Coming': Inside Black America* (1943: Houghton Mifflin), 341–42. Gunnar Myrdal, *An American Dilemma: The Negro Problem and Modern Democracy* (1944: Harper & Row), 815, 1016; the opinion poll is in ibid., 1400.

39. On the Japanese ties to black militants, see Erdmann Benyon, "The Voodoo Cult among Negro Migrants in Detroit," *American Journal of Sociology* 43.6 (May 1938): esp. 904; C. Eric Lincoln, *The Black Muslims in America* (1961: Beacon Press), 16, 26, 187–88; Ottley, chap. 22 (entitled "Made in Japan"). *Time* reported on these links and stated that through Smyth the Japanese had also invested in *Current History* and the *Saturday Review of Literature*; September 14, 1942, 46. *Henry L. Stimson Diaries*, reel 7: 741.

40. On segregated blood plasma, which caused considerable discomfort to the Red Cross, see Foster Rhea Dulles, *The Red Cross: A History* (1950: Harper & Brothers), 419–21; Charles Hurd, *The Compact History of the American Red Cross* (1959: Hawthorn Books), 236–37; and the protest against this practice by the Committee on Race Relations of the American Association of Physical Anthropologists, published in *Science*, (July 3, 1942); 8. The policy of segregating plasma was approved by Norman Davis (the head of the Red Cross), the surgeon generals of both the Army and Navy, and the secretaries of War and the Navy; cf. *New York Times*, January 18, 27, and 29, 1942. All parties responsible for the decision to segregate white and Negro plasma agreed there was no scientific reason to do so; but to fail to do so, they argued, would cause an uproar among Americans. In the final analysis, racists thus determined the policy, and their line of argument was exemplified by Congressman John Rankin of Mississippi, who denounced the argument that the blood of whites and blacks was interchangeable as a Communist plot to "mongrelize America." Rankin also made it clear that vigilance against such miscegenation-by-transfusion, as it were, had to extend to Oriental blood as well, for what the blood-bank conspirators were really trying to do was "to pump Negro or Japanese blood into the veins of our wounded white boys regardless of the dire effect it might have on their children"; *Atlantic Monthly*, January 1943, 95; Rayford F. Logan, ed., *What the Negro Wants* (1944: University of North Carolina Press), 311.

41. On apes and children, cf. Walter White, *A Rising Wind* (1945: Doubleday, Doran & Co.), 17, 99–100, 139. For the black experience in the military, see Jack D. Foner, *Blacks and the Military in American History: A New Perspective* (1974: Praeger).

42. Wilkins is quoted in Richard Polenberg, *War and Society: The United States, 1941–1945* (1972: Lippincott), 101. The dialogue appears in *Survey Graphic*, November 1942, 482.

43. "Fighting for White Folk?" *The Nation*, September 26, 1942, 267–68; *Atlantic Monthly*, January 1943, 99; *Survey Graphic*, November 1942, 482; *Asia and the Americas*, January 1943, 5.

44. Herbert Garfinkel, *When Negroes March: The March on Washington Movement in the Organizational Politics for FEPC* (1959: Free Press), 31, 93, 137.

45. White, 154–55. Randolph was one of the most radical of the black leaders who saw the war as "a war to continue 'white supremacy'," as well as "a war between the imperialism of Fascism and Nazism and imperialism of monopoly capitalistic democracy." His vision of a global union of "the darker races" emerging out of World War Two was clear and precise—as was his argument that "the colored people of Asia, Africa, and Latin America will measure the genuineness of our declarations about a free world to the extent that we create a free world within our own borders"; see his essay in Logan, esp. 133–35, 139, 152–53, 161–62.

CHAPTER 8: THE PURE SELF

1. For some Japanese reactions to the scientific racism of the West, see the observations of Inoue Tetsujirō and Miyake Setsurei cited in Kenneth B. Pyle, *The New Generation in Meiji Japan: Problems in Cultural Identity, 1885–1895* (1969: Stanford University Press), 110, 152; the treatment of white supremacism and Yellow Peril sentiments by the famous writer and scientist Mori Ōgai in 1903, reprinted in *Mori Ōgai Zenshū* (1952: Iwanami Shoten), 19: 377–466; and the citation to Adachi Buntarō in n. 32 below.

The feeling that the Japanese military forced British and Americans to suffer indignities in retaliation for past discrimination against nonwhites was expressed by U.S. General Jonathan M. Wainwright after Japan's surrender. As a prisoner of war, Wainwright himself was physically beaten by Japanese enlisted men on a number of occasions. "We were struck with particular reason—just to demonstrate how superior a Japanese was to any American citizen or British subject, however high his rank," Wainwright told newsmen in September 1945. "It is my measured opinion," he went on, "and I have thought about it a great deal, as you may guess, that the Japanese military authorities bore down on us because they felt before the war that we were arrogant. They were trying to demonstrate their superiority over the Anglo-Saxon races. Theirs was a studied procedure. They ordered private soldiers to strike generals because that fits into their pattern of thought. It was their way of showing that they were not arrogant, merely superior"; *New York Times*, September 18, 1945, 3.

2. Uchikawa Yoshimi, ed., *Gendai Shiryō 41: Masu Media Tōsei (2)*. [Contemporary Documents 41: Control of Mass Media, 2] (1975: Misuzu Shobō), 367–71.

3. Kōsaka Masaaki et al., "Tōa Kyōeiken no Ronrisei to Rekishisei" [The Logical and Historical Nature of the East Asia Co-Prosperity Sphere], *Chūō Kōron* 57.4 (April 1942): 120–61, esp. 141. See also n. 46 below.

4. Ben-Ami Shillony, *Politics and Culture in Wartime Japan* (1981: Oxford University Press), 151–56; Milan Hauner, *India in Axis Strategy* (1981: Klett-Cotta), 30–31, 435–36; Erich von Ludendorff, *The Nation at War,* translated from the German (1937: Hutchinson & Co.), 35, 42–43; Otto D. Tolischus, *Tokyo Record* (1943: Reynal & Hitchcock), 218–20 on Haushofer; Adolf Hitler, *Mein Kampf,* translated from the German by Ralph Manheim (1962: Houghton Mifflin), 290–91; Adolf Hitler, *Hitler's Secret Conversations, 1941–1944* (1953: Farrar, Straus & Young), 123, 130–31, 147, 155, 396; Mohan Singh, *Soldiers' Contribution to Indian Independence: The Epic of the Indian National Army* (1974: Army Educational Stores, New Delhi), 127–29, on Japanese military distrust of Germany; Anton Pettenkofer, "Hitler Means to *Destroy* Japan," *Asia,* November 1941, 653–60; Robert Bellaire, "Why the Japs Hate the Nazis," *Collier's,* January 23, 1943; *Time,* March 1, 1943, 18, on *The Great Dictator.*

5. Peter Duus, "Nagai Ryūtarō and the 'White Peril,' " *Journal of Asian Studies* 31 (November 1971): 41–48; cf. Kodama Kota and Kuno Takeshi, eds., *Nihonshi Zuroku 4: Meiji-Gendai* [Pictorial Record of Japanese History 4: Meiji to Contemporary] (1964: Kobunkan), 142.

6. "Kichiku Bei-Ei" in *Manga Nippon,* October 1944, 10–11; editorial in *Manga,* March 1943, 7.

7. *Osaka Puck,* November 1942, 25.

8. See the special issue of *Daedalus* devoted to "Color and Race" (Spring 1967), esp. Roger Bastide, "Color, Racism, and Christianity," 312–27, on traditional color symbolism in the West.

9. Hiroshi Wagatsuma, "The Social Perception of Skin Color in Japan," *Daedalus,* Spring 1967, 407–43; Wagatsuma Hiroshi and Yoneyama Toshinao, *Henken no Kōzō: Nihonjin no Jinshukan* [The Structure of Prejudice: Japanese Perceptions of Race] (1967: NHK Books #55), esp. chap. 1.

10. Kōseishō, Jinkō Minzokubu [Ministry of Health and Welfare, Population and Race Section], "Yamato Minzoku o Chūkaku to suru Sekai Seisaku no Kentō" [An Investigation of Global Policy with the Yamato Race as Nucleus], vol. 6 of *Minzoku Jinkō Seisaku Kenkyū Shiryō: Senjika in okeru Kōseishō Kenkyūbu Jinkō Minzokubu Shiryō* [Research Documents on Race and Population Policy: Wartime Documents of the Population and Race Section of the Research Bureau of the Ministry of Health and Welfare] (1982: Busei Shoin), 2436–54. See chap. 10, n. 1 below for a description of this source.

11. Konishi Shirō, *Nishikie: Bakumatsu Meiji no Rekishi* ["Brocade Pictures": A History of Bakumatsu and Meiji Japan] (1977: Kodansha), vol. 11; Donald Keene, "The

Sino-Japanese War of 1894–95 and Japanese Culture," *Landscapes and Portraits: Appreciations of Japanese Culture* (1971: Secker & Warburg), 259–99; Shumpei Okamoto, ed., *Impressions of the Front: Woodcuts of the Sino-Japanese War* (1983: Philadelphia Museum of Art).

12. Wagatsuma and Yoneyama, 109.

13. Cf. *Osaka Puck*, June 1942, 5, and July 1942, 24–26.

14. Michio Kitahara, "Popular Culture in Japan: A Psychoanalytic Interpretation," *Journal of Popular Culture* 17.1 (Summer 1983): 103–10.

15. *Manga*, March 1943, 7.

16. Ogushi Toyoo, "Nippon Minzoku Sekaikan no Kakuritsu" [Establishing a Japanese Racial World View], *Bungei Shunjū* 20.1 (January 1942): 24–33.

17. The cleansing experience, or sense of relief and sudden clarity of purpose, which many Japanese men of letters felt upon hearing of the outbreak of war with the United States is summarized in Donald Keene, "Japanese Writers and the Greater East Asian War," in his *Landscapes and Portraits*, 300–305; in Japanese see Odagiri Susumu's two-part "Record of December Eighth" in *Bungaku* 29 (December 1961) and 30 (April 1962). As Keene reveals elsewhere, the vocabulary of purification also was used by former Japanese leftists who recanted and adopted a nationalistic stance in the 1930s. Thus, we find the famous writer Hayashi Fusao equating the Western leftist intellectual tradition with Yomi, the polluted underworld of the ancient myths, while the unique spirit of service to the Japanese emperor represented the world of spiritual purity. The merciful gods of Japan, Hayashi declared in a book published in 1941, "have commanded a people which has strayed into Yomi, the land of sin and pollution, to return from Yomi, to come back to life, and to be purified in the clear waters of the traditions of our nation"; quoted in Donald Keene, "Japanese Literature and Politics in the 1930s," *Journal of Japanese Studies* 2.2 (Summer 1976): 243. The nomenclature of Imperial Navy ships is summarized in Paul S. Dull, *Battle History of the Imperial Japanese Navy (1941–1945)* (1978: Naval Institute Press), 351.

18. Mainichi Shimbunsha, ed., *Shōwa Ryūkōka Shi: Bessatsu—Ichiokunin no Shōwa Shi* [History of Popular Songs of the Shōwa Period—Special Volume of "History of the Hundred Million People of the Shōwa Period"] (1979: Mainichi Shimbunsha), 112. It is intriguing to note that while Japanese popular songs tended to be characterized by an abstractness and sentimentality that contrasts to the coarse lyrics of many American war songs, established Japanese poets, on the other hand, condemned the enemy with bloodthirsty verses that have no real counterpart in the wartime writings of Anglo-American poets and serious men of letters; cf. Donald Keene, "The Barren Years: Japanese War Literature," *Monumenta Nipponica* 33.1 (Spring 1978): 90–93. See also chap. 9, n. 35 below.

19. Mainichi Shimbunsha, *Shōwa Ryūkōka Shi*, 137. See also the cartoon in *Osaka Puck*, April 1942, 6.

20. Komota Nobuo et al., *Nihon Ryūkōka Shi* [History of Japanese Popular Songs] (1970: Shakai Shisōsha), 333.

21. Komota, 320.

22. Komota, 321.

23. Komota, 334.

24. Komota, 335.

25. Komota, 338.

26. *Osaka Puck*, December 1941 through July 1942. I have not been able to obtain the August 1942 issue. From September, the marginal slogans were dropped. The reference to Chiang appeared in the June 1942 issue.

27. *Asahi Shimbun* (evening), December 9, 1941. The Japanese is *susume ichioku hi no tama da.*

28. For the 1934 pamphlet, see Kenneth W. Colegrove, *Militarism in Japan* (1936: World Peace Foundation), 52–53; the pamphlet was titled *Principles of National Defense*

and Proposals for Its Augmentation (Kokubō no Hongi to Sono Kyōka no Teishō). See also the commentary on the Kyoto Gakuha in Takeuchi Yoshimi, *Takeuchi Yoshimi Zenshū* [Collected Works of Takeuchi Yoshimi] (1980: Chikuma Shobō), 8: 40–46. The key article on this subject was a roundtable discussion published under the title "Sōryokusen no Tetsugaku" [The Philosophy of Total War] in *Chūō Kōron* 58.1 (January 1943): 54–112. See also n. 46 below, and chap. 9, n. 33.

29. Naikaku Sōryokusen Kenkyūjo [Cabinet Institute for the Study of Total War], *Chōkisen Kenkyū* [A Study of Protracted War], March 1945, 41.

30. Tsurumi Shunsuke, ed., *Nihon no Hyakunen 3: Hateshinaki Sensen* [Japan's Hundred Years 3: The Endless War Front] (1967: Chikuma Shobō), 180.

31. In addition to the U.S. Army propaganda film *Know Your Enemy—Japan* discussed in chap. 2, see such wartime publications as Otto D. Tolischus, ed., *Through Japanese Eyes* (1945: Reynal & Hitchcock); Robert O. Ballou, *Shinto, the Unconquered Enemy: Japan's Doctrine of Racial Superiority and World Conquest* (1945: Viking); and Saul K. Padover, "Japanese Race Propaganda," *Public Opinion Quarterly* 7.2 (Summer 1943): 191–204. The historian E. Herbert Norman, writing in 1943, called attention to many instruments of indoctrination in Japan "which monotonously preach a morbid nationalism and a chauvinism both as potent and poisonous as Nazi racism"; *Pacific Affairs* 16.4 (December 1943): 475.

32. Adachi Buntarō, *Zōho Nipponjin Taishitsu no Kenkyū* [Studies in the Physical Constitution of the Japanese People, (rev. ed.)] (1944: Ogiwara Seibunkan). See esp. 1–3, 35–46, 69–75; the quotation is on 73.

33. Kiyono Kenji, *Nippon Jinshuron no Hensen Shi* [A History of Changing Theories about the Japanese Race] (1944: Koyama Shoten); see esp. 66–72.

34. Ishida Shuzō, *Seibutsu no Shinka* [Evolution of Life] (1942: Hata Shoten); see esp. 1–3, 189–201.

35. See the English translation by John O. Gauntlett, edited by Robert K. Hall: *Kokutai no Hongi: Cardinal Principles of the National Entity of Japan* (1949: Harvard University Press), esp. 54, 66, 79, 82, 91, 100, 101, 130, 132, 133.

36. Gauntlett and Hall, 105.

37. Guantlett and Hall, 129–33.

38. Gauntlett and Hall, 126–27, 138. The reference is to the ancient *uji* ("clans") and *be* ("subordinate groups").

39. Koya Nakamura, *History of Japan* (1939: Board of Tourist Industries, Japanese Government Railways); reprinted in Ballou, 188–89.

40. *Japan Times and Mail*, February 11, 1940.

41. Tokutomi Iichirō, *Hisshō Kokumin Tokuhon* [A Citizen's Reader for Certain Victory] (1944: Mainichi Shimbunsha).

42. Tokutomi, 9–18.

43. Tokutomi, 41–47, 61–62.

44. Tokutomi, 69–71, 139–40.

45. The official English translation of Fujisawa's pamphlet is reproduced in Tolischus, *Tokyo Record*, 429–49; see also 398–400.

46. The Kyoto Gakuha published three major articles in the monthly *Chūō Kōron*: "Sekaishiteki Tachiba to Nippon" [Japan and the Perspective of World History] (January 1942); "Tōa Kyōeiken no Ronrisei to Rekishisei" [The Logical and Historical Nature of the East Asia Co-Prosperity Sphere] (April 1942); and "Sōryokusen no Tetsugaku" [The Philosophy of Total War] (January 1943). Their discussion of "transcending the modern" (*kindai no chōkoku*) was published in the September and October 1942 issues of *Bungakukai*. See also Kōsaka Masaaki, "Dai Tōa Kyōeiken e no Michi" [The Road to the Greater East Asia Co-Prosperity Sphere], *Kaizō* 24.1 (January 1942): 16–37. A good short summary is provided in *Takeuchi Yoshimi Zenshū*, cited in n. 28 above.

47. For the Kyoto School's use of "world-historical race" *(sekaishiteki minzoku)*, see *Kaizō*, January 1942, 30; an example of the school's use of the Taiwa concept appears in

Chūō Kōron, January 1943, 67, and the concept in general is discussed in *Takeuchi Yoshimi Zenshū*, 8:46. For Taiwa in *Kokutai no Hongi*, see Gauntlett and Hall, 94–95. In the *Senjinkun*, this is introduced in the second section. In English, Taiwa is variously rendered as Great Harmony, Great Peace, or Universal Peace. The adoption of the same two ideographs used to write Taiwa to designate Yamato probably occurred in the eighth century, and appears to have been based on phonological considerations rather than considerations of meaning; cf. *Nihon Rekishi Daijiten* [Encyclopedia of Japanese History] (1969: Kawada Shobō Shinsha), 9:388, and the *Kojien* dictionary (1955: Iwanami Shoten), 2149.

In Suzuki's *Tōyōteki "Ichi"* (1942: Daitō Shuppansha), see esp. 1–27. His attempt to balance advocacy of Japan's mission, Asia's "oneness," and coexistence between Orient and Occident resembles the cultural ideology of "Asia is One" that was propounded at the turn of the century by Okakura Tenshin (author of the famous *Book of Tea*, which he wrote in English), and worked to death by Japanese nationalists during World War Two; cf. Keene, "The Barren Years," 91–92, and "Japanese Writers and the Greater East Asia War," 310.

48. Cf. Gauntlett and Hall, 82; Fujisawa in Tolischus, 440; Shillony, 141–51.

49. *Osaka Puck*, December 1941, 16–17.

50. *Osaka Puck*, April 1942, 8, and September–October 1942, 29.

51. *Osaka Puck*, February 1942, 4; cf. ibid., 5.

52. *Osaka Puck*, December 1942, 19.

53. *Osaka Puck*, July 1942, 11.

54. *Osaka Puck*, February 1942, 8; November 1942, cover.

55. *Osaka Puck*, November 1942, 3.

56. *Manga*, May 1942, 17.

57. Mainichi Shimbunsha, ed., *Shōwa Manga Shi—Bessatsu, Ichiokunin no Shōwa Shi* [History of Cartoons of the Shōwa Period—Special Volume of "History of the Hundred Million People of the Shōwa Period"] (1977: Mainichi Shimbunsha), 110.

58. The slogan "Extravagance is the enemy" (*Zeitaku wa teki da*) dated from 1938; Wakamori Tarō, ed., *Gunkoku kara Minshūka e* [From Military State to Democratization], vol. 10 in Wakamori, ed., *Nihon Seikatsu Bunka Shi* [History of Daily Life and Culture in Japan] (1975: Kawade Shobo), vii. For the "Monday, Monday . . ." slogan, cf. ibid., 88; also Komota, 325.

59. Nyozekan Hasegawa, "Our 'Emaciated Endurance'," *Contemporary Japan* 12.5 (May 1943): 570–76. In the same journal, cf. 11.2 (February 1942): 281; 11.7 (July 1942): 1103–6; 11.9 (September 1942): 1365–68; 12.8 (August 1943): 1054–59. Yoshimoto Takaaki, *Takemura Kotarō* (1966: Shunjusha), 138–40.

60. Samuel Eliot Morison, *History of United States Naval Operations in World War II* (1951: Little, Brown) 7: 49–51; *Time*, July 5, 1943, 28–29; *Reader's Digest*, September 1943, 74.

61. Iizuka Koji, *Nihon no Guntai* [The Japanese Military] (1968: Hyōronsha; reprint of 1950 ed. by Tokyo Daigaku Kyōdō Kumiai Shuppansha), 68–69; the former officer was Kobayashi Junichi. The conventional interpretation of *gyokusai* appears to have been that it was better to die gloriously, like a shattered gem, than to live meaninglessly, like a mundane roof tile; cf. Morohashi Tetsuji, *Dai Kanwa Jiten* [Great Mandarin Dictionary] (1958: Taishukan Shoten), 7: 793. In even plainer terms, the standard Japanese-English dictionary translates the key passage as "A man of honor would rather die with his name unstained than survive with disgrace," and renders *gyokusai* itself as meaning to "prefer death to dishonor"; *Kenkyūsha's New Japanese-English Dictionary* (1954: Kenkyūsha), 355. One of the most revered tragic heroes of modern Japan, Saigō Takamori, used the *gyokusai* image in a Chinese-style poem written several years before his death in futile battle in 1877; Okawa Nobuyoshi, ed., *Dai Saigō Zenshū* [Collected Works of the Great Saigō] (1927: Heibonsha), 3: 1126–28. The phrase *Attu gyokusai* was first used on May 31, 1943.

62. Rikihei Inoguchi and Tadashi Nakajima, with Roger Pineau, *The Divine Wind: Japan's Kamikaze Force in World War II* (1958; 1968: Ballantine), 19, 161. Cf. also the classic letters in this source, esp. 177–79, 185. These Japanese concerns with youth, purity, and intuition were the mirror images of the Western view of the enemy. The emphasis on youth reinforced Western contempt for the "childish." The fixation on purity emerged in Western analyses as a fixation on cleanliness and symptomatic of a deep national neurosis. And the intuitive sense of the young men, manifested in their willingness to die, became further evidence of the enemy's fundamental "irrationality" (although some Westerners discerned "superhuman" qualities here as well.)

63. Hino Ashihei's poem appears in the *Asahi Shimbun,* June 5, 1945. For the *ichioku Tokkō* slogan, see *Asahi Shimbun,* December 28, 1944. The phrase was introduced in the Diet by the Army and Navy, and received strong support in a front-page *Asahi* editorial. On January 30, 1945, the Japanese cabinet approved an "information policy" which included the recommendation that *ichioku Tokkō* be promoted as a major policy; Uchikawa, 528.

64. Konishi Shirō and Hayashi Shigeru, eds., *Nihon no Rekishi, Bessatsu 4: Zuroku, Isshin kara Gendai* [History of Japan, Special Volume 4: Illustrated Record, From the Restoration to Modern Times] (1967: Chūō Kōronsha).

CHAPTER 9: THE DEMONIC OTHER

1. Masao Yamaguchi, "Kingship, Theatricality, and Marginal Reality in Japan," in Ravindra K. Jain, ed., *Text and Context: The Social Anthropology of Tradition* (1977: Institute for the Study of Human Issues), 151–79; the quotation is on 152. See also Yamaguchi Masao, *Bunka to Ryōgisei* [The Double Meaning of Culture] (1975: Iwanami Shoten), esp. 80–83; Teigo Yoshida, "The Stranger As God: The Place of the Outsider in Japanese Folk Religion," *Ethnology* 20.2 (April 1981): 87–99. The linkages between "inside-outside" and concepts of purity and pollution in Japan are examined in Emiko Ohnuki-Tierney, *Illness and Culture in Contemporary Japan: An Anthropological View* (1984: Cambridge University Press), esp. chap. 2.

2. On the Japanese perception of spirits, see Robert Smith, *Ancestor Worship in Contemporary Japan* (1974: Cornell University Press), esp. chap. 2. In addition to the *marebito* and *goryō*, the powerful and ambiguous gods of ancient times were known by such names as *araburukami, chihayaburukami,* etc.; cf. Wakamori Tarō, *Shōmin no Seishin Shi* [History of the Spirit of the Common People] (1965: Kawade Shobo), 171–73.

3. These class divisions and inside-outside (*uchi-soto*) orientations are discussed in all serious general histories and sociocultural studies of Japan.

4. On the outcastes—variously known over the course of Japanese history as *hinin, eta,* and *burakumin*—see Shigeaki Ninomiya, "An Inquiry Concerning the Origin, Development, and Present Situation of the Eta in Relation to the History of Social Classes in Japan," *Transactions of the Asiatic Society of Japan,* 2nd ser., 10 (December 1933): 47–154; Keiji Nagahara, "The Medieval Origins of the *Eta-Hinin," Journal of Japanese Studies* 5.2 (1979): 385–403; George De Vos and Hiroshi Wagatsuma, *Japan's Invisible Race: Caste in Culture and Personality* (1966: University of California Press).

5. Yamaguchi in Jain, 164; Ohnuki-Tierney, 43–50.

6. Some of the most interesting work on Japanese attitudes toward foreigners, in both Japanese and English, has been done by Wagatsuma Hiroshi. In Japanese, see Wagatsuma Hiroshi and Yoneyama Toshinao, *Henkan no Kōzō: Nihonjin no Jinshukan* [The Structure of Prejudice: Japanese Perceptions of Race] (1967: NHK Books #55). Professor Wagatsuma's writings in English include "The Social Perception of Skin Color in Japan," *Daedalus,* Spring 1967, 407–43, and a useful brief summary of "Foreigners, attitude toward" in the *Kodansha Encyclopedia of Japan* (1983: Kodansha), 2: 311–13. In the discussion that follows, it should be kept in mind that the Japanese perception of the outsider as possessing inferior and dangerous qualities but also potentially powers of a

superior nature is, of course, similar to Western perceptions of the Other, including Orientals, where attractive and ominous "spiritual," sexual, intellectual, or physical powers are often seen as commingling with inferior qualities.

7. John O. Gauntlett, trans., and Robert K. Hall, ed., *Kokutai no Hongi: Cardinal Principles of the National Entity of Japan* (1949: Harvard University Press), 74. On Ebisu, see Yoshida, "The Stranger as God," 90–94; *Kodansha Encyclopedia of Japan,* 2: 143 (where Ebisu is treated as a *marebito*).

8. In addition to Yoshida, see George Elison, *Deus Destroyed: The Image of Christianity in Early Modern Japan* (1973: Harvard University Press), esp. 144, 214–16, 450–51.

9. Elison, 125, 232–33, 321, 457. This interesting monograph includes a translation of the 1639 text. The *tengu* is another classic figure possessing both harmful and beneficial powers in Japanese folklore.

10. Elison, 215, 450; Yoshida, 89.

11. Donald Keene, *The Japanese Discovery of Europe, 1720–1830,* rev. ed. (1969: Stanford University Press), chap. 7, esp. 170; Wagatsuma, "The Social Perception of Skin Color in Japan," 438. In Ryusaku Tsunoda et al., *Sources of Japanese Tradition* (1958: Columbia University Press); cf. the excerpts from Hirata Atsutane (540–51) and also expressions of Japanese superiority by Satō Nobuhiro (575–78) and Aizawa Seishisai (595–603).

12. Elison, 450 (n. 5); 496.

13. Tsunoda, 595–96.

14. Mainichi Shimbunsha, ed., *Shōwa Ryūkōka Shi: Bessatsu—Ichiokunin no Shōwa Shi* [History of Popular Songs of the Shōwa Period—Special Volume of "History of the Hundred Million People of the Shōwa Period"] (1979: Mainichi Shimbunsha), 137. Mainichi Shimbusha, ed. *Nihon News Eiga Shi: Bessatsu—Ichiokunin no Shōwa Shi* [History of Japanese Newsreels—Special Volume of "History of the Hundred Million People of the Shōwa Period"] (1977: Mainichi Shimbunsha), 487. Komota Nobuo et al., *Nihon Ryūkōka Shi* [History of Japanese Popular Songs] (1970: Shakai Shisōsha), 336.

15. Cf. *Manga,* January 1942, 16, 40; April 1942, 18–19; May 1942, 16, 23; October 1942, 3; February 1943, 4. Also *Osaka Puck,* January 1942, 15; September–October 1942, cover.

16. *Osaka Puck,* February 1942, 8 and 15; ibid., July 1942, 12; *Manga,* July 1942, 8; *Osaka Puck,* February 1942, 20; *Manga,* September 1944, 21; *Osaka Puck,* July 1942, 13; Willard Price, *Japan and the Son of Heaven* (1945: Duell, Sloan, & Pearce), 11, 86.

17. Kiyosawa Kiyoshi, *Ankoku Nikki* [Diary of Darkness] (1954: Tōyō Keizai Shimpōsha), 13. Another visual pun on *Mei-ri-ken* was "rice-profit dog"; cf. Ben-Ami Shillony, *Politics and Culture in Wartime Japan* (1981: Oxford University Press), 204. Shillony's study draws together much useful information on the wartime scene in Japan; see esp. chap. 6 on "East versus West." Otto D. Tolischus, ed., *Through Japanese Eyes* (1945: Reynal & Hitchcock), 152. Cf. *Manga,* June 1944, 5.

18. *Osaka Puck,* June 1942, 8. See also Shimizu Isao, ed., *Taiheiyō Sensōki Manga* [Cartoons of the Pacific War Period] (1971: Bijutsu Dōjinsha), 10, for another rendering of Chiang as a monkey, alongside human depictions of Roosevelt, Churchill, and the Dutch. Rare, random renderings of the Americans and British as apes appear in *Osaka Puck,* December 1942, cover; *Manga,* March 1944, 18, and April 1942, 24; and Shimizu, 35.

19. *Manga,* May 1982, 28, and March 1943, 32; ibid., January 1942, 22–23.

20. Asahi Shimbun, ed., *The Pacific Rivals: A Japanese View of Japanese-American Relations* (1972: Weatherhill/Asahi; originally published in 1971 in Japanese by Asahi Shimbunsha under the title *Nihon to Amerika*), 106. L.D. Meo, *Japan's Radio War on Australia, 1941–1945* (1968: Melbourne University Press), 111. On the change in ideographs, see *Japan Times and Advertiser,* October 1, 1942; Shillony, 145. The practice of using the more "bestial" ideographs for the United States and Britain was only sporadically

followed, however. By mere happenstance, moreover, the standard ideograph used to designate Germany already contained the same "beast" radical.

21. Ryūdō Shuppansha, ed., *Fukurokuban Shōwa Daizasshi: Senchūhen* [Reproductions from Major Shōwa Magazines: Wartime] (1978: Ryūdō Shuppansha), 282–92; the article was published in December 1944, but the source is not indicated.

22. Ryūdō Shuppansha, *Fukurokuban*, 232–33. Cf. *Manga*, October 1944, 3–5, on the bombing of the hospital ship *Buenos Aires*, and the cartoon on the same incident in *Manga*, October 1943, 6. Wartime Japanese studies of race problems in the United States include Kawamura Tadao, *Beikoku Kokujin no Kenkyū* [A Study of the American Negro] (1943: Fuji Shoten), and Inahara Katsuji, *Amerika Minzoku Dan* [On the American People] (1943: Ryūhinsha); cf. *Contemporary Japan* 13.1 (January 1944): 112–15 and 12.9 (September 1943): 1191–94.

23. The elaborations appear in Donald Keene, "The Barren Years: Japanese War Literature," *Monumenta Nipponica* 33.1 (Spring 1978): 90–91. The first reference appeared in a poem by Satō Haruo celebrating the fall of Singapore. "The heads of the hobgoblins have dropped," Satō exulted, "under the keen Japanese swords." Hino Ashihei's 1944 poem "Laughable Enemies," describing Allied deaths in the Pacific, stated "The swarms of hairy, twisted-nosed savages / Sank and rotted idiotically / In the equatorial waters." For Matsuoka, *Shōwa Ishin* (Shōwa Restoration, 1938), quoted in Tolischus, *Through Japanese Eyes*, 66; cf. ibid. 84.

24. *Manga*, April 1941, 9.

25. *Manga*, February 1942, 18–19; ibid., July 1944, 16. Shimizu, 39; cf. 40, depicting Roosevelt and Churchill as fox and badger.

26. For Katō Etsurō's graphics, see *Osaka Puck*, February 1942, cover and 19; also ibid., December 1942, 3; Katō's heirs have refused to allow these illustrations to be reproduced. For other references, cf. *Asahi Shimbun*, December 28, 1941, and January 25, April 19, and October 20, 1942; Kodama Kota and Kuno Takeshi, eds., *Nihonshi Zuroku 4: Meiji-Gendai* [Illustrated History of Japan 4: From Meiji to the Present] (1964: Yoshikawa Kobunkan), 141; *Manga*, June 1943, 6, 11.

27. Uchikawa Yoshimi, ed., *Gendai Shiryō 41: Masu Media Tōsei (2)* [Contemporary Documents 41: Control of the Mass Media, 2] (1975: Misuzu Shobō), 523–25, 528–29.

28. *Manga Nippon*, October 1944, 10–11, 15.

29. Shillony, 145–46.

30. *Manga*, July 1944, 8, and October 1944, 3–5, 18. *Asahi Shimbun*, January 14, March 11, and April 24, 1945 (the statement about the "inhuman" nature of the air raids was by Foreign Minister Tōgō). Mainichi Shimbunsha, *Nihon News Eiga Shi*, 477, on Iwo Jima.

31. *Hinode*, November 1944, esp. 2–10, 20–37, 50–54. For a contemporary American account of "Japanese hunting licenses," cf. *Time*, December 22, 1941, 13.

32. See, for example, the purifying sun motif in *Osaka Puck*, July 1942, 12, and August 1942, 35; and in *Manga*, January 1942, 22–23, and July 1942, 8. For the sword (or bayonet) of righteousness, cf. *Osaka Puck*, February 1942, cover, 3, 19; also *Hinode*, November 1944, 10, 63. Other abstract renderings of Japan included images of the disembodied "hand of God" and of Mount Fuji; cf. *Osaka Puck*, December 1942, 18; *Manga*, October 1944, 6; and *Hinode*, November 1944, 10.

33. Cf. Carmen Blacker's entry on *"oni"* in *Kodansha Encyclopedia of Japan*, 6:106; the encyclopedia *Daihyakka Jiten* (1937: Heibonsha), 4, 1: 169–71, esp. 170; and the previously mentioned *Hinode*, November 1944, 20–25.

34. Kaigo Tokiomi, ed., *Nihon Kyōkasho Taikei, Kindai-hen, Dai-8-kan: Kokugo 5* [Outline of Japanese Textbooks, Modern Period, vol. 8: Japanese Language 5] (1964: Kodansha), 348–53. Yanagita Kunio, *Momotarō no Tanjō* [The Birth of Momotarō] (1944: Sanseido). Shogo Koide, "Our Juvenile Stories," *Contemporary Japan* 10.7 (July 1941): 922–30; ibid., 13.7–9 (July–September 1944), 817–21.

35. *Manga,* February 1942, 32. Ariga Hiroshi, *Nikki* [Diary], entry for July 30, 1943; in archives of the Japanese Defense Agency. Anthony Reid, "Indonesia: From Briefcase to Samurai Sword," in Alfred W. McCoy, ed., *Southeast Asia Under Japanese Rule* (1980: Yale University, Southeast Asian Studies Monograph Series, no. 22), 24; in this Indonesian adaptation, Momotarō's three loyal followers were identified as Indonesia, China, and the Philippines.

36. Both *Momotarō of the Sky* (*Sora no Momotarō*) and *Momotarō and the Eagles of the Ocean* (*Momotarō no Umiwashi*) are in the Japanese film collection in the Library of Congress. An advertisement for the latter appeared in *Manga,* December 1942, 11. *Momotarō—Divine Troops of the Ocean* (*Momotarō—Umi no Shimpei*) cost 270,000 yen, a large sum at the time, and was prepared by a staff of about seventy individuals associated with the Shōchiku Animated Film Research Institute (Shōchiku Dōga Kenky ūjo). Although completed in December 1944, the film was not released until April 1945, by which time the war situation had become so perilous that few Japanese were able to attend the movies. After Japan's surrender, U.S. occupation authorities ordered that the film be destroyed, and for many years it was believed to have been completely lost. Around 1984, however, the negative was discovered in the Shōchiku archives, and in August of that year *Divine Troops of the Ocean* was reissued in Japan with a fair amount of publicity —including flyers from which the information given here is taken. The discussion that follows is based on the video release.

37. Thus: *shin seiji taisei* (new political structure), *shin keizai taisei* (new economic structure), *sekai shinchitsujo* (new world order), *shin zaibatsu* (new zaibatsu), *shin kanryō* (new bureaucrats), *shin haiku* (new poetry), *shinkō fujin* (new woman), etc. For a specific cultural example, the "new photography," cf. John W. Dower, "Ways of Seeing, Ways of Remembering," in Dower and Japan Photographers Association, eds., *A Century of Japanese Photography* (1980: Pantheon), esp. 16–20.

38. For graphic examples of the naturalized Momotarō type, see *Manga,* March 1943, 32, and *Osaka Puck,* February 1942, 15, March 1942, 27, April 1942, 6, June 1942, 5, September–October 1942, 42. For the "man-on-man," cf. *Osaka Puck,* April 1942, 4–5, and August 1942, 89; *Manga,* April 1942, 33.

39. *Manga,* June 1943, 6. For the complex Western perception of internal demons, see Edward J. Dudley and Maximillian E. Novak, eds., *The Wild Man Within: An Image in Western Thought from the Renaissance to Romanticism* (1973: University of Pittsburgh Press).

40. Meo, 111; cf. Joel V. Berreman, "Assumptions about America in Japanese War Propaganda to the United States," *American Journal of Sociology* 54.2 (September 1948): 108–17.

41. For Don Quixote: *Manga,* February 1942, 24; *Shūkan Asahi,* June 27, 1943, 18–19; Shimizu, 18 (with Chiang Kai-shek as Don Quixote). Other examples of lunacy are found in *Manga,* April 1941, 34; January 1943, 23; and January 1944, 18. Also *Osaka Puck,* April 1942, 37, and July 1942, 4–5; and Shimizu, 10. For the Napoleonic pose: *Manga,* May 1942, 18–19, and January 1944, 18. For gangsters, see Mainichi Shimbunsha, *Shōwa Manga Shi,* 92, 93; *Osaka Puck,* September–October 1942, 17. For pirates: *Osaka Puck,* December 1942, 19. For drunkenness and depravity: *Osaka Puck,* February 1942, 21, 24–25; *Manga,* January 1942, 35, 41, and February 1943, 3; Shimizu, 38; *Manga Nippon,* October 1944, 10–11. Excellent samples of graphics of European and American colonial oppression appear in *Osaka Puck,* December 1941, 3, February 1942, 3, 24, 25, September–October 1942, 30–33, December 1942, 16–18; *Manga,* January 1942, 40, and May 1942, 18–19. See also the "Train of Aggression" in *Osaka Puck,* July 1942, 8–9, and "History of Asia" in *Manga,* June 1944, 12–13.

42. Anti-Semitic graphics appear in *Manga,* February 1941, 22, January 1942, 17, 21 (Onō Saseo), 22–23, and February 1942, 34; also Shimizu, 5. See also anti-Semitism in chap. 10, n. 5 below.

43. The "Pietà" appeared in *Manga,* April 1941, 26, and is reproduced in Shimizu,

39. For the crucifixion, see *Manga*, April 1942, 29, and an even more grotesque rendering in Shimizu, 31. Other anti-Christian graphics appear in *Manga*, October 1944, 4; *Osaka Puck*, July 1942, 27; and Mainichi Shimbunsha, *Shōwa Manga Shi*, 91.

44. Michael Barnhart, "Japanese Intelligence before the Second World War; 'Best Case' Analysis," in Ernest R. May, ed., *Knowing One's Enemies: Intelligence Assessment before the Two World Wars* (1984: Princeton University Press), 424–55, esp. 429, 441, 446, 454.

45. Ronald H. Spector, *Eagle Against the Sun: The American War with Japan* (1984: Free Press), 48, 486. The definitive study of the submarine war is Clay Blair, Jr., *Silent Victory: The U.S. Submarine War Against Japan* (1975: J. B. Lippincott).

46. Spector, 166.

CHAPTER 10: "GLOBAL POLICY WITH THE YAMATO RACE AS NUCLEUS"

1. Only one volume of this eight-volume report was found in a used-book store in 1981. This discovery led to the disclosure of the full report in the archives of the current Ministry of Health and Welfare, which permitted it to be photocopied and reprinted in full by the publisher Bunsei Shoin in 1982. The collective title of the reprint edition is *Minzoku Jinkō Seisasku Kenkyū Shiryō: Senjika in okeru Kōseishō Kenkyūbu Jinkō Minzokubu Shiryō* [Research Documents on Race and Population Policy: Wartime Documents of the Population and Race Section of the Research Bureau of the Ministry of Health and Welfare]. The first two parts of the study, dealing with the demographic influences of war, total 807 pages. The final six volumes—*Yamato Minzoku o Chūkaku to suru Sekai Seisaku no Kentō* [An Investigation of Global Policy with the Yamato Race as Nucleus]—begin again at page 1, and are cumulatively numbered through the six volumes. In the citations which follow, these six volumes are identified with the abbreviation *YM*, followed by the page number. I am greatly indebted to Herbert Bix for calling this valuable document to my attention shortly after it was discovered, and to Takako Kishima for research assistance in surveying the contents.

2. See esp. *YM*, 2148–77.

3. *YM*, 2319–20, 2369. Cf. chap. 8, n. 16.

4. The theoretical definitions are presented most concisely in *YM*, 27–58. On the necessity of avoiding race-war concepts, cf. *YM*, 2422.

5. In their technical discussions of the concept of "race," the ministry researchers referred in passing to a dozen or so Western scientists and social scientists; *YM*, 27–58. Elsewhere they devoted several hundred pages to a summation of Nazi racial policies and "the Jewish problem"; *YM*, 1608–1870. For general discussions of Japanese attitudes toward the Jews, see Ben-Ami Shillony, *Politics and Culture in Wartime Japan* (1981: Oxford University Press), 156–71; David Kranzler, "Japanese Policy Toward the Jews, 1938–1941," *Japan Interpreter* 11.4 (1977): 493–527; Kranzler's *Japanese, Nazis, and Jews: the Jewish Refugee Community of Shanghai, 1938–1945* (1976: Yeshiva University Press); Tetsu Kohno, "Debates on the Jewish Question in Japan," *Hōsei Daigaku Kyōyōbu Kiyō* 46 (January 1983): 1–33; Marvin Tokayer and Mary Swartz, *The Fugu Plan: The Untold Story of the Japanese and the Jews During World War II* (1979: Paddington Press).

The notorious *Protocols of the Elders of Zion*, which purported to be the minutes of a secret Zionist meeting plotting world conquest (and which had an anti-Japanese counterpart in the fabricated Tanaka Memorial of the late 1920s) were translated into Japanese in 1924 and 1938 (and again in 1959); Kohno, 7, 12. The two standard Japanese translations of *Mein Kampf* which were available during the war years deleted those portions of the work which denigrated the Japanese as a "culture-carrying" but not "culture-creating" race, although these passages had been made available in Japanese in a 1931 study; Kohno, 134, Shillony, 153. Anti-Semitic rhetoric is found in a number of the internal policy documents pertaining to the Co-Prosperity Sphere; cf. Harry J. Benda,

James K. Irikura, and Koichi Kishi, eds., *Japanese Military Administration in Indonesia: Selected Documents* (1965: Yale University Southeast Asian Studies, Translation Series no. 6), 107, 112–14, 115. See also L. D. Meo, *Japan's Radio War on Australia 1941–1945* (1968: Melbourne University Press), 111–14; Otto Tolischus, ed., *Through Japanese Eyes* (1945: Reynal & Hitchcock), 88–92, 140; Tokutomi Iichirō, *Hisshō Kokumin Tokuhon* [A Citizen's Reader for Certain Victory] (1944: Mainichi Shimbunsha), 71. Although most commentators now regard anti-Semitism as a peripheral and aberrant current in the wartime ideology of the Japanese, at the time at least one American interpreted it as decidedly practical. In this interpretation, Japanese attacks on the Jews were inseparable from Japanese ambitions in the Middle East and attempts to win the support of Arab peoples and Moslems throughout the world; see Saul K. Padover, "Japanese Race Propaganda," *Public Opinion Quarterly* 7.2 (Summer 1943): 203–4.

    6. *YM*, 29–36.

    7. *YM*, 36–47.

    8. Cf. *YM*, 47–58, 308, 363.

    9. *YM*, 2162, 304–5; see also n. 36 below.

    10. *YM*, 312, 2296.

    11. *YM*, 50–52, 2202.

    12. *Asahi Shimbun*, August 3, 1941, 5.

    13. *YM*, 311–12.

    14. *YM*, 2044–50, 2294–95, 2350–51. At one point the researchers also stated that the essence of Japanism was to be found in the Imperial Rescript on Education issued in 1890; *YM*, 3078. It should be noted that the most sophisticated Japanese apologetics for the war—notably the argument offered by the small Kyoto School (Kyoto Gokuha) of intellectuals associated with Kyoto Imperial University—explicitly rejected this approach. Instead of stressing Japan's role as a synthesizer of East and West, they argued that Japan, by its current struggle, was in fact "transcending the modern" (*kindai no chōkoku*) and creating an entirely new level of civilization and morality. Cf. Takeuchi Yoshimi, "Kindai no Chōkoku" [Transcending the Modern] in *Takeuchi Yoshimi Zenshū* (1980: Chikuma Shobō), 8: 3–67. The Kyoto School's discussion of "transcending the modern" was published in the September and October 1942 issues of *Bungakukai*.

    15. See, for example, *YM*, 2347–48, 2424, 2430, 3081.

    16. *YM*, 57–58, 2349.

    17. *YM*, 386–93, 2307, 2348–49.

    18. On social-welfare legislation, which was an important and often neglected legacy of the war years to the postwar era, cf. Thomas R. H. Havens, *Valley of Darkness: The Japanese People and World War Two* (1978: Norton), 46–49. The population policy announced in early 1941 is covered in detail in *Asahi Shimbun*, January 23, 1941. See also the encyclopedia *Nihon Hyakka Daijiten* (1963), 5: 353 on mobilization of marriage-counseling agencies to improve eugenics through arranged marriages. For the "propagate and multiply movement" (*umeyo fuyaseyo undō*) and healthy-baby contests, cf. Ogi Shinzō, *Shōwa Shōmin Bunka Shi* [History of the Culture of the Common People in the Shōwa Period] (1971: Nihon Hōsō Shuppan Kyōkai) 2: 340; also Morosawa Yōko, "Jōsei no Kyōgū" [The Circumstances of Women], in Wakamori Tarō, ed., *Gunkoku kara Minshūkae* [From Military State to Democratization], vol. 10 in Wakamori, ed., *Nihon Seikatsu Bunka Shi* [History of Daily Life and Culture in Japan] (1975: Kawade Shobō), 140. For further information on demographic policies and trends, cf. Havens, 134–38, 142–47; also Irene B. Tauber, *The Population of Japan* (1958: Princeton University Press), esp. chap. 16, "The Demography of War."

    19. *YM*, 63, 2061.

    20. *YM*, 101–2. They had in mind particularly a 1937 publication of the Royal Institute of International Affairs entitled *The Colonial Problem*.

    21. On the repudiation of "Far East," cf. *Asahi Shimbun*, October 25, 1942, evening

ed. The official rectification of names also attempted to alter the usual Japanese rendering for the peoples of Asia, who were conventionally spoken of as "natives," or literally "people of the soil" (*domin* or *dojin;* another common and mildly pejorative way of referring to the "natives" was *genjūmin*). Such phrases smacked of Western-style imperialism, the government announced in 1942, and henceforth the other people of Asia should be spoken of as *jūnin* or "inhabitants"; ibid. Letters from soldiers in the field indicate that the condescending old usages persisted; cf. the letters from peasant conscripts collected in Iwate-ken Nōson Bunka Kondankai, ed., *Senbotsu Nōmin Heishi no Tegami* [Letters of Peasant Conscripts Killed in Battle] (1961: Iwanami Shinsho #424). Komaki's Japanese writings are cited in John J. Stephan, *Hawaii Under the Rising Sun: Japan's Plans for Conquest after Pearl Harbor* (1984: University of Hawaii Press), 127–28, 154–55, 212. For the Western response to Komaki's frenetic cartography, cf. Sidney C. Menefee, "Japan's Global Conceit," *Asia and the Americas,* July 1943, 330–32; Padover, "Japanese Race Propaganda," 194–96

22. *YM,* 2025–29.

23. *YM,* 2334–35. This section of the report bears earmarks of having been drafted in the early part of 1942, since by mid-1943 (when the full report presumedly was completed) the Philippines were under Japan's control, while Australia and New Zealand, of course, were not. The sensational Stage 4 is not mentioned again. Nor does the report mention acquisition of Hawaii, although the recent research of John Stephan (n. 21 above) has revealed that this was briefly on the Japanese drawing boards between their victory at Pearl Harbor and defeat at Midway in mid-1942. On the other hand, the geography textbooks issued by the Ministry of Education in December 1943 and January 1944 for fifth and sixth graders included under Greater East Asia not only the areas already occupied by Japan but also Australia, New Zealand, India, West and Central Asia, Siberia, and the Pacific islands, including the Aleutians and Hawaii. These areas either already had been awakened by Japan's power and leadership, the students were told, or were about to be so awakened. It was Japan's mission to revitalize and unify these various peoples as "a Great East Asia race, each in its proper place" (*Dai Tōa minzoku to shite yomigaerase, ono ono sono tokoro o esaseru koto*). Once such a Greater East Asia had been established under the emperor, Japan would go on to bring peace to all peoples of the world. Mombushō [Ministry of Education], *Shotōka Chiri* [Elementary Geography], 2 vols., reproduced in Kaigo Tokiomi, ed., *Nihon Kyōkasho Taikei, Kindai-hen, Dai-17-kan: Chiri 3* [Outline of Japanese Textbooks, Modern Period, vol. 17: Geography 3] (1966: Kodansha), 54–99 (esp. 57, 99), 624–25.

24. *YM,* 2335.

25. *YM,* 3078, 3087.

26. *YM,* 3091.

27. *YM,* 6. The creation of a "new world order" (*sekai shinchitsujo*) was one of the basic avowed objectives of the Japanese government, emphasized in propaganda policy and in such ideological tracts as *The Way of the Family* [*Ie no Michi*], issued in 1942; cf. Uchikawa Yoshimi, ed., *Gendai Shiryō, 41: Masu Media Tōsei 2* [Contemporary Documents 41: Control of Mass Media 2] (1975: Misuzu Shobō), 368, where the propaganda policy adopted on December 8, 1941, emphasizes "creation of a new world order" based on assigning every nation its "proper place"; also Isono Fujiko, ed., *Ie: Gendai no Esprit* [Family: The Spirit of Modern Times] (1965: Shibundō), 132. In a three-volume *Study of Protracted War* prepared in March 1945 by the government's Institute for the Study of Total War, Japanese strategic planners even at this late date continued to speak about "exercising the unique power of the race" and "realizing *hakkō ichiu* throughout the world." The current conflict belonged to that category of "wars for world domination" (*sekai seihasen*) which had been seen previously in history. Such conflicts, involving incompatible worldviews, almost always ended in the triumph of one worldview, the destruction of the defeated nation, and the decline of the losing race. See Naikaku

Sōryokusen Kenkyūjo [Cabinet Institute for the Study of Total War], *Chōkisen Kenkyū* [A Study of Protracted War], March 1945, 36, 41, 74–75, 83–90.

28. *YM,* 2433–34. The numbers add up to 12,080,000 settlers rather than 12,090,000, but the latter is the figure used in the text.

29. *YM,* 76, 303–31, 363, 2181–83, 2362–64, 2430–32. In their detailed discussion of racial intermarriage (303–31), the researchers as usual cite numerous Western authorities.

30. Furuya Yoshio, *Nippon Hyōron,* July 1943; summarized under the title "Racial Integrity and Population Factor" in the government-supported English monthly *Contemporary Japan* 12.8 (August 1943): 1054–57.

31. *YM,* 303–4. "Blood and soil" was identified as a Nazi concept in the early pages of the report; *YM,* 27.

32. *YM,* 2486–87. On Indonesian mixed-bloods, see M. Z. Aziz, *Japan's Colonialism and Indonesia* (1955: Martinus Nijhoff, The Hague), 172.

33. *YM,* 2368–71; cf. 13 ff., 2307, 2322. German occupation policies are described in 2371–2421. For more abstruse rationalizations of Japan's destiny to create a new *Lebensraum,* cf. Kōsaka Masaaki's theories of "life space" (*seimei kūkan*) and "historical space" (*rekishiteki kūkan*) in "Dai Tōa Kyōeiken e no Michi" [The Road to the Greater East Asia Co-Prosperity Sphere], *Kaizō* 24.1 (January 1942): 16–37; also Sakaeda Yoshitaka's discussion of "composed space" (*kōsei kūkan*)—incorporating both "fated space" (*unmei kūkan*) and "controlled space" (*shihai kūkan*) such as colonies—and "subsidiary space" (*josei kūkan*), in "Kyōei Kūkan no Kōseitaironteki Haaku" [Comprehending the Structure of Co-Prosperity Space], *Chūō Kōron* 57.5 (May 1942): 22–33.

34. *YM,* 2181, 2307–8.

35. Cf. *YM,* 2197, 2300, 2321, 2329, 2332–33, 2369.

36. *Cf. YM,* 2183, 2197–98, 2300, 2310, 2323, 2329, 2332–33.

37. *YM,* 2198 (racial consanguinity), 2162 (collective racialism), 2322 ("heart" and "love"). The multiracial organization sponsored by the Japanese in Manchukuo was known as the Kyōwakai, formally translated into English as "Concordia Association."

38. On the family system in modern Japanese history, see Kawashima Takeyoshi, *Ideorogi to Shite no Kazoku Seidō* [The Family System As Ideology] (1975: Iwanami Shoten). Cf. Sumiya Mikio, "The Emergence of Modern Japan," in Kazuo Okochi, Bernard Karsh, and Solomon Levine, eds., *Workers and Employers in Japan: The Japanese Employment Relations System* (1974: Princeton University Press), 15–48.

39. John O. Gauntlett, trans., and Robert K. Hall, ed., *Kokutai no Hongi: Cardinal Principles of the National Entity of Japan* (1949: Harvard University Press), 97–98. An English translation of *The Way of the Subject* (or *The Way of Subjects*) prepared by the Japanese government is included as an appendix in Otto Tolischus, *Tokyo Record* (1943: Reynal & Hitchcock), 405–27.

40. U.S. Department of State, *Foreign Relations of the United States: Japan, 1931–1941* (1943: Government Printing Office), 2: 111.

41. U.S. Department of State, *Peace and War: United States Foreign Policy, 1931–1941* (1943: Government Printing Office), 573.

42. Kawashima, 64; the text of the imperial rescript appears in *Asahi Shimbun,* September 28, 1940.

43. Kaigo Tokiomi, ed., *Nihon Kyōkasho Taikei, Kindai-hen, Dai 20-kan: Rekishi 3* [Outline of Japanese Textbooks, Modern Period, vol. 20: History 3] (1962: Kodansha), 234.

44. *YM,* 2294–97.

45. *YM,* 2312–16; cf. 3077, 3078 (*ono ono sono tokoro*). "Proper place" was also rendered as *fusawashii chii* (2315). Another version was "appropriate burden" *(sōtō no futan);* 2423.

46. *YM,* 2315–16.

NOTES FOR PAGES 283–286 ▸ 361

47. YM, 2366, 2422. *Oni* (stern justice) was one of the moral values emphasized in the *Senjinkun* (Field Service Code) issued to Japanese servicemen.

48. Saitō Tadashi, Ono Seiichirō (or Kiyoichirō), and Matsushita Masahisa (or Masatoshi), "Dai Tōa Sengen no Shingi" [The True Meaning of the Declaration of the Greater East Asia War], *Kaizō* 26.3 (March 1944): 4–25. Matsushita described the Eastern moral order as the rule of man rather than the rule of law, and Ono argued that "familyism" (*kazokushugi*) had been the basis of Greek and Roman society before being supplanted by individualism. The participants in this roundtable discussion suggested that family-oriented morality was universalistic, while the rule of law was a latterday development unique to the West. See also Ogushi Toyoo, "Nippon Minzoku Sekaikan no Kakuritsu" [Establishing a Japanese Racial Worldview], *Bungei Shunjū* 20.1 (January 1942): 27–28.

49. Kaigo, 3: 432; Harold J. Wray, "A Study in Contrasts: Japanese School Textbooks of 1903 and 1941–5," *Monumenta Nipponica* 28.1 (1973): 85; Mombushō, ed., *Dai Tōa Sensō to Warera* [The Greater East Asia War and Ourselves] (1942), 11.

50. YM, 776 for Manchukuo as a "branch family" and 2422 for the model of elder and younger brothers. For Manchukuo as a "child country," cf. Tsurumi Shunsuke, ed., *Nihon no Hyakunen 3: Hateshinaki Sensen* [Japan's Hundred Years 3: The Endless War Front] (1967: Chikuma Shobō), 183. Wartime geography texts explained that the relationship between Japan and Manchukuo was as between parent and child (*oya-ko*); Kaigo, 17: 66. For Manchukuo as the model for Japan's relationships with other countries in the Co-Prosperity Sphere, cf. Willard H. Elsbree, *Japan's Role in South-East Asian Nationalist Movements* (1953: Harvard University Press), 26–29; and for "universal brotherhood" as appropriate English for *hakkō ichiu*, see Arita Hachirō in *Contemporary Japan* 10.1 (January 1941), reprinted in Joyce C. Lebra, ed. *Japan's Greater East Asia Co-Prosperity Sphere in World War II: Selected Readings and Documents* (1975: Oxford University Press), 74. For the kindergarten reference, see YM, 2368–70.

51. YM, 2368–70.

52. Lebra, 122–31; Louis M. Allen, "Fujiwara and Suzuki: Patterns of Asian Liberation," in William H. Newell, ed., *Japan in Asia* (1981: Singapore University Press), 83–103; Mohan Singh, *Soldiers' Contribution to Indian Independence: The Epic of the Indian National Army* (1974: Army Educational Stores, New Delhi). For the affectionate recollection of Japanese female teachers in Indonesia, see Yohanna Johns, "The Japanese as Educators in Indonesia: A Personal View," in Newell, 25–31.

53. Changsoo Lee and George De Vos, *Koreans in Japan: Ethnic Conflict and Accomodation* (1981: University of California Press), esp. 21–28; 31–57. For a recent appraisal of Japanese colonialism, focusing primarily on developments prior to establishment of the Co-Prosperity Sphere, see Ramon H. Meyers and Mark R. Peattie, eds., *The Japanese Colonial Empire, 1895–1945* (1984: Princeton University Press). This provides a historical background for many of the points emphasized in the 1942–43 Ministry of Health and Welfare study, including the assumption of Japanese racial superiority, buttressed by imperial mythohistory; the policy of permanent economic and cultural domination of subordinate peoples (especially in the case of Koreans and Formosans); the early policies of "acculturation" or "Japanization"; and the application abroad of domestic class concepts, such as *kanson mimpi* ("respect superiors, despise inferiors") and *mibun sōō* ("appropriate social status"). Mark Peattie also introduces in this work (110–13) an earlier sustained endeavor to base Japanese colonial policy on racial distinctions, published in 1925 by the colonial administrator Tōgō Minoru under the title *Colonial Policy and Racial Consciousness* (*Shokumin Seisaku to Minzoku Shinri*). This study went through four printings between 1925 and 1937. For an outstanding brief statement of Japan's "nationality policy," see the "Plan for Leadership of Nationalities in Greater East Asia" of August 6, 1942, in Lebra, 118–21.

54. Mark R. Peattie, *Ishiwara Kanji and Japan's Confrontation with the West* (1966: Princeton University Press), 287; Michael A. Barnhart, "Japanese Intelligence before the

Second World War: 'Best Case' Analysis," in Ernest R. May, ed., *Knowing One's Enemies: Intelligence Assessment before the Two World Wars* (1984: Princeton University Press), 432, 435.

55. Ba Maw, *Breakthrough in Burma: Memoirs of a Revolution, 1939–1946* (1968: Yale University Press), 155–56, 180–81, 185.

56. Cf. Aziz, 174–82; Benda et al., 33.

57. Benda et al., 17–25, 26–46.

58. Cf. *YM,* 680 for the Han Chinese; 1107–8 for the overseas Chinese; 1033, 1098, 1113 for southern peoples; 1123–32 for Filipinos.

59. *YM,* 2360–62.

60. *YM,* 2351, 2365–66.

61. *YM,* 2340–42, 2350, 3083, 3093, 3105.

62. *YM,* 2340, 3088, 1106–08.

63. *YM,* 2350–51. For general statements of economic policy, cf. ibid., 2339–42, 2349–57, 3077–94, and 3105–07.

64. Benda et al., 187; cf. the 1944 Foreign Ministry statement in ibid., 243.

CHAPTER 11: FROM WAR TO PEACE

1. For general estimates of World War Two casualties and deaths see Robert Goralski, *World War II Almanac: 1931–1945* (1981: Putnam), 425–29; Hans Dollinger, *The Decline and Fall of Nazi Germany and Imperial Japan* (1968: Crown; a translation of *Die Letzen Hundert Tage,* 1965), 422; R. Ernest Dupuy, *World War II: A Compact History* (1969: Hawthorn Books), 318 for "global costs" and throughout for individual battles.

2. United Nations, Economic and Social Council, *Report of the Working Group for Asia and the Far East,* Suppl. 10, 1947, 6–7; George Blakeslee, *The Far Eastern Commission: A Study in International Cooperation, 1945 to 1952* (1953: U.S. Department of State Publications, no. 5138), 145; Chang Hsin–hai, "The Treaty with Japan: A Chinese View," *Foreign Affairs* 26.3 (April 1948); 506. The usual estimate of Chinese military casualties from 1937 to 1945 is 3.2 million, of which 1.3 million died, but higher estimates are available; cf. the *New York Times,* November 5, 1947, where Chinese military dead from 1941 to 1945 are estimated to have been 2,850,000 men.

3. *Report of the Working Group for Asia and the Far East,* 13–14, 18. On Europeans imprisoned in the Dutch East Indies, see also M. Z. Aziz, *Japan's Colonialism and Indonesia* (1955: Martinus Nijhoff, The Hague), 170. See also chap. 3, n. 39 above.

4. *Report of the Working Group for Asia and the Far East,* 9–10, 13–15, for Malaya, Burma, and India. For Filipino losses, see *New York Times,* July 29, 1946. For the French in Indochina, see *The Far Eastern Commission,* 146; the famine is discussed in Chieu N. Vu, "Political and Social Change in Viet-Nam Between 1940 and 1946," Ph.D. dissertation in history, University of Wisconsin-Madison, 1984. For Korean deaths, see chap. 3, n. 38 above.

5. Basic figures are from the Keizai Antei Honbu (Japanese Economic Stabilization Board) compilations of 1949, reprinted in Ōkurashō Zaisei Shi Shitsu, ed., *Shōwa Zaisei Shi: Shūsen kara Heiwa made* [Shōwa Financial History: From War's End to the Peace Settlement] (1978: Tōyō Keizai Shimbun), 19 (Tokei): 22–23. Figures for the China war are also from the Keizai Antei Honbu, cited in Tōyami Shigeki, Imai Seiichi, and Fujiwara Akira, *Shōwa Shi,* [Shōwa History] rev. ed. (1959: Iwanami Shoten), 241. Figures for Hiroshima and Nagasaki follow the Committee for the Compilation of Materials on Damage Caused by the Atomic Bombs in Hiroshima and Nagasaki, *Hiroshima and Nagasaki: The Physical, Medical, and Social Effects of the Atomic Bombings* (1981: Basic Books; translated from the 1979 Iwanami publication), esp. 113–15. NOTE: A standard error which has crept into many English sources concerning the number of Japanese killed in air raids is the use of the figure 668,000 (or 665,000); the error derives from the 1947

Japanese report on air-raid "casualties," which included wounded and missing as well as killed. The bombing victims include 10,000 to 15,000 Koreans who were in Hiroshima and Nagasaki when the atomic bombs were dropped.

6. On mortality from hunger and illness, see Bernd Martin, "Japan und der Krieg in Ostasien: Kommentierender Bericht über das Schrifttum," *Historische Zeitschrift*, Sonder-haft (Special Issue) 8, 1980, 79–219. The figures for illness among repatriated troops were released by the Japanese government in 1945: Tsuji Kiyoaki, ed., *Shiryō: Sengo Nijūnen Shi* [Documents: Twenty Years of Postwar History] (1966: Nihon Hyōronsha), 1: 15; *Contemporary Japan* 14.4–12 (April–December 1945): 176. Known deaths of Japanese troops awaiting repatriation in Allied (non-Soviet) hands were listed as 81,090 by U.S. authorities, but most figures for Japanese surrenders were "adjusted" by the United States to coincide with actual repatriations, thus obscuring the controversial issue of Japanese deaths after surrender. See *Reports of General MacArthur*, vol. 1, Supplement, *MacArthur in Japan: The Occupation: Military Phase* (1966: Government Printing Office), 130, 149.

7. For Saipan, see *Kindai Nihon Sōgo Nempyō* [Comprehensive Chronology of Modern Japan] (1968: Iwanami Shoten), 338. For Okinawa: Ōta Masahide, *Sōshi: Okinawa-sen* [Comprehensive History of the Battle of Okinawa] (1982: Iwanami Shoten), 219. Japanese soldiers in post-1945 China are discussed in Donald G. Gillin with Charles Etter, "Staying On: Japanese Soldiers and Civilians in China, 1945–1949," *Journal of Asian Studies* 42.3 (May 1983): 497–518.

Repatriation figures are given in *Reports of General MacArthur*, 1, Supplement, chaps. 5 and 6. The Japanese prisoners of the Soviet Union became one of the most emotional and controversial issues of the early cold war. As of October 1948, the U.S.S.R. had repatriated 877,015 Japanese. The following May, the Soviet government announced that only 95,000 prisoners remained (plus some accused Japanese war criminals), and they were repatriated by November 1949. The Japanese government claimed that 374,041 Japanese remained unaccounted for (including approximately 60,000 civilians); ibid., 159–61, 179–86. See also Robert A. Fearey, *The Occupation of Japan: Second Phase, 1948–50* (1950: Macmillan Co.), 14–16. The Japanese government calculated that 111,-250 Japanese nationals died in Manchuria in the winter of 1945–46, and some accounts put the figure at more than 135,000: U.S. Department of State, *Foreign Relations of the United States, 1946*, 8: 306; Gillin and Etter, 503.

8. These estimates are compiled from various sources including Dupuy; Goralski; John Costello, *The Pacific War, 1941–1945* (1981: Quill Trade Paperbacks); and the Army and Navy casualty tables cited in the following note. Some calculations indicate that Japanese war dead in the Philippines may have been close to 400,000; cf. *Reports of General MacArthur*, 1: 358; 1, Supplement: 168; and 2, 2: 560.

9. Army and Air Forces statistics are from Statistical and Accounting Branch, Office of the Adjutant General, U.S. Department of the Army, *Army Battle Casualties and Nonbattle Deaths in World War II: Final Report, 7 December 1941–31 December 1946*, adapted from 42–43. Navy and Marine casualty figures are from U.S. Department of the Navy, Bureau of Medicine and Surgery, Division of Medical Statistics, *The History of the Medical Department of the United States Navy in World War II*, vol. 3, *The Statistics of Diseases and Injuries* (1950: Navmed P-1318), adapted from 171–74.

Army casualties and deaths include 25,697 Americans who were captured in May 1942, of whom 10,957 died. This accounts for a large percentage of Army casualties and deaths listed as occurring prior to July 1944. It should be noted that there are inconsistencies within the official U.S. statistics themselves. The same basic Adjutant General's report, for example, elsewhere gives higher estimates for the total number of U.S. Army and Air Forces deaths in the Pacific, notably 53,221 (pp. 94–95) and 57,286 (pp. 76–77). The Navy Department also offers slightly lower casualty figures for Navy and Marine deaths in the same medical report, notably 29,263 Navy and 19,163 Marine deaths (pp. 78, 84). The standard itemization for total U.S. deaths in World War Two uses the higher estimates and is as follows:

	European Theater	Asia and the Pacific	Total Military Deaths
Army and Air Forces	177,549	57,286	234,874
Navy	7,225	31,032	38,257
Marines	405	19,585	19,990

(The Army and Air Forces total includes 39 deaths in unspecified locales.)

10. B. B. A. Roling and C. F. Ruter, eds., *The Tokyo Judgment: The International Military Tribunal for the Far East (I.M.T.F.E.), 29 April 1946–November 1948,* vol. 1 (1977: APA-University Press Amsterdam BV), 395; Wesley Frank Craven and James Lea Cate, eds., *The Army Air Forces in World War II* (1953: Office of Air Force History), 5: 732–33.

11. *Newsweek,* September 3, 1945, 23.

12. Cf. Frank D. Morris, "Seventy Million Problem Children," *Collier's,* December 1, 1945. For postsurrender Western cartoons of the Japanese as children and pupils, see Sodei Rinjirō and Fukushima Jurō, *Makkāsā: Sengo Nihon no Genten* [MacArthur: The Origins of Postwar Japan] (1982: Nihon Hōsō Shuppan Kyōkai), 233. Also *New York Times,* April 13 and June 1, 1947, March 16, 1952.

13. U.S. Senate, Committee on Armed Services and Committee on Foreign Relations, 82nd Cong., 1st sess., *Hearings to Conduct an Inquiry into the Military Situation in the Far East and the Facts Surrounding the Relief of General of the Army Douglas MacArthur from His Assignments in that Area,* 1951, pt. 1: 312–13. I am indebted to Sodei Rinjirō for the account of plans to build a MacArthur statue in Tokyo Bay. The "Parent States" concept is discussed in William Roger Louis, *Imperialism at Bay, 1941–1945: The United States and the Decolonialization of the British Empire* (1977: Oxford University Press), 211–24, 229, 244–45, 251.

14. J. W. Dower, *Empire and Aftermath: Yoshida Shigeru and the Japanese Experience, 1878–1954* (1979: Harvard University Press), 312–13.

15. Kinbara Samon and Takemae Eiji, *Shōwa Shi* [Shōwa History] (1982: Yukihaku), 243–44.

16. Dulles was fond of referring to a conversation between Stalin and Foreign Minister Matsuoka Yōsuke in April 1941, on which occasion the Soviet dictator allegedly told the Japanese emissary, "You are an Asian, so am I." As early as 1938, Kennan was writing about Russia as an "Oriental Byzantium," and in his famous long dispatch of 1946 he spoke of the U.S.S.R. as an explosive mixture of traditional Russian insecurity, Communist ideology, and "Oriental secretiveness and conspiracy." See C. Ben Wright, "George F. Kennan, Scholar-Diplomat: 1926–1946," Ph.D. dissertation in history, University of Wisconsin-Madison, 1972, 124–26; Walter LaFeber, *America, Russia, and the Cold War, 1945–1966* (1967: Wiley), 53. On Churchill and "the threat from the East," see Montgomery Cunningham Meigs, "Managing Uncertainty: Vannevar Bush, James B. Conant and the Development of the Atomic Bomb, 1940–1945," Ph.D. dissertation in history, University of Wisconsin-Madison, 1982, 160–63.

17. The Chinese Communists were called blue ants by Westerners because of the color of their clothing. Clubb's comment is cited in Michael Schaller, *The American Occupation of Japan: The Origins of the Cold War in Asia* (1985: Oxford University Press), 253.

18. Howard Schonberger, "John Foster Dulles and the China Question in the Making of the Japanese Peace Treaty," in Thomas W. Burkman, ed., *The Occupation of Japan: The International Context* (1984: MacArthur Foundation), 242, 248.

19. U.S. Department of State, *Foreign Relations of the United States, 1951* (Government Printing Office), 6.1: 825–26. The manner in which the United States perceived its postoccupation military and economic relationship with Japan as simultaneously a

partnership and a way of institutionalizing long-term control over the recent enemy is addressed in Dower, *Empire and Aftermath.*

20. Watanabe Takeshi, *Senryōka no Nihon Zaisei Oboegaki* [Recollections of Japanese Finance under the Occupation] (1966: Nihon Keizai Shimbunsha), 292–93.

21. *Manchester Guardian Weekly,* July 21, 1985; *Wisconsin State Journal,* October 20, 1985 (quoting Representative John Dingell, White House Chief of Staff Donald Regan, and Senator Donald Riegle); Howard H. Baker, Jr., in *New York Times,* August 21, 1985; *Washington Post National Weekly Edition,* July 30, 1984, and July 29, 1985; *U.S. News and World Report,* April 1, 1985; Theodore White, "The Danger from Japan," *New York Times Magazine,* August 11, 1985; Russell Braddon, *Japan Against the World, 1941–2041: The 100-Year War for Supremacy* (1983: Stein & Day); *Wall Street Journal,* November 19 and December 7, 1982; *New York Times,* August 17, 1983; *Japan Christian Activity News* 603 (November 18, 1983) and 616 (December 20, 1984); William R. Burkhardt, "Institutional Barriers, Marginality, and Adaptation Among the American-Japanese Mixed Bloods in Japan," *Journal of Asian Studies* 42.3 (May 1983): 519–44.

BIBLIOGRAPHY

Adachi, Buntarō. *Zōho Nipponjin Taishitsu no Kenkyū* [Studies in the Physical Constitution of the Japanese People]. Rev. ed. Ogiwara Seibunkan, 1944.
Allen, Louis. *The End of the War in Asia*. Hart-Davis, MacGibbon, 1976.
————. "The Indian National Army," *Purnell's History of the Second World War, 107:* 2984–86. Purnell, n.d.
————. *Singapore, 1941–1942*. Davis-Poynter, 1977.
Anderson, B. R. O'G. "Japan: 'The Light of Asia'." In Josef Silverstein, ed., *Southeast Asia in World War II: Four Essays*, 13–39. Yale University Southeast Asia Studies, Monograph Series no. 7, 1966.
Anderson, Joseph L., and Donald Ritchie. *The Japanese Film: Art and Industry*. Expanded ed. Princeton University Press, 1982.
Andrew, George S., Jr. "The 41st Didn't Take Prisoners." *Saturday Evening Post,* July 27, 1946.
Annan, Noel. "Patriot." *New York Review of Books.* September 24, 1981.
Asahi Shimbun, ed. *The Pacific Rivals: A Japanese View of Japanese-American Relations.* John Weatherhill, 1972.
Aziz, M. Z. *Japan's Colonialism and Indonesia.* Martinus Nijhoff, The Hague, 1955.
Australia, Director General of Public Relations under the authority of General Sir Thomas Blamey, Commander in Chief, Australian Military Forces. *The Jap Was Thrashed: An Official Story of the Australian Soldier—First Victor of the "Invincible" Jap, New Guinea, 1942–43.* Australian Military Forces, 1944.
Ba Maw. *Breakthrough in Burma: Memoirs of a Revolution, 1939–1946.* Yale University Press, 1968.
Bahr, Howard M., Bruce A. Chadwick, and Joseph H. Stauss. "Race and Race Thinking." Chap 6 in their *American Ethnicity*. D. C. Heath & Co., 1979.
Bailey, Tom. *Tarawa.* Monarch Books, 1962.
Baldwin, Hanson W. "This Is the Army We Have to Defeat." *New York Times Magazine,* July 29, 1945.
Ballhatchet, Kenneth. *Race, Sex and Class under the Raj: Imperial Attitudes and Politics and Their Critics, 1793–1905.* St. Martin's, 1980.

Ballou, Robert O. *Shinto, the Unconquered Enemy: Japan's Doctrine of Racial Superiority and World Conquest.* Viking, 1945.

Barber, Noel. *Sinister Twilight: The Fall and Rise Again of Singapore.* William Collins Sons & Co., 1968.

Barnhart, Michael A. "Japanese Intelligence before the Second World War: 'Best Case' Analysis." In Ernest R. May, ed., *Knowing One's Enemies: Intelligence Assessment before the Two World Wars.* 424–55. Princeton University Press, 1984.

Barnouw, Victor. *Culture and Personality.* Dorsey Press, 1963.

Bastide, Roger. "Color, Racism, and Christianity." *Daedalus,* Spring 1967, 312–27.

Batchelder, Robert. *The Irreversible Decision, 1939–1950.* Houghton Mifflin, 1961.

Bateson, Gregory, and Margaret Mead. *Balinese Character: A Photographic Analysis.* Special Publications of the New York Academy of Sciences, vol. 11, 1942.

Beaufort, John, and Clinton Green. "Japs Don't Want to Die." *Collier's,* October 21, 1944.

Bellaire, Robert. "Why the Japs Hate the Nazis." *Collier's,* January 23, 1943.

Benda, Harry J. *The Crescent and the Rising Sun: Indonesian Islam under the Japanese Occupation, 1942–1945.* W. van Hoeve, The Hague and Bandung, 1958.

———, James K. Irikura, and Koichi Kishi, eds. *Japanese Military Administration in Indonesia: Selected Documents.* Yale University Southeast Asia Studies, Translation Series no. 6, 1965.

Benedict, Ruth. *The Chrysanthemum and the Sword.* Houghton Mifflin, 1946.

———. "The Japanese Are So Simple." *Asia and the Americas* November 1946, 500–503.

———. *Race: Science and Politics.* Rev ed. Viking, 1945.

Bennett, John W., and Michio Nagai. "The Japanese Critique of the Methodology of Benedict's *Chrysanthemum and the Sword.*" *American Anthropologist* 55.3 (August 1953): 404–11.

Benyon, Erdmann. "The Voodoo Cult among Negro Migrants in Detroit." *American Journal of Sociology* 43.6 (May 1938): 894–907.

Berkhofer, Robert F., Jr. *The White Man's Indian: Images of the American Indian from Columbus to the Present.* Knopf, 1978.

Berreman, Joel V. "Assumptions about America in Japanese War Propaganda to the United States." *American Journal of Sociology* 54.2 (September 1948): 108–17.

Berrey, Lester V., and Melvin Van Den Bark. *The American Thesaurus of Slang.* 2nd ed. Crowell, 1953.

Berry, Henry. *Semper Fi, Mac: Living Memories of the U.S. Marines in World War Two.* Arbor House, 1982.

Bishop, Robert Lee. *The Overseas Branch of the Office of War Information.* Ph.D. dissertation in Mass Communications, University of Wisconsin-Madison, 1966.

Blair, Clay, Jr. *Silent Victory: The U.S. Submarine War against Japan.* Lippincott, 1975.

Blakefield, William J. "A War Within: The Making of *Know Your Enemy—Japan.*" *Sight and Sound: International Film Quarterly* 52.2 (Spring 1983): 128–33.

Blakeslee, George. *The Far Eastern Commission: A Study in International Cooperation, 1945–1952.* U.S. Department of State Publications 5138, 1953.

Bohn, Thomas William. *An Historical and Descriptive Analysis of the "Why We Fight" Series.* Arno Press, 1977.

Bolte, Charles G. "This Is the Face of War." *The Nation,* March 3, 1945.

Borg, Dorothy, and Shumpei Okamoto, eds. *Pearl Harbor As History: Japanese-American Relations, 1931–1941.* Columbia University Press, 1973.

Boxer, Charles R. *The Christian Century in Japan, 1549–1650.* University of California Press, 1961.

———. "The Color Question in the Portuguese Empire." *Proceedings of the British Academy 47* (1962): 113–38.

Braddon, Russell. *Japan against the World, 1941–2041: The 100-Year War for Supremacy.* Stein & Day, 1983.

Brittain, Vera. "Massacre by Bombing: The Facts behind the British-American Attack on Germany." *Fellowship* 10.3 (March 1944): 50–64.

Brown, Cecil. *Suez to Singapore*. Halcyon House Publications, 1942.

Buck, Pearl. "An Appeal to California." *Asia and the Americas*, January 1944, 21–23.

———. "Postwar China and the United States." *Asia and the Americas*, November 1943, 613–15.

———. *The Promise. Asia* magazine, 1942–43; Sun Dial Press, 1945.

———. "The Race Barrier 'That Must Be Destroyed.' " *New York Times Magazine*, May 31, 1942.

———. "Tinder for Tomorrow." *Asia* March 1942, 153–56.

———. "Western Weapons in the Hands of the Reckless East." *Asia* October 1937, 672–73.

Burgess, John. "Rewriting the 'Rape of Nanking.' " *Washington Post National Weekly Edition*, February 11, 1985.

Burkhardt, William R. "Institutional Barriers, Marginality, and Adaptation among the American-Japanese Mixed Bloods in Japan." *Journal of Asian Studies* 42.3 (May 1983): 519–44.

Butow, Robert J. C. *Tojo and the Coming of the War*. Stanford University Press, 1961.

Byas, Hugh. "How Tough Are the Japanese?" *New York Times Magazine*, May 2, 1943.

———. *The Japanese Enemy: His Power and His Vulnerability*. Knopf, 1942.

Caidin, Martin. *The Ragged, Rugged Warriors*. Dutton, 1966.

Calvocoressi, Peter, and Guy Wint. *Total War: Causes and Courses of the Second World War*. Pelican, 1972.

Cantril, Hadley, ed. *Public Opinion, 1935–1946*. Princeton University Press, 1951.

Capra, Frank. *The Name above the Title: An Autobiography*. Macmillan Co., 1971.

Cater, Harold Dean, comp. *Henry Adams and His Friends: A Collection of His Unpublished Letters*. Houghton Mifflin, 1947.

Catton, Bruce. *The War Lords of Washington*. Harcourt, Brace & Co., 1948.

Chamberlin, William Henry. *Modern Japan*. Edited by Maxwell S. Stewart. American Council, Institute of Pacific Affairs and Webster Publishing Co., 1942.

Chang Hsin-hai. "The Treaty With Japan: A Chinese View." *Foreign Affairs* 26.3 (April 1948): 505–14.

Chennault, Claire Lee. *Way of a Fighter: The Memoirs of Claire Lee Chennault*. Edited by Robert Holz. Putnam, 1949.

Chicago Tribune. *War Cartoons by McCutcheon, Orr, Parrish, Somdal: December 8, 1941–September 28, 1942*. Chicago Tribune, 1942.

Chuman, Frank F. *The Bamboo People: The Law and Japanese-Americans*. Publisher's Inc., 1976.

Churchill, Winston. *The Grand Alliance*. Houghton Mifflin, 1950.

———. *Triumph and Tragedy*. Houghton Mifflin, 1953.

Clausen, Walter. "The Showdown in the Pacific." *Science Digest* 14.6 (December 1943): 88–91.

Clear, Warren J. "Close-Up of the Jap Fighting Man," *Reader's Digest*, November 1942, 124–30.

Cobbe, Frances Power. "Criminals, Idiots, Women, and Minors: Is the Classification Sound?" *Fraser's Magazine*, December 1868.

Colegrove, Kenneth W. *Militarism in Japan*. World Peace Foundation, 1936.

Commission on Wartime Relocation and Internment of Civilians. *Personal Justice Denied*. U.S. Government Printing Office, December 1982.

The Committee for the Compilation of Materials on Damage Caused by the Atomic Bombs in Hiroshima and Nagasaki. *Hiroshima and Nagasaki: The Physical, Medical, and Social Effects of the Atomic Bombings*. Basic Books, 1981; originally published in Japanese in 1979 by Iwanami Shoten.

Conn, Stetson. "The Decision to Evacuate the Japanese from the Pacific Coast (1942).

"In Kent Roberts Greenfield, ed., *Command Decisions.* 88–109. Harcourt, Brace & Co. for the Office of the Chief of Military History, 1959.

————, Rose C. Engelman, and Byron Fairchild. *Guarding the United States and Its Outposts.* Office of the Chief of Military History, Department of the Army, 1964.

Connell, Evan S. *Son of the Morning Star: Custer and the Little Bighorn.* North Point Press, 1984.

Cooper, Michael, S.J., ed. *They Came to Japan: An Anthology of European Reports on Japan, 1543–1640.* University of California Press, 1965.

Costello, John. *The Pacific War, 1941–1945.* Quill, 1981.

Craigie, Robert. *Behind the Japanese Mask.* Hutchinson & Co., 1946.

Craven, Welsey Frank, and James Lea Cate, eds. *The Army Air Forces in World War II.* 5 vols. University of Chicago Press and U.S. Office of Air Force History, 1948–53.

Creel, George. "To Understand Japan Consider Toyama." *Reader's Digest,* January 1945, 87–88.

Crow, Carl, ed. *Japan's Dream of World Empire: The Tanaka Memorial.* Harper & Brothers, 1942.

Culbert, David. " 'Why We Fight': Social Engineering for a Democratic Society at War." In K. R. M. Short, ed., *Film and Radio Propaganda in World War II.* 173–91. University of Tennessee Press, 1983.

Curtis, L. Perry, Jr. *Apes and Angels: The Irishman in Victorian Caricature.* Smithsonian Institution, 1971.

Dabney, Virginius. "Nearer and Nearer the Precipice." *Atlantic Monthly,* January 1943, 94–100.

Dai, Bingham. "Some Chinese Fears." *Asia and the Americas* November 1943, 611–19.

Daihyakka Jiten [Great Encyclopedia]. Heibonsha, 1937.

Daniels, Gordon. "Japanese Domestic Radio and Cinema Propaganda." In K. R. M. Short, ed., *Film and Radio Propaganda in World War II.* 293–318. University of Tennessee Press, 1983.

Daniels, Roger. *Concentration Camps USA: Japanese-Americans and World War II.* Holt, Rinehart & Winston, 1971.

————. *The Decision to Relocate the Japanese Americans.* Lippincott, 1975.

————. *The Politics of Prejudice.* Atheneum, 1968.

Daugherty, William E., and Morris Janowitz, eds. *A Psychological Warfare Casebook.* John Hopkins University Press, for the U.S. Operations Research Office, 1958.

de Las Casas, Bartolomé. *In Defense of the Indians: The Defense of the Most Reverend Lord, Don Fray Bartolomé de Las Casas of the Order of Preachers, Late Bishop of Chiapa, Against the Persecuters and Slanderers of the Peoples of the New World Discovered Across the Seas.* Translated and edited by Stafford Poole. Northern Illinois University Press, 1974.

De Mendelssohn, Peter. *Japan's Political Warfare.* George Allen & Unwin, 1944.

De Vos, George, and Hiroshi Wagatsuma. *Japan's Invisible Race: Caste in Culture and Personality.* University of California Press, 1966.

Dilks, David, ed. *The Diaries of Sir Alexander Cadogan, 1938–1945.* Cassell & Co., 1971.

Djilas, Milovan. *Conversations with Stalin.* Pelican, 1969.

Dollinger, Hans. *The Decline and Fall of Nazi Germany and Imperial Japan* (a translation of *Die Letzen Hundert Tage*). Crown, 1965.

Dower, John W. *Empire and Aftermath: Yoshida Shigeru and the Japanese Experience, 1878–1954.* Council on East Asian Studies, Harvard University, 1979.

————. "Rethinking World War Two in Asia." *Reviews in American History* 12.2 (June 1984): 155–69.

————. "Ways of Seeing, Ways of Remembering." In Dower and Japan Photographers Association, eds., *A Century of Japanese Photography.* Pantheon, 1980.

————, and John Junkerman, eds. *The Hiroshima Murals: The Art of Iri Maruki and Toshi Maruki.* Kodansha International, 1985.

Drinnon, Richard. *Facing West: The Metaphysics of Indian-Hating and Empire-Building.* New American Library, 1980.

Dudley, Edward J., and Maximillian E. Novak, eds. *The Wild Man Within: An Image in Western Thought from the Renaissance to Romanticism.* University of Pittsburgh Press, 1973.

Dull, Paul S. *Battle History of the Imperial Japanese Navy (1941–1945).* Naval Institute Press, 1978.

Dulles, Foster Rhea. *The Red Cross: A History.* Harper & Brothers, 1950.

Dupuy, R. Ernest. *World War II: A Compact History.* Hawthorn Books, 1969.

Duus, Peter. "Nagai Ryutarō and the 'White Peril,' 1905–1944." *Journal of Asian Studies* 31 (November 1971): 41–48.

Eden, Anthony. *The Eden Memoirs: The Reckoning.* Cassell & Co., 1965.

The Editors of *Fortune*, eds. *Japan and the Japanese: A Military Power We Must Defeat, A Pacific Problem We Must Solve.* Infantry Journal Press, 1944.

Eichelberger, Robert. *Dear Miss Em: General Eichelberger's War in the Pacific, 1942–1945.* Edited by Jay Luvaas. Greenwood Press, 1972.

Elison, George. *Deus Destroyed: The Image of Christianity in Early Modern Japan.* Harvard University Press, 1973.

Elsbree, Willard H. *Japan's Role in South-East Asian Nationalist Movements.* Harvard University Press, 1953.

Embree, John. "Anthropology and the War." *Bulletin of the American Association of University Professors* 32.3 (Autumn 1946): 485–95.

————. "Applied Anthropology and its Relationship to Anthropology." *American Anthropologist* 47.4 (October-December 1945): 635–37.

————. "Democracy in Postwar Japan." *American Journal of Sociology* 50.3 (November 1944): 205–7.

————. *The Japanese.* Smithsonian Institution War Background Studies no. 7, January 23, 1943.

————. "A Note on Ethnocentrism in Anthropology." *American Anthropologist* 52.3 (July-September 1950): 430–32.

————. "Resistance to Freedom—An Administrative Problem." *Applied Anthropology* (July-September 1943): 10–14.

————. "Standardized Error and Japanese Character: A Note on Political Interpretation." *World Politics* 2.3 (April 1950): 439–43.

Fahey, James J. *Pacific War Diary, 1942–1945.* Houghton Mifflin, 1963.

Farago, Ladislas. *Burn after Reading: The Espionage History of World War II.* Walker & Co., 1961.

Fearey, Robert A. *The Occupation of Japan: Second Phase, 1948–50.* Macmillan Co., 1950.

Fellers, Bonner F. Bonner Frank Fellers Collection. Hoover Institution.

Fleisher, Wilfrid. *What to Do with Japan.* Doubleday, Doran & Co., 1945.

Foner, Jack D. *Blacks and the Military in American History: A New Perspective.* Praeger, 1974.

Ford, Worthington Chauncey, ed. *Letters of Henry Adams (1858–1891).* Houghton Mifflin, 1930.

Foreign Morale Analysis Division, Bureau of Overseas Intelligence, Office of War Information, Record Group 208, National Archives. *The Attitudes of Japanese Prisoners of War: An Overall View.* Report no. 31, December 29, 1945.

————. *Bibliography of Articles and Books Relating to Japanese Psychology.* Report no. 24, August 25, 1945.

————. *Current Psychological and Social Tensions in Japan.* Special Report 5, June 1, 1945).

————. *Japanese Behavior Patterns.* Report no. 25, September 15, 1945.

————. *The Japanese Emperor.* Report no. 27, October 31, 1945.

————. *Japanese Personality and Reactions As Seen in Soldier's Diaries.* Report no. 30, December 19, 1945.

————. *Japanese Use of American Statements and Acts, Real or Alleged, in Propaganda to Create Fear.* Report no. 21, June 15, 1945.

————. *Principle Findings Regarding Japanese Morale During the War.* Report no. 26, September 20, 1945.

————. *Pro-American Sentiment among the Japanese During the War.* Report no. 32, December 31, 1945.

————. *Wartime Analysis of Japanese Morale.* 1946.

Foster, George M. *Applied Anthropology.* Little, Brown, 1969.

Foxx, Colonel A. G. "Your Enemy: The Jap." *Infantry Journal,* March 1945, 23–24.

Fried, Morton H. *The Study of Anthropology.* Crowell, 1972.

Fukukita, Yasunosuke, ed. *Japan's Innate Virility: Selections from Okakura and Nitobe.* Hokuseido, 1943.

Furuya, Yoshio. "Racial Integrity and Population Factor." *Contemporary Japan* 12.8 (August 1943): 1054–57.

Garfinkel, Herbert. *When Negroes March: The March on Washington Movement in the Organizational Politics for FEPC.* Free Press, 1959.

Gassner, John, and Dudley Nichols, eds. *Best Film Plays of 1943–1944.* Crown, 1945.

Gauntlett, John O., trans., and Robert K. Hall, ed. *Kokutai no Hongi: Cardinal Principles of the National Entity of Japan.* Harvard University Press, 1949.

Gillin, Donald G., and Charles Etter. "Staying On: Japanese Soldiers and Civilians in China, 1945–1949." *Journal of Asian Studies* 42.3 (May 1983), 497–518.

Gilman, Sander L. "Jews and Mental Illness: Medical Metaphors, Anti-Semitism, and the Jewish Response." *Journal of the History of the Behavioral Sciences* 20 (April 1984): 150–59.

Girdner, Audrie, and Anne Loftis. *The Great Betrayal: The Evacuation of the Japanese-Americans During World War II.* Macmillan Co., 1969.

Goette, John. *Japan Fights for Asia.* Harcourt, Brace & Co., 1943.

Goldschmidt, Walter, ed. *The Uses of Anthropology.* American Anthropological Association, 1979.

Goodman, Jack, ed. *While You Were Gone: A Report on Wartime Life in the United States.* Simon & Schuster, 1946.

Goralski, Robert. *World War II Almanac: 1931–1941.* Putnam, 1981.

Gorer, Geoffrey. "Themes in Japanese Culture." *Transactions of the New York Academy of Sciences,* Series II, 5.1 (November 1943): 106–24.

Gossett, Thomas F. *Race: The History of an Idea in America.* Southern Methodist University Press, 1963.

Gould, Stephen Jay. *The Mismeasure of Man.* Norton, 1981.

————. *The Panda's Thumb: More Reflections in Natural History.* Norton, 1980.

Gray, J. Glenn. *The Warriors: Reflections on Men in Battle.* Harper & Row, 1959.

Great Britain, Ministry of Information. *A Diagnosis of Japanese Psychology.* April 27, 1945.

————. *Japan: The Place and the Population.* April 1942.

————. *The Japanese People.* 1943.

Greater East Asia War Inquiry Commission, ed. *The American-British Challenge Directed against Nippon.* Mainichi Publishing Co., 1943.

Greenbie, Sydney. "Misconceptions about the Japanese," *American Mercury,* May 1944, 533–38.

Grew, Joseph C. "The People of Japan." In U.S. Office of Education, *Introducing the Peoples of the Far East.* Bulletin no. 7, 1945.

————. *Report From Tokyo.* Simon & Schuster, 1942.

————. *Ten Years in Japan.* Simon & Schuster, 1944.
Hagedorn, Hermann. *Roosevelt in the Badlands.* Houghton Mifflin, 1921.
Halsey, William F., and Joseph Bryan III. *Admiral Halsey's Story.* McGraw-Hill, 1947.
Hamerow, Theodore S. "The Hidden Holocaust." *Commentary,* March 1985, 32–42.
Hanke, Lewis. *All Mankind Is One: A Study of the Disputation between Bartolomé de Las Casas and Juan Ginés de Sepúlveda in 1550 on the Intellectual and Religious Capacity of the American Indian.* Northern Illinois University Press, 1974.
Haring, Douglas Gilbert. *Blood on the Rising Sun.* Macrae Smith Co., 1943.
————. *Personal Character and Cultural Milieu: A Collection of Readings.* 3rd rev. ed. Syracuse University Press, 1956.
Harris, Marvin. *The Rise of Anthropological Theory.* Crowell, 1968.
Hasegawa, Nyozekan. "Our 'Emaciated Endurance.'" *Contemporary Japan* 12.5 (May 1943): 570–76.
Hassler, R. Alfred. "Slaughter of the Innocent." *Fellowship* 10.2 (February 1944): 19–21.
Hastings, Max. *Bomber Command.* Dial, 1979.
Hauner, Milan. *India in Axis Strategy: Germany, Japan, and Indian Nationalists in the Second World War.* Klett-Cotta, Stuttgart, 1981.
Havens, Thomas R. H. *Valley of Darkness: The Japanese People and World War Two.* Norton, 1978.
Hayashida, Cullen Tadao. *Identity, Race and the Blood Ideology of Japan.* Ph.D. dissertation in sociology, University of Washington, Seattle, 1976.
Heinrichs, Waldo. *American Ambassador: Joseph C. Grew and the Development of the United States Diplomatic Tradition.* Little, Brown, 1966.
Herzog, Kristin. *Women, Ethnics, and Exotics: Images of Power in Mid-Nineteenth-Century Fiction.* University of Tennessee Press, 1983.
Hill, Milton. "The Lessons of Bataan." *Science Digest* 12.6 (December 1942): 52–56.
Hitler, Adolf. *Hitler's Secret Conversations, 1941–1944.* Farrar, Straus & Young, 1953.
————. *Mein Kampf.* Translated by Ralph Manheim. Houghton Mifflin, 1962.
Hogden, Margaret T. *Early Anthropology in the Sixteenth and Seventeenth Centuries.* University of Pennsylvania Press, 1964.
Hopkins, George F. "Bombing and the American Conscience During World War II." *The Historian* 28.3 (May 1966): 451–73.
Horikoshi, Jirō. *Eagles of Mitsubishi: The Story of the Zero Fighter.* University of Washington Press, 1980; translated from the 1970 Japanese edition by Kappa Books.
Hurd, Charles. *The Compact History of the American Red Cross.* Hawthorn Books, 1959.
Hutchinson, E. P. *Legislative History of American Immigration Policy, 1798–1965.* University of Pennsylvania Press, 1981.
Ienaga, Saburō. *The Pacific War, 1931–1945.* Pantheon, 1978.
————. *Sensō Sekinin* [War Responsibility]. Iwanami Shoten, 1985.
Iglehart, Charles. "America's War Casualties." *Fellowship* 11.7 (July 1945): 119–22.
Iizuka Koji. *Nihon no Guntai* [The Japanese Military]. Hyōronsha; reprint of 1950 ed. published by Tokyo Daigaku Kyōdō Kumiai Shuppansha, 1968.
Ike, Nobutake, trans. and ed. *Japan's Decision for War: Records of the 1941 Policy Conferences.* Stanford University Press, 1967.
Inahara Katsuji. *Amerika Minzoku Dan* [On the American People]. Ryūhinsha, 1943.
Inoguchi, Rikihei, and Tadashi Nakajima, with Roger Pineau. *The Divine Wind: Japan's Kamikaze Force in World War II.* Ballantine, 1958.
Institute of Pacific Relations Collection. Butler Library, Columbia University. Especially box 92 for "Provisional Analytic Summary of Institute of Pacific Relations Conference on Japanese Character Structure," December 16–17, 1944.
Iriye, Akira. *Pacific Estrangement: Japanese and American Expansion, 1897–1911.* Harvard University Press, 1972.
————. *Power and Culture: The Japanese-American War, 1941–1945.* Harvard University Press, 1981.

————, ed. *Mutual Images: Studies in American-Japanese Relations*. Harvard University Press, 1975.

Ishida Shuzō. *Seibutsu no Shinka* [Evolution of Life]. Hata Shoten, 1942.

Isono Fujiko, ed. *Ie: Gendai no Esprit* [Family: The Spirit of Modern Times]. Shibundō, 1965.

Iwate-ken Nōson Bunka Kondankai, ed. *Senbotsu Nōmin Heishi no Tegami* [Letters of Peasant Conscripts Killed in Battle]. Iwanami Shinsho no. 424, 1961.

Janeway, Eliot. "Fighting a White Man's War." *Asia and the Americas* January 1943, 5.

Japan, Bureau of Publicity, Department of General Affairs, Japanese Military Administration [Philippines], ed. *The Official Journal of the Japanese Military Administration*. Vol. 3. May 11, 1942.

————. Kōseishō, Jinkō Minzokubu [Ministry of Health and Welfare, Population and Race Section]. *Sensō no Jinkō ni oyobosu Eikyō* [The Influence of War on Population] and *Yamato Minzoku o Chū kaku to suru Sekai Seisaku no Kentō* [Investigation of Global Policy with the Yamato Race as Nucleus], originally prepared in 1942–43 and reprinted as *Minzoku Jinkō Seisaku Kenkyū Shiryō* [Research Documents on Race and Population Policy]. 7 vol. Bunsei Shoin, 1982.

————. Mombushō [Ministry of Education], ed. *Dai Tōa Sensō to Warera* [The Greater East Asia War and Ourselves]. 1942.

————. Naikaku Sōryokusen Kenkyūjo [Cabinet Institute for the Study of Total War]. *Chōkisen Kenkyū* [A Study of Protracted War]. March 1945.

————. Ōkurashō Zaisei Shishitsu [Ministry of Finance, Financial History Section], ed. *Shōwa Zaisei Shi: Shūsen kara Heiwa made* [Financial History of the Shōwa Period: From the End of the War to the Peace Treaty]. Vol. 19, *Tōkei* [Statistics]. Tōyō Keizai Shimbun, 1978.

Jensen, J. Vernon. "British Voices on the Eve of the American Revolution: Trapped by the Family Metaphor." *Quarterly Journal of Speech* 63 (February 1977): 43–50.

Johnson, Chalmers. *Peasant Nationalism and Communist Power: The Emergence of Revolutionary China, 1937–1945*. Stanford University Press, 1962.

Johnson, John J. *Latin America in Caricature*. University of Texas Press, 1980.

Johnson, Sheila K. *American Attitudes toward Japan, 1941–1975*. American Enterprise Institute and Hoover Institution, 1975.

Johnston, Eric. "America's World Chance." *Reader's Digest*, June 1945, 5–9.

Johnston, George H. *New Guinea Diary*. Angus & Robertson, 1944.

————. *Pacific Partner*. Duell, Sloan & Pearce, 1944.

————. *The Toughest Fighting in the World*. Duell, Sloan & Pearce, 1943.

Jones, Edgar L. "Fighting with Words: Psychological Warfare in the Pacific." *Atlantic Monthly*, August 1945, 47–51.

————. "One War Is Enough." *Atlantic Monthly*, February 1946, 48–53.

Jordan, Winthrop D. *White over Black: American Attitudes toward the Negro, 1550–1812*. University of North Carolina Press, 1968.

Kai, Kenzo. *Sakura no Kaori: The Fragrance of Cherry Blossoms*. Foreign Affairs Association of Japan, 1933.

Kaigo Tokiomi, ed. *Nihon Kyōkasho Taikei, Kindai-hen* [Outline of Japanese Textbooks, Modern Period]. Kodansha, esp. vol. 8 on Japanese language (*Kokygo 5*, 1964), vol. 17 on geography (*Chiri 3*, 1966), and vol. 20 on history (*Rekishi 3*, 1962).

Kawahara Hiroshi and Fujii Shōzō, eds. *Ni-Chū Kankei Shi no Kiso Chishiki* [Basic Knowledge of the History of Sino-Japanese Relations]. Yūhikaku, 1974.

Kawamura Tadao. *Beikoku Kokujin no Kenkyū* [A Study of the American Negro]. Fuji Shoten, 1943.

Kawashima Takeyoshi. *Ideorogi to Shite no Kazoku Seidō* [The Family System As Ideology]. Iwanami Shoten, 1975.

Keene, Donald. "The Barren Years: Japanese War Literature." *Monumenta Nipponica* 33.1 (Spring 1978): 67–112.

———. *The Japanese Discovery of Europe, 1720–1830.* Rev. ed. Stanford University Press, 1969.

———. "Japanese Literature and Politics in the 1930s." *Journal of Japanese Studies* 2.2 (Summer 1976): 225–48.

———. "Japanese Writers and the Greater East Asia War." In his *Landscapes and Portraits: Appreciations of Japanese Culture,* 300–321. Martin Secker & Warburg, 1971.

Kiernan, V. G. *The Lords of Humankind: Black Man, Yellow Man and White Man in an Age of Empire.* Little, Brown, 1969.

Kinbara Samon and Takemae Eiji. *Shōwa Shi* [Shōwa History]. Yūhikaku, 1982.

King, Ernest J., and Walter Muir Whitehall. *Fleet Admiral King: A Naval Record.* Norton, 1952.

Kipling, Rudyard. *Rudyard Kipling's Verse: Definitive Edition.* Doubleday, Doran & Co., 1940.

Kirby, Stanley W. *Singapore: The Chain of Disaster.* Cassell & Co., 1971.

———. *The War against Japan.* Her Majesty's Stationery Office, 1957.

Kitahara, Michio. "Popular Culture in Japan: A Psychoanalytic Interpretation," *Journal of Popular Culture* 17.1 (Summer 1983): 103–10.

Kiyono Kenji. *Nippon Jinshuron no Hensen Shi* [A History of Changing Theories about the Japanese Race]. Koyama Shoten, 1944.

Kiyosawa Kiyoshi. *Ankoku Nikki* [Diary of Darkness]. Tōyō Keizai Shimpōsha, 1954.

Kluckhohn, Clyde. *Mirror for Man: The Relation of Anthropology to Modern Life.* McGraw-Hill, 1949.

Knox, Donald. *Death March: The Survivors of Bataan.* Harcourt Brace Jovanovich, 1981.

Kodama Kota and Kuno Takeshi, eds. *Nihonshi Zuroku 4: Meiji-Gendai* [Illustrated History of Japan 4: From Meiji to the Present]. Yoshikawa Kobunkan, 1964.

The Kodansha Encyclopedia of Japan. 8 vols. Kodansha, 1983.

Kogan, Herman. "These Nips Are Nuts." *American Legion Magazine* 139 (February 1945): 88–89.

Kohno, Tetsu. "Debates on the Jewish Question in Japan." *Hōsei Daigaku Kyōyōbu Kiyō* 46 (January 1983): 1–33.

Koide, Shogo. "Our Juvenile Stories." *Contemporary Japan* 10.7 (July 1941): 922–30.

Komota Nobuo et al. *Nihon Ryūkōka Shi* [History of Japanese Popular Songs]. Shakai Shisōsha, 1970.

Kong, Walter. "How We Grill the Chinese." *Asia* September 1942, 520–23.

Konishi Shirō. *Nishikie: Bakumatsu Meiji no Rekishi* [Brocade Pictures: A History of Bakumatsu and Meiji Japan] vol. 11. Kodansha, 1977.

——— and Hayashi Shigeru, eds. *Nihon no Rekishi, Bessatsu 4: Zuroku, Isshin kara Gendai* [History of Japan, Special Volume 4: Illustrated Record, From the Restoration to Modern Times]. Chūō Kōronsha, 1967.

Kōsaka Masaaki. "Dai Tōa Kyōeiken e no Michi" [The Road to the Greater East Asia Co-Prosperity Sphere]. *Kaizō* 24.1 (January 1942): 16–37.

———. et al. "Sōryokusen no Tetsugaku" [The Philosophy of Total War]. *Chūō Kōron* 58.1 (January 1943): 54–112.

———. "Tōa Kyōeiken no Rinrisei to Rekishisei" [The Historical and Moral Nature of the East Asia Co-Prosperity Sphere]. *Chūō Kōron* 57.4 (April 1942): 120–61.

Kranzler, David. *Japanese, Nazis, and Jews: The Jewish Refugee Community of Shanghai, 1938–1945.* Yeshiva University Press, 1976.

———. "Japanese Policy toward the Jews, 1938–1941." *Japan Interpreter* 11.4 (1977): 493–527.

Kroeber, A. L., ed. *Anthropology Today: An Encyclopedic Inventory.* University of Chicago Press, 1953.

La Barre, Weston. "Some Observations on Character Structure in the Orient." *Psychiatry: Journal of Biology and the Pathology of Interpersonal Relations* 8.3 (August 1945): 319–42.

La Farge, John. *Reminiscences of the South Seas*. Doubleday, Page & Co., 1916.

Lamott, Willis. *Nippon: The Crime and Punishment of Japan*. John Day Co., 1944.

———. "What Not to Do with Japan." *Reader's Digest*, (August 1945), 23–26.

Landau, Ellen G. *Artists for Victory: An Exhibition Catalog*. Library of Congress, 1983.

Lea, Homer. *The Valor of Ignorance*. Harper & Brothers, 1942 (originally 1909).

Leahy, William D. *I Was There: The Personal Story of the Chief of Staff to Presidents Roosevelt and Truman Based on His Notes and Diaries Made at the Time*. McGraw-Hill, 1950.

Lebow, Richard Ned. *White Britain and Black Ireland: The Influence of Stereotypes on Colonial Policy*. Ishi Institute for the Study of Human Issues, 1976.

Lebra, Joyce C., ed. *Japan's Greater East Asia Co-Prosperity Sphere in World War II: Selected Readings and Documents*. Oxford University Press, 1975.

Lebra, Takie Sugiyama. *Japanese Patterns of Behavior*. University of Hawaii Press, 1976.

Lee, Bradford A. *Britain and the Sino-Japanese War, 1937–1939*. Stanford University Press and Oxford University Press, 1973.

Lee, Changsoo, and George De Vos. *Koreans in Japan: Ethnic Conflict and Accomodation*. University of California Press, 1981.

LaFeber, Walter. *America, Russia, and the Cold War, 1945–1966*. Wiley, 1967.

Leighton, Alexander. *Human Relations in a Changing World: Observations on the Use of the Social Sciences*. Dutton, 1949.

———, and Morris Opler. "Psychological Warfare and the Japanese Emperor." In Robert Hunt, ed., *Personalities and Culture: Readings in Psychological Anthropology*, 251–60. Natural History Press, 1967 (originally published in 1946).

LeMay, Curtis E., with MacKinlay Kantor. *Mission with LeMay: My Story*. Doubleday, 1965.

Lerner, Daniel, and Harold D. Lasswell, eds. *The Policy Sciences: Recent Developments in Scope and Method*. Stanford University Press, 1951.

Lin Yutang. *Between Tears and Laughter*. John Day Co., 1948.

Lincoln, C. Eric. *The Black Muslims in America*. Beacon Press, 1961.

Lindbergh, Charles A. *Autobiography of Values*. Harcourt Brace Jovanovich, 1978.

———. *The Wartime Journals of Charles A. Lindbergh*. Harcourt Brace Jovanovich, 1970.

Lindesmith, Alfred R., and Anselm L. Strauss. "A Critique of Culture-Personality Writings." *American Sociological Review* 15.5 (October 1950): 587–600.

Linebarger, Paul. M. A. *Psychological Warfare*. Infantry Journal Press, 1948.

Linenthal, Edward Tabor. *Changing Images of the Warrior Hero in America: A History of Popular Symbolism*. Edwin Mellen Press, 1982.

Logan, Rayford F., ed. *What the Negro Wants*. University of North Carolina Press, 1944.

Louis, William Roger. *Imperialism at Bay, 1941–1945: The United States and the Decolonialization of the British Empire*. Oxford University Press, 1977.

Lovejoy, Arthur O. *The Great Chain of Being: A Study of the History of an Idea*. Harvard University Press, 1961.

Low, David. *Years of Wrath*. Simon & Schuster, 1946.

Lowenheim, Francis L., et al., eds. *Roosevelt and Churchill: Their Secret Wartime Correspondence*. Saturday Review Press, 1975.

Löwith, Karl. "The Japanese Mind." *Fortune* December 1943, 132–35, 230–35.

Mainichi Shimbunsha, ed. *Nihon News Eiga Shi—Bessatsu, Ichiokunin no Shōwa Shi* [History of Japanese News Reels—Special Volume of "History of the Hundred-Million People of the Shōwa Period"]. Mainichi Shimbunsha, 1977.

———, ed. *Shōwa Manga Shi—Bessatsu, Ichiokunin no Shōwa Shi* [History of Cartoons of the Shōwa Period—Special Volume of "History of the Hundred-Million People of the Shōwa Period"]. Mainichi Shimbunsha, 1977.

————, ed. *Shōwa Ryūkōka Shi—Bessatsu, Ichiokunin no Shōwa Shi* [History of Popular Songs of the Shōwa Period—Special Volume of "History of the Hundred-Million People of the Shōwa Period"). Mainichi Shimbunsha, 1979.

Manchester, William. *American Caesar: Douglas MacArthur, 1880–1964.* Dell, 1978.

————. *Goodbye, Darkness: A Memoir of the Pacific War.* Dell, 1980.

Marcu, Valeriu. "American Prophet of Total War." *American Mercury* April 1942, 473–78.

Marquand, J. P. *Thank You, Mr. Moto and Mr. Moto Is So Sorry.* Curtis Publishing Co., 1977.

————. "These People Are Like Ourselves." *Asia* July 1941, 361–64.

Martin, Bernd. "Japan und der Krieg in Ostasien: Kommentierender Bericht über das Schrifttum." *Historische Zeitschrift,* Sonderhaft (Special Issue) 8, 1980, 79–219.

Mashbir, Sidney Forrester. *I Was an American Spy.* Vantage Press, 1953.

May, Ernest R., ed. *Knowing One's Enemies: Intelligence Assessment before the Two World Wars.* Princeton University Press, 1984.

McCoy, Alfred W., ed. *Southeast Asia under Japanese Rule.* Yale University Southeast Asia Studies, Monograph Series no. 22, 1980.

McGinnis, H. C. "Which War Comes Next?" *Catholic World,* July 1945, 329–35.

McLaine, Ian. *Ministry of Morale: Home Front Morale and the Ministry of Information in World War II.* George Allen & Unwin, 1979.

McWilliams, Carey. *Prejudice: Japanese Americans—Symbol of Racial Intolerance.* Little, Brown, 1944.

Mead, Margaret. *Ruth Benedict.* Columbia University Press, 1974.

————, and Rhoda Metraux, eds. *The Study of Culture at a Distance.* University of Chicago Press, 1953.

Mears, Helen. *Mirror for Americans: Japan.* Houghton Mifflin, 1948.

Meigs, Montgomery Cunningham. *Managing Uncertainty: Vannevar Bush, James B. Conant and the Development of the Atomic Bomb, 1940–1945.* Ph.D. dissertation in history, University of Wisconsin-Madison, 1982.

Menefree, Sidney C. "Japan's Global Conceit." *Asia and the Americas,* July 1943, 330–32.

Meo, L. D. *Japan's Radio War on Australia, 1941–1945.* Melbourne University Press, 1968.

Merrill, James M. *A Sailor's Admiral: A Biography of William F. Halsey.* Crowell, 1976.

Meyers, Ramon H., and Mark R. Peattie, eds. *The Japanese Colonial Empire, 1895–1945.* Princeton University Press, 1984.

Miller, Stuart Creighton. *"Benevolent Assimilation": The American Conquest of the Philippines, 1899–1903.* Yale University Press, 1982.

————. *The Unwelcome Immigrant: The American Image of the Chinese, 1785–1882.* University of California Press, 1969.

Minear, Richard H. "Cross-Cultural Perception and World War II: American Japanists of the 1940s and Their Images of Japan." *International Studies Quarterly* 24.4 (December 1980): 555–80.

————. "Helen Mears, Asia, and American Asianists." Occasional Papers Series no. 7, Asian Studies Committee, International Area Studies Program, University of Massachusetts at Amherst, 1981.

————. "The Wartime Studies of Japanese National Character." *Japan Interpreter,* Summer 1980, 36–59.

Modell, Judith Schachter. *Ruth Benedict: Patterns of a Life.* University of Pennsylvania Press, 1983.

Mori Ōgai. *Mori Ōgai Zenshū* [Collected Works of Mori Ōgai]. Iwanami Shoten, 1952.
Morimura Seiichi. *Akuma no Hōshoku* [The Devil's Gluttony]. Kobunsha, 1981.
Morison, Samuel Eliot. *History of United States Naval Operations in World War II.* Little, Brown, 1951.
Morosawa Yoko. "Jōsei no Kyōgū" [The Circumstances of Women]. In Wakamori Tarō, ed., *Gunkoku kara Minshuka e* [From Military State to Democratization], vol. 10 in Wakamori, ed., *Nihon Seikatsu Bunka Shi* [History of Daily Life and Culture in Japan]. Kawade Shobō, 1975.
Morris, Ivan. *The Nobility of Failure: Tragic Heroes in the History of Japan.* Meridian, 1976.
Morrison, Ian. "New Light on the Japanese." *Science Digest* 15.3 (March 1944): 54–56.
———. *Our Japanese Foe.* Putnam, 1943.
Mosse, George L. *Toward the Final Solution: A History of European Racism.* University of Wisconsin Press, 1984.
Murphy, William Thomas. "The Method of *Why We Fight.*" *Journal of Popular Film* 1 (1972): 185–96.
Muzumdar, Haridas T. "Asians Ask Some Questions." *Asia* July 1942, 416–18.
Myers, Debs, Jonathan Kilbourn, and Richard Harrity, eds. *Yank—the GI Story of the War.* Duell, Sloan & Pearce, 1947.
Myrdal, Gunnar. *An American Dilemma: The Negro Problem and Modern Democracy.* Harper & Row, 1944.
Nagahara, Keiji. "The Medieval Origins of the *Eta-Hinin.*" *Journal of Japanese Studies* 5.2 (1979): 385–403.
Nahm, Andrew C., ed. *Korea under Japanese Colonial Rule.* Center for Korean Studies, Western Michigan University, 1973.
Nakamura, Koya. *History of Japan.* Board of Tourist Industries, Japanese Government Railways, 1939.
Namikawa, Ryō. "Japanese Overseas Broadcasting: a Personal View." In K. R. M. Short, ed., *Film and Radio Propaganda in World War II*, 319–33. University of Tennessee Press, 1983.
Naruhashi Hitoshi et al., eds. *Taiheiyō Sensō Meigashū* [The Pacific War Art Collection]. Nobel Shobō, 1967.
Nash, Ernest T. "Japan's Schizophrenia." *Asia* September 1942, 526–28.
Nelson, Donald M. "China Can Also Help Us." *Collier's,* May 12, 1945.
Nevins, Allan. "How We Felt About the War." In Jack Goodman, ed., *While You Were Gone: A Report on Wartime Life in the United States.* Simon & Schuster, 1946.
Newell, William H., ed., *Japan in Asia.* Singapore University Press, 1981.
Nichols, H. G., ed., *Washington Despatches, 1941–1945: Weekly Political Reports from the British Embassy.* University of Chicago Press, 1981.
Ninomiya, Shigeaki. "An Inquiry Concerning the Origin, Development, and Present Situation of the Eta in Relation to the History of Social Classes in Japan." *Transactions of the Asiatic Society of Japan* 10 (2nd Series, December 1933): 47–154.
Ogi Shinzō. *Shōwa Shomin Bunka Shi* [History of the Culture of the Common People in the Shōwa Period]. NHK Books, 1971.
Ōgushi Toyoo. "Nippon Minzoku Sekaikan no Kakuritsu" [Establishing a Japanese Racial Worldview]. *Bungei Shunjū* 20.1 (January 1942), 24–33.
Ohnuki-Tierney, Emiko. *Illness and Culture in Contemporary Japan: An Anthropological View.* Cambridge University Press, 1984.
Okamoto, Shumpei, ed. *Impressions of the Front: Woodcuts of the Sino-Japanese War.* Philadelphia Museum of Art, 1983.
Okawa Nobuyoshi, ed. *Dai Saigo Zenshū* [Collected Works of the Great Saigo]. Heibonsha, 1927.
O'Neill, Richard. *Suicide Squads.* Ballantine, 1981.

Ono, Setsuko. *A Western Image of Japan: What Did the West See through the Eyes of Loti and Hearn?* Thèse no. 235, Institut Universitaire de Haute Études Internationales, Université de Genève, 1972.

Ōta Masahide. *Sōshi: Okinawa-sen* [Complete History of the Battle of Okinawa]. Iwanami Shoten, 1982.

Ottley, Roi. *'New World A-Coming': Inside Black America.* Houghton Mifflin, 1943.

Overy, R. J. *The Air War, 1939–1945.* Europa Publications, 1980.

Padover, Saul K. "Japanese Race Propaganda." *Public Opinion Quarterly* 7.2 (Summer 1943): 191–204.

Pagden, Anthony. *The Fall of Natural Man: The American Indian and the Origins of Comparative Ethnology.* Cambridge University Press, 1982.

Pal, Radhabinod. *International Military Tribunal for the Far East, Dissentient Judgment.* Sanyal & Co., Calcutta, 1953.

Peattie, Mark R. *Ishiwara Kanji and Japan's Confrontation with the West.* Princeton University Press, 1966.

Peffer, Nathaniel. "Japanese Superman? That, Too, Is a Fallacy." *New York Times Magazine,* March 22, 1942.

Pelz, Stephen E. *Race to Pearl Harbor: The Failure of the Second London Conference and the Onset of World War II.* Harvard University Press, 1974.

Perrett, Geoffrey. *Days of Sadness, Years of Triumph: The American People, 1939–1945.* Coward, McCann & Geoghegan, 1973.

Perry, Glen C. H. *"Dear Bart": Washington Views of World War II.* Greenwood Press, 1982.

Pettenkofer, Anton. "Hitler Means to Destroy Japan." *Asia* November 1941, 653–60.

Piccigallo, Philip R. *The Japanese on Trial: Allied War Crimes Operations in the East, 1945–1951.* University of Texas Press, 1979.

Polenberg, Richard. *War and Society: The United States, 1941–1945.* Lippincott, 1972.

Powell, John W. "Japan's Biological Weapons, 1930–1945: A Hidden Chapter in History." *Bulletin of Concerned Asian Scholars* 12.4 (October–December 1980): 2–17.

———. "Japan's Germ Warfare: The U.S. Cover-Up of a War Crime." *Bulletin of Concerned Asian Scholars* 12 (1980): 2–17.

Prange, Gordon W. *At Dawn We Slept: The Untold Story of Pearl Harbor.* McGraw-Hill, 1981.

Pratt, Fletcher. *Sea Power and Today's War.* Harrison-Hilton Books, 1939.

Pratt, Sir John T. *War and Politics in China.* Jonathan Cape, 1943.

Price, Janet. *The Black Book of Villains.* David & Charles, 1975.

Price, Willard. *Japan and the Son of Heaven.* Duell, Sloan & Pearce, 1945.

Pritchard, R. John, and Sonia Magbanua Zaide, eds. *The Tokyo War Crimes Trial: The Complete Transcripts of the Proceedings of the International Military Tribunal for the Far East.* 21 vols. Garland Publishing, 1981.

Purcell, Victor. *The Chinese in Southeast Asia.* Oxford University Press, 1951.

Pyle, Ernie. *Last Chapter.* Henry Holt & Co., 1945.

Pyle, Kenneth B. *The New Generation in Meiji Japan: Problems in Cultural Identity, 1885–1895.* Stanford University Press, 1969.

Ramsdell, Daniel B. "Asia Askew: U.S. Best-Sellers on Asia, 1931–1980." *Bulletin of Concerned Asian Scholars* 15.4 (October-December 1983): 2–25.

Reid, Anthony. "Indonesia: From Briefcase to Samurai Sword." In Alfred W. McCoy, ed., *Southeast Asia under Japanese Rule.* Yale University Southeast Asia Studies, Monograph Series no. 22, 1980.

Rhodes, Anthony. *Propaganda, the Art of Persuasion: World War II.* Chelsea House Publishers, 1976.

Richards, Denis, and Hilary St. George Saunders. *Royal Air Force, 1939–1945.* Her Majesty's Stationery Office, 1954.

Roling, B. B. A., and C. F. Ruter, eds. *The Tokyo Judgment: The International Military*

Tribunal for the Far East (I.M.T.F.E.), 29 April 1946—12 November 1948. Vol. 1. APA-University Press Amsterdam BV, 1977.

Romulo, Carlos P. *I See the Philippines Rise.* Doubleday, 1946.

Roosevelt, Franklin D. *The Public Papers and Addresses of Franklin D. Roosevelt, 1939 Volume: War—and Neutrality.* Macmillan Co., 1941.

Rosenberg, Bruce A. *Custer and the Epic of Defeat.* University of Pennsylvania Press, 1974.

Rosenfarb, Joseph. *Highway to Tokyo.* Little, Brown, 1943.

Rosinger, Lawrence K. "China As a Post-War Market." *Foreign Policy Report* 20.20 (January 1, 1945), 250–63.

Roskill, Stephen. *Hankey: Man of Secrets, Volume II, 1919–1931.* William Collins Sons & Co., 1972.

———. *Naval Policy between the Wars.* Wm. Collins & Co., 1976.

Rostow, Eugene V. "The Japanese American Cases—A Disaster." *Yale Law Journal* 54.3 (June 1945): 489–533.

Roth, Andrew. *Dilemma in Japan.* Little, Brown, 1945.

Royal Institute of International Affairs. *Japan in Defeat: A Report by a Chatham House Study Group.* Oxford University Press, 1945.

Russell, Edward Frederick Langley (Lord Russell of Liverpool). *The Knights of Bushido.* Berkley Medallion, 1958.

Ryūdō Shuppan, ed. *Fukurokuban: Shōwa Daizasshi: Senchūhen* [Reproductions from Major Shōwa Magazines: Wartime]. Ryūdō, 1978.

Said, Edward. *Orientalism.* Pantheon, 1978.

Saitō Tadashi, Ōno Seiichirō (or Kiyoichirō), and Matsushita Masahisa (or Masatoshi). "Dai Tōa Sengen no Shingi" [The True Meaning of the Declaration of the Greater East Asia War]. *Kaizō* 26.3 (March 1944): 4–25.

Sakaeda Yoshitaka. "Kyōei Kūkan no Kōseitaironteki Haaku" [Comprehending the Structure of Co-Prosperity Space]. *Chūō Kōron* 57.5 (May 1942): 22–33.

Sansom, George. *The Western World and Japan.* Knopf, 1950.

Schaffer, Ronald. "American Military Ethics in World War II: The Bombing of German Civilians." *Journal of American History* 67.2 (September 1980): 318–34.

Schonberger, Howard. "John Foster Dulles and the China Question in the Making of the Japanese Peace Treaty." In Thomas W. Burkman, ed., *The Occupation of Japan: The International Context.* MacArthur Foundation, 1984.

Sherrod, Robert. "Civilian Suicides on Saipan." *Reader's Digest,* October 1944, 83–84.

———. "Perhaps He Is Human." *Reader's Digest,* September 1943, 74.

Shillony, Ben-Ami. *Politics and Culture in Wartime Japan.* Oxford University Press, 1981.

Shimizu Isao, ed. *Taiheiyō Sensōki Manga* [Cartoons of the Pacific War Period]. Bijitsu Dōjinsha, 1971.

Shindler, Colin. *Hollywood Goes to War: Films and American Society, 1939–1952.* Routledge & Kegan Paul, 1979.

Short, K. R. M., ed. *Film and Radio Propaganda in World War II.* University of Tennessee Press, 1983.

Silberpfennig, Judith. "Psychological Aspects of Current Japanese and German Paradoxa." *Psychoanalytic Review* 32.1 (January 1945): 73–85.

Silberstein, Josef, ed. *Southeast Asia in World War II: Four Essays.* Yale University Southeast Asia Studies, Monograph Series no. 7, 1966.

Singh, Mohan. *Soldiers' Contribution to Indian Independence: The Epic of the Indian National Army.* Army Educational Stores, New Delhi, 1974.

Sledge, E. B. *With the Old Breed at Peleliu and Okinawa.* Presidio Press, 1981.

Slim, William. *Defeat into Victory.* David McKay Co., 1961.

Slotkin, Richard. "Dreams and Genocide: The American Myth of Regeneration through Violence." *Journal of Popular Culture* 5.1 (Summer 1971): 38–59.

————. *Regeneration through Violence: The Mythology of the American Frontier, 1600–1860.* Wesleyan University Press, 1973.

Smith, Kingsbury. "Our Government's Plan for a Defeated Japan." *American Mercury* January 1944, 29–36.

Smith, Robert. *Ancestor Worship in Contemporary Japan.* Cornell University Press, 1974.

Smith, S. E., ed. *The United States Marine Corps in World War II.* Random House, 1969.

Snow, Edgar. *The Battle for Asia.* World Publishing Co., 1942.

Sodei Rinjirō and Fukushima Jūrō. *Makkāsā: Sengo Nihon no Genten* [MacArthur: The Origins of Postwar Japan]. Nihon Hōsō Shuppan Kyōkai, 1982.

Spector, Ronald H. *Eagle against the Sun: The American War with Japan.* Free Press, 1984.

Spinks, Charles Nelson. "Repeal Chinese Exclusion!" *Asia* February 1942, 92–94.

Spitzer, Hermann M. "Psychoanalytic Approaches to the Japanese Character." *Psychoanalysis and the Social Sciences* 1 (1947): 131–56.

Stanton, William. *The Leopard's Spots: Scientific Attitudes toward Race in America, 1815–59.* University of Chicago Press, 1960.

Steadman, John M. *The Myth of Asia.* Simon & Schuster, 1969.

Steele, Richard W. " 'The Greatest Gangster Movie Ever Filmed': *Prelude to War.*" *Prologue* 11.4 (Winter 1979): 221–35.

Steinberg, Rafael, et al. *Return to the Philippines.* Time-Life Books, 1979.

Steiner, Jesse. *Behind the Japanese Mask.* Macmillan Co., 1943.

Stephan, John J. *Hawaii under the Rising Sun: Japan's Plans for Conquest after Pearl Harbor.* University of Hawaii Press, 1984.

————. "The Tanaka Memorial (1927): Authentic or Spurious?" *Modern Asian Studies* 7.4 (1973): 733–45.

Stevenson, Robert Louis. *The Travels and Essays of Robert Louis Stevenson.* Scribner, 1924.

Stimson, Henry L. *Henry L. Stimson Diaries.* Yale University Libraries Microfilm.

Stonequist, Everett. "How the Japs Got That Way." *Science Digest* 12.5 (November 1942): 33–36.

Sukarno, as told to Cindy Adams. *Sukarno: An Autobiography.* Bobbs-Merrill, 1965.

Sumiya, Mikio. "The Emergence of Modern Japan." In Kazuo Okochi, Bernard Karsh, and Solomon Levine, eds., *Workers and Employers in Japan: The Japanese Employment Relations System,* 15–48. Princeton University Press, 1974.

Suzuki Akira and Yamamoto Akira, eds. *Hiroku: Boryaku Senden Bira—Taiheiyō Sensō no Kami Bakudan* [Propaganda Leaflets—Paper Bullets of the Pacific War]. Kodansha, 1977.

Suzuki, D. T. *Tōyōteki "Ichi"* [Asian "Oneness"]. Daitō Shuppansha, 1942.

Suzuki, Peter T. "Anthropologists in the Wartime Camps for Japanese Americans: A Documentary Study." *Dialectical Anthropology* 6.1 (August 1981): 23–60.

————. "A Retrospective Analysis of a Wartime 'National Character' Study." *Dialectical Anthropology* 5.1 (May 1980): 33–46.

Takeuchi Yoshimi. "Kindai no Chōkoku" [Transcending the Modern]. In *Takeuchi Yoshimi Zenshū* [Collected Works of Takeuchi Yoshimi], vol. 8. Chikuma Shobo, 1980.

Tauber, Irene B. *The Population of Japan.* Princeton University Press, 1958.

Taylor, A. Marjorie. *The Language of World War II.* Rev. ed. H. W. Wilson Co., 1948.

Terkel, Studs. *"The Good War": An Oral History of World War Two.* Pantheon, 1984.

Thorne, Christopher. *Allies of a Kind: The United States, Britain, and the War against Japan, 1941–1945.* Oxford University Press, 1978.

————. "Britain and the Black G.I.s: Racial Issues and Anglo-American Relations in 1942." *New Community: Journal of the Community Relations Commission* 3.3 (Summer 1974): 262–71.

————. "Racial Aspects of the Far Eastern War of 1941–1945." *Proceedings of the British Academy* 66 (1980): 329–77.

Timperley, H. J. *Japanese Terror in China.* Modern Age Books, 1938.

Tinker, Hugh. *Race, Conflict and the International Order: From Empire to United Nations.* St. Martin's, 1977.

Todorov, Tzvetan. *The Conquest of America: The Question of the Other.* Translated by Richard Howard. Harper & Row, 1982.

Tokayer, Marvin, and May Swartz. *The Fugu Plan: The Untold Story of the Japanese and the Jews During World War II.* Paddington Press, 1979.

Tokutomi Iichirō. *Hisshō Kokumin Tokuhon* [A Citizen's Reader for Certain Victory]. Mainichi Shimbunsha, 1944.

Toland, John. *The Rising Sun: The Decline and Fall of the Japanese Empire, 1936–1945.* Random House, 1970.

Tolischus, Otto D., ed. *Through Japanese Eyes.* Reynal & Hitchcock, 1945.

————. *Tokyo Record.* Reynal & Hitchcock, 1943.

Tregaskis, Richard. *Guadalcanal Diary.* Random House, 1942.

Trotsky, Leon. *Writings of Leon Trotsky, 1939–1940.* Pathfinder Press, 1973.

Tsuji, Masanobu. *Singapore: The Japanese Version.* Constable & Co., 1962.

Tsunoda, Ryusaku, et al. *Sources of Japanese Tradition.* Columbia University Press, 1958.

Tsurumi, Kazuko. *Social Change and the Individual: Japan before and after Defeat in World War II.* Princeton University Press, 1970.

Tsurumi Shunsuke, ed. *Nihon no Hyakunen 3: Hateshinaki Sensen* [Japan's Hundred Years, 3: The Endless War Front]. Chikuma Shobo, 1967.

Tuchman, Barbara. *Practicing History: Selected Essays.* Knopf, 1981.

Uchikawa Yoshimi, ed. *Gendai Shiryō 41: Masu Media Tōsei 2* [Contemporary Documents 41: Control of Mass Media 2]. Misuzu Shobō, 1975.

United Nations, Economic and Social Council, 2nd Year, 4th Session. *Report of the Working Group for Asia and the Far East.* Supplement no. 10, 1947.

U.S. Army. *Reports of General MacArthur.* 4 vols. Government Printing Office, 1966.

————. Statistical and Accounting Branch, Office of the Adjutant General. *Army Battle Casualties and Nonbattle Deaths in World War II: Final Report, 7 December 1941 —31 December 1946.* Government Printing Office, 1953.

U.S. Department of State. *Foreign Relations of the United States: Conferences at Washington, 1941–1942, and Casablanca, 1943.* Government Printing Office, 1968.

————. *Foreign Relations of the United States: Japan 1931–1941.* Government Printing Office, 1943.

————. *Foreign Relations of the United States, 1946.* Government Printing Office, 1971.

U.S. Navy, Bureau of Medicine and Surgery, Division of Medical Statistics. *The History of the Medical Department of the United States Navy in World War II, Volume 3, The Statistics of Diseases and Injuries.* Navmed P-1318, 1950.

————. Commander in Chief, Pacific Fleet and Pacific Ocean Areas. *Guide to Japan.* CINCPAC-CINPOA Bulletin no. 209–45, September 1, 1945.

U.S. Office of War Information. See Foreign Morale Analysis Division.

Van Ash, Cay, and Elizabeth Sax Rohmer. *Master of Villainy: A Biography of Sax Rohmer.* Bowling Green University Popular Press, 1972.

von Ludendorff, Eric. *The Nation at War.* Hutchinson & Co., 1937.

Vu, Chieu. *Political and Social Change in Vietnam between 1940 and 1946.* Ph.D. dissertation in history, University of Wisconsin-Madison, 1984.

Wagatsuma Hiroshi and Yoneyama Toshinao. *Henken no Kōzō: Nihonjin no Jinshukan* [The Structure of Prejudice: Japanese Perceptions of Race]. NHK Books no. 55, 1967.

Wagatsuma, Hiroshi. "The Social Perception of Skin Color in Japan," *Daedalus,* Spring 1967, 407–43.

Wakamori Tarō. *Shōmin no Seishin Shi* [History of the Spirit of the Common People]. Kawade Shobō, 1965.

———, ed. *Nihon Seikatsu Bunka Shi* [History of Daily Life and Culture in Japan]. Kawade Shobō, 1975.

Wallace, Henry A. *The Price of Vision: The Diary of Henry A. Wallace, 1942–1946.* Edited by John Morton Blum. Houghton Mifflin, 1973.

Waller, George. *Singapore Is Silent.* Harcourt, Brace & Co., 1943.

Ward, Robert S. "Can Japan Win By Losing?" *Asia and the Americas* May 1945, 234–38.

Warner, Denis, and Peggy Warner. *The Sacred Warriors: Japan's Suicide Legions.* Avon, 1982.

Watanabe Takeshi. *Senryōka no Nihon Zaisei Oboegaki* [Recollections of Japanese Finance under the Occupation]. Nihon Keizai Shimbunsha, 1966.

Weigley, Russell F. *The American Way of War: A History of United States Military Strategy and Policy.* Indiana University Press, 1973.

Wentworth, Harold, and Stuart Berg Flexner, eds. *Dictionary of American Slang.* 2nd ed. Crowell, 1975.

Wertheim [Tuchman], Barbara. "Japan: A Clinical Note," *Foreign Affairs* 14.3 (April 1936): 520–22.

Wertheim, W. F. *Indonesian Society in Transition: A Study of Social Change.* W. Van Hoeve, The Hague and Bandung, 1956.

West, W. J., ed. *Orwell: The War Broadcasts.* British Broadcasting Co./Duckworth, 1985.

Weston, Rubin Francis. *Racism in U.S. Imperialism: The Influence of Racial Assumptions on American Foreign Policy, 1893–1946.* University of South Carolina Press, 1972.

White, Theodore. "The Danger from Japan." *New York Times Magazine,* August 11, 1985.

White, Walter. *A Rising Wind.* Doubleday, Doran & Co. 1945.

Wilkins, Ford. "Close-Up Report on the Japanese." *New York Times Magazine,* March 4, 1945.

Wilmott, H. P. *Empires in the Balance: Japanese and Allied Pacific Strategies to April 1942.* Naval Institute Press, 1982.

———. "Zero." In *Classic Aircraft of World War II;* 204–63. Bison Books, 1981.

Winkler, Allan M. *The Politics of Propaganda: The Office of War Information, 1942–1945.* Yale University Press, 1978.

Wray, Harold J. "A Study in Contrasts: Japanese School Textbooks of 1903 and 1941–1945." *Monumenta Nipponica* 28.1 (1973): 69–86.

Wright, C. Ben. *George F. Kennan, Scholar-Diplomat: 1926–1946.* Ph.D. dissertation in history, University of Wisconsin-Madison, 1972.

Wu, William F. *The Yellow Peril: Chinese Americans in American Fiction, 1850–1940.* Archon Books, 1982.

Wyman, David S. *The Abandonment of the Jews: America and the Holocaust, 1941–1945.* Pantheon, 1984.

Yamaguchi, Masao. "Kinship, Theatricality, and Marginal Reality in Japan." In Ravindra K. Jain, ed., *Text and Context, the Social Anthropology of Tradition,* 151–79. Institute for the Study of Human Issues, 1977.

———. *Bunka to Ryōgisei* [Culture and Double Meaning]. Iwanami Shoten, 1975.

Yanagita Kunio. *Momotarō no Tanjō* [The Birth of Momotarō]. Sanseidō, 1944.

Yoshida Teigo. "The Stranger As God: The Place of the Outsider in Japanese Folk Religion." *Ethnology* 20.2 (April 1981): 87–99.

Yoshimoto Takaaki. *Takemura Kotarō.* Shunjūsha, 1966.

Young, James R. "Japan Risks Destruction." *Reader's Digest,* November 1941, 29–33.

Yuzuru Sanematsu, ed. *Gendai Shiryō 35: Taiheiyō Sensō 2* [Contemporary Documents 35: Pacific War 2]. Misuzu Shobō, 1969.

Zacharias, Ellis M. *Secret Missions: The Story of an Intelligence Officer.* Putnam, 1946.

MAGAZINES AND NEWSPAPERS

Amerasia, American Legion Magazine, American Mercury, American Rifleman, Asahi Shimbun, Asia (title changed to *Asia and the Americas* in October 1942), *Asiatic Review, The Atlantic Monthly, Bungei Shunjū, Catholic World, Chicago Tribune, Christian Century, Chūō Kōron, Collier's, Commonweal, Fellowship: The Journal of the Fellowship of Reconciliation, Fortune, Infantry Journal, Kaizō, Leatherneck, Life, The Nation, The New Republic, The New York Times, The New Yorker, Newsweek, Reader's Digest, The Saturday Evening Post, Science Digest, Survey Graphic, United States News.*

PICTURE CREDITS

Grateful acknowledgment is made to copyright holders for permission to reprint the following graphics (the numbered illustrations appear on pages 181–200):

"Men or Beasts?" (page 88) and "Let the Punishment Fit the Crime" (figure 7). Copyright © 1945/48 by the New York Times Company. Reprinted by permission.

"Throwing In an Extra Charge" (figure 1), "The Heroic Role" (figure 11), and "Out for Vengeance!" (figure 12). Reprinted by permission of the *Chicago Tribune*.

"East or West?" (figure 2). David Low cartoon supplied by permission of *The Standard* (London Express News and Feature Services).

"Mimic," (figure 3). © *The Washington Post*. Reprinted by permission.

"The Monkey Folk" (figure 4). Reproduced by permission of *Punch*.

"Knock Him Off That Springboard" (figure 5). Reprinted by permission of the *Philadelphia Inquirer*.

"Louseous Japanicas" (figure 8) and the *Leatherneck* cover of September 1945 (figure 9). Reprinted by permission of the Marine Corps Association.

"How Tough Are the Japanese?" (figure 10). Originally published in the *London Daily Mail* and reproduced by permission of Associated Newspapers Group PLC.

"Another Puzzler for World Scholars" (figure 14). Reprinted by permission of the *Detroit News*, a division of Evening News Association, copyright 1985.

The following Japanese graphics have been reprinted with the kind permission of the artists or their heirs:

"Purging One's Head of Anglo-Americanism" (figure 15), by Sugiura Yukio.
"Horse's Legs, Badger's Tail" and "Vespers" (figures 18 and 19), by Kondō Hidezō.
"Grieving Statue of Liberty" (figure 20), by Ono Saseo.
Demon removing Roosevelt mask (figure 22), Saso Yoshikuni.
Demonic Roosevelt and Churchill in sight of Mount Fuji (figure 23), by Shishido Sako.
"Kill the Enemy by Increasing Production" (figure 26), by Nasu Ryōsuke.
"Establish the East Asia Co-Prosperity Sphere" (figure 27), by Sugiura Yukio.

. . .

INDEX

NOTE: Page numbers in italics refer to illustrations.

AAA Movement, 6
"ABCD" encirclement, 59–60, *192*, 241
Across the Pacific, 343 *n.* 11
Adachi Buntarō, 217–19
Adams, Henry, 155–56, 343 *n.* 11
Aitape, 69
Aizawa Seishisai, 239–40
Alamo, 12, 73
Amaterasu Omikami (Sun Goddess),
    222–23
"American-British Challenge Directed
    Against Nippon, The," 59
American Federation of Labor, 170
American Indians, 26, 33, 60, 73, 145,
    148–54, 330 *n.* 103; Japanese
    perceptions of, 26
American Legion, 170
American Legion Magazine, 87, 91, 141,
    144
American Mercury, 109, 143
American Rifleman, 158
Anglo-Japanese Alliance, 59
Anti-communism, 16–17, 27, 43, 309–10,

Anti-Semitism, 4–5; Japanese, *192*, *194*,
    225, 241–44, 258, 267, 358 *n.* 5;
    Western, 4, 34–35, 120, 320 *n.* 8.
    See also German extermination
    campaign
Aristotle, 10, 150, 153, 264
Arita Hachirō, 59
Asahi, 232, 269, 301
Asia and the Americas, 141, 142
"Asiatic barred zone," 165. *See also*
    United States immigration policy
Assembly of the Greater East Asiatic
    Nations, 6
Atlantic Monthly, 64, 173–74
Atomic bombs, 38, 47, 58, 138, 300;
    American attitudes toward, 54, 142;
    as an atrocity, 37–38, 324 *n.* 13;
    casualties resulting from, 298, 325 *n.*
    21
Atrocities, 10–12, 33–73, *182;* Allied,
    61–71, 141–42, 330 *n.* 95, 330–31
    n. 104; German, 34–35, 48;
    Japanese, 7, 12, 18, 33–52, 61, 64,

Atrocities (*continued*)
66, 144, 238, 261, 285–88, 300, 327
n. 39, 349 n. 1
Attu, 87, *184*, 231
Axis alliance, 206–7, 280–81

Baelz, Erwin, 269
Baker, Howard H., 313–14
Baldwin, Hanson, 162
Baltimore Sun, 65
Ba Maw, 6, 7, 46, 286
Banzai charges, 12, 45, 52, 144. *See also*
Japanese attitudes toward death
Barnhart, Michael, 259
Bataan, 112, 260, 321 n. 10; Death
March, 22, 44, 51–52, 61, 328 n.
47
Bateson, Gregory, 119, 133
Battle of China, The, 17–18, 321 n. 6
Bayonet, 43–45, *196–7*, 245–46, 249,
250
Benedict, Ruth, 55, 119, 120, 134
Berlin, Isaiah, 90
Bismarck Sea, battle of, 67
Bisson, T. A., 57
Black Muslim movement, 174
Blacks: and early racism, 148–49, 153,
155; in Japanese propaganda, 26,
198–99, 208, 218, 247–48; and
World War Two, 5, 120, 173–80,
348 n. 4
Blakeslee, George, 55
Blamey, Thomas, 53, 71, 72, 73, 77
"Blood and soil," 265–66, 274, 276–77
Blood for the Emperor, 161
Boas, Franz, 119–20, 154
Bombing of civilians, 11, 38–39, 294;
Allied, 12, 38, 40–41, 48–50, 60,
184, 298, 300–301; Allied
condemnation of, 38–40, 41–42,
325–26 n. 22; casualties resulting
from, 41, 298, 325 n. 21, 362–63 n.
5; German, 39–40; incendiary
bombing, 40–41, 246, 325 n. 21;

Japanese, 41–42; Japanese
condemnation of, 9, 12, 24, 34, 40,
41, 49, 58, 60, 72, 246, 248
Bond, Lionel, 100
Borneo, 44
Borton, Hugh, 55
Bougainville, 63, 66
Bowles, Gordon, 132
Boxer Rebellion, 156
Bridge on the River Kwai, The, 47–48
British evaluations of the Japanese: prior
to the fall of Singapore, 99–108; by
Ministry of Information, 140–41,
143–44. *See also* Cadogan,
Churchill, Slim
British Foreign Office, 39, 54
Brooke-Popham, Robert, 99
Brown, Cecil, 100–101, 111
Buddhism, 106, 227
Buck, Pearl, 7, 39, 160, 178, 345 n. 17
Bugs Bunny Nips the Nips, 84
Bungei Shunjū, 211, 213
Burma, 6, 44, 46, 53, 83, 100, 112, 288
Burma-Siam "railroad of death," 47, 296,
327 n. 39
Burmese Independence Army, 6, 285
Bushido (Way of the Warrior), 157. *See
also* Samurai tradition
Byas, Hugh, 110, 144

Cabral, Francisco, 95
Cadogan, Sir Alexander, 84
Cairo Conference, 60
Cape Esperance, 115
Capra, Frank, 15–19, 30, 35, 322 n. 8
*Cardinal Principles of the National Polity
(Kokutai no Hongi)*, 221–22, 225,
227, 228, 280
Cartography, 272–73, 359 n. 23
Casualties. *See* World War Two casualty
figures
Cato the Elder, 54
Chamberlin, William Henry, 98
Chan, Charlie, 159

Chaplin, Charlie, 207
Chennault, Claire, 104
Chiang Kai-shek, 59, 168, 172, *192*, 215, 241
Chicago Tribune, 181, 188, 189
China and the Chinese: attitudes toward the West, 5, 167–69; Japanese actions toward, 25, 38, 39, 42–43, 46, 47, 98, 101–2, 109, 284–86, 288; Western attitudes toward, 10, 14, 17–18, 39, 154–59, 164–73, 207, 309–10, 343 *n.* 12. *See also* United States Immigration policy
China Incident of 1937, 22, 271
China market, 171–72, 347 *n.* 34
Christianity: Japanese attitudes toward, *193*, 238–39, 245, 258, 326 *n.* 32; Western perception of threat to, 21, 156, 162–63 169. *See also* World War Two as a moral war
Chrysanthemum and the Sword, The (Benedict), 120
Chūō Kōron, 228
Churchill, Winston, 12, 39, 40, 55, 82, 100–101, 142, 161–62, 168, *192–93, 195–96, 198–99*, 293, 309, 321 *n.* 10, 321 *n.* 2
Clubb, O. Edmund, 309
Cold war, 14
Collier's, 56, 87, 158, 170, *184*
Color symbolism, 156–63, 205–15. *See also* "Yellow Peril"
"Combining benevolence and stern justice" *(oni heiyō)*, 283
Commonweal, 169
Confucianism, 266, 282. *See also* Japanese perceptions of the family system as metaphor
Conquest of Canäan, The (Dwight), 150
Contemporary Japan, 230
Coral Sea, 115
Craigie, Robert, 95
Curtis, Carl, 168
Custer, George Armstrong, 12, 73

Dazai Osamu, 242
Declaration of Independence, 150
de Las Casas, Bartolomé, 150
Derr Biggers, Earl, 159
de Sepúlveda, Juan Ginés, 150
Destination Tokyo, 90
Detroit Free Press, 65
Detroit News, 190
Development of Our Own, 174
De Witt, John L., 80–81
Dingell, John, 313
Dirkson, Everett, 310
Doolittle, James, 48–49
Doolittle raid, 48–50, 60, 86, *184–85*, 246, 302, 329 *n.* 72
Drinnon, Richard, 149
Dulles, John Foster, 309–12, 364 *n.* 16

"Ear mound," 20, 65
Eckstein, Gustav, 96
Eden, Anthony, 44
Eichelberger, Robert, 86
Eliot, George Fielding, 54
"Emaciated endurance" *(yase-gaman)*, 230
Embree, John, 95, 128–29, 338 *n.* 5
Emperor Hirohito, 281–82, 176, 306–7. *See also* Imperial institution
Emperor Jimmu, 205, 214, 217, 222, 223, 228, 268, 282
Evolution, theory of in Japan, 217–21
Executive Order 9066, 79–80
"Expert" opinion: about the Japanese, 94–96, 102, 103, 113, 118–46: about other nonwhites, 155
Exterminationist sentiments, 29; Allied, 9, 11, 17, 23, 29, 36–37, 40, 50, 52–57, 70–71, 73, 79, 81–83, 85, 90–92, 157, *184–85*, 243, 293, 328 *n.* 52; Japanese, 11, 72–73, *196–97*, 232–33, 245, 247–49, 255; Western toward nonwhites, 150–52

F Agency (F Kikan), 285
Fellers, Bonner F., 41
Field Service Code (Senjinkun), 26, 61, 227
Flamethrowers, 91–92
Fleisher, Wilfrid, 322 *n.* 9
Flynn, Errol, 12
Foreign Affairs, 96
Formosa, 22, 23, 46, 147, 284–86, 289
Fortune, 54, 96, 110
Freudian analysis of Japanese behavior, 123–24, 129–31
Fujisawa Chikao, 225–28
Fujiwara Iwaichi, 285
Fu Manchu, 157–59, 163, 344 *n.* 15
Furuya Yoshio, 275–76

Gandhi, Mohandas K., 177
Genocidal attitudes. *See* Exterminationist sentiments
German-American Bund, 79
German extermination campaign, 4, 34–35, 48, 52; Allied perception of, 4, 35, 323 *n.* 3
Germany and the Germans, 34, 35, 37, 39–41, 46, 48, 50, 52, 54, 56, 66, 78–80, 83, 87, 140
"Goettge patrol," 64
Gorer, Geoffrey, 119, 124–31, 134, 136
Gray, J. Glenn, 62, 69
Great Dictator, The, 207
"Great Chain of Being," 150, 153, 264, 266 *n.* 47
Great Shinto Purification Ritual and the Divine Mission of Japan, The (Fujisawa), 225–28
Greater East Asia Co-Prosperity Sphere, 7, 8, 163, *200*, 211, 220, 262–92, 274–75; financial and economic policy for, 287–88
Greater East Asia War Inquiry Commission, 59–60, 329 *n.* 71
Grew, Joseph, 83, 96–97, 113, 142, 163
Gripsholm, the, 113

Griswold, A. Whitney, 60
Guadalcanal, 45, 52, 64, 89–91, 115, 249
Guadalcanal Diary (Tregaskis), 64
Gunther, John, 126
Gyokusai, 231–33, 352 *n.* 61

Hakko ichiū ("eight corners of the world under one roof"), 20, 223, 274, 284, 359 *n.* 27
Halifax, Lord, 162
Halsey, William, 36, 55, 56, 79, 85, 115
Haring, Douglas, 134–35, 340 *n.* 18
Hart, Thomas, 56–57
Hasegawa Nyozekan, 230
Haushofer, Karl, 207, 269
Hay, John, 156
Hayashi Fusao, 350 *n.* 17
Hayashi Razan, 237
Hearn, Lafcadio, 119, 142
Hearst newspapers, 7, 157, 161
Hideyoshi, 20, 21, 65
Hino Ashihei, 232
Hinode, 244, 249, 251
Hirata Atsutane, 239
Hirohito. *See* Emperor Hirohito
Hiss, Alger, 57
Hitler, Adolf, 88, 176, 207, 269
Hong Kong, 42, 44, 99, 105
Horikoshi Jirō, 104
Horney, Karen, 134–35
"Hundred-year war," 56, 57, 163, 314, 329 *n.* 68
Hunting metaphors: Allied use of, 89–93, 231; Japanese use of, 255. *See also* Stereotypes, animal imagery *and* Exterminationist sentiments

Ichioku Tokkō ("the hundred million as a Special Attack Force"), 232–33
Ichioku gyokusai ("the shattering of the hundred million like a beautiful jewel"), 233
Ikeda Eiji, *192*

Imperial institution: Allied perceptions of, 18–21, 130, 322 *n.* 8; Allied recommendations for treatment of, 18–19, 121–22, 127–28, 136, 138, 338 *n.* 4, 350 *n.* 17; Japanese attitudes toward, 27, 31, 222, 225–28, 236, 282, 283, 306–8

Imperial Precepts to Soldiers and Sailors, 61

Imperial Rule Assistance Association, 225–26

"Imperial Way," 8, 61, 163, 225, 280

Imperialism: Japanese, 8, 21, 22, 30, 147–48, 264–65, 272, 279–81; Japanese attitudes toward Western, 24, 29–30, 236, 242, 253, 268, 270, 274–77, 283; Western, 4, 29, 148–50, 166, 172–73

India, 165, 167, 347 *n.* 35

Indian National Army, 6, 285

Indians of Western Hemisphere. *See* American Indians

Indonesia and East Indies, 6, 36, 42, 44–47, 84–87, 296

Infantry Journal, 86, 152

Institute of Pacific Relations, 98; conference on "Japanese character structure," 131–33

International Military Tribunal for the Far East (IMTFE), 37, 41, 58, 324 *n.* 11

Isolationism, 15, 114

Itō Shinsui, 249

Ivens, Joris, 18–19

Iwo Jima, 57, 91, 92, 248–49, 299

"Japan bashing," 313

Japan Institute, 97

Japan Times and Mail, 223

Japanese-Americans, 5, 79–82, 92, 112, 114, 131, 135–36

Japanese attitudes toward death, 9, 11, 12, 25–26, 57, 67–68, 72, 103, 215–16, 231–33, 246–49, 261,

305–6; Western response to, 72, 89, 113, 163, 231–32. *See also* Banzai charges *and* Special Attack Forces

Japanese battle cries, 341 *n.* 33

Japanese behavior toward other Asians, 7, 12, 18, 30, 38–39, 41–47, 133, 178, 203, 241, 242, 254, 261, 263–64, 266, 275–76, 278–90. *See also* Atrocities, Japanese

Japanese belief in their divine origin, 46, 205, 216–25, 241, 255

Japanese belief in their inherent superiority, 5, 8, 9, 72, 111, 179, *200,* 203–33, 260, 261–92, 301, 311, 314–15

Japanese "Caucasianization," 209–10

Japanese challenge of Western racism, 5–6, 208

Japanese child-rearing, 123–28, 129, 130, 132, 136, 248

Japanese class system, 31, 46–47, 235–36, 308–9

Japanese colonization, 264–65, 270, 272–78, 285–90

Japanese culture: as basis for "national character" studies, 121–23, 133, 145, 154; as perceived by the West, 97–98, 110, 128, 133, 153

Japanese hated more than Germans, 8, 33–35, 37, 48, 50, 52, 77–81, 140

Japanese impressed labor: 7, 47–48, 287–88, 327 *n.* 38

Japanese material deprivation, 228–31

Japanese military planning, 59

Japanese morale, 137–38. *See also* Office of War Information

Japanese perceptions of: "brightness," 206, 210–15, 221; collective purity, 9, 215–16, 268–69, 315; color, 203, 207–14, 267; divine origin, 46, 205, 216–17, 221, 224, 225, 241, 255 (*see also* Emperor Jimmu); family system as a metaphor, 279–85, 301, 361 *n.* 5 (*see also* "Proper place"); inherent superiority, 5, 8, 9, 46, 72,

Japanese perceptions of (*continued*)
111, 179, 203–33, 260, 261–92, 301,
311, 314–15; "national character,"
269–70; national unity or
homogeneity, 31, 180, 205, 215–17,
221–23, 236, 301, 306, 315;
outsiders or strangers, 10, 203,
233–40, 251, 315; purity, 9, 10,
72–73, 180, *191*, 203–33, 234–36,
248, 268–69, 300, 305–6, 315, 350
n. 17; their uniqueness, 31–32, 180,
203, 204–5, 216–17, 221;
tradition/history, 25, 27, 205,
212–13, 214, 215, 221–24, 225, 226,
236, 256, 268, 279, 281–82, 305;
war as purifying, 215–16, 225–26,
245–46, 255, 350 *n.* 17; Western
history, 224–25, 258–59; Western
racism, 242–44, 247–48, 249, 260;
Westerners (pre-20th century),
237–40
Japanese population policies, 270–78
Japanese postwar challenge of white
(Western) supremacy, 315–17
Japanese principles of war, 26–27
Japanese purge of Western influences,
228–29, 257, 287, 305
Japanese soldier as the supreme Japanese
weapon: to Japan, 22, 111; to the
West, 22
Japanese suicide, 45–46. *See also*
Japanese attitudes toward death
Japanese toilet training, 123–30
Japanese value system in Western eyes,
125–26, 127, 132, 138–39
Japanese war objectives, 14, 24–25, 26,
29, 58–59, 224–25, 243, 248, 268,
270, 277–78, 358 *n.* 14, 359 *n.* 27
Japanese worldview as male/female
oriented, 126, 129, 130
Japanese writing system, 107–8
"Japanization," 7, 284–87
Jefferson, Thomas, 149, 150
Jesuits, 94–95
Jimmu. *See* Emperor Jimmu

Jones, Edgar L., 137
Jordan, Robert O., 175
Jordan, Winthrop, 149
Judd, Walter, 168, 169
Jung, Carl, 106

Kamikaze. *See* Special Attack Forces
Katō Etsurō, 245–46
Kempeitai (military police), 46, 143, 327
n. 37
Kennan, George, 309, 364 *n.* 16
"Kill or be killed," 10, 12, 60, 64, 67,
77, 243
King, Ernest, 6, 58, 109
Kipling, Rudyard, 95, 151, 155,
183
Kiyono Kenji, 219–20
Kluckhohn, Clyde, 55, 119, 138
Know Your Enemy—Japan, 18–23, 27,
28, 31, 84, 254, 316, 321 *n.* 7, 322
n. 8
Knox, Frank, 110
Kobayashi Junichi, 352 *n.* 61
Koiso Kuniaki, 248
*Kokutai no Hongi. See Cardinal
Principles of the National Polity*
Komaki Tsunekichi, 273
Kondō Hidezō, *193*, 245
Konjaku Monogatari, 250
Konoe Fumimaro, 95, 333 *n.* 4
Koo, Wellington, 310
Korea and the Koreans, 20, 22, 42, 46,
47, 147, 284, 285–86, 289, 315, 363
n. 5
"Korea Clique," 286
Korean War, 310
Kōsaka Masaaki, 226
Kōyama Iwao, 226
Kyoto School (Kyoto Gakuha), 206, 216,
226–27

La Barre, Weston, 135–36
Lamott, Willis, 97, 135

Lea, Homer, 113–14, 157–58, 344 *n.* 14
"Leading race" *(shidō minzoku),* 8, 203,
206, 217, 221, 223–28, 261, 262–92
League for Industrial Democracy, 161
League of Nations, 22, 98, 204
Leahy, William, 6–7, 54, 110, 141–42
Leatherneck, 65, 66, 79, 91, *184–85,*
186, 302
Lebensraum ("expansion of living
space"), 277–78
Leighton, Alexander, 119, 138, 139
LeMay, Curtis, 40–41, 116
Life, 65, 81, 90, 111, 141, *189,* 224, 330
n. 90
Lindbergh, Charles, 69–71
Lin Yutang, 7, 160, 161, 345 *n.* 17
London Daily Mail, 187
Los Angeles Times, 80, 112
Low, David, 87, *182,* 302
Luce, Clare Boothe, 158

MacArthur, Arthur, 152
MacArthur, Douglas, 12, 18, 44, 105,
111, 139, 303–4, 321 *n.* 10, 338
n. 4
Macartney, Sir Halliday, 155
Madama Butterfly, 97
Mainichi, 301
Malaya, 42, 115
Manchester, William, 63
Manchuria and Manchukuo, 22, 25,
42, 46, 59, 98, 283–84, 285–86,
299
Manga, 191, 192, 221, 229, 253, 257
Manila, 22, 44–45, 61, 111, 112, 326 *n.*
32
Mansfield, Mike, 168
Marquand, John, 159
Marshall, George C., 15, 40, 109, 141,
173
Maruki Iri, 45–46
Maruki Toshi, 45–46
Mashbir, Sidney, 61
Mason, Noah, 171

Master-race theory, 4, 5, 16, 175, 266
Matsuoka Yōsuke, 244–45, 280–81
McCloy, John J., 80
McGinnis, H. C., 172
McNutt, Paul V., 55
Mead, Margaret, 119, 132, 133, 143
Mears, Helen, 133–34
Mein Kampf (Hitler), 22, 207, 267, 357
n. 5
Midway, 115, 261
Mikado, The, 97, *184–85*
Miller, Stuart Creighton, 151–52
Moby Dick (Melville), 208
Momotarō, 10, *198,* 251–57, 306
Momotarō and the Eagles of the Ocean,
253
Momotarō—Divine Troops of the Ocean,
253–54, 316, 356 *n.* 36
Momotarō of the Sky, 253
Monroe Doctrine, 59
"Monroe Doctrine for Asia,"
147–48
Mori Ōgai, 107
Morton, Samuel George, 155
Mr. Moto, 159, 344, 345 *n.* 16
Muhammed, Elijah, 175
Museum of Modern Art (New York),
189
Myrdal, Gunnar, 174

Nagumo Chūichi, 261
Nakajima Chikuhei, 217, 221
Nakasone Yasuhiro, 315
Nation, The, 91, 176
"National character" studies, 9, 118–46,
338 *n.* 5, 339 *n.* 5, 339–40 *n.* 14
National Eugenics Law, 269
"Natural slavery," 150, 153, 155, 343 *n.*
11
Negro News Syndicate, 175
Nelson, Donald, 347 *n.* 34
Nevins, Allan, 33
New Guinea, 50–51, 67, 69, 70, 71
"New Guinea diary," 50–51, 62, 67

"New" Japan, 256–57, 259, 306
"New world order" *(sekai shinchitsujo)*, 27, 205, 226–27, 229, 263, 274, 277–83, 306, 359 *n.* 27
New York Times, 50, 51, 87–88, 92, 96, 115, *184–85, 190,* 302
New York Times Magazine, 115, 129, 143, 152–53, *187*
New Yorker, 37, 85, 302
Newsweek, 95, 97, 142, 302
Nippon Hyōron, 276
Nishitani Keiji, 226
Norman, E. H., 106

Occupation policy and programs, 13, 23, 139, 303–5, 310. *See also* Purge of Japanese militarists
Office of War Information, Foreign Morale Analysis Division (OWI-FMAD), 55, 68, 118, 124, 134, 137–38, 301, 336–37 *n.* 1
Okinawa, 45–46, 61, 63, 105–6, 298, 299
"One hundred million" *(ichioku),* 30, 31, 215, 241, 306, 323 *n.* 17
Ōnishi Takijirō, 232
Ono Saseo, *194,* 258
Oriental exclusion laws. *See* United States immigration policy
Orr, Carey, *182, 188*
Orwell, George, 46
Osaka Puck, 208, 228–29, 246

Pal, Radhabinod, 37–38, 42
Pakenham, Compton, 95, 142, 333 *n.* 4
Pan-Asianism, 6, 7, 8, 25, 180, 207, 265, 289; Western perceptions of, 6, 163, 171
Paris Peace Conference (Versailles), 22, 59, 147
Parkman, Francis, 150–51
Parsons, Talcott, 132

Pearl Harbor, 10, 22, 33, 35, 36–37, 49, 101, 105, 108, 111, 112, 161, 176, 259–60, 316, 319 *n.* 1
Peleliu, 63, 299
Pence, H. L., 55
Percival, A. E., 100
Perry, Matthew, 21, 239
Philadelphia Inquirer, 184
Philippine Sea, battle of, 90
Philippines, 6, 34, 35, 36, 105, 143, 167, 299; U. S. conquest of, 148–49, 151–52
Phillips, William, 7, 171, 347 *n.* 35
Plasma segregation, 348 *n.* 40
Postwar: economic conversion, 170–71; recommendations for reform, 129, 133; repatriation, 363 *nn.* 6 and 7
Pratt, Fletcher, 102–4
Pratt, Sir John, 140
Prelude to War, 15, 16, 17, 314
Price, Willard, 142
Prince of Wales, the, 100–2, 111, 112
Prisoners of war: Allied attitudes toward, 60–71; Japanese attitudes toward, 35, 48–52. *See also* Surrender
Promise, The (Buck), 160
Propaganda, 15–32; Allied, 42–43, 44, 48–52, 114, 322 *n.* 8; Japanese, 5, 12, 24–25, 49, 61–62, 175, 207, 208, 242, 243, 246–47, 249, 250; sources for, 16, 19, 22, 28, 30, 41–43
"Propagate and multiply movement," 271–72. *See also* Japanese population policies
"Proper place," 9–10, 27, *200,* 205–6, 211, 220–21, 226–28, 254, 259, 261, 264–66, 278–84, 305, 308
"Psychological purge" argument. *See* Exterminationist sentiment
Psychological warfare campaign, 77, 137–38, 340 *n.* 22
Punch, 84, *183,* 302
Purge of Japanese militarists, 306–8

"Purity of blood," 275–77. See also
Japanese perceptions of purity
Purple Heart, The, 50, 91, 327–28
n. 44
Pyle, Ernie, 78, 82, 85

Quebec Conference, 40
Quigley, Harold, 56

Races of Mankind, The, 120
Racial code words and formulaic
expressions, 8–10, 27–32, 71–73,
116–17, 144–48, 203–5, 301–16. See
also Stereotypes
"Racial virility," 230, 276
Radford, Arthur, 55
Ramspeck, Robert, 169
Randolph, A. Philip, 177, 348 n. 45
Rankin, John, 81, 348 n. 40
Rape of Nanking, 22, 43, 61, 326 n. 26
Read This and the War Is Won (Kore
dake Yomeba Ware wa Kateru),
23–27, 207–8
Reader's Digest, 85, 109, 141, 143, 162
Recapitulationist theory, 153–55
Records of the Legitimate Succession of
the Divine Sovereign (Jinnō Shōtōki),
222
Red Badge of Courage, The (Crane), 211
"Red Peril," 14, 172, 177, 309
Regan, Donald, 313
Report from Tokyo (Grew), 113
Repulse, the 100–2, 111, 112
Riegle, Donald, 314
Rising Wind, A (White), 177
Rohmer, Sax, 157–59
Romulo, Carlos, 44–45
Roosevelt, Archie, 115
Roosevelt, Eleanor, 178
Roosevelt, Elliott, 55
Roosevelt, Franklin D., 3, 7, 15, 38, 39,
40, 49, 52, 65, 69, 79, 81, 108, 142,

150, 164, 167, 170, 172, 192–96,
198–99, 224, 330 n. 90
Roosevelt, Theodore, 151
Russo-Japanese War, 22, 59, 126,
147

Saipan, 45, 61, 246, 249, 298–99
Samurai tradition: Japanese perception
of, 51, 279; Western perception of,
20, 51, 56
Sansom, George, 95
Saturday Evening Post, 158, 161, 168
Science Digest, 143
"Scientific antiracism:" Japanese, 218–20;
Western, 4, 119–20, 154, 338 n. 3
"Scientific racism," 119, 148, 153–55,
204
Senjinkun. See Field Service Code
Serres, Etienne, 153
Shinto, 209, 212, 225, 229, 230, 252;
Western perception of, 20, 21,
125–26, 140–41
Shōchiku, 253, 254
Silberpfennig, Judith, 130–31
Singapore, 35, 36, 43, 44, 84, 87, 99,
100–1, 105, 109, 111–12, 143, 207,
213, 260, 321 n. 10
Singapore Is Silent, 54
Singh, Mohan, 207, 285
Sino-Japanese War, 21, 39, 156, 209,
282, 286
Sledge, E. B., 63, 65
Slim, William, 44, 53, 83, 90, 112
Slogans: Allied, 36, 53, 55, 92; black,
177; Japanese, 214–15, 230, 231–33
Smyth, Joseph Hilton, 175
Snow, Edgar, 133, 141
Society for International Cultural
Relations (Kokusai Bunka
Shinkōkai), 97
Songs. See War songs
Southern Agency (Minami Kikan), 285
"Souvenir-hunting" by Allied soldiers, 12,

"Souvenir-hunting" (*continued*)
61–66, 70–71; Japanese attitudes
toward, 12, 34, 224, 249
Soviet Union. *See* U.S.S.R.
Special Attack Forces (Tokkōtai), 12,
52–53, 212, 232–33, 256, 300, 308;
Allied attitudes toward, 22, 52–53,
300, 328 *n.* 51; casualty figures, 331
n. 105
"Spiritual cleansing," 225–26
Spiritual Culture Institute, 31
Stalin, Joseph, 83, 105, 172
Stereotypes, 15–32
Stereotypes, Allied: animal imagery,
81–93, 161–62, 312; animal
imagery, apes, 37, 71, 73, 77, 84–88,
115, 157, 162, 167, *182–86,* 302;
animal imagery, dogs, 20, 68, 82–83,
162, 313; animal imagery, insects,
83, 90–91, 332 *n.* 11; animal
imagery, subhuman/beast, 9, 49,
52–53, 69, 78, 89, 99, 155, 231;
animal imagery, vermin, 71, 73, 78,
80, 84, 90–92, *184–85;* Japanese as
bent on world conquest, 17, 20, 22,
113, 127, 128, 136, 274; Japanese as
"borrowers," 34, 37, 98, 110, 128,
312; Japanese as children, 9, 97,
109, 117, 122–24, 128–34, 139,
142–45, 155, 167, *190,* 302, 303,
343 *n.* 11; Japanese as comical, 110,
343 *n.* 11; Japanese as complete
opposites, 29, 91–93, 95, 96, 97,
135, 139; Japanese as deranged or
neurotic, 9, 20, 23, 56, 72, 95–97,
105–6, 111, 117, 122–35, 139,
143–45, *190,* 304, 309; Japanese as
homogeneous, 8, 17–21, 30–31,
79–84, 92–94, 105, 118–46, 322 *n.*
8, 322 *n.* 9; Japanese as imperialists,
22; Japanese as inherently inferior,
9, 20, 71–72, 98, 103–4, 111, 123,
133, *190,* 312; Japanese as intuitive
or spiritually powerful, 106–7,

116–17, 312–13; Japanese as
inscrutable, 94–95, 96, 97, 113;
Japanese as physiologically inferior,
98, 101–5, 107, 108, 140–41,
142–43, *190,* 335 *n.* 15; Japanese as
primitive or barbaric, 9, 38, 39, 48,
51, 53, 57, 71, 106–7, 117, 122–26,
129, 134, 139–43, 155, *190,* 304;
Japanese as supermen, 9, 98–99,
112–17, *187, 188,* 260–61, 312–13;
Japanese as treacherous, 20, 33,
36–37, 87, 152–53, *181,* 323 *n.* 4,
333 *n.* 24; Japanese as unique, 10,
31–32, 35, 48, 95–97, 312–13;
Japanese history as basis for, 20–22,
51, 73, 127.
Stereotypes common to Allies and
Japanese, 11, 29–32
Stereotypes, dehumanizing aspects of: 9,
11, 17, 19–22, 28, 30, 31–32, 82,
89, 99, 116, 216, 242, 294
Stereotypes, distorting, leading to
misassessment of the enemy: 11, 36,
56, 94–117, 203, 259–61, 286, 319
n. 1
Stereotypes, existing independently of the
war in Asia: 9–10, 13–14, 17, 29,
82, 86, 116–17, 145–46, 147–80,
236–40, 251, 253–58, 259, 264, 288,
301–17, 320 *n.* 8, 342 *n.* 1, 343 *n.*
12
Stereotypes, Japanese: animal
imagery/bestiality/inhumanity, 11,
24, 34, 49, 72, 216, 224, 235,
237–49; use of American history to
create stereotypes, 24, 26–27, 29–30,
59–60, 72; Westerners as
decadent/female/soft, 24, 36,
126–27, *194,* 257–61; Westerners as
demons, 9, 13, 72–73, 179, *194–96,*
198, 203–33, 300, 305; Westerners
as deranged or mad, *192,* 242–43,
255–58; Westerners as egotistical,
materialistic, 24, 26, 30, 36, 221,

228, 243, 248, 258–61; Westerners as imperialists, 24–26, 29–30, 59–60, *192*, 205, 224–25, 241, 249, 258; Westerners as old, 259; Westerners as unclean, 216, 221, 228–30; white arrogance, 24–25, 111, 264
Stereotypes, leading to atrocities, 11, 13
Stereotypes, postwar reinterpretation of, 13, 14, 255–56, 301–5, 306–17
Stereotypes, stemming from atrocities, 9, 11–13, 24, 38, 51–52, 86
Stereotypes, Western toward nonwhites, 149–55, 158–63, 175, 304 *n.* 17
Stevenson, Robert Louis, 154
Stimson, Henry, 80, 82, 109, 113, 138, 158, 173, 175, 313, 344 *n.* 14
Sukarno, 46
Surrender: Allied attitudes toward, 12, 321 *n.* 10; Allied reluctance to take prisoners, 11, 35, 53, 57, 60, 64, 67–71, 137–38; Allied attempts to encourage, 145, 345 *n.* 22 (*see also* Office of War Information, Foreign Morale Analysis Division); Allied demand for unconditional, 36, 56, 57, 60, 139, 329 *n.* 69; difficulty of, 10–12, 35–36, 68–69, 137–38; Japanese as prisoners, 77, 139; Japanese expectations about, 68, 77, 243–44; Japanese refusal to, 35, 45, 52–53, 56–57, 67–68, 144
Suzuki Daisetz, 106, 227, 352 *n.* 47
Suzuki Kantarō, 305
Suzuki Keiji, 285
Suzuki Shigetaka, 226
"Symbolic incidents," 28, 35–36, 48–53

Takahashi Satakata, 174
Takamura Kōtarō, 230
Tale of Genji, 209
Tale of the Christians (Kirishitan Monogatari), 238

Tanaka Memorial, 22, 323 *n.* 22
Tannenbaum, Frank, 132
Tarawa, 68, 71, 91
Technological progress, 93, 294
Tenaru River, 115
They Died with Their Boots On, 12
"Thirty Comrades," 285
Thorne, Christopher, 108, 169
"Three-all" policy *(sankō seisaku),* 43
Time, 37, 67, 79, 81, 87, 111, 113, 124, 158, 161, 231
Tōjō Hideki, 26, 60, 87, 141
Tokutomi Iichirō, 223–25
Tokyo Rose, 69
Tolischus, Otto, 78, 96, 106, 141
Total War Research Bureau, 216
Tregaskis, Richard, 64
Trotsky, Leon, 323 *n.* 10
Truman, Harry, 142, 301, 303
Tsuji Masanobu, 23, 323 *n.* 12, 324 *n.* 5
Tuchman, Barbara, 96

Umi Yukaba (Across the Sea), 25
Unequal treaties, 163–64, 204
United States immigration policy, 5, 35; Japanese propaganda concerning, 167; toward the Chinese, 154, 164–70, 346 *n.* 27; toward the Japanese, 204
United States–Japan security alliance, 311
United States News, 56, 59, 60
United States War Relocation Authority, 131
U.S.S.R., 34, 35, 36, 295, 309

Valignano, Alessandro, S. J., 95, 97, 238
Valor of Ignorance, The (Lea), 113–14, 157–59; Japanese translation of, 344 *n.* 14
Veterans of Foreign Wars, 170

"Victory disease," 260–61
von Ludendorff, Erich, 207
von Ranke, Leopold, 227
Vorys, John, 168

Wainwright, Jonathan M., 349 n. 1
Wakde Island, 69
Wallace, Henry, 16, 110
Wang Ching-wei, 6
War cartoons, 181–200; Allied, 34, 91,
    302, 303; Japanese, 228–29, 238,
    240–50, 253, 256–59, 309–10
War songs: Allied, 25, 81, 162; Japanese,
    213–14, 250 n. 18
"War words," 148–49, 151, 155, 162–63.
    See also Racial code words and
    formulaic expressions
Ward, Robert S., 172
Warner, Dennis, 63
Washington Conference (1921–1922), 59
Washington Post, 182
Wavell, Archibald, 321 n. 10
Way of the Family, The (Ie no Michi or
    Senji Katei Kyōiku Shidō Yōkō),
    280
Way of the Subject, The (Shinmin no
    Michi), 24, 26, 27, 31, 280
Western postwar fears of Japan's
    trustworthiness, 310–11
White, Theodore, 314
White, Walter, 177–78
"White Peril," 207
White supremacism, 6, 25, 147–80,
    264
Why We Fight, 15–18, 23, 35
Wilkins, Roy, 176
Williams, Roger, 150
Wilson, Woodrow, 82, 165
Wolfert, Ira, 333 n. 21
Wood, Lawson, 87, 184

World War One, 16, 27, 42; lessons of,
    56
World War Two and changes in racial
    consciousness: American, 4, 5, 120,
    163–65, 168, 172–78; Asian, 5, 7,
    120, 163–67, 168, 172–73
World War Two as a moral war:
    Japanese perceptions of, 25, 27, 205,
    206, 217, 218, 224–25, 227–28, 243,
    245, 248, 281, 282, 283; Western
    perceptions of, 3, 7, 16–17
World War Two casualty figures, 48, 53,
    294–300; China, 295–96; final year
    of the war, 299–301; India, 297;
    Indochina, 296–97; Indonesia, 296;
    Japan, 297–99, 363 n. 8; Korea,
    297; Malaya, 296; Philippines, 296;
    U.S., 299, 300, 363–64 n. 9;
    U.S.S.R. and the West, 295

Xavier, Francis, 94

Yamaguchi Masao, 234, 236
Yamamoto Isoroku, 36, 161, 260
Yamashita Tomoyuki, 84
Yanagita Kunio, 252
Yank, 83, 112
"Yellow Peril," 10, 37, 39, 60, 69,
    84, 85, 93, 113, 117, 155–63,
    168, 171, 172–73, 188, 189,
    309–10, 313
Yoshida Shigeru, 305
Yu-Pin, Paul, 169

Zacharias, Ellis, 55, 96
Zen. See Buddhism
Zero (aircraft), 104, 112, 115,
    240

ABOUT THE AUTHOR

John W. Dower, born in 1938, holds the Joseph Naiman Endowed Chair in Japanese Studies at the University of California, San Diego. He is the author of *Empire and Aftermath: Yoshida Shigeru and the Japanese Experience, 1878–1954* and *The Elements of Japanese Design*, and is the editor of *The Origins of the Japanese State: Selected Writings of E. H. Norman* and coeditor of *The Hiroshima Murals: The Art of Iri Maruki and Toshi Maruki*.